CompTIA®
Linux+ Study Guide
Fifth Edition

CompTIA®
Linux+ Study Guide
Exam XK0-005
Fifth Edition

Richard Blum

Christine Bresnahan

SYBEX®
A Wiley Brand

Acknowledgments

First, all glory and praise go to God, who through His Son, Jesus Christ, makes all things possible and gives us the gift of eternal life.

Many thanks go to the fantastic team of people at Sybex for their outstanding work on this project. Thanks to Kenyon Brown, the senior acquisitions editor, for offering us the opportunity to work on this book. Also thanks to Kim Wimpsett, the development editor, for keeping things on track and making the book more presentable. Thanks, Kim, for all your hard work and diligence. The technical proofreader, David Clinton, did a wonderful job of double-checking all of the work in the book in addition to making suggestions to improve the content. Thanks also goes to the young and talented Daniel Anez (`theanez.com`) for his illustration work. We would also like to thank Carole Jelen at Waterside Productions, Inc., for arranging this opportunity for us and for helping us out in our writing careers.

Rich would particularly like to thank his wife Barbara for enduring his grouchy attitude during this project and helping to keep up his spirits with baked goods.

About the Authors

Richard Blum, CompTIA Linux+ ce, CompTIA Security+ ce, LPIC-1, has also worked in the IT industry for more than 35 years as both a system and network administrator, and he has published numerous Linux and open source books. Rich is an online instructor for Linux and web programming courses that are used by colleges and universities across the United States. When he is not being a computer nerd, Rich enjoys spending time with his wife Barbara and his two daughters, Katie and Jessica.

Christine Bresnahan, CompTIA Linux+, LPIC-1, started working with computers more than 35 years ago in the IT industry as a system administrator. Christine is an adjunct professor at Ivy Tech Community College, where she teaches Linux certification and Python programming classes. She also writes books and produces instructional resources for the classroom.

About the Technical Editor

David Clinton is a Linux Server Professional and an Amazon Web Services (AWS) solutions architect with 10 years' experience teaching technology subjects. Besides his books (Wiley/Sybex, Manning, and independently published), he's created dozens of video courses for Pluralsight. He works with Linux administration, AWS, data analytics, security, and server virtualization.

Contents at a Glance

Contents

Table of Exercises

Introduction

Linux has become one of the fastest-growing operating systems used in server environments. Most companies utilize some type of Linux system within their infrastructure, and Linux is one of the major players in the cloud computing world. The ability to build and manage Linux systems is a skill that many companies are now looking for. The more you know about Linux, the more marketable you'll become in today's computer industry.

The purpose of this book is to provide you with the knowledge and skills you need to succeed in the Linux world.

What Is Linux+?

The CompTIA Linux+ exam has become a benchmark in the computer industry as a method of demonstrating skills with the Linux operating system. Obtaining CompTIA Linux+ certification means that you're comfortable working in a Linux environment and have the skills necessary to install and maintain Linux systems.

Previously, CompTIA had partnered with the Linux Professional Institute (LPI) to produce the Linux+ certification exams. However, with the release of exam XK0-004 in 2019 CompTIA moved to creating its own exam, and has continued that with the updated XK0-005 exam. The updated Linux+ certification is still a single exam that covers hands-on components of operating a Linux system. The updated Linux+ exam focuses on four areas of Linux:

- System management
- Security
- Scripting, containers, and automation
- Troubleshooting

The XK0-005 exam uses performance-based, multiple-choice, and multiple-answer questions to identify employees who can perform the job of Linux system administrator. The exam covers tasks associated with all major Linux distributions, not focusing on any one specific distribution. It consists of 90 questions, and you will have 90 minutes to complete it.

Why Become Linux Certified?

With the growing popularity of Linux (and the increase in Linux-related jobs) comes hype. With all of the hype that surrounds Linux, it's become hard for employers to distinguish employees who are competent Linux administrators from those who just know the buzzwords. This is where Linux+ certification comes in.

With a Linux+ certification, you will establish yourself as a Linux administrator who is familiar with the Linux platform and can install, maintain, and troubleshoot any type of Linux system. By changing the exam to be more performance based, CompTIA has established the new Linux+ exam as a way for employers to have confidence in knowing their employees who pass the exam will have the skills necessary to get the job done.

How to Become Certified

The Linux+ certification is available for anyone who passes the XK0-005 exam. There are no prerequisites to taking the exam, but CompTIA recommends having either the A+ and Network+ certifications or a similar amount of experience, along with at least 12 months of hands-on Linux administrator experience.

Pearson VUE administers the exam. The exam can be taken at any Pearson VUE testing center. To register for the exam, call Pearson VUE at (877) 619-2096, or register online at http://home.pearsonvue.com/comptia.

After you take the exam, you will be immediately notified of your score. If you pass, you will get a certificate in the mail showing your Linux+ certification credentials along with a verification number that employers can use to verify your credentials online.

The Linux+ exam is part of CompTIA's Continuing Education (CE) track of exams. It's valid for three years, but it can be renewed by acquiring an appropriate number of continuing education units (CEUs) and paying a yearly fee.

Who Should Buy This Book

While anyone who wants to pass the Linux+ certification exams would benefit from this book, that's not the only reason for purchasing it. This book covers all the material someone new to the Linux world would need to know to start out in Linux. After you've become familiar with the basics of Linux, the book will serve as an excellent reference for quickly finding answers to everyday Linux questions.

The book is written with the assumption that you have a familiarity with basic computer and networking principles. No experience with Linux is required to benefit from this book, but it will help if you know your way around a computer in either the Windows or macOS world, such as how to use a keyboard, use optical disks, and work with USB thumb drives.

It will also help to have a Linux system available to follow along with. Many chapters contain a simple exercise that will walk you through the basic concepts presented in the chapter. This provides the crucial hands-on experience that you'll need to both pass the exam and do well in the Linux world.

While the CompTIA Linux+ exam is Linux distribution neutral, it's impossible to write exercises that work in all Linux distributions. That said, the exercises in this book assume you have either Ubuntu 20.04 LTS or Rocky Linux 8 available. You can install either or both of these Linux distributions in a virtual environment using the Oracle VirtualBox software, available at https://virtualbox.org.

How This Book Is Organized

This book consists of 30 chapters organized around the different objective areas of the Linux+ exam:

- Chapter 1, "Preparing Your Environment," helps you with finding and installing a Linux distribution to use for experimenting with Linux and working on the exercises in the book.

- Chapter 2, "Introduction to Services," introduces you to the different server applications and uses you'll commonly see in Linux.

- Chapter 3, "Managing Files, Directories, and Text," covers the basic Linux commands for working with files and directories from the command line.

- Chapter 4, "Searching and Analyzing Text," discusses the different tools Linux provides for working with text files.

- Chapter 5, "Explaining the Boot Process," takes you into the inner processes of how the Linux operating system starts, showing you how to customize the Linux boot process.

- Chapter 6, "Maintaining System Startup and Services," walks you through how the Linux system starts applications at boot time by discussing the two methods used for controlling program startups.

- Chapter 7, "Configuring Network Connections," shows how to get your Linux system working on a local area network, along with the tools available to help troubleshoot network problems on your Linux system.

- Chapter 8, "Comparing GUIs," discusses the graphical desktop environments available in Linux.

- Chapter 9, "Adjusting Localization Options," shows how to change the character set and date/time formats for your Linux system to accommodate the different formats used in various countries.

- Chapter 10, "Administering Users and Groups," explores how Linux handles user accounts and how you can assign users to groups to manage access to files and directories.

- Chapter 11, "Handling Storage," examines the storage methods and formats available in the Linux system.

- Chapter 12, "Protecting Files," dives into the world of data backups, archiving, and restoring.

- Chapter 13, "Governing Software," explains how Linux manages software applications and how to install software packages on the various Linux distribution types.

- Chapter 14, "Tending Kernel Modules," discusses how Linux uses kernel modules to support hardware and how you can manage the kernel modules on your Linux system.

- Chapter 15, "Applying Ownership and Permissions," explores the multiple methods available for protecting files and directories on a Linux system. It discusses the standard Linux-style permissions as well as the more advanced SELinux and AppArmor applications used to provide more advanced security for Linux systems.

- Chapter 16, "Looking at Access and Authentication Methods," explores the methods Linux can use to authenticate user accounts, both locally and in network environments.

- Chapter 17, "Implementing Logging Services," shows how Linux logs system events and how you can use the Linux system logs for troubleshooting problems on your Linux system.

- Chapter 18, "Overseeing Linux Firewalls," walks you through how to protect your Linux system in a network environment.

- Chapter 19, "Embracing Best Security Practices," discusses various common methods you can implement to make your Linux environment more secure.

- Chapter 20, "Analyzing System Properties and Remediation," explores the methods you have available to troubleshoot different types of Linux problems. This includes network issues, storage issues, and operating system issues.

- Chapter 21, "Optimizing Performance," discusses how Linux handles running applications and the tools you have available to control how those applications behave.

- Chapter 22, "Investigating User Issues," explores how to troubleshoot and fix common user-related issues, such as the inability to access specific files or directories on the system.

- Chapter 23, "Dealing with Linux Devices," walks you through the types of hardware devices Linux supports and how best to get them working on your Linux system.

- Chapter 24, "Troubleshooting Application and Hardware Issues," focuses on troubleshooting methods for solving storage, application, and network problems that may occur on your Linux system.

- Chapter 25, "Deploying Bash Scripts," discusses how to create your own scripts to automate common tasks in Linux.

- Chapter 26, "Automating Jobs," follows up on the topic of Bash scripts by showing you how to schedule your scripts to run at specific times of the day, week, month, or year.

- Chapter 27, "Controlling Versions with Git," explores the world of software version control and demonstrates how you can use the common Git version control software to manage your own applications and scripts.

- Chapter 28, "Understanding Cloud and Virtualization Concepts," walks you through the basics of what the cloud is and how to use Linux to create your own cloud computing environment.

- Chapter 29, "Inspecting Cloud and Virtualization Services," demonstrates how to implement cloud computing software in Linux.

- Chapter 30, "Orchestrating the Environment," discusses how you can use containers and orchestration engines in your Linux environment to control application development environments and deploy applications in controlled environments.

What's Included in the Book

We've included several study learning tools throughout the book:

- **Assessment Test.** At the end of this introduction is an assessment test that you can take to check your level of Linux skills. Take the test before you start reading the book; it will help you determine the areas in which you need extra help. The answers to the questions appear on a separate page after the last question in the test. Each answer includes an explanation and a note telling you the chapter in which the material appears.

- **Objective Map and Opening List of Objectives.** An objective map shows you where each of the Linux+ exam objectives is covered in this book. Also, each chapter opens with a note as to which objective it covers. Use these to see exactly where each of the exam topics is covered.

- **Exam Essentials.** At the end of each chapter, after the summary, is a list of exam essentials covered in the chapter. These are the key topics you should take from the chapter as you prepare for the exam.

- **Chapter Review Questions.** To test your knowledge as you progress through the book, there are review questions at the end of each chapter. As you finish each chapter, answer the review questions, and then check your answers against the answers provided in Appendix. You can then go back and reread any sections that detail the topics of the questions you missed.

> The assessment test, review questions, and other testing elements included in this book are not derived from the actual Linux+ exam questions, so don't memorize the answers to these questions and assume you will pass the exam. You should learn the underlying topics, as described in the text of the book. This will help you answer the questions provided with this book and pass the exam. Learning the underlying topics is also the approach that will serve you best in the workplace, the ultimate goal of the certification.

To get the most out of this book, you should read each chapter from start to finish and then check your memory and understanding with the chapter review questions. Even if you're already familiar with a topic, it will help to review the material in the chapter. In Linux there are often multiple ways to accomplish a task. Become familiar with the different methods to help with the Linux+ exam.

Interactive Online Learning Environment and Test Bank

The interactive online learning environment that accompanies the book provides a test bank with study tools to help you prepare for the certification exam and increase your chances of passing it the first time. The test bank includes the following:

- **Sample Tests.** All of the questions in this book are provided, including the assessment test, which you'll find at the end of this introduction, and the chapter tests that include the review questions at the end of each chapter. In addition, there is a practice exam.

Use these questions to test your knowledge of the study guide material. The online test bank runs on multiple devices.

- **Flashcards.** Questions are provided in digital flashcard format (a question followed by a single correct answer). You can use the flashcards to reinforce your learning and provide last-minute test prep before the exam.

- **Other Study Tools.** A glossary of key terms from this book and their definitions are available as a fully searchable PDF.

 Like all exams, the Linux+ certification from CompTIA is updated periodically and may eventually be retired or replaced. At some point after CompTIA is no longer offering this exam, the old editions of our books and online tools will be retired. If you have purchased this book after the exam was retired, or you are attempting to register in the Sybex online learning environment after the exam was retired, please know that we make no guarantees that this exam's online Sybex tools will be available once the exam is no longer available.

Go to www.wiley.com/go/sybextestprep to register and gain access to this interactive online learning environment and test bank with study tools.

Conventions Used in This Book

This book uses certain typographic styles in order to help you quickly identify important information and avoid confusion over the meaning of words such as onscreen prompts. In particular, look for the following styles:

- *Italicized text* indicates key terms that are described at length for the first time in a chapter. (Italics are also used for emphasis.)

- A `monospaced font` indicates the contents of configuration files, messages displayed at text-mode Linux shell prompts, filenames, text-mode command names, and Internet URLs.

- *`Italicized monospace text`* indicates a variable, or information that differs from one system or command run to another, such as the name of a file or a process ID number.

- **`Bold monospace text`** is information that you're to type into the computer, usually at a Linux shell prompt. This text can also be italicized to indicate that you should substitute an appropriate value for your system. (When isolated on their own lines, commands are preceded by nonbold monospace $ or # command prompts, denoting regular user or system administrator user, respectively.)

In addition to these text conventions, which can apply to individual words or entire paragraphs, a few conventions highlight segments of text, as in the following examples:

A note indicates information that's useful or interesting but that's somewhat peripheral to the main text. A note might be relevant to a small number of networks, for instance, or it may refer to an outdated feature.

 A tip provides information that can save you time or frustration and that may not be entirely obvious. A tip might describe how to get around a limitation or how to use a feature to perform an unusual task.

 Warnings describe potential pitfalls or dangers. If you fail to heed a warning, you may end up spending a lot of time recovering from a bug, or you may even end up restoring your entire system from scratch.

A sidebar is like a note but longer. The information in a sidebar is useful, but it doesn't fit into the main flow of the text.

A case study is a real-world scenario, a type of sidebar that describes a task or an example that's particularly grounded in the real world. This may be a situation we or somebody we know has encountered, or it may be advice on how to work around problems that are common in real-world, working Linux environments.

EXERCISE

An exercise is a procedure that you should try on your own computer to help you learn about the material in the chapter. Don't limit yourself to the procedures described in the exercises, though. Try other commands and procedures to truly learn about Linux.

The Exam Objectives

The exam objectives define the topics you can expect to find on the CompTIA Linux+ exam. The exam developers have determined that these topics are relevant to the skills necessary to become a competent Linux administrator and have based the exam questions on your ability to demonstrate your knowledge in these topics. The official CompTIA Linux+ XK0-005 exam topics are listed here, along with references to where you can find them covered in the book.

1.0 System Management

1.1 Summarize Linux fundamentals. (Chapters 5, 8, 11, and 23)

- Filesystem Hierarchy Standard (FHS)
- Basic boot process
- Kernel panic
- Device types in /dev
- Basic package compilation from source
- Storage concepts
- Listing hardware information

1.2 Given a scenario, manage files and directories. (Chapters 3, 4, and 12)

- File editing
- File compression, archiving, and backup
- File metadata
- Soft and hard links
- Copying files between systems
- File and directory operations

1.3 Given a scenario, configure and manage storage using the appropriate tools. (Chapter 11)

- Disk partitioning
- Mounting local and remote devices
- Filesystem management
- Monitoring storage space and disk usage
- Creating and modifying volumes using Logical Volume Manager (LVM)
- Inspecting RAID implementations
- Storage area network (SAN)/network-attached storage (NAS)
- Storage hardware

1.4 Given a scenario, configure and use the appropriate processes and services. (Chapters 6, 21, and 26)

- System services
- Scheduling services
- Process management

1.5 Given a scenario, use the appropriate networking tools or configuration files. (Chapters 7 and 20)

- Interface management
- Name resolution
- Network monitoring
- Remote networking tools

1.6 Given a scenario, build and install software. (Chapter 13)

- Package management
- Sandboxed applications
- System updates

1.7 Given a scenario, manage software configurations. (Chapters 9, 14, and 17)

- Updating configuration files
- Configure kernel options
- Configure common system services

2.0 Security

2.1 Summarize the purpose and use of security best practices in a Linux environment. (Chapters 16 and 19)

- Managing public key infrastructure (PKI) certificates
- Certificate use cases
- Authentication
- Linux hardening

2.2 Given a scenario, implement identity management (Chapters 10 and 16)

- Account creation and deletion
- Account management

2.3 Given a scenario, implement and configure firewalls. (Chapter 18)

- Firewall use cases
- Common firewall technologies
- Key firewall features

2.4 Given a scenario, configure and execute remote connectivity for system management. (Chapter 16)

- SSH
- Executing commands as another user

2.5 Given a scenario, apply the appropriate access controls. (Chapter 15)

- File permissions
- Security-enhanced Linux (SELinux)
- AppArmor
- Command-line utilities

3.0 Scripting, Containers, and Automation

3.1 Given a scenario, create simple shell scripts to automate common tasks. (Chapters 4 and 25)

- Shell script elements
- Standard stream redirection
- Common script utilities
- Environment variables

3.2 Given a scenario, perform basic container operations. (Chapter 28)

- Container management
- Container image operations

3.3 Given a scenario, perform basic version control using Git. (Chapter 27)

- Common Git uses
- Git commands

3.4 Summarize common infrastructure as code technologies. (Chapters 27 and 30)

- File formats
- Utilities
- Continuous integration/continuous deployment (CI/CD)
- Advanced Git topics

3.5 Summarize container, cloud, and orchestration concepts. (Chapters 28, 29, and 30)

- Kubernetes benefits and application use cases
- Single-node, multicontainer use cases
- Container persistent storage
- Container networks
- Service mesh
- Bootstrapping
- Container registries

4.0 Troubleshooting

4.1 Given a scenario, analyze and troubleshoot storage issues. (Chapters 20 and 24)

- High latency
- Low throughput
- Input/output operations per second (IOPS) scenarios
- Capacity issues
- Filesystem issues
- I/O scheduler
- Device issues
- Mount options problems

4.2 Given a scenario, analyze and troubleshoot network resource issues. (Chapters 7 and 20)

- Network configuration issues
- Firewall issues
- Interface errors
- Bandwidth limitations
- Name resolution issues
- Testing remote systems

4.3 Given a scenario, analyze and troubleshoot central processing unit (CPU) and memory issues. (Chapters 7, 20, 21, and 24)

- Runaway processes
- Zombie processes
- High CPU utilization
- High load average
- High run queues
- CPU times
- CPU process priorities
- Memory exhaustion
- Out of memory (OOM)
- Swapping
- Hardware

4.4 Given a scenario, analyze and troubleshoot user access and file permissions. (Chapter 22)

- User login issues
- User file access issues
- Password issues
- Privilege escalation
- Quota issues

4.5 Given a scenario, use systemd to diagnose and resolve common problems with a Linux system. (Chapter 6)

- Unit files
- Common systemd problems

How to Contact the Publisher

If you believe you've found a mistake in this book, please bring it to our attention. At John Wiley & Sons, we understand how important it is to provide our customers with accurate content, but even with our best efforts an error may occur.

In order to submit your possible errata, please email it to our Customer Service Team at wileysupport@wiley.com with the subject line "Possible Book Errata Submission."

Assessment Test

1. What software package allows a Linux server to share folders and printers with Windows and Mac clients?

    A. Postfix

    B. Apache

    C. Samba

    D. Kerberos

    E. Docker

2. Which software package allows developers to deploy applications using the exact same environment in which they were developed?

    A. Postfix

    B. Apache

    C. Samba

    D. Kerberos

    E. Docker

3. The `cat -n File.txt` command is entered at the command line. What will be the result?

    A. The text file `File.txt` will be displayed.

    B. The text file `File.txt` will be displayed along with any special hidden characters in the file.

    C. The text file `File.txt` will be displayed along with any special symbols representing end-of-line characters.

    D. The text file `File.txt` will be displayed along with line numbers.

    E. The text file `File.txt` will be displayed in reverse order.

4. Which of the following are stream editors? (Choose all that apply.)

    A. `vim`

    B. `sed`

    C. `awk`

    D. `gawk`

    E. `nano`

5. Which command in GRUB2 defines the location of the /boot folder to the first partition on the first hard drive on the system?

    A. `set root=hd(0,1)`

    B. `set root=hd(1,0)`

    C. `set root=hd(1,1)`

    D. `set root=hd(0,0)`

    E. `set root=first`

6. If you see read or write errors appear in the system log, what tool should you use to correct any bad sections of the hard drive?

    A. `mount`

    B. `unmount`

    C. `fsck`

    D. `dmesg`

    E. `mkinitrd`

7. The `init` program is started on a Linux system and has a process ID number. What typically is that process's ID number?

    A. 0

    B. 1

    C. 2

    D. 10

    E. Unknown

8. You need to determine the default target of a systemd system. Which of the following commands should you use?

    A. `grep initdefault /etc/inittab`

    B. `runlevel`

    C. `systemctl is-enabled`

    D. `systemd get-target`

    E. `systemctl get-default`

9. The Cinnamon desktop environment uses which window manager?

    A. Mutter

    B. Muffin

    C. Nemo

    D. Dolphin

    E. LightDM

10. Your X11 session has become hung. What keystrokes do you use to restart the session?

    A. Ctrl+C

    B. Ctrl+Z

    C. Ctrl+Q

    D. Ctrl+Alt+Delete

    E. Ctrl+Alt+Backspace

11. What folder contains the time zone template files in Linux?

A. /etc/timezone

B. /etc/localtime

C. /usr/share/zoneinfo

D. /usr/share/timezone

E. /usr/share/localtime

12. What systemd command allows you to view and change the time, date, and time zone?

A. timedatectl

B. localectl

C. date

D. time

E. locale

13. Which of the following files contain user account creation directives used by the useradd command? (Choose all that apply.)

A. The /etc/default/useradd file

B. The /etc/useradd file

C. The /etc/adduser.conf file

D. The /etc/login.defs file

E. The /etc/login.def file

14. You need to display the various quotas on all your filesystems employing quota limits. Which of the following commands should you use?

A. edquota -t

B. quotaon -a

C. quotacheck -cu

D. quotacheck -cg

E. repquota -a

15. What drive and partition does the raw device file /dev/sdb1 reference?

A. The first partition on the second SCSI storage device

B. The second partition on the first SCSI storage device

C. The first partition on the second PATA storage device

D. The second partition on the first PATA storage device

E. The second partition on the second SATA storage device

16. What tool creates a logical volume from multiple physical partitions?

   A. mkfs

   B. pvcreate

   C. lvcreate

   D. fdisk

   E. vgcreate

17. Which of the following can be used as backup utilities? (Choose all that apply.)

   A. The gzip utility

   B. The zip utility

   C. The tar utility

   D. The rsync utility

   E. The dd utility

18. A system administrator has created a backup archive and transferred the file to another system across the network. Which utilities can be used to check the archive files integrity? (Choose all that apply.)

   A. The rsync utility

   B. The md5sum utility

   C. The sftp utility

   D. The scp utility

   E. The sha512sum utility

19. What tool should you use to install a DEB package file?

   A. dpkg

   B. tar

   C. gcc

   D. rpm

   E. gzip

20. What tool do you use to install an RPM package file?

   A. dpkg

   B. tar

   C. gcc

   D. rpm

   E. gzip

21. The `lsmod` utility provides the same information as what other utility or file(s)?

    A. The `modinfo` utility

    B. The `/proc/modules` file

    C. The `/etc/modules.conf` file

    D. The `insmod` utility

    E. The `/run/modprobe.d/*.conf` files

22. Which utility should be used to remove a module along with any dependent modules?

    A. The `rmmod` utility

    B. The `modinfo` utility

    C. The `cut` utility

    D. The `depmod` utility

    E. The `modprobe` utility

23. What special bit should you set to prevent users from deleting shared files created by someone else?

    A. SUID

    B. GUID

    C. Sticky bit

    D. Read

    E. Write

24. What command can you use to change the owner assigned to a file?

    A. `chmod`

    B. `chown`

    C. `chage`

    D. `ulimit`

    E. `chgrp`

25. Which directory contains the various PAM configuration files?

    A. The `/etc/pam/` directory

    B. The `/etc/pam_modules/` directory

    C. The `/etc/modules/` directory

    D. The `/etc/pam.d/` directory

    E. The `/etc/pam_modules.d/` directory

26. Which of the following can override the settings in the `~/.ssh/config` file?

    A. The settings in the `/etc/ssh/ssh_config` file.

    B. The `ssh` utility's command-line options.

    C. You cannot override the settings in this file.

    D. The settings in the `/etc/ssh/sshd_config` file.

    E. The settings in the `sshd` daemon's configuration file.

27. What command can you use to display new entries in a log file in real time as they occur?
    A. head
    B. tail
    C. tail -f
    D. head -f
    E. vi

28. What command do you use to display entries in the systemd-journald journal?
    A. journalctl
    B. syslogd
    C. klogd
    D. systemd-journald
    E. vi

29. The /etc/services file may be used by firewalls for what purpose?
    A. To designate what remote services to block
    B. To store their ACL rules
    C. To map a service name to a port and protocol
    D. To determine if the port can be accessed
    E. To designate what local services can send out packets

30. Which of the following is true about netfilter? (Choose all that apply.)
    A. It is used by firewalld.
    B. It is used by UFW.
    C. It provides code hooks into the Linux kernel for firewall technologies to use.
    D. It is used by iptables.
    E. It provides firewall services without the need for other applications.

31. Which of the following is a measurement of the maximum amount of data that can be trans-
    ferred over a particular network segment?
    A. Bandwidth
    B. Throughput
    C. Saturation
    D. Latency
    E. Routing

32. Which tool will allow you to view disk I/O specific to swapping?
    A. ipcs -m
    B. cat /proc/meminfo
    C. free
    D. swapon -s
    E. vmstat

33. What command-line command allows you to view the applications currently running on the Linux system?

   A. lsof

   B. kill

   C. ps

   D. w

   E. nice

34. What command-line commands allow you to send process signals to running applications? (Choose two.)

   A. renice

   B. pkill

   C. nice

   D. kill

   E. pgrep

35. Annika puts the file line PS1="My Prompt: " into her account's $HOME/.bash_profile file. This setting changes her prompt the next time she logs into the system. However, when she starts a subshell, it is not working properly. What does Annika need to do to fix this issue?

   A. Add the file line to the $HOME/.profile file instead.

   B. Nothing. A user's prompt cannot be changed in a subshell.

   C. Add export prior to PS1 on the same line in the file.

   D. Change her default shell to /bin/dash for this to work.

   E. Change the last field in her password record to /sbin/false.

36. A user, who is not the owner or a group member of a particular directory, attempts to use the ls command on the directory and gets a permission error. What does this mean?

   A. The directory does not have display (d) set for other permissions.

   B. The directory does not have execute (x) set for other permissions.

   C. The directory does not have write (w) set for other permissions.

   D. The directory does not have list (l) set for other permissions.

   E. The directory does not have read (r) set for other permissions.

37. Which directories contain dynamic files that display kernel and system information? (Choose two.)

   A. /dev

   B. /proc

   C. /etc

   D. /sys

   E. /dev/mapper

38. What directory contains configuration information for the X Windows System in Linux?

   A. /dev

   B. /proc

   C. /etc/X11

   D. /sys

   E. /proc/interrupts

39. How would you fix a "mount point does not exist" problem?

   A. Employ the fsck utility to fix the bad disk sector.

   B. Employ the badblocks utility to fix the bad disk sector.

   C. Use super user privileges, if needed, and create the directory via the vgchange command.

   D. Use super user privileges, if needed, and create the directory via the mkdir command.

   E. Use super user privileges, if needed, and create the directory via the mountpoint command.

40. Peter is trying to complete his network application, Spider, but is running into a problem with accessing a remote server's files and there are no network problems occurring at this time. He thinks it has something to do with the remote server's ACLs being too restrictive. You need to investigate this issue. Which of the following might you use for troubleshooting this problem? (Choose all that apply.)

   A. The firewall-cmd command

   B. The ufw command

   C. The iptables command

   D. The getacl command

   E. The setacl command

41. Which Bash shell script command allows you to iterate through a series of data until the data is complete?

   A. if

   B. case

   C. for

   D. exit

   E. $()

42. Which environment variable allows you to retrieve the numeric user ID value for the user account running a shell script?

   A. $USER

   B. $UID

   C. $BASH

   D. $HOME

   E. $1

43. What does placing an ampersand sign (&) after a command on the command line do?

    A. Disconnects the command from the console session

    B. Schedules the command to run later

    C. Runs the command in background mode

    D. Redirects the output to another command

    E. Redirects the output to a file

44. When will the cron table entry 0 0 1 * * myscript run the specified command?

    A. At 1 a.m. every day

    B. At midnight on the first day of every month

    C. At midnight on the first day of every week

    D. At 1 p.m. every day

    E. At midnight every day

45. Which of the following packages will provide you with the utilities to set up Git VCS on a system?

    A. git-vcs

    B. GitHub

    C. gitlab

    D. Bitbucket

    E. git

46. If you do not tack on the -m option with an argument to the git commit command, what will happen?

    A. The command will throw an error message and fail.

    B. The commit will take place, but no tracking will occur.

    C. You are placed in an editor for the COMMIT_EDITMSG file.

    D. Your commit will fail, and the file is removed from the index.

    E. Nothing. This is an optional switch.

47. At a virtualization conference, you overhear someone talking about using blobs on their cloud-based virtualization service. Which virtualization service are they using?

    A. Amazon Web Services

    B. KVM

    C. Digital Ocean

    D. GitHub

    E. Microsoft Azure

48. What is a networking method for controlling and managing network communications via software that consists of a controller program as well as two APIs?

   A. Thick provisioning

   B. Thin provisioning

   C. SDN

   D. NAT

   E. VLAN

49. Your company decides it needs an orchestration system (also called an engine). Which of the following is one you could choose? (Choose all that apply.)

   A. Mesos

   B. Kubernetes

   C. Splunk

   D. Swarm

   E. AWS

50. Which of the following is used in container orchestration? (Choose all that apply.)

   A. Automated configuration management

   B. Self-healing

   C. DevOps

   D. Agentless monitoring

   E. Build automation

51. What type of cloud service provides the full application environment so that everyone on the Internet can run it?

   A. PaaS

   B. Private

   C. Public

   D. SaaS

   E. Hybrid

52. What type of hypervisor is the Oracle VirtualBox application?

   A. PaaS

   B. SaaS

   C. Type II

   D. Type I

   E. Private

53. What file should you place console and terminal filenames in to prevent users from logging into the Linux system as the root user account from those locations?

   A. /etc/cron.deny

   B. /etc/hosts.deny

   C. /etc/securetty

   D. /etc/login.warn

   E. /etc/motd

54. What Linux program logs user file and directory access?

   A. chroot

   B. LUKS

   C. auditd

   D. klist

   E. kinit

55. You've moved your present working directory to a new location in the Linux virtual directory structure and need to go back to the previous directory where you were just located. Which command should you employ?

   A. cd

   B. exit

   C. cd ~

   D. cd -

   E. return

56. To copy a directory with the cp command, which option do you need to use?

   A. -i

   B. -R

   C. -v

   D. -u

   E. -f

Answers to Assessment Test

1. C. The Samba software package allows Linux servers and clients to communicate with Windows and Mac clients or servers using the Microsoft SMB protocol, so option C is correct. The Postfix software package provides email service for Linux servers, not Windows services, so option A is incorrect. The Apache package is a web server; it doesn't allow Linux servers to share folders with Windows and Mac clients, so option B is incorrect. The Kerberos package provides authentication services; it does not allow Linux servers to share folders, so option D is incorrect. The Docker package provides container services for deploying applications on a Linux server; it does not allow the Linux server to share folders with Windows or Mac clients, so option E is incorrect.

2. E. The Docker package provides a method for developers to capture the entire development environment for an application and deploy it into a production environment as a container, so option E is correct. The Postfix package provides email services for a Linux server; it doesn't deploy applications, so option A is incorrect. The Apache package provides web server services for a Linux server; it doesn't deploy application environments, so option B is incorrect. The Samba package allows a Linux server to interact in a Windows network with Windows clients and servers; it does not provide an environment for deploying applications, so option C is incorrect. The Kerberos package provides authentication services for Linux servers; it doesn't deploy applications, so option D is incorrect.

3. D. The `cat -n File.txt` command will display the `File.txt` text file along with line numbers. Therefore, option D is correct. The command in option A will simply display the `File.txt` file. Thus, option A is a wrong answer. To see any special hidden characters within the `File.txt` file, you would need to enter the command `cat -A File.txt`. Therefore, option B is an incorrect choice. End-of-line characters need a different `cat` command option, such as the `-E` switch. Therefore, option C is a wrong choice. The `cat` command does not have a switch that will allow a text file's contents to be displayed in reverse order. Thus, option E is an incorrect choice.

4. B, C, D. The `sed`, `awk`, and `gawk` utilities are all stream editors. Therefore, options B, C, and D are correct. Both `vim` and `nano` are considered to be text editors. Therefore, options A and E are incorrect choices.

5. A. GRUB2 identifies the hard drives starting at 0, but the partitions start at 1, so the first partition on the first hard drive would be 0,1 and option A is correct. Option B (1,0) defines the second hard drive and an incorrect partition number, so it is incorrect. Option C defines the first partition but the second hard drive, so it is incorrect. Option D defines the first hard drive but an incorrect partition, so it is incorrect. Option E uses the keyword `first`, which is not recognized by GRUB2, so it is incorrect.

6. C. The `fsck` program can perform a filesystem check and repair multiple types of filesystems on partitions, so option C is correct. The `mount` program is used to append a partition to a virtual directory; it can't correct a partition that contains errors, so option A is incorrect. The `unmount` command removes a partition from the virtual directory, so option B is incorrect. Option D (the `dmesg` command) displays boot messages, and option E (the `mkinitrd` command) creates an initrd RAM disk, so both are incorrect.

7. B. The `init` program is typically started immediately after the Linux system has traversed the boot process, and it has a process ID (PID) number of 1. Therefore, option B is the correct answer. The Linux kernel has the 0 PID number, and thus, option A is a wrong answer. Options C, D, and E are also incorrect choices.

8. E. The `systemctl get-default` command will display a systemd system's default target. Therefore, option E is the correct answer. The `grep initdefault /etc/inittab` command will extract the default runlevel for a SysV init system. Thus, option A is a wrong answer. The `runlevel` command will display a SysV init system's previous and current runlevel. Therefore, option B is an incorrect answer. The `systemctl is-enabled` command shows whether or not a particular service, whose name is passed as a command argument, is configured to start at system boot. Thus, option C is a wrong choice. Option D is a made-up command and therefore the wrong answer.

9. B. The Cinnamon desktop environment uses the Muffin window manager. Therefore, option B is the correct answer. Mutter is the window manager for the GNOME Shell desktop environment, though Muffin did fork from that project. Thus, option A is a wrong answer. Nemo is the file manager for Cinnamon, and therefore, option C is a wrong choice. Dolphin is the file manager for the KDE Plasma desktop environment. Thus, option D is a wrong choice. LightDM is the display manager for Cinnamon, and therefore, option E is also an incorrect choice.

10. E. The Ctrl+Alt+Backspace will kill your X11 session and then restart it, putting you at the login screen (display manager.) Therefore, option E is the correct answer. The Ctrl+C combination sends an interrupt signal but does not restart an X11 session. Thus, option A is a wrong answer. The Ctrl+Z keystroke combination sends a stop signal, but it will not restart the X11 session. Therefore, option B is also an incorrect answer. The Ctrl+Q combination will release a terminal that has been paused by Ctrl+S. However, it does not restart an X11 session, so it too is a wrong choice. The Ctrl+Alt+Delete keystroke combination can be set to do a number of tasks, depending on your desktop environment. In some cases, it brings up a shutdown, logout, or reboot menu. However, it does not restart the X11 session, so option D is an incorrect choice.

11. C. Both Debian-based and Red Hat–based Linux distributions store the time zone template files in the `/usr/share/zoneinfo` folder, so option C is correct. The `/etc/timezone` and `/etc/localtime` files contain the current time zone file for Debian- and Red Hat–based systems, not the time zone template files, so options A and B are incorrect. The `/usr/share/timezone` and `/usr/share/localtime` folders don't exist in either Debian-based or Red Hat–based Linux distributions, so options D and E are also incorrect.

12. A. The `timedatectl` program is part of the systemd package and allows you to both view and change the current time, date, and time zone for the Linux system, so option A is correct. The `localectl` program is also part of the systemd package, but it handles localization information and not time and date information, so option B is incorrect. The `date` command allows you to view and change the time and date but not the time zone setting, so option C is incorrect. The `time` command displays the elapsed CPU time used by an application, not the current time, date, and time zone, so option D is incorrect. The `locale` command allows you to view the localization settings for the Linux system, not the time, date, or time zone, so option E is also incorrect.

13. A, D. The /etc/default/useradd file and /etc/login.defs file are files that contain user account creation directives used by the useradd command. Therefore, options A and D are the correct answers. Option B's /etc/useradd file is a made-up file name, and thus option B is a wrong choice. The /etc/adduser.conf file is only on Linux distributions that use the adduser utility to create accounts. Thus, option C is an incorrect answer. The /etc/login.def file is a made-up file name, and thus option E is also an incorrect choice.

14. E. The repquota -a command will display the various quotas on all your filesystems employing quota limits. Therefore, option E is the correct answer. The edquota -t command will edit quota grace periods for the system. Therefore, option A is a wrong answer. The quotaon -a command will automatically turn on quotas for all mounted non-NFS filesystems in the /etc/fstab file, but it does not display filesystems' quotas. Thus, option B is an incorrect choice. The quotacheck utility creates either the aquota.group file, if the -cg options are used, or the aquota.user file, if the -cu switches are used, or both files if -cug is employed. However, it does nothing for displaying filesystems' quotas. Thus, options C and D are incorrect answers.

15. A. Option A is the correct answer because Linux uses the /dev/sdxx format for SCSI and SATA raw devices. The device is represented by a letter, starting with a, and the partition is represented by a number, starting at 1. So /dev/sdb1 references the first partition on the second SCSI or SATA device. Option B would be referenced by the /dev/sda2 file, so it is incorrect. Option C would be referenced by the /dev/hdb1 file, so it is incorrect. Option D would be referenced by /dev/hda2, so option D is incorrect, and option E would be referenced by /dev/sdb2, so it is incorrect.

16. C. The lvcreate program creates a logical volume from multiple partitions that you can use as a single logical device to build a file system and mount it to the virtual directory, so option C is correct. The mkfs program creates a filesystem on a partition but doesn't create a logical volume, so option A is incorrect. The pvcreate program identifies a physical volume from a partition but doesn't create the logical volume, so option B is incorrect. The fdisk program creates and modifies physical partitions, not logical volumes, so option D is incorrect. The vgcreate program creates a volume group for grouping physical partitions but doesn't create the logical volume, so option E is incorrect.

17. B, C, D, E. The zip, tar, rsync, and dd utilities all can be used to create data backups. Therefore, options B, C, D, and E are correct answers. The gzip utility can be used after a backup is created or employed through tar options to compress a backup, so option A is the only wrong choice.

18. B, E. Both the md5sum and sha512sum utilities produce hashes on files, which can be compared to determine if file corruption occurred, such as when transferring a file over the network. Therefore, options B and E are the correct answers. The utilities mentioned in options A, C, and D will allow you to securely transfer files but not check a file's integrity. Therefore, options A, C, and D are incorrect choices.

19. A. The dpkg program is used for installing and removing Debian-based packages that use the DEB file format, so option A is correct. The tar program is used for creating and extracting tape archive formatted files that use the .tar file extension, so option B is incorrect. The gcc program is used for compiling source code into executable programs, so option

C is incorrect. The rpm program is used for installing and removing Red Hat–based packages that use the RPM file format, so option D is incorrect. The gzip program compresses files and adds the .gz file extension to them, so option E is incorrect.

20. D. The rpm program is used for installing and removing Red Hat–based packages that use the RPM file format, so option D is correct. The dpkg program is used for installing and removing Debian-based packages that use the DEB file format, so option A is incorrect. The tar program is used for creating and extracting tape archive formatted files that use the .tar file extension, so option B is incorrect. The gcc program is used for compiling source code into executable programs, so option C is incorrect. The gzip program compresses files and adds the .gz file extension to them, so option E is incorrect.

21. B. The /proc/modules file has the same information that is displayed by the lsmod utility (though the lsmod utility formats it much nicer). Therefore, option B is the correct answer. The modinfo utility provides detailed module data, whereas lsmod shows only brief information. Thus, option A is a wrong answer. The /etc/modules.conf file is a kernel module configuration file, and it does not provide the same information as the lsmod utility. Therefore, option C is also an incorrect answer. The insmod command is used to dynamically load kernel modules, and thus it is a wrong answer. The /run/modprobe.d/*.conf files are kernel module configuration files, and they do not provide the same information as the lsmod utility. Therefore, option E is also an incorrect choice.

22. E. The modprobe utility along with its -r switch is the utility to employ for removing (unloading) a kernel module along with any of its dependencies. Therefore, option E is the correct answer. The rmmod utility will remove a kernel module but not any of its dependencies. Thus, option A is a wrong answer. The modinfo command does not unload kernel modules but instead displays detailed information concerning a specified module. Therefore, option B is an incorrect choice. The cut utility is used to filter text files and display the filtered text to STDOUT. It is not involved in kernel module removal, and thus option C is a wrong choice. The depmod utility is used to create a list of modules and their dependencies, but it is not used to remove modules. Therefore, option D is an incorrect choice.

23. C. The sticky bit assigned to a directory restricts all of the files in that directory so that only the file owner can delete the file, even if a user account is in the group that has write permissions, so option C is correct. The SUID bit allows a standard user to run an application with the file owner permissions but doesn't block users from deleting shared files, so option A is incorrect. The GUID bit is used on a directory to ensure that all files created in the directory have the same group as the directory, but it doesn't prevent users in that group from deleting files, so option B is incorrect. The Read and Write standard permission bits control access to read to a file or write to a file, but they don't block users from deleting a file, so options D and E are both incorrect.

24. B. The chown command allows you to set both the owner and group assigned to a file, so option B is correct. The chmod command allows you to change the permissions for the file, but not the owner of the file, so option A is incorrect. The chage command manages password aging for user accounts, not owners of files, so option C is incorrect. The ulimit command allows the administrator to restrict system resources assigned to users but doesn't assign users to files, so option D is incorrect. The chgrp command allows you to change the group assigned to a file but not the owner, so option E is incorrect.

25. D. The /etc/pam.d/ directory contains the various PAM configuration files. Therefore, option D is the correct answer. The other directory names are made up. Thus, options A, B, C, and E are incorrect answers.

26. B. The settings within the ~/.ssh/config file can be overridden by various ssh utility options provided at the command line. Therefore, option B is the correct answer. The settings in the /etc/ssh/ssh_config file can be overridden by both the settings in the ~/.ssh/ config file and the ssh utility's command-line options, so option A is a wrong answer. The /etc/ssh/sshd_config file is the sshd daemon's configuration file, and it deals with providing the SSH services, not in setting the configuration for the SSH client. Therefore, both options D and E are incorrect choices.

27. C. The -f option of the tail command displays new additions to a file in real time, so option C is correct. The head and tail commands by themselves just list the existing entries in a file, so options A and B are incorrect. The head command doesn't support the -f option, so option D is incorrect. The vi editor also only displays existing data in a file and not newly added data, so option E is incorrect.

28. A. The systemd-journald application uses its own binary file format for the journal file and requires the journalctl file to read it, so option A is correct. The syslogd and klogd applications are syslog loggers and not able to read the systemd-journald journal file, so options B and C are incorrect. The systemd-journald application itself only adds event messages to the journal and doesn't read it, so option D is incorrect. Since the journal file is in binary format, you can't read it using standard text editor programs, so option E is incorrect.

29. C. The /etc/services file may be used by a firewall, such as UFW, to map a particular service name to its port and protocol. Thus, option C is the correct answer. The file is not used to designate remote services to block or store a firewall's ACL rules. Therefore, options A and B are wrong answers. The Linux firewall applications do not use the /etc/ services file to determine if a port can be accessed or what local services can send out packets. Thus, options D and E are incorrect choices.

30. A, B, C, D. Used by firewalld, UFW, and iptables, netfilter provides code hooks into the Linux kernel for firewall technologies to use in order to implement fully functional firewall capabilities. Therefore, options A, B, C, and D are all correct answers. Unfortunately, netfilter cannot provide firewall services on its own. Thus, option E is the only incorrect choice.

31. A. Bandwidth is a measurement of the maximum data amount that can be transferred between two network points over a period of time. Therefore, option A is the correct answer. Throughput is a measurement of the actual data amount that is transferred between two network points, and thus option B is a wrong answer. Saturation occurs when network traffic exceeds capacity, but it is not a measurement. Thus, option C is an incorrect answer. Latency is the time between a source sending a packet and the packet's destination receiving it. Therefore, option D is a wrong choice. Routing is the process of forwarding IP packets to the appropriate destination. Thus, option E is also an incorrect answer.

32. E. The vmstat utility provides a lot of memory statistics, including disk I/O specific to swapping. Therefore, option E is the correct answer. The ipcs -m command allows you to see shared memory segments instead of disk I/O specific to swapping. Thus, option A is the wrong answer. The cat /proc/meminfo command displays detailed information concerning a system's RAM. Therefore, option B is an incorrect answer. The free command shows memory items such as free memory, used memory, and buffer/cache usage. Thus, option C is a wrong choice. The swapon -s command displays swap space elements such as type, name, and priority. Therefore, option D is also an incorrect choice.

33. C. The ps command with the proper options displays the active applications running on the Linux system, so option C is correct. The lsof command displays the files currently open by applications but not all of the running applications, so option A is incorrect. The kill command stops a running application based on its process ID; it doesn't display all of the running applications, so option B is incorrect. The w command displays all of the current users on the system but not all of the running applications, so option D is incorrect. The nice command allows you to start a new application with a specified priority level, but it doesn't allow you to display the currently running applications, so option E is incorrect.

34. B, D. The pkill and kill commands allow you to send Linux process signals to running applications, so options B and D are correct. The renice command allows you to change the priority level of a running application but not send process signals to it, so option A is incorrect. The nice command allows you to start an application with a specified priority level but not send process signals to applications that are already running, so option C is incorrect. The pgrep command allows you to display running applications, but it doesn't send process signals to them, so option E is incorrect.

35. C. The problem is directly related to a missing export command prior to the PS1="My Prompt: " in Annika's environment file. When this environment variable is exported and when it is set, it will be set in any started subshells. Thus, option C is the correct answer. Since Annika's environment file exists, the $HOME/.profile file is not used. Thus, option A is a wrong answer. A user prompt can be changed in a subshell, so option B is also an incorrect answer. Changing Annika's default shell will not fix this issue, so option D is a wrong choice. If Annika changes the last field in her password record to /sbin/false, she will no longer be able to log into the system using her account. Therefore, option E is an incorrect choice.

36. E. In order for a user to list files in a directory, the directory needs to have read (r) set for other permissions if the user is not the directory's owner or does not belong to the directory's set group. Therefore, option E is the correct answer. There is no display (d) permission setting, so option A is a wrong answer. The execute (x) permission allows a user to change their present working directory to that directory as long as all the parent directories also have that permission set. Thus, option B is a wrong choice. The write (w) permission allows a user to create files within that directory, so option C is an incorrect answer. There is no list (l) permission setting, so option D is also an incorrect choice.

37. B, D. The Linux kernel uses the /proc and /sys directories to produce dynamic files that contain information about the kernel and system, so options B and D are correct. The /dev folder contains files for communicating with devices, not kernel and system information, so option A is incorrect. The /etc directory contains application configuration files, not files created by the kernel for displaying kernel and system information, so option C is incorrect. The /dev/mapper directory is used for virtual files mapped to physical device files for LVM and LUKS, not kernel information, so option E is incorrect.

38. C. The /etc/X11 directory contains configuration files used by both the X.org and XFree86 applications for controlling the X Windows graphical environment on the Linux system, so option C is correct. The /dev directory contains device files used to send and receive data from devices, not the X Windows configuration files, so option A is incorrect. The kernel uses the /proc and /sys directories to create dynamic files that show kernel and system information, not contain X Windows configuration files, so options B and D are incorrect. The /proc/interrupts file contains information about hardware interrupts currently used by hardware devices on the system, not X Windows configuration files, so option E is incorrect.

39. D. This problem concerns a missing directory. Therefore, to fix it, use super user privileges, if needed, and create the directory via the mkdir command. Thus, option D is the correct answer. The problem does not concern a bad disk sector (and you cannot fix bad disk sectors with the badblocks utility), so options A and B are wrong answers. You would employ the vgchange command for a missing volume in a logical volume but not a missing directory. Therefore, option C is an incorrect answer. While the mountpoint command does allow you to see if a particular directory is a mount point, it does not allow you to create a missing directory. Thus, option E is an incorrect choice as well.

40. A, B, C. Since the problem involves a remote server, you need to investigate the firewall access control lists (ACLs) on both the local and remote systems. Therefore, depending on the firewall employed, you can use the firewall-cmd, ufw, or iptables command in the troubleshooting process. Thus, options A, B, and C are the correct answers. The getacl and setacl commands deal with file inheritance issues, and therefore options D and E are incorrect choices.

41. C. The for command allows you to iterate through a series of data one by one until the data set is exhausted, so option C is correct. The if and case statements perform a single test on an object to determine if a block of commands should be run; they don't iterate through data, so options A and B are incorrect. The exit command stops the shell script and exits to the parent shell, so option D is incorrect. The $() command redirects the output of a command to a variable in the shell script, so option E is incorrect.

42. B. The $UID environment variable contains the numeric user ID value of the user account running the shell script, so option B is correct. The $USER environment variable contains the text user name of the user account running the shell script, not the numerical user ID value, so option A is incorrect. The $BASH environment variable contains the path to the executable Bash shell, so option C is incorrect. The $HOME environment variable contains the location of the home directory of the user account running the shell, so option D is incorrect. The $1 positional variable contains the first parameter listed on the command-line command when the shell script was run, so option E is incorrect.

43. C. The ampersand sign (&) tells the shell to run the specified command in background mode in the console session, so option C is correct. The nohup command is used to disconnect the command from the console session, so option A is incorrect. The at command is used to schedule a command to run later, so option B is incorrect. The pipe symbol (|) redirects the output from the command to another command, so option D is incorrect. The greater-than symbol (>) redirects the output from the command to a file, so option E is incorrect.

44. B. The cron table format specifies the times to run the script by minute, hour, day of month, month, and day of week. Thus the format 0 0 1 * * will run the command at 00:00 (midnight) on the first day of the month for every month. That makes option B correct, and options A, C, D, and E incorrect.

45. E. This git package provides utilities to set up Git VCS on a system, so option E is the correct answer. The git-vcs package is made up, so option A is a wrong answer. The GitHub, gitlab, and Bitbucket packages are also made up, but they have similar names as cloud-based remote repositories used with Git (GitHub, GitLab, BitBucket). Therefore, options B, C, and D are also incorrect choices.

46. C. If the -m option with an argument is not tacked onto the git commit command, you are placed into the vim editor to edit the COMMIT_EDITMSG file. Thus, option C is the correct answer. All the other options are made up and therefore incorrect.

47. E. The Microsoft Azure cloud-based virtualization service provides blobs, which are large unstructured data storage that is offered over the Internet and can be manipulated with .NET code. Therefore, option E is the correct answer. Amazon Web Services (AWS) and Digital Ocean are both cloud-based virtualization services, but they do not employ storage called blob, so options A and C are wrong answers. KVM is a hypervisor, not a cloud-based virtualization service, so option B is an incorrect answer. GitHub is a cloud-based remote repository used in version control, so option D is also an incorrect choice.

48. C. A software-defined network (SDN) is a networking method for controlling and managing network communications via software that consists of a controller program as well as two APIs. Thus, option C is the correct answer. Thick provisioning and thin provisioning refer to virtual storage configurations, not networking methods, so options A and B are wrong answers. Network address translation (NAT) is a virtualization network adapter configuration, which operates similarly to a NAT router in a network. Therefore, option D is an incorrect answer. A VLAN is a virtual (logical) LAN configuration, and thus, option E is an incorrect choice as well.

49. B, D. Only Kubernetes and Swarm are orchestration systems. Therefore, options B and D are correct answers. Mesos needs Marathon to implement an orchestration engine, so option A is a wrong answer. Splunk can be used as a monitoring tool in an orchestrated environment, but it is not an orchestration system, so option D is also a wrong choice. Amazon Web Services (AWS) is cloud-based virtualization services on which you can use orchestration tools, but it is not an orchestration engine. Thus, option E is also an incorrect choice.

50. A, B, D, E. The concepts listed in options A, B, D, and E are all used in container orchestration. While DevOps benefits from container orchestration and often employs it, it is not used within container orchestration. Thus, option C is an incorrect choice.

51. D. The software-as-a-service (SaaS) cloud service type provides full applications, allowing anyone to connect to your application, so option D is correct. The platform-as-a-service (PaaS) cloud service type doesn't include an application; you must provide it yourself, so option A is incorrect. Private, public, and hybrid are all methods of implementing cloud services, not cloud service types, so options B, C, and E are all incorrect.

52. C. The Oracle VirtualBox hypervisor installs on top of a host operating system, making it a Type II hypervisor, so option C is correct. PaaS and SaaS are types of cloud services, not hypervisors, so options A and B are incorrect. A private cloud service is a method for implementing cloud services in an internal network, not a type of hypervisor, so option E is incorrect.

53. C. The `/etc/securetty` file provides a list of locations from which users can't log in using the root user account, so option C is correct. The `/etc/cron.deny` file prevents users from scheduling jobs, not logging in as the root user account, so option A is incorrect. The `/etc/hosts.deny` file blocks access from remote network hosts; it doesn't block root access from local terminals or the console, so option B is incorrect. The `/etc/login.warn` and `/etc/motd` files contain messages that are displayed at login time; they don't block users from logging in as the root user account, so options D and E are incorrect.

54. C. The `auditd` program monitors system activity, including user file and directory access, and logs events based on rules you create. Thus, option C is correct. The `chroot` utility restricts applications to a specific location in the virtual filesystem but doesn't log user file and directory access, so option A is incorrect. The LUKS system encrypts disk partitions but doesn't log user file and directory access, so option B is incorrect. The `klist` and `kinit` programs are used for Kerberos user authentication, not logging user file and directory access, so options D and E are both incorrect.

55. D. The `cd -` command will return your process to its previous directory in the virtual directory system, so option D is the correct answer. The `cd` and `cd ~` commands both return your process to your home directory, which was not necessarily the previous directory. Therefore, options A and C are wrong answers. The `exit` command causes your process to exit its current shell, not return to the previous directory, so option B is also an incorrect answer. The `return` command is used in Bash shell scripts to return from a function or return from a sourced script. Thus, option E is also an incorrect choice.

56. B. The `-R` option used with the `cp` command allows you to copy a directory's contents. You can also employ the `-r` or `--recursive` option to achieve the same results. Therefore, option B is the correct answer. The `-i` option will ask before overwriting a preexisting directory but not copy recursively, so option A is a wrong answer. The `-v` option will provide verbose information for the copy, which is helpful but does not allow a recursive copy to occur. Thus, option C is also an incorrect answer. The `-u` option is handy in that it will only allow the `cp` command to overwrite preexisting files with the same name, if the files being copied are newer. However, it is not used to recursively copy, so option D is also an incorrect answer. The `-f` option forces a copy to occur and overwrites any preexisting files with the same name but does not force a recursive copy. Thus, option E is an incorrect choice.

Gathering Your Tools

PART

I

Chapter

1

Preparing Your Environment

Before beginning your journey to successfully pass the CompTIA Linux+ certification exam, you need a learning space. A *learning space* consists of Linux systems (virtual or physical), where you can actively try out, practice, and explore various Linux commands and utilities. Besides reading this book, having a private space to work freely will assist in your success.

You may already have experience working with Linux in your enterprise environment. However, most likely you are using only one Linux distribution. Training with more than one distribution is needed to pass the Linux+ exam.

In addition, your employer may frown upon any risky behavior on their systems. You need to feel free to try out Linux commands that may cause a system to crash. Your own learning space, containing various Linux distributions and their assorted tools, is a key factor in successfully passing the Linux+ exam.

This chapter begins by looking at a few items concerning the setup of your learning space environment. We will also explore various Linux distributions for your learning space. At the chapter's end, we'll cover a method for accessing the Linux command line.

Setting Up a Learning Space

Your learning space needs to be an environment where you can freely explore Linux and its various distributions (called *distros* for short) and utilities. Whereas some companies may have a spare Linux server available for you to fully use, many of us are not so lucky. Even if you are a student, with a nice lab environment already set up and available for your use, you may want your own space, where you can explore without restrictions.

Although there are many different ways to set up your personal learning space, we will focus on only a few, such as setting up Linux on an old laptop, implementing a virtualized environment, and using the cloud. Hopefully the ideas here will spur you on to setting up a helpful exploration and study environment.

Using That Old Laptop

If you've got a spare or old laptop sitting around, repurposing it as your Linux learning space may work well for you. This is especially useful if you like to move your study environment, such as, for example, moving to a different and quieter location in your home when things get a little loud and crazy. An old desktop will also work, but you will be less mobile.

Whatever system you choose, ensure that it has enough capacity to handle the minimum hardware requirements for a learning space. If you plan on installing multiple Linux distributions on a single system, booting them individually, and not using a virtualized environment, then Table 1.1 will serve as your requirements guide.

TABLE 1.1   Hardware requirements for using a single distribution at a time

Resource	Minimum	Recommended
Memory	2 GB	>= 4 GB
Free disk space	25 GB	>= 30 GB
Processor	2 GHz dual core	> 2 GHz dual core

Although you can use this learning space, it is certainly not ideal. In addition, you can expect this type of Linux learning environment to boot and operate slowly. This learning space environment should be used only if you have no other options.

Creating a Virtualized Environment

Creating a virtualized environment for your Linux learning space is ideal. This setting will allow you to boot multiple Linux distributions at the same time, enable you to move quickly between them, and provide compare and contrast experiences. In addition, you can explore networking utilities more thoroughly in such an environment.

If you are unfamiliar with a virtualized environment, do not despair. Not only are there many resources on the Internet that can get you up to speed, but we also cover virtualization concepts in Chapter 28, "Understanding Cloud and Virtualization Concepts."

There are several excellent and free virtualization products (called *hypervisors* or *virtual machine managers*) that you can install. They include the following:

Oracle VirtualBox   This actively developed open source software is available at www.virtualbox.org. It can run on Linux, Windows, Macintosh, and even Solaris. You can use VirtualBox to run multiple Linux distributions at the same time, assuming your hardware has enough resources. The website is loaded with helpful documentation and has community forums to help you create your Linux learning space.

VMware Workstation Player   VMware Workstation Pro is a proprietary closed source virtualization product. VMware offers a free version called Workstation Player, which is available at www.vmware.com/products/workstation-player.html. This free version does have its limits. Workstation Player will only allow you to run a single virtual machine at time. Also, if you want to install it at your company's site, you must pay a fee to do so.

If you are using a Mac, VMware Workstation Player will not work on your system. Instead, VMware offers a separate virtualization product called VMware Fusion. It is available at www.vmware.com/products/fusion .html. Unfortunately, Fusion is not free, but you can try it out for free.

Microsoft Hyper-V Server 2019   This closed source virtualization product is available on many current Windows 64-bit versions, such as Windows 10 Professional and Enterprise. However, Windows 10 Home edition does not support it. You can use Hyper-V to run multiple Linux distributions at the same time, assuming your hardware has enough resources.

Please don't feel limited by this list. It includes only a few suggested hypervisors for you to investigate. If you have found a virtualization product that works better for your environment, use it for your learning space.

Prior to selecting and installing a particular hypervisor, determine if your laptop or chosen system has enough capacity to handle the entire learning space's minimum hardware requirements. If you plan on installing and running multiple Linux distributions at the same time, use Table 1.2 as a guide for your needed hardware resources. However, be aware that the virtualization products' websites may provide more detailed information.

TABLE 1.2   Hardware requirements for using a virtualization product

Resource	Minimum	Recommended
Memory	8 GB	>= 8 GB
Free disk space	70 GB	>= 100 GB
Processor	x86_64 2 GHz dual core	x86_64 > 2 GHz dual core

Using a virtualized learning space is very flexible. Figure 1.1 shows an example of this type of elastic learning space environment.

FIGURE 1.1 Learning space using Oracle VirtualBox

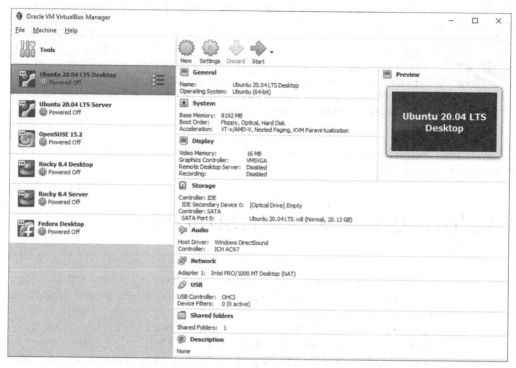

Notice in the learning space depicted in Figure 1.1 that there are two installations of both the Ubuntu and Rocky Linux distributions. These distributions provide the ability to install either a server-oriented environment or a graphical desktop-oriented environment. With VirtualBox you can easily install both environments and compare them!

Hopefully you are starting to gather some ideas of how you want to configure your private learning space. Before you do, there is one more platform category we need to explore.

Jumping to the Cloud

If you do not own a laptop or desktop with enough resources to provide a multiple Linux distribution learning space, consider the cloud. While cloud servers have become increasingly popular for large environments, they can also provide an easy way to run just a single Linux system.

There are many cloud service providers where you can start up various Linux distribution virtual machines, such as Amazon Web Services (AWS), Microsoft Azure, and DigitalOcean. Cloud services change rapidly, so you may not be able to find the Linux distribution versions you need. However, it is worth your time to take a look at the various offerings from cloud service providers. The cloud just might be a cheaper option for your learning space than a new computer.

If you choose to use a cloud service, the service may not give you a way to explore certain CompTIA Linux+ objectives, such as, for example, modifying how a Linux server boots via BIOS versus UEFI. Keep this in mind as you explore your learning space venue.

Before you settle on the location for your learning space, consider the various recommended Linux distributions and their versions. These are additional components of your successful learning space environment.

Exploring Linux Distributions

The CompTIA Linux+ certification is vendor neutral. In practical terms, that means no particular Linux distribution is the focus of the exam. If you have experience with Red Hat Enterprise Linux (RHEL), you need to learn more about utilities and features on Ubuntu and openSUSE distributions, and vice versa.

It is tempting to think that Linux distributions are all the same and that few differences exist between them. Unfortunately, this is a fallacy. We like to compare the Linux kernel to a car's engine and a distribution to a car's features. If you have ever rented a car, the car's features are often rather different than the features of the car you normally drive. When you get into the rented car, you have to take a few minutes to adjust the seat, view the various car controls, and figure out how to use them prior to taking off onto the roadway. This is also true with learning new distributions. The good news is that if you have lots of previous experience with Linux, learning a new distribution is not that difficult.

Linux distributions are often based on other distributions or distribution forks. Two popular distribution groups, which contain distributions helpful to passing the Linux+ exam, are Red Hat based and Debian based. Differences between these two groups include software packages, names, and their management tools; configuration filenames and/or locations; software release schedules; firewall configuration utilities; and so on. Red Hat Inc. tends to focus on businesses and enterprise computing, whereas the Debian Project focuses on free software. Due to these various differences, it is necessary to use distributions from both groups in your learning space.

It is important to understand which Linux distros will help you in successfully passing the CompTIA Linux+ certification exam. In addition, you should know which particular distribution versions are helpful.

Looking at Red Hat Enterprise Linux

The original Red Hat Linux started life in 1995 as an open source project. It gained in popularity to the point where it was at one time the most popular Linux distribution, used in educational environments, in corporate environments, and even by casual Linux hobbyists.

However, in 2003 Red Hat discontinued the Red Hat Linux project in favor of the Red Hat Enterprise Linux (RHEL) project. The RHEL project is primarily focused on business Linux environments. RHEL is a commercial package; thus under most situations you must purchase a license to use it. In return, Red Hat provides full customer support to help with setting up and troubleshooting the Linux system, unlike most other Linux distributions.

Fortunately for Linux hobbyists, there is an alternative way to run RHEL. Since Linux is an open source software package, Red Hat is required to release the source code for RHEL. A few other Linux distributions have popped up using the RHEL source code. The most popular had been the Community Enterprise Operating System (CentOS). It was nearly an exact duplicate of RHEL, and a great free study resource for the CompTIA Linux+ certification exam.

However, as is often the case in the fast-moving Linux world, things have changed. In 2014 CentOS joined Red Hat's Open Source and Standards team, and in 2020 Red Hat replaced the original CentOS project with a new development version called CentOS Stream. Although you can still freely obtain CentOS Stream, it's no longer an exact duplicate of the current RHEL version, but rather a testing ground for new concepts, making it less beneficial as a study resource.

But have no fear, the original developers of CentOS have started yet another distribution, named Rocky Linux. Rocky Linux has gone back to the origins of CentOS—it's an exact duplicate of the latest RHEL version. You can obtain a Rocky Linux distribution ISO from the Rocky website at www.rockylinux.org. Be aware that this distribution, like many others, comes in multiple flavors. We recommend you obtain the Rocky BaseOS download package, in the 8.x version series (at the time of this writing, at version 8.5).

As time goes on, new Rocky distribution versions will be available. Although it is always tempting to get the latest and greatest version, it is not beneficial to use it in your learning space. Remember that the CompTIA Linux+ objectives are static until the next time the certification exam is updated. Therefore, it is wise to use the distribution versions that were available at the certification exam's creation time.

As you install Rocky Linux, you'll be prompted for the environment you want to install. For learning Linux, it's usually best to install a graphical desktop environment, because that provides the easiest way to access all of the Linux features you'll need to learn about.

After you install your Rocky Linux version 8.x BaseOS distribution, you should update the software packages. Do this by logging into the root account using the password you set up during installation and issuing the commands shown in Listing 1.1.

Listing 1.1: Updating software on Rocky Linux

```
# sudo dnf update
Loaded plugins: fastestmirror
[...]
Upgrade  3 Packages

Total download size: 1.3 M
Is this ok [y/d/N]: y
[...]
Complete!
#
```

While RHEL (and its derivatives) is a popular distro, you also need a distribution in the Debian camp. Next, we'll explore the Ubuntu distribution.

Looking at Ubuntu

The Ubuntu Linux distribution is managed by Canonical LTD and has been around since 2004. This free and popular Linux distro is based on the Debian distribution and is a must-have in your personal Linux learning space.

You can obtain the Ubuntu distro ISO from www.ubuntu.com. There are several flavors of Ubuntu, and if you'd like to ensure that you can follow the examples in this book, we recommend you download the Ubuntu Desktop version 20.04 LTS.

The LTS in the Ubuntu version name stands for Long-Term Support. This is an indicator Canonical uses to show that it will provide maintenance and security updates for an extended time period. In the case of 20.04 LTS, you can count on these updates through April 2025.

If you are unfamiliar with Ubuntu, you need to be aware of a few important items. By default, you cannot log into the root account. Instead, when you need to use super user privileges, log into the account you set up at installation and put the command **sudo** in front of your command-line commands. An example is shown in Listing 1.2.

Listing 1.2: Using sudo on Ubuntu

```
$ sudo grep root /etc/shadow
root:!:17737:0:99999:7:::
$
```

If you have never issued command-line commands in a terminal, it is recommended you read this entire chapter prior to attempting to do so. You will read more about terminals later in this chapter.

Another important item concerns installing Ubuntu. If you are connected to a network, you can automatically update the distribution's software when you install the distribution. You will see this option listed in the installation process as `Download updates during the installation` with a check box next to it. If you choose to not install updates during the installation, you can update the software via the command line later on by manually issuing the commands shown in Listing 1.3 in a terminal, using super user privileges.

Listing 1.3: Updating software on Ubuntu

```
$ sudo apt-get update
[sudo] password for Christine:
Hit:1 http://us.archive.ubuntu.com/ubuntu bionic InRelease
Get:2 http://us.archive.ubuntu.com/ubuntu bionic-updates InRelease
[88.7 kB]
[...]
Fetched 1,053 kB in 2s (631 kB/s)
Reading package lists... Done
$
$ sudo apt-get dist-upgrade
Reading package lists... Done
Building dependency tree
Reading state information... Done
Calculating upgrade... Done
The following packages will be upgraded:
[...]
Do you want to continue? [Y/n] Y
[...]
$
```

If you have room for only two Linux distros, Rocky Linux and Ubuntu make fine choices. If you have additional resources, it would be worthwhile to add another distribution, openSUSE.

Looking at openSUSE

The openSUSE distro had its first release in 1994, under a different name, SUSE Linux. There have been many companies involved in supporting it, with the Germany-based company SUSE being the original.

This distro has a very loyal and solid following. Not only is the openSUSE distribution strongly supported by community developers, the openSUSE users love it as well. One of its unique and popular utilities is the Yet another Setup Tool (YaST). YaST, which can be thought of as a command center utility, allows you to control many system services from one interface.

You can obtain the openSUSE distribution ISO from `https://software.opensuse .org`. This distro comes in two primary flavors, Leap and Tumbleweed. We recommend you select openSUSE Leap in the version 15.x series.

 The openSUSE community changed its distribution's version numbering scheme in 2017. The version before 15.0 was 42.3. Be aware of this dramatic change when you go to obtain openSUSE Leap.

Once you have successfully installed openSUSE, it is a good idea to update all the software prior to exploring this distro. To update the software via the command line, manually issue the commands shown in Listing 1.4 in a terminal, using super user privileges.

Listing 1.4: Updating software on openSUSE

```
$ sudo zypper patch
[sudo] password for root:
Loading repository data...
Reading installed packages...
Resolving package dependencies...
[...]
    Note: System reboot required.
Continue? [y/n/...? shows all options] (y): y
[...]
Warning: One of the installed patches requires a
reboot of your machine. Reboot as soon as possible.
There are some running programs that might use files
deleted by recent upgrade. You may wish to check and
restart some of them. Run 'zypper ps -s' to list these programs.
$
```

You may have noticed that the last three distros use different commands for updating software. This is another reason you need to have access to multiple distributions in your learning space. We'll look at one more important distro next.

Looking at Fedora

Fedora is maintained by the Fedora Project, which is sponsored by Red Hat. Innovative and sometimes bleeding-edge software is one of this distribution's great features. If you want to try something new, Fedora is for you. This distro, like the others, comes in multiple flavors, which are called *editions* by the Fedora Project. We recommend Fedora 34 Workstation edition. You can get a copy of this Fedora ISO at `https://getfedora.org`.

Be aware that this particular distro updates its versions every six months. Therefore, you may need to retrieve Fedora 34 Workstation from this location instead: https://dl.fedoraproject.org/pub/fedora/ linux/releases/34/Workstation.

The Fedora distro comes not only in multiple flavors, but also in multiple spins. A spin is an extra special flavor of Fedora. For example, if you are not happy with the default GUI that comes prepackaged with Fedora, you can opt for a spin that has a different GUI. If you want to browse the various Fedora spins available, take a look at the Fedora Project spins' website, https://spins.fedoraproject.org.

Similar to the Ubuntu distro, by default you cannot log into the root account. Instead, when you need to use super user privileges, log into the account you set up at installation, and put the command **sudo** in front of your command-line commands.

Once you've got Fedora Workstation successfully installed, update the software. To update the software via the command line, log into the account you set up at installation, and manually issue the commands shown in Listing 1.5 in a terminal, using super user privileges.

Listing 1.5: Updating software on Fedora

```
$ sudo su -c 'dnf upgrade'
[sudo] password for Christine:
[...]
Install     4 Packages
Upgrade   161 Packages

Total download size: 295 M
Is this ok [y/N]: y
Downloading Packages:
[...]
Complete!
$
```

If very few packages get updated, you may need to add an additional option to your command. Issue the command **sudo su -c 'dnf upgrade -refresh'** in a command-line terminal.

If you have spent your time on Linux in the GUI or are fairly new to Linux, you may be unfamiliar with how to access a command-line terminal. The next section will help. If you are a seasoned command-line user, you can skip this section.

Locating a Terminal

For exploring Linux and preparing to take the CompTIA Linux+ certification exam, you need to spend some time at the command line. The terminal is your gateway to the command line. Once you understand how to locate and use this terminal, you can start progressing through the rest of this book's contents.

The simplest way to reach a terminal in most distributions is by pressing the key combination Ctrl+Alt plus one of the function keys (usually F2 or F3) after the system boots. This will take you to a terminal named tty2. After entering the username and password you created during the Linux distribution's installation, you will be provided with a prompt. Figure 1.2 shows a tty3 terminal on the openSUSE distribution.

FIGURE 1.2   openSUSE tty3 terminal

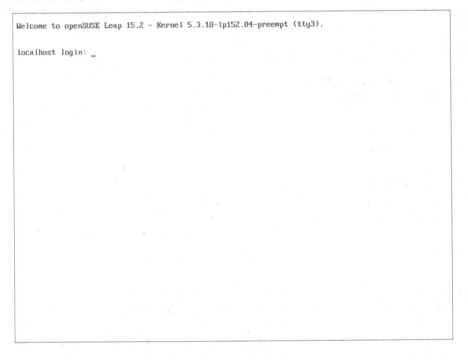

```
Welcome to openSUSE Leap 15.2 - Kernel 5.3.18-lp152.84-preempt (tty3).

localhost login: _
```

At the terminal prompt, you can start entering commands. If you have newly installed the distro, go ahead and update its software as directed earlier in this chapter. To leave this terminal, simply type in the command **exit**.

If you're using a graphical desktop environment, you can also access the command line by using a terminal application.

Summary

A learning space is a virtual or physical Linux system where you can explore, practice, and try out various Linux commands and utilities. A private learning space is a necessity to be successful in passing the CompTIA Linux+ certification exam. You can set up a learning space on an old laptop, on a current laptop using a hypervisor, or within the cloud.

Having multiple Linux distributions in your learning space is also essential. Because the distributions have differences, it is important to have them readily available to explore those differences.

Once you have your Linux learning space set up, you can start to dive into the CompTIA Linux+ certification objectives. We'll begin covering those objectives in the next chapter.

Chapter 2

Introduction to Services

Previous versions of the CompTIA Linux+ certification exam included an objective on Linux server services, such as web servers, file servers, and database servers. The XK0-005 exam has dropped that as a formal objective, but there are other objectives that assume you know what Linux server services are and how they accept connections from clients. While Linux has had a rough time breaking into the desktop market, it has thrived in the server market, so it is important to know how Linux servers work and what server software packages are popular these days.

The popularity of Linux servers has much to do with their versatility, performance, and cost. This chapter helps get you up to speed in how Linux servers operate and covers the most common server software packages you can install and run in Linux to provide services to your network clients.

What Is a Linux Server?

Before we dive into Linux server details, we will first explain what we mean by a Linux server and show how a Linux server differs from a Linux desktop.

Both Linux desktops and Linux servers use the same Linux kernel, run the same shells, and even have the ability to run the same programs. The difference comes in which programs they primarily run and how those programs run on the system.

Linux desktops primarily focus on personal programs that you run from a graphical desktop interface, such as when you browse the Internet or edit a document. The graphical desktop provides an easy interface for users to interact with the operating system and all files and programs. You start programs by selecting them from a menu system or clicking a desktop icon. In the desktop world, everything is interactive.

Linux servers primarily operate without any human interaction. There's no one sitting at a desktop launching applications (and in fact, many servers don't even have a dedicated monitor and keyboard).

The server runs programs that provide shared resources (called *services*) to multiple users (clients), normally in a network environment. Many services run all the time, even when no clients are actively using them.

Server programs seldom rely on a graphical interface. Instead, they almost always utilize the Linux shell's command-line interface (CLI) to interact with a server administrator, and often, the administrator connects to the server from a remote client to perform any interactive work with the services.

Since there's little interaction with a human operator, servers must know how to launch the programs that provide the services to clients on their own. How the server runs those services can differ from server to server and service to service. The following sections describe how Linux servers start services and how they provide access to those services to clients.

Launching Services

There are two primary ways Linux servers run service programs:

- As a background process, running at all times and listening for requests
- As a process spawned by a parent program that listens for the requests

When a Linux service program runs continually as a background process, it's called a *daemon*. Linux servers often utilize scripts to launch service daemons as soon as the server boots up (see Chapter 6, "Maintaining System Startup and Services").

Linux daemon programs often end with the letter *d* to indicate they're daemon processes. Listing 2.1 shows an example of the MySQL database server daemon running in the background on a server.

Listing 2.1: Listing the MySQL database server daemon process

```
$ ps ax | grep mysql
 5793 ?          Sl      0:00 /usr/sbin/mysqld --daemonize --pid
file=/run/mysqld/mysqld.pid
 5900 pts/0     S+      0:00 grep --color=auto mysql
$
```

The mysqld daemon program listens for network connections from clients. When the daemon receives a request from a client, it processes the request and returns data to the client via the same network channel.

 Note that the name for a background program running in Linux is "daemon" and not "demon," as it is often confused with. Daemons are from Greek mythology and were supernatural beings that provided help to humans when needed.

The more services a Linux server supports, the more daemons it must have running in the background, waiting for client requests. Each daemon requires memory resources on the server, even when it's just listening for clients. While today's servers have lots of memory at their disposal, that wasn't always the case in the old days of Linux. Thus came the necessity of *super-servers*.

Super-servers are programs that listen for network connections for several different applications. When the super-server receives a request for a service from a client, it spawns the appropriate service program.

The original super-server program created for Linux was the *internet daemon (inetd)* application. The inetd program ran as a daemon, listening for specific requests from clients and launching the appropriate service program when needed. The inetd program uses the /etc/inetd.conf configuration file to allow you to define the services for which it handles requests.

The *extended internet daemon (xinetd)* application is an advanced version of inetd. It too launches service programs as requested by clients, but it contains additional features, such as access control lists (ACLs), more advanced logging features, and the ability to set schedules to turn services on and off at different times of the day or week.

 Linux systems that utilize the Systemd startup method (see Chapter 6) can utilize systemd unit files to replace the functionality provided by inetd or xinetd.

Listening for Clients

A standard Linux server supports lots of services. Usually, a single Linux server will support multiple services at the same time. This means multiple clients will be making requests to the server for multiple services. The trick is in getting requests from clients to the correct server service.

Each service, whether it's running as a daemon or running from a super-server, uses a separate network protocol to communicate with its clients. Common service protocols are standardized by the Internet Engineering Task Force (IETF) and published as Request for Comments (RFC) documents. Each server software program communicates with its clients using the protocol specified for its service, such as a web server using HTTP or an email server using SMTP.

The network protocol for a service defines exactly how network clients communicate with the service, using preassigned network *ports*. Ports are defined within the TCP and UDP standards to help separate network traffic going to the same IP address. The IETF assigns different services to different ports for communication. This works similarly to telephone extensions used in a large business. You enter a single phone number to reach the business and then select a separate extension to get to a specific individual within the office. With services, clients use a common IP address to reach a server and then different ports to reach individual services.

The IETF has defined a standard set of ports to common services used on the Internet. These are called *well-known ports*. Table 2.1 shows just a few of the more common well-known ports assigned.

A host of Linux services are available for serving applications to clients on the network. The /etc/services file contains all of the ports defined on a Linux server.

The following sections explore the different types of services you will find on Linux servers as well as common Linux applications that provide those services.

TABLE 2.1   Common Internet well-known port numbers

Port number	Protocol	Description
20 and 21	FTP	File Transfer Protocol (FTP) is used for sending files to and from a server.
22	SSH	The Secure Shell (SSH) protocol is used for sending encrypted data to a server.
23	Telnet	Telnet is an unsecure protocol for providing an interactive interface to the server shell.
25	SMTP	The Simple Mail Transport Protocol (SMTP) is used for sending email between servers.
53	DNS	The Domain Name System (DNS) provides a name service to match IP addresses to computer names on a network.
67	DHCP	The Dynamic Host Configuration Protocol (DHCP) enables client computers to obtain a valid IP address on a network automatically.
80	HTTP	The Hypertext Transfer Protocol (HTTP) allows clients to request web pages from servers.
109 and 110	POP	The Post Office Protocol (POP) allows clients to communicate with a mail server to read messages in their mailbox.
137–139	SMB	Microsoft servers use the Server Message Block (SMB) protocol for file and print sharing with clients.
143, 220	IMAP	The Internet Message Access Protocol (IMAP) provides advanced mailbox services for clients.
389	LDAP	The Lightweight Directory Access Protocol (LDAP) provides access to directory services for authenticating users, workstations, and other network devices.
443	HTTPS	The secure version of HTTP provides encrypted communication with web servers.
2049	NFS	The Network File System (NFS) provides file sharing between Unix and Linux systems.

Serving the Basics

There are some basic Internet services that Linux servers are known to do well and that have become standards across the Internet. The three Internet services Linux servers provide are as follows:

- Web services
- Database services
- Email services

The following sections discuss each of these types of Linux services and show you the open source software packages commonly used to support them.

Web Servers

By far the most popular use of Linux servers on the Internet is as a web server. Linux-based web servers host the majority of websites, including many of the most popular websites.

As is true for many Linux applications, there are multiple programs that you can use to build a Linux web server. These are the most popular ones you'll run into and should know about.

The Apache Server

Over the years, the *Apache* web server has become one of the most popular web servers on the Internet. It was developed from the first web server software package created by the National Center for Supercomputing Applications (NCSA) at the University of Illinois.

The Apache web server has become popular due to its modularity. Each advanced feature of the Apache server is built as a plug-in module. When features are incorporated as modules, the server administrator can pick and choose just which modules a particular server needs for a particular application. This helps reduce the amount of memory required to run the Apache server daemons on the system.

The nginX Server

The *nginX* web server (pronounced like "engine-X") is the relatively new kid on the block. Released in 2004, nginX was designed as an advanced replacement for the Apache web server, improving on performance and providing some additional features, such as working as a web proxy, mail proxy, web page cache, and even load-balancing server. While the Apache web server can be configured to provide some of these features by using modules, such as load balancing, the nginX web server was designed to have these features built in to increase performance.

The core nginX program has a smaller memory footprint than the larger Apache program, making it ideal for high-volume environments. It's capable of handling over 10,000 simultaneous network client connections.

While still relatively new, the nginX web server is gaining in popularity, especially in high-traffic web environments. One configuration that's becoming popular is to use a combination of the nginX web server as a load-balancing front end to multiple Apache web servers on the backend. This takes advantage of the nginX server's capabilities of handling large traffic volumes and the Apache web server's versatility in handling dynamic web applications.

The lighthttpd Package

On the other end of the spectrum, there may be times you need a lightweight web server to process incoming client requests for a network application. The *lighthttpd* package provides such an environment.

The lighthttpd web server is known for low memory usage and low CPU usage, making it ideal for smaller server applications, such as in embedded systems. It also incorporates a built-in database, allowing you to combine basic web and database services in a single package.

Database Servers

Storing and retrieving data is an important feature for most applications. Although the use of standard text files is often enough for simple data storage applications, there are times when more advanced data storage techniques are required.

The advent of the relational database allowed applications to quickly store and retrieve data. Relational database servers allowed multiple clients to access the same data from a centralized location. The Structured Query Language (SQL) provides a common method for clients to send requests to the database server and retrieve the data.

Many popular commercial database servers are available for Unix and Windows (and even Linux); a few high-quality open source databases have risen to the top in the Linux world. These database server packages offer many (if not most) of the same features as the expensive commercial database packages and can sometimes even outperform the commercial packages.

The following sections discuss the three most popular open source database servers you'll encounter when working in the Linux environment.

The PostgreSQL Server

The *PostgreSQL* database server started out as a university project and became an open source package available to the public in 1996. The goal of the PostgreSQL developers was to implement a complete object-relational database management system to rival the popular commercial database servers of the day.

PostgreSQL is known for its advanced database features. It follows the standard atomicity, consistency, isolation, and durability (ACID) guidelines used by commercial databases and supports many of the fancy features you'd expect to find in a commercial relational database server, such as transactions, updatable views, triggers, foreign keys, functions, and stored procedures.

PostgreSQL is very versatile, but with versatility comes complexity. In the past the PostgreSQL database had a reputation for being somewhat slow, but it has made vast improvements in performance. Unfortunately, old reputations are hard to shake, and PostgreSQL still struggles to gain acceptance in the web world.

The MySQL Server

Unlike the PostgreSQL package, the *MySQL* database server didn't originally try to compete with commercial databases. Instead, it started out as a project to create a simple but fast database system. No attempt was made to implement fancy database features; it just offers basic features that performed quickly.

Because of its focus on speed, the MySQL database server became the de facto database server used in many high-profile Internet web applications. The combination of a Linux server running the Apache web server and the MySQL database server and utilizing the PHP programming language became known as the LAMP platform and can be found in Linux servers all over the world.

Since its inception, the MySQL database has added features that can rival those found in PostgreSQL and commercial databases. However, staying true to its roots, MySQL still maintains the option of utilizing the faster storage engine that it became famous for.

 In 2008 the MySQL project was acquired by Sun Microsystems. In 2010, when Oracle purchased Sun Microsystems, by default it also took control over MySQL development. This concerned many in the open source community, and shortly after the purchase a group of MySQL developers left Oracle to start the MariaDB project. MariaDB is a replica of MySQL, using the same source code and having the same features (with some new features added). Many Linux distributions now use MariaDB by default instead of MySQL, so don't be alarmed if you see that.

The MongoDB Server

With the rising popularity of object-oriented programming and application design, the use of object-oriented databases has also risen. Currently one of the most popular object-oriented methods of storing data is called *NoSQL*.

As its name suggests, a NoSQL database system stores data differently than the traditional relational database systems using SQL. A NoSQL database doesn't create tables but instead stores data as individual documents. Unlike relational tables, each NoSQL document can contain different data elements, with each data element being independent from the other data elements in the database.

One NoSQL database package that is gaining in popularity is the *MongoDB* package. MongoDB was released in 2009 as a full NoSQL-compliant database management system. It stores data records as individual *JavaScript Object Notation (JSON)* elements, making each data document independent of the others.

The MongoDB database server supports many relational database features, such as indexes, queries, replication, and even load balancing. It allows you to incorporate JavaScript in queries, making it a very versatile tool for querying data.

The MongoDB server installs with a default of no security—anyone can connect to the server to add and retrieve data records. This "gotcha" has been a problem for even some high-profile websites where data has been breached. Please be careful when using a MongoDB database for your web applications.

Mail Servers

At one time, email was the backbone of the Internet. Just about everyone had an email address, and it was crucial to be plugged into an email server to communicate with the world. While these days newer technology is taking over (such as texting, tweeting, and messaging), email is still a vital operation for most Internet users. Just about every Linux server installation uses some type of email server package.

Instead of having one monolithic program that handles all of the pieces required for sending and receiving mail, Linux uses multiple small programs that work together in the processing of email messages. Figure 2.1 shows you how most open source email software modularizes email functions in a Linux environment.

FIGURE 2.1   The Linux modular email environment

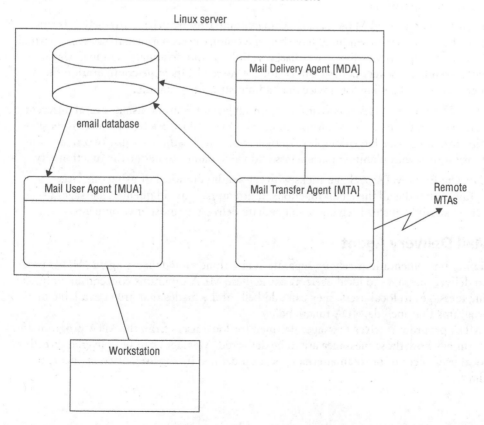

As you can see in Figure 2.1, the Linux email server is normally divided into three separate functions:

- The mail transfer agent (MTA)
- The mail delivery agent (MDA)
- The mail user agent (MUA)

MUA is the program that interacts with end users, allowing them to view and manipulate email messages. Therefore, the MUA programs don't usually run on the server side but rather on the client side. Graphical applications such as Evolution and K-Mail are popular for reading email in Linux desktop environments. The MTA and MDA functions are found on the Linux server. The following sections show the more common MTA and MDA applications you'll see in Linux.

The Mail Transfer Agent

The *mail transfer agent (MTA)* is responsible for handling both incoming and outgoing email messages on the server. For each outgoing message, the MTA determines the destination host of the recipient address. If the destination host is a remote mail server, the MTA must establish a communication link with another MTA program on the remote host to transfer the message.

There are quite a few MTA software packages for the Linux environment, but the Linux+ exam focuses on three of them:

- *sendmail*: The sendmail MTA package gained popularity by being extremely versatile. Many of the features in sendmail have become synonymous with email systems—virtual domains, message forwarding, user aliases, mail lists, and host masquerading. Unfortunately, sendmail is very complex to configure correctly. Its large configuration file is sometimes overwhelming for novice mail administrators to handle.

- *Postfix*: The Postfix MTA was written as a modular application, using several different programs to implement the MTA functionality. One of Postfix's best features is its simplicity. Instead of one large complex configuration file, Postfix uses just two small configuration files with plaintext parameters and value names to define the functionality.

- *Exim*: The Exim MTA package sticks with the sendmail model of using one large program to handle all the email functions. It attempts to avoid queuing messages as much as possible, instead relying on immediate delivery in most environments.

The Mail Delivery Agent

Often, Linux implementations rely on separate stand-alone *mail delivery agent (MDA)* programs to deliver messages to local users. Because these MDA programs concentrate only on delivering messages to local users, they can add bells and whistles that aren't available in MTA programs that include MDA functionality.

The MDA program receives messages destined for local users from the MTA program and then determines how those messages are to be delivered. Messages can be delivered directly to the local user account or to an alternate location defined by the user, often by incorporating filters.

There are two common MDA programs used in Linux:

- *Binmail:* The binmail program is the most popular MDA program used in Linux. Its name comes from its normal location in the system, `/bin/mail`. It has become popular thanks to its simplicity. By default, it can read email messages stored in the standard `/var/spool/mail` directory, or you can point it to an alternative mailbox.

- *Procmail:* The procmail program was written by Stephen R. van den Berg and has become so popular that many Linux implementations install it by default. The popularity of procmail comes from its versatility in creating user-configured recipes that allow a user to direct how the server processes received mail. A user can create a personal `.procmailrc` file in their `$HOME` directory to direct messages based on regular expressions to separate mailbox files, forward messages to alternative email addresses, or even send messages directly to the `/dev/null` file to trash unwanted email automatically.

Serving Local Networks

Besides running large Internet web and database applications, Linux servers are also commonly used in local network environments to provide simple network services. Running a local network requires lots of behind-the-scenes work, and the Linux server is up to the task. This section walks through the most common services you'll find used on all sizes of local networks.

File Servers

These days, the sharing of files has become a necessity in any business environment. Allowing multiple employees to create and edit files in a common folder can greatly improve collaboration efforts in any project.

While sharing files via a web server is common in a wide area network environment, there are easier ways to do that within a local network. There are two basic methods for sharing files in a local network environment:

- Peer-to-peer
- Client-server

In a peer-to-peer network, one workstation enables another workstation to access files stored locally on its hard drive. This method allows collaboration between two employees on a small local network but becomes somewhat difficult if you need to share data between more than two people.

The client-server method of file sharing utilizes a centralized *file server* for sharing files that multiple clients can access and modify as needed. However, with the centralized file server, an administrator must control who has access to which files and folders, protecting them from unauthorized access.

In the Linux world, there are two common server software packages used for sharing files: NFS and Samba.

NFS

The *Network File System (NFS)* is a protocol used to share folders in a network environment. With NFS, a Linux system can share a portion of its virtual directory on the network to allow access by clients as well as other servers.

In Linux, the software package used to accomplish this is *nfs-utils*. The nfs-utils package provides the drivers to support NFS as well as the underlying client and server software to both share local folders on the network and connect to remote folders shared by other Linux systems on the local network. Using nfs-utils, your Linux system can mount remotely shared NFS folders almost as easily as if they were on a local hard drive partition.

Samba

These days, Microsoft Windows workstations and servers have become the norm in many business environments. While Windows workstations and servers can use NFS, the default file sharing method used in Windows is the *System Message Block (SMB)* protocol, created by Microsoft. Although Microsoft servers use proprietary software, Microsoft has released the SMB protocol as a network standard, so it's possible to create open source software that can interact with Windows servers and clients using SMB.

The *Samba* software package (note the clever use of embedding SMB in the name) was created to allow Linux systems to interact with Windows clients and servers. With Samba, your Linux system can act either as a client, connecting to Windows server shared folders, or as a server, allowing Windows workstations to connect to shared folders on the Linux system. Samba does take some work in configuring the correct parameters to manage access to your shared folders.

Print Servers

In a business environment, having a printer for every person in the office is somewhat of a wasted expense. The ability to share network printers has become a requirement for most offices and has also become popular in many home environments.

The standard Linux print sharing software package is called the *Common Unix Printing System (CUPS)*. The CUPS software allows a Linux system to connect to any printer resource, either locally or via a network, by using a common application interface that operates over dedicated printer drivers. The key to CUPS is the printer drivers. Many printer manufacturers create CUPS drivers for their printers, so Linux systems can connect with their printers. For connecting to network printers, CUPS uses the *Internet Printing Protocol (IPP)*.

Besides connecting to a network printer, the CUPS system also allows you to share a locally attached printer with other Linux systems. This allows you to connect a printer to a Linux server and share it among multiple users in a local network.

The Samba software package can also interact with printers shared on Microsoft networks. You can connect your Linux workstation to printers shared on Windows networks using Samba, or you can even share your own locally attached Linux printer with Windows workstations.

Network Resource Servers

Running a local network requires quite a few different resources to keep clients and servers in sync. This is especially true for larger networks where network administrators must manage many different types of clients and servers.

Fortunately, Linux provides a few different service packages that network administrators can use to make their lives easier. The following sections walk through some of the basic network-oriented services that you may see on a Linux server.

IP Addresses

Every device on a local network must have a unique IP address to interact with other devices on the network. For a small home network, that may not be too difficult to manage, but for large business networks, that task can be overwhelming.

To help simplify that requirement, developers have created the *Dynamic Host Configuration Protocol (DHCP)*. Clients can request a valid IP address for the network from a DHCP server. A central DHCP server keeps track of the IP addresses assigned, ensuring that no two clients receive the same IP address.

These days you can configure many different types of devices on a network to be a DHCP server. Most home broadband routers provide this service, as well as most server-oriented operating systems, such as Windows servers and, of course, Linux servers.

The most popular Linux DHCP server package is maintained by the Internet Systems Consortium (ISC) and is called *DHCPd*. Just about all Linux server distributions include this in their software repositories.

Once you have the DHCPd server running on your network, you'll need to tell your Linux clients to use it to obtain their network addresses. This requires a DHCP client software package. For Linux DHCP clients, there are three popular packages that you can use:

- dhclient
- dhcpcd
- pump

Most Debian- and Red Hat–based distributions use the *dhclient* package and even install it by default when a network card is detected during the installation process. The dhcpcd and pump applications are less known, but you may run into them.

Logging

Linux maintains log files that record various key details about the system as it runs. The log files are normally stored locally in the /var/log directory, but in a network environment it can come in handy to have Linux servers store their system logs on a remote logging server.

The remote logging server provides a safe backup of the original log files, plus a safe place to store logs in case of a system crash or a break-in by an attacker.

There are two main logging packages used in Linux, and which one a system uses depends on the startup software it uses (see Chapter 6):

- *rsyslogd*: The SysVinit and Upstart systems utilize the rsyslogd service to accept logging data from remote servers.

- *journald*: The Systemd system utilizes the journald service for both local and remote logging of system information.

Both rsyslogd and journald use configuration files that allow you to define just how data is logged and what clients the server accepts log messages from.

Name Servers

Using IP addresses to reference servers on a network is fine for computers, but humans usually require some type of text to remember addresses. Enter the Domain Name System (DNS). DNS maps IP addresses to a host naming scheme on networks. A DNS server acts as a directory lookup to find the names of servers on the local network.

Linux servers use the *BIND* software package to provide DNS naming services. The BIND software package was developed in the very early days of the Internet (the early 1980s) at the University of California, Berkeley, and is released as open source software.

The main program in BIND is *named*, the server daemon that runs on Linux servers and resolves hostnames to IP addresses for clients on the local network. The beauty of DNS is that one BIND server can communicate with other DNS servers to look up an address on remote networks. This allows clients to point to only one DNS name server and be able to resolve any IP address on the Internet!

The DNS protocol is text based and is susceptible to attacks, such as hostname spoofing. The DNSSEC protocol incorporates a layer of encryption around the standard DNS packets to help provide a layer of security in the hostname lookup process. Ensure that your BIND installation supports DNSSEC for the proper security.

Network Management

Being responsible for multiple hosts and network devices for an organization can be an overwhelming task. Trying to keep up with what devices are active or which servers are running at capacity can be a challenge. Fortunately for administrators, there's a solution.

The *Simple Network Management Protocol (SNMP)* provides a way for an administrator to query remote network devices and servers to obtain information about their configuration, status, and even performance. SNMP operates in a simple client/server paradigm. Network devices and servers run an SNMP server service that listens for requests from SNMP client packages. The SNMP client sends requests for data from the SNMP server.

The SNMP standards have changed somewhat drastically over the years, mainly to help add security and boost performance. The original SNMP version 1 (called SNMPv1) provided for only simple password authentication of clients and passed all data as individual plaintext records. SNMP version 2 (called SNMPv2) implemented a basic level of security and provided for the bulk transmission of monitoring data to help reduce the network traffic required to monitor devices. The current version (SNMPv3) utilizes both strong authentication and data encryption capabilities and provides a more streamlined management system.

The most popular SNMP software package in Linux is the open source *net-snmp* package. This package has SNMPv3 compatibility, allowing you to securely monitor all aspects of a Linux server remotely.

Time

For many network applications to work correctly, both servers and clients need to have their internal clocks coordinated with the same time. The *Network Time Protocol (NTP)* accomplishes this. It allows servers and clients to synchronize on the same time source across multiple networks, adding or subtracting fractions of a second as needed to stay in sync.

For Linux systems, the *ntpd* program synchronizes a Linux system with remote NTP servers on the Internet. It's common to have a single Linux server use ntpd to synchronize with a remote time standard server and then have all other servers and clients on the local network sync their times to the local Linux server.

Implementing Security

These days, security is at the top of every system administrator's list of worries. With a seemingly endless supply of people trying to break into servers, implementing security is a vital role for every Linux administrator.

Fortunately, Linux provides several layers of security that you can implement in your Linux server environment. The following sections walk through the server software packages that you may run into as you implement security in your Linux servers.

Authentication Server

The core security for Linux servers is the standard userid and password assigned to each individual user on the system and stored in either the /etc/passwd (on non-secure legacy systems) or the /etc/shadow file. Each Linux server maintains its own list of valid user accounts that have access on that server.

For a large network environment where users may have to access resources on multiple Linux servers, trying to remember multiple userids and passwords can be a challenge. Fortunately, there are a few different methods for sharing user account databases across multiple Linux servers on a network.

NIS

The *Network Information System (NIS)* is a directory service that allows both clients and servers to share a common naming directory. The NIS naming directory is often used as a common repository for user accounts, hostnames, and even email information on local networks. The NIS+ protocol expands on NIS by adding security features.

The *nis-utils* package is an open source project for implementing an NIS or NIS+ directory in a Linux environment. It's included in most Linux distribution repositories.

 The NIS system was originally designed at Sun Microsystems and released under the clever name Yellow Pages (YP). However, due to trademark infringement, the name had to be changed to the more boring NIS.

Kerberos

Kerberos was developed at MIT as a secure authentication protocol. It uses symmetric-key cryptography to securely authenticate users with a centralized server database. The entire authentication process is encrypted, making it a secure method of logging into a Linux server.

You can use the Kerberos authentication system for more than simple server logins. Many common Linux server applications provide plug-in modules to interface with a Kerberos database for authenticating application users.

LDAP

Network authentication systems have taken off in the commercial networking world. Microsoft's Active Directory system is by far the most popular network authentication system used today. However, the open source world isn't too far behind, creating its own network directory system.

The *Lightweight Directory Access Protocol (LDAP)* was created at the University of Michigan to provide simple network authentication services to multiple applications and devices on a local network. The most popular implementation of LDAP in the Linux world is the *OpenLDAP* package.

OpenLDAP allows you to design a hierarchical database to store objects in your network. In the hierarchical database, objects are connected in a treelike fashion to one another, as shown in Figure 2.2.

The hierarchical databases allows you to group objects by types, such as users and servers, or by location, or both. This provides a flexible way of designing authentication for your local network.

The OpenLDAP package consists of both client and server programs. The client program allows systems to access an OpenLDAP server to authenticate requests made by clients or other network objects.

FIGURE 2.2   A sample LDAP directory tree

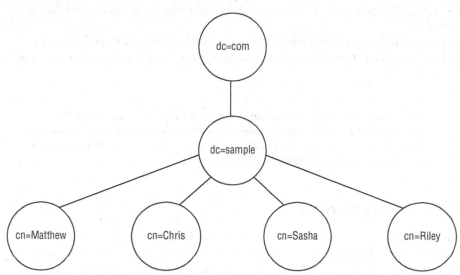

Certificate Authority

The days of assigning every user on your server a userid and password are nearing an end (if it hasn't already come). The userid/password method of logging into a server is fraught with security issues—sharing user accounts, simple passwords, and even accounts with no passwords assigned.

A better method of authenticating users is using *certificates*. A certificate is an encrypted key that implements a two-factor authentication method. To log into a server, a user must have two things:

- Something they possess, such as the certificate file
- Something they know, such as a PIN

A certificate identifies a specific user on the network. Only one user should have the certificate and know the PIN required to access the certificate. However, it's important that the server trusts the certificate as well. For that, you need a certificate authority.

The *OpenSSL* package provides standard certificate functions for both servers and clients. You can set up your Linux server to create certificates for clients and then authenticate them for network applications.

Access Server (SSH)

Remotely accessing servers in today's environment is risky. There are plenty of people around snooping on networks, looking for information they can steal. Logging into a server from a remote location using a plaintext protocol such as Telnet or FTP is not a good idea anymore.

Instead, you should use a remote access protocol that incorporates encryption between the client and server. The *Secure Shell (SSH)* provides a layer of encryption around data sent across the network.

The most popular software package that implements SSH in the Linux environment is the *OpenSSH* package. The OpenSSH package provides secure Telnet, FTP, and even remote copy features using SSH.

> The OpenSSH program also supports a feature called tunneling. With tunneling, you can wrap any type of network transaction with an encryption layer, thus protecting any type of network application even if it's not directly supported by the OpenSSH software.

Virtual Private Networks

Remotely connecting to servers on your local network via the Internet can be a dangerous thing. Your network traffic takes many hops between many intermediary networks before getting to your servers, providing lots of opportunities for prying eyes to snoop on your data.

The solution to remotely connecting to resources on a local network is the *virtual private network (VPN)* protocol. The VPN protocol creates a secure point-to-point tunnel between a remote client or server and a VPN server on your local network. This provides a secure method for remotely accessing any server on your local network.

In Linux, a popular VPN solution is the *OpenVPN* package. The OpenVPN package runs as a server service on a Linux server on your local network. Remote clients can use OpenVPN to connect with the OpenVPN server to establish connectivity to the server and then, once on the server, gain access to the rest of your local network.

Proxy Server

A *web proxy server* allows you to intercept web requests from local network clients. By intercepting the web requests, you have control of how clients interact with remote web servers. The web proxy server can block websites you don't want your network clients to see, and the server can cache common websites so that future requests for the same pages load faster.

The most popular web proxy server in Linux is the *Squid* package. You can configure it to work both as a filter and as a caching server. The nginX web server package discussed earlier also has the ability to work as a web proxy server and is starting to gain in popularity.

Monitoring

If you have multiple Linux servers on your network, trying to keep up with what they're all doing can be a challenge. It's always a good idea for system administrators to peek in on a server's performance and log files just to be aware if anything bad is about to happen or has already happened.

There are several monitoring tools available in the Linux world. The *Nagios* software package is quickly becoming a popular tool, especially in cloud Linux systems. Nagios uses SNMP to monitor the performance and logs of Linux servers and provide results in a simple graphical window environment.

Improving Performance

Developers and administrators of high-volume Linux applications are always looking for ways to improve the performance of the applications. There are three common methods for improving performance that all Linux administrators should be aware of. This section covers these methods.

Clustering

A computer *cluster* improves application performance by dividing application functions among multiple servers. Each server node in the cluster is configured the same and can perform the same functions, but the cluster management software determines how to split the application functions among the servers. Since each server in the cluster is working on only part of the application, you can use less powerful servers within the cluster than if you had to run the entire application on a single server.

The cluster management software is the key to the performance of the cluster. One of the earliest attempts at creating clusters of inexpensive Linux servers was the Beowulf cluster. The Beowulf cluster relied on parallel processing libraries, such as the *Parallel Virtual Machine (PVM)* library, to distribute an application's library calls between multiple Linux servers.

Newer versions of clustering include the *Apache Hadoop* project and the *Linux Virtual Server (LVS)* project.

Load Balancing

Load balancing is a special application of clustering. A load balancer redirects entire client requests to one of a cluster of servers. While a single server processes the entire request, the client load is distributed among the multiple servers automatically.

Common Linux load-balancing packages include *HAProxy*, the Linux Virtual Server (LVS), and even the nginX web server.

Containers

One of the biggest problems for application developers is creating a development environment that mirrors the actual server environment the applications run in. All too often a developer will get an application working just fine in a workstation development environment only to see it crash and burn when ported to the server.

Linux *containers* help solve this problem by creating a self-contained environment to encapsulate applications. A container packages all of the necessary application files, library files, and operating system libraries into a bundle that you can easily move between environments.

Several Linux server packages are available that support containers. Currently, the two most popular ones are *Docker* and *Kubernetes*. You can use these packages to easily port application containers to any Linux server, whether it's a physical server, a virtual server, or in the cloud.

Summary

Linux servers provide network applications that support both clients and network devices. Server applications are called services and are launched by the Linux server without human intervention. When a Linux server can launch services directly, they're called daemons. The daemon runs in the background and listens for client connection requests. A super-server runs in the background and listens for client connection requests for multiple services. When a connection request is accepted, the super-server launches the appropriate service.

Linux supports services for all types of applications. The Apache and nginX services provide web server applications for Linux. For database applications, PostgreSQL, MySQL, and MongoDB are the most popular. If you're looking to run an email server, the sendmail, Postfix, or Exim application should do the trick. Linux also works well as a server for a local network environment. There are open source packages for file, print, and network server resources as well as packages for security authentication and certificate applications.

Finally, you can configure Linux servers for fault tolerance by clustering a large group of small servers together to create one large server. The clustering software can either work to split an application to run over several servers simultaneously or assign individual clients to specific servers to implement load balancing. To support application development, Linux servers also support containers. Containers allow developers to migrate the same environment used to develop an application to a production environment, ensuring that applications will work the same in both development and production.

Exam Essentials

Describe the ways to start server programs in Linux.   Server programs in Linux can either run continually in the background as a daemon process or be started from a super-server daemon when requested by a client.

Explain how clients know how to contact a server program.   Server applications listen for client connections on well-known ports. Clients must send a connection request to the server on the well-known port for the application they want to interact with.

Explain the components commonly used in a LAMP stack.   The LAMP stack uses the Linux operating system, the Apache web server, the MySQL database server, and the PHP programming language to provide a platform for web applications.

Describe the difference between a relational database and a NoSQL database.   A relational database stores data records in individual data tables. Each data type consists of one or more data fields that contain individual data elements. A data record is an instance of data for each data field in a table. A NoSQL database stores data values in documents. Each document is independent of all of the other documents in the database. Each document can also contain different data elements.

Understand the ways a Linux server can share files in a local network.   Linux servers can use the nfs-utils package to communicate with other Linux servers to share folders using NFS. The local Linux server can mount folders from the remote Linux server as if they were local disks. Linux servers can also use the Samba package to share files on Windows local networks with Windows clients and servers as well as map folders located on Windows servers.

Understand which server packages are commonly used to support network features on a local network.   The DHCPd package provides DHCP server services to assign IP addresses to clients. The BIND package provides DNS server services to both clients and servers on a local network for hostname resolution. The net-snmp package allows you to implement remote device management using SNMP, and you can use the ntpd package to create an NTP time server for the local network.

Describe how to create a network directory server using Linux.   The OpenLDAP package allows you to create an LDAP directory of users and devices on the local network. Clients and other servers can use the LDAP directory to authenticate users and devices on the network.

Explain how to improve the performance of a network application.   For network applications in a high-volume environment, you can improve performance by implementing either a cluster or load balancing environment. In a cluster, you can split application functions between multiple servers by using a cluster package such as Apache Hadoop. With load balancing, you can distribute client connections between multiple servers using packages such as HAProxy and Linux Virtual Server (LVS).

Review Questions

1. Which web server is used in the popular LAMP stack?

    A. nginX

    B. Apache

    C. Lighthttpd

    D. PostgreSQL

2. A _____ runs in the background and listens for client connection requests for a single application.

    A. Daemon

    B. Super-server

    C. Shell

    D. Graphical desktop

3. Which open source database provided fast performance and became a popular choice for web applications?

    A. MongoDB

    B. PostgreSQL

    C. MySQL

    D. NoSQL

4. How does a server know what client request is sent to which application daemon?

    A. IP addresses

    B. Ports

    C. Ethernet addresses

    D. Services

5. What popular open source web servers can also perform as a load balancer?

    A. nginX

    B. Apache

    C. PostgreSQL

    D. Lighthttpd

6. What format does MongoDB use to store data elements in the database?

    A. Relational

    B. YaML

    C. JSON

    D. Encrypted

7. Which part of the Linux mail process is responsible for sending emails to remote hosts?

   A. MUA

   B. MTA

   C. MDA

   D. Evolution

8. Which part of the Linux mail process allows you to create filters to automatically redirect incoming mail messages?

   A. MUA

   B. MTA

   C. MDA

   D. Evolution

9. What protocol should you use to mount folders from remote Linux servers on your local Linux server?

   A. SNMP

   B. NTP

   C. DHCP

   D. NFS

10. The _____ software package allows your Windows workstations to mount a folder stored on a Linux server.

    A. ntpd

    B. Samba

    C. DHCPd

    D. Evolution

11. Which two software packages are used in Linux to maintain log files? (Choose two.)

    A. rsyslogd

    B. journald

    C. ntpd

    D. DHCPd

12. Which software program should you load on your Linux server to synchronize its time with a standard time server?

    A. DHCPd

    B. BIND

    C. ntpd

    D. Samba

13. What software package allows a Linux server to print to a network printer?

   A. DHCPd

   B. BIND

   C. ntpd

   D. CUPS

14. If you see the named program running in the background on your Linux server, what service does it provide?

   A. Network time

   B. Hostname resolution

   C. Dynamic IP address allocation

   D. Printing

15. Which authentication package used to be called by the name "Yellow Pages"?

   A. Samba

   B. Kerberos

   C. NIS

   D. BIND

16. What package do you need to install to allow your Linux server to provide IP addresses to clients on your local network?

   A. DHCPd

   B. BIND

   C. ntpd

   D. Evolution

17. The _____ package allows you to create a secure tunnel across a private network to access your local network remotely.

   A. BIND

   B. ntpd

   C. OpenSSH

   D. OpenSSL

18. What server role should you implement to block your local network clients from accessing sports websites during business hours?

   A. A DHCP server

   B. A web server

   C. A web proxy

   D. A container

19. What server role should you implement to increase performance on your company's website?

    A. A load balancer

    B. A web proxy

    C. A DHCP server

    D. A container

20. A _____ allows your developers to easily deploy applications between development, test, and production.

    A. web proxy

    B. DHCP server

    C. container

    D. cluster

Chapter

3

Managing Files, Directories, and Text

✓ **Objective 1.2: Given a scenario, manage files and directories**

In the original Linux years, to get anything done you had to work with the *Gnu/Linux shell*. The shell is a special interactive utility that allows users to run programs, manage files, handle processes, and so on. The shell provides a command-line interface, which furnishes a prompt at which you can enter text-based commands. These commands are actually programs. There are literally thousands of commands you can enter at the command line. However, you need to use only a few hundred commands on a regular basis in your daily job.

While it is highly likely that you have had multiple exposures to many of the commands in this chapter, you may not know all of them. In addition, there may be some shell commands you are using in an ineffective manner. Our purpose in this chapter is to improve your Linux command-line tool belt. We'll cover the basics of managing files and directories, reviewing text files, and finding information. The simple and oft-used `ls` command is covered as well as the interesting `diff` utility. Commands and concepts in this chapter will be built upon and used in later chapters.

Handling Files and Directories

Files on a Linux system are stored within a single directory structure, called a *virtual directory*. The virtual directory contains files from all the computer's storage devices and merges them into a single directory structure. This structure has a single base directory called the *root directory*, which is often simply called *root*.

Often one of the first skills learned at the command line is how to navigate the virtual directory structure as well as how to create directories and remove them. Viewing files, creating them, copying and moving them, and deleting them are also important skills. The following sections describe how to use commands at the command line to accomplish these various tasks.

Viewing and Creating Files

The most basic command for viewing a file's name and its various *metadata* is the list (`ls`) command. Metadata is information that describes and provides additional details about data.

To issue the list command, you type **ls** and any needed options or arguments. The basic syntax structure for the list command is:

```
ls [OPTION]... [FILE]...
```

In the list command's syntax structure, [*OPTION*] means there are various options (also called *switches*) you can add to display different file metadata. The brackets indicate that switches are optional. The [*FILE*] argument shows that you can add a directory or filename to the command's end to look at metadata for either specific files or files within other virtual directory structure locations. It too is optional, as denoted by the brackets.

Syntax structure is depicted for many command-line commands within the Linux system's manual pages, also called the *man pages*. To find a particular command's syntax structure, view its man page (e.g., man ls) and look in the Synopsis section.

When you issue the ls command with no additional arguments or options, it displays all the files' and subdirectories' names within the *present working directory*, as shown in Listing 3.1.

Listing 3.1: Using the ls and pwd commands

```
$ ls
Desktop     Downloads  Pictures      Public     Videos
Documents   Music      Project47.txt Templates
$
$ pwd
/home/Christine
$
```

Your present working directory is your login process's current location within the virtual directory structure. You can determine this location's directory name by issuing the pwd command, which is also shown in Listing 3.1.

To display more than file and directory name metadata, you need to add various options to the list command. Table 3.1 shows a few commonly used options.

Table 3.1 has the best ls command options to memorize, because you will use them often. However, it is worthwhile to try all the various ls command options and option combinations. Take time to peruse the ls command's options in its man pages. You can, for example, try the -lh option combination, as shown in Listing 3.2, which makes the file size more human-readable. When you experiment with various command options, not only will you be better prepared for the Linux+ certification exam, you'll also find combinations that work well for your particular needs.

TABLE 3.1   The `ls` command's commonly used options

Short	Long	Description
-a	--all	Display all file and subdirectory names, including hidden files' names.
-d	--directory	Show a directory's own metadata instead of its contents.
-F	--classify	Classify each file's type using an indicator code (*,/,=,>,@, or |).
-i	--inode	Display all file and subdirectory names along with their associated index number.
-l	N/A	Display file and subdirectory metadata, which includes file type, file access permissions, hard link count, file owner, file's group, modification date and time, and filename.
-R	N/A	Show a directory's contents, and for any subdirectory within the original directory tree, consecutively show their contents as well (recursively).

Listing 3.2: Exploring the `ls -lh` command

```
$ pwd
/home/Christine/Answers
$
$ ls -l
total 32
drwxrwxr-x. 2 Christine Christine     6 Aug 19 17:34 Everything
drwxrwxr-x. 2 Christine Christine     6 Aug 19 17:34 Life
-rw-r--r--. 1 Christine Christine 29900 Aug 19 17:37 Project42.txt
drwxrwxr-x. 2 Christine Christine     6 Aug 19 17:34 Universe
$
$ ls -lh
total 32K
drwxrwxr-x. 2 Christine Christine   6 Aug 19 17:34 Everything
drwxrwxr-x. 2 Christine Christine   6 Aug 19 17:34 Life
-rw-r--r--. 1 Christine Christine 30K Aug 19 17:37 Project42.txt
drwxrwxr-x. 2 Christine Christine   6 Aug 19 17:34 Universe
$
```

Be aware that some distributions include, by default, an *alias* for the `ls -l` command. It is `ll` (two lowercase *L* characters) and is demonstrated on a CentOS distribution in Listing 3.3. An alias at the Linux command line is simply a short command that represents another, typically complicated, command. You can view all the current aliases your process has by typing **alias** at the command line.

Listing 3.3: Exploring the ll command

```
$ ls -l
total 32
drwxrwxr-x. 2 Christine Christine     6 Aug 19 17:34 Everything
drwxrwxr-x. 2 Christine Christine     6 Aug 19 17:34 Life
-rw-r--r--. 1 Christine Christine 29900 Aug 19 17:37 Project42.txt
drwxrwxr-x. 2 Christine Christine     6 Aug 19 17:34 Universe
$
$ ll
total 32
drwxrwxr-x. 2 Christine Christine     6 Aug 19 17:34 Everything
drwxrwxr-x. 2 Christine Christine     6 Aug 19 17:34 Life
-rw-r--r--. 1 Christine Christine 29900 Aug 19 17:37 Project42.txt
drwxrwxr-x. 2 Christine Christine     6 Aug 19 17:34 Universe
$
```

If you're working with lots of files and directories, sometimes it helps to see a graphical overview of things. If you don't have access to a graphical desktop, you can still view things on the command line in a pseudo-graphical format using the tree command, as shown in Figure 3.1.

FIGURE 3.1   The tree command output

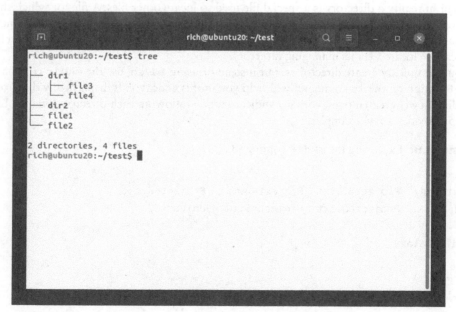

The output from the `tree` command creates a tiered structure, showing which files are associated with which directory, making it easier to sort things out.

The `touch` command will allow you to create empty files on the fly. This command's primary purpose in life is to update a file's timestamps—access and modification. However, for studying purposes, it is useful in that you can quickly create files with which to experiment, as shown in Listing 3.4.

Listing 3.4: Using the `touch` command

```
$ touch Project43.txt
$
$ ls
Everything  Life  Project42.txt  Project43.txt  Universe
$
$ touch Project44.txt Project45.txt Project46.txt
$
$ ls
Everything  Project42.txt  Project44.txt  Project46.txt
Life        Project43.txt  Project45.txt  Universe
$
```

Notice in Listing 3.4 that with the `touch` command you can create a single file or multiple files at a time. To create multiple files, just list the files' names after the command, separated by a space.

Directories are sometimes called *folders*. From a user perspective, a directory contains files, but in reality a directory is a special file used to locate other files. A file for which the directory is responsible has some of its metadata stored within the directory file. This metadata includes the file's name along with the file's associated index (inode) number. Therefore, a file can be located via its managing directory.

You can quickly create directories, but instead of using `touch`, use the `mkdir` command. The `-F` option on the `ls` command will help you in this endeavor. It displays any directories, including newly created ones, with a / indicator code following each directory's name. Listing 3.5 provides a few examples.

Listing 3.5: Exploring the `mkdir` command

```
$ ls -F
Everything/  Project42.txt  Project44.txt  Project46.txt
Life/        Project43.txt  Project45.txt  Universe/
$
$ mkdir Galaxy
$
$ ls -F
Everything/  Life/         Project43.txt  Project45.txt  Universe/
```

```
Galaxy/        Project42.txt  Project44.txt  Project46.txt
$
$ pwd
/home/Christine/Answers
$
$ mkdir /home/Christine/Answers/Galaxy/Saturn
$
$ ls -F Galaxy
Saturn/
$
```

To create a subdirectory in your present working directory, you simply enter the mkdir command followed by the subdirectory's name, as shown in Listing 3.5. If you want to build a directory in a different location than your present working directory, you can use an absolute directory reference, as was done for creating the Saturn directory in Listing 3.5.

If you are creating directories and moving into them from your present working directory, it is easy to become lost in the directory structure. Quickly move back to your previous present working directory using the cd – command or back to your home directory using just the cd command with no options.

Be aware when building directories that a few problems can occur. Specifically this can happen when attempting to create a directory tree, such as the example shown in Listing 3.6.

Listing 3.6: Avoiding problems with the mkdir command

```
$ ls -F
Everything/  Life/          Project43.txt  Project45.txt  Universe/
Galaxy/       Project42.txt  Project44.txt  Project46.txt
$
$ mkdir Projects/42/
mkdir: cannot create directory 'Projects/42/': No such file or directory
$
$ mkdir -p Projects/42/
$
$ ls -F
Everything/  Life/          Project43.txt  Project45.txt  Projects/
Galaxy/       Project42.txt  Project44.txt  Project46.txt  Universe/
$
$ ls -F Projects
42/
$
```

Notice that an error occurs when you attempt to use the mkdir command to build the directory Projects and its 42 subdirectory. A subdirectory (42) cannot be created without its parent directory (Projects) preexisting. The mkdir command's -p option allows you to overwrite this behavior, as shown in Listing 3.6, and successfully create directory trees.

    It is tedious to enter the ls -F command after each time you issue the mkdir command to ensure that the directory was built. Instead, use the -v option on the mkdir command to receive verification that the directory was successfully constructed.

Copying and Moving Files

Copying, moving, and renaming files and directories are essential skills. There are several nuances between the commands to complete these tasks that are important for you to know.

To copy a file or directory locally, use the cp command. To issue this command, you use cp along with any needed options or arguments. The basic syntax structure for the command is:

```
cp [OPTION]... SOURCE DEST
```

The command options, as shown in the structure, are not required. However, the source (SOURCE) and destination (DEST) are required, as shown in a basic cp command example within Listing 3.7.

Listing 3.7: Using the cp command

```
$ pwd
/home/Christine/SpaceOpera/Emphasis
$
$ ls
melodrama.txt
$
$ cp melodrama.txt space-warfare.txt
$
$ ls
melodrama.txt  space-warfare.txt
$
$ cp melodrama.txt
cp: missing destination file operand after 'melodrama.txt'
Try 'cp --help' for more information.
$
```

In Listing 3.7, the first time the cp command is used, both the source file and its destination are specified. Thus no problems occur. However, the second time the cp command is used the destination file's name is missing. This causes the source file to not be copied and generates an error message.

There are several useful cp command options. Many will help protect you from making a grievous mistake, such as accidentally overwriting a file or its permissions. Table 3.2 shows a few commonly used options.

TABLE 3.2   The cp command's commonly used options

Short	Long	Description
-a	--archive	Perform a recursive copy and keep all the files' original attributes, such as permissions, ownership, and timestamps.
-f	--force	Overwrite any preexisting destination files with the same name as *DEST*.
-i	--interactive	Ask before overwriting any preexisting destination files with the same name as *DEST*.
-n	--no-clobber	Do not overwrite any preexisting destination files with the same name as *DEST*.
-R, -r	--recursive	Copy a directory's contents, and for any subdirectory within the original directory tree, consecutively copy its contents as well (recursive).
-u	--update	Only overwrite preexisting destination files with the same name as *DEST* if the source file is newer.
-v	--verbose	Provide detailed command action information as command executes.

To copy a directory, you need to add the -R (or -r) option to the cp command. This option enacts a recursive copy. A recursive copy will not only create a new directory (DEST), but it also copies any files the source directory manages, source directory subdirectories, and their files as well. Listing 3.8 shows an example of how to do a recursive copy as well as how *not* to do one.

Listing 3.8: Performing a recursive copy with the cp command

```
$ pwd
/home/Christine/SpaceOpera
$
$ ls -F
Emphasis/
$
```

```
$ cp Emphasis Story-Line
cp: omitting directory 'Emphasis'
$
$ ls -F
Emphasis/
$
$ cp -R Emphasis Story-Line
$
$ ls -F
Emphasis/  Story-Line/
$
$ ls -R Emphasis
Emphasis:
chivalric-romance.txt        melodrama.txt
interplanetary-battles.txt   space-warfare.txt
$
$ ls -R Story-Line/
Story-Line/:
chivalric-romance.txt        melodrama.txt
interplanetary-battles.txt   space-warfare.txt
$
```

Notice that the first time the cp command is used in Listing 3.8, the -R option is not used, and thus the source directory is not copied. The error message generated, cp: omitting directory, can be a little confusing, but essentially it is telling you that the copy will not take place. When the cp -R command is used to copy the source directory in Listing 3.8, it is successful. The recursive copy option is one of the few command options that can be uppercase, -R, or lowercase, -r.

To move or rename a file or directory locally, you use a single command: mv. The command's basic syntax is nearly the same as the cp command:

mv [OPTION]... SOURCE DEST

The commonly used mv command options are similar to cp command options. However, you'll notice in Table 3.3 that there are fewer typical mv command options than common cp options. As always, be sure to view the mv utility's man pages, using the man mv command, to review all the options for certification studying purposes and explore uncommon options, which may be useful to you.

The move command is simple to use. A few examples of renaming a file as well as employing the -i option to avoid renaming a file to a preexisting file are shown in Listing 3.9.

TABLE 3.3   The mv command's commonly used options

Short	Long	Description
-f	--force	Overwrite any preexisting destination files with the same name as *DEST*.
-i	--interac-tive	Ask before overwriting any preexisting destination files with the same name as *DEST*.
-n	--no-clobber	Do not overwrite any preexisting destination files with the same name as *DEST*.
-u	--update	Only overwrite preexisting destination files with the same name as *DEST* if the source file is newer.
-v	--verbose	Provide detailed command action information as the command executes.

Listing 3.9: Using the mv command

```
$ ls
chivalric-romance.txt        melodrama.txt
interplanetary-battles.txt   space-warfare.txt
$
$ mv space-warfare.txt risk-taking.txt
$
$ ls
chivalric-romance.txt        melodrama.txt
interplanetary-battles.txt   risk-taking.txt
$
$ mv -i risk-taking.txt melodrama.txt
mv: overwrite 'melodrama.txt'? n
$
```

When renaming an entire directory, there are no additional required command options. Just issue the mv command as you would for renaming a file, as shown in Listing 3.10.

Listing 3.10: Renaming a directory using the mv command

```
$ pwd
/home/Christine/SpaceOpera
$
$ ls -F
Emphasis/  Story-Line/
```

```
$
$ mv -i Story-Line Story-Topics
$
$ ls -F
Emphasis/   Story-Topics/
$
```

You can move a file and rename it all in one simple mv command, as shown in Listing 3.11. The *SOURCE* uses the file's current directory reference and current name. The *DEST*
uses the file's new location as well as its new name.

Listing 3.11: Moving and renaming a file using the mv command

```
$ pwd
/home/Christine/SpaceOpera
$
$ ls
Emphasis   Story-Topics
$
$ ls Emphasis/
chivalric-romance.txt          melodrama.txt
interplanetary-battles.txt  risk-taking.txt
$
$ ls Story-Topics/
chivalric-romance.txt          melodrama.txt
interplanetary-battles.txt  space-warfare.txt
$
$ mv Emphasis/risk-taking.txt Story-Topics/risks.txt
$
$ ls Emphasis/
chivalric-romance.txt   interplanetary-battles.txt   melodrama.txt
$
$ ls Story-Topics/
chivalric-romance.txt          melodrama.txt   space-warfare.txt
interplanetary-battles.txt  risks.txt
$
```

In Listing 3.11, the file risk-taking.txt is located in the Emphasis directory. Employing a single mv command, it is moved to the Story-Topics directory and renamed to
risks.txt at the same time.

For lightning-fast copies of big files or when you are copying large groups of files, the
remote sync utility is rather useful. This tool is often used to create backups, can securely
copy files over a network, and is accessed via the rsync command.

When you're copying files over a network to a remote host, the file transfer process typically needs protection via encryption methods. The rsync command can be tunneled through OpenSSH to provide data privacy. Also, the scp command can be employed to provide a secure file copy mechanism. Both of these methods are covered in Chapter 12, "Protecting Files."

To quickly copy a file locally, the rsync command syntax is similar to the mv command's syntax. It is as follows:

rsync [OPTION]... SOURCE DEST

Certain rsync options will assist you in making quick file copies. Certain switches are helpful for copying large files or creating backups locally, so it's a good idea to review the commonly used rsync options listed in Table 3.4.

TABLE 3.4 The rsync command's commonly used local copy options

Short	Long	Description
-a	--archive	Use archive mode.
-D	N/A	Retain device and special files.
-g	--group	Retain file's group.
-h	--human-readable	Display any numeric output in a human-readable format.
-l	--links	Copy symbolic links as symbolic links.
-o	--owner	Retain file's owner.
-p	--perms	Retain file's permissions.
N/A	--progress	Display progression of file copy process.
-r	--recursive	Copy a directory's contents, and for any subdirectory within the original directory tree, consecutively copy its contents as well (recursive).
N/A	--stats	Display detailed file transfer statistics.
-t	--times	Retain file's modification time.
-v	--verbose	Provide detailed command action information as command executes.

Archive mode, turned on by the -a (or --archive) switch, is an interesting feature. Using this one switch is equivalent to using the option combination of -rlptgoD, which is a popular rsync command option set for creating directory tree backups.

An example of using the rsync utility to copy a large file is shown in Listing 3.12. Notice that when the copy is complete, the utility outputs useful information, such as the data transfer rate. If you want additional file transfer statistics, add the --stats option to your command.

Listing 3.12: Moving and renaming a file using the rsync command

```
# ls -sh /media/USB/Parrot-full-3.7_amd64.iso
3.6G /media/USB/Parrot-full-3.7_amd64.iso
#
# rsync -v /media/USB/Parrot-full-3.7_amd64.iso /home/Christine/
Parrot-full-3.7_amd64.iso

sent 3,769,141,763 bytes  received 35 bytes  3,137,030.21 bytes/sec
total size is 3,768,221,696  speedup is 1.00
#
# ls -sh /home/Christine/Parrot-full-3.7_amd64.iso
3.6G /home/Christine/Parrot-full-3.7_amd64.iso
#
```

The remote sync utility will often display a speedup rating in its output. This rating is related to conducting synchronized backups. If you are using the rsync command to conduct periodic backups of a particular directory to another directory location, the speedup rating lets you know how many files did not need to be copied because they had not been modified and were already backed up. For example, if 600 of 600 files had to be copied to the backup directory location, the speedup is 1.00. If only 300 of 600 files had to be copied, the speedup is 2.00. Thus, whenever you are using the rsync command to copy a single file to a new location, the speedup will always be 1.00.

Removing Files

Tidying up an entire filesystem or simply your own directory space often starts with deleting unneeded files and directories. Understanding the commands and their switches to do so is paramount to avoid mistakes in removing these items.

The most flexible and heavily used deletion utility is the remove tool. It is employed via the rm command, and the basic syntax is:

```
rm [OPTION]... FILE
```

There are many useful options for the rm utility, so be sure to view its man pages to see them all. However, the most commonly used options are listed in Table 3.5.

TABLE 3.5   The rm command's commonly used options

Short	Long	Description
-d	--dir	Delete any empty directories.
-f	--force	Continue on with the deletion process, even if some files designated by the command for removal do not exist, and do not ask prior to deleting any existing files.
-i	--interactive	Ask before deleting any existing files.
-I	N/A	Ask before deleting more than three files, or when using the -r option.
-R,-r	--recursive	Delete a directory's contents, and for any subdirectory within the original directory tree, consecutively delete its contents and the subdirectory as well (recursive).
-v	--verbose	Provide detailed command action information as command executes.

To simply delete a single file, you can use the rm command designating the filename to remove and not use any switches. However, it is always a good idea to use the -i (or --interactive) option to ensure that you are not deleting the wrong file, as demonstrated in Listing 3.13.

Listing 3.13: Deleting a file using the rm command

```
$ ls Parrot-full-3.7_amd64.iso
Parrot-full-3.7_amd64.iso
$
$ rm -i Parrot-full-3.7_amd64.iso
rm: remove write-protected regular file 'Parrot-full-3.7_amd64.iso'? y
$
$ ls Parrot-full-3.7_amd64.iso
ls: cannot access Parrot-full-3.7_amd64.iso: No such file or directory
$
$ rm -i Parrot-full-3.7_amd64.iso
rm: cannot remove 'Parrot-full-3.7_amd64.iso': No such file or directory
$
$ rm -f Parrot-full-3.7_amd64.iso
$
```

Notice also in Listing 3.13 that when the file has been deleted, if you reissue the `rm -i` command, an error message is generated, but if you issue the `rm -f` command, it is silent concerning the missing file. The `-f` (or `--force`) switch is useful when you are deleting many files and desire for no error messages to be displayed.

Removing a directory tree or a directory full of files can be tricky. If you just issue the `rm -i` command, you will get an error message, as shown in Listing 3.14. Instead, you need to add the `-R` or `-r` option in order for the directory and the files it is managing to be deleted.

Listing 3.14: Deleting a directory containing files using the `rm` command

```
$ cd SpaceOpera/
$
$ ls -F
Emphasis/  Story-Topics/
$
$ rm -i Emphasis/
rm: cannot remove 'Emphasis/': Is a directory
$
$ rm -ir Emphasis
rm: descend into directory 'Emphasis'? y
rm: remove regular empty file 'Emphasis/melodrama.txt'? y
rm: remove regular empty file 'Emphasis/interplanetary-battles.txt'? y
rm: remove regular empty file 'Emphasis/chivalric-romance.txt'? y
rm: remove directory 'Emphasis'? y
$
$ ls -F
Story-Topics/
$
```

If you have lots of files to delete, want to ensure that you are deleting the correct files, and don't want to have to answer **y** for every file to delete, employ the `-I` option instead of the `-i` switch. It will ask before deleting more than three files as well as when you are deleting a directory full of files and are using one of the recursive switches, as shown in Listing 3.15.

Listing 3.15: Employing the `rm` command's `-I` option

```
$ ls -F
Story-Topics/
$
$ rm -Ir Story-Topics/
rm: remove 1 argument recursively? y
$
$ ls -F
$
```

Deleting an empty directory, a directory containing no files, is simple. Use the remove empty directories tool by issuing the `rmdir` command. You'll find that adding the -v (or --verbose) switch is helpful as well, as shown in Listing 3.16.

Listing 3.16: Using the `rmdir` command

```
$ mkdir -v EmptyDir
mkdir: created directory 'EmptyDir'
$
$ rmdir -v EmptyDir/
rmdir: removing directory, 'EmptyDir/'
$
```

If you want to remove a directory tree, which is free of files but contains empty subdirectories, you can also employ the `rmdir` utility. The -p (or --parents) switch is required along with providing the entire directory tree name as an argument. An example is shown in Listing 3.17.

Listing 3.17: Using the `rmdir` command to delete an empty directory tree

```
$ mkdir -vp EmptyDir/EmptySubDir
mkdir: created directory 'EmptyDir'
mkdir: created directory 'EmptyDir/EmptySubDir'
$
$ rmdir -vp EmptyDir/EmptySubDir
rmdir: removing directory, 'EmptyDir/EmptySubDir'
rmdir: removing directory, 'EmptyDir'
$
```

You may have a situation where you need to remove only empty directories from a directory tree. In this case, you will need to use the `rm` command and add the -d (or --dir) switch, as shown in Listing 3.18.

Listing 3.18: Using the `rm` command to delete empty directories in a tree

```
$ mkdir -v EmptyDir
mkdir: created directory 'EmptyDir'
$
$ mkdir -v NotEmptyDir
mkdir: created directory 'NotEmptyDir'
$
$ touch NotEmptyDir/File42.txt
$
$ rm -id EmptyDir NotEmptyDir
rm: remove directory 'EmptyDir'? y
rm: cannot remove 'NotEmptyDir': Directory not empty
$
```

An important skill is understanding the commands used to create and remove directories along with the various commands to view, create, copy, move, rename, and delete files. Also, having a firm grasp on the commonly used command options is vital knowledge. This expertise is a valuable tool in your Linux command-line tool belt.

Linking Files and Directories

Understanding file and directory links is an essential part of your Linux journey. While many quickly pick up how to link files, they do not necessarily understand the underlying link structure. And that can be a problem. In this section, we'll explore linking files as well as their implications.

There are two types of links. One is a symbolic link, which is also called a *soft link*. The other is a hard link, and we'll take a look at it first.

Establishing a Hard Link

A hard link is a file or directory that has one index (inode) number but at least two different filenames. Having a single inode number means that it is a single data file on the filesystem. Having two or more names means the file can be accessed in multiple ways. Figure 3.2 shows this relationship. In this diagram, a hard link has been created. The hard link has two file names, one inode number, and therefore one filesystem location residing on a disk partition. Thus, the file has two names but is physically one file.

FIGURE 3.2   Hard link file relationship

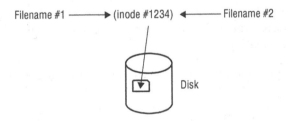

A hard link allows you to have a pseudo-copy of a file without truly copying its data. This is often used in file backups where not enough filesystem space exists to back up the file's data. If someone deletes one of the file's names, you still have another filename that links to its data.

To create a hard link, use the `ln` command. For hard links, the original file must exist prior to issuing the `ln` command. The linked file must not exist. It is created when the command is issued. Listing 3.19 shows this command in action.

Listing 3.19: Using the `ln` command to create a hard link

```
$ touch OriginalFile.txt
$
$ ls
OriginalFile.txt
$
$ ln OriginalFile.txt HardLinkFile.txt
$
$ ls
HardLinkFile.txt  OriginalFile.txt
$
$ ls -i
2101459 HardLinkFile.txt  2101459 OriginalFile.txt
$
$ touch NewFile.txt
$
$ ls -og
total 0
-rw-rw-r--. 2 0 Aug 24 18:09 HardLinkFile.txt
-rw-rw-r--. 1 0 Aug 24 18:17 NewFile.txt
-rw-rw-r--. 2 0 Aug 24 18:09 OriginalFile.txt
$
```

In Listing 3.19, a new blank and empty file, `OriginalFile.txt`, is created via the `touch` command. It is then hard-linked to `HardLinkFile.txt` via the `ln` command. Notice that `OriginalFile.txt` was created prior to issuing the `ln` command and `HardLinkFile.txt` was created *by* issuing the `ln` command. The inode numbers for these files are checked using the `ls -i` command, and you can see that the numbers are the same for both files.

Also in Listing 3.19, after the hard link is created and the inode numbers are checked, a new empty file is created, called `NewFile.txt`. This was done to compare link counts. Using the `ls -og` command, the file's metadata is displayed, which includes file type, permissions, link counts, file size, creation dates, and filenames. This command is similar to `ls -l` but omits file owners and groups. You can quickly find the link counts in the command output. They are right next to the files' sizes, which are all 0 since the files are empty. Notice that both `OriginalFile.txt` and `HardLinkFile.txt` have a link count of 2. This is because they are both hard-linked to one other file. `NewFile.txt` has a link count of 1 because it is *not* hard-linked to another file.

If you want to remove a linked file but not the original file, use the `unlink` command. Just type **unlink** at the command line and include the linked filename as an argument.

When creating and using hard links, there are a few important items to remember:

- The original file must exist before you issue the ln command.
- The second file listed in the ln command must *not* exist prior to issuing the command.
- An original file and its hard links share the same inode number.
- An original file and its hard links share the same data.
- An original file and any of its hard links can exist in different directories.
- An original file and its hard links must exist on the same filesystem.

Constructing a Soft Link

Typically, a soft link file provides a pointer to a file that may reside on another filesystem. The two files do not share inode numbers because they do not point to the same data. Figure 3.3 illustrates the soft link relationship.

FIGURE 3.3   Soft-link file relationship

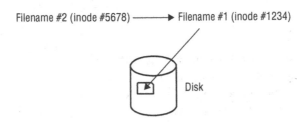

To create a symbolic link, the ln command is used with the –s (or ––symbolic) option. An example is shown in Listing 3.20.

Listing 3.20: Using the ln command to create a soft link

```
$ touch OriginalSFile.txt
$
$ ls
OriginalSFile.txt
$
$ ln -s OriginalSFile.txt SoftLinkFile.txt
$
$ ls -i
2101456 OriginalSFile.txt  2101468 SoftLinkFile.txt
$
$ ls -og
total 0
-rw-rw-r--. 1  0 Aug 24 19:04 OriginalSFile.txt
lrwxrwxrwx. 1 17 Aug 24 19:04 SoftLinkFile.txt -> OriginalSFile.txt
$
```

Similar to a hard link, the original file must exist prior to issuing the `ln -s` command. The soft-linked file must not exist. It is created when the command is issued. In Listing 3.20, you can see via the `ls -i` command that soft-linked files do not share the same inode number, unlike hard-linked files. Also, soft-linked files do not experience a link count increase. The `ls -og` command shows this, and it also displays the soft-linked file's pointer to the original file.

> Sometimes you have a soft-linked file that points to another soft-linked file. If you want to quickly find the final file, use the `readlink -f` command and pass one of the soft-linked filenames as an argument to it. The `readlink` utility will display the final file's name and directory location.

When creating and using soft links, keep a few things in mind:

- The original file must exist before you issue the `ln -s` command.
- The second file listed in the `ln -s` command must not exist prior to issuing the command.
- An original file and its soft links do not share the same inode number.
- An original file and its soft links do not share the same data.
- An original file and any of its soft links can exist in different directories.
- An original file and its soft links can exist in different filesystems.

> Stale links can be a serious security problem. A stale link, sometimes called a *dead link*, is when a soft link points to a file that was deleted or moved. The soft-linked file itself is not removed or updated. If a file with the original file's name and location is created, the soft link now points to that new file. If a malicious file is put in the original file's place, your server's security could be compromised. Use symbolic links with caution and employ the `unlink` command if you need to remove a linked file.

File and directory links are easy to create. However, it is important that you understand the underlying structure of these links in order to use them properly.

Reading Files

Linux systems contain many text files. They include configuration files, log files, data files, and so on. Understanding how to view these files is a basic but important skill. In the following sections, we'll explore several utilities you can use to read text files.

Reading Entire Text Files

The basic utility for viewing entire text files is the concatenate (`cat`) command. Though this tool's primary purpose in life is to join together text files and display them, it is often used just to display a single small text file. To view a small text file, use the `cat` command with the basic syntax that follows:

```
cat [OPTION]... [FILE]...
```

The `cat` command is simple to use. You just enter the command followed by any text file you want to read, as shown in Listing 3.21.

Listing 3.21: Using the `cat` command to display a file

```
$ cat numbers.txt
42
2A
52
0010 1010
*
$
```

The `cat` command simply spits out the entire text file to your screen. When you get your prompt back (shown as the $ in Listing 3.21), you know that the line above the prompt is the file's last line.

> There is a handy new clone of the `cat` command called bat. Its developer calls it "cat with wings" because of the bat utility's many additional features. You can read about its features at https://github.com/sharkdp/bat.

One `cat` command option that is useful is the `-n` (or `--number`) switch. Using this option will display line numbers along with the file text, as shown in Listing 3.22.

Listing 3.22: Employing the `cat -n` command to display a file

```
$ cat -n numbers.txt
     1  42
     2  2A
     3  52
     4  0010 1010
     5  *
$
```

Another useful command to view entire text files is the `pr` command. Its original use was to format text files for printing. However, nowadays it is far more useful for displaying a file when you need some special formatting. To view a small text file, use the `pr` command with the basic syntax that follows:

```
pr [OPTION]... [FILE]...
```

The special formatting options are what set this command apart from simply using the cat command. Table 3.6 shows some useful pr utility options for displaying a file.

TABLE 3.6   The pr command's useful file display options

Short	Long	Description
-n	--columns=n	Display the file(s) in column format, using *n* columns.
-l *n*	--length=n	Change the default 66-line page length to *n* lines long.
-m	--merge	When displaying multiple files, display them in parallel, with one file in each column, and truncate the files' lines.
-s *c*	--separator=c	Change the default column separator from tab to *c*.
-t	--omit-header	Do not display any file header or trailers.
-w *n*	--width=n	Change the default 72-character page width to *n* characters wide. The −s option overrides this setting.

To display one file, you need to use the page length option, -l (or --length), to shorten the page length. If you do not use this switch and have a very short file, the text will scroll off the screen. Also the -t (or --omit-header) option is useful if you only want to see what text is in the file. Listing 3.23 shows the pr command in action.

Listing 3.23: Employing the pr command to display a file

```
$ pr -tl 15 numbers.txt
42
2A
52
0010 1010
*
$
```

Where the pr utility really shines is displaying two short text files at the same time. You can quickly view the files side by side. In this case, it is useful to employ the -m (or --merge) option, as shown in Listing 3.24.

Listing 3.24: Using the pr command to display two files

```
$ pr -mtl 15 numbers.txt random.txt
42                                    42
2A                                    Flat Land
52                                    Schrodinger's Cat
0010 1010                             0010 1010
*                                     0000 0010
$
```

 If you want to display two files side by side and you do not care how sloppy the output is, you can use the paste command. Just like school paste, it will glue them together but not necessarily be pretty.

When a text file is larger than your output screen, if you use commands such as cat and pr, text may scroll off the screen. This can be annoying. Fortunately, there are several utilities that allow you to read portions of a text file, which are covered next.

Reading Text File Portions

If you just want to read a single file line or a small portion of a file, it makes no sense to use the cat command. This is especially true if you are dealing with a large text file.

The grep utility can help you find a file line (or lines) that contain certain text strings. While this utility, covered in more detail later, is primarily used to search for text patterns within a file, it is also very useful in searching for a single string. The basic syntax for the grep command is as follows:

```
grep [OPTIONS] PATTERN [FILE...]
```

When searching for a particular text string, you use the string for *PATTERN* in the command's syntax and the file you are searching as *FILE*. Listing 3.25 shows an example of using the *grep* command.

Listing 3.25: Using the grep command to find a file line

```
$ grep christine /etc/passwd
$
$ grep -i christine /etc/passwd
Christine:x:1001:1001::/home/Christine:/bin/bash
$
```

Be aware that the grep utility pays attention to case. If the string you enter does not match a string exactly (including case) within the file, the grep command will return nothing, as happened for the first command in Listing 3.25. If you employ the -i (or --ignore-case) switch, grep will search for any instance of the string disregarding case, as shown in Listing 3.25's second command.

Another handy tool for displaying portions of a text file is the head utility. The head command's syntax is as follows:

head [*OPTION*]... [*FILE*]...

By default, the head command displays the first 10 lines of a text file. An example is shown in Listing 3.26.

Listing 3.26: Employing the head command

```
$ head /etc/passwd
root:x:0:0:root:/root:/bin/bash
bin:x:1:1:bin:/bin:/sbin/nologin
daemon:x:2:2:daemon:/sbin:/sbin/nologin
adm:x:3:4:adm:/var/adm:/sbin/nologin
lp:x:4:7:lp:/var/spool/lpd:/sbin/nologin
sync:x:5:0:sync:/sbin:/bin/sync
shutdown:x:6:0:shutdown:/sbin:/sbin/shutdown
halt:x:7:0:halt:/sbin:/sbin/halt
mail:x:8:12:mail:/var/spool/mail:/sbin/nologin
operator:x:11:0:operator:/root:/sbin/nologin
$
```

A good command option to try allows you to override the default behavior of only displaying a file's first 10 lines. The switch to use is either -n (or --lines=), followed by an argument. The argument determines the number of file lines to display, as shown in Listing 3.27.

Listing 3.27: Using the head command to display fewer lines

```
$ head -n 2 /etc/passwd
root:x:0:0:root:/root:/bin/bash
bin:x:1:1:bin:/bin:/sbin/nologin
$
$ head -2 /etc/passwd
root:x:0:0:root:/root:/bin/bash
bin:x:1:1:bin:/bin:/sbin/nologin
$
```

Notice in Listing 3.27 that the -n 2 switch and argument used with the head command display only the file's first two lines. However, the second command eliminates the n portion of the switch, and the command behaves just the same as the first command.

You can also eliminate the file's bottom lines by using a negative argument with the -n (or --lines=) switch. This is demonstrated in Listing 3.28.

Listing 3.28: Using the head command to not display bottom lines

```
$ head -n -40 /etc/passwd
root:x:0:0:root:/root:/bin/bash
bin:x:1:1:bin:/bin:/sbin/nologin
daemon:x:2:2:daemon:/sbin:/sbin/nologin
adm:x:3:4:adm:/var/adm:/sbin/nologin
$
$ head --40 /etc/passwd
head: unrecognized option '--40'
Try 'head --help' for more information.
$
```

Notice in Listing 3.28 that the -n switch's argument is negative this time (-40). This tells the head command to display all the file's lines except the last 40 lines. If you try to use a negative argument without using the -n switch, as you can do with a positive argument, you'll get an error message, as shown in Listing 3.28.

If you want to display the file's last lines instead of its first lines, employ the tail utility. Its general syntax is similar to the head command's syntax:

```
tail [OPTION]... [FILE]...
```

By default, the tail command will show a file's last 10 text lines. However, you can override that behavior by using the -n (or --lines=) switch with an argument. The argument tells tail how many lines from the file's bottom to display. If you add a plus sign (+) in front of the argument, the tail utility will start displaying the file's text lines starting at the designated line number to the file's end. There are three examples of using tail in these ways shown in Listing 3.29.

Listing 3.29: Employing the tail command

```
$ tail /etc/passwd
saslauth:x:992:76:Saslauthd user:/run/saslauthd:/sbin/nologin
pulse:x:171:171:PulseAudio System Daemon:/var/run/pulse:/sbin/nologin
gdm:x:42:42::/var/lib/gdm:/sbin/nologin
setroubleshoot:x:991:985::/var/lib/setroubleshoot:/sbin/nologin
rpcuser:x:29:29:RPC Service User:/var/lib/nfs:/sbin/nologin
nfsnobody:x:65534:65534:Anonymous NFS User:/var/lib/nfs:/sbin/nologin
sssd:x:990:984:User for sssd:/:/sbin/nologin
gnome-initial-setup:x:989:983::/run/gnome-initial-setup/:/sbin/nologin
tcpdump:x:72:72::/:/sbin/nologin
avahi:x:70:70:Avahi mDNS/DNS-SD Stack:/var/run/avahi-daemon:/sbin/nologin
$
$ tail -n 2 /etc/passwd
tcpdump:x:72:72::/:/sbin/nologin
```

```
avahi:x:70:70:Avahi mDNS/DNS-SD Stack:/var/run/avahi-daemon:/sbin/nologin
$
$ tail -n +42 /etc/passwd
gnome-initial-setup:x:989:983::/run/gnome-initial-setup/:/sbin/nologin
tcpdump:x:72:72::/:/sbin/nologin
avahi:x:70:70:Avahi mDNS/DNS-SD Stack:/var/run/avahi-daemon:/sbin/nologin
$
```

One of the most useful `tail` utility features is its ability to watch log files. Log files typically have new messages appended to the file's bottom. Watching new messages as they are added is handy. Use the `-f` (or `--follow`) switch on the `tail` command and provide the log filename to watch as the command's argument. You will see a few recent log file entries immediately. As you keep watching, additional messages will display as they are being added to the log file.

 Some log files have been replaced on various Linux distributions, and now the messages are kept in a journal file managed by `journald`. To watch messages being added to the journal file, use the `journalctl --follow` command.

To end your monitoring session using `tail`, you must use the Control+C key combination. An example of watching a log file using the `tail` utility is shown snipped in Listing 3.30.

Listing 3.30: Watching a log file with the `tail` command

```
$ sudo tail -f /var/log/auth.log
[sudo] password for Christine:
Aug 27 10:15:14 Ubuntu1804 sshd[15662]: Accepted password [...]
Aug 27 10:15:14 Ubuntu1804 sshd[15662]: pam_unix(sshd:sess[...]
Aug 27 10:15:14 Ubuntu1804 systemd-logind[588]: New sessio[...]
Aug 27 10:15:50 Ubuntu1804 sudo: Christine : TTY=pts/1 ; P[...]
Aug 27 10:15:50 Ubuntu1804 sudo: pam_unix(sudo:session): s[...]
Aug 27 10:16:21 Ubuntu1804 login[10703]: pam_unix(login:se[...]
Aug 27 10:16:21 Ubuntu1804 systemd-logind[588]: Removed se[...]
^C
$
```

 If you are following along on your own system with the commands in your book, your Linux distribution may not have the /var/log/auth.log file. Try the /var/log/secure file instead.

Reading Text File Pages

One way to read through a large file's text is by using a *pager*. A pager utility allows you to view one text page at a time and move through the text at your own pace. The two commonly used pagers are the more and less utilities.

Though rather simple, the more utility is a nice little pager utility. You can move forward through a text file by pressing the spacebar (one page down) or the Enter key (one line down). However, you cannot move backward through a file. An example of using the more command is shown in Figure 3.4.

FIGURE 3.4   Using the more pager

```
#
# /etc/nsswitch.conf
#
# An example Name Service Switch config file. This file should be
# sorted with the most-used services at the beginning.
#
# The entry '[NOTFOUND=return]' means that the search for an
# entry should stop if the search in the previous entry turned
# up nothing. Note that if the search failed due to some other reason
# (like no NIS server responding) then the search continues with the
# next entry.
#
# Valid entries include:
#
#       nisplus             Use NIS+ (NIS version 3)
#       nis                 Use NIS (NIS version 2), also called YP
#       dns                 Use DNS (Domain Name Service)
#       files               Use the local files
#       db                  Use the local database (.db) files
#       compat              Use NIS on compat mode
#       hesiod              Use Hesiod for user lookups
#       [NOTFOUND=return]   Stop searching if not found so far
#

# To use db, put the "db" in front of "files" for entries you want to be
# looked up first in the databases
#
# Example:
#passwd:    db files nisplus nis
#shadow:    db files nisplus nis
#group:     db files nisplus nis

passwd:     files sss
shadow:     files sss
--More--(59%)
```

The output displayed in Figure 3.4 was reached by issuing the command more /etc/nsswitch.conf at the command line. Notice that the more pager utility displays at the screen's bottom how far along you are in the file. At any time you wish to exit from the more pager, you must press the q key. This is true even if you have reached the file's last line.

A more flexible pager is the less utility. While similar to the more utility in that you can move through a file a page (or line) at a time, this pager utility also allows you to move backward. Yet the less utility has far more capabilities than just that, which leads to the famous description of this pager, "less is more."

Figure 3.5 shows using the less utility on the /etc/nsswitch.conf text file. Notice that the display does not look that dissimilar from Figure 3.4, but don't let that fool you.

FIGURE 3.5   Using the `less` pager

```
#
# /etc/nsswitch.conf
#
# An example Name Service Switch config file. This file should be
# sorted with the most-used services at the beginning.
#
# The entry '[NOTFOUND=return]' means that the search for an
# entry should stop if the search in the previous entry turned
# up nothing. Note that if the search failed due to some other reason
# (like no NIS server responding) then the search continues with the
# next entry.
#
# Valid entries include:
#
#       nisplus                 Use NIS+ (NIS version 3)
#       nis                     Use NIS (NIS version 2), also called YP
#       dns                     Use DNS (Domain Name Service)
#       files                   Use the local files
#       db                      Use the local database (.db) files
#       compat                  Use NIS on compat mode
#       hesiod                  Use Hesiod for user lookups
#       [NOTFOUND=return]       Stop searching if not found so far
#

# To use db, put the "db" in front of "files" for entries you want to be
# looked up first in the databases
#
# Example:
#passwd:    db files nisplus nis
#shadow:    db files nisplus nis
#group:     db files nisplus nis

passwd:     files sss
shadow:     files sss
/etc/nsswitch.conf
```

The `less` page utility allows faster file traversal because it does not read the entire file prior to displaying the file's first page. You can also employ the up and down arrow keys to traverse the file as well as the spacebar to move forward a page and the Esc+V key combination to move backward a page. You can search for a particular word within the file by pressing the ? key, typing in the word you want to find, and pressing Enter to search backward. Replace the ? key with the / key and you can search forward. As with the `more` pager, you do need to use the q key to exit.

> By default, the Linux man page utility uses `less` as its pager. Learning the `less` utility's commands will allow you to search through various man pages with ease.

The `less` utility has amazing capabilities. It would be well worth your time to peruse the `less` pager's man pages and play around using its various file search and traversal commands on a large text file.

Finding Information

There are many ways to find various types of information on your Linux system. These methods are important to know so that you can make good administrative decisions and/or solve problems quickly. They will save you time as you perform your administrative tasks, as well as help you pass the certification exam. In the following sections, we'll explore several tools that assist in finding information.

Viewing File Information

It's not uncommon to look through a directory and see files that you're not familiar with, or perhaps even forgot why they're there. Linux has a couple of handy commands that can help you out with that.

The `file` command can provide basic information about the file type of a specified file, as shown in Listing 3.31.

Listing 3.31: Using the `file` command

```
$ file mytest
mytest: Bourne-Again shell script, ASCII text executable
$
```

The output from the `file` command shows that Linux recognizes the `mytest` file as a shell script file, in ASCII text format, and as an executable file.

If you'd like to see information about when a file was created, modified, or last accessed, use the `stat` command, as shown in Listing 3.32.

Listing 3.32: Using the `stat` command

```
$ stat mytest
  File: mytest
  Size: 1016  Blocks: 8 IO Block: 4096 regular file
Device: 805h/2053d    Inode: 1054186      Links: 1
Access: (0764/-rwxrw-r--)
Uid: ( 1000/    rich)
Gid: ( 1000/    rich)
Access: 2021-11-06 09:18:23.856584608 -0500
Modify: 2021-10-31 11:25:22.048406517 -0500
Change: 2021-10-31 11:25:22.048406517 -0500
 Birth: -
$
```

As seen in Listing 3.32, the output from the `stat` command provides basic information about the file, such as the file's name, size, inode number, and the physical device it's stored on. But it also provides some harder-to-find information, such as the last time the file was accessed and modified.

Exploring File Differences

A handy command to explore text file differences is the `diff` command. It allows you to make comparisons between two files, line by line. The basic syntax for the command is:

```
diff [OPTION]... FILES
```

With the diff utility you can perform a variety of comparisons. In addition, you can format the output to make the results easier for viewing. Table 3.7 shows a few commonly used options.

TABLE 3.7   The diff command's commonly used options

Short	Long	Description
-e	--ed	Create an ed script, which can be used to make the first file compared the same as the second file compared.
-q	--brief	If files are different, issue a simple message expressing this.
-r	--recursive	Compare any subdirectories within the original directory tree, and consecutively compare their contents and the subdirectories as well (recursive).
-s	--report-identical-files	If files are the same, issue a simple message expressing this.
-W n	--width n	Display a width maximum of n characters for output.
-y	--side-by-side	Display output in two columns.

To simply see if differences exist between two text files, you enter the diff command with the -q switch followed by the filenames. An example is shown in Listing 3.33. To help you see the exact file differences, the pr command is employed first to display both files side by side in a column format.

Listing 3.33: Quickly comparing files using the diff -q command

```
$ pr -mtw 35 numbers.txt random.txt
42                      42
2A                      Flat Land
52                      Schrodinger's Cat
0010 1010               0010 1010
*                       0000 0010
$
$ diff -q numbers.txt random.txt
Files numbers.txt and random.txt differ
$
```

For just a quick view of differences between files, modify the diff command's output to display the files in a column format. Use the -y (or --side-by-side) option along with the -W (or --width) switch for an easier display to read, as shown in Listing 3.34. The pipe symbol (|) designates the second file's lines, which are different from those in the first file.

Listing 3.34: Using the diff command for quick file differences

```
$ diff -yW 35 numbers.txt random.txt
42                 42
2A               | Flat Land
52               | Schrodinger's
0010 1010          0010 1010
*                | 0000 0010
$
```

The diff utility provides more than just differences; it also denotes what needs to be appended, changed, or deleted to make the first file identical to the second file. To see the exact differences between the files and any needed modifications, remove the -q switch. An example is shown in Listing 3.35.

Listing 3.35: Employing the diff command

```
$ diff numbers.txt random.txt
2,3c2,3
< 2A
< 52
---
> Flat Land
> Schrodinger's Cat
5c5
< *
---
> 0000 0010
$
```

The diff command's output can be a little confusing. In Listing 3.35, the first output line displays 2,3c2,3. This output tells you that to make the first file, numbers.txt, just like the second file, random.txt, you will need to change the numbers.txt file's lines 2 through 3 to match the random.txt file's lines 2 through 3. The output's next six lines show each file's text content that does not match, separated by a dashed line. Next, the 5c5 designates that line 5 in numbers.txt needs to be changed to match line 5 in the random.txt file.

The diff command is rather powerful. Not only can it tell you the differences between text file lines, but it can also create a script for you to use. The script allows you to modify the first compared text file and turn it into a twin of the second text file. This function is demonstrated in the next chapter.

The letter c in the diff utility's output denotes that changes are needed. You may also see an a for any needed additions or d for any needed deletions.

Using Simple Pinpoint Commands

Commands that quickly locate (pinpoint) files are very useful. They allow you to determine if a particular utility is installed on your system, locate a needed configuration file, find helpful documentation, and so on. The beauty of the commands covered here is that they are simple to use.

The which command shows you the full path name of a shell command passed as an argument. Listing 3.36 shows examples of using this utility.

Listing 3.36: Using the which command

```
$ which diff
/usr/bin/diff
$
$ which shutdown
/usr/sbin/shutdown
$
$ which line
/usr/bin/which: no line in (/usr/local/bin:/usr/bin:/usr/local/sbin:
/usr/sbin:/home/Christine/.local/bin:/home/Christine/bin)
$
$ echo $PATH
/usr/local/bin:/usr/bin:/usr/local/sbin:/usr/sbin:
/home/Christine/.local/bin:/home/Christine/bin
$
```

In the first example in Listing 3.36, the which command is used to find the diff command's program location. The command displays the full path name of /usr/bin/diff. The shutdown utility is located in a sbin directory. However, the line program is not installed on this system, and the which utility displays all the directories it searched to find the program. It uses the PATH environment variable, whose contents are also displayed in Listing 3.36, to determine which directories to search.

Environment variables are configuration settings that modify your process's environment. When you type in a command (program) name, the PATH variable sets the directories Linux will search for the program binary. It is also used by other commands, such as the which utility. Note that directory names are separated by a colon (:) in the PATH list.

The which command is also handy for quickly determining if a command is using an alias. Listing 3.37 shows an example of this.

Listing 3.37: Using the which command to see a command alias

```
$ which ls
alias ls='ls --color=auto'
        /usr/bin/ls
$
$ unalias ls
$
$ which ls
/usr/bin/ls
$
```

When the which utility is used on the ls command in Listing 3.37, it shows that currently the ls command has an alias. Thus, when you type ls, it is as if you have typed in the ls --color=auto command. After employing the unalias command on ls, the which utility only shows the ls program's location.

Another simple pinpoint command is the whereis utility. This utility allows you to not only locate any command's program binaries but also locate source code files as well as any man pages. Examples of using the whereis utility are shown in Listing 3.38.

Listing 3.38: Employing the whereis command

```
$ whereis diff
diff: /usr/bin/diff /usr/share/man/man1/diff.1.gz
/usr/share/man/man1p/diff.1p.gz
$
$ whereis line
line:
$
```

The first command issued in Listing 3.38 searches for program binaries, source code files, and man pages for the diff utility. In this case, the whereis command finds a binary file as well as two man page files. However, when whereis is used to locate files for the fictitious line utility, nothing is found on the system.

A handy and simple utility to use in finding files is the locate program. This utility searches a database, mlocate.db, which is located in the /var/lib/mlocate/ directory, to determine if a particular file exists on the local system. The basic syntax for the locate command is as follows:

```
locate [OPTION]... PATTERN...
```

Notice in the syntax that the locate utility uses a pattern list to find files. Thus, you can employ partial filenames and regular expressions and, with the command options, ignore case. Table 3.8 shows a few commonly used locate command options.

TABLE 3.8   The locate command's commonly used options

Short	Long	Description
-A	--all	Display filenames that match all the patterns, instead of displaying files that match only one pattern in the pattern list.
-b	--basename	Display only file names that match the pattern and do not include any directory names that match the pattern.
-c	--count	Display only the number of files whose name matches the pattern instead of displaying file names.
-i	--ignore-case	Ignore case in the pattern for matching filenames.
-q	--quiet	Do not display any error messages, such as permission denied, when processing.
-r	--regexp R	Use the regular expression, R, instead of the pattern list to match filenames.
-w	--wholename	Display filenames that match the pattern and include any directory names that match the pattern. This is default behavior.

To find a file with the locate command, just enter **locate** followed by the filename. If the file is on your system and you have permission to view it, the locate utility will display the file's directory path and name. An example of this is shown in Listing 3.39.

Listing 3.39: Using the locate command to find a file

```
$ locate Project42.txt
/home/Christine/Answers/Project42.txt
$
```

Using the locate command *PATTERN* can be a little tricky, due to default pattern *file globbing*. File globbing occurs when you use wildcards, such as an asterisk (*) or a question mark (?), added to a filename argument in a command, and the filename is expanded into multiple names. For example, passw*d could be expanded into the filename password or passwrd.

If you don't enter any wildcards into your pattern, the locate command, by default, adds wildcards to the pattern. So if you enter the pattern, **passwd**, it is automatically turned into ***passwd***. Thus, if you just want to search for the base name passwd, with no file globbing, you must add quotation marks (single or double) around the pattern and precede the pattern with the \ character. A few examples of this are shown in Listing 3.40.

Listing 3.40: Using the locate command with no file globbing

```
$ locate -b passwd
/etc/passwd
/etc/passwd-
/etc/pam.d/passwd
/etc/security/opasswd
/usr/bin/gpasswd
[...]
/usr/share/vim/vim74/syntax/passwd.vim
$
$ locate -b '\passwd'
/etc/passwd
/etc/pam.d/passwd
/usr/bin/passwd
/usr/share/bash-completion/completions/passwd
$
```

The first example in Listing 3.40 shows what would happen if you allow the default file globbing to occur. Many more files are displayed than those named passwd. So many files are displayed that the listing had to be snipped to fit. However, in the second example, file globbing is turned off with the use of quotation marks and the \ character. Using this pattern with the locate utility provides the desired results of displaying files named passwd.

If you do not have permission to view a directory's contents, the locate command cannot show files that match your *PATTERN*, which are located in that directory. Thus, you may have some files missing from your display.

Keep in mind that the locate command's *PATTERN* is really a pattern list. So, you can add additional patterns. Just be sure to separate them with a space, as shown in Listing 3.41.

Listing 3.41: Using the locate command with a pattern list

```
$ locate -b '\passwd' '\group'
/etc/group
/etc/passwd
/etc/iproute2/group
/etc/pam.d/passwd
```

```
/usr/bin/passwd
/usr/share/X11/xkb/symbols/group
/usr/share/bash-completion/completions/passwd
$
```

Another problem you can run into deals with newly created or downloaded files. The locate utility is really searching the mlocate.db database as opposed to searching the virtual directory structure. This database is typically updated only one time per day via a cron job. Therefore, if the file is newly created, locate won't find it.

The mlocate.db database is updated via the updatedb utility. You can run it manually using super user privileges if you need to find a newly created or downloaded file. Be aware that it may take a while to run.

Using Intricate Pinpoint Commands

While using simple commands to locate files is useful, they don't work in situations where you need to find files based on things such as metadata. Thankfully, there are more complex commands that can help.

The find command is flexible. It allows you to locate files based on data, such as who owns the file, when the file was last modified, permission set on the file, and so on. The basic command syntax is:

```
find  [PATH...] [OPTION] [EXPRESSION]
```

The PATH argument is a starting point directory, because you designate a starting point in a directory tree and find will search through that directory and all its subdirectories (recursively) for the file or files you seek. You can use a single period (.) to designate your present working directory as the starting point directory.

 There are also options for the find command itself that handle such items as following or not following links and debugging. In addition, you can have a file deleted or a command executed if a particular file is located. See the *find* utility's man page for more information on these features.

The EXPRESSION command argument and its preceding OPTION control what type of metadata filters are applied to the search as well as any settings that may limit the search. Table 3.9 shows the more commonly used OPTION and EXPRESSION combinations.

The find utility has many features. Examples help clarify the use of this command. Listing 3.42 provides a few.

TABLE 3.9   The find command's commonly used options and expressions

Option	Expression	Description
-cmin	*n*	Display names of files whose status changed *n* minutes ago.
-empty	N/A	Display names of files that are empty and are a regular text file or a directory.
-gid	*n*	Display names of files whose group id is equal to *n*.
-group	*name*	Display names of files whose group is *name*.
-inum	*n*	Display names of files whose inode number is equal to *n*.
-maxdepth	*n*	When searching for files, traverse down into the starting point directory's tree only *n* levels.
-mmin	*n*	Display names of files whose data changed *n* minutes ago.
-name	*pattern*	Display names of files whose name matches *pattern*. Many regular expression arguments may be used in the *pattern* and need to be enclosed in quotation marks to avoid unpredictable results. Replace -name with -iname to ignore case.
-nogroup	N/A	Display names of files where no group name exists for the file's group ID.
-nouser	N/A	Display names of files where no username exists for the file's user ID.
-perm	*mode*	Display names of files whose permissions matches *mode*. Either octal or symbolic modes may be used.
-size	*n*	Display names of files whose size matches *n*. Suffixes can be used to make the size more human readable, such as G for gigabytes.
-user	*name*	Display names of files whose owner is *name*.

Listing 3.42: Employing the find command

```
$ find . -name "*.txt"
./Project47.txt
./Answers/Project42.txt
```

```
./Answers/Everything/numbers.txt
./Answers/Everything/random.txt
./Answers/Project43.txt
./Answers/Project44.txt
./Answers/Project45.txt
./Answers/Project46.txt
./SpaceOpera/OriginalSFile.txt
./SpaceOpera/SoftLinkFile.txt
$
$ find . -maxdepth 2 -name "*.txt"
./Project47.txt
./Answers/Project42.txt
./Answers/Project43.txt
./Answers/Project44.txt
./Answers/Project45.txt
./Answers/Project46.txt
./SpaceOpera/OriginalSFile.txt
./SpaceOpera/SoftLinkFile.txt
$
```

The first example in Listing 3.42 is looking for files in the present working directory's tree with a txt file extension. Notice that the -name option's *pattern* uses quotation marks to avoid unpredictable results. In the second example, a -maxdepth option is added so that the find utility searches only two directories: the current directory and one subdirectory level down.

The find command is handy for auditing your system on a regular basis as well as when you are concerned that your server has been hacked. The -perm option is useful for one of these audit types, and an example is shown in Listing 3.43.

Listing 3.43: Using the find command to audit a server

```
$ find /usr/bin -perm /4000
/usr/bin/newgrp
/usr/bin/chsh
/usr/bin/arping
/usr/bin/gpasswd
/usr/bin/chfn
/usr/bin/traceroute6.iputils
/usr/bin/pkexec
/usr/bin/passwd
/usr/bin/sudo
$
```

In Listing 3.43, the /usr/bin directory is being audited for the potentially dangerous SUID permission by using the find utility and its -perm option. The expression used is /4000, which will ask the find utility to search for SUID settings (octal code 4) and, due to the forward slash (/) in front of the number, ignore the other file permissions (octal codes 000). The resulting filenames all legitimately use SUID, and thus, nothing suspicious is going on here.

 On older Linux systems, to enact a search as shown in Listing 3.41, you would enter **+4000** to designate the permission. The plus sign (+) is now deprecated for this use and has been replaced by the forward slash (/) symbol for the find command.

Earlier in this chapter we briefly covered the grep command for the purpose of reading a portion of a text file. You can also use this clever utility to search for files on your system.

Suppose it has been a while since you last modified your /etc/nsswitch.conf configuration file. A problem arises that requires you to make a change to the hosts: setting within the file and you can't remember its exact name. Instead of digging around using the ls command, just employ the grep command as shown in Listing 3.44 and quickly find the file's name.

Listing 3.44: Using the grep command to find a file

```
$ sudo grep -d skip hosts: /etc/*
/etc/nsswitch.conf:hosts:          files [...]
$
```

In Listing 3.44, the grep command is used to search all the files within the /etc/ directory for the hosts: setting. The -d skip option is used to skip any directory files in order to eliminate messages concerning them. The grep utility displays the configuration filename, followed by a colon (:) and the file's line where the setting is located. If you are not sure where in the /etc/ directory tree the configuration file is placed, you can tack on the -R (or -r, or --recursive) option to recursively search through the specified directory tree. If you don't have permission to search through various files, the grep command will issue annoying error messages. You'll learn in the next chapter how to redirect those error messages.

Quickly finding files as well as various types of information on your Linux server can help you be a more effective and efficient system administrator. It is a worthwhile investment to try any of this section's commands or their options that are new to you.

Summary

Being able to effectively and swiftly use the right commands at the shell command line is important for your daily job. It allows you to solve problems, manage files, gather information, peruse text files, and so on.

This chapter's purpose was to improve your Linux command-line tool belt. Not only will this help you in your day-to-day work life, but it will also help you successfully pass the CompTIA Linux+ certification exam.

Exam Essentials

Explain basic commands for handling files and directories.   Typical basic file and directory management activities include viewing and creating files, copying and moving files, and deleting files. For viewing and creating files and directories, use the `ls`, `touch`, and `mkdir` commands. When needing to duplicate, rename, or move files, employ one of the `mv`, `cp`, or `rsync` commands. For local large file copies, the `rsync` utility is typically the fastest. You can quickly delete an empty directory using the `rmdir` utility, but for directories full of files, you will need to use the `rm -r` command. Also, if you need to ensure that you are removing the correct files, be sure to use the `-i` option on the `rm` utility.

Describe both structures and commands involved in linking files.   Linking files is easy to do with the `ln` command. However, it is important for you to describe the underlying link structure. Hard-linked files share the same inode number, whereas soft-linked files do not. Soft or symbolic links can be broken if the file they link to is removed. It is also useful to understand the `readlink` utility to help you explore files that have multiple links.

Summarize the various utilities that can be employed to read text files.   To read entire text files, you can use the `cat`, `bat`, and `pr` utilities. Each utility has its own special features. If you need to read only the first or last lines of a text file, employ either the `head` or `tail` command. For a single text line out of a file, the `grep` utility is useful. For reviewing a file a page at a time, you can use either the `less` or the `more` pager utility.

Describe how to find information on your Linux system.   To determine two text files' differences, the `diff` utility is helpful. With this utility, you can also employ redirection and modify the files to make them identical. When you need to quickly find files on your system and want to use simple tools, the `which`, `whereis`, and `locate` commands will serve you well. Keep in mind that the `locate` utility uses a database that is typically updated only one time per day, so you may need to manually update it via the `updatedb` command. When simple file location tools are not enough, there are more complex searching utilities, such as `find` and `grep`. The `grep` command can employ regular expressions to assist in your search.

Review Questions

1. You are looking at a directory that you have not viewed in a long time and need to determine which files are actually directories. Which command is the best one to use?

   A. `mkdir -v`

   B. `ls`

   C. `ls -F`

   D. `ls -i`

   E. `ll`

2. You are using the `ls` command to look at a directory file's metadata but keep seeing metadata for the files within it instead. What command option will rectify this situation?

   A. `-a`

   B. `-d`

   C. `-F`

   D. `-l`

   E. `-R`

3. You have just created an empty directory called `MyDir`. Which command did you most likely use?

   A. `mkdir -v MyDir`

   B. `touch MyDir`

   C. `cp -R TheDir MyDir`

   D. `mv -r TheDir MyDir`

   E. `rmdir MyDir`

4. You have a file that is over 10 GB in size, and it needs to be backed up to a locally attached drive. What is the best utility to use in this situation?

   A. `readlink -f`

   B. `mv`

   C. `cp`

   D. `scp`

   E. `rsync`

5. A long-time server administrator has left the company, and now you are in charge of her system. Her old user account directory tree, /home/Zoe/, has been backed up. Which command is the best one to use to quickly remove her files and still indicate that you are removing the correct directory, but without forcing you to confirm every file deletion?

   A. `cp -R /home/Zoe/ /dev/null/`

   B. `mv -R /home/zoe/ /dev/null/`

   C. `rm -Rf /home/Zoe/`

   D. `rm -ri /home/Zoe/`

   E. `rm -rI /home/Zoe`

6. There is a large directory structure that needs to be renamed. What mv command options should you consider employing? (Choose all that apply.)

   A. `-f`

   B. `-i`

   C. `-n`

   D. `-r`

   E. `-v`

7. You are trying to decide whether to use a hard link or a symbolic link for a data file. The file is 5 GB, has mission-critical data, and is accessed via the command line by three other people. What should you do?

   A. Create a hard link so that the file can reside on a different filesystem for data protection.

   B. Create three hard links and provide the links to the three other people for data protection.

   C. Create three symbolic links and protect the links from the three other people for data protection.

   D. Create a symbolic link so that the file can reside on a different filesystem.

   E. Create a symbolic link so that the links can share an inode number.

8. A short text-based control file is no longer working properly with the program that reads it. You suspect the file was accidentally corrupted by a control code update you performed recently, even though the file's control codes are all correct. Which command should you use next on the file in your problem investigation?

   A. `cat -v`

   B. `cat -z`

   C. `cat -n`

   D. `cat -s`

   E. `cat -E`

9. You have two short text files that have maximum record lengths of 15 characters. You want to review these files side by side. Which of the following commands would be the best to use?

    A. pr -m

    B. pr -tl 20

    C. cat

    D. pr -mtl 20

    E. pr -ml 20

10. You have a lengthy file named FileA.txt. What will the head -15 FileA.txt command do?

    A. Display all but the last 15 lines of the file.

    B. Display all but the first 15 lines of the file.

    C. Display the first 15 lines of the file.

    D. Display the last 15 lines of the file.

    E. Generate an error message.

11. You have issued the command grep Hal on a text file you generated using information from a failed login attempts file. It returns nothing, but you just performed a test case by purposely failing to log into the Hal account prior to generating the text file. Which of the following is the best choice as your next step?

    A. Employ the tail command to peruse the text file.

    B. Employ the cat command to view the text file.

    C. Delete the text file and regenerate it using information from the failed login attempts file.

    D. Issue the grep -d skip Hal command on the text file.

    E. Issue the grep -i Hal command on the text file.

12. You are trying to peruse a rather large text file. A coworker suggests you use a pager. Which of the following best describes what your coworker is recommending?

    A. Use a utility that allows you to view the first few lines of the file.

    B. Use a utility that allows you to view one text page at time.

    C. Use a utility that allows you to search through the file.

    D. Use a utility that allows you to filter out text in the file.

    E. Use a utility that allows you to view the last few lines of the file.

13. Which of the following does not describe the less utility?

    A. It does not read the entire file prior to displaying the file's first page.

    B. You can use the up and down arrow keys to move through the file.

    C. You press the spacebar to move forward a page.

    D. You can use the Esc+V key combination to move backward a page.

    E. You can press the X key to exit from the utility.

14. Which diff option is the best option to allow you to quickly determine if two text files are different from one another?

   A. -e

   B. -q

   C. -s

   D. -W

   E. -y

15. You are working on a Linux server at the command line, and you try to issue a diff command and receive a response stating that the command was not found. What is the next best step to take in order to start the troubleshooting process?

   A. Hit your up arrow key and press Enter.

   B. Log out, log back in, and retry the command.

   C. Enter the which diff command.

   D. Enter the whereis diff command.

   E. Reboot the server and retry the command.

16. You are trying to find a file on your Linux server whose name is conf. Employing the locate conf command for your search shows many directories that contain the letters conf. What is the best description for why this is happening?

   A. The locate utility searches for only for directory names.

   B. You did not employ the -d skip switch.

   C. It is most likely because the locate database is corrupted.

   D. You did not employ the appropriate regular expression.

   E. It is due to file globbing on the pattern name.

17. You downloaded a large important file, fortytwo.db, from your company's local website to your Linux server but got interrupted by an emergency. Now you cannot remember where you stored the file. What is the best first step to fixing this problem?

   A. Issue the sudo updatedb command.

   B. Issue the locate -b fortytwo.db command.

   C. Issue the locate -b 'fortytwo.db' command.

   D. Download the file from the company's local website again.

   E. Issue the locate fortytwo.db command.

18. You want to search for a particular file, `main.conf`, using the `find` utility. This file most likely is located somewhere in the `/etc/` directory tree. Which of the following commands is the best one to use in this situation?

    A. `find -r /etc -name main.conf`

    B. `find / -name main.conf`

    C. `find /etc -maxdepth -name main.conf`

    D. `find /etc -name main.conf`

    E. `find main.conf /etc`

19. Yesterday a coworker, Michael, was fired for nefarious behavior. His account and home directory were immediately deleted. You need to audit the server to see if he left any files out in the virtual directory system. Which of the following commands is the best one to use in this situation?

    A. `find / -name Michael`

    B. `find / -user Michael`

    C. `find / -mmin 1440`

    D. `find ~ -user Michael`

    E. `find / -nouser`

20. You need to figure out what configuration file(s) hold a hostname directive. Which of the following commands is the best one to use?

    A. `which`

    B. `whereis`

    C. `grep`

    D. `locate`

    E. `find`

Chapter

4

Searching and Analyzing Text

✓ **Objective 1.2: Given a scenario, manage files and directories**

✓ **Objective 3.1: Given a scenario, create simple shell scripts to automate common tasks**

Managing a Linux server involves many important steps and decisions based on data. Trying to gather the information you need in an agile and efficient manner is crucial. There are many Linux structures and tools that can help you uncover the knowledge you seek quickly.

In this chapter, we'll add more items to your Linux command-line tool belt. We'll cover filtering and formatting text and the basics of redirection, all the way to editing text. Commands and concepts in this chapter will be built upon and used in later chapters.

Processing Text Files

Once you have found or created a text file, you may need to process it in some way to extract needed information. Understanding how to filter and format text will assist you in this endeavor. In the following sections, we'll take a look at tools and methods that will aid you in processing text files.

Filtering Text

To sift through the data in a large text file, it helps to quickly extract small data sections. The cut utility is a handy tool for doing this. It will allow you to view particular fields within a file's records. The command's basic syntax is as follows:

cut *OPTION*... *[FILE]*...

Before we delve into using this command, here are a few basics you should understand about the cut command:

Text File Records   A text file record is a single file line that ends in a newline linefeed, which is the ASCII character LF. You can see if your text file uses this end-of-line character via the cat -E command. It will display every newline linefeed as a $. If your text file records end in the ASCII character NUL, you can also use cut on them, but you must use the -z option.

Text File Record Delimiter   For some of the cut command options to be properly used, fields must exist within each text file record. These fields are not database-style fields but instead data that is separated by some *delimiter*. A delimiter is one or more characters that create a boundary between different data items within a record. A single space can be a delimiter. The password file, /etc/passwd, uses colons (:) to separate data items within a record.

Text File Changes   Contrary to its name, the cut command does not change any data within the text file. It simply copies the data you wish to view and displays it to you. Rest assured that no modifications are made to the file.

The cut utility has a few options you will use on a regular basis. These options are listed in Table 4.1.

TABLE 4.1   The cut command's commonly used options

Short	Long	Description
-c nlist	--characters nlist	Display only the record characters in the nlist (e.g., 1-5).
-b blist	--bytes blist	Display only the record bytes in the blist (e.g., 1-2).
-d d	--delimiter d	Designate the record's field delimiter as d. This overrides the Tab default delimiter. Put d within quotation marks to avoid unexpected results.
-f flist	--fields flist	Display only the record's fields denoted by flist (e.g., 1,3).
-s	--only-delimited	Display only records that contain the designated delimiter.
-z	--zero-terminated	Designate the record end-of-line character as the ASCII character NUL.

A few cut commands in action will help demonstrate its capabilities. Listing 4.1 shows a few cut utility examples.

Listing 4.1: Employing the cut command

```
$ head -2 /etc/passwd
root:x:0:0:root:/root:/bin/bash
bin:x:1:1:bin:/bin:/sbin/nologin
$
$ cut -d ":" -f 1,7 /etc/passwd
root:/bin/bash
bin:/sbin/nologin
[...]
$
```

```
$ cut -c 1-5 /etc/passwd
root:
bin:x
[...]
$
```

In Listing 4.1, the head command is used to display the password file's first two lines. This text file employs colons (:) to delimit the fields within each record. The first use of the cut command designates the colon delimiter using the -d option. Notice that the colon is encased in quotation marks to avoid unexpected results. The -f option is used to specify that only fields 1 (username) and 7 (shell) should be displayed.

The second example in Listing 4.1 uses the -c option. In this case, the nlist argument is set to 1-5, so every record's first five characters are displayed.

Occasionally it is worthwhile to save a cut command's output. You can do this by redirecting standard output, which is covered later in this chapter.

Another nice tool for filtering text is our old friend the grep command. The grep command is powerful in its use of regular expressions, which will really help with filtering text files. But before we cover those, peruse Table 4.2 for commonly used grep utility options.

TABLE 4.2   The grep command's commonly used options

Short	Long	Description
-c	--count	Display a count of text file records that contain a *PATTERN* match.
-d *action*	--directories=*action*	When a file is a directory, if *action* is set to read, read the directory as if it were a regular text file; if *action* is set to skip, ignore the directory; and if *action* is set to recurse, act as if the - R, -r, or --recursive option was used.
-E	--extended-regexp	Designate the *PATTERN* as an extended regular expression.
-i	--ignore-case	Ignore the case in the *PATTERN* as well as in any text file records.
-R, -r	--recursive	Search a directory's contents, and for any subdirectory within the original directory tree, consecutively search its contents as well (recursively).
-v	--invert-match	Display only text files records that do *not* contain a *PATTERN* match.

Many commands use *regular expressions*. A regular expression is a pattern template you define for a utility, such as grep, which uses the pattern to filter text. Basic regular expressions (BREs) include characters, such as a dot followed by an asterisk (.*), to represent multiple characters and a single dot (.) to represent one character. They also may use brackets to represent multiple characters, such as [a,e,i,o,u], or a range of characters, such as [A-z]. To find text file records that begin with particular characters, you can precede them with a caret (^) symbol. For finding text file records where particular characters are at the record's end, append a dollar sign ($) symbol to them.

> You will see in documentation and technical descriptions different names for regular expressions. The name may be shortened to *regex* or *regexp*.

Using a BRE pattern is fairly straightforward with the grep utility. Listing 4.2 shows some examples.

Listing 4.2: Using the grep command with a BRE pattern

```
$ grep daemon.*nologin /etc/passwd
daemon:x:2:2:daemon:/sbin:/sbin/nologin
[...]
daemon:/dev/null:/sbin/nologin
[...]
$
$ grep root /etc/passwd
root:x:0:0:root:/root:/bin/bash
operator:x:11:0:operator:/root:/sbin/nologin
$
$ grep ^root /etc/passwd
root:x:0:0:root:/root:/bin/bash
$
```

In the first snipped grep example within Listing 4.2, the grep command employs a pattern using the BRE .* characters. In this case, the grep utility will search the password file for any instances of the word daemon within a record and display that record if it also contains the word nologin after the word daemon.

The next two grep examples in Listing 4.2 are searching for instances of the word root within the password file. Notice that the first command displays two lines from the file. The second command employs the BRE ^ character and places it before the word root. This regular expression pattern causes grep to display only lines in the password file that begin with root.

The -v option is useful when auditing your configuration files with the grep utility. It produces a list of text file records that do not contain the pattern. Listing 4.3 shows an example of finding all the records in the password file that *do not* end in nologin. Notice that the BRE pattern puts the $ at the end of the word. If you were to place the $ before the word, it would be treated as a variable name instead of a BRE pattern.

Listing 4.3: Using the grep command to audit the password file

```
$ grep -v nologin$ /etc/passwd
root:x:0:0:root:/root:/bin/bash
sync:x:5:0:sync:/sbin:/bin/sync
[...]
Christine:x:1001:1001::/home/Christine:/bin/bash
$
```

Extended regular expressions (EREs) allow more complex patterns. For example, a vertical bar symbol (|) allows you to specify two possible words or character sets to match. You can also employ parentheses to designate additional subexpressions.

 If you would like to get a better handle on regular expressions, there are several good resources. Our favorite is Chapter 20 in the book *Linux Command Line and Shell Scripting Bible, 4th Edition* by Richard Blum and Christine Bresnahan (Wiley, 2021).

Using ERE patterns can be rather tricky. A few examples employing grep with EREs are helpful, such as the ones shown in Listing 4.4.

Listing 4.4: Using the grep command with an ERE pattern

```
$ grep -E "^root|^dbus" /etc/passwd
root:x:0:0:root:/root:/bin/bash
dbus:x:81:81:System message bus:/:/sbin/nologin
$
$ egrep "(daemon|s).*nologin" /etc/passwd
bin:x:1:1:bin:/bin:/sbin/nologin
daemon:x:2:2:daemon:/sbin:/sbin/nologin
[...]
$
```

In the first example, the grep command uses the -E option to indicate that the pattern is an extended regular expression. If you did not employ the -E option, unpredictable results would occur. Quotation marks around the ERE pattern protect it from misinterpretation. The command searches for any password file records that start with either the word root or the word dbus. Thus, a caret (^) is placed prior to each word, and a vertical bar (|) separates the words to indicate that the record can start with either word.

In Listing 4.4's second example, notice that the egrep command is employed. The egrep command is equivalent to using the grep -E command. The ERE pattern here uses quotation marks to avoid misinterpretation and employs parentheses to issue a subexpression. The subexpression consists of a choice, indicated by the vertical bar (|), between the word daemon and the letter s. Also in the ERE pattern, the .* symbols are used to indicate there can be anything in between the subexpression choice and the word nologin in the text file record.

Take a deep breath. That was a lot to take in. However, as hard as BRE and ERE patterns are, they are worth using with `grep` to filter out data from your text files.

Formatting Text

Often to understand the data within text files, you need to reformat file data in some way. There are a couple of simple utilities you can use to do this.

The `sort` utility sorts a file's data. Keep in mind it makes no changes to the original file. Only the output is sorted. The basic syntax of this command is as follows:

```
sort [OPTION]... [FILE]...
```

If you want to order a file's content using the system's standard sort order, simply enter the `sort` command followed by the name of the file you wish to sort. Listing 4.5 shows an example of this.

Listing 4.5: Employing the `sort` command

```
$ cat alphabet.txt
Alpha
Tango
Bravo
Echo
Foxtrot
$
$ sort alphabet.txt
Alpha
Bravo
Echo
Foxtrot
Tango
$
```

If a file contains numbers, the data may not be in the order you desire using the `sort` utility. To obtain proper numeric order, add the `-n` option to the command, as shown in Listing 4.6.

Listing 4.6: Using the `sort -n` command

```
$ cat counts.txt
105
8
37
42
54
$
```

```
$ sort counts.txt
105
37
42
54
8
$ sort -n counts.txt
8
37
42
54
105
$
```

In Listing 4.6, notice that the file has different numbers listed in an unsorted order. The second example attempts to numerically order the file, using the sort command with no options. This yields incorrect results. However, the third example uses the sort -n command, which properly orders the file numerically.

There are several useful options for the sort command. Commonly used switches are shown in Table 4.3.

TABLE 4.3   The sort command's commonly used options

Short	Long	Description
-c	--check	Check if file is already sorted. Produces no output if file is sorted. If file is not sorted, it displays the file name, the line number, the keyword disorder, and the first unordered line's text.
-f	--ignore-case	Consider lowercase characters as uppercase characters when sorting.
-k n1 [,n2]	--key=n1 [,n2]	Sort the file using the data in the n1 field. May optionally specify a second sort field by following n1 with a comma and specifying n2. Field delimiters are spaces by default.
-M	--month-sort	Display text in month of the year order. Months must be listed as standard three-letter abbreviations, such as JAN, FEB, MAR, and so on.
-n	--numeric-sort	Display text in numerical order.
-o file	--output=file	Create a new sorted file named file.
-r	--reverse	Display text in reverse sort order.

The sort utility is handy for formatting a small text file to help you understand the data it contains. Another useful command for formatting small text files is one we've already touched on: the cat command.

The cat command's original purpose in life was to concatenate files for display. That is where it gets its name. However, it is typically used to display a single file. Listing 4.7 is an example of concatenating two files to display their text contents one after the other.

Listing 4.7: Using the cat command to concatenate files

```
$ cat numbers.txt random.txt
42
2A
52
0010 1010
*
42
Flat Land
Schrodinger's Cat
0010 1010
0000 0010
$
```

Both files displayed in Listing 4.7 have the number 42 as their first line. This is the only way you can tell where one file ends and the other begins, because the cat utility does not denote a file's beginning or end in its output.

Unfortunately, often the cat utility's useful formatting options go unexplored. Table 4.4 has a few commonly used switches.

TABLE 4.4 The cat command's commonly used options

Short	Long	Description
-A	--show-all	Equivalent to using the option -vET combination.
-E	--show-ends	Display a $ when a newline linefeed is encountered.
-n	--number	Number all text file lines and display that number in the output.
-s	--squeeze-blank	Do not display repeated blank empty text file lines.
-T	--show-tabs	Display a ^I when a Tab character is encountered.
-v	--show-nonprinting	Display nonprinting characters when encountered using either ^ and/or M- notation.

Being able to display nonprinting characters with the cat command is handy. If a text file is causing some sort of odd problem when you're processing it, you can quickly see if any nonprintable characters are embedded. Listing 4.8 contains an example of this method.

Listing 4.8: Using the cat command to display nonprintable characters

```
$ cat bell.txt

$ cat -v bell.txt
^G
$
```

In Listing 4.8, the first cat command displays the file, and it appears to simply contain a blank line. However, by employing the -v option, you can see that a nonprintable character exists within the file. The ^G is in caret notation and indicates that the nonprintable Unicode character BEL is embedded in the file. This character causes a bell sound when the file is displayed.

Another handy set of utilities for formatting text are the pr and printf commands. The pr utility was covered in Chapter 3, "Managing Files, Directories, and Text," so let's explore the printf command. Its entire purpose in life is to format and display text data. It has the following basic syntax:

```
printf FORMAT [ARGUMENT]...
```

The basic idea is that you provide text formatting via *FORMAT* for the *ARGUMENT*. A simple example is shown in Listing 4.9.

Listing 4.9: Employing the printf command

```
$ printf "%s\n" "Hello World"
Hello World
$
```

In Listing 4.9, the printf command uses the %s\n as the formatting description. It is enclosed within quotation marks to prevent unexpected results. The %s tells printf to print the string of characters listed in the *ARGUMENT*, which in this example is Hello World. The \n portion of the *FORMAT* tells the printf command to print a newline character after printing the string. This allows the prompt to display on a new line, instead of at the displayed string's end.

While the pr utility can handle formatting entire text files, the printf command is geared toward formatting the output of a single text line. You must incorporate other commands and write a Bash shell script for it to process a whole text file with it.

The formatting characters for the printf command are not too difficult once you have reviewed them. A few common ones are listed in Table 4.5.

TABLE 4.5   The `printf` command's commonly used *FORMAT* settings

FORMAT	Description
%c	Display the first *ARGUMENT* character.
%d	Display the *ARGUMENT* as a decimal integer number.
%f	Display the *ARGUMENT* as a floating-point number.
%s	Display the *ARGUMENT* as a character string.
\%	Display a percentage sign.
\"	Display a double quotation mark.
\\	Display a backslash.
\f	Include a form feed character.
\n	Include a newline character.
\r	Include a carriage return.
\t	Include a horizontal tab.

In Listing 4.10 the `printf` command is used to print a floating-point number, which has three digits after the decimal point. Only two are desired, so the `%.2f` format is used.

Listing 4.10: Using the `printf` command to format a floating-point number

```
$ printf "%.2f\n" 98.532
98.53
$
```

Formatting text data can be useful in uncovering information. Be sure to play around with all these commands to get some worthwhile experience.

Determining Word Count

Besides formatting data, gathering statistics on various text files can also be helpful when you are managing a server. The easiest and most common utility for determining counts in a text file is the wc utility. The command's basic syntax is as follows:

```
wc [OPTION]... [FILE]...
```

When you issue the wc command with no options and pass it a filename, the utility will display the file's number of lines, words, and bytes in that order. Listing 4.11 shows an example.

Listing 4.11: Employing the wc command

```
$ wc random.txt
 5  9 52 random.txt
$
```

There a few useful and commonly used options for the wc command. These are shown in Table 4.6.

TABLE 4.6   The wc command's commonly used options

Short	Long	Description
-c	--bytes	Display the file's byte count.
-L	--max-line-length	Display the byte count of the file's longest line.
-l	--lines	Display the file's line count.
-m	--chars	Display the file's character count.
-w	--words	Display the file's word count.

An interesting wc option for troubleshooting configuration files is the -L switch. Generally speaking, configuration file line length will be under 150 bytes, though there are exceptions. Thus, if you have just edited a configuration file and that service is no longer working, check the file's longest line length. A longer-than-usual line length indicates you might have accidentally merged two configuration file lines. An example is shown in Listing 4.12.

Listing 4.12: Using the wc command to check line length

```
$ wc -L /etc/nsswitch.conf
72 /etc/nsswitch.conf
$
```

In Listing 4.12, the file's line length shows a normal maximum line length of 72 bytes. This wc command switch can also be useful if you have other utilities that cannot process text files exceeding certain line lengths.

Redirecting Input and Output

When processing text and text files to help you to gather data, you may want to save that data. In addition, you may need to combine multiple refinement steps to obtain the information you need.

Handling Standard Output

It is important to know that Linux treats every object as a file. This includes the output process, such as displaying a text file on the screen. Each file object is identified using a *file descriptor*, an integer that classifies a process's open files. The file descriptor that identifies output from a command or script file is 1. It is also identified by the abbreviation STDOUT, which describes standard output.

By default, STDOUT directs output to your current terminal. Your process's current terminal is represented by the /dev/tty file.

A simple command to use when discussing standard output is the echo command. Issue the echo command along with a text string, and the text string will display to your process's STDOUT, which is typically the terminal screen. An example is shown in Listing 4.13.

Listing 4.13: Employing the echo command to display text to STDOUT

```
$ echo "Hello World"
Hello World
$
```

The neat thing about STDOUT is that you can redirect it via *redirection operators* on the command line. A redirection operator allows you to change the default behavior of where input and output are sent. For STDOUT, you redirect the output using the > redirection operator, as shown in Listing 4.14.

Listing 4.14: Employing a STDOUT redirection operator

```
$ grep nologin$ /etc/passwd
bin:x:1:1:bin:/bin:/sbin/nologin
daemon:x:2:2:daemon:/sbin:/sbin/nologin
[...]
$ grep nologin$ /etc/passwd > NologinAccts.txt
$
$ less NologinAccts.txt
bin:x:1:1:bin:/bin:/sbin/nologin
daemon:x:2:2:daemon:/sbin:/sbin/nologin
[...]
$
```

In Listing 4.14, the password file is being audited for all accounts that use the /sbin/ nologin shell via the grep command. The grep command's output is lengthy and was snipped in the listing. It would be so much easier to redirect STDOUT to a file. This was done in Listing 4.14 by issuing the same grep command but tacking on a redirection operator, >, and a filename to the command's end. The effect was to send the command's output to the file NologinAccts.txt instead of the screen. Now the data file can be viewed using the less utility.

 WARNING   If you use the > redirection operator and send the output to a file that already exists, that file's current data will be deleted. Use caution when employing this operator.

To append data to a preexisting file, you need to use a slightly different redirection operator. The >> operator will append data to a preexisting file. If the file does not exist, it is created and the outputted data is added to it. Listing 4.15 shows an example of using this redirection operator.

Listing 4.15: Using a STDOUT redirection operator to append text

```
$ echo "Nov 16, 2019" > AccountAudit.txt
$
$ wc -l /etc/passwd >> AccountAudit.txt
$
$ cat AccountAudit.txt
Nov 16, 2019
44 /etc/passwd
$
```

The first command in Listing 4.15 puts a date stamp into the AccountAudit.txt file. Because that date stamp needs to be preserved, the next command appends STDOUT to the file using the >> redirection operator. The file can continue to be appended to using the >> operator for future commands.

Redirecting Standard Error

Another handy item to redirect is standard error. The file descriptor that identifies a command or script file error is 2. It is also identified by the abbreviation STDERR, which describes standard error. STDERR, like STDOUT, is by default sent to your terminal (/dev/tty).

The basic redirection operator to send STDERR to a file is the 2> operator. If you need to append the file, use the 2>> operator. Listing 4.16 shows an example of redirecting standard error.

Listing 4.16: Employing a STDERR redirection operator

```
$ grep -d skip hosts: /etc/*
grep: /etc/anacrontab: Permission denied
grep: /etc/audisp: Permission denied
[...]
$
$ grep -d skip hosts: /etc/* 2> err.txt
/etc/nsswitch.conf:#hosts:      db files nisplus nis dns
/etc/nsswitch.conf:hosts:       files dns myhostname
[...]
$
$ cat err.txt
grep: /etc/anacrontab: Permission denied
grep: /etc/audisp: Permission denied
[...]
$
```

The first command in Listing 4.16 was issued to find any files within the /etc/ directory that contain the hosts: directive. Unfortunately, since the user does not have super user privileges, several permission denied error messages are generated. This clutters up the output and makes it difficult to see what files contain this directive.

To declutter the output, the second command in Listing 4.16 redirects STDERR to the err.txt file using the 2> redirection operator. This makes it much easier to see what files contain the hosts: directive. If needed, the error messages can be reviewed because they reside now in the err.txt file.

> Sometimes you want to send standard error and standard output to the same file. In these cases, use the &> redirection operator to accomplish the goal.

If you don't care to keep a copy of the error messages, you can always throw them away. This is done by redirecting STDERR to the /dev/null file, as shown snipped in Listing 4.17.

Listing 4.17: Using an STDERR redirection operator to remove error messages

```
$ grep -d skip hosts: /etc/* 2> /dev/null
/etc/nsswitch.conf:#hosts:      db files nisplus nis dns
/etc/nsswitch.conf:hosts:       files dns myhostname
[...]
$
```

The /dev/null file is sometimes called the *black hole*. This name comes from the fact that anything you put into it, you cannot retrieve.

Regulating Standard Input

Standard input, by default, comes into your Linux system via the keyboard or other input devices. The file descriptor that identifies an input into a command or script file is 0. It is also identified by the abbreviation STDIN, which describes standard input.

As with STDOUT and STDERR, you can redirect STDIN. The basic redirection operator is the < symbol. The tr command is one of the few utilities that require you to redirect standard input. An example is shown in Listing 4.18.

Listing 4.18: Employing a STDIN redirection operator

```
$ cat Grades.txt
89 76 100 92 68 84 73
$
$ tr " " "," < Grades.txt
89,76,100,92,68,84,73
$
```

In Listing 4.18, the file Grades.txt contains various integers separated by a space. The second command utilizes the tr utility to change those spaces into a comma (,). Because the tr command requires the STDIN redirection symbol, it is also employed in the second command followed by the filename. Keep in mind that this command did not change the Grades.txt file. It only displayed to STDOUT what the file would look like with these changes.

It's nice to have a concise summary of the redirection operators. Therefore, we have provided one in Table 4.7.

A practical example of redirecting STDOUT and STDIN involves the diff utility, covered in Chapter 3. The diff utility allows you to discover any disparities between two text files and change the differing text file so that the two files are identical. It involves a few steps. The first ones are shown in Listing 4.19 along with extra explanatory commands.

Listing 4.19: Using diff with redirection operators

```
$ pr -mtl 15 numbers.txt random.txt
42                          42
2A                          Flat Land
52                          Schrodinger's Cat
0010 1010                   0010 1010
*                           0000 0010
$
$ cp numbers.txt n.txt
$
$ diff -e n.txt random.txt > switch.sh
$
```

TABLE 4.7 Commonly used redirection operators

Operator	Description
>	Redirect STDOUT to specified file. If file exists, overwrite it. If it does not exist, create it.
>>	Redirect STDOUT to specified file. If file exists, append to it. If it does not exist, create it.
2>	Redirect STDERR to specified file. If file exists, overwrite it. If it does not exist, create it.
2>>	Redirect STDERR to specified file. If file exists, append to it. If it does not exist, create it.
&>	Redirect STDOUT and STDERR to specified file. If file exists, overwrite it. If it does not exist, create it.
&>>	Redirect STDOUT and STDERR to specified file. If file exists, append to it. If it does not exist, create it.
<	Redirect STDIN from specified file into command.
<>	Redirect STDIN from specified file into command and redirect STDOUT to specified file.

In Listing 4.19, the pr utility displays the two files numbers.txt and random.txt side by side. You can see that differences exist between these two files. A new copy of the numbers.txt file is created, so any changes are only made to the new file, n.txt, in case anything goes wrong. The diff command uses the -e switch to create an ed script. This script will make the n.txt file the same as the random.txt file.

Prior to enacting the created script, a few additional items must be added to it. In Listing 4.20, the echo command is used two times to append letters to the script.

Listing 4.20: Update an ed script via redirection operators

```
$ echo w >> switch.sh
$ echo q >> switch.sh
$
$ cat switch.sh
5c
0000 0010
.
```

```
2,3c
Flat Land
Schrodinger's Cat
.
w
q
$
```

In Listing 4.20, the last command displays the ed script, switch.sh, to standard output. This script will modify the n.txt file, as shown in Listing 4.21.

Listing 4.21: Modifying a file via an ed script

```
$ diff -q n.txt random.txt
Files n.txt and random.txt differ
$
$ ed n.txt < switch.sh
21
52
$
$ diff -q n.txt random.txt
$
```

In Listing 4.21, the diff command does a simple comparison between the two files. Notice that it sends a message to STDOUT that the files are different. Then the ed utility is employed. To enact the script created by the diff command in Listing 4.21, the STDIN redirection operator is used. The last command in Listing 4.21 shows that there are now no differences between these two files.

Piping Commands

If you really want to enact powerful and quick results at the Linux command line, you need to explore pipes. The pipe is a simple redirection operator represented by the ASCII character 124 (|), which is called the vertical bar, vertical slash, or vertical line.

 Be aware that some keyboards and text display the vertical bar not as a single vertical line. Instead, it looks like a vertical double dash.

With the pipe, you can redirect STDOUT, STDIN, and STDERR between multiple commands all on one command line. Now that is powerful redirection.

The basic syntax for redirection with the pipe symbol is as follows:

command 1 | command 2 [| command n]...

The syntax for pipe redirection shows that the first command, command1, is executed. Its STDOUT is redirected as STDIN into the second command, command2. Also, you can pipe more commands together than just two. Keep in mind that any command in the pipeline has its STDOUT redirected as STDIN to the next command in the pipeline. Listing 4.22 shows a simple use of pipe redirection.

Listing 4.22: Employing pipe redirection

```
$ grep /bin/bash$ /etc/passwd | wc -l
3
$
```

In Listing 4.22, the first command in the pipe searches the password file for any records that end in /bin/bash. This is essentially finding all user accounts that use the Bash shell as their default account shell. The output from the first command in the pipe is passed as input into the second command in the pipe. The wc -l command will count how many lines have been produced by the grep command. The results show that there are only three accounts on this Linux system that have the Bash shell set as their default shell.

You can get creative using pipe redirection. Listing 4.23 shows a command employing over four different utilities in a pipeline to audit accounts using the /sbin/nologin default shell.

Listing 4.23: Employing pipe redirection for several commands

```
$ grep /sbin/nologin$ /etc/passwd | cut -d ":" -f 1 | sort | less
abrt
adm
avahi
bin
chrony
[...]
:
```

In Listing 4.23, the output from the grep command is fed as input into the cut command. The cut utility removes only the first field from each password record, which is the account username. The output of the cut command is used as input into the sort command, which alphabetically sorts the usernames. Finally, the sort utility's output is piped as input into the less command for leisurely perusing through the account usernames.

In cases where you want to keep a copy of the command pipeline's output as well as view it, the tee command will help. Similar to a tee pipe fitting in plumbing, where the water flow is sent in multiple directions, the tee command allows you to both save the output to a file and display it to STDOUT. Listing 4.24 contains an example of this handy command.

Listing 4.24: Employing the tee command

```
$ grep /bin/bash$ /etc/passwd | tee BashUsers.txt
root:x:0:0:root:/root:/bin/bash
user1:x:1000:1000:Student User One:/home/user1:/bin/bash
Christine:x:1001:1001::/home/Christine:/bin/bash
$
$ cat BashUsers.txt
root:x:0:0:root:/root:/bin/bash
user1:x:1000:1000:Student User One:/home/user1:/bin/bash
Christine:x:1001:1001::/home/Christine:/bin/bash
$
```

The first command in Listing 4.24 searches the password file for any user account records that end in /bin/bash. That output is piped into the tee command, which displays the output as well as saves it to the BashUsers.txt file. The tee command is handy when you are installing software from the command line and want to see what is happening as well as keep a log file of the transaction for later review.

Creating Here Documents

Another form of STDIN redirection can be accomplished using a *here document*, which is sometimes called here text or heredoc. A here document allows you to redirect multiple items into a command. It can also modify a file using a script, create a script, keep data in a script, and so on.

A here document redirection operator is << followed by a keyword. This keyword can be anything, and it signals the beginning of the data as well as the data's end. Listing 4.25 shows an example of using the sort command along with a here document.

Listing 4.25: Employing a here document with the sort command

```
$ sort <<EOF
> dog
> cat
> fish
> EOF
cat
dog
fish
$
```

In Listing 4.25, the sort command is entered followed by the << redirection operator and a keyword, EOF. The Enter key is pressed, and a secondary prompt, >, appears, indicating that more data can be entered. Three words to be sorted are entered. The keyword,

EOF, is entered again to denote that data entry is complete. When this occurs, the `sort` utility alphabetically sorts the words and displays the results to STDOUT.

Creating Command Lines

Creating command-line commands is a useful skill. There are several different methods you can use. One such method is using the `xargs` utility. The best thing about this tool is that you sound like a pirate when you pronounce it, but it has other practical values as well.

By piping STDOUT from other commands into the `xargs` utility, you can build command-line commands on the fly. Listing 4.26 shows an example of doing this.

Listing 4.26: Employing the `xargs` command

```
$ find tmp -size 0
tmp/EmptyFile1.txt
tmp/EmptyFile2.txt
tmp/EmptyFile3.txt
$
$ find tmp -size 0 | xargs /usr/bin/ls
tmp/EmptyFile1.txt   tmp/EmptyFile2.txt   tmp/EmptyFile3.txt
$
```

In Listing 4.26, the first command finds any files in the `tmp` subdirectory that are empty (`-size 0`). The second command does the same thing, except this time, the output from the `find` command is piped as STDIN into the `xargs` utility. The `xargs` command uses the `ls` command to list the files. Notice that `xargs` requires not only the `ls` command's name but also its program's location in the virtual directory tree.

While Listing 4.26's commands are educational, they are not practical, because you get the same information just using the `find` utility. Listing 4.27 shows a functional use of employing the `xargs` utility.

Listing 4.27: Using the `xargs` command to delete files

```
$ find tmp -size 0 | xargs -p /usr/bin/rm
/usr/bin/rm tmp/EmptyFile1.txt tmp/EmptyFile2.txt tmp/EmptyFile3.txt
?...y
$
```

The `xargs` command used in Listing 4.27 uses the `-p` option. This option causes the `xargs` utility to stop and ask permission before enacting the constructed command-line command. Notice that the created command is going to remove all three empty files with one `rm` command. After you type **y** and press the Enter key, the command is enacted, and the three files are deleted. This is a pretty handy way to find and remove unwanted files.

The other methods to create command-line commands on the fly use shell expansion. The first method puts a command to execute within parentheses and precedes it with a dollar sign. An example of this method is shown in Listing 4.28.

Listing 4.28: Using the $() method to create commands

```
$ touch tmp/EmptyFile1.txt
$ touch tmp/EmptyFile2.txt
$ touch tmp/EmptyFile3.txt
$
$ ls $(find tmp -size 0)
tmp/EmptyFile1.txt  tmp/EmptyFile2.txt   tmp/EmptyFile3.txt
$
```

In Listing 4.28, the find command is again used to locate any empty files in the tmp subdirectory. Because the command is encased by the $() symbols, it does not display to STDOUT. Instead, the filenames are passed to the ls utility, which does display the files to STDOUT. Of course, it would be more useful to delete those files, but they are needed in the next few examples.

The next method puts a command to execute within backticks (`). Be aware that backticks are not single quotation marks. You can typically find the backtick on the same keyboard key as the tilde (~) symbol. An example of this method is shown in Listing 4.29.

Listing 4.29: Using the backtick method to create commands

```
$ ls `find tmp -size 0`
tmp/EmptyFile1.txt  tmp/EmptyFile2.txt   tmp/EmptyFile3.txt
$
```

Notice in Listing 4.29 that the created command-line command behaves exactly as the constructed command in Listing 4.28. The command between the backticks executes and its output is passed as input to the ls utility.

Backticks are not very popular anymore. While they perform the same duty as do the $() symbols for creating commands, they are harder to see and are often confused with single quotation marks.

Another method for creating commands is brace expansion. This handy approach allows you to cut down on typing at the command line. Listing 4.30 provides a useful example of brace expansion.

Listing 4.30: Using brace expansion to create commands

```
$ rm -i tmp/EmptyFile{1,3}.txt
rm: remove regular empty file 'tmp/EmptyFile1.txt'? y
rm: remove regular empty file 'tmp/EmptyFile3.txt'? y
$
```

Notice in Listing 4.30 that two files are deleted. Instead of typing out the entire filenames, you can employ curly braces ({}). These curly braces contain two numbers separated by a comma. This causes the `rm` utility to substitute a 1 in the braces' location for the first filename and a 3 for the second file's name. In essence, the brace expansion method allows you to denote multiple substitutions within a command argument. Thus, you can get very creative when building commands on the fly.

Editing Text Files

Manipulating text is performed on a regular basis when managing a Linux system. You may need to employ either a stream editor or a full-fledged interactive text editor to accomplish the task. In the following sections, we'll cover both types of editors.

Appreciating Text Editors

Whether you need to modify a configuration file or create a shell script, being able to use an interactive text file editor is an important skill. Also, it is a good idea to know more than just one. Therefore, we'll cover both the `nano` and the `vim` text editors.

The nano editor is a good text editor to start using if you have never dealt with an editor or have only used GUI editors. To start using the nano text editor, type **nano** followed by the name of the file you wish to edit or create. Figure 4.1 shows a nano text editor screen in action.

FIGURE 4.1 Using the nano text editor

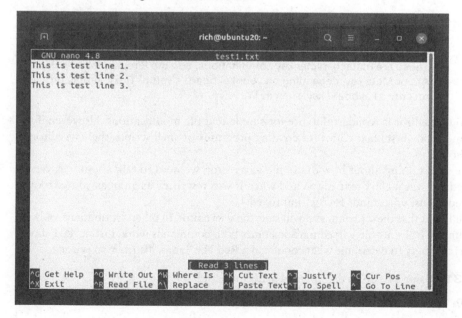

In Figure 4.1 you can see the four main sections of the nano text editor. They are as follows:

Title Bar   The title bar is at the nano text editor window's top line. It shows the current editor version as well as the name of the file you are presently editing. In Figure 4.1, the file being edited is the test1.txt file. If you simply typed **nano** and did not include a filename, you would see New Buffer in the title bar.

Main Body   The nano text editor's main body is where you perform the editing. If the file already contains text, its first lines are shown in this area. If you need to view text that is not in the main body, you can use either arrow keys, the Page Up or Page Down key, and/or the page movement shortcut key combinations to move through the text.

Status Bar   The status bar does not always contain information. It only displays status information for certain events. For example, in Figure 4.1, the text file has just been opened in nano, so the status bar area displays [Read 3 lines] to indicate that three text lines were read into the editor.

Shortcut List   The shortcut list is one of the editor's most useful features. By glancing at this list at the window's bottom, you can see the most common commands and their associated shortcut keys. The caret (^) symbol in this list indicates that the Ctrl key must be used. For example, to remove text from the file, you highlight the text first, then press and hold the Ctrl key and then press the K key. To see additional commands, press the Ctrl+G key combination for help.

> Within the nano text editor's help subsystem, you'll see some key com-
> binations denoted by M-k. An example is M-W for repeating a search.
> These are metacharacter key combinations, and the M represents the Esc,
> Alt, or Meta key, depending on your keyboard's setup. The k simply rep-
> resents a keyboard key, such as W.

The nano text editor is wonderful to use for simple text file modifications. However, if you need a more powerful text editor for creating programs or shell scripts, the vim editor is a popular choice.

Before we start talking about how to use the vim editor, we need to talk about vim versus vi. The vi editor was a Unix text editor, and when it was rewritten as an open source tool, it was improved. Thus, vim stands for "vi improved."

Often you'll find that the vi command will start the vim editor. In other distributions, only the vim command will start the vim editor. Sometimes both commands work. Listing 4.31 shows using the which utility to determine what command a Red Hat Linux distribution is using.

Listing 4.31: Using which to determine which command

```
$ which vim
/usr/bin/vim
$
```

```
$ which vi
alias vi='vim'
        /usr/bin/vim
$
```

Listing 4.31 shows that this Red Hat Linux distribution has aliased the vi command to point to the vim command. Thus, for this distribution, both the vi and vim commands will start the vim editor.

WARNING   Some distributions, such as Ubuntu, do not have the vim editor installed by default. Instead, they use an alternative, called vim.tiny, which will not allow you to try all the various vim commands discussed here. You can check your distribution to see if vim is installed by obtaining the vim program filename. Type **type vi** and press Enter, and if you get an error or an alias, then enter **type vim**. Once you receive the program's directory and filename, type the command **readlink -f** and follow it up with the directory and filename. For example: readlink -f /usr/bin/ vi. If you see /usr/bin/vi.tiny, you need to either switch to a different distribution to practice the vim commands or install the vim package (see Chapter 13, "Governing Software").

To start using the vim text editor, type **vim** or **vi**, depending on your distribution, followed by the name of the file you wish to edit or create. Figure 4.2 shows a vim text editor screen in action.

FIGURE 4.2   Using the vim text editor

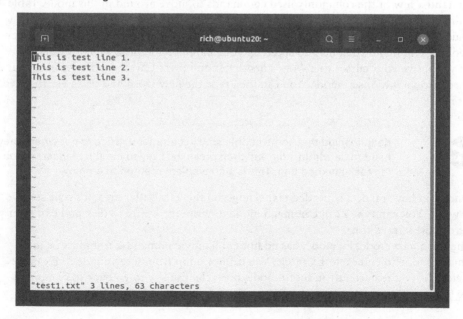

In Figure 4.2 the file being edited is the `test1.txt` file again. The `vim` editor loads the file data in a memory buffer, and this buffer is displayed on the screen. If you open `vim` without a filename or the filename you entered doesn't yet exist, `vim` starts a new buffer area for editing.

The `vim` editor has a message area near the bottom line. If you have just opened an already created file, it will display the filename along with the number of lines and characters read into the buffer area. If you are creating a new file, you will see `[New File]` in the message area.

The `vim` editor has three standard modes as follows:

Command Mode   This is the mode `vim` uses when you first enter the buffer area; this is sometimes called normal mode. Here you enter keystrokes to enact commands. For example, pressing the J key will move your cursor down one line. This is the best mode to use for quickly moving around the buffer area.

Insert Mode   Insert mode is also called edit or entry mode. This is the mode where you can perform simple editing. There are not many commands or special mode keystrokes. You enter this mode from command mode, by pressing the I key. At this point, the message `--Insert--` will display in the message area. You leave this mode by pressing the Esc key.

Ex Mode   This mode is sometimes also called *colon commands* because every command entered here is preceded by a colon (`:`). For example, to leave the `vim` editor and not save any changes you type **:q** and press the Enter key.

Since you start in command mode when entering the `vim` editor's buffer area, it's good to understand a few of the commonly used commands to move around in this mode. Table 4.8 contains several moving commands for your perusal.

Quickly moving around in the `vim` editor buffer is useful. However, there are also several editing commands that help to speed up your modification process. For example, when you move your cursor to a word's first letter and press CW, the word is deleted, and you are thrown into insert mode. You can then type the new word and press Esc to leave insert mode.

Keep in mind that some people stay in command mode to get where they need to be within a file and then press the I key to jump into insert mode for easier text editing. This is a convenient method to employ.

Once you have made any needed text changes in the `vim` buffer area, it's time to save your work. You can type **ZZ** in command mode to write the buffer to disk and exit your process from the `vim` editor.

The third `vim` mode, Ex mode, has additional handy commands. You must be in command mode to enter into Ex mode. You cannot jump from insert mode to Ex mode. Therefore, if you're currently in insert mode, press the Esc key to go back to command mode first.

TABLE 4.8   Commonly used `vim` command mode moving commands

Keystroke	Description
h	Move cursor left one character.
l	Move cursor right one character.
j	Move cursor down one line (the next line in the text).
k	Move cursor up one line (the previous line in the text).
w	Move cursor forward one word to front of next word.
e	Move cursor to end of current word.
b	Move cursor backward one word.
^	Move cursor to beginning of line.
$	Move cursor to end of line.
gg	Move cursor to the file's first line.
G	Move cursor to the file's last line.
nG	Move cursor to file line number n.
Ctrl+B	Scroll up almost one full screen.
Ctrl+F	Scroll down almost one full screen.
Ctrl+U	Scroll up half of a screen.
Ctrl+D	Scroll down half of a screen.
Ctrl+Y	Scroll up one line.
Ctrl+E	Scroll down one line.

Table 4.9 shows several Ex commands that can help you manage your text file. Notice that all the keystrokes include the necessary colon (:) to use Ex commands.

After reading through the various mode commands, you may see why some people despise the `vim` editor. There are a lot of obscure commands to know. However, some people love the `vim` editor because it is so powerful.

TABLE 4.9   Commonly used vim Ex mode commands

Keystrokes	Description
:x	Write buffer to file and quit editor.
:wq	Write buffer to file and quit editor.
:wq!	Write buffer to file and quit editor (overrides protection).
:w	Write buffer to file and stay in editor.
:w!	Write buffer to file and stay in editor (overrides protection).
:q	Quit editor without writing buffer to file.
:q!	Quit editor without writing buffer to file (overrides protection).
:! *command*	Execute shell *command* and display results, but don't quit editor.
:r! *command*	Execute shell *command* and include the results in editor buffer area.
:r *file*	Read *file* contents and include them in editor buffer area.

Some distributions have a vim tutorial installed by default. This is a handy way to learn to use the vim editor. To get started, just type **vimtutor** at the command line. If you need to leave the tutorial before it is complete, just type in the Ex mode command **:q** to quit.

It's tempting to learn only one text editor and ignore the other. This, of course, won't help you pass the CompTIA Linux+ certification exam. But, in addition, knowing at least two text editors is useful in your day-to-day Linux work. For simple modifications, the nano text editor shines. For more complex editing, the vim editor is king. Both are worth your time to master.

Learning about Stream Editors

There are times where you will want to edit text files without having to pull out a full-fledged text editor. In these cases, learning about two very popular *stream editors* is worth-while. A stream editor modifies text that is passed to it via a file or output from a pipeline. The editor uses special commands to make text changes as the text "streams" through the editor utility.

The first stream editor we'll explore is called the *stream editor*. The command to invoke it is sed. The sed utility edits a stream of text data based on a set of commands you supply ahead of time. It is a quick editor because it makes only one pass through the text to apply the modifications.

The sed editor changes data based on commands either entered into the command line or stored in a text file. The process the editor goes through is as follows:

- Reads one text line at a time from the input stream
- Matches that text with the supplied editor commands
- Modifies the text as specified in the commands
- Outputs the modified text to STDOUT

After the sed editor matches all the prespecified commands against a text line, it reads the next text line and repeats the editorial process. Once sed reaches the end of the text lines, it stops.

Before looking at some sed examples, it is important to understand the command's basic syntax. It is as follows:

```
sed  [OPTIONS] [SCRIPT]... [FILENAME]
```

By default, sed will use the text from STDIN to modify according to the prespecified commands. An example is shown in Listing 4.32.

Listing 4.32: Using sed to modify STDIN text

```
$ echo "I like cake." | sed 's/cake/donuts/'
I like donuts.
$
```

Notice in Listing 4.32 that the text output from the echo command is piped as input into the stream editor. The sed utility's s command (substitute) specifies that if the first text string, cake, is found, it is changed to donuts in the output. Note that the entire command after sed is considered to be the *SCRIPT*, and it is encased in single quotation marks. Also notice that the text words are delimited from the s command, the quotation marks, and each other by the forward slashes (/).

Keep in mind that just using the s command will not change all instances of a word within a text stream. Listing 4.33 shows an example of this.

Listing 4.33: Using sed to globally modify STDIN text

```
$ echo "I love cake and more cake." | sed 's/cake/donuts/'
I love donuts and more cake.
$
$ echo "I love cake and more cake." | sed 's/cake/donuts/g'
I love donuts and more donuts.
$
```

In the first command in Listing 4.33, only the first occurrence of the word cake was modified. However, in the second command a g, which stands for global, was added to the sed script's end. This caused all occurrences of cake to change to donuts.

You can also modify text stored in a file. Listing 4.34 shows an example of this.

Listing 4.34: Using sed to modify file text

```
$ cat cake.txt
Christine likes chocolate cake.
Rich likes lemon cake.
Tim only likes yellow cake.
Samantha does not like cake.
$
$ sed 's/cake/donuts/' cake.txt
Christine likes chocolate donuts.
Rich likes lemon donuts.
Tim only likes yellow donuts.
Samantha does not like donuts.
$
$ cat cake.txt
Christine likes chocolate cake.
Rich likes lemon cake.
Tim only likes yellow cake.
Samantha does not like cake.
$
```

In Listing 4.34, the file contains text lines that contain the word cake. When the cake .txt file is added as an argument to the sed command, its data is modified according to the script. Notice that the data in the file is not modified. The stream editor only displays the modified text to STDOUT.

The stream editor has some rather useful command options. Commonly used ones are displayed in Table 4.10.

TABLE 4.10   The sed command's commonly used options

Short	Long	Description
-e *script*	--expression=*script*	Add commands in *script* to text processing. The *script* is written as part of the sed command.
-f *script*	--file=*script*	Add commands in *script* to text processing. The *script* is a file.
-r	--regexp-extended	Use extended regular expressions in script.

A handy option to use is the -e option. This allows you to employ multiple scripts in the sed command. An example is shown in Listing 4.35.

Listing 4.35: Using sed -e to use multiple scripts

```
$ sed -e 's/cake/donuts/ ; s/like/love/' cake.txt
Christine loves chocolate donuts.
Rich loves lemon donuts.
Tim only loves yellow donuts.
Samantha does not love donuts.
$
```

Pay close attention to the syntax change in Listing 4.35. Not only is the -e option employed, but the script is slightly different too. Now the script contains a semicolon (;) between the two script commands. This allows both commands to be processed on the text stream.

If you have a lot of sed script commands, you can store them in a file. This is convenient because you can use the script file over and over again. Listing 4.36 shows an example of using a sed script one time.

Listing 4.36: Using sed -f to use a script file

```
$ cat script.sed
s/cake/donuts/
s/like/love/
$
$ sed -f script.sed cake.txt
Christine loves chocolate donuts.
Rich loves lemon donuts.
Tim only loves yellow donuts.
Samantha does not love donuts.
$
```

In Listing 4.36, notice that the sed script has single sed commands on each file line. No single quotation marks are employed here. Once the sed command is used along with the -f option and script file argument, the changes are applied to the file data and displayed STDOUT.

The gawk utility is also a stream editor, but it provides a more powerful editing process through its programming language. With the gawk programming language, you can do the following:

- Define variables to store data.
- Use arithmetic and string operators to work on data.
- Use programming structures, such as loops, to add logic to your processing.
- Create formatted reports from data.

The gawk programming language is popular for creating formatted reports from large datasets. You can create gawk programs and store them in files for repeated use.

A little confusion exists between awk and gawk, so let's address that before delving further into the gawk utility. The awk program was created for the Unix operating system, so when the GNU project rewrote it, they named it GNU awk, or gawk for short. However, on many distributions you can use either command, but they both actually call the gawk program. Listing 4.37 shows an example of this on an Ubuntu distribution.

Listing 4.37: Looking at the awk and gawk commands

```
$ which awk
/usr/bin/awk
$
$ readlink -f /usr/bin/awk
/usr/bin/gawk
$
$ which gawk
/usr/bin/gawk
$
```

In Listing 4.37, you can see that the awk command exists on this distribution. However, when you follow the soft link trail to the actual program used, it points to the gawk program. The gawk command exists as well.

Before looking at some gawk examples, it is important to understand the command's basic syntax. It is as follows:

```
gawk   [OPTIONS] [PROGRAM]... [FILENAME]
```

Similar to sed, you can provide the program on the same command line as the gawk command. It also employs the use of single quotation marks to enclose the script. However, unlike sed, the gawk utility requires you to put your programming language commands between two curly braces. An example is shown in Listing 4.38.

Listing 4.38: Using gawk to modify STDIN text

```
$ echo "Hello World" | gawk '{print $0}'
Hello World
$
$ echo "Hello World" | gawk '{print $1}'
Hello
$
$ echo "Hello World" | gawk '{print $2}'
```

World
$

The print command displays text to STDOUT, but notice that different parts of STDIN are shown, as you can see in Listing 4.38. This is accomplished through the gawk utility's defined data field variables. They are defined as follows:

- The $0 variable represents the entire text line.
- The $1 variable represents the text line's first data field.
- The $2 variable represents the text line's second data field.
- The $n variable represents the text line's nth data field.

The gawk utility can also process text data from a file. An example of this is shown in Listing 4.39.

Listing 4.39: Using gawk to modify file text

```
$ cat cake.txt
Christine likes chocolate cake.
Rich likes lemon cake.
Tim only likes yellow cake.
Samantha does not like cake.
$
$ gawk '{print $1}' cake.txt
Christine
Rich
Tim
Samantha
$
```

The gawk programming language is rather powerful and allows you to use many typical structures employed in other programming languages. In Listing 4.40, an attempt is made to change the word cake in the output to donut.

Listing 4.40: Using gawk structured commands to modify file text

```
$ gawk '{$4="donuts"; print $0}' cake.txt
Christine likes chocolate donuts
Rich likes lemon donuts
Tim only likes donuts cake.
Samantha does not donuts cake.
$
```

```
$ gawk '{if ($4 == "cake.") {$4="donuts"; print $0}}' cake.txt
Christine likes chocolate donuts
Rich likes lemon donuts
$
```

In Listing 4.40, the first attempt to substitute the words does not work properly. That is a result of two text file lines having the word cake in data field $5 instead of data field $4. The second gawk attempt employs an if statement to check if data field $4 is equal to the word cake. If the statement returns true, the data field is changed to donuts and the text line is displayed on STDOUT. Otherwise, the text line is ignored.

Using complex programming structures in gawk can be tricky on the command line. It's much better to put those commands in a file. However, you need to know a few common gawk options prior to doing this. Table 4.11 has some typical gawk switches.

TABLE 4.11   The gawk command's commonly used options

Short	Long	Description
-F *d*	--field-separator*d*	Specify the delimiter that separates the data file's fields.
-f *file*	--file=*file*	Use program in *file* for text processing.
-s	--sandbox	Execute gawk program in sandbox mode.

Using the field separator option is very handy when the data file's fields are separated by commas or colons. An example of pulling data from the password file using this switch is shown in Listing 4.41.

Listing 4.41: Using gawk structured commands to extact file data

```
$ gawk -F : '{print $1}' /etc/passwd
root
bin
daemon
[...]
$
```

You can put complex gawk programs into files to keep them for reuse. Listing 4.42 shows an example of this.

Listing 4.42: Using a gawk program file

```
$ cat cake.txt
Christine likes chocolate cake.
Rich likes lemon cake.
Tim only likes yellow cake.
Samantha does not like cake.
$
$ cat script.gawk
{if ($4=="cake.")
  {$4="donuts"; print $0}
else if ($5=="cake.")
  {$5="donuts"; print $0}}
$
$ gawk -f script.gawk cake.txt
Christine likes chocolate donuts
Rich likes lemon donuts
Tim only likes yellow donuts
Samantha does not like donuts
$
```

In Listing 4.42, a more complex if structure statement is written using the gawk programming language and saved to a file, script.gawk. This script not only employs an if statement, it also incorporates an else if structure. Notice also that no single quotation marks are needed when the gawk program is stored in a file. Using the -f switch, the program is enacted on the cake.txt file, and the appropriate word is changed in every line.

Summary

Being able to process data to make agile decisions is important for administering your Linux system. There are many Linux structures and tools, which can help you in uncovering the information you need.

This chapter's purpose was to continue to improve your Linux command-line tool belt. The tools and structures added in this chapter will allow you to search and analyze text in order to uncover knowledge in an efficient manner.

Exam Essentials

Summarize the various utilities used in processing text files.   Filtering text file data can be made much easier with utilities such as grep, egrep, and cut. Once that data is filtered, you may want to format it for viewing using sort, pr, printf, or even the cat utility. If you need some statistical information on your text file, such as the number of lines it contains, the wc command is handy.

Explain both the structures and commands for redirection.   Employing STDOUT, STDERR, and STDIN redirection allows rather complex filtering and processing of text. The echo command can assist in this process as well as here documents. You can also use pipelines of commands to perform redirection and produce excellent data for review.

Describe the various methods used for editing text files.   Editing text files is part of a system administrator's life. You can use full-screen editors such as the rather complicated vim text editor or the simple and easy-to-use nano editor. For fast and powerful text stream editing, employ sed and its scripts or the gawk programming language.

Review Questions

1. The `cat -E MyFile.txt` command is entered, and at the end of every line displayed is a $. What does this indicate?

   A. The text file has been corrupted somehow.

   B. The text file records end in the ASCII character NUL.

   C. The text file records end in the ASCII character LF.

   D. The text file records end in the ASCII character $.

   E. The text file records contain a $ at their end.

2. The `cut` utility often needs delimiters to process text records. Which of the following best describes a delimiter?

   A. One or more characters that designate the beginning of a line in a record

   B. One or more characters that designate the end of a line in a record

   C. One or more characters that designate the end of a text file to a command-line text processing utility

   D. A single space or a colon (:) that creates a boundary between different data items in a record

   E. One or more characters that create a boundary between different data items in a record

3. Which of the following utilities change text within a file? (Choose all that apply.)

   A. `cut`

   B. `sort`

   C. `vim`

   D. `nano`

   E. `sed`

4. You have a text file, `monitor.txt`, which contains information concerning the monitors used within the data center. Each record ends with the ASCII LF character and fields are delimited by a comma (,). A text record has the monitor ID, manufacture, serial number, and location. To display each data center monitor's monitor ID, serial number, and location, you'd use which `cut` command?

   A. `cut -d "," -f 1,3,4 monitor.txt`

   B. `cut -z -d "," -f 1,3,4 monitor.txt`

   C. `cut -f "," -d 1,3,4 monitor.txt`

   D. `cut monitor.txt -d "," -f 1,3,4`

   E. `cut monitor.txt -f "," -d 1,3,4`

5. The grep utility can employ regular expressions in its *PATTERN*. Which of the following best describes a regular expression?

   A. A series of characters you define for a utility, which uses the characters to match the same characters in text files

   B. ASCII characters, such as LF and NUL, that a utility uses to filter text

   C. Wildcard characters, such as * and ?, that a utility uses to filter text

   D. A pattern template you define for a utility, which uses the pattern to filter text

   E. Quotation marks (single or double) used around characters to prevent unexpected results

6. You are a system administrator on a Red Hat Linux server. You need to view records in the /var/log/messages file that start with the date May 30 and end with the IPv4 address 192.168.10.42. Which of the following is the best grep command to use?

   A. `grep "May 30?192.168.10.42" /var/log/messages`

   B. `grep "May 30.*192.168.10.42" /var/log/messages`

   C. `grep -i "May 30.*192.168.10.42" /var/log/messages`

   D. `grep -i "May 30?192.168.10.42" /var/log/messages`

   E. `grep -v "May 30.*192.168.10.42" /var/log/messages`

7. Which of the following is a BRE pattern that could be used with the grep command? (Choose all that apply.)

   A. `Sp?ce`

   B. `"Space, the .*frontier"`

   C. `^Space`

   D. `(lasting | final)`

   E. `frontier$`

8. You need to search through a large text file and find any record that contains either Luke or Laura at the record's beginning. Also, the phrase Father is must be located somewhere in the record's middle. Which of the following is an ERE pattern that could be used with the egrep command to find this record?

   A. `"Luke$|Laura$.*Father is"`

   B. `"^Luke|^Laura.Father is"`

   C. `"(^Luke|^Laura).Father is"`

   D. `"(Luke$|Laura$).* Father is$"`

   E. `"(^Luke|^Laura).*Father is.*"`

9. A file data.txt needs to be sorted numerically and its output saved to a new file newdata.txt. Which of the following commands can accomplish this task? (Choose all that apply.)

    A. sort -n -o newdata.txt data.txt

    B. sort -n data.txt > newdata.txt

    C. sort -n -o data.txt newdata.txt

    D. sort -o newdata.txt data.txt

    E. sort data.txt > newdata.txt

10. Which of the following commands can display the data.txt and datatoo.txt files' content one after the other to STDOUT? (Choose all that apply.)

    A. ls data.txt datatoo.txt

    B. sort -n data.txt > datatoo.txt

    C. cat -n data.txt datatoo.txt

    D. ls -l data.txt datatoo.txt

    E. sort data.txt datatoo.txt

11. A text file, StarGateAttacks.txt, needs to be specially formatted for review. Which of the following commands is the best command to accomplish this task quickly?

    A. printf

    B. wc

    C. pr

    D. paste

    E. nano

12. You need to format the string 42.777 into the correct two-digit floating number. Which of the following printf command *FORMAT* settings is the correct one to use?

    A. "%s\n"

    B. "%.2s\n"

    C. "%d\n"

    D. "%.2c\n"

    E. "%.2f\n"

13. A Unicode-encoded text file, MyUCode.txt, needs to be perused. Before you decide what utility to use in order view the file's contents, you employ the wc command on it. This utility displays 2020 6786 11328 to STDOUT. Which of the following is true? (Choose all that apply.)

    A. The file has 2,020 lines in it.

    B. The file has 2,020 characters in it.

    C. The file has 6,786 words in it.

    D. The file has 11,328 characters in it.

    E. The file has 11,328 lines in it.

14. Which of the following best defines a file descriptor?

   A. A letter that represents the file's type

   B. A number that represents a process's open files

   C. Another term for the file's name

   D. A six-character name that represents standard output

   E. A symbol that indicates the file's classification

15. By default, STDOUT goes to what item?

   A. `/dev/tty`*n*, where *n* is a number

   B. `/dev/null`

   C. `>`

   D. `/dev/tty`

   E. `pwd`

16. Which of the following commands will display the file `SpaceOpera.txt` to output as well as save a copy of it to the file `SciFi.txt`?

   A. `cat SpaceOpera.txt | tee SciFi.txt`

   B. `cat SpaceOpera.txt > SciFi.txt`

   C. `cat SpaceOpera.txt 2> SciFi.txt`

   D. `cp SpaceOpera.txt SciFi.txt`

   E. `cat SpaceOpera.txt &> SciFi.txt`

17. Which of the following commands will put any generated error messages into the black hole?

   A. `sort SpaceOpera.txt 2> BlackHole`

   B. `sort SpaceOpera.txt &> BlackHole`

   C. `sort SpaceOpera.txt > BlackHole`

   D. `sort SpaceOpera.txt 2> /dev/null`

   E. `sort SpaceOpera.txt > /dev/null`

18. Which of the following commands will determine how many records in the file `Problems.txt` contain the word `error`?

   A. `grep error Problems.txt | wc -b`

   B. `grep error Problems.txt | wc -w`

   C. `grep error Problems.txt | wc -l`

   D. `grep Problems.txt error | wc -w`

   E. `grep Problems.txt error | wc -l`

19. You want to find any file named `42.tmp`, which exists somewhere in your current directory's tree structure and display its contents to STDOUT. Which of the following will allow you to build a command to do this? (Choose all that apply.)

   A. `xargs (find . -name 42.tmp) cat`

   B. `cat ʼfind . -name 42.tmpʼ`

   C. `cat $(find . -name 42.tmp)`

   D. `cat {find . -name 42.tmp}`

   E. `find . -name 42.tmp | xargs cat`

20. You want to edit the file `SpaceOpera.txt` and decide to use the `vim` editor to complete this task. Which of the following are `vim` modes you might employ? (Choose all that apply.)

   A. Insert

   B. Change

   C. Command

   D. Ex

   E. Edit

Starting Up and Configuring Your System

PART

II

Chapter

5

Explaining
the Boot Process

✓ **Objective 1.1: Summarize Linux fundamentals.**

Before you can log in and start using your Linux system, a complicated process of booting the operating system must take place. A lot happens behind the scenes in the Linux boot process. It helps to know just what all goes on in case something goes wrong.

This chapter examines the boot and startup processes in Linux systems. First, we'll look at the role the computer firmware plays in getting the process started, and then we'll discuss Linux bootloaders and how to configure them. Next, the chapter discusses the Linux initialization process, showing how Linux decides which background applications to start at bootup. The chapter ends by taking a look at some system recovery options you have available to help salvage a system that won't boot.

The Linux Boot Process

When you turn on the power to your Linux system, it triggers a series of events that eventually leads to the login prompt. Normally you don't worry about what happens behind the scenes of those events; you just log in and start using your applications.

However, there may be times when your Linux system doesn't boot quite correctly, or perhaps an application you expected to be running in background mode isn't. In those cases, it helps to have a basic understanding of just how Linux boots the operating system and starts programs so you can troubleshoot the problem.

The following sections walk through the steps of the boot process and how you can watch the boot process to see what steps failed.

Following the Boot Process

The Linux boot process can be split into three main steps:

1. The workstation firmware starts, performing a quick check of the hardware (called a *Power-On Self-Test, or POST*) and then looks for a bootloader program to run from a bootable device.

2. The bootloader runs and determines what Linux kernel program to load.

3. The kernel program loads into memory and starts the necessary background programs required for the system to operate (such as a graphical desktop manager for desktops or web and database servers for servers).

While on the surface these three steps may seem simple, a ballet of operations happens to keep the boot process working. Each step performs several actions as they prepare your system to run Linux.

Viewing the Boot Process

You can monitor the Linux boot process by watching the system console screen as the system boots. You'll see lots of informative messages scroll by as the system detects hardware and loads software.

 Some graphical desktop Linux distributions hide the boot messages in a separate console window when they start up. Often you can press either the Esc key or the Ctrl+Alt+F1 key combination to view those messages.

Usually the boot messages scroll by quickly and it's hard to see what's happening. If you need to troubleshoot boot problems, you can review the boot time messages using the dmesg command. Most Linux distributions copy the boot kernel messages into a special ring buffer in memory, called the *kernel ring buffer*. The buffer is circular and set to a predetermined size. As new messages are logged in the buffer, older messages are rotated out.

The dmesg command displays the most recent boot messages that are currently stored in the kernel ring buffer, as shown in Listing 5.1.

Listing 5.1 The dmesg command output from an Ubuntu workstation

```
$ dmesg
[    0.000000] Linux version 5.11.0-40-generic (buildd@lgw01-amd64-
010) (gcc (Ubuntu 9.3.0-17ubuntu1~20.04) 9.3.0, GNU ld (GNU Binutils
 for Ubuntu) 2.34) #44~20.04.2-Ubuntu SMP Tue Oct 26 18:07:44 UTC 2021
 (Ubuntu 5.11.0-40.44~20.04.2-generic 5.11.22)
[    0.000000] Command line: BOOT_IMAGE=/boot/vmlinuz-5.11.0-40-
generic root=UUID=5423117e-4aaf-4416-ada7-01e07073b2e1 ro quiet splash
[    0.000000] KERNEL supported cpus:
[    0.000000]   Intel GenuineIntel
[    0.000000]   AMD AuthenticAMD
[    0.000000]   Hygon HygonGenuine
[    0.000000]   Centaur CentaurHauls
[    0.000000]   zhaoxin   Shanghai
[    0.000000] x86/fpu: Supporting XSAVE feature 0x001: 'x87 floating point
registers'
[    0.000000] x86/fpu: Supporting XSAVE feature 0x002: 'SSE registers'
[    0.000000] x86/fpu: Supporting XSAVE feature 0x004: 'AVX registers'
[    0.000000] x86/fpu: xstate_offset[2]:  576, xstate_sizes[2]:   256
[    0.000000] x86/fpu: Enabled xstate features 0x7, context size is 832
bytes, using 'standard' format.
[    0.000000] BIOS-provided physical RAM map:
[    0.000000] BIOS-e820: [mem 0x0000000000000000-0x000000000009fbff] usable
[    0.000000] BIOS-e820: [mem 0x000000000009fc00-0x000000000009ffff] reserved
```

```
[    0.000000] BIOS-e820: [mem 0x00000000000f0000-0x00000000000fffff] reserved
[    0.000000] BIOS-e820: [mem 0x0000000000100000-0x00000000dffefff] usable
[    0.000000] BIOS-e820: [mem 0x00000000dfff0000-0x00000000dfffffff] ACPI data
[    0.000000] BIOS-e820: [mem 0x00000000fec00000-0x00000000fec00fff] reserved
[    0.000000] BIOS-e820: [mem 0x00000000fee00000-0x00000000fee00fff] reserved
[    0.000000] BIOS-e820: [mem 0x00000000fffc0000-0x00000000ffffffff] reserved
[    0.000000] BIOS-e820: [mem 0x0000000100000000-0x000000021fffffff] usable
[    0.000000] NX (Execute Disable) protection: active
[    0.000000] SMBIOS 2.5 present.
[    0.000000] DMI: innotek GmbH VirtualBox/VirtualBox, BIOS VirtualBox
12/01/2006
[    0.000000] Hypervisor detected: KVM
[    0.000000] kvm-clock: Using msrs 4b564d01 and 4b564d00
[    0.000000] kvm-clock: cpu 0, msr 109001001, primary cpu clock
[    0.000000] kvm-clock: using sched offset of 3933158608 cycles
[    0.000001] clocksource: kvm-clock: mask: 0xffffffffffffffff max_cycles:
0x1cd42e4dffb, max_idle_ns: 881590591483 ns
[    0.000003] tsc: Detected 1497.589 MHz processor
```

Most Linux distributions also store the boot messages in a log file, usually in the /var/log folder. For both Debian-based and Red Hat–based systems, the file is usually /var/log/boot.log, but some legacy Linux systems may use /var/log/boot.

While it helps to be able to see the different messages generated during boot time, it is also helpful to know what generates those messages. This chapter discusses each of these three boot steps and goes through some examples showing just how they work.

The Firmware Startup

All IBM-compatible workstations and servers utilize some type of built-in firmware to control how the installed operating system starts. On older workstations and servers, this firmware was called the *Basic Input/Output System (BIOS)*. On newer workstations and servers, a method called the *Unified Extensible Firmware Interface (UEFI)* maintains the system hardware status and launches an installed operating system.

The BIOS Startup

The BIOS firmware had a simplistic menu interface that allowed you to change some settings to control how the system found hardware and define what device the BIOS should use to start the operating system.

One limitation of the original BIOS firmware was that it could read only one sector's worth of data from a hard drive into memory to run. That's not enough space to load an entire operating system. To get around that limitation, most operating systems (including Linux and Microsoft Windows) split the boot process into two parts.

First, the BIOS runs a *bootloader* program, a small program that initializes the necessary hardware to find and run the full operating system program. It's often found at another location on the same hard drive but sometimes on a separate internal or external storage device.

The bootloader program usually has a configuration file, so you can tell it where to find the actual operating system file to run or even to produce a small menu allowing the user to boot between multiple operating systems.

To get things started, the BIOS must know where to find the bootloader program on an installed storage device. Most BIOS setups allow you to load the bootloader program from several locations:

- An internal hard drive
- An external hard drive
- A CD or DVD drive
- A USB memory stick
- An ISO file
- A network server using either NFS, HTTP, or FTP

When booting from a hard drive, you must designate the hard drive, and the partition on the hard drive, from which the BIOS should load the bootloader program. This is done by defining a *Master Boot Record (MBR)*.

The MBR is the first sector on the first hard drive partition on the system. There is only one MBR for the computer system. The BIOS looks for the MBR and reads the program stored there into memory. Since the bootloader program must fit in one sector, it must be very small, so it can't do too much. The bootloader program mainly points to the location of the actual operating system kernel file, stored in a boot sector of a separate partition installed on the system. There are no size limitations on the kernel boot file.

 The bootloader program isn't required to point directly to an operating system kernel file; it can point to any type of program, including another bootloader program. You can create a primary bootloader program that points to a secondary bootloader program, which provides options to load multiple operating systems. This process is called *chainloading*.

The UEFI Startup

As operating systems became more complicated, it eventually became clear that a new boot method needed to be developed.

Intel created the *Extensible Firmware Interface (EFI)* in 1998 to address some of the limitations of BIOS. By 2005, the idea caught on with other vendors, and the Universal EFI (UEFI) specification was adopted as a standard. These days just about all IBM-compatible desktop and server systems utilize the UEFI firmware standard.

Instead of relying on a single boot sector on a hard drive to hold the bootloader program, UEFI specifies a special disk partition, called the *EFI System Partition (ESP)*, to store bootloader programs. This allows for any size of bootloader program, plus the ability to store multiple bootloader programs for multiple operating systems.

The ESP setup utilizes the old Microsoft File Allocation Table (FAT) filesystem to store the bootloader programs. On Linux systems, the ESP is typically mounted in the /boot/efi directory, and the bootloader files are typically stored using the .efi filename extension, such as linux.efi.

The UEFI firmware utilizes a built-in mini-bootloader (sometimes referred to as a *boot manager*) that allows you to configure which bootloader program file to launch.

WARNING Not all Linux distributions support the UEFI firmware. If you're using a UEFI system, ensure that the Linux distribution you select supports it. Also, many UEFI systems utilize a *secure boot* feature, which when enabled only loads bootloader programs digitally signed by a known signing certificate. Many of these systems only recognize Microsoft certificates, making it complicated, but not impossible, to boot a Linux system. To get around this most Linux distributions use chainloading to first load a shim bootloader, signed by Microsoft, which then points to the real Linux bootloader.

With UEFI, you need to register each individual bootloader file you want to appear at boot time in the boot manager interface menu. You can then select the bootloader to run each time you boot the system.

Once the firmware finds and runs the bootloader, its job is done. The bootloader step in the boot process can be somewhat complicated. The next section dives into covering that.

Linux Bootloaders

The bootloader program helps bridge the gap between the system firmware and the full Linux operating system kernel. In Linux there are several choices of bootloaders to use. However, the main bootloader programs that have been used by default in Linux distributions are as follows:

- Linux Loader (LILO)
- Grand Unified Bootloader (GRUB) Legacy
- GRUB2

In the original versions of Linux, the *Linux Loader (LILO)* bootloader was the only bootloader program available. It was extremely limited in what it could do, but it accomplished its purpose—loading the Linux kernel from the BIOS startup. The LILO configuration file is stored in a single file, /etc/lilo.conf, which defines the systems to boot.

Unfortunately, LILO doesn't work with UEFI systems, so it has limited use on modern systems and is quickly fading into history.

The first version of the GRUB bootloader (now called *GRUB Legacy*) was created in 1999 to provide a more robust and configurable bootloader to replace LILO. GRUB quickly became the default bootloader for all Linux distributions, whether they were run on BIOS or UEFI systems.

GRUB2 was created in 2005 as a total rewrite of the GRUB Legacy system. It supports advanced features, such as the ability to load hardware driver modules and using logic statements to dynamically alter the boot menu options, depending on conditions detected on the system (such as if an external hard drive is connected).

Since UEFI can load any size of bootloader program, it's now possible to load a Linux operating system kernel directly without a special bootloader program. This feature was incorporated in the Linux kernel starting with version 3.3.0. However, this method isn't common, as bootloader programs can provide more versatility in booting, especially when working with multiple operating systems.

The following sections walk through the basics of both the GRUB Legacy and GRUB2 bootloaders, which should cover just about every Linux distribution that you'll run into these days.

GRUB Legacy

The GRUB Legacy bootloader was designed to simplify the process of creating boot menus and passing options to kernels. GRUB Legacy allows you to select multiple kernels and/or operating systems using both a menu interface and an interactive shell. You configure the menu interface to provide options for each kernel or operating system you want to boot with. The interactive shell provides a way for you to customize boot commands on the fly.

Both the menu and the interactive shell utilize a set of commands that control features of the bootloader. The following sections walk through how to configure the GRUB Legacy bootloader, how to install it, and how to interact with it at boot time.

Configuring GRUB Legacy

When you use the GRUB Legacy interactive menu, you need to tell it what options to show using special GRUB *menu commands*.

The GRUB Legacy system stores the menu commands in a standard text configuration file called menu.lst. This file is stored in the /boot/grub folder (while not a requirement, some Linux distributions create a separate /boot partition on the hard drive). Red Hat–derived Linux distributions (such as CentOS and Fedora) use grub.conf instead of menu.lst for the configuration file.

The GRUB Legacy configuration file consists of two sections:

- Global definitions
- Operating system boot definitions

The global definitions section defines commands that control the overall operation of the GRUB Legacy boot menu. The global definitions must appear first in the configuration file. There are only a handful of global settings that you can make; Table 5.1 shows these settings.

TABLE 5.1   GRUB Legacy global commands

Setting	Description
color	Specifies the foreground and background colors to use in the boot menu
default	Defines the default menu option to select
fallback	A secondary menu selection to use if the default menu option fails
hiddenmenu	Doesn't display the menu selection options
splashimage	Points to an image file to use as the background for the boot menu
timeout	Specifies the amount of time to wait for a menu selection before using the default

For GRUB Legacy, to define a value for a command, you list the value as a command-line parameter:

```
default 0
timeout 10
color white/blue yellow/blue
```

The color command defines the color scheme for the menu. The first pair defines the foreground/background pair for normal menu entries, while the second pair defines the foreground/background pair for the selected menu entry.

After the global definitions, you place definitions for the individual operating systems that are installed on the system. Each operating system should have its own definition section. There are a lot of boot definition settings that you can use to customize how the bootloader finds the operating system kernel file. Fortunately, only a few commands are required to define the operating system. The ones to remember are listed here:

- title—The first line for each boot definition section; this is what appears in the boot menu.
- root—Defines the disk and partition where the GRUB /boot folder partition is on the system.

- `kernel`—Defines the kernel image file stored in the /boot folder to load.
- `initrd`—Defines the initial RAM disk file, which contains drivers necessary for the kernel to interact with the system hardware.
- `rootnoverify`—Defines non-Linux boot partitions, such as Windows.

The `root` command defines the hard drive and partition that contains the /boot folder for GRUB Legacy. Unfortunately, GRUB Legacy uses a somewhat odd way of referencing those values:

(hd*drive*, *partition*)

Also, unfortunately, GRUB Legacy doesn't refer to hard drives the way Linux does; it uses a number system to reference both disks and partitions, starting at 0 instead of 1. For example, to reference the first partition on the first hard drive on the system, you'd use (hd0,0). To reference the second partition on the first hard drive, you'd use (hd0,1).

The `initrd` command is another important feature in GRUB Legacy. It helps solve a problem that arises when using specialized hardware or filesystems as the root drive. The `initrd` command defines a file that's mounted by the kernel at boot time as a RAM disk, also called the *initrd*. The kernel can then load modules from the `initrd` RAM disk, which then allows it to access hardware or filesystems not compiled into the kernel itself. The `initrd` RAM disk file, located in the /boot directory, is called `initrd.img-`*kversion*, where *kversion* is the kernel version number.

> If you install new hardware on your system that's required to be visible at boot time, you'll need to modify the `initrd` file. You can create a new `initrd` RAM disk image containing modules for the new hardware using the `mkinitrd` command in Red Hat–based systems. For Debian-based systems, the file is called `initramfs`, and you create it using the `mkinitramfs` command. Alternatively, you can use the `dracut` utility, which creates the `initramfs` image from a framework and copies files from the installed modules.

Listing 5.2 shows a sample GRUB configuration file that defines both a Windows and a Linux partition for booting.

Listing 5.2 Sample GRUB Legacy configuration file

```
default 0
timeout 10
color white/blue yellow/blue

title Ubuntu Linux
root (hd1,0)
kernel (hd1,0)/boot/vmlinuz
```

```
initrd /boot/initrd

title Windows
rootnoverify (hd0,0)
```

This example shows two boot options—one for an Ubuntu Linux system and one for a Windows system. The Ubuntu system is installed on the first partition of the second hard drive, whereas the Windows system is installed on the first partition of the first hard drive. The Linux boot selection specifies the kernel file to load as well as the `initrd` image file to load into memory.

> You may have noticed that the kernel filename in the Listing 5.2 example was called `vmlinuz`. No, that's not a typo—the z at the end of the file-name indicates that the kernel file is compressed using the bzImage com-pression method, a very common method in most Linux distributions. For kernel files that aren't compressed, the kernel image file is usually called `vmlinux`.

Installing GRUB Legacy

Once you build the GRUB Legacy configuration file, you must install the GRUB Legacy program in the MBR. The command to do this is `grub-install`.

The `grub-install` command uses a single parameter—the partition on which to install GRUB. You can specify the partition using either Linux or GRUB Legacy format. For example, to use Linux format you'd use

```
# grub-install /dev/sda
```

to install GRUB on the MBR of the first hard drive. To use GRUB Legacy format, you must enclose the hard drive format in quotes:

```
# grub-install '(hd0)'
```

If you're using the chainloading method and prefer to install a copy of GRUB Legacy on the boot sector of a partition instead of to the MBR of a hard drive, you must specify the partition, again using either Linux or GRUB format:

```
# grub-install /dev/sda1
# grub-install 'hd(0,0)'
```

You don't need to reinstall GRUB Legacy in the MBR after making changes to the config-uration file. GRUB Legacy reads the configuration file each time it runs.

Interacting with GRUB Legacy

When you boot a system that uses the GRUB Legacy bootloader, you'll see a menu that shows the boot options you defined in the configuration file. If you wait for the timeout to expire, the default boot option will process. Alternatively, you can use the arrow keys to select one of the boot options and then press the Enter key to select it.

You can also edit boot options on the fly from the GRUB menu. First, arrow to the boot option you want to modify and then press the E key. Use the arrow key to move the cursor to the line you need to modify and then press the E key to edit it. Press the B key to boot the system using the new values. You can also press the C key at any time to enter an interactive shell mode, allowing you to submit commands on the fly.

GRUB2

Since the GRUB2 system was intended to be an improvement over GRUB Legacy, many of the features are the same, with a few twists. For example, the GRUB2 system changes the configuration file name to `grub.cfg` and stores it in the `/boot/grub/` folder (this allows you to have both GRUB Legacy and GRUB2 installed at the same time). Some Red Hat–based Linux distributions also make a symbolic link to this file in the `/etc/grub2.cfg` file for easy reference.

Configuring GRUB2

There are also a few changes to the commands used in GRUB2. For example, instead of the `title` command, GRUB2 uses the `menuentry` command, and you must also enclose each individual boot section with braces immediately following the `menuentry` command. Here's an example of a sample GRUB2 configuration file:

```
menuentry "Ubuntu Linux" {
    set root=(hd1,1)
    linux /boot/vmlinuz
    initrd /initrd
}
menuentry"Windows" {
    set root=(hd0,1)
}
```

Notice that GRUB2 uses the `set` command to assign values to the `root` keyword and an equal sign to assign the device. GRUB2 utilizes environment variables to configure settings instead of commands.

GRUB2 also changes the numbering system for partitions. While it still uses 0 for the first hard drive, the first partition is set to 1. So, to define the `/boot` folder on the first partition of the first hard drive, you now need to use

```
set root=hd(0,1)
```

In addition, notice that the `rootnoverify` and `kernel` commands are not used in GRUB2. Non-Linux boot options are defined the same as Linux boot options using the `root` environment variable, and you define the kernel location using the `linux` command.

The configuration process for GRUB2 is also different. While the `/boot/grub/grub.cfg` file is the configuration file that GRUB2 uses, you should never modify that file. Instead, there are separate configuration files stored in the `/etc/grub.d` folder. This allows you (or the system) to create individual configuration files for each boot option installed on your system (for example, one configuration file for booting Linux and another for booting Windows).

For global commands, use the /etc/default/grub configuration file. The format for some of the global commands has changed from the GRUB Legacy commands, such as GRUB_TIMEOUT instead of just timeout.

Most Linux distributions generate the new grub.cfg configuration file automatically after certain events, such as upgrading the kernel. Usually the distribution will keep a boot option pointing to the old kernel file just in case the new one fails.

Installing GRUB2

Unlike with GRUB Legacy, you don't need to install GRUB2; you simply rebuild the main installation file by running the grub2-mkconfig program.

The grub2-mkconfig program reads configuration files stored in the /etc/grub.d folder and assembles the commands into the single grub.cfg configuration file.

You can update the configuration file manually by running the grub2-mkconfig command:

```
# grub2-mkconfig -o /boot/grub2/grub.cfg
```

Notice that you must use the -o command-line option to redirect the output of the grub2-mkconfig program to the grub.cfg configuration file. By default the grub2-mkconfig program just outputs the new configuration file commands to standard output.

 Debian-based Linux distributions, such as Ubuntu, use GRUB2 but compile the programs to match the GRUB Legacy command names, such as the grub-mkconfig command instead of grub2-mkcondig. Needless to say, this can cause lots of confusion. You can tell which version of GRUB is being used by using the command grub-mkconfig -V.

There may be situations where you do need to reinstall GRUB2 on the boot drive. To do that, after creating the grub.cfg configuration file you can install it onto the primary hard disk using the grub2-install command:

```
# grub2-install /dev/sda
```

 Instead of running both the grub2-mkconfig and grub2-install commands, you can use the update-grub2 command (sometimes referred to as grub2-update), which is a front end that performs both operations from a single script.

Interacting with GRUB2

The GRUB2 bootloader produces a boot menu similar to the GRUB Legacy method. You can use arrow keys to switch between boot options, the E key to edit a boot entry, or the C key to bring up the GRUB2 command line to submit interactive boot commands. Figure 5.1 shows editing an entry in the GRUB2 boot menu on an Ubuntu system.

FIGURE 5.1   Editing an Ubuntu GRUB2 menu entry

```
                          GNU GRUB  version 2.04

setparams 'Ubuntu'

        recordfail
        load_video
        gfxmode $linux_gfx_mode
        insmod gzio
        if [ x$grub_platform = xxen ]; then insmod xzio; insmod lzopio; \
fi
        insmod part_msdos
        insmod ext2
        set root='hd0,msdos5'
        if [ x$feature_platform_search_hint = xy ]; then
            search --no-floppy --fs-uuid --set=root --hint-bios=hd0,msdos5\
--hint-efi=hd0,msdos5 --hint-baremetal=ahci0,msdos5  5423117e-4aaf-4416\
-ada7-01e07073b2e1                                                     ↓

    Minimum Emacs-like screen editing is supported. TAB lists
    completions. Press Ctrl-x or F10 to boot, Ctrl-c or F2 for a
    command-line or ESC to discard edits and return to the GRUB
    menu.
```

 Some graphical desktops (such as Ubuntu) hide the GRUB boot menu behind a graphical interface. Usually if you hold down the Shift key when the system first boots, that will display the GRUB boot menu.

Alternative Bootloaders

While GRUB Legacy and GRUB2 are the most popular Linux bootloader programs in use, you may run into a few others, depending on which Linux distributions you use.

The *Syslinux project* includes five separate bootloader programs that have special uses in Linux:

- SYSLINUX: A bootloader for systems that use the Microsoft FAT filesystem (popular for booting from USB memory sticks)

- EXTLINUX: A mini-bootloader for booting from an ext2, ext3, ext4, or btrfs filesystem

- ISOLINUX: A bootloader for booting from a LiveCD or LiveDVD

- PXELINUX: A bootloader for booting from a network server

- MEMDISK: A utility to boot older DOS operating systems from the other SYSLINUX bootloaders

The ISOLINUX bootloader is popular for distributions that release a LiveDVD version. The bootloader requires two files: `isolinux.bin`, which contains the bootloader program image, and `isolinux.cfg`, which contains the configuration settings.

The PXELINUX bootloader uses the *Pre-boot eXecution Environment (PXE)* standard, which defines how a network workstation can boot and load an operating system from a central network server. PXE uses DHCP to assign a network address to the workstation and BOOTP to load the bootloader image from the server. The network server must support the TFTP protocol to transfer the boot image file to the workstation.

To utilize PXELINUX, the TFTP server needs to have the PXELINUX bootloader program, stored as /tftpboot/pxelinux.0, available for the workstations to download. Each workstation must also have a configuration file available in the /tftpboot/pxelinux.cfg directory. The files are named based on the MAC address of the workstation and contain specific configuration settings required for that workstation.

Although PXE was designed to use TFTP to load the boot image, it has been modified to also load the bootloader image stored on a network server using NFS, HTTP, or even FTP.

System Recovery

There's nothing worse than starting up your Linux system and not getting a login prompt. Plenty of things can go wrong in the Linux startup process, but most issues come down to two categories:

- Kernel failures
- Drive failures

The following sections walk through some standard troubleshooting practices you can follow to attempt to recover a Linux system that fails to boot.

Kernel Failures

Kernel failures are when the Linux kernel stops running in memory, causing the Linux system to crash. This is commonly referred to as a *kernel panic*. Kernel panics often are a result of a software change, such as installing a new kernel without the appropriate module or library changes or starting (or stopping) a program at a new runlevel. Often these types of boot errors can be fixed by starting the system using an alternative method and editing the necessary files to change the system.

Selecting Previous Kernels at Boot

One of the biggest culprits to a failed boot is when you upgrade the Linux kernel, either on your own or from a packaged distribution upgrade. When you install a new kernel file, it's always a good idea to leave the old kernel file in place and create an additional entry in the GRUB boot menu to point to the new kernel.

By creating multiple kernel entries in the GRUB boot menu, you can select which kernel version to boot. If the new kernel fails to boot properly, you can reboot and select the older kernel version.

Most Linux distributions do this automatically when adding a new kernel, keeping the most recent older kernel available in the boot menu, as shown in Figure 5.2.

FIGURE 5.2   The Rocky Linux Grub boot menu with multiple kernel options

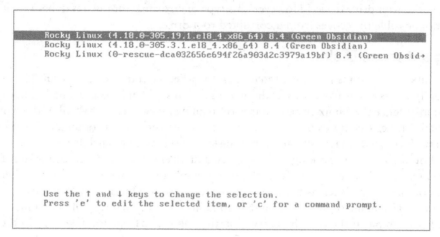

```
Rocky Linux (4.18.0-305.19.1.el8_4.x86_64) 8.4 (Green Obsidian)
Rocky Linux (4.18.0-305.3.1.el8_4.x86_64) 8.4 (Green Obsidian)
Rocky Linux (0-rescue-dca032656e694f26a903d2c3979a19bf) 8.4 (Green Obsid+




        Use the ↑ and ↓ keys to change the selection.
        Press 'e' to edit the selected item, or 'c' for a command prompt.
```

Single-User Mode

At times you may need to perform some type of system maintenance, such as adding a new hardware module or library file to get the system to boot properly. In these situations, you want the system to boot up without allowing multiple users to connect, especially in a server environment. This is called *single-user mode*.

The GRUB menu allows you to start the system in single-user mode by adding the `single` command to the `linux` line in the boot menu commands. To get there, press the E key on the boot option in the GRUB boot menu.

When you add the `single` command, the system will boot into `runlevel 1` (or for systems using the Systemd startup method, the `runlevel-1` target), which creates a single login for the root user account. Once you log in as the root user account, you can modify the appropriate modules, init scripts, or GRUB boot menu options necessary to get your system started correctly.

Passing Kernel Parameters

Besides the single-user mode trick, you can add other kernel parameters to the `linux` command in the GRUB boot menu. The kernel accepts parameters that alter the hardware modules it activates or the hardware settings it looks for with specific devices (this is especially true for sound and network cards). You can specify the different hardware settings as additional parameters to the kernel in the `linux` command and then boot from that entry in the GRUB menu.

Root Drive Failure

Perhaps the worst feeling for a Linux system administrator is seeing that the bootloader can't read the root drive device. However, this type of error may not be fatal, because it is sometimes possible to recover from a corrupted root drive.

Using a Rescue Disk

Many Linux distributions provide a *rescue disk* for when fatal disk errors occur. The rescue disk usually boots either from the CD drive or as a USB stick and loads a small Linux system into memory. Since the Linux system runs entirely in memory, it can leave all of the workstation hard drives free for examination and repair. From the system command-line prompt, you can perform some diagnostic and repair tasks on your system hard drives.

The tool of choice for checking and fixing hard drive errors is the `fsck` command. The `fsck` command isn't a program; it's an alias for a family of commands specific to different types of filesystems (such as ext2, ext3, and ext4). You need to run the `fsck` command against the device name of the partition that contains the root directory of your Linux system. For example, if the root directory is on the `/dev/sda1` partition, you'd run the following command:

```
# fsck /dev/sda1
```

The `fsck` command will examine the inode table along with the file blocks stored on the hard drive and attempt to reconcile them. If any errors occur, you will be prompted on whether to repair them or not. If there are a lot of errors on the partition, you can add the `-y` parameter to automatically answer yes to all the repair questions. After a successful repair, it's a good idea to run the `fsck` command once more to ensure that all errors have been found and corrected. Continue running the `fsck` command until you get a clean run with no errors.

Mounting a Root Drive

When the `fsck` repair is complete, you can test the repaired partition by mounting it into the virtual directory created in memory. Just use the `mount` command to mount it to an available mount directory:

```
# mount /dev/sda1 /media
```

You can examine the filesystem stored in the partition to ensure that it's not corrupted. Before rebooting, you should unmount the partition using the `umount` command:

```
# umount /dev/sda1
```

After successfully unmounting the partition, you can reboot your Linux system using the standard bootloader and attempt to boot using the standard kernel and runlevels.

While booting Linux in single-user mode isn't used all that often, it comes in handy to know how to do it "just in case." Exercise 5.1 walks though the steps to help you get some practice in booting up a Linux system in single user mode.

EXERCISE 5.1

Using Rescue Mode

This exercise will demonstrate how to start your Linux distribution in single-user mode to examine filesystems and configurations without performing a complete bootup. To use single-user mode, follow these steps:

1. First, start your Linux distribution as normal, and log in on the standard login prompt (either the graphical desktop or the command-line login) as your normal user account.

2. Type **runlevel** to determine the default runlevel for your system. The first character returned refers to the previous runlevel (N denotes no previous runlevel since the system booted). The second character is the current runlevel. This is likely to be 2 on Debian-based systems or 3 on command-line Red Hat–based systems or 5 on graphical desktop Red Hat–based systems.

3. Now reboot your system, and press an arrow key when the GRUB2 menu appears to stop the countdown timer. If you're using a Linux distribution that hides the GRUB2 menu (such as Ubuntu), hold down the Shift key when the system boots to display the GRUB2 menu.

4. At the GRUB2 menu, use the arrow keys to go to the default menu entry (usually the first entry in the list) and then press the **E** key. This takes GRUB2 into edit mode.

5. Look for either the linux or linux16 menu command lines. These define the kernel used to start the session.

6. Go to the end of the linux or the linux16 line, and add the word single. Press Ctrl+X to temporarily save the change and start your system using that menu entry.

7. The Linux system will boot into single-user mode. Depending on your Linux distribution, it may prompt you to enter the root user account or to press Ctrl+D to continue with the normal boot. Enter the root user account password to enter single-user mode.

8. Now you are at the root user command prompt. Enter the command **runlevel** to view the current runlevel. It should show runlevel 1. From here you can modify configuration files, check filesystems, and change user accounts.

9. Reboot the system by typing **reboot**.

10. You should return to the standard boot process and GRUB2 menu options as before. Select the standard GRUB2 menu option to boot your system and then log in.

11. At a command-line prompt, type **runlevel** to ensure that you are back to the normal default runlevel for your Linux system.

Summary

Although Linux distributions are designed to boot without any user intervention, it helps to know the Linux boot process in case anything does go wrong. Most Linux systems use either the GRUB Legacy or GRUB2 bootloader program. These programs both reside in the BIOS Master Boot Record or in the ESP partition on UEFI systems. The bootloader loads the Linux kernel program, which then runs the SysV init or Systemd programs to start individual background programs required for the Linux system.

No discussion on Linux startup is complete without examining system recovery methods. If your Linux system fails to boot, the most likely cause is either a kernel issue or a root device issue. For kernel issues, you can often modify the GRUB menu to add additional kernel parameters, or even boot from an older version of the kernel. For root drive issues you can try to boot from a rescue mode into a version of Linux running in memory and then use the `fsck` command to repair a damaged root drive.

Exam Essentials

Describe the Linux boot process.   The BIOS or UEFI starts a bootloader program from the Master Boot Record, which is usually the Linux GRUB Legacy or GRUB2 program. The bootloader program loads the Linux kernel into memory, which in turn looks for the `init` program to run. The `init` program starts individual application programs and starts either the command-line terminals or the graphical desktop manager.

Describe the Linux GRUB Legacy and GRUB2 bootloaders.   The GRUB Legacy bootloader stores files in the `/boot/grub` folder and uses the `menu.lst` or `grub.conf` configuration file to define commands used at boot time. The commands can create a boot menu, allowing you to select between multiple boot locations, options, or features. You must use the `grub-install` program to install the GRUB Legacy bootloader program into the Master Boot Record. The GRUB2 bootloader also stores files in the `/boot/grub` folder, but it uses the `grub.cfg` configuration file to define the menu commands. You don't edit the `grub.cfg` file directly but instead store files in the `/etc/default/grub` file or individual configuration files in the `/etc/grub.d` folder. Run the `grub-mkconfig` program to generate the GRUB2 configuration from the configuration files and then redirect the output to the `/etc/grub.cfg` file.

Describe alternative Linux bootloaders.   The LILO bootloader is used on older Linux systems. It uses the `/etc/lilo.conf` configuration file to define the boot options. The Syslinux project has created the most popular alternative Linux bootloaders. The SYSLINUX bootloader provides a bootloader that runs on FAT filesystems, such as floppy disks and USB memory sticks. The ISOLINUX bootloader is popular on LiveCD distributions, as it can boot from a CD or DVD. It stores the bootloader program in the `isolinux.bin` file and configuration settings in the `isolinux.cfg` file. The PXELINUX bootloader program allows a network workstation to boot from a network server. The server must contain the `pxelinux.0` image file along with the `pxelinux.cfg` directory, which contains separate configuration files for each workstation. The EXTLINUX bootloader is a small bootloader program that can be used on smaller embedded Linux systems.

Describe how to recover from a kernel panic.   The GRUB bootloaders provide you with options that can help if your Linux system fails to boot or stops due to a kernel panic issue. You can press the E key at the GRUB boot menu to edit any boot menu entry, then add any additional kernel parameters, such as placing the system in single-user mode. You can also use a rescue disk to boot Linux into memory, then use the `fsck` command to repair any corrupted hard drives, and finally use the `mount` command to mount them to examine the files.

Review Questions

1. What program does the workstation firmware start at boot time?
   A. A bootloader
   B. The `fsck` program
   C. The Windows OS
   D. The `mount` command
   E. The `mkinitrd` program

2. Where does the firmware first look for a Linux bootloader program?
   A. The `/boot/grub` folder
   B. The Master Boot Record (MBR)
   C. The `/var/log` folder
   D. A boot partition
   E. The `/etc` folder

3. The _____ command allows us to examine the most recent boot messages.
   A. `fsck`
   B. `init`
   C. `mount`
   D. `dmesg`
   E. `mkinitrd`

4. What folder do most Linux distributions use to store boot logs?
   A. `/etc`
   B. `/var/messages`
   C. `/var/log`
   D. `/boot`
   E. `/proc`

5. Where does the workstation BIOS attempt to find a bootloader program? (Choose all that apply.)
   A. An internal hard drive
   B. An external hard drive
   C. A DVD drive
   D. A USB memory stick
   E. A network server

6. Where is the Master Boot Record located? (Choose all that apply.)

A. The first sector of the first hard drive on the system

B. The boot partition of any hard drive on the system

C. The last sector of the first hard drive on the system

D. Any sector on any hard drive on the system

E. The first sector of the second hard drive on the system

7. The EFI System Partition (ESP) is stored in the _____ directory on Linux systems.

A. /boot

B. /etc

C. /var

D. /boot/efi

E. /boot/grub

8. What file extension do UEFI bootloader files use?

A. .cfg

B. .uefi

C. .lst

D. .conf

E. .efi

9. Which was the first bootloader program used in Linux?

A. GRUB Legacy

B. LILO

C. GRUB2

D. SYSLINUX

E. ISOLINUX

10. Where are the GRUB Legacy configuration files stored?

A. /boot/grub

B. /boot/efi

C. /etc

D. /var

E. /proc

11. Where are GRUB2 configuration files stored? (Choose all that apply.)

A. /proc

B. /etc/grub.d

C. /boot/grub

D. /boot/efi

E. /var

12. You must run the _____ command to generate the GRUB2 `grub.cfg` configuration file.

   A. `mkinitrd`

   B. `mkinitramfs`

   C. `grub-mkconfig`

   D. `grub-install`

   E. `fsck`

13. What command must you run to save changes to a GRUB Legacy boot menu?

   A. `mkinitrd`

   B. `mkinitramfs`

   C. `grub-mkconfig`

   D. `grub-install`

   E. `fsck`

14. The ____ firmware method has replaced BIOS on most modern IBM-compatible computers.

   A. FTP

   B. UEFI

   C. PXE

   D. NFS

   E. HTTPS

15. What memory area does Linux use to store boot messages?

   A. BIOS

   B. The GRUB bootloader

   C. The MBR

   D. The initrd RAM disk

   E. The kernel ring buffer

16. What command parameter would you add to the end of the GRUB2 `linux` command to force a Linux system to start in single-user mode?

   A. `single`

   B. `fsck`

   C. `mkinitrd`

   D. `mkinitramfs`

   E. `dmesg`

17. What is the term commonly used for when the Linux system halts due to a system error?

   A. Kernel panic

   B. Kernel ring buffer

   C. initrd RAM disk

   D. Bootloader

   E. Firmware

18. The _____ command generates the GRUB2 configuration used for booting.
   A. mkinitrd
   B. grub-mkconfig
   C. grub-install
   D. mkinitramfs
   E. dmesg

19. What program allows you to fix corrupted hard drive partitions?
   A. mount
   B. umount
   C. fsck
   D. dmesg
   E. mkinitrd

20. Which command allows you to append a partition to the virtual directory on a running Linux system?
   A. mount
   B. umount
   C. fsck
   D. dmesg
   E. mkinitramfs

Chapter

6

Maintaining System Startup and Services

✓ **Objective 1.4: Given a scenario, configure and use the appropriate processes and services**

✓ **Objective 4.5: Given a scenario, use systemd to diagnose and resolve common problems with a Linux system**

After your Linux system has traversed the boot process, it enters final system initialization, where it needs to start various services. A service, or daemon, is a program that performs a particular duty. Several services were covered in Chapter 2, "Introduction to Services."

The initialization daemon (init) determines which services are started and in what order. This daemon also allows you to stop and manage the various system services.

The SysV init (SysV) was based on the Unix System V initialization daemon. While it's not used by many major Linux distributions anymore, you still may find it lurking around that older Linux server at your company.

The systemd initialization method is the new kid on the block. Started around 2010, it is now the most popular system service initialization and management mechanism. This daemon reduces initialization time by starting services in a parallel manner.

Beyond initialization, these daemons are also responsible for managing these services well past boot time. We'll explore these concepts in this chapter.

Looking at *init*

Before we start examining the various service management methods, it's a good idea to take a look at the init program itself. Classically, service startups are handled by the init program. This program can be located in the /etc/, the /bin/, or the /sbin/ directory. Also, it typically has a process ID (PID) of 1.

The init program or systemd is the parent process for every service on a Linux system. If your system has the pstree program installed, you can see a diagram depicting this relationship by typing in **pstree -p 1** at the command line.

This information will assist you in determining which system initialization method your current Linux distribution is using, systemd or SysV init. First find the init program's location, using the which command. An example is shown in Listing 6.1.

Listing 6.1 Finding the init program file location

```
# which init
/sbin/init
#
```

Now that you know the init program's location, using super user privileges, you can use the readlink -f command to see if the program is linked to another program, as shown in Listing 6.2.

Listing 6.2 Checking the `init` program for links

```
# readlink -f /sbin/init
/usr/lib/systemd/systemd
#
```

You can see in Listing 6.2 that this system is actually using systemd. You can verify this by taking a look at PID 1, as shown in Listing 6.3.

Listing 6.3 Checking PID 1

```
# ps -p 1
  PID TTY          TIME CMD
    1 ?        00:00:06 systemd
#
```

In Listing 6.3, the `ps` utility is used. This utility allows you to view processes. A process is a running program. The ps command shows you what program is running for a particular process in the CMD column. In this case, the systemd program is running. Thus, this Linux system is using systemd.

Keep in mind that these discovery methods are not foolproof. Also, there are other system initialization methods, such as the now-defunct Upstart. The following brief list shows a few Linux distribution versions that used Upstart:

- Fedora v9–v14
- openSUSE v11.3–v12.2
- RHEL v6
- Ubuntu v6.10–v15.04

If you are using the distribution versions recommended in Chapter 1, "Preparing Your Environment," be aware that those distributions are all systemd systems.

Managing systemd Systems

The systemd approach introduced a major paradigm shift in how Linux systems manage services. Services can now be started when the system boots, when a particular hardware component is attached to the system, when certain other services are started, and so on. Some services can be started based on a timer.

In the following sections, we'll focus on starting, stopping, and controlling systemd managed services. We'll walk you through the systemd technique's structures, commands, and configuration files.

Exploring Unit Files

The easiest way to start exploring systemd is through the *systemd units*. A unit defines a service, a group of services, or an action. Each unit consists of a name, a type, and a configuration file. There are currently 12 different systemd unit types, as follows:

- automount
- device
- mount
- path
- scope
- service
- slice
- snapshot
- socket
- swap
- target
- timer

The `systemctl` utility is the main gateway to managing systemd and system services. Its basic syntax is as follows:

```
systemctl [OPTIONS...] COMMAND [NAME...]
```

You can use the `systemctl` utility to provide a list of the various units currently loaded in your Linux system. A snipped example is shown in Listing 6.4.

Listing 6.4 Looking at systemd units

```
$ systemctl list-units
UNIT                      LOAD   ACTIVE SUB      DESCRIPTION
[...]
smartd.service            loaded active running  Self Monitor[...]
sshd.service              loaded active running  OpenSSH serv[...]
sysstat.service           loaded active exited   Resets Syste[...]
[...]
graphical.target          loaded active active   Graphical I[...]
[...]
$
```

In Listing 6.4 you can see various units as well as additional information. Units are identified by their name and type using the format *name.type*. System services (daemons) have unit files with the `.service` extension. Thus, the secure shell (SSH) daemon, sshd, has a unit filename of `sshd.service`.

Many displays from the systemctl utility use the less pager by default. Thus, to exit the display, you must press the Q key. If you want to turn off the systemctl utility's use of the less pager, tack the --no-pager option on the command.

Groups of services are started via target unit files. At system startup, the default.target unit is responsible for ensuring that all required and desired services are launched at system initialization. It is set up as a symbolic link to another target unit file, as shown in Listing 6.5 on an Ubuntu distribution.

Listing 6.5 Looking at the default.target link

```
$ find / -name default.target 2>/dev/null
/usr/lib/systemd/system/default.target
[...]
$ readlink -f /usr/lib/systemd/system/default.target
/usr/lib/systemd/system/graphical.target
$ systemctl get-default
graphical.target
$
```

First, in Listing 6.5, the default.target unit's full filename is located via the find utility. The readlink command is then employed to find the actual target file, which determines what services to start at system boot. In this case, the target unit file is graphical.target.

Also notice in Listing 6.5 that the systemctl command is much easier to use than the other two commands. It is simply systemctl get-default, and it displays the actual target file. Due to the default.target file being located in different directories on the different distros, it is always best to use the systemctl utility. Table 6.1 shows the more commonly used system boot target unit files.

TABLE 6.1 Commonly used system boot target unit files

Name	Description
graphical .target	Provides multiple users access to the system via local terminals and/or through the network. Graphical user interface (GUI) access is offered.
multi-user .target	Provides multiple users access to the system via local terminals and/or through the network. No GUI access is offered.
network-online .target	Provides a target that runs after the system has established a connection to the network. This is useful for starting applications that require the network to be present.
runlevel$n$ .target	Provides backward compatibility to SysV init systems, where n is set to 1–5 for the desired SysV runlevel equivalence.

In Table 6.1, you'll notice that systemd provides backward compatibility to the classic SysV init systems. The SysV runlevels will be covered later in this chapter.

The master systemd configuration file is the /etc/systemd/system. conf file. In this file you will find all the default configuration settings commented out via a hash mark (#). Viewing this file is a quick way to see the current systemd configuration. If you need to modify the configuration, just edit the file. However, it would be wise to peruse the file's man page first by typing **man systemd-system.conf** at the command line.

Focusing on Service Unit Files

Service unit files contain information, such as which environment file to use, when a service must be started, what targets want this service started, and so on. These configuration files are located in different directories.

Keep in mind that a unit configuration file's directory location is critical, because if a file is found in two different directory locations, one will have precedence over the other. The following list shows the directory locations in ascending priority order:

1. /etc/systemd/system/

2. /run/systemd/system/

3. /usr/lib/systemd/system/

To see the various service unit files available, you can again employ the systemctl utility. However, a slightly different command is needed than when viewing units, as shown in Listing 6.6.

Listing 6.6 Looking at systemd unit files

```
$ systemctl list-unit-files
UNIT FILE                           STATE
[...]
dev-hugepages.mount                 static
dev-mqueue.mount                    static
proc-fs-nfsd.mount                  static
[...]
nfs.service                         disabled
nfslock.service                     static
ntpd.service                        disabled
ntpdate.service                     disabled
[...]
ctrl-alt-del.target                 disabled
default.target                      static
emergency.target                    static
[...]
$
```

Besides the unit file's base name, you can also see a unit file's state in Listing 6.6. Their states are called enablement states and refer to when the service is started. There are at least 12 different enablement states, but you'll commonly see these three:

- `enabled`: Service starts at system boot.
- `disabled`: Service does not start at system boot.
- `static`: Service starts if another unit depends on it. Can also be manually started.

To see what directory or directories store a particular systemd unit file(s), use the `systemctl` utility. An example on an Ubuntu distribution is shown in Listing 6.7.

Listing 6.7 Finding and displaying a systemd unit file

```
$ systemctl cat cron.service
# /lib/systemd/system/cron.service
[Unit]
Description=Regular background program processing daemon
Documentation=man:cron(8)
After=remote-fs.target nss-user-lookup.target

[Service]
EnvironmentFile=-/etc/default/cron
ExecStart=/usr/sbin/cron -f $EXTRA_OPTS
IgnoreSIGPIPE=false
KillMode=process
Restart=on-failure

[Install]
WantedBy=multi-user.target
$
```

Notice in Listing 6.7 that the first displayed line shows the `cron.service` unit file's base name and directory location. The next several lines are the unit configuration file's contents.

For service unit files, there are three primary configuration sections:

- `[Unit]`
- `[Service]`
- `[Install]`

Within the service unit configuration file's `[Unit]` section, there are basic *directives*. A directive is a setting that modifies a configuration, such as the `After` setting shown in Listing 6.7. Commonly used `[Unit]` section directives are described in Table 6.2.

TABLE 6.2 Commonly used service unit file [Unit] section directives

Directive	Description
After	Sets this unit to start after the designated units.
Before	Sets this unit to start before the designated units.
Description	Describes the unit.
Documen-tation	Sets a list of Uniform Resource Identifiers (URIs) that point to documentation sources. The URIs can be web locations, particular system files, info pages, and man pages.
Conflicts	Sets this unit to *not* start with the designated units. If any of the designated units start, this unit is not started. (Opposite of Requires.)
Requires	Sets this unit to start together with the designated units. If any of the designated units do not start, this unit is *not* started. (Opposite of Conflicts.)
Wants	Sets this unit to start together with the designated units. If any of the designated units do not start, this unit is *still* started.

There is a great deal of useful information in the man pages for systemd and unit configuration files. Just type **man -k systemd** to find several items you can explore. For example, explore the service type unit file directives and more with the man systemd.service command. You can find information on all the various directives by typing **man systemd.directives** at the command line.

The [Service] directives within a unit file set configuration items, which are specific to that service. Commonly used [Service] section directives are described in Table 6.3.

TABLE 6.3 Commonly used service unit file [Service] section directives

Directive	Description
ExecReload	Indicates scripts or commands (and options) to run when unit is reloaded.
ExecStart	Indicates scripts or commands (and options) to run when unit is started.
ExecStop	Indicates scripts or commands (and options) to run when unit is stopped.
Environment	Sets environment variable substitutes, separated by a space.

Directive	Description
Environment File	Indicates a file that contains environment variable substitutes.
RemainAfterExit	Set to either no (default) or yes. If set to yes, the service is left active even when the process started by ExecStart terminates. If set to no, then ExecStop is called when the process started by ExecStart terminates.
Restart	Service is restarted when the process started by ExecStart terminates. Ignored if a systemctl restart or systemctl stop command is issued. Set to no (default), on-success, on-failure, on-abnormal, on-watchdog, on-abort, or always.
Type	Sets the startup type.

The [Service] Type directive needs a little more explanation than what is given in Table 6.3. This directive can be set to at least six different specifications, of which the most typical are listed here:

- forking: ExecStart starts a parent process. The parent process creates the service's main process as a child process and exits.

- simple: (Default) ExecStart starts the service's main process.

- oneshot: ExecStart starts the service's main process, which is typically a configuration setting or a quick command, and the process exits.

- idle: ExecStart starts the service's main process, but it waits until all other start jobs are finished.

 You will only find a unit file [Service] section in a service unit file. This middle section is different for each unit type. For example, in auto mount unit files, you would find an [Automount] section as the middle unit file section.

Another [Service] configuration setting that needs additional explanation is the Environment directive. Linux systems use a feature called *environment variables* to store information about the shell session and working environment (thus the name *environment variable*). If you want to ensure that a particular environment variable is set properly for your service, you will want to employ the Environment directive. A snipped example on a Rocky Linux distribution is shown in Listing 6.8.

Listing 6.8 Viewing a service unit file's Environment directive

```
$ echo $PATH
/usr/local/bin:/usr/bin:/usr/local/sbin:/usr/sbin:[...]
$
```

```
$ systemctl --no-pager cat anaconda.service
# /usr/lib/systemd/system/anaconda.service
[Unit]
Description=Anaconda
[...]
[Service]
Type=forking
Environment=HOME=/root MALLOC_CHECK_=2 MALLOC_PERTURB_=204 PATH=/usr/bin:/
bin:/sbin:/usr/sbin:/mnt/sysimage/bin: [...]
LANG=en_US.UTF-8 [...]
[...]
$
```

In Listing 6.8, you can see that the PATH environment variable's contents are displayed. This environment variable is a colon-separated list of directories where the process looks for commands. The anaconda.service unit file uses the Environment directive to set particular environment variables to its own desired environment parameters. These parameters are separated by a space. You can see in Listing 6.8 that one of those parameters set by the Environment directive is PATH.

 Some service type unit files use the EnvironmentFile directive, instead of the Environment directive. This directive points to a file containing environment parameters. The cron.service unit file shown in Listing 6.7 does just that.

The [Install] directives within a unit file determine what happens to a particular service if it is enabled or disabled. An *enabled service* is one that starts at system boot. A *disabled service* is one that does *not* start at system boot. Commonly used [Install] section directives are described in Table 6.4.

TABLE 6.4   Commonly used service unit file [Install] section directives

Directive	Description
Alias	Sets additional names that can be used to denote the service in systemctl commands.
Also	Sets additional units that must be enabled or disabled for this service. Often the additional units are socket type units.
RequiredBy	Designates other units that require this service.
WantedBy	Designates which target unit manages this service.

Focusing on Target Unit Files

For systemd, you need to understand the service unit files as well as the target unit files. The primary purpose of target unit files is to group together various services to start at system boot time. The default target unit file, `default.target`, is symbolically linked to the target unit file used at system boot. In Listing 6.9, the default target unit file is located and displayed using the `systemctl` command.

Listing 6.9 Finding and displaying the systemd target unit file

```
$ systemctl get-default
graphical.target
$
$ systemctl cat graphical.target
# /usr/lib/systemd/system/graphical.target
[...]
[Unit]
Description=Graphical Interface
Documentation=man:systemd.special(7)
Requires=multi-user.target
Wants=display-manager.service
Conflicts=rescue.service rescue.target
After=multi-user.target rescue.service rescue.target display-manager.service
AllowIsolate=yes
$
```

Notice in Listing 6.9 that the `graphical.target` unit file has many of the same directives as a service unit file. These directives were described back in Table 6.2. Of course, these directives apply to a target type unit file instead of a service type unit file. For example, the `After` directive in the `graphical.target` unit file sets this target unit to start after the designated units, such as `multi-user.target`. Target units, similar to service units, have various target dependency chains as well as conflicts.

In Listing 6.9, there is one directive we have not covered yet. The `AllowIsolate` directive, if set to `yes`, permits this target file to be used with the `systemctl isolate` command. This command is covered later in this chapter.

 Real World Scenario

Modifying Systems Configuration Files

Occasionally you may need to change a particular unit configuration file for your Linux system's requirements or add additional components. However, be careful when doing this task. You should not modify any unit files in the `/lib/systemd/system/` or `/usr/lib/systemd/system/` directory.

To modify a unit configuration file, copy the file to the `/etc/systemd/system/` directory and modify it there. This modified file will take precedence over the original unit file left in the original directory. Also, it will protect the modified unit file from software updates.

If you just have a few additional components, you can extend the configuration. Using super user privileges, create a new subdirectory in the `/etc/systemd/system/` directory named *service.service-name*`.d`, where *service-name* is the service's name. For example, for the OpenSSH daemon, you would create the `/etc/systemd/system/service.sshd.d` directory. This newly created directory is called a drop-in file directory, because you can drop in additional configuration files. Create any configuration files with names like *description*`.conf`, where *description* describes the configuration file's purpose, such as `local` or `script`. Add your modified directives to this configuration file.

After making these modifications, there are a few more needed steps. Find and compare any unit file that overrides another unit file by issuing the `systemd-delta` command. It will display any unit files that are duplicated, extended, redirected, and so on. Review this list. It will help you avoid any unintended consequences from modifying or extending a service unit file.

To have your changes take effect, issue the `systemctl daemon-reload` command for the service whose unit file you modified or extended. After you accomplish that task, issue the `systemctl restart` command to start or restart the service. These commands are explained in the next section.

Looking at *systemctl*

You may have noticed that while there are various commands to manage systemd and system services, it is easier and faster to employ the `systemctl` utility.

There are several basic `systemctl` commands available for you to manage system services. One that is often used is the `status` command. It provides a wealth of information. A couple of snipped examples on an Ubuntu distro are shown in Listing 6.10.

Listing 6.10 Viewing a service unit's status via `systemctl`

```
$ systemctl status cron
 cron.service - Regular background program processing daemon
     Loaded: loaded (/lib/systemd/system/cron.service; disabled; vendor
preset: >
     Active: inactive (dead) since Sat 2021-11-20 14:28:12 EST; 5s ago
       Docs: man:cron(8)
    Process: 593 ExecStart=/usr/sbin/cron -f $EXTRA_OPTS (code=killed,
signal=T>
   Main PID: 593 (code=killed, signal=TERM)
```

```
Nov 20 14:13:44 ubuntu20 systemd[1]: Started Regular background program
process>
Nov 20 14:13:44 ubuntu20 cron[593]: (CRON) INFO (pidfile fd = 3)
Nov 20 14:13:44 ubuntu20 cron[593]: (CRON) INFO (Running @reboot jobs)
Nov 20 14:17:01 ubuntu20 CRON[2329]: pam_unix(cron:session): session opened
for>
Nov 20 14:17:01 ubuntu20 CRON[2330]: (root) CMD (   cd / & & run-parts
--report >
Nov 20 14:17:01 ubuntu20 CRON[2329]: pam_unix(cron:session): session closed
for>
Nov 20 14:28:12 ubuntu20 systemd[1]: Stopping Regular background program
proces>
Nov 20 14:28:12 ubuntu20 systemd[1]: cron.service: Succeeded.
Nov 20 14:28:12 ubuntu20 systemd[1]: Stopped Regular background program
process>
$ systemctl status sshd
 ssh.service - OpenBSD Secure Shell server
     Loaded: loaded (/lib/systemd/system/ssh.service; enabled; vendor preset: e>
     Active: active (running) since Sat 2021-11-20 14:13:45 EST; 12min ago
       Docs: man:sshd(8)
             man:sshd_config(5)
   Main PID: 686 (sshd)
      Tasks: 1 (limit: 9469)
     Memory: 2.3M
     CGroup: /system.slice/ssh.service
             └686 sshd: /usr/sbin/sshd -D [listener] 0 of 10-100 startups

Nov 20 14:13:44 ubuntu20 systemd[1]: Starting OpenBSD Secure Shell server...
Nov 20 14:13:45 ubuntu20 sshd[686]: Server listening on 0.0.0.0 port 22.
Nov 20 14:13:45 ubuntu20 sshd[686]: Server listening on :: port 22.
Nov 20 14:13:45 ubuntu20 systemd[1]: Started OpenBSD Secure Shell server.
$
```

In Listing 6.10, the first `systemctl` command shows the status of the `cron` service. Notice the third line in the utility's output. It states that the service is `disabled`. The fourth line states that the service is `inactive`. In essence, this means that the `cron` service is not running (`inactive`) and is not configured to start at system boot time (`disabled`). Another item to look at within the `cron` service's status is the `Loaded` line. Notice that the unit file's complete filename and directory location are shown.

The status of the `sshd` service is also displayed, showing that `sshd` is running (`active`) and configured to start at system boot time (`enabled`).

There are several simple commands you can use with the `systemctl` utility to manage systemd services and view information regarding them. Common commands are listed in Table 6.5. These `systemctl` commands generally use the following syntax:

`systemctl COMMAND UNIT-NAME...`

TABLE 6.5 Commonly used `systemctl` service management commands

Command	Description
daemon-reload	Load the unit configuration file of the running designated unit(s) to make unit file configuration changes without stopping the service. Note that this is different from the `reload` command.
disable	Mark the designated unit(s) to *not* be started automatically at system boot time.
enable	Mark the designated unit(s) to be started automatically at system boot time.
mask	Prevent the designated unit(s) from starting. The service cannot be started using the `start` command or at system boot. Use the `--now` option to immediately stop any running instances as well. Use the `--running` option to mask the service only until the next reboot or unmask is used.
restart	Stop and immediately restart the designated unit(s). If a designated unit is not already started, this will simply start it.
start	Start the designated unit(s).
status	Display the designated unit's current status.
stop	Stop the designated unit(s).
reload	Load the service configuration file of the running designated unit(s) to make service configuration changes without stopping the service. Note that this is different from the `daemon-reload` command.
unmask	Undo the effects of the `mask` command on the designated unit(s).

Notice the difference in Table 6.5 between the `daemon-reload` and the `reload` command. This is an important difference. Use the `daemon-reload` command if you need to load systemd unit file configuration changes for a running service. Use the `reload` command to load a service's modified configuration file. For example, if you modified the ntpd service's configuration file, /etc/ntp.conf, and wanted the new configuration to take immediate effect, you would issue the command **systemctl reload ntpd** at the command line.

Use caution when employing the `systemctl mask` command on a service. This links the service to the /dev/null (black hole) to prevent any kind of service startup. This has been described as the "third level of off." You will not be able to start the service manually. Also, the service will *not* start at boot time if you did not employ the `--running` option when you used mask on it. You can reenable the ability to start the service by using the `systemctl unmask` command on it.

Besides the commands in Table 6.7, there are some other handy `systemctl` commands you can use for managing system services. An example on a CentOS distro is shown in Listing 6.11.

Listing 6.11 Determining if a service is running by using `systemctl`

```
# systemctl stop sshd
#
# systemctl is-active sshd
inactive
#
# systemctl start sshd
#
# systemctl is-active sshd
active
#
```

In Listing 6.11, the OpenSSH daemon (`sshd`) is stopped using `systemctl` and its `stop` command. Instead of the `status` command, the `is-active` command is used to quickly display that the service is stopped (`inactive`). The OpenSSH service is started back up and again the `is-active` command is used, showing that the service is now running (`active`). Table 6.6 describes these useful service status checking commands.

TABLE 6.6 Convenient `systemctl` service status commands

Command	Description
is-active	Displays `active` for running services and `failed` for any service that has reached a failed state
is-enabled	Displays `enabled` for any service that is configured to start at system boot and `disabled` for any service that is *not* configured to start at system boot
is-failed	Displays `failed` for any service that has reached a failed state and `active` for running services

Services can fail for many reasons: for hardware issues, a missing dependency set in the unit configuration file, an incorrect permission setting, and so on. You can employ the `systemctl` utility's `is-failed` command to see if a particular service has failed. An example is shown in Listing 6.12.

Listing 6.12 Determining if a service has failed by using `systemctl`

```
$ systemctl is-failed NetworkManager-wait-online.service
failed
$
$ systemctl is-active NetworkManager-wait-online.service
failed
$
```

In Listing 6.12, you can see that this particular service has failed. Actually, it was a failure forced by disconnecting the network cable prior to boot, so you could see a service's `failed` status. If the service was not in failed state, the `is-failed` command would show an `active` status.

The `systemctl` program is a handy tool to use when troubleshooting systemd issues, such as unit name resolution problems and services not starting on time. Since the systemd startup method can control so many aspects of your Linux system, it's a good idea to have a handle on just what `systemctl` can do for you.

Examining Special systemd Commands

The `systemctl` utility has several commands that go beyond service management. Also, systemd has some special commands. You can manage what targets (groups of services) are started at system boot time, jump between various system states, and even analyze your system's boot time performance. We'll look at these various commands in this section.

One special command to explore is the `systemctl is-system-running` command. An example of this command is shown in Listing 6.13.

Listing 6.13 Determining a system's operational status

```
$ systemctl is-system-running
running
$
```

You may think the status returned here is obvious, but it means all is well with your Linux system currently. Table 6.7 shows other useful statuses.

TABLE 6.7 Operational statuses provided by `systemctl is-system-running`

Status	Description
running	System is fully in working order.
degraded	System has one or more failed units.
maintenance	System is in emergency or recovery mode.
initializing	System is starting to boot.
starting	System is still booting.
stopping	System is starting to shut down.

The `maintenance` operational status will be covered shortly in this chapter. If you receive `degraded` status, however, you should review your units to see which ones have failed and take appropriate action. Use the `systemctl --failed` command to find the failed unit(s), as shown snipped in Listing 6.14.

Listing 6.14 Finding failed units

```
$ systemctl is-system-running
degraded
$
$ systemctl --failed
  UNIT            LOAD   ACTIVE SUB     DESCRIPTION
• rngd.service loaded failed failed Hardware RNG Entropy Gatherer Daemon
[...]
$
```

Other useful `systemctl` utility commands deal with obtaining, setting, and jumping the system's target. They are as follows:

- `get-default`
- `set-default`
- `isolate`

You've already seen the `systemctl get-default` command in action within Listing 6.5. This command displays the system's default target. As you may have guessed, you can set the system's default target with super user privileges via the `systemctl set-target` command.

The `isolate` command is handy for jumping between system targets. When this command is used along with a target name for an argument, all services and processes not enabled in the listed target are stopped. Any services and processes enabled and not running in the listed target are started. A snipped example is shown in Listing 6.15.

Listing 6.15 Jumping to a different target unit

```
# systemctl get-default
graphical.target
#
# systemctl isolate multi-user.target
#
# systemctl status graphical.target
[...]
   Active: inactive (dead) since Thu 2018-09-13 16:57:00 EDT; 4min 24s ago
     Docs: man:systemd.special(7)

Sep 13 16:54:41 localhost.localdomain systemd[1]: Reached target Graphical
In...
Sep 13 16:54:41 localhost.localdomain systemd[1]: Starting Graphical
Interface.
Sep 13 16:57:00 localhost.localdomain systemd[1]: Stopped target Graphical
In[...]
Sep 13 16:57:00 localhost.localdomain systemd[1]: Stopping Graphical
Interface.
[...]
#
```

In Listing 6.15, using super user privileges, the `systemctl isolate` command caused the system to jump from the default system target to the multiuser target. Unfortunately, there is no simple command to show your system's current target in this case. However, the `systemctl status` command is useful. If you use the command and give it the previous target's name (`graphical.target` in this case), you should see that it is no longer active and thus is not the current system target. Notice that a short history of the graphical target's starts and stops is also shown in the status display.

 The `systemctl isolate` command can only be used with certain targets. The target's unit file must have the `AllowIsolate=yes` directive set.

Two extra special targets are rescue and emergency. These targets, sometimes called modes, are described here:

Rescue Target   When you jump your system to the rescue target, the system mounts all the local filesystems, only the root user is allowed to log into the system, networking services are turned off, and only a few other services are started. The systemctl is-system-running command will return the maintenance status. Running disk utilities to fix corrupted disks is a useful task in this particular target.

Emergency Target   When your system goes into emergency mode, the system only mounts the root filesystem, and it mounts it as read-only. Similar to rescue mode, it only allows the root user to log into the system, networking services are turned off, and only a few other services are started. The systemctl is-system-running command will return the maintenance status. If your system goes into emergency mode by itself, there are serious problems. This target is used for situations where even rescue mode cannot be reached.

Be aware that if you jump into either rescue or emergency mode, you'll only be able to log into the root account. Therefore, you need to have the root account password. Also, your screen may go blank for a minute, so don't panic. An example of jumping into emergency mode is shown in Listing 6.16.

Listing 6.16 Jumping to the emergency target unit

```
# systemctl isolate emergency
Welcome to emergency mode! After logging in, type "journalctl -xb" to view
system logs, "systemctl reboot" to reboot, "systemctl default" or ^D to
try again to boot into default mode.
Give root password for maintenance
(or type Control-D to continue):
#
# systemctl is-system-running
maintenance
#
# systemctl list-units --type=target
UNIT              LOAD     ACTIVE  SUB     DESCRIPTION
emergency.target  loaded   active  active  Emergency Mode
[...]
#
# systemctl default
#
```

In Listing 6.16, the systemctl command is used to jump into emergency mode. Notice that you do not have to add the .target extension on the emergency target unit's filename. This is true with all systemd targets. Once you reach emergency mode, you must enter the root password at the prompt. Once you reach the command line, you can enter commands listed in the welcome display or try some additional systemctl commands.

Other targets you can jump to include reboot, poweroff, and halt. For example, just type **systemctl isolate reboot** to reboot your system.

Notice in Listing 6.16 that when the systemctl is-system-running command is issued, the response is maintenance instead of running. Also, when the list-units command is employed, it shows that the emergency.target is active. The systemctl default command will cause the system to attempt to jump into the default target.

If you are using GRUB2 as your bootloader, you can reach a different target via the bootloader menu. Just move your cursor to the menu option that typically boots your system and press the E key to edit it. Scroll down and find the line that starts with the linux16 command. Press the End key to reach the line's end. Press the spacebar and type **systemd.unit=*target-name*.target**, where *target-name* is the name of the target you want your system to activate. This is useful for emergency situations.

A handy systemd component is the systemd-analyze utility. With this utility, you can investigate your system's boot performance and check for potential system initialization problems. Table 6.8 contains common commands you can use with the systemd-analyze utility.

TABLE 6.8 Common systemd-analyze commands

Command	Description
blame	Displays the amount of time each running unit took to initialize. Units and their times are listed starting from the slowest to the fastest.
time	Displays the amount of time system initialization spent for the kernel, and the initial RAM filesystem, as well as the time it took for normal system user space to initialize. (Default)
critical-chain	Displays time-critical units in a tree format. Can pass it a unit file argument to focus the information on that particular unit.
dump	Displays information concerning all the units. The display format is subject to change without notice, so it should be used only for human viewing.
verify	Scans unit files and displays warning messages if any errors are found. Will accept a unit file name as an argument, but follows directory location precedence.

Be aware that some of the longer `systemd-analyze` displays are piped into the `less` pager utility. You can turn that feature off by using the `--no-pager` option. In Listing 6.17, using super user privileges, a few of these `systemd-analyze` commands are shown in action.

Listing 6.17 Employing the `systemd-analyze` utility

```
# systemd-analyze verify
#
# systemd-analyze verify sshd.service
#
# systemd-analyze time
Startup finished in 665ms (kernel) +
3.285s (initrd) + 58.319s (userspace) = 1min 2.269s
#
# systemd-analyze --no-pager blame
        30.419s NetworkManager-wait-online.service
[...]
        4.848s kdump.service
        4.707s firewalld.service
        4.565s tuned.service
        4.390s libvirtd.service
        4.221s lvm2-monitor.service
[...]
         632ms NetworkManager.service
         607ms network.service
[...]
           9ms sys-kernel-config.mount
#
```

The first command used in Listing 6.17 allows you to check all your system's unit files for problems. The second one only checks the `sshd.service` unit file. If you just receive a prompt back from those two commands, it indicates there were no errors found.

The third command in Listing 6.17 provides time information concerning your system's initialization. Note that you could leave off the `time` keyword, and the `systemd-analyze` utility would still display the system initialization time because that is the default utility action.

The last command in Listing 6.17 employs the `blame` command. This display starts with those units that took the longest to initialize. At the bottom of the list are the units that initialized the fastest. It is a handy guide for troubleshooting initialization problems. Now if only you could use `systemd-analyze blame` to analyze your friends who are always late.

The systemd initialization approach is flexible and reliable for operating Linux systems and their services. The preceding sections provided an overview of the methods and commands for managing systemd initialized systems.

Managing SysV init Systems

Many server administrators have gone through the process of moving from a SysV init system to a systemd system. Recall that systemd is backward compatible with SysV init, so understanding SysV init is important.

First, if you want to experiment with the original SysV init commands without interference from systemd or the now defunct Upstart, find a Linux distribution that uses the SysV init initialization method. One way to find one is to visit the DistroWatch website and use their search tool at `https://distrowatch.com/search.php`. Scroll down to the Search by Distribution Criteria section, and for Init software, select SysV. Any Linux distributions still using SysV init will display in the search results.

To get clean SysV init listings for this book, we used a blast from the Linux distribution past, Fedora 7. To grab an ISO copy of this old distribution, visit `https://archives.fedoraproject.org/pub/archive/fedora/linux/releases`.

WARNING   Using any older and no-longer-supported Linux distribution can open up your system to a whole host of problems. If you do choose to take this risk, minimize your exposure by putting the Linux distribution in a virtualized environment; do not install any network interface cards (NICs) for the virtual machine, and turn off access to the host machine's filesystem.

The next section should provide you with enough of a SysV init understanding to help in the Linux server migration process to systemd.

Understanding Runlevels

At system boot time, instead of targets to determine what groups of services to start, SysV init uses runlevels. These runlevels are defined in Table 6.9 and Table 6.10. Notice that different distributions use different runlevel definitions.

TABLE 6.9   Red Hat–based distribution SysV init runlevels

Runlevel	Description
0	Shut down the system.
1, s, or S	Single-user mode used for system maintenance.
2	Multiuser mode without networking services enabled.
3	Multiuser mode with networking services enabled.

Runlevel	Description
4	Custom.
5	Multiuser mode with GUI available.
6	Reboot the system.

Note that runlevels 0 and 6 are not runlevels by definition. Instead, they denote a transition from the current system state to the desired state. For example, a running system currently operating at runlevel 5 is transitioned to a powered-off state via runlevel 0.

TABLE 6.10 Debian-based distribution SysV init runlevels

Runlevel	Description
0	Shut down the system.
1	Single-user mode used for system maintenance.
2	Multiuser mode with GUI available.
6	Reboot the system.

To determine your system's current and former runlevel, you employ the `runlevel` command. The first number or letter displayed indicates the previous runlevel (N indicates that the system is newly booted), and the second number indicates the current runlevel. An example is shown in Listing 6.18 of a newly booted Red Hat–based SysV init system, which is running at runlevel 5.

Listing 6.18 Employing the `runlevel` command

```
# runlevel
N 5
#
```

Instead of using a default target like systemd, SysV init systems employ a configuration file, `/etc/inittab`. This file used to start many different services, but in later years it only started terminal services and defined the default runlevel for a system. The file line defining the default runlevel is shown in Listing 6.19.

Listing 6.19 The /etc/inittab file line that sets the default runlevel

```
# grep :initdefault: /etc/inittab
id:5:initdefault:
#
```

Within Listing 6.19, notice the number 5 between the id: and the :initdefault: in the /etc/inittab file record. This indicates that the system's default runlevel is 5. The initdefault is what specifies the runlevel to enter after the system boots.

 Look back at Table 6.1 in this chapter. You'll see that systemd provides backward compatibility to SysV init via runlevel targets, which can be used as the default target and/or in switching targets with the systemctl isolate command.

Setting the default runlevel is the first step in configuring certain services to start at system initialization. Next, each service must have an initialization script located typically in the /etc/init.d/ directory. Listing 6.20 shows a snipped example of the various scripts in this directory. Note that the -1F options are used on the ls command to display the scripts in a single column and tack on a file indicator code. The * file indicator code denotes that these files are executable programs (Bash shell scripts in this case).

Listing 6.20 Listing script files in the /etc/init.d/ directory

```
# ls -1F  /etc/init.d/
anacron*
atd*
[...]
crond*
cups*
[...]
ntpd*
[...]
ypbind*
yum-updatesd*
#
```

These initialization scripts are responsible for starting, stopping, restarting, reloading, and displaying the status of various system services. The program that calls these initialization scripts is the rc script, and it can reside in either the /etc/init.d/ or the /etc/rc.d/ directory. The rc script runs the scripts in a particular directory. The directory picked depends on the desired runlevel. Each runlevel has its own subdirectory in the /etc/rc.d/ directory, as shown in Listing 6.21.

Listing 6.21 Runlevel subdirectories in the /etc/rc.d/ directory

```
# ls /etc/rc.d/
init.d  rc0.d  rc2.d  rc4.d  rc6.d     rc.sysinit
rc      rc1.d  rc3.d  rc5.d  rc.local
#
```

Notice in Listing 6.21 that there are seven subdirectories named rc*n*.d, where *n* is a number from 0 to 6. The rc script runs the scripts in the rc*n*.d subdirectory for the desired runlevel. For example, if the desired runlevel is 3, all the scripts in the /etc/rc.d/rc3.d/ directory are run. Listing 6.22 shows a snippet of the scripts in this directory.

Listing 6.22 Files in the /etc/rc.d/rc3.d directory

```
# ls -1F /etc/rc.d/rc3.d/
K01smolt@
K02avahi-dnsconfd@
K02NetworkManager@
[...]
K99readahead_later@
S00microcode_ctl@
S04readahead_early@
[...]
S55cups@
S99local@
S99smartd@
#
```

Notice in Listing 6.22 that the script names start with either a K or an S, are followed by a number, and then have their service name. The K stands for kill (stop), and the S stands for start. The number indicates the order in which this service should be stopped or started for that runlevel. This is somewhat similar to the After and Before directives in the systemd service type unit files.

The files in the /etc/rc.d/rc*n*.d/ directories are all symbolic links to the scripts in the /etc/init.d/ directory. Listing 6.23 shows an example of this.

Listing 6.23 Displaying the /etc/rc.d/rc3.d/S55cups link

```
# readlink -f /etc/rc.d/rc3.d/S55cups
/etc/rc.d/init.d/cups
#
```

The rc script goes through and runs all the K scripts first, passing a stop argument to each script. It then runs all the S scripts, passing a start argument to each script. This not only ensures that the proper services are started for a particular runlevel, it also allows jumping between runlevels after system initialization and thus stopping and starting certain services for that new runlevel.

> If you need to enact certain commands or run any scripts as soon as system initialization is completed, there is a file for that purpose. The /etc/rc.local script allows you to add additional scripts and or commands. Just keep in mind that this script is not run until all the other SysV init scripts have been executed.

Scripts are central to the SysV init process. To understand SysV init scripts, be sure to read through Chapter 25, "Deploying Bash Scripts," first. That chapter will help you understand Bash shell script basics, which in turn will help you understand the SysV init script contents.

Investigating SysV init Commands

The various SysV init commands help in starting and stopping services, managing what services are deployed at various runlevels, and jumping between runlevels on an already running Linux system. We cover the various SysV init commands in this section.

Jumping between runlevels is a little different than jumping between systemd targets. It uses the `init` or the `telinit` utility to do so. These two utilities are essentially twins and can be interchanged for each other. To jump between runlevels on a SysV init system, the basic syntax is as follows:

```
init Destination-Runlevel
telinit Destination-Runlevel
```

Listing 6.24 shows an example of jumping on a SysV init system from the current runlevel 5 to the destination runlevel 3. Note that the `runlevel` command is used to show the previous and current runlevels.

Listing 6.24 Jumping from runlevel 5 to runlevel 3

```
# runlevel
N 5
#
# init 3
#
# runlevel
5 3
#
```

Keep in mind that you can shut down a SysV init system by entering **init 0** or **telinit 0** at the command line as long as you have the proper privileges. You can also reboot a SysV init system by typing **init 6** or **telinit 6** at the command line.

To view a SysV init managed service's status and control whether or not it is currently running, use the `service` utility. This utility has the following basic syntax:

```
service SCRIPT COMMAND [OPTIONS]
```

The `SCRIPT` in the `service` utility refers to a particular service script within the `/etc/init.d/` directory. The `service` utility executes the script, passing it the designated `COMMAND`. Service scripts typically have the same name as the service. Also, you only have to provide a script's base name and not the directory location. As an example, for the NTP service script, `/etc/init.d/ntpd`, you only need to use the `ntpd` base name.

Table 6.11 describes the various commonly used items you can employ for the `COMMAND` portion of the service utility. Keep in mind that if the `COMMAND` is not handled by the script or handled differently than it's commonly handled, you'll get an unexpected result.

TABLE 6.11 Commonly used `service` utility commands

Command	Description
restart	Stop and immediately restart the designated service. Note that if a designated service is not already started, a `FAILED` status will be generated on the stop attempt, and then the service will be started.
start	Start the designated service.
status	Display the designated service's current status.
stop	Stop the designated service. Note that if a designated service is already stopped, a `FAILED` status will be generated on the stop attempt.
reload	Load the service configuration file of the running designated service. This allows you to make service configuration changes without stopping the service. Note that if you attempt the reload command on a stopped service, a `FAILED` status will be generated.

It helps to see examples of the `service` utility in action. Listing 6.25 provides a few for your review.

Listing 6.25 Employing the `service` utility

```
# service httpd status
httpd is stopped
#
```

```
# service httpd start
Starting httpd:                       [  OK  ]
#
# service httpd status
httpd (pid 14124 14123 [...]) is running...
#
# service httpd stop
Stopping httpd:                       [  OK  ]
#
# service httpd status
httpd is stopped
#
# service --status-all
anacron is stopped
atd (pid 2024) is running...
[...]
ypbind is stopped
yum-updatesd (pid 2057) is running...
#
```

The last service utility example in Listing 6.25 is worth pointing out. This command allows you to view all the services on your system along with their current status. Keep in mind that this list will scroll by quickly, so it's a good idea to redirect its STDOUT to the less pager utility so that you can view the display more comfortably.

 While some SysV init commands have been modified to work with systemd utilities, others, such as service --status-all, might produce unpredictable or confusing results. As tempting as it is to hang on to past commands, those habits may cause you problems in the future. It is best to learn native systemd commands and employ them instead.

To configure various services to start at different runlevels, there are two different commands you can use. The one you employ depends on which distribution you are using. For Red Hat–based distros using SysV init, you'll want to use the chkconfig utility. For Debian-based Linux distributions using SysV init, the update-rc.d program is the one to use.

The chkconfig utility has several different formats. They allow you to check what runlevels a service will start or not start on. Also, you can enable (start at system boot) or disable (not start at system boot) a particular service for a particular runlevel. Table 6.12 describes these various commonly used chkconfig utility formats.

TABLE 6.12 Commonly used chkconfig utility formats

Command	Description
chkconfig *service*	Check if the *service* is enabled at the current runlevel. If yes, the command returns a true (0). If no, the command returns a false (1).
chkconfig *service* on	Enable the *service* at the current runlevel.
chkconfig *service* off	Disable the *service* at the current runlevel.
chkconfig --add *service*	Enable this *service* at runlevels 0–6.
chkconfig --del *service*	Disable this *service* at runlevels 0–6.
chkconfig --levels [*levels*] *service* on/off	Enable (on) or disable (off) this *service* at runlevels *levels*, where *levels* can be any number from 0 through 6.
chkconfig --list *service*	Display the runlevels and whether or not the *service* is enabled (on) or disabled (off) for each one.

The first command in Table 6.12 can be a little confusing. Be aware that when the utility checks if the service is enabled at the current runlevel, a true or false is returned in the ? variable. Listing 6.26 shows an example of using this command and displaying the variable results.

Listing 6.26 Using the chkconfig utility to check service status

```
# runlevel
3 5
#
# chkconfig --list sshd
sshd            0:off   1:off   2:on    3:on    4:on    5:on    6:off
#
# chkconfig sshd
# echo $?
0
# chkconfig --list ntpd
ntpd            0:off   1:off   2:off   3:off   4:off   5:off   6:off
#
```

```
# chkconfig ntpd
# echo $?
1
#
```

Notice in Listing 6.26 that the system's current runlevel is 5. The sshd service is checked using the chkconfig --list command, and you can see from the display that this service does start on runlevel 5, indicated by the 5:on shown. Therefore, the chkconfig sshd command should return a true. As soon as the command is entered and the prompt is returned, an echo $? command is entered. This displays a 0, which indicates a true was returned. Yes, 0 means true. That is confusing!

For the ntpd service in Listing 6.26, the service is not started at runlevel 5. Therefore, the chkconfig ntpd command returns a false, which is a 1.

To enable services at multiple runlevels, you'll need to employ the --level option. For this option, the runlevel numbers are listed one after the other with no delimiter in between. An example is shown in Listing 6.27.

Listing 6.27 Using the chkconfig utility to enable/disable services

```
# chkconfig --list ntpd
ntpd            0:off   1:off   2:off   3:off   4:off   5:off   6:off
#
# chkconfig --level 35 ntpd on
#
# chkconfig --list ntpd
ntpd            0:off   1:off   2:off   3:on    4:off   5:on    6:off
#
# chkconfig --level 35 ntpd off
#
# chkconfig --list ntpd
ntpd            0:off   1:off   2:off   3:off   4:off   5:off   6:off
#
```

If you are using a Debian-based Linux SysV init distribution, instead of the chkconfig utility, you'll need to employ the update-rc.d utility. It has its own set of options and arguments.

To start a program at the default runlevel, just use the following format:

update-rc.d *service* defaults

To remove the program from starting at the default runlevel, use the following format:

update-rc.d *service* remove

If you want to specify what runlevels the program starts and stops in, you'll need to use the following format:

```
update-rc.d -f service start 40 2 3 4 5 . stop 80 0 1 6 .
```

The 40 and 80 specify the relative order within the runlevel when the program should start or stop (from 0 to 99). This allows you to customize exactly when specific programs are started or stopped during the boot sequence.

As you can see, managing the SysV init scripts and their associated runlevels can be tricky. However, if you have to take care of one of these systems, you now understand the tools that can help you.

Digging Deeper into systemd

Though handling storage and various issues such as mounting filesystems are thoroughly covered in Chapter 11, "Handling Storage," we want to look at systemd's mount and auto-mount units while systemd is still fresh in your mind. We feel this will help you better retain this important certification information.

Looking at systemd Mount Units

Distributions using systemd have additional options for persistently attaching filesystems. Filesystems can be specified either within the /etc/fstab file or within a mount unit file. A mount unit file provides configuration information for systemd to mount and control designated filesystems.

On Linux servers using systemd, if you only use the /etc/fstab file, systemd still manages these filesystems. The mount points listed in /etc/fstab are converted into native units when either the server is rebooted or systemd is reloaded. In fact, using /etc/fstab for persistent filesystems is the preferred method over manually creating a mount unit file. For more information on this process, type **man** **systemd-fstab-generator** at the command line.

A single mount unit file is created for each mount point, and the filename contains the mount point's absolute directory reference. However, the absolute directory reference has its preceding forward slash (/) removed, subsequent forward slashes are converted to dashes (-), and any trailing forward slash is removed. Mount unit filenames also have a .mount extension. For example, the mount point /home/temp/ would have a mount unit file named home-temp.mount.

A mount unit file's contents mimic other systemd unit files, with a few special sections and options. In Listing 6.28, using the /home/temp/ mount point, an example mount unit file is shown.

Listing 6.28 Displaying an example systemd mount unit file

```
# cat /etc/systemd/system/home-temp.mount
[Unit]
Description=Test Mount Units

[Mount]
What=/dev/sdo1
Where=/home/temp
Type=ext4
Options=defaults
SloppyOptions=on
TimeOutSec=4

[Install]
WantedBy=multi-user.target
#
```

Notice that the file has the typical three sections for a unit file, with the middle section, [Mount], containing directives specific to mount type unit files. The What directive can use the device filename or a universally unique identifier (UUID), such as /dev/disk/by-uuid/*UUID*.

The SloppyOptions directive is helpful in that if set to on, it ignores any mount options not supported by a particular filesystem type. By default, it is set to off. Another helpful directive is TimeOutSec. If the mount command does not complete by the number of designated seconds, the mount is considered a failed operation.

Be sure to include the [Install] section and set either the WantedBy or the RequiredBy directive to the desired target. If you do not do this, the filesystem will not be mounted upon a server boot.

You can manually mount and unmount the unit using the standard systemctl utility commands. Listing 6.29 contains an example of deploying the home-temp.mount unit file.

Listing 6.29 Deploying a systemd mount unit file

```
# systemctl daemon-reload home-temp.mount
#
# systemctl start home-temp.mount
#
# ls /home/temp
lost+found
#
```

In Listing 6.29, the first command loads the newly configured mount unit file. The second command has systemd mount the filesystem using the `home-temp.mount` unit file. The second command is similar to how a service is started in that it uses the `start` command. While you don't have to have the `home-temp.mount` argument and the command will work without it, (a) the argument does add clarity/education to the situation being discussed, and (b) the argument prevents other services from being reloaded, which if other services were restarted could prove problematic.

To ensure that the filesystem is properly mounted, like a service unit, you use the `systemctl` utility to obtain a mounted filesystem's status. An example is shown in Listing 6.30.

Listing 6.30 Checking a systemd mount unit's status

```
# systemctl status home-temp.mount
• home-temp.mount - Test Mount Units
   Loaded: loaded (/etc/systemd/system/home-temp.mount; [...])
   Active: active (mounted) since Sat 2019-09-14 16:34:2[...]
    Where: /home/temp
     What: /dev/sdo1
  Process: 3990 ExecMount=/bin/mount /dev/sdo1 /home/temp[...]
[...]
#
```

One additional step is required. To ensure that systemd will mount the filesystem persistently, the mount unit file must be enabled to start at boot, as other systemd units are enabled. An example is shown in Listing 6.31.

Listing 6.31 Enabling a systemd mount unit

```
# systemctl enable home-temp.mount
Created symlink from
/etc/systemd/system/multi-user.target.wants/home-temp.mount to
/etc/systemd/system/home-temp.mount.
#
```

This should all look very familiar! Keep in mind that you should only use mount unit files if you need to tweak the persistent filesystem configuration. If you do not, it's best to use an `/etc/fstab` record to persistently mount the filesystem.

Exploring Automount Units

With systemd, you can also configure on-demand mounting as well as mounting in parallel using automount units. In addition, you can set filesystems to automatically unmount upon lack of activity.

An automount unit file operates similarly to a mount unit file. The naming convention is the same, except that the filename extension is `.automount`.

Within an automount unit file, for the [Automount] section, only the following three directives are available:

- Where
- DirectoryMode
- TimeOutIdleSec

The Where directive is required. It is configured the exact same way as it is in mount unit files. With this directive, you set the mount point.

The DirectoryMode directive is not a required option. This setting determines the permissions placed on any automatically created mount point and parent directories. By default it is set to the 0755 octal code.

 You can also configure an automount point in the /etc/fstab file. However, keep in mind that if an automount point is configured in the /etc/fstab file and it has a unit file, the unit file configuration will take precedence.

The TimeOutIdleSec directive is also not required. This particular directive allows you to set the maximum amount of time (in seconds) a mounted filesystem can be idle. Once the time limit is reached, the filesystem is unmounted. By default this directive is disabled.

Focusing on Timer Unit Files

Timer unit files allow you to define events that occur at specific dates or times, similar to how the cron program works (see Chapter 26, "Automating Jobs"). The timer unit files allow you to fine-tune exactly when a program starts.

Timer unit files are designated by a .timer file extension and include a [Timer] section to define the directives required to determine when to start the event. Table 6.13 describes these directives.

TABLE 6.13   Commonly used timer unit file [Timer] section directives

Directive	Description
AccuracySec	Specifies the accuracy of the timer. The default is one minute.
OnActiveSec	Defines the timer relative to the moment the timer is activated.
OnBootSec	Defines the timer relative to when the system was booted.
OnCalendar	Defines the timer as a specific date/time value.
OnStartupSec	Defines the timer relative to when the systemd program started.
OnUnitActiveSec	Defines the timer relative to when the timer unit was last activated.

Directive	Description
OnUnitInactiveSec	Defines the timer relative to when the timer unit was last deactivated.
Persistent	When set, the time the timer unit was last triggered is stored on disk.
RandomizedDelaySec	Delays the timer activation by a random amount of time.
RemainAfterElapse	When set, the expired timer unit remains loaded, allowing you to query its status using systemctl.
Unit	Defines the unit file to start when the timer elapses.
WakeSystem	When set, the timer unit will cause the system to resume from being suspended.

As you can see from Table 6.13, timer units provide several options for how to set the timer. This allows you to choose exactly when a program should start on the system.

Summary

Managing your server's final system initialization phase is the job of the initialization daemon. This daemon must determine what services to start from the information you provide within the appropriate configuration files. In addition, the daemon can manage services while the system is running.

The classic system initialization daemon, SysV init, is still around, though typically only on older distributions. The popular and modern systemd is heavily used among current Linux distributions. It not only allows faster server boot times, it offers additional services as well, such as automounting filesystems. Often system administrators find themselves migrating from SysV init systems to systemd servers, and thus it is important to understand both system initialization methods.

Exam Essentials

Describe the init program.   Either the init program or systemd is the parent process for every service on a Linux system. It typically has a PID of 1. The program is located in the /etc/, the /bin/, or the /sbin/ directory. On systemd servers, this program is a symbolic link to /usr/lib/systemd/systemd.

Summarize systemd unit concepts.   A systemd unit defines a service, a group of services, or an action, and there are currently 12 different systemd unit types. To view load units, use the systemctl list-units command. The four systemd units to focus on are service, target, mount, and automount.

Explain systemd service units and their files.   Service units control how services are started, stopped, and managed. Their unit files contain configuration information via directives in one of the three primary unit file sections: [Unit], [Service], and [Install]. Directives, such as After and Before, configure when a service will be started. While the [Unit] and [Install] file sections are common to all unit files, the [Service] section and its directives are unique to services. Unit files may exist in one of three directory locations, and their location is important because if multiple files exist for a particular unit, one takes precedence over the other depending on its whereabouts.

Explain systemd target units and their files.   Target units are responsible for starting groups of services. At system initialization, the default.target unit ensures that all required and desired services are launched. It is set up as a symbolic link to another target unit file. The primary target units used for system initialization are graphical.target, multi-user .target, and runleveln.target, where n = 1–5 for the desired SysV init runlevel experience. There are additional target units, which handle system power off, halt, and reboot as well as emergency and rescue modes. The target type unit files are similar to service unit files, but they typically contain fewer directives.

Demonstrate how to manage systemd systems via commands.   The systemctl utility contains many commands that allow you to manage and control systemd units. You can jump between targets using the systemctl isolate command. You can set particular services to start at system boot time via the systemctl enable command and vice versa via the systemctl disable command. Additional commands allow you to start, stop, restart, and reload units as well as reload their unit files via the systemctl daemon-reload command. Helpful commands such as systemctl is-system-running and systemctl get-default aid you in assessing your current systemd system. You can employ the systemd-analyze series of commands to evaluate your server's initialization process and find ways to improve it.

Summarize SysV init concepts.   The classic SysV init method consists of the /etc/inittab file, which sets the default runlevel via the initdefault record. Runlevels determine what services are started, and the default runlevel determines what services are started at system initialization. The rc script starts and stops services depending on what runlevel is chosen. It executes the scripts in the appropriate runlevel directory and passes the appropriate stop or start parameter. The scripts located in the various runlevel directories are symbolic links to the files within the /etc/init.d/ directory.

Demonstrate how to manage SysV init systems via commands.   You can determine a SysV init system's previous and current runlevel via the runlevel command. Runlevels can be jumped into via the init or telinit command. Services can have their status checked; have their configuration files be reloaded; or be stopped, started, or restarted with the status command. You can view all currently loaded services on a SysV init system by using the service --status-all command. Services are enabled or disabled through either the chkconfig or the update-rc.d command, depending on your distribution.

Describe systemd mount and automount unit files.   If your server employs systemd, besides managing system initialization, it can also persistently attach filesystems. These filesystems can be mounted or automounted via their associated unit files. Mount and automount unit filenames are based on the filesystem mount point but use the `.mount` or `.automount` filename extension, respectively. Their unit file contents have three sections, similar to service unit files, except the mount unit file's middle section is [Mount], whereas the automount unit file's middle section is [Automount]. Each unit file has its own special directives that designate what partition is supposed to be mounted at the mount point and other items such as, for automount units, how long a filesystem must be idle before it can be unmounted.

Review Questions

1. The init program may be located in which of the following directories? (Choose all that apply.)

    A. /etc/rc.d/

    B. /etc/

    C. /sbin/

    D. /usr/lib/systemd/

    E. /bin/

2. Which of the following is true concerning systemd service units? (Choose all that apply.)

    A. Services can be started at system boot time.

    B. Services can be started in parallel.

    C. A service can be started based on a timer.

    D. A service can be started after all other services are started.

    E. A service can be prevented from starting at system boot time.

3. Which of the following is not a systemd target unit?

    A. runlevel7.target

    B. emergency.target

    C. graphical.target

    D. multi-user.target

    E. rescue.target

4. You need to modify a systemd service unit configuration. Where should the modified file be located?

    A. /etc/system/systemd/

    B. /usr/lib/system/systemd/

    C. /etc/systemd/system/

    D. /usr/lib/systemd/system/

    E. /run/system/systemd/

5. On your server, you need Service-B to start immediately before Service-A. Within the systemd Service-A unit configuration file, what directive should you check and potentially modify?

    A. Conflicts

    B. Wants

    C. Requires

    D. Before

    E. After

6. For setting environment parameters within a unit configuration file, which directives should you potentially employ? (Choose all that apply.)

   A. Type

   B. Environment

   C. EnvironmentParam

   D. EnvironmentFile

   E. PATH

7. You attempt to jump to a systemd target using the systemctl isolate command, but it will not work. You decide to look at the target unit file. What might you see there that is causing this problem?

   A. static

   B. AllowIsolate=yes

   C. Type=oneshot

   D. AllowIsolate=no

   E. disabled

8. You have modified an OpenSSH service's configuration file, /etc/ssh/ssh_config. The service is already running. What is the best command to use with systemctl to make this modified file take immediate effect?

   A. reload

   B. daemon-reload

   C. restart

   D. mask

   E. unmask

9. Your system uses systemd and has a service currently set to not start at system boot. You want to change this behavior and have it start. What systemctl command should you employ for this service?

   A. restart

   B. start

   C. isolate

   D. disable

   E. enable

10. You need to change the system's default target. What systemctl command should you use to accomplish this task?

    A. get-default

    B. set-default

    C. isolate

    D. is-enabled

    E. is-active

11. Your systemd system is taking a long time to boot and you need to reduce the boot time. Which `systemd-analyze` command is the best to start narrowing down which units need to be investigated first?

- **A.** `time`
- **B.** `dump`
- **C.** `failure`
- **D.** `blame`
- **E.** `verify`

12. Your older Debian-based Linux distribution system uses SysV init. It will soon be upgraded to a Debian-based distro that uses systemd. To start some analysis, you enter the `runlevel` command. Which of the following are results you may see? (Choose all that apply.)

- **A.** N 5
- **B.** 3 5
- **C.** N 2
- **D.** 2 3
- **E.** 1 2

13. You've recently become the system administrator for an older Linux server, which still uses SysV init. You determine that its default runlevel is 3. What file did you find that information in?

- **A.** `/etc/inittab`
- **B.** `/etc/rc.d`
- **C.** `/etc/init.d/rc`
- **D.** `/etc/rc.d/rc`
- **E.** `/etc/rc.local`

14. Which directory on an old SysV init system stores the service startup scripts?

- **A.** `/usr/lib/systemd/system/`
- **B.** `/etc/rc.d/rcn.d/`
- **C.** `/etc/init.d/`
- **D.** `/etc/systemd/system/`
- **E.** `/run/systemd/system/`

15. You are managing a SysV init system and need to perform some emergency maintenance at runlevel 1. To do this, you need to jump runlevels. What command could you employ? (Choose all that apply.)

- **A.** `telinit S`
- **B.** `telinit 1`
- **C.** `init one`
- **D.** `init s`
- **E.** `init 1`

16. A customer has complained that a service on your SysV init system is not working. Which of the following commands is the best command to use to check the service?

   A. `service start`

   B. `service status`

   C. `service --status-all`

   D. `service stop`

   E. `service reload`

17. You need to enable the DHCP service on your Red Hat–based SysV init system for runlevels 3 and 5. Which of the following commands should you use?

   A. `service enable dhcp 3,5`

   B. `chkconfig --levels 3,5 dhcp on`

   C. `chkconfig --levels 35 on dhcp`

   D. `chkconfig --levels 35 dhcp on`

   E. `service enable dhcp 35`

18. You need to enable the DHCP service on your Debian-based SysV init system for the default runlevels. Which of the following commands should you use?

   A. `update-rc.d dhcp default`

   B. `chkconfig --default dhcp on`

   C. `update-rc.d default dhcp`

   D. `update-rc.d defaults dhcp`

   E. `update-rc.d dhcp defaults`

19. Which of the following would be the appropriate base name for a mount unit file that mounts a filesystem at the `/var/log/` mount point?

   A. `/var/log.mount`

   B. `/var/log.unit`

   C. `var-log.mount`

   D. `var-log.unit`

   E. `var/log.mount`

20. You are managing a systemd system and need to create an automount unit file. Which of the following directives should you review to possibly include in this file's `[Automount]` section? (Choose all that apply.)

   A. `Where`

   B. `Options`

   C. `DirectoryMode`

   D. `TimeOutIdleSec`

   E. `What`

Chapter

7

Configuring Network Connections

✓ **Objective 1.5: Given a scenario, use the appropriate networking tools or configuration files**

✓ **Objective 4.2: Given a scenario, analyze and troubleshoot network resource issues**

These days it's almost a necessity to have your Linux system connected to some type of network. Whether it's because of the need to share files and printers on a local network or the need to connect to the Internet to download updates and security patches, most Linux systems have some type of network connection.

This chapter looks at how to configure your Linux system to connect to a network as well as how to troubleshoot network connections if things go wrong. There are a few different methods for configuring network settings in Linux, and you'll need to know them all for the Linux+ exam. First, we'll cover the common locations for the configuration files in Linux distributions. Next, we'll examine the different tools you have at your disposal that help make configuring the network settings easier. After that, the chapter discusses some simple network troubleshooting techniques you can use to help find the problem if anything goes wrong.

Configuring Network Features

There are five main pieces of information you need to configure in your Linux system to interact on a network:

- The host address
- The network subnet address
- The default router (sometimes called gateway)
- The system hostname
- A DNS server address for resolving hostnames

There are three different ways to configure this information in Linux systems:

- Manually editing network configuration files
- Using a graphical tool included with your Linux distribution
- Using command-line tools

The following sections walk through each of these methods.

Network Configuration Files

Every Linux distribution uses network configuration files to define the network settings required to communicate on the network. However, there's not a single standard configuration file that all distributions use.

Instead, different distributions use different configuration files to define the network settings. Table 7.1 shows the most common network configuration files that you'll run into.

TABLE 7.1 Linux network configuration files

Distribution	Network Configuration Location
Debian based	`/etc/network/interfaces` file
Red Hat based	`/etc/sysconfig/network-scripts` directory
openSUSE	`/etc/sysconfig/network` file

While each of the Linux distributions uses a different method of defining the network settings, they all have similar features. Most configuration files define each of the required network settings as separate values in the configuration file. Listing 7.1 shows an example from a Debian-based Linux system.

Listing 7.1: Sample Debian network static configuration settings

```
auto eth0
iface eth0 inet static
    address 192.168.1.77
    netmask 255.255.255.0
    gateway 192.168.1.254
iface eth0 inet6 static
    address 2003:aef0::23d1::0a10:00a1
    netmask 64
    gateway 2003:aef0::23d1::0a10:0001
```

The example shown in Listing 7.1 assigns both an IP and an IPv6 address to the wired network interface designated as `eth0`.

Listing 7.2 shows how to define the IP network settings automatically using a DHCP server on the network.

Listing 7.2: Sample Debian network DHCP configuration settings

```
auto eth0
iface eth0 inet dhcp
iface eth0 inet6 dhcp
```

If you just want to assign an IPv6 *link local address*, which uniquely identifies the device on the local network, but not retrieve an IPv6 address from a DHCP server, replace the `inet6` line with this:

```
iface eth0 inet6 auto
```

The `auto` attribute tells Linux to assign the link local address, which allows the Linux system to communicate with any other IPv6 device on the local network but not a global address.

 Since version 17.04, the Ubuntu distribution has deviated from the standard Debian method and utilizes the Netplan tool to manage network settings. Netplan uses simple YAML text files in the /etc/netplan folder to define the network settings for each network interface installed on the system. By default, Netplan just passes the network settings off to the Network Manager tool, so you don't need to worry about how the Netplan configuration files are set.

For Red Hat–based systems, you'll need to define the network settings in multiple files, one for each network interface. The format of each file is:

```
ifcfg-interface
```

where `interface` is the device name for the network adapter, such as `ifcfg-enp0s3`. Listing 7.3 shows an example from a Rocky Linux system.

Listing 7.3: Sample Rocky network interface configuration settings

```
TYPE=Ethernet
PROXY_METHOD=none
BROWSER_ONLY=no
BOOTPROTO=dhcp
DEFROUTE=yes
IPV4_FAILURE_FATAL=no
IPV6INIT=yes
IPV6_AUTOCONF=yes
IPV6_DEFROUTE=yes
IPV6_FAILURE_FATAL=no
IPV6_ADDR_GEN_MODE=stable-privacy
NAME=enp0s3
UUID=c8752366-3e1e-47e3-8162-c0435ec6d451
```

```
DEVICE=enp0s3
ONBOOT=yes
IPV6_PRIVACY=no
```

This configuration indicates that the workstation is using the DHCP process to automatically retrieve network information from a network server. For static IP addresses, you can set the IP address, default gateway, and subnet mask in the configuration file.

Most Linux distributions use the /etc/hostname file to store the local hostname of the system; however, some use /etc/HOSTNAME instead. You will also need to define a DNS server so that the system can use DNS hostnames. Fortunately, this is a standard that all Linux systems follow and is handled in the /etc/resolv.conf configuration file:

```
domain mydomain.com
search mytest.com
nameserver 192.168.1.1
```

The domain entry defines the domain name assigned to the network. By default the system will append this domain name to any hostnames you specify. The search entry defines any additional domains used to search for hostnames. The nameserver entry is where you specify the DNS server assigned to your network. Some networks can have more than one DNS server; just add multiple nameserver entries in the file.

For systems using the systemd startup method, you can use the hostnamectl command to view or change the hostname information. Also, to help speed up connections to commonly used hosts, you can manually enter their hostnames and IP addresses into the /etc/hosts file on your Linux system. The /etc/nsswitch.conf file defines whether the Linux system checks this file before or after using DNS to look up the hostname.

Graphical Tools

The *Network Manager* tool is a popular program used by many Linux distributions to provide a graphical interface for defining network connections. The Network Manager tool starts automatically at boot time and appears in the system tray area of the desktop as an icon.

If your system detects a wired network connection, the icon appears as a mini-network with blocks connected together. If your system detects a wireless network connection, the icon appears as an empty radio signal. When you click the icon, you'll see a list of the available wireless networks detected by the network card (as shown in Figure 7.1).

Click your access point to select it from the list. If your access point is encrypted, you'll be prompted to enter the password to gain access to the network.

FIGURE 7.1   Network Manager showing a wireless network connection

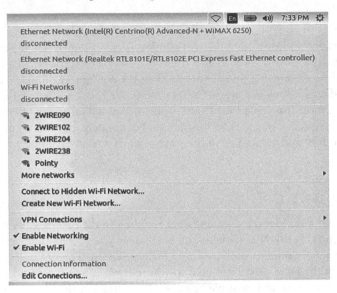

Once your system is connected to a wireless access point, the icon appears as a radio signal. Click the icon, and then select Edit Connections to edit the network connection settings for the system, shown in Figure 7.2.

FIGURE 7.2   The Network Connections window

You can select the network connection to configure (either wireless or wired) and then click the Edit button to change the current configuration.

The Network Manager tool allows you to specify all four of the network configuration values by using the manual configuration option or to set the configuration to use DHCP to determine the settings. The Network Manager tool automatically updates the appropriate network configuration files with the updated settings.

Command-Line Tools

If you're not working with a graphical desktop client environment, you'll need to use the Linux command-line tools to set the network configuration information. Quite a few command-line tools are at your disposal. The following sections cover the ones you're most likely to run into (and that you'll likely see on the Linux+ exam).

Network Manager Command-Line Tools

The Network Manager tool also provides two different types of command-line tools:

- nmtui provides a simple text-based menu tool.
- nmcli provides a text-only command-line tool.

Both tools help guide you through the process of setting the required network information for your Linux system. The *nmtui* tool displays a stripped-down version of the graphical tool where you can select a network interface and assign network properties to it, as shown in Figure 7.3.

FIGURE 7.3 The Network Manager nmtui command-line tool

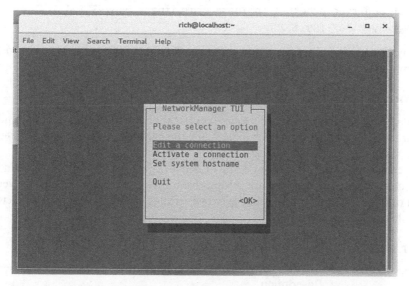

The *nmcli* tool doesn't attempt to use any type of graphics capabilities; it just provides a command-line interface where you can view and change the network settings. By default, the command displays the current network devices and their settings, as shown in Listing 7.4.

Listing 7.4: The default output of the nmcli command

```
$ nmcli
enp0s3: connected to enp0s3
        "Intel 82540EM Gigabit Ethernet Controller (PRO/1000 MT Desktop
 Adapter)
        ethernet (e1000), 08:00:27:73:1C:6D, hw, mtu 1500
        ip4 default
        inet4 10.0.2.15/24
        route4 0.0.0.0/0
        route4 10.0.2.0/24
        inet6 fe80::5432:eddb:51ea:fb44/64
        route6 ff00::/8
        route6 fe80::/64
        route6 fe80::/64
```

The nmcli command uses command-line options to allow you to set the network settings:

```
# nmcli con add type ethernet con-name eth1 ifname enp0s3 ip4
10.0.2.10/24 gw4 192.168.1.254
```

This way, you can set all of the necessary network configuration features in a single nmcli command.

The iproute2 Utilities

The *iproute2 package* is a newer open source project that contains a set of command-line utilities for managing network connections. While the package contains several different programs, the ip program is the most used.

The ip command is the Swiss army knife of network programs, and it's becoming a popular method for defining network settings from the command line. It uses several command options to display the current network settings or define new network settings. Table 7.2 shows these commands.

TABLE 7.2   The ip utility command options

Parameter	Description
address	Display or set the IPv4 or IPv6 address on the device.
addrlabel	Define configuration labels.
l2tp	Tunnel Ethernet over IP.
link	Define a network device.

Parameter	Description
maddress	Define a multicast address for the system to listen to.
monitor	Watch for netlink messages.
mroute	Define an entry in the multicast routing cache.
mrule	Define a rule in the multicast routing policy database.
neighbor	Manage ARP or NDISC cache entries.
netns	Manage network namespaces.
ntable	Manage the neighbor cache operation.
route	Manage the routing table.
rule	Manage entries in the routing policy database.
tcpmetrics	Manage TCP metrics on the interface.
token	Manage tokenized interface identifiers.
tunnel	Tunnel over IP.
tuntap	Manage TUN/TAP devices.
xfrm	Manage IPSec policies for secure connections.

Each command option utilizes parameters to define what to do, such as display network settings or modify existing network settings. Listing 7.5 demonstrates how to display the current network settings using the show parameter.

Listing 7.5: The ip address output

```
$ ip address show
1: lo: <LOOPBACK,UP,LOWER_UP> mtu 65536 qdisc noqueue state UNKNOWN group
default qlen 1000
    link/loopback 00:00:00:00:00:00 brd 00:00:00:00:00:00
    inet 127.0.0.1/8 scope host lo
       valid_lft forever preferred_lft forever
    inet6 ::1/128 scope host
```

```
        valid_lft forever preferred_lft forever
2: enp0s3: <BROADCAST,MULTICAST,UP,LOWER_UP> mtu 1500 qdisc pfifo_fast
state UP group default qlen 1000
    link/ether 08:00:27:73:1c:6d brd ff:ff:ff:ff:ff:ff
    inet 10.0.2.15/24 brd 10.0.2.255 scope global noprefixroute dynamic
enp0s3
        valid_lft 84411sec preferred_lft 84411sec
    inet6 fe80::5432:eddb:51ea:fb44/64 scope link noprefixroute
        valid_lft forever preferred_lft forever
$
```

This example shows two network interfaces on the Linux system:

- lo is the local loopback interface.

- enp0s3 is a wired network interface.

The *local loopback interface* is a special virtual network interface. Any local program can use it to communicate with other programs just as if they were across a network. That can simplify transferring data between programs.

The enp0s3 network interface is the wired network connection for the Linux system. The ip command shows the IP address assigned to the interface (there's both an IP and an IPv6 link local address assigned), the netmask value, and some basic statistics about the packets on the interface.

If the output doesn't show a network address assigned to the interface, you can use the ip command to specify the host address and netmask values for the interface:

```
# ip address add 10.0.2.15/24 dev enp0s3
```

Then use the ip command with the route option to set the default router for the network interface:

```
# ip route add default via 192.168.1.254 dev enp0s3
```

Then make the network interface active by using the link option:

```
# ip link set enp0s3 up
```

With the single ip command, you can manage just about everything you need for your network connections.

The net-tools Legacy Tool

If you need to work on an older Linux distribution, the *net-tools package* may be all you have to work with. The net-tools package was the original method in Linux for managing individual aspects of the network configuration. There are four main command-line tools that you need to use:

- ethtool displays Ethernet settings for a network interface.

- ifconfig displays or sets the IP address and netmask values for a network interface.

- iwconfig sets the SSID and encryption key for a wireless interface.

- route sets the default router address.

The *ethtool command* allows you to peek inside the network interface card Ethernet settings and change any properties that you may need to communicate with a network device, such as a switch.

By default, the ethtool command displays the current configuration settings for the network interface, as shown in Listing 7.6.

Listing 7.6: Output from the ethtool command

```
$ ethtool enp0s3
Settings for enp0s3:
        Supported ports: [ TP ]
        Supported link modes:   10baseT/Half 10baseT/Full
                                100baseT/Half 100baseT/Full
                                1000baseT/Full
        Supported pause frame use: No
        Supports auto-negotiation: Yes
        Supported FEC modes: Not reported
        Advertised link modes:  10baseT/Half 10baseT/Full
                                100baseT/Half 100baseT/Full
                                1000baseT/Full
        Advertised pause frame use: No
        Advertised auto-negotiation: Yes
        Advertised FEC modes: Not reported
        Speed: 1000Mb/s
        Duplex: Full
        Port: Twisted Pair
        PHYAD: 0
        Transceiver: internal
        Auto-negotiation: on
        MDI-X: off (auto)
Cannot get wake-on-lan settings: Operation not permitted
        Current message level: 0x00000007 (7)
                               drv probe link
        Link detected: yes
$
```

You can change features such as speed, duplex, and whether or not the network interface attempts to auto-negotiate features with the switch.

The *ifconfig command* is a legacy command that allows you to set the network address and subnet mask for a network interface:

```
$ sudo ifconfig enp0s3 down 10.0.2.10 netmask 255.255.255.0
```

You can also use the ifconfig command to view the current statistics for a network interface, as shown in Listing 7.7.

Listing 7.7: The network interface stats from the ifconfig command

```
$ ifconfig
enp0s3: flags=4163<UP,BROADCAST,RUNNING,MULTICAST>  mtu 1500
        inet 10.0.2.15  netmask 255.255.255.0  broadcast 10.0.2.255
        inet6 fe80::a00:27ff:fe55:dfbd  prefixlen 64  scopeid 0x20<link>
        ether 08:00:27:55:df:bd  txqueuelen 1000  (Ethernet)
        RX packets 19067  bytes 28092762 (26.7 MiB)
        RX errors 0  dropped 0  overruns 0  frame 0
        TX packets 6431  bytes 414153 (404.4 KiB)
        TX errors 0  dropped 0 overruns 0  carrier 0  collisions 0

lo: flags=73<UP,LOOPBACK,RUNNING>  mtu 65536
        inet 127.0.0.1  netmask 255.0.0.0
        inet6 ::1  prefixlen 128  scopeid 0x10<host>
        loop  txqueuelen 1000  (Local Loopback)
        RX packets 4  bytes 240 (240.0 B)
        RX errors 0  dropped 0  overruns 0  frame 0
        TX packets 4  bytes 240 (240.0 B)
        TX errors 0  dropped 0 overruns 0  carrier 0  collisions 0

virbr0: flags=4099<UP,BROADCAST,MULTICAST>  mtu 1500
        inet 192.168.122.1  netmask 255.255.255.0  broadcast 192.168.122.255
        ether 52:54:00:10:7a:b8  txqueuelen 1000  (Ethernet)
        RX packets 0  bytes 0 (0.0 B)
        RX errors 0  dropped 0  overruns 0  frame 0
        TX packets 0  bytes 0 (0.0 B)
        TX errors 0  dropped 0 overruns 0  carrier 0  collisions 0

$
```

Using the ifconfig command, you can see the link status of a network interface, whether it is receiving or transmitting packets, and whether there were any dropped packets or collisions. This can be a handy network troubleshooting tool.

Each command option utilizes parameters to define what to do, such as display network settings or modify existing network settings. Listing 7.7 demonstrates how to display the current network settings by using the ifconfig command without specifying a command-line parameter.

With the net-tools package you must also set the default router using the separate route command:

```
# route add default gw 192.168.1.254
```

You can also use the route command by itself to view the current default router config-ured for the system:

```
$ route
Kernel IP routing table
Destination     Gateway          Genmask          Flags Metric Ref Use Iface
default         192.168.1.254    0.0.0.0          UG    0      0   0   enp0s3
192.168.1.0     *                255.255.255.0    U     1      0   0   enp0s3
$
```

The default router defined for this Linux system is 192.168.1.254 and is available from the enp0s3 network interface. The output also shows that to get to the 192.168.1.0 net-work, you don't need a gateway because that's the local network the Linux system is connected to.

If your network is connected to multiple networks via multiple routers, you can manually create the routing table in the system by using the add or del command-line option for the route command. The format for that is:

route [add] [del] *target* gw *gateway*

where *target* is the target host or network and *gateway* is the router address.

If you're working with a wireless network card, you must assign the wireless SSID and encryption key values using the iwconfig command:

```
# iwconfig wlp6s0 essid "MyNetwork" key s:mypassword
```

The essid parameter specifies the access point SSID name, and the key parameter spec-ifies the encryption key required to connect to it. Notice that the encryption key is preceded by an s:. That allows you to specify the encryption key in ASCII text characters; otherwise you'll need to specify the key using hexadecimal values.

If you don't know the name of a local wireless connection, you can use the iwlist command to display all of the wireless signals your wireless card detects. Just specify the name of the wireless device, and use the scan option:

```
$ sudo iwlist wlp6s0 scan
```

Once you've set the wireless network card configuration, you can proceed to assign it an IP address and default route the same as you would a wired network card.

You can fine-tune networking parameters for a network interface using the /etc/sysctl.conf configuration file, or files stored in the /etc/sysctl.d or /usr/lib/sysctl.d directories. This file defines kernel parameters that the Linux system uses when interacting with the network interface. This has become a popular method to use for setting advanced security features, such as to disable responding to ICMP messages by setting the icmp_echo_ignore_broadcasts value to 1, or if your system has multiple network interface cards, to disable packet forward-ing by setting the ip_forward value to 0.

Additional Network Features

If your network uses DHCP, you'll need to ensure that a proper DHCP client program is running on your Linux system. The DHCP client program communicates with the network DHCP server in the background and assigns the necessary IP address settings as directed by the DHCP server. There are three common DHCP programs available for Linux systems:

- dhcpcd
- dhclient
- pump

The dhcpcd program is becoming the most popular of the three, but you'll still see the other two used in some Linux distributions.

When you use your Linux system's software package manager utility to install the DHCP client program, it sets the program to automatically launch at boot time and handle the IP address configuration needed to interact on the network.

 If you're working with a Linux server that acts as a DHCP server, the /etc/dhcpd.conf file contains the IP address settings that the server offers to DHCP clients. The file contains a section for each subnet the DHCP server services:

```
subnet 10.0.2.0 netmask 255.255.255.0 {
        option routers                  192.168.1.254;
        option subnet-mask              255.255.255.0;

        option domain-name              "mynetwork.com";
        option domain-name-servers      192.168.1.254;

        option time-offset              -18000;
# Eastern Standard Time

    range 10.0.2.1 10.0.2.100;
}
```

One final network configuration setting you may run into has to do with network interface *bonding*. Bonding allows you to aggregate multiple interfaces into one virtual network device.

You can then tell the Linux system how to treat the virtual network device using three different bonding types:

- *Load balancing*: Network traffic is shared between two or more network interfaces.
- *Aggregation*: Two or more network interfaces are combined to create one larger network pipe.

- *Active/passive*: One network interface is live while the other is used as a backup for fault tolerance.

There are seven different bonding modes you can choose from, as shown in Table 7.3.

TABLE 7.3 Network interface bonding modes

Mode	Name	Description
0	balance-rr	Provides load balancing and fault tolerance using interfaces in a round-robin approach
1	active-backup	Provides fault tolerance using one interface as the primary and the other as a backup
2	balance-xor	Provides load balancing and fault tolerance by transmitting on one interface and receiving on the second
3	broadcast	Transmits all packets on both interfaces
4	802.3ad	Aggregates the interfaces to create one connection combining the interface bandwidths
5	balance-tlb	Provides load balancing and fault tolerance based on the current transmit load on each interface
6	balance-alb	Provides load balancing and fault tolerance based on the current receive load on each interface

To initialize network interface bonding, you must first load the bonding module in the Linux kernel:

```
$ sudo modprobe bonding
```

This creates a bond0 network interface, which you can then define using the `ip` utility:

```
$ sudo ip link add bond0 type bond mode 4
```

Once you've defined the bond type, you can add the appropriate network interfaces to the bond using the `ip` utility:

```
$ sudo ip link set eth0 master bond0
$ sudo ip link set eth1 master bond0
```

The Linux system will then treat the bond0 device as a single network interface using the load balancing or aggregation method you defined.

> If you have multiple network interface cards on your Linux system and choose to connect them to separate networks, you can configure your Linux system to act as a bridge between the two networks. The `brctl` command allows you to control how the bridging behaves. To do this, though, you must set the `ip_forward` kernel parameter in the /etc/sysctl.conf file to 1 to enable bridging.

Command-Line Networking Tool

Linux provides a wealth of networking tools for connecting to remote hosts, but none is more versatile than the *netcat* program. The netcat program can act as either a network server or network client, sending and receiving data packets using either TCP or UDP. This section provides some examples of the versatility of the netcat program.

Depending on your Linux distribution, the netcat program may be available as either `netcat`, or just `nc`. The format of the command is simply:

```
nc host port
```

where `host` is the IP address or hostname of the remote server and `port` is the port number for the connection. By default netcat will attempt to establish a TCP connection with the remote server. To establish a UDP connection, add the `-u` option.

There are lots of different options available to customize the connection. Table 7.4 lists the netcat options.

TABLE 7.4 The netcat command options

Option	Description
-4	Use only IPv4 addresses
-6	Use only IPv6 addresses
-C	Use a carriage return/linefeed combination at the end of each line
-D	Enable socket debugging
-d	Do not read from STDIN
-h	Displays the netcat help document
-i	Specify a delay interval between text sent and received
-k	Continuing listing for an incoming connection after the current connection terminates

Option	Description
-l	Listing for an incoming connection instead of initializing a new connection
-n	Do not use DNS lookups for hostnames
-p	Specifies the port used for the connection
-r	Use a random source and/or destination port
-S	Enables the MD5 signature option
-s	Specify the IP address of the network interface used for sending packets
-T	Specify the IP Type of Service (ToS) used for the connection
-t	Reply to Telnet protocol options send from servers
-U	Uses Unix domain sockets instead of network sockets
-u	Use UDP instead of TCP
-v	Enable verbose mode to display more information
-w	Specify a timeout value for inactivity disconnections
-X	Use SOCK or HTTP proxy server protocols
-x	Specify the proxy server to use for the connection
-z	Scan for listening applications rather than attempting to connect

A great troubleshooting feature of nc is the ability to send HTTP requests directly to servers and see the HTTP response as well as the HTML code returned. Listing 7.8 shows an example of the output you would see.

Listing 7.8: Using netcat to retrieve HTTP data

```
$ printf "GET / HTTP/1.0\r\n\r\n" | nc richblum.com 80
HTTP/1.1 200 OK
Date: Mon, 04 Dec 2021 16:14:35 GMT
Server: Apache
Vary: Accept-Encoding
Connection: close
```

```
Content-Type: text/html

,,,

<!DOCTYPE html PUBLIC "-//W3C//DTD XHTML 1.0 Transitional//EN"
"http://www.w3.org/TR/xhtml1/DTD/xhtml1-transitional.dtd">
<html xmlns="http://www.w3.org/1999/xhtml">
<head>
<link rel="stylesheet" type="text/css" href="main/mystyle.css" />
<link rel="stylesheet" media="print" type="text/css"
href="main/print.css" />
<title>Rich Blum's Blog</title>
</head>

,,,
$
```

The output in Listing 7.8 shows the HTTP options sent by the server, followed by the HTML code for the web page.

You can also create a simple chat dialogue between two systems from the command-line. On one system, just start nc in listen mode using the -l option:

```
$ nc -l 8000
```

Then on the other system, connect to that port on the remote system:

```
$ nc hostname 8000
```

Now any text you type in one side displays on the other side! To break the connection, just press Ctrl+C on either side of the connection.

Finally, another great use of the netcat program is as a quick way to transfer a file from one system to another. Just redirect the output of the listening host to a file:

```
$ nc -l 8000 > filename.txt
```

Then on the sending host, redirect the file as input to the sending nc command:

```
$ nc hostname 8000 < myfile.txt
```

When the file transfer completes, both sides of the connection will automatically terminate, and the new file will be available on the receiving host. This makes moving files between systems a breeze!

If you need to test secure SSL connections with a network server, the s_client package allows you to do that. It can utilize certificates to establish connections with secure servers.

Basic Network Troubleshooting

Once you have a Linux kernel installed, there are a few things you can do to check to make sure things are operating properly. The following sections walk through the commands you should know to monitor the network activity, including watching what processes are listening on the network and what connections are active from your system.

Sending Test Packets

One way to test network connectivity is to send test packets to known hosts. Linux provides the ping and ping6 commands to do that. The ping and ping6 commands send *Internet Control Message Protocol (ICMP)* packets to remote hosts using either the IP (*ping*) or IPv6 (*ping6*) protocol. ICMP packets work behind the scenes to track connectivity and provide control messages between systems. If the remote host supports ICMP, it will send a reply packet back when it receives a ping packet.

The basic format for the ping command is to specify the IP address of the remote host:

```
$ ping 10.0.2.2
PING 10.0.2.2 (10.0.2.2) 56(84) bytes of data.
64 bytes from 10.0.2.2: icmp_seq=1 ttl=63 time=14.6 ms
64 bytes from 10.0.2.2: icmp_seq=2 ttl=63 time=3.82 ms
64 bytes from 10.0.2.2: icmp_seq=3 ttl=63 time=2.05 ms
64 bytes from 10.0.2.2: icmp_seq=4 ttl=63 time=0.088 ms
64 bytes from 10.0.2.2: icmp_seq=5 ttl=63 time=3.54 ms
64 bytes from 10.0.2.2: icmp_seq=6 ttl=63 time=3.97 ms
64 bytes from 10.0.2.2: icmp_seq=7 ttl=63 time=0.040 ms
^C
--- 10.0.2.2 ping statistics ---
7 packets transmitted, 7 received, 0% packet loss, time 6020ms
rtt min/avg/max/mdev = 0.040/4.030/14.696/4.620 ms
$
```

The ping command continues sending packets until you press Ctrl+C. You can also use the -c command-line option to specify a set number of packets to send and then stop.

For the ping6 command, things get a little more complicated. If you're using an IPv6 link local address, you also need to tell the command which interface to send the packets out on:

```
$ ping6 -c 4 fe80::c418:2ed0:aead:cbce%enp0s3
PING fe80::c418:2ed0:aead:cbce%enp0s3(fe80::c418:2ed0:aead:cbce) 56 data
bytes
```

```
64 bytes from fe80::c418:2ed0:aead:cbce: icmp_seq=1 ttl=128 time=1.47 ms
64 bytes from fe80::c418:2ed0:aead:cbce: icmp_seq=2 ttl=128 time=0.478 ms
64 bytes from fe80::c418:2ed0:aead:cbce: icmp_seq=3 ttl=128 time=0.777 ms
64 bytes from fe80::c418:2ed0:aead:cbce: icmp_seq=4 ttl=128 time=0.659 ms

--- fe80::c418:2ed0:aead:cbce%enp0s3 ping statistics ---
4 packets transmitted, 4 received, 0% packet loss, time 3003ms
rtt min/avg/max/mdev = 0.478/0.847/1.475/0.378 ms
$
```

The %enp0s3 part tells the system to send the ping packets out the enp0s3 network interface for the link local address.

Yet another useful tool is the traceroute command. The traceroute command uses
a feature of ICMP packets that restrict the number of network "hops" they can make. By
manipulating that value in the packet, the traceroute command allows you to see the network routers used to get the packets from the client to the server.

Finally, the mtr program is a package that utilizes data retrieved from ping and
traceroute commands to document network availability and latency in a real-time chart.
Figure 7.4 shows the output of the mtr command tracing the connectivity to the linux
.org server.

FIGURE 7.4   Using mtr to monitor network connectivity to a server

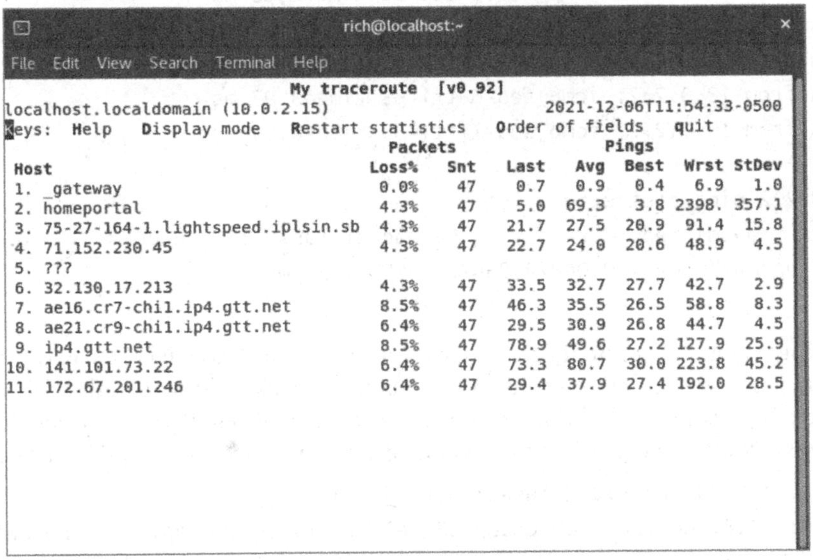

WARNING Unfortunately, these days many hosts don't support ICMP packets because they can be used to create a denial-of-service (DOS) attack against the host. Don't be surprised if you try to ping a remote host and don't get any responses.

Finding Host Information

Sometimes the problem isn't with network connectivity but with the DNS hostname system. You can test a hostname using the *host* command:

```
$ host www.linux.org
www.linux.org is an alias for linux.org.
linux.org has address 107.170.40.56
linux.org mail is handled by 20 mx.iqemail.net.
$
```

The `host` command queries the DNS server to determine the IP addresses assigned to the specified hostname. By default it returns all IP addresses associated with the hostname. Some hosts are supported by multiple servers in a load balancing configuration. The `host` command will show all of the IP addresses associated with those servers:

```
$ host www.yahoo.com
www.yahoo.com is an alias for atsv2-fp-shed.wg1.b.yahoo.com.
atsv2-fp-shed.wg1.b.yahoo.com has address 98.138.219.231
atsv2-fp-shed.wg1.b.yahoo.com has address 72.30.35.9
atsv2-fp-shed.wg1.b.yahoo.com has address 72.30.35.10
atsv2-fp-shed.wg1.b.yahoo.com has address 98.138.219.232
atsv2-fp-shed.wg1.b.yahoo.com has IPv6 address 2001:4998:58:1836::10
atsv2-fp-shed.wg1.b.yahoo.com has IPv6 address 2001:4998:58:1836::11
atsv2-fp-shed.wg1.b.yahoo.com has IPv6 address 2001:4998:44:41d::3
atsv2-fp-shed.wg1.b.yahoo.com has IPv6 address 2001:4998:44:41d::4
$
```

You can also specify an IP address for the `host` command, and it will attempt to find the hostname associated with it:

```
$ host 98.138.219.231
231.219.138.98.in-addr.arpa domain name pointer media-router-
fp1.prod1.media.vip.ne1.yahoo.com.
$
```

Notice, though, that often an IP address will resolve to a generic server hostname that hosts the website and not the website alias, as is the case here with the www.linux.org IP address.

Another great tool to use is the *dig* command. The dig command displays all of the DNS data records associated with a specific host or network. For example, you can look up the information for a specific hostname:

```
$ dig www.linux.org

; <<>> DiG 9.9.4-RedHat-9.9.4-18.el7_1.5 <<>> www.linux.org
;; global options: +cmd
;; Got answer:
;; ->>HEADER<<- opcode: QUERY, status: NOERROR, id: 45314
;; flags: qr rd ra; QUERY: 1, ANSWER: 2, AUTHORITY: 0, ADDITIONAL: 1

;; OPT PSEUDOSECTION:
; EDNS: version: 0, flags:; udp: 4096
;; QUESTION SECTION:
;www.linux.org.          IN     A

;; ANSWER SECTION:
www.linux.org.       14400   IN    CNAME  linux.org.
linux.org.       3600    IN    A    107.170.40.56

;; Query time: 75 msec
;; SERVER: 192.168.1.254#53(192.168.1.254)
;; WHEN: Sat Feb 06 17:44:29 EST 2016
;; MSG SIZE  rcvd: 72

$
```

Or you can look up DNS data records associated with a specific network service, such as a mail server:

```
$ dig linux.org MX

; <<>> DiG 9.9.5-3ubuntu0.5-Ubuntu <<>> linux.org MX
;; global options: +cmd
;; Got answer:
;; ->>HEADER<<- opcode: QUERY, status: NOERROR, id: 16202
;; flags: qr rd ra; QUERY: 1, ANSWER: 1, AUTHORITY: 0, ADDITIONAL: 1
```

```
;; OPT PSEUDOSECTION:
; EDNS: version: 0, flags:; udp: 4096
;; QUESTION SECTION:
;linux.org.                IN    MX

;; ANSWER SECTION:
linux.org.        3600    IN    MX    20  mx.iqemail.net.

;; Query time: 75 msec
;; SERVER: 127.0.1.1#53(127.0.1.1)
;; WHEN: Tue Feb 09 12:35:43 EST 2016
;; MSG SIZE  rcvd: 68

$
```

If you need to look up DNS information for multiple servers or domains, the *nslookup* command provides an interactive interface where you can enter commands:

```
$ nslookup
> www.google.com
Server:        192.168.1.254
Address:       192.168.1.254#53

Non-authoritative answer:
Name:    www.google.com
Address: 172.217.2.228
> www.wikipedia.org
Server:        192.168.1.254
Address:       192.168.1.254#53

Non-authoritative answer:
Name:    www.wikipedia.org
Address: 208.80.153.224
> exit

$
```

You can also dynamically specify the address of another DNS server to use for the name lookups, which is a handy way to determine if your default DNS server is at fault if a name resolution fails.

One final tool that can be useful is the whois command. The whois command attempts to connect to the centralized Internet domain registry at http://whois .networksolutions.com and retrieve information about who registered the requested domain name. Listing 7.9 shows a partial output from the whois command.

Listing 7.9: Partial output from the whois command

```
$ whois linux.com
   Domain Name: LINUX.COM
   Registry Domain ID: 4245540_DOMAIN_COM-VRSN
   Registrar WHOIS Server: whois.1api.net
   Registrar URL: http://www.1api.net
   Updated Date: 2021-03-18T15:40:08Z
   Creation Date: 1994-06-02T04:00:00Z
   Registry Expiry Date: 2022-06-01T04:00:00Z
   Registrar: 1API GmbH
   Registrar IANA ID: 1387
   Registrar Abuse Contact Email: abuse@1api.net
   Registrar Abuse Contact Phone: +49.68949396850
   Domain Status: clientTransferProhibited
https://icann.org/epp#clientTransferProhibited
   Name Server: NS1.DNSIMPLE.COM
   Name Server: NS2.DNSIMPLE.COM
   Name Server: NS3.DNSIMPLE.COM
   Name Server: NS4.DNSIMPLE.COM
...
```

Theoretically the registry contains complete contact information for the owner of the domain, but these days due to privacy concerns that information is usually blocked. But there is usually a contact email address for the domain in case you need to report suspected abuse from the domain.

Advanced Network Troubleshooting

Besides the simple network tests shown in the previous section, Linux has some more advanced programs that can provide more detailed information about the network environment. Sometimes it helps to be able to see just what network connections are active on a Linux system. There are two ways to troubleshoot that issue: the netstat command and the ss command.

The *netstat* Command

The *netstat* command is part of the net-tools package and can provide a wealth of network information for you. By default, it lists all of the open network connections on the system:

```
# netstat
Active Internet connections (w/o servers)
Proto Recv-Q Send-Q Local Address          Foreign Address          State
```

```
Active UNIX domain sockets (w/o servers)
Proto RefCnt Flags       Type        State      I-Node  Path
unix  2      [ ]         DGRAM                  10825
  @/org/freedesktop/systemd1/notify
unix  2      [ ]         DGRAM                  10933
  /run/systemd/shutdownd
unix  6      [ ]         DGRAM                  6609
  /run/systemd/journal/socket
unix  25     [ ]         DGRAM                  6611    /dev/log
unix  3      [ ]         STREAM      CONNECTED  25693
unix  3      [ ]         STREAM      CONNECTED  20770
  /var/run/dbus/system_bus_socket
unix  3      [ ]         STREAM      CONNECTED  19556
unix  3      [ ]         STREAM      CONNECTED  19511
unix  2      [ ]         DGRAM                  24125
unix  3      [ ]         STREAM      CONNECTED  19535
unix  3      [ ]         STREAM      CONNECTED  18067
  /var/run/dbus/system_bus_socket
unix  3      [ ]         STREAM      CONNECTED  32358
unix  3      [ ]         STREAM      CONNECTED  24818
  /var/run/dbus/system_bus_socket
...
```

The netstat command produces lots of output because there are normally lots of programs that use network services on Linux systems. You can limit the output to just TCP or UDP connections by using the -t command-line option for TCP connections or -u for UDP connections:

```
$ netstat -t
Active Internet connections (w/o servers)
Proto Recv-Q Send-Q Local Address       Foreign Address          State
tcp   1      0 10.0.2.15:58630          productsearch.ubu:https CLOSE_WAIT
tcp6  1      0 ip6-localhost:57782      ip6-localhost:ipp       CLOSE_WAIT
$
```

You can also get a list of what applications are listening on which network ports by using the -l option:

```
$ netstat -l
Active Internet connections (only servers)
Proto Recv-Q Send-Q Local Address          Foreign Address        State
tcp   0      0 ubuntu02:domain           *:*                    LISTEN
tcp   0      0 localhost:ipp             *:*                    LISTEN
tcp6  0      0 ip6-localhost:ipp         [::]:*                 LISTEN
```

```
udp        0        0 *:ipp              *:*
udp        0        0 *:mdns             *:*
udp        0        0 *:36355            *:*
udp        0        0 ubuntu02:domain    *:*
udp        0        0 *:bootpc           *:*
udp        0        0 *:12461            *:*
udp6       0        0 [::]:64294         [::]:*
udp6       0        0 [::]:60259         [::]:*
udp6       0        0 [::]:mdns          [::]:*
...
```

As you can see, just a standard Linux workstation still has lots of things happening in the background, waiting for connections.

Yet another great feature of the netstat command is that the -s option displays statistics for the different types of packets the system has used on the network:

```
# netstat -s
Ip:
    240762 total packets received
    0 forwarded
    0 incoming packets discarded
    240747 incoming packets delivered
    206940 requests sent out
    32 dropped because of missing route
Icmp:
    57 ICMP messages received
    0 input ICMP message failed.
    ICMP input histogram:
        destination unreachable: 12
        timeout in transit: 38
        echo replies: 7
    7 ICMP messages sent
    0 ICMP messages failed
    ICMP output histogram:
        echo request: 7
IcmpMsg:
        InType0: 7
        InType3: 12
        InType11: 38
```

```
        OutType8: 7
Tcp:
    286 active connections openings
    0 passive connection openings
    0 failed connection attempts
    0 connection resets received
    0 connections established
    239933 segments received
    206091 segments send out
    0 segments retransmited
    0 bad segments received.
    0 resets sent
Udp:
    757 packets received
    0 packets to unknown port received.
    0 packet receive errors
    840 packets sent
    0 receive buffer errors
    0 send buffer errors
UdpLite:
TcpExt:
    219 TCP sockets finished time wait in fast timer
    15 delayed acks sent
    26 delayed acks further delayed because of locked socket
    Quick ack mode was activated 1 times
    229343 packet headers predicted
    289 acknowledgments not containing data payload received
    301 predicted acknowledgments
    TCPRcvCoalesce: 72755
IpExt:
    InNoRoutes: 2
    InMcastPkts: 13
    OutMcastPkts: 15
    InOctets: 410722578
    OutOctets: 8363083
    InMcastOctets: 2746
    OutMcastOctets: 2826
#
```

The netstat statistics output can give you a rough idea of how busy your Linux system is on the network or if there's a specific issue with one of the protocols installed.

Examining Sockets

The netstat tool provides a wealth of network information, but it can often be hard to determine just which program is listening on which open port. The *ss* command can come to your rescue for that.

A program connection to a port is called a *socket*. The ss command can link which system processes are using which network sockets that are active:

```
$ ss -anpt
State     Recv-Q Send-Q Local Address:Port          Peer Address:Port
LISTEN    0      100    127.0.0.1:25                    *:*
LISTEN    0      128          *:111               *:*
LISTEN    0      5      192.168.122.1:53                   *:*
LISTEN    0      128          *:22                *:*
LISTEN    0      128    127.0.0.1:631                   *:*
LISTEN    0      100         ::1:25               :::*
LISTEN    0      128         :::111               :::*
LISTEN    0      128         :::22                :::*
LISTEN    0      128         ::1:631              :::*
ESTAB     0      0           ::1:22               ::1:40490
ESTAB     0      0           ::1:40490            ::1:22
users:(("ssh",pid=15176,fd=3))
$
```

The -anpt option displays both listening and established TCP connections and the process they're associated with. This output shows that the ssh port (port 22) has an established connection and is controlled by process ID 15176, the ssh program.

Monitoring the Network

Often when troubleshooting network applications it helps to see what's going on "behind the scenes" in the network. Knowing what TCP or UDP packets are being sent between the client and server can be crucial in determining what's going wrong. Fortunately, Linux has a few different tools that can help with that:

- tcpdump—the legacy command-line tool for watching network packets
- wireshark—a graphical tool for watching network packets and performing advanced network analysis
- tshark—the command-line version of Wireshark

The tcpdump program is a legacy tool that's been around for a long time, but it can still be useful if that's all you have to work with. It provides simple capturing of network data on the system and can do rudimentary decoding of the packets to break out the different data contained within the network packet.

The `tcpdump` program also provides basic filtering capabilities so that you can limit the capture to a single host, client, or even network session.

The `wireshark` package is an open source graphical tool for performing advanced network analysis of packets. Not only will `wireshark` capture and decode network packets, but it also provides color coding of traffic types and can display groups of packets based on applications. Figure 7.5 shows a sample `wireshark` display of simple network traffic.

FIGURE 7.5 The `wireshark` network analysis window

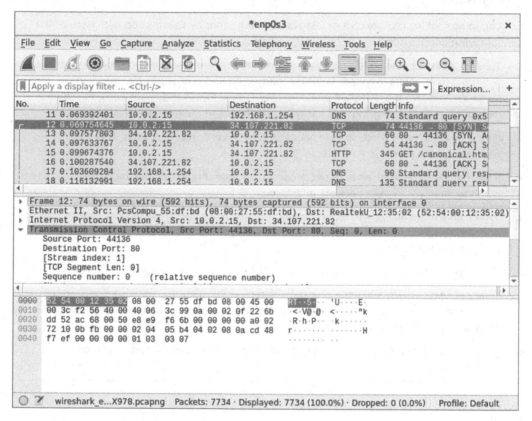

If you don't have a graphical desktop environment on your Linux system, you can still use the power of `wireshark` from the command line with `tshark`. The `tshark` program provides many of the same network analysis tools as `wireshark`, but in a more rudimentary display format on the command line.

WARNING To see all network traffic on a network interface, you must have administrator privileges on your system. That usually means either logging in with the root user account or using the `sudo` command from a normal account to gain root privileges.

EXERCISE 7.1

Determining the Network Environment

This exercise will demonstrate how to quickly assess the network configuration and programs for your Linux system without you having to dig through lots of configuration files. To document your system network information, follow these steps (depending on your distribution you may need to first install the netstat and iwlist programs from the software repository):

1. Log in as root, or acquire root privileges by using su or by using sudo with each of the following commands.

2. Type **ip address show** to display the current network interfaces on your system. You will most likely see a loopback interface (named l0) and one or more network interfaces. Write down the IP (called inet) and IPv6 (called inet6) addresses assigned to each network interface along with the hardware address and the network mask address.

3. If your system has a wireless network card, type **iwlist wlan0 scan** to view the wireless access points in your area.

4. If your system has a wireless network card, type **iwconfig** to display the current wireless settings for your network interface.

5. Type **route** to display the routes defined on your system. Note the default gateway address assigned to your system. It should be on the same network as the IP address assigned to the system.

6. Type **cat /etc/resolv.conf** to display the DNS settings for your system.

7. Type **netstat -l** to display the programs listening for incoming network connections. The entries marked as unix are using the loopback address to communicate with other programs internally on your system.

8. Type **ss -anpt** to display the processes that have active network ports open on your system.

Summary

Connecting Linux systems to networks can be painless if you have the correct tools. To connect the Linux system, you'll need an IP address, a netmask address, a default router, a hostname, and a DNS server. If you don't care what IP address is assigned to your Linux system, you can obtain those values automatically using DHCP. However, if you are running a Linux server that requires a static IP address, you may need to configure these values manually.

Linux stores network connection information in configuration files. You can either manually modify the files to store the appropriate network information or use a graphical or command-line tool to do that. The Network Manager tool is the most popular graphical tool used by Linux distributions. It allows you to configure both wired and wireless network settings from a graphical window. The Network Manager icon in the system tray area shows network connectivity as well as basic wireless information for wireless network cards.

If you must configure your network settings from the command line, you'll need a few different tools. For wireless connections, use the iwconfig command to set the wireless access point and SSID key. For both wireless and wired connections, use the ifconfig or ip command to set the IP address and netmask values for the interface. You may also need to use the route command to define the default router for the local network.

To use hostnames instead of IP addresses, you must define a DNS server for your network. You do that in the /etc/resolv.conf configuration file. You will also need to define the hostname for your Linux system in either the /etc/hostname or the /etc/HOSTNAME file.

Once your network configuration is complete, you may have to do some additional troubleshooting for network problems. The ping and ping6 commands allow you to send ICMP packets to remote hosts to test basic connectivity. If you suspect issues with hostnames, you can use the host and dig commands to query the DNS server for hostnames.

For more advanced network troubleshooting, you can use the netstat and ss commands to display what applications are using which network ports on the system.

Exam Essentials

Describe the command-line utilities required to configure and manipulate Ethernet network interfaces. To set the network address on a network interface you can use the nmtui, nmcli, ip, or ifconfig commands. The nmtui and nmcli commands are available on systems that utilize the Network Manager tool for managing network interfaces. The ip command is from the iproute2 package, and the ifconfig command is from the legacy net-tools package. If you use the ifconfig command you'll also need to use the route command to set the default router (or gateway) for the network.

Explain how to configure basic access to a wireless network. Linux uses the iwlist command to list all wireless access points detected by the wireless network card. You can configure the settings required to connect to a specific wireless network using the iwconfig command. At a minimum, you'll need to configure the access point SSID value and most likely specify the encryption key value to connect to the access point.

Describe how to manipulate the routing table on a Linux system. For legacy systems use the route command to display the existing router table used by the Linux system. You can add a new route by using the add option or remove an existing route by using the del option. You can specify the default router (gateway) used by the network by adding the default keyword to the command. For systems that utilize the iproute2 package, you use the ip route command to display and manipulate the routing table.

Summarize the tools you would need to analyze the status of network devices.   The `nmtui`, `nmcli`, `ifconfig` and `ip` commands display the current status of all network interfaces on the system. You can also use the `netstat` or `ss` command to display statistics for all listening network ports.

Describe how Linux initializes the network interfaces.   Debian-based Linux systems use the `/etc/network/interfaces` file to configure the IP address, netmask, and default router. Red Hat–based Linux systems use files in the `/etc/sysconfig/network-scripts` folder. The `ifcfg-emp0s3` file contains the IP address and netmask settings, while the `network` file contains the default router settings. These files are examined at bootup to determine the network interface configuration. Newer versions of Ubuntu use the Netplan tool, which stores the network configuration in the `/etc/netplan` folder.

Explain how to test network connectivity.   The `ping` and `ping6` commands allow you to send ICMP messages to remote hosts and display the response received. The `traceroute` command allows you to view the network path used to reach a specific remote host. The `mtr` command provides real-time connectivity and response statistics for a specific remote host.

Describe one graphical tool used to configure network settings in Linux.   The Network Manager tool provides a graphical interface for changing settings on the network interfaces. The Network Manager appears as an icon in the desktop system tray area. If your Linux system uses a wireless network card, the icon appears as a radio signal, while for wired network connections it appears as a mini-network. When you click the icon, it shows the current network status, and for wireless interfaces, it shows a list of the access points detected. When you open the Network Manager interface, it allows you to either set static IP address information or configure the network to use a DHCP server to dynamically set the network configuration.

Review Questions

1. Which two commands can be used to set the IP address, subnet mask, and default router information on an interface using the command line?
    A. netstat
    B. ping
    C. nmtui
    D. ip
    E. route

2. Which tool does newer versions of Ubuntu use to set network address information?
    A. netstat
    B. Netplan
    C. iwconfig
    D. route
    E. ifconfig

3. Which command displays the duplex settings for an Ethernet card?
    A. ethtool
    B. netstat
    C. iwconfig
    D. iwlist
    E. route

4. Which command displays what processes are using which ports on a Linux system?
    A. iwconfig
    B. ip
    C. ping
    D. nmtui
    E. ss

5. If your Linux server doesn't have a graphical desktop installed, what two tools could you use to configure network settings on a wired network card from the command line?
    A. nmcli
    B. iwconfig
    C. ip
    D. netstat
    E. ping

6.   What network setting defines the network device that routes packets intended for hosts on remote networks?

   A.   Default router

   B.   Netmask

   C.   Hostname

   D.   IP address

   E.   DNS server

7.   What device setting defines a host that maps a host name to an IP address?

   A.   Default router

   B.   Netmask

   C.   Hostname

   D.   IP address

   E.   DNS server

8.   What is used to automatically assign an IP address to a client?

   A.   Default router

   B.   DHCP

   C.   ARP table

   D.   Netmask

   E.   `ifconfig`

9.   What type of address is used so local applications can use network protocols to communicate with each other?

   A.   Dynamic address

   B.   Loopback address

   C.   Static address

   D.   Hostname

   E.   MAC address

10.   Which command would you use to find the mail server for a domain?

   A.   `dig`

   B.   `netstat`

   C.   `ping6`

   D.   `host`

   E.   `ss`

11. What command would you use to find out what application was using a specific TCP port on the system?

    A. ip

    B. ss

    C. host

    D. dig

    E. ifconfig

12. What directory do Red Hat–based systems use to store network configuration files?

    A. /etc/sysconfig/network-scripts

    B. /etc/network

    C. /etc/ifcfg-eth0

    D. /etc/ifconfig

    E. /etc/iwconfig

13. Which configuration line sets a dynamic IP address for a Debian system?

    A. iface eth0 inet static

    B. iface eth0 inet dhcp

    C. auto eth0

    D. iface eth0 inet6 auto

    E. BOOTPROTO=dynamic

14. Which file contains a list of DNS servers the Linux system can use to resolve hostnames?

    A. /etc/dhcpd.conf

    B. /etc/resolv.conf

    C. /etc/nsswitch.conf

    D. /etc/network/interfaces

    E. /etc/sysctl.conf

15. Which ifconfig format correctly assigns an IP address and netmask to the eth0 interface?

    A. ifconfig eth0 up 192.168.1.50 netmask 255.255.255.0

    B. ifconfig eth0 255.255.255.0 192.168.1.50

    C. ifconfig up 192.168.1.50 netmask 255.255.255.0

    D. ifconfig up

    E. ifconfig down

16. What command displays all of the available wireless networks in your area?

    A. iwlist

    B. iwconfig

    C. ifconfig

    D. ip

    E. arp

17. What option sets the wireless access point name in the `iwconfig` command?

    A. `key`

    B. `netmask`

    C. `address`

    D. `essid`

    E. `channel`

18. What command can you use to both display and set the IP address, netmask, and default router values?

    A. `ifconfig`

    B. `iwconfig`

    C. `router`

    D. `ifup`

    E. `ip`

19. What tool allows you to send ICMP messages to a remote host to test network connectivity?

    A. `netstat`

    B. `ifconfig`

    C. `ping`

    D. `iwconfig`

    E. `ss`

20. You have a network application that fails to connect to a remote server. What command-line tool should you use to watch the network packets that leave your system to ensure that they use the correct network port?

    A. `nc`

    B. `tcpdump`

    C. `ping`

    D. `traceroute`

    E. `mtr`

Chapter

8

Comparing GUIs

✓ **Objective 1.1: Summarize Linux fundamentals**

A *graphical user interface (GUI)* is a set of programs that allow a user to interact with the computer system via icons, windows, and various other visual elements. While some believe that you should only administer a system via the text-based command line, it is still important to understand the Linux GUI (pronounced "gooey"). You may need to use certain GUI utilities to administer the system and its security.

Different Linux distributions come with various default desktop environments, which you may need to install and manage for users who prefer a graphical-based UI. Administering the underlying software is necessary too. In addition, you need to understand remote desktops and their client-server model. Remote desktop interactions that travel over the network are prone to privacy problems, so it is crucial to secure these GUI transmissions.

Access to the various GUI desktops should provide universal access for all. A GUI desktop environment needs to be configured to work appropriately for any person who has problems with vision, hearing, hand and finger control, and so on. Thus, we are pleased to present a section on accessibility in this chapter.

Focusing on the GUI

With some operating systems, your GUI is fairly rigid. You may be able to move or add a few icons, change a background picture, or tweak a few settings. However, with Linux, the GUI choices are almost overwhelming and the flexibility is immense.

On Linux, a GUI is a series of components that work together to provide the graphical setting for the user interface (UI). One of these components is the *desktop environment.* A desktop environment provides a predetermined look and feel to the GUI. It is typically broken up into the following graphical sections and functions:

Desktop Settings   Desktop settings consist of programs that allow you to make configuration changes to the desktop environment. For example, you may want desktop windows to activate when the cursor hovers over them instead of when you click them.

Display Manager   The desktop environment's login screen is where you choose a username and enter a password to gain system access. If multiple desktop environments are installed on the system, the display manager allows you to choose between them prior to logging in. These login screens are often modified by corporations to contain a legal statement about appropriate use of the system and/or a company logo.

File Manager   This program allows you to perform file maintenance activities graphically. Often a folder icon is shown for directories within the manager program. You can perform such tasks as moving a file, viewing directory contents, copying files, and so on.

Icons   An icon is a picture representation of a file or program. It is activated via mouse clicks, finger touches (if the screen is a touchscreen), voice commands, and so on.

Favorites Bar   This window area contains popular icons, which are typically used more frequently. These icons can be removed or added as desired. Some desktop environments update the bar automatically as you use the system to reflect your regularly used icons.

Launch   This program allows you to search for applications and files. It can also allow certain actions, such as start or open, to be performed on the search results.

Menus   These window areas are typically accessed via an icon. They contain files and/or programs list as well as sublists of additional files and/or program selections.

Panels   Panels are slim and typically rectangular areas that are located at the very top or bottom of a desktop environment's main window. They can also be at the desktop's far left or right. They often contain notifications, system date and/or time, program icons, and so on.

System Tray   A system tray is a special menu, commonly attached to a panel. It provides access to programs that allow a user to log out, lock their screen, manage audio settings, view notifications, shut down or reboot the system, and so on.

Widgets   Widgets are divided into applets, screenlets, desklets, and so on. They are programs that provide to the user information or functionality on the desktop. For example, current sports news may be displayed continually to a screenlet. Another example is a sticky note applet that allows the user to put graphical windows that look like sticky notes on their desktop and add content to them.

Window Manager   These client programs determine how the windows (also called *frames*) are presented on the desktop. These programs control items such as the size and appearance of the windows. In addition, they manage how additional windows can be placed, such as either next to each other or overlapping.

Many Linux users are very passionate about the desktop environment they use and for good reason. There are several excellent ones from which you can choose. We'll cover a few of these desktop environments in the following sections and look at universal accessibility to them as well.

Getting to Know GNOME

The GNOME desktop environment, created around the late 1990s, is very popular and found by default on Linux distributions such as CentOS and Ubuntu. Currently a large volunteer group that belongs to the GNOME Foundation maintains it. For more about the GNOME project, visit `www.gnome.org`.

GNOME 2 was a more traditional desktop user interface, and when GNOME 3 (now formally called GNOME Shell) was released in 2011, with its nontraditional interface, many users reacted strongly. This spurred a few GNOME project forks. However, over time and with a few changes, GNOME Shell gained ground. For those who still prefer the traditional GNOME 2 environment, the GNOME Classic desktop is available.

Figure 8.1 shows a GNOME Shell desktop environment on an Ubuntu distribution.

FIGURE 8.1   The GNOME Shell desktop environment

In Figure 8.1, notice the panel at the frame's top, containing a clock and a system tray on the far right. The Activities button on the panel's far left allows you to switch between windows and provides the Search bar. The favorites bar on the UI frame's left side shows various application icons as well as a multidot icon, which is the Apps button. The Apps button displays various application icons that allow you to quickly access a desired program.

 Keep in mind that a default desktop environment may be modified slightly for each Linux distribution. For example, GNOME Shell on Rocky Linux does not have a favorites bar displaying unless you click Activities in the panel, whereas GNOME Shell on Ubuntu automatically displays the favorites bar.

The best way to understand a graphical interface is to try a desktop environment for yourself. However, to help you with memorizing the assorted components that make up these different desktops, we are providing tables. Some of the GNOME Shell's various components are briefly described in Table 8.1.

TABLE 8.1   GNOME shell desktop environment default components

Name	Program Name and/or Description
Display manager	GNOME Display Manager (GDM).
File manager	GNOME Files (sometimes just called Files). Formerly called Nautilus.
Favorites bar	GNOME Shell Dash (sometimes called the Dock).
Panels	A single panel located at GNOME Shell frame's top.
System tray	Located on the right side of the single panel.
Window manager	Mutter.

An interesting feature of GNOME Shell is that the panel, which contains the system tray, is available on the Display Manager as well as within the GNOME Shell.

Probing KDE Plasma

The Kool Desktop Environment (KDE) got its start in 1996, with its first version released in 1998. Through time the name KDE was no longer just referring to a desktop environment, but instead it specified the project's organization and the strong community that supported it. KDE had many additional software projects besides its famous desktop environment. Thus in 2009, KDE's desktop environment was rebranded as KDE Plasma. For more about the KDE group, visit www.kde.org.

Figure 8.2 shows a KDE Plasma desktop environment on an openSUSE LEAP distribution.

In Figure 8.2, the panel is located at the primary UI frame's bottom. This is a more traditional panel location used on older systems and one of the reasons KDE Plasma is known for being a good desktop environment for those who are new to Linux. On this panel, the system tray, which contains notifications, the time, and various other plasmoids (widgets), is located on the panel's right side. The Application Menu, a launcher for various programs in addition to containing the favorites bar, is on the panel's far-left side. Table 8.2 briefly describes some of the KDE Plasma components.

TABLE 8.2   KDE Plasma desktop environment default components

Name	Program Name and/or Description
Display manager	SDDM (Simple Desktop Display Manager)
File manager	Dolphin
Favorites bar	Displayed inside Application Menu
Panels	A single panel located at the Plasma frame's bottom
System tray	Located on the right side of the single panel
Widgets	Called plasmoids
Window manager	Kwin

FIGURE 8.2   The KDE Plasma desktop environment

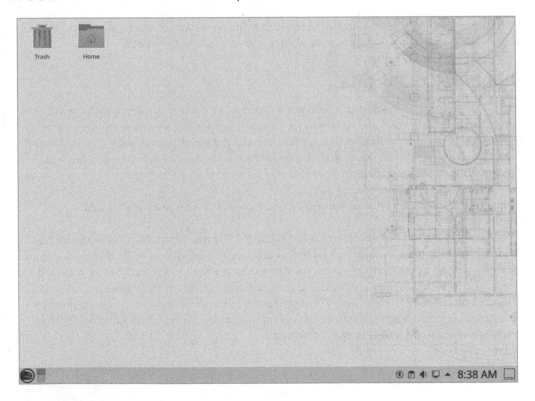

To help those users familiar with accessing files via folder icons, KDE Plasma offers a folder view. Folders appear in the default UI on the openSUSE Leap distribution in Figure 8.2. These icons on the primary desktop window allow you to launch the Dolphin file manager and jump straight to the directory named on the folder icon.

Many desktop environments have multiple UIs called *workspaces* available for each user. Workspaces are individual desktops. For example, you can have two GUI apps open on one workspace and just a terminal emulator open on the other workspace. Switching between the workspaces can be done via mouse clicks or keystroke combinations, such as Ctrl+Alt+Up Arrow/Down Arrow on Fedora 28's Wayland desktop environment. Using multiple workspaces can be very handy, especially if you need to quickly look productive at work when your boss walks by.

Considering Cinnamon

The Cinnamon desktop environment got its start in 2011 when many users reacted strongly to the release of GNOME 3 (now GNOME Shell). Developers of the Linux Mint distribution began creating Cinnamon as a fork of GNOME 3. It was officially "GNOME-free" as of late 2013. Cinnamon is still managed by the Mint development team, and you can find out more at their website, www.linuxmint.com.

Cinnamon, like KDE Plasma, is known for being a good UI for those who are new to Linux. Figure 8.3 shows a Cinnamon desktop environment on a Fedora Workstation distribution.

Notice the primary UI frame's bottom panel on the right side. It has the system tray containing audio controls, the time, and various other widgets. The Menu, a launcher for various programs that also contains the favorites bar, is on the panel's far left. Note that the Cinnamon panel also contains icons for quick launching.

If you want to install a Cinnamon desktop environment on one of the distributions you installed in Chapter 1, "Preparing Your Environment," we recommend you try it on Fedora 34 Workstation. Use an account that has super user privileges. This is typically the account you set up during the system installation. Access a terminal and enter the command **sudo dnf groupinstall -y "Cinnamon Desktop"** at the command line. Be sure to include the command's quotation marks. When the installation is complete, reboot your system. You can access the Cinnamon desktop environment through a menu provided by the system's display manager's gear icon.

FIGURE 8.3   The Cinnamon desktop environment

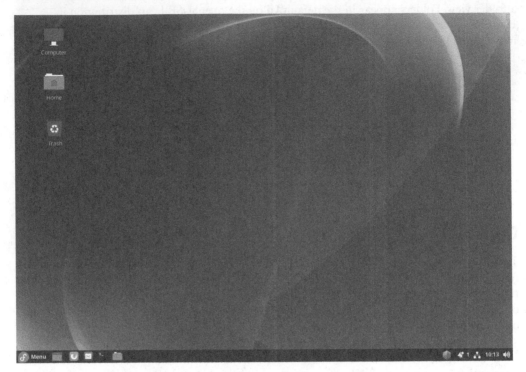

The Cinnamon desktop environment layout should be somewhat familiar because it is similar to the KDE Plasma default layout. They both have folder icons on the main UI windows. Table 8.3 briefly describes some of the Cinnamon components.

TABLE 8.3   Cinnamon desktop environment default components

Name	Program name and/or description
Display manager	LightDM
File manager	Nemo (a fork of Nautilus)
Favorites bar	Displayed inside Application Menu
Panels	A single panel (called the Cinnamon panel) located at the Cinnamon frame's bottom
System tray	Located on the right side of the single panel
Widgets	Cinnamon Spices
Window manager	Muffin (a fork of GNOME Shell's Mutter)

The Cinnamon Spices go beyond just applets and desklets for modifying your desktop environment. They also include themes and extensions that you can download and install to make your Cinnamon UI experience truly unique. The official Cinnamon Spices repository is at `https://cinnamon-spices.linuxmint.com`.

Making Acquaintance with MATE

The MATE desktop environment also got its start in 2011, when GNOME 3 (now called GNOME Shell) was released. It was started by an Arch Linux distribution user in Argentina. Pronounced "ma-tay," this desktop environment was officially released only two months after it was announced and was derived from GNOME 2. The desktop environment is available on a wide variety of Linux distributions, such as Arch Linux, Debian, Fedora, Ubuntu, Linux Mint, and so on.

MATE is named after a tea made from a plant's dried leaves. The plant (*Ilex paraguariensis*) is native to South America. Mate tea is the national drink of Argentina. It is purported to have the health benefits of tea as well as provide mental alertness similar to the benefit of drinking coffee.

If you've ever used the old GNOME 2 desktop environment, MATE will feel familiar. Figure 8.4 shows a MATE desktop environment on an Ubuntu Desktop distribution.

FIGURE 8.4   The MATE desktop environment

There are two panels in the MATE desktop environment: one is at the primary UI frame's top, and the other is at its bottom. The system tray, which contains audio controls, the time, and various other widgets, is located on the top panel's right side. Applications, a menu-driven launcher for various programs, is on the top panel's far-left side. Note that this top panel also contains icons for quick launching.

 If you want to install a MATE desktop environment on one of the distributions you installed in Chapter 1, we recommend you try it on Ubuntu Desktop 20.04. Use an account that has super user privileges. This is typically the account you set up during the system installation. Access a terminal and enter **sudo apt-get update** at the command line to update your system's repositories. When you get a prompt back, install the `tasksel` program. The `tasksel` program is a graphical utility that installs multiple related packages as a harmonized process. In other words, it makes installing certain packages with lots of dependencies easier. To install it, type **sudo apt-get install tasksel** at the command line. Then you can install the MATE desktop environment by entering **sudo tasksel install ubuntu-mate-desktop**. When the installation is complete, reboot your system. You can access the MATE desktop environment through a menu provided by the system's display manager's gear icon.

On the bottom panel of the MATE desktop environment, in the lower-left corner is the Show Desktop Button icon. This is handy if you have several windows open in the main UI frame. Just click the Show Desktop Button, and all the windows currently open will be hidden to the lower panel. You can restore all the windows on the lower panel by clicking Show Desktop Button again. Table 8.4 briefly describes some of the MATE components.

TABLE 8.4   MATE desktop environment default components

Name	Program name and/or description
Display manager	LightDM.
File manager	Caja (a fork of Nautilus).
Favorites bar	A Favorites menu is used instead and is accessed via the Applications menu-driven launcher.
Panels	One panel is located at the MATE frame's bottom and the other panel occupies the top of the MATE UI.
System tray	Located on the right side of the top panel.
Windows manager	Marco (a fork of Metacity).

You can add additional widgets to your MATE UI's top panel. Just right-click the panel, and from the drop-down context menu, select Add To Panel. This will open a window of applets you can install.

Setting Up Accessibility

In a GUI environment, accessibility deals with a user's ability to use the desktop environment. While the default desktop environment provided by a Linux distribution works for many people, accessibility settings accommodate all potential users. This includes individuals who may have vision impairment, challenges using the mouse, finger movement issues, and so on. It's important to know the desktop environment configurations concerning these accommodations so that you can help provide access for all.

Each desktop environment will provide slightly different methods for configuring accessibility. But most settings can be accomplished through desktop environment control panels, such as the Universal Access panel in GNOME Shell settings.

> Even though most desktop environments provide accessibility control panels of different names, you can usually find the panels using the environment's search facilities. Good search terms include "universal access," "accessibility," and "assistive technologies."

Figure 8.5 shows the Universal Access menu opened from the Ubuntu login window. You can find more accessibility settings in the access control panel by searching for "universal access" in the GNOME Shell's search feature.

For users with serious visual impairments or just poor eyesight, several accessibility settings may help. Table 8.5 describes common visual impairment settings.

TABLE 8.5   Common visual impairment accessibility settings

Name	Description
Cursor Blinking	Modifies the cursor blink rate to make it easier to locate the cursor on the screen.
Cursor Size	Modifies the cursor size.
High Contrast	Increases the brightness of windows and buttons and darkens window edges as well as text and the cursor.
Large Text	Modifies the font size.
Screen Reader	Uses a screen reader to read the UI aloud. Popular choices include Orca screen reader and Emacspeak.
Sound Keys	Beeps when Caps Lock or Num Lock is turned on (off). Also called *toggle keys*.
Zoom	Amplifies the screen or a screen portion to different magnification levels.

FIGURE 8.5   Universal Access top panel menu in GNOME Shell

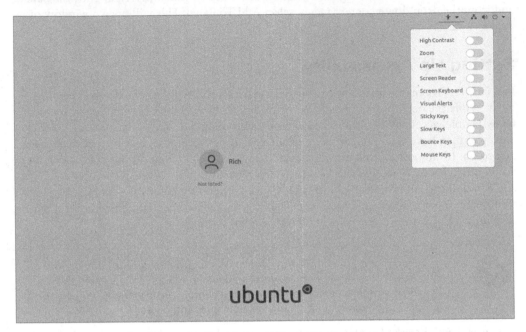

If a blind user has access to a braille display, you can install the BRLTTY package, which is available in most Linux distribution's repositories. BRLTTY operates as a Linux daemon and provides console (text mode) access via a braille display. You can find out more about this software at its official headquarters, http://mielke.cc/brltty. Be aware that you can also use the Orca screen reader with a refreshable braille display.

If you are not able to hear sound alerts on your Linux system, you can enable visual alerts. Thus, if something occurs that normally produces a sound, a visual flash is performed instead. You can set the visual alert to flash a single window or flash the entire display.

For users with hand and/or finger impairments, several accessibility settings allow full functional system use. Common settings are listed in Table 8.6.

TABLE 8.6   Common hand and finger impairment accessibility settings

Name	Description
Bounce Keys	Keyboard option that helps compensate for single keys accidentally pressed multiple times.
Double-Click Delay	Mouse option that modifies the amount of time allowed between double mouse clicks.
Gestures	Mouse option that activates programs and/or options via combining both mouse clicks and keyboard presses.

Name	Description
Hover Click	Mouse option that triggers a mouse click when the pointer is hovered over an item.
Mouse Keys	Mouse option that allows you to use keyboard keys to emulate the mouse functions.
Repeat Keys	Keyboard option that modifies how long a key must be pressed down as well as a delay to acknowledge the key repeat. Also called *keyboard repeat rate*.
Screen Keyboard	Keyboard option that displays a visual keyboard on the UI that can be manipulated by a mouse or other pointing device to emulate key strokes.
Simulated Secondary Click	Mouse option that sets a primary key to be pressed along with a mouse click to emulate secondary mouse clicks.
Slow Keys	Keyboard option that modifies how long a key must be pressed down to acknowledge the key.
Sticky Keys	Keyboard option that sets keyboard modifier keys, such as Ctrl and Shift, to maintain their pressed status until a subsequent key is pressed.

AccessX was a program that provided many of the options in Table 8.6. Thus, you will often see it referred to in the accessibility control panels, such as in the Typing Assist (AccessX) option. One interesting AccessX setting is Enable By Keyboard, which allows you to turn on or off accessibility settings via keystrokes on the keyboard.

Serving Up the GUI

Many players are involved in providing a Linux system user interface. The desktop environment components are only a piece of this puzzle. Figure 8.6 is a rudimentary depiction of serving a GUI to a user.

In Figure 8.6, notice that the window manager is an intermediary in this scenario. A window manager is a program that communicates with the display server (sometimes called a window manager) on behalf of the UI. Each particular desktop environment has its own default window manager, such as Mutter, Kwin, Muffin, Marco, and Metacity.

In the following sections, we will focus on the *display server*, a program that uses a communication protocol to transmit the desires of the UI to the operating system, and vice versa. The communication protocol is called the *display server protocol* and can operate over a network.

FIGURE 8.6 Serving the GUI components

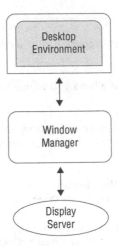

Another member in the display server team is the *compositor*. A compositor program arranges various display elements within a window to create a screen image to be passed back to the client.

Before computers printed documents, compositors were people. Physical frames (called *chases*) held wooden blocks with letters or images carved on them. A compositor arranged the wooden blocks into the frames to make words and/or images. The compositor handed the frames to the printer, who was also a person. The printer inked the blocks and then pressed the frames onto paper, which resulted in a printed document. A compositor program operates in a similar manner, except it uses multiple elements composed into a single screen image and handed off to the client.

Figuring Out Wayland

Wayland is a replacement for the X11 display server (described later). It was designed to be simpler, more secure, and easier to develop and maintain. Wayland specifically defines the communication protocol between a display server and its various clients. However, Wayland is also an umbrella term that covers the compositor, the window server, and the display server.

The Wayland protocol was initially released back in 2009, and it is now used by many current Linux desktop environments, such as GNOME Shell and KDE Plasma. If you want to dig down into Wayland, visit its website at https://wayland.freedesktop.org.

Exercise 8.1 helps walk you through the display environment in your Linux distribution by using a couple of command-line commands to show the display settings.

Checking Your Display Server

You can quickly determine what display server your desktop uses, X11 or Wayland, with the following steps:

1. Log into your system's GUI. This will start a GUI session for you.

2. Open a terminal emulator application.

3. Type **echo $WAYLAND_DISPLAY** at the command line and press the Enter key. If you get no response and just a command-line prompt back, most likely your system is using X11. If you receive a response, then your desktop environment is probably using Wayland. An additional test will help you ensure what is in use.

4. You need to get the GUI session number, so type **loginctl** and press Enter. Note the session number.

5. Type the command **loginctl show-session** *session-number* **-p Type** at the command line, where *session-number* is the number you obtained in the previous step. If you receive Type=Wayland, then your desktop environment is using Wayland. If instead you receive Type=X11, then your system is using the X11 display server.

The Wayland compositor is Weston, which provides a rather basic desktop experience. It was created as a Wayland compositor reference implementation, which is a compositor requirements example for developers who want to create their own Wayland compositor. Thus, Weston's core focus is correctness and reliability.

Wayland's compositor is swappable. In other words, you can use a different compositor if you need a more full-featured desktop experience. Several compositors are available for use with Wayland, including Arcan, Sway, Lipstick, and Clayland. However, you may not need to go out and get a Wayland compositor. Many desktop environments create their own Wayland compositors, which are typically embedded within their window manager. For example, Kwin and Mutter both fully handle Wayland compositor tasks.

> If you have any legacy X11 applications that will not support Wayland, do not despair. The XWayland software is available in the Weston package. XWayland allows X-dependent applications to run on the X server and display via a Wayland session.

If your UI is using Wayland but you are having GUI issues, you can try a few troubleshooting techniques. The following list steps through some basic approaches.

Try the GUI without Wayland. If your Linux distribution has multiple flavors of the desktop environment (with Wayland or with X11), log out of your GUI session and pick the desktop environment without Wayland. If your UI problems are resolved, then you know it has most likely something to do with Wayland.

If you do not have multiple flavors of the desktop environment and you are using the GNOME Shell user interface, turn off Wayland. Do this by using super user privileges and editing the /etc/gdm3/custom.conf file. Remove the # from the #WaylandEnable=false line and save the file. Reboot the system and log into a GUI session and see if the problems are gone.

Check your system's graphics card.   If your system seems to be running fine under X11 but gets problematic when under Wayland, check your graphics card. Go to the graphics card vendor's website and see if its drivers support Wayland. Many do, but there are a few famous holdouts that shall go unnamed here.

Use a different compositor.   If you are using a desktop environment's built-in compositor or one of the other compositors, try installing and using the Weston compositor package instead. Remember that Weston was built for reliability. If Weston is not in your distribution's software repository, you can get it from https://github.com/wayland-project/Weston. This site also contains helpful documentation. If using Weston solves your GUI problem, then you have narrowed down the culprit.

Be aware that some desktop environment commands won't work when you have a Wayland session. For example, if you are using GNOME Shell, the gnome-shell --replace command will do nothing but generate the message Window manager warning: Unsupported session type.

Examining X11

The X Window System (X for short) has been around since the 1980s, so it has endured the test of time. On Linux the dominant server implementing X was XFree86 until 2004, when a licensing change occurred. This change caused many Linux distributions to switch to the X.org foundation's implementation of X.

The X.Org's server implements the X Window System version 11. Thus, you will see a wide variety of names about the Linux X display server, such as X.org-X11, X, X11, X.Org Server, and so on. We'll use either X or X11 in this chapter.

Currently X11 is being rapidly replaced by Wayland. Not only does Wayland provide better security, but it is far easier to maintain. There are many old and obscure options in the older X11 configuration. However, you still may have distributions using X11, so it is important to understand its basics.

If for some reason your X11 session becomes hung, you can quickly kill it off; go back to the display manager screen and log back on to the system. Just press the Ctrl+Alt+Backspace key combination. The X11 session will stop and then restart for you, providing the display manager screen so you can log on.

The X11 primary configuration file is /etc/X11/xorg.conf, though it sometimes is stored in the /etc/ directory. Typically this file is no longer used. Instead, X11 creates a session configuration on the fly using runtime autodetection of the hardware involved with each GUI's session.

However, in some cases, autodetect might not work properly and you need to make X11 configuration changes. In those cases, you can create the configuration file. To do this, shut down the X server, open a terminal emulator, and using super user privileges, generate the file via the Xorg -configure command. The file, named xorg.conf.new, will be in your local directory. Make any necessary tweaks, rename the file, move the file to its proper location, and restart the X server.

The xorg.conf file has several sections. Each section contains important configuration information as follows:

- Input Device: Configures the session's keyboard and mouse
- Monitor: Sets the session's monitor configuration
- Modes: Defines video modes
- Device: Configures the session's video card(s)
- Screen: Sets the session's screen resolution and color depth
- Module: Denotes any modules that need to be loaded
- Files: Sets file path names, if needed, for fonts, modules, and keyboard layout files
- Server Flags: Configures global X server options
- Server Layout: Links together all the session's input and output devices

Keep in mind that many desktop environments also provide dialog boxes in their UI, which allow you to configure your GUI X sessions. Most likely you will have little to no need to ever create or tweak the X11 configuration file. However, if you want to dig into the X11 configuration file's details, view its man page by issuing the **man 5 xorg.conf** command.

 While most desktop environments use their own display manager, the X display manager is a basic one available for use. It employs the X Display Manager Control Protocol (XDMCP). The main configuration file is /etc/X11/xdm/xdm-config.

If you need to troubleshoot X problems, two utilities can help: xdpyinfo and xwininfo. The xdpyinfo command provides information about the X server, including the different screen types available, the default communication parameter values, protocol extension information, and so on.

The xwininfo utility is focused on providing window information. If no options are given, an interactive utility asks you to click the window for which you desire statistics. The displayed stats include location information, the window's dimensions (width and height), color map ID, and so on.

Be aware that the `xwininfo` command will hang if you are running a Wayland session instead of an X session. Press Ctrl+C to exit out of the hung command.

Although Wayland is replacing X as the default display server on many Linux systems, the X server will be around for a while. Thus, understanding them both is invaluable not only for certification purposes but also to work effectively.

Using Remote Desktops

Sitting down at a monitor directly attached to your Linux server is a rarity nowadays. Most servers are either rack-mounted systems in condition-controlled environments or virtual machines running on those rack-mounted systems. To access these servers, a user from a desktop in another room typically employs the text-based OpenSSH utility. However, there are times you need a fully functional desktop environment.

Remote desktop software uses a client-server model. The server runs on the remote Linux system, and the client runs on the local system. For example, say you need to access a Linux virtual machine located on a server somewhere else in the office building. You could use your laptop, which is running the remote desktop client software, to log into the Linux virtual machine, which is running the remote desktop server software, and get a full-fledged desktop experience over the network.

In the following sections we'll take a look at some common remote desktop implementations for Linux. They include VNC, Xrdp, NX, and SPICE.

Viewing VNC

Virtual Network Computing (VNC) was developed by the Olivetti & Oracle Research Lab. It is multiplatform and employs the Remote Frame Buffer (RFB) protocol. This protocol allows a user on the client side to send GUI commands, such as mouse clicks, to the server. The server sends desktop frames back to the client's monitor. RealVNC Ltd., which consists of the original VNC project team developers, now trademarks VNC.

If you are using KVM virtual machines (covered in Chapters 28 and 29), then typically, by default, you access their desktop environment via VNC. However, there are other options available, such as SPICE, which is covered later in this chapter.

The VNC server offers a GUI service at TCP port 5900 + n, where n equals the display number, usually 1 (port 5901). On the command line, you point the VNC client (called a *viewer*) to the VNC server's hostname and TCP port. Alternatively, you can use the display number instead of the whole TCP port number. The client user is required to enter a predetermined password, which is for the VNC server, not Linux system authentication. Once the client user has authenticated with VNC, the user is served up the desktop environment's display manager output so that system authentication can take place.

The VNC server is flexible in that you can also use a Java-enabled web browser to access it. It provides that service at TCP port 5800 + *n*. HTML5 client web browsers are supported as well.

Two types of desktop UIs are available for VNC clients: persistent and static. Persistent desktops are UIs that do not change when presented. This is similar to a local desktop experience; the user has certain windows open, the user locks the screen and engages in an activity away from the local system, the user comes back and unlocks the screen, and the user finds the GUI in the exact same state it was left in. Persistent desktops are available only via web browser access. Static desktops do not provide a saved-state GUI.

The following are positive benefits when using VNC:

- It has lots of flexibility in providing remote desktops.
- Desktops are available for multiple users.
- Both persistent and static desktops are available.
- It can provide desktops on an on-demand basis.
- A SSH tunnel can be employed via `ssh` or a client viewer command-line option to encrypt traffic.

The following are potential difficulties or concerns with VNC:

- The VNC server only handles mouse movements and keystrokes. It does not deal with file and audio transfer or printing services for the client.
- VNC, by default, does not provide traffic encryption, so you must employ another means of protection, such as tunneling through OpenSSH.
- The VNC server password is stored as plain text in a server file.

Besides VNC, there are alternatives that implement the VNC technology. A popular implementation of VNC for Linux is TigerVNC (`https://tigervnc.org`). It also works on Windows, so you can connect to either a remote Linux or remote Windows system. For installing the server on a Linux system, use the `tigervnc-server` package name. You'll need to perform some setup to prepare for clients and configure the server to provide the proper client requirements. There are several excellent tutorials on the web. If you want to install the VNC client, just use the `tigervnc` package name.

When accessing a remote desktop via commands at the command line, be sure to use a terminal emulator in the GUI environment. If you attempt to use a text-mode terminal outside the GUI to issue these commands, you will not be successful.

Once you have the TigerVNC server installed, you control it with the `vncserver` and `vncconfig` commands. After making the appropriate server firewall modifications, the client can use the `vncviewer` command to connect to the server system and get a remote desktop. For example, say a server (`example.com`) has been configured properly to serve a remote desktop to you at display number 1. You would access the desktop from another system via the `vncviewer example.com:1` command. Figure 8.7 shows a TigerVNC connection from a Fedora system into a CentOS server, which is providing the user with a GNOME Shell desktop environment.

FIGURE 8.7   Using TigerVNC

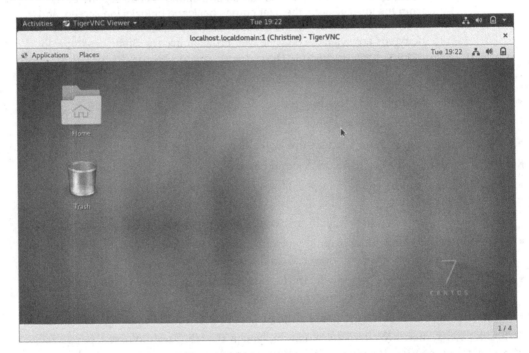

When configuring your VNC server, be sure to employ OpenSSH port forwarding for the VNC server ports (covered later in this chapter.) Also configure your firewalls to allow traffic through port 22 (or whatever port number you are using for SSH traffic).

Grasping Xrdp

Xrdp is an alternative to VNC. It supports the Remote Desktop Protocol (RDP). It uses X11rdp or Xvnc to manage the GUI session.

Xrdp provides only the server side of an RDP connection. It allows access from several RDP client implementations, such as rdesktop, FreeFDP, and Microsoft Remote Desktop Connection.

Xrdp comes systemd ready, so you can simply install, enable, and start the server using the `systemctl` commands. The package name on Linux is `xrdp`. Note that it may not be in your Linux distribution's standard repositories.

After installing and starting the Xrdp server, adjust the firewall so that traffic can access the standard RDP port (TCP 3389). Now direct your RDP client choice to the server via its hostname or IP address and, if necessary, provide the client with the RDP port number.

Depending on your RDP client, you may be presented with a screen that denotes that the server is not trusted. If this is the server you just set up, you are fine to continue. You will need to enter the Linux system's user authentication information, but the login screen depends on the Xrdp client software you are using. An example of Xrdp in action is shown in Figure 8.8.

FIGURE 8.8   Using Xrdp

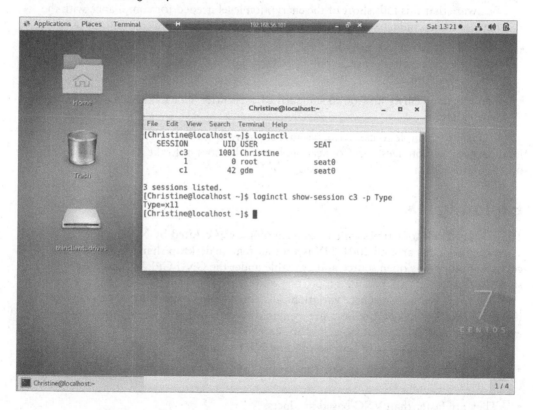

Figure 8.8 shows a connection from a Windows 10 system to a CentOS 7 Linux server, which is running the Xrdp server. Notice the output from the commands run in the terminal emulator. You can see that an X11 session is being deployed.

The following are positive benefits of using Xrdp:

- Xrdp uses RDP, which encrypts its traffic using TLS.

- A wide variety of open source RDP client software is available.

- You can connect to an already existing connection to provide a persistent desktop.

- Xrdp Server handles mouse movements and keystrokes as well as audio transfers and mounting of local client drives on the remote system.

You can determine the various Xrdp configuration settings in the `/etc/xrdp/xrdp.ini` file. An important setting in this file is the `security_layer` directive. If set to `negotiate`, the default, the Xrdp server will negotiate with the client for the security method to use. Three methods are available:

- `tls` provides SSL (TLS 1.0) encryption for server authentication and data transfer. Be aware that this falls short of the encryption level needed for compliance with the Payment Card Industry (PCI) standards.

- `negotiate` sets the security method to be the highest the client can use. This is problematic if the connection is over a public network and the client must use the Standard RDP Security method.

- `rdp` sets the security method to standard RDP Security. This method is not safe from network attacks.

Xrdp is fairly simple to use. Also, because so many Windows-oriented users are already familiar with Remote Desktop Connection, it typically does not take long to employ it in the office environment.

Exploring NX

The NX protocol, sometimes called NX technology, was created by NoMachine (www .nomachine.com) around 2001. NX is another remote desktop sharing protocol. Its v3.5 core technology was open source and available under the GNU GPL2 license. Yet when version 4 was released, NX became proprietary and closed source.

However, several open source variations are available based on the NX3 technology, including FreeNX and X2Go. Both are available on various Linux distributions but not necessarily in their default software repositories.

The following are positive benefits of using NX products:

- They provide excellent response times, even over low-bandwidth connections that have high-latency issues.

- They are faster than VNC-based products.

- They use OpenSSH tunneling by default, so traffic is encrypted.

- They support multiple simultaneous users through a single network port.

NX technology compresses the X11 data so that there is less data to send over the network, which improves response times. It also heavily employs caching data to provide an improved remote desktop experience.

Studying SPICE

Another interesting remote connection protocol is Simple Protocol for Independent Computing Environments (SPICE). Originally it was a closed source product developed by Qumranet in 2007. However, Red Hat purchased Qumranet in 2008 and made SPICE open source. Its website is at `www.spice-space.org`.

SPICE (sometimes written as Spice) was developed to provide a good remote desktop product that would allow connections to your various virtual machines. Now, typically SPICE is used primarily for providing connections with KVM virtual machines, moving into VNC's territory.

 Both VNC and Spice provide remote desktop connections to KVM virtual machines. Virtual machines are covered in more detail in Chapters 28 and 29.

SPICE is platform independent and has some nice additional features as well:

- SPICE's client side uses multiple data socket connections, and you can have multiple clients.

- It delivers desktop experience speeds similar to a local connection.

- It consumes low amounts of CPU so that you can use it with various servers that have multiple virtual machines and not adversely affect their performance.

- It allows high-quality video streaming.

- It provides live migration features, which means there are no connection interruptions if the virtual machine is being migrated to a new host.

While SPICE has a single server implementation, it has several client implementations. These include remote-viewer and GNOME Boxes.

Another benefit of employing SPICE is its strong security features. Transmitted data can either be sent plain text or have its traffic encrypted using TLS. Authentication between the SPICE client and remote SPICE server is implemented using Simple Authentication and Security Layer (SASL). This framework allows various authentication methods, as long as they are supported by SASL. Kerberos is a supported method.

If you are still dealing with X11, you can use Xspice. X.Org-created Xspice acts as a stand-alone SPICE server as well as an X server.

Forwarding

Providing data access to only those who are authorized is imperative. Whether it's sending plaintext data or remote desktop GUI client-server interaction information, both need to be secured across the network.

One way to provide security is via *SSH port forwarding*, sometimes called *SSH tunneling*. SSH port forwarding allows you to redirect a connection from one particular network port to port 22, where the SSH service is waiting to receive it. This allows data traffic to move back and forth through a secure encrypted tunnel, similar to a virtual private network (VPN).

To use SSH port forwarding, you must have the OpenSSH service installed and enabled on your Linux system. Fortunately, most distributions come with this service already available. You can check to see if it is running by using the `systemctl` command, covered in Chapter 6, "Maintaining System Startup and Services." In Listing 8.1, a check of the OpenSSH service on a system is conducted. It shows that OpenSSH is `active` (running) as well as `enabled` (will start at boot time).

Listing 8.1 Checking the OpenSSH service status

```
$ systemctl is-active sshd
active
$ systemctl is-enabled sshd
enabled
$
```

If your system does not have the OpenSSH server, you can typically install both the server and client via the openssh package. Chapter 13, "Governing Software," discusses installing and managing Linux packages.

Another item to check before attempting SSH port forwarding is the OpenSSH configuration file, `/etc/ssh/sshd_config`. The directive `AllowTcpForwarding` should be set to yes. If the directive is set to no, you must modify it to employ SSH port forwarding. In Listing 8.2, a check is performed on the configuration file for this directive on an openSUSE distribution.

Listing 8.2 Checking the `AllowTCPForwarding` directive

```
$ sudo grep "AllowTcpForwarding yes" /etc/ssh/sshd_config
#AllowTcpForwarding yes
$
```

Notice in Listing 8.2 that the directive is commented out by a pound sign (#). This is not a problem because, by default, `AllowTcpFowarding` is set to yes.

SSH port forwarding comes in the following three flavors:

- Local
- Remote
- Dynamic

Each of these varieties allows you to perform various types of tunneled traffic. However, since we are focusing on the GUI environment, we'll only cover local and remote SSH port forwarding for remote desktops.

Local

Local port forwarding sends traffic from the OpenSSH client on your system to the client's OpenSSH server. The client's OpenSSH server then forwards that traffic on to the destination server through a secured tunnel. In other words, the outbound traffic is rerouted to a different outbound port and tunneled through OpenSSH before leaving the client system.

To enact this on the command line, the `-L` option of the `ssh` command is used along with some additional arguments. Concerning remote desktops, the command has the following syntax:

```
ssh -L local-port:127.0.0.1:remote-port -Nf user@destination-host
```

In the command's syntax are the following arguments:

- `destination-host` is the computer you are logging into in order to use the desktop environment residing there.
- `user` is the desktop host username you wish to use to authenticate so that the secure tunnel can be established.
- `local-port` is the application's port number you are employing on the client side.
- `remote-port` is the port where the application is listening on the destination host.
- `127.0.0.1` designates that you are using a local SSH port forwarding method.

Keep in mind that this command only establishes the tunnel; it does not provide a remote desktop connection. Therefore, there are two additional important command options: the `-N` option lets OpenSSH know that no remote terminal process is desired, and the `-f` option indicates that after the user is authenticated to the server, the `ssh` command should move into the background. These two options allow the user to issue additional commands, such as a remote desktop command, after the secured tunnel is established.

A practical example can be described using VNC. Recall that VNC uses port $5900 + n$, where n equals the display number. Thus, if on the remote system your desktop is available at display 2, you can issue the following command to use SSH port forwarding and forward your local VNC port 5901 to the remote hosts' port 5902:

```
ssh -L 5901:127.0.0.1:5902 -Nf Doug@example.com
```

Once the tunnel is established, you can use the VNC remote desktop commands to access and view your desktop environment on the remote host. Keep in mind that you will need to perform some firewall configurations to allow access to the remote host.

Fortunately TigerVNC provides a much simpler method for local SSH port forwarding. Just employ the `-via localhost` option on the `vncviewer` command, as shown in Figure 8.9.

FIGURE 8.9   Using local SSH port forwarding with TigerVNC

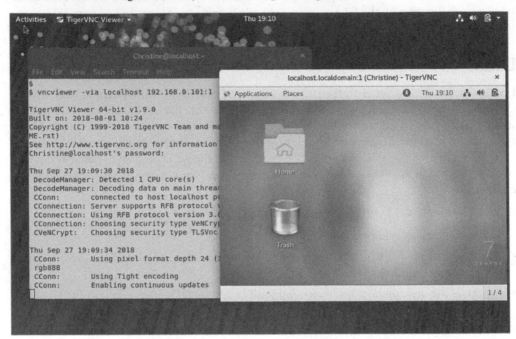

The `-via localhost` option used in conjunction with the `vncviewer` command forces the connection to use local SSH port forwarding. The last command argument is the destination host's IPv4 address (you could also use a hostname), followed by a colon and the remote desktop's display number (1). This is far easier to use and certainly requires fewer commands and options.

Remote

The remote SSH port forwarding method starts at the destination host (server), as opposed to the remote client. Therefore, on the destination host, you create the remote desktop secure tunnel with the following command syntax:

```
ssh -R local-port:127.0.0.1:remote-port -Nf user@client-host
```

There are some important differences in this command from the local method:

- The `-R` option is used instead of the `-L` option.
- *client-host* is the remote client's IP address or hostname (where you will issue the remote desktop commands).
- *local-port* is the port number you use on the *client-host* with the `vncviewer` command.
- *remote-port* is on the remote desktop server.

Tunneling Your X11 Connection

Another method that provides remote GUI interactions within a secure tunnel is *X11 forwarding*. X11 forwarding allows you to interact with various X11-based graphical utilities on a remote system through an encrypted network connection. This method is also enacted using the OpenSSH service.

First you need to see if X11 forwarding is permitted. This setting is in the OpenSSH configuration file, /etc/ssh/sshd_config. The directive X11Forwarding should be set to yes in the remote system's configuration file. If the directive is set to no, then you must modify it to employ X11 forwarding. In Listing 8.3, a check is performed on the configuration file for this directive on a CentOS distribution.

Listing 8.3 Checking the AllowTCPForwarding directive

```
# grep "X11Forwarding yes" /etc/ssh/sshd_config
X11Forwarding yes
#
```

Once you have made any necessary configuration file modifications, the command to use is ssh -X *user@remote-host*. Similar to earlier ssh command uses, *user* is the user account that resides on the *remote-host* system. *remote-host* has the GUI utilities you wish to employ and can be designated via an IP address or a hostname. Figure 8.10 shows connecting from a remote Fedora client to a CentOS server and using a graphical utility on that server.

FIGURE 8.10   Forwarding X11

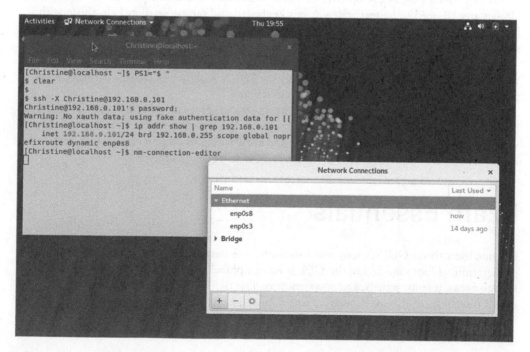

It's always a good idea to check your IP address to ensure that you have successfully reached the remote system. In Figure 8.10, the `ip addr show` command is employed for this purpose. Once you have completed your work, just type **exit** to log out of the X11 forwarding session.

WARNING   You may read about using X11 forwarding via the `ssh -Y` command, which is called trusted X11. This does not mean the connection is more secure. In fact, it is quite the opposite. When employing this command, you are treating the remote server as a trusted system. This can cause many security issues and should be avoided.

Summary

Creating, managing, and troubleshooting a GUI environment for yourself and the system's users involves an important skill set. You need to understand the distinct desktop environments, their supporting frameworks, and how to transmit them safely and securely across the network.

The various desktop environments, such as GNOME Shell, KDE Plasma, MATE, Cinnamon, and Unity, provide many various environments to meet different needs and tastes. The currently evolving world of display servers, which include primarily Wayland and the older X11, support these GUI desktops.

Linux provides GUI desktop environments with many accessibility features, which allow almost any UI need to be met. The various keyboard and mouse settings help those with hand or finger difficulties. There are also many utilities for the vision impaired, including screen readers and zoom features.

Accessing a GUI across the network is accomplished through remote desktop software. VNC, Xrdp, and NX are a few examples. SPICE is unique in that its primary focus is providing remote desktop access to virtual machines.

Whether you are accessing a rack-mounted physical server or a virtual machine running on that server, it is important to secure the remote desktop connection. This is accomplished with SSH port forwarding and, if needed, X11 forwarding. If employed correctly, both allow an encrypted tunnel for data and GUI interactions to travel securely.

Exam Essentials

Outline the various GUI sections and functions.   A desktop environment provides a predetermined look and feel to the GUI. It has graphical sections, such as a favorites bar, launch areas, menus, panels, and a system tray. The GUI also has typical functions like desktop settings, a display manager, a file manager, icons to access programs, widgets, and a window manager.

Describe the various GUI desktop environments.   The primary desktop environments used for current Linux distributions include GNOME Shell, KDE Plasma, MATE, and Cinnamon.

Summarize available universal access utilities.   The distinct accessibility tools are located in menus or panels. These panels have various locations around the desktop environments and have names like Universal Access, Accessibility, Assistive Technologies, and so on. It is best to use a desktop environment's search feature to locate them. The various access tools for vision-impaired users include cursor blinking, cursor size, contract modifications, text size enlargement, sound keys, zoom functions, and screen readers. For those individuals who need access to braille technologies, the `brltty` software is available. Displayed windows can be set to flash instead of providing a sound alert for those who are hearing impaired. When someone has trouble using the keyboard, there are many settings available, such as bounce keys, repeat keys, screen keyboard, slow keys, and sticky keys. For mouse use difficulties, the tools to explore are double-click delays, gestures, hover clicks, mouse keys, and simulated secondary clicks.

Explain the display servers' role.   A display server is a program or program group that uses a communication protocol to convey information between the GUI and the operating system. The communication protocol is called the display server protocol and can operate over a network. One critical program used with the display server is the compositor. The compositor arranges display elements within a window to create a screen image. Two important display servers are Wayland and X11. X11 is an older display server, which has been around for a while. Wayland is a newer display server, which adds many needed security features and is easier to maintain.

Describe the available remote desktop software.   Remote desktop software provides a fully functioning desktop environment over the network from a remote server. It uses a client-server model, and there are several packages from which to choose. They include VNC, Xrdp, NX, and SPICE.

Summarize SSH port and X11 forwarding.   SSH port forwarding, sometimes called SSH tunneling, redirects a connection from one particular network port to the SSH service at port 22. This allows data traffic to move back and forth through a secure encrypted tunnel, similar to a virtual private network (VPN). SSH port forwarding has three distinct methods: local, remote, and dynamic. Besides SSH port forwarding, X11 forwarding is also available. It also provides a secure tunnel for GUI interactions. However, instead of a full desktop environment, you can start X11-based graphical utilities from the remote system's command line.

Review Questions

1. Which of the following best describes a desktop environment?
   A. A set of programs that allow a user to interact with the system via icons, windows, and various other visual elements
   B. A screen where you choose a username and enter a password to gain system access
   C. A series of components that work together to provide the graphical setting for the user interface
   D. A program that allows you to perform file maintenance activities graphically
   E. A set of programs that determine how the windows are presented on the desktop

2. Which of the following are GUI components? (Choose all that apply.)
   A. Favorites bar
   B. File manager
   C. Icons
   D. Command line
   E. System tray

3. Which of the following is not used by default within GNOME Shell?
   A. SDDM
   B. Files
   C. Mutter
   D. GDM
   E. Dock

4. Which of the following is the KDE Plasma files manager?
   A. Nautilus
   B. Plasmoid
   C. Dolphin
   D. Kwin
   E. Nemo

5. Which of the following is true concerning the MATE desktop environment? (Choose all that apply.)
   A. MATE is a GNOME Shell fork.
   B. MATE uses Metacity as its window manager.
   C. MATE's display manager is LightDM.
   D. MATE's file manager is Caja.
   E. MATE is no longer being developed.

6. Which of the following describes the sound keys accessibility setting?

    A. Sounds are made when the Caps Lock or Num Lock key is turned on or off.

    B. A program that reads the GUI aloud, such as Orca.

    C. A cursor blink rate modification to make it easier to locate the cursor on the screen.

    D. Output to a refreshable braille display that is provided by the Orca screen reader.

    E. The screen or a screen portion is amplified to different magnification levels.

7. A blind coworker who is programming on the Linux server is suddenly having odd problems with his braille display device. You determine that you need to restart the braille service. Assuming the appropriate systemd unit file is available, which command would you use?

    A. `systemctl restart braille`

    B. `systemctl reload braille`

    C. `systemctl restart brailled`

    D. `systemctl restart brltty`

    E. `systemctl reload brltty`

8. Which of the following best describes the slow keys accessibility setting?

    A. A keyboard option that modifies how long a key must be pressed down to acknowledge the key

    B. A keyboard option that sets keyboard modifier keys, such as Ctrl and Shift, to maintain their pressed status until a subsequent key is pressed

    C. A keyboard option that modifies how long a key must be pressed down and that defines a delay to acknowledge the key repeat

    D. A keyboard option that sets a primary key to be pressed along with a mouse click to emulate secondary mouse clicks

    E. A keyboard option that displays a visual keyboard on the UI that can be manipulated by a mouse or other pointing device to emulate keystrokes

9. Which of the following communicates with the Linux operating system to transmit the UI wants and needs?

    A. Window manager

    B. Display manager

    C. Desktop environment

    D. Windows server

    E. Display server

10. Which of the following is true of a compositor? (Choose all that apply.)

    A. A compositor arranges various display elements within a window to create a screen image.

    B. Wayland is a compositor.

    C. Mutter contains a compositor.

    D. Kwin contains a compositor.

    E. Weston is a compositor.

11. Which of the following are true concerning Wayland? (Choose all that apply.)
    A. Currently X11 is more secure than Wayland.
    B. Wayland uses the $WAYLAND_DISPLAY environment variable.
    C. Wayland's only compositor is Weston.
    D. XWayland supports legacy X11 programs.
    E. Set WaylandDisable to true to disable Wayland in GNOME Shell.

12. Which of the following commands will help you determine whether your display server is Wayland or X11?
    A. $WAYLAND_DISPLAY
    B. echo $AccessX
    C. loginctl
    D. echo $X11
    E. runlevel

13. You use the command gnome-shell --replace at the command line and receive an error message from the utility. What does this indicate?
    A. The X11 display server is hung. You need to reboot the server.
    B. The --replace option should be swapped for the -R option.
    C. Your display server is Wayland.
    D. XWayland is currently being used.
    E. Wayland has been disabled for this session.

14. Which of the following is true concerning X11? (Choose all that apply.)
    A. XFree86 is the dominant X server.
    B. X.Org foundation develops an X server.
    C. The X server is being replaced by Wayland.
    D. X11 means a user can have 11 sessions.
    E. X is short for X Window System.

15. Your system is running an X display server and a user's graphical user interface is not acting properly. Which of the following commands can you use first to diagnose potential problems? (Choose all that apply.)
    A. xwininfo
    B. Xorg -configure
    C. xcpyinfo
    D. xdpyinfo
    E. loginctl

16. Which of the following are remote desktops? (Choose all that apply.)

    A. SPICE

    B. NX

    C. Xrdp

    D. VNC

    E. Caja

17. Which of the following are remote desktops typically used with virtual machines? (Choose all that apply.)

    A. SPICE

    B. NX

    C. Xrdp

    D. VNC

    E. All of the above

18. Which of the following protocols does Xrdp employ?

    A. Remote Frame Buffer protocol

    B. Wayland protocol

    C. NX technology protocol

    D. Simple protocol for ICEs

    E. Remote Desktop Protocol

19. You want to employ SSH port forwarding and use its local mode. Which `ssh` command switches should you employ? (Choose all that apply.)

    A. `-N`

    B. `-X`

    C. `-f`

    D. `-R`

    E. `-L`

20. You (username Samantha) are logged into a laptop (IP address 192.168.0.42) running a Linux GNOME Classic desktop environment at your company desk in Building A. A problem has occurred on a rack-mounted Linux system (IP address 192.168.0.7) in Building C. You need to securely access a GUI application on the remote system that uses X11. What command should you use?

    A. `ssh -Y Samantha@192.168.0.7`

    B. `ssh -X Samantha@192.168.0.7`

    C. `ssh -Y Samantha@192.168.0.42`

    D. `ssh -X Samantha@192.168.0.42`

    E. `ssh -L Samantha@192.168.0.42`

Chapter

9

Adjusting Localization Options

✓ **Objective 1.7: Given a scenario, manage software configurations**

Linux has become a worldwide phenomenon. You'll find Linux desktops and servers all over the world, in many different kinds of environments. However, because of its worldwide popularity, Linux must support a wide variety of languages, date and time formats, and monetary formats.

This chapter walks through how to configure your Linux system to blend in with the local environment where it's running. First, the chapter discusses how Linux handles different language characters, including how it formats monetary values. Then it moves on to how Linux handles times and dates as used in different countries.

Understanding Localization

The world is full of different languages. Not only does each country have its own language (or sometimes, sets of languages), each country has its own way for people to write numerical values, monetary values, and the time and date. For a Linux system to be useful in any specific location, it must adapt to the local way of doing all those things.

Localization is the ability to adapt a Linux system to a specific locale. To accomplish this, the Linux system must have a way to identify how to handle the characters contained in the local language. The following sections discuss just how Linux does that.

Character Sets

At their core, computers work with ones and zeros, and Linux is no different. However, for a computer to interact with humans, it needs to know how to speak our language. This is where character sets come in.

A *character set* defines a standard code used to interpret and display characters in a language. There are quite a few different character sets used in the world for representing characters. Here are the most common ones you'll run into (and the ones you'll see on the Linux+ exam):

- *ASCII:* The American Standard Code for Information Interchange (ASCII) uses 7 bits to store characters found in the English language.

- *Unicode:* An international standard that uses a 3-byte code and can represent every character known to be in use in all countries of the world.

- *UTF:* The Unicode Transformation Format (UTF), which transforms the long Unicode values into either 1-byte (*UTF-8*) or 2-byte (*UTF-16*) simplified codes. For work in English-speaking countries, the UTF-8 character set is replacing ASCII as the standard.

Once you've decided on a character set for your Linux system, you'll need to know how to configure your Linux system to use it, which is shown in the following section.

Environment Variables

Linux stores locale information in a special set of environment variables (see Chapter 25, "Deploying Bash Scripts"). Programs that need to determine the locale of the Linux system just need to retrieve the appropriate environment variable to see what character set to use.

Linux provides the *locale* command to help you easily display these environment variables. Listing 9.1 shows the locale environment variables as set on a Rocky Linux system installed in the United States.

Listing 9.1 The Linux locale environment variables

```
$ locale
LANG=en_US.UTF-8
LC_CTYPE="en_US.UTF-8"
LC_NUMERIC="en_US.UTF-8"
LC_TIME="en_US.UTF-8"
LC_COLLATE="en_US.UTF-8"
LC_MONETARY="en_US.UTF-8"
LC_MESSAGES="en_US.UTF-8"
LC_PAPER="en_US.UTF-8"
LC_NAME="en_US.UTF-8"
LC_ADDRESS="en_US.UTF-8"
LC_TELEPHONE="en_US.UTF-8"
LC_MEASUREMENT="en_US.UTF-8"
LC_IDENTIFICATION="en_US.UTF-8"
LC_ALL=
$
```

The output of the `locale` command defines the localization information in this format:

language_country.character set

In the example shown in Listing 9.1, the Linux system is configured for United States English, using the UTF-8 character set to store characters.

Each *LC_* environment variable itself represents a category of more environment variables that relate to the locale settings. You can explore the environment variables contained within a category by using the `-ck` option, along with the category name, as shown in Listing 9.2.

Listing 9.2 The detailed settings for the `LC_MONETARY` localization category

```
$ locale -ck LC_MONETARY
LC_MONETARY
int_curr_symbol="USD "
```

```
currency_symbol="$"
mon_decimal_point="."
mon_thousands_sep=","
mon_grouping=3;3
positive_sign=""
negative_sign="-"
. . .
monetary-decimal-point-wc=46
monetary-thousands-sep-wc=44
monetary-codeset="UTF-8"
$
```

The environment variables shown in Listing 9.2 control what characters and formats are used for representing monetary values. Programmers can fine-tune each of the individual environment variables to customize exactly how their programs behave within the locale.

Setting Your Locale

As shown in Listing 9.1, there are three components to how Linux handles localization. A locale defines the language, the country, and the character set the system uses. Linux provides a few different ways for you to change each of these localization settings.

Installation Locale Decisions

When you first install the Linux operating system, one of the prompts available during the installation process is for the default system language. Figure 9.1 shows the prompt from a Rocky Linux 8 installation.

When you select a language from the menu, the Linux installation script automatically sets the localization environment variables appropriately for that country and language to include the character set necessary to represent the required characters. Often that's all you need to do to set up your Linux system to operate correctly in your locale.

Changing Your Locale

After you've already installed the Linux operating system, you can still change the localization values that the system uses. There are two methods available to do that. You can manually set the LC_ environment variables, or you can use the localectl command.

FIGURE 9.1   The language option in a Rocky Linux 8 installation

FIGURE 9.1   The language option in a Rocky Linux 8 installation

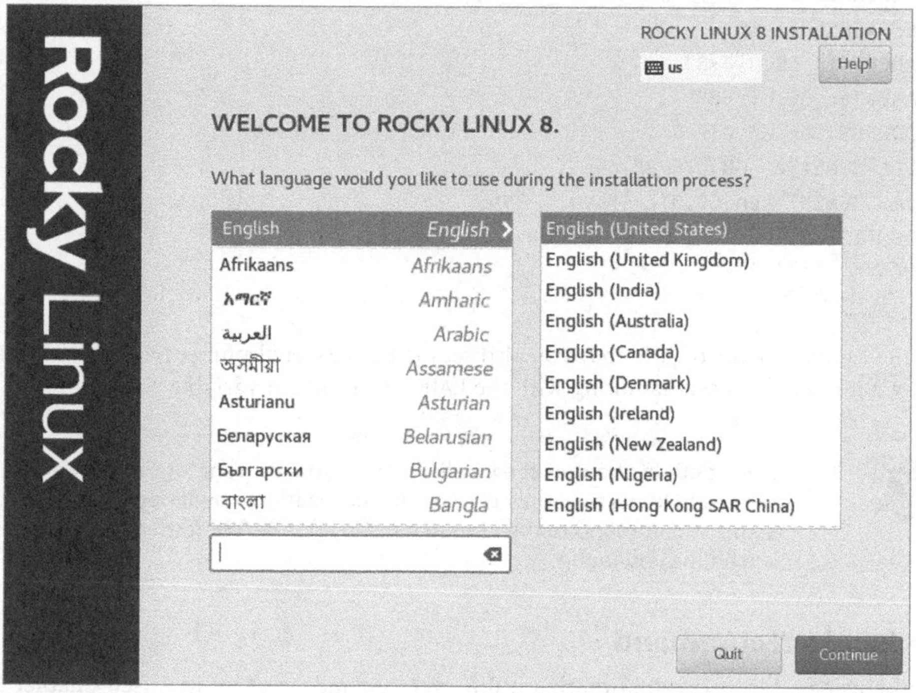

Manually Changing the Environment Variables

For the manual method, change the individual LC_ localization environment variables just as you would any other environment variable, by using the export command:

```
$ export LC_MONETARY=en_GB.UTF-8
```

That works well for changing individual settings, but it would be tedious if you wanted to change all the localization settings for the system.

Instead of having to change all of the LC_ environment variables individually, the LANG environment variable controls all of them at one place:

```
$ export LANG=en_GB.UTF-8
$ locale
LANG=en_GB.UTF-8
LC_CTYPE="en_GB.UTF-8"
LC_NUMERIC="en_GB.UTF-8"
LC_TIME="en_GB.UTF-8"
```

```
LC_COLLATE="en_GB.UTF-8"
LC_MONETARY="en_GB.UTF-8"
LC_MESSAGES="en_GB.UTF-8"
LC_PAPER="en_GB.UTF-8"
LC_NAME="en_GB.UTF-8"
LC_ADDRESS="en_GB.UTF-8"
LC_TELEPHONE="en_GB.UTF-8"
LC_MEASUREMENT="en_GB.UTF-8"
LC_IDENTIFICATION="en_GB.UTF-8"
LC_ALL=
$
```

Some Linux systems require that you also set the LC_ALL environment variable, so it's usually a good idea to set that along with the LANG environment variable.

 This method changes the localization for your current login session. If you need to permanently change the localization, you'll need to add the export command to the .bashrc file in your $HOME folder so that it runs each time you log in.

The *localectl* command

If you're using a Linux distribution that utilizes the systemd set of utilities (see Chapter 6, "Maintaining System Startup and Services"), you have the localectl command available. By default, the *localectl* command just displays the current localization settings:

```
$ localectl
   System Locale: LANG=en_US.UTF-8
       VC Keymap: us
      X11 Layout: us
$
```

Not only does it show the LANG environment variable setting, it also shows the keyboard layout mapping as well as the X11 graphical environment layout.

The localectl command supports many options, but the most common are to list all the locales installed on your system with the list-locales option and to change the localization by using the set-locale option:

```
$ localectl set-locale LANG=en_GB.utf8
```

That makes for an easy way to change the localization settings for your entire Linux system.

Looking at Time

The date and time associated with a Linux system are crucial to the proper operation of the system. Linux uses the date and time to keep track of running processes, to know when to start or stop jobs, and in logging important events that occur. Having your Linux system coordinated with the correct time and date for your location is a must.

Linux handles the time as two parts—the time zone associated with the location of the system and the actual time and date within that time zone. The following sections walk through how to change both values.

Working with Time Zones

One of the most important aspects of time is the *time zone*. Each country selects one or more time zones, or offsets from the standard Coordinated Universal Time (UTC) time, to determine time within the country. If your Linux environment includes having servers located in different time zones, knowing how to set the proper time zone is a must.

Most Debian-based Linux systems define the local time zone in the */etc/timezone* file, while most Red Hat–based Linux systems use */etc/localtime*. These files are not in a text format, so you can't simply edit the /etc/timezone or /etc/localtime file to view or change your time zone. Instead, you must link that file to a template file stored in the */usr/share/zoneinfo* folder.

To determine the current time zone setting for your Linux system, use the date command, with no options:

```
$ date
Sat Dec  4 08:20:23 EST 2021
$
```

The time zone appears as the standard three-letter code at the end of the date and time display, before the year.

To view the current time zone template file that the system is using, just use the ls command to display the active time zone file:

```
$ ls -al /etc/localtime
lrwxrwxrwx. 1 root root 38 Nov 30 09:06 /etc/localtime -> ../usr/share/
zoneinfo/America/New_York
$
```

To change the time zone for a Linux system, link the appropriate time zone template file from the /usr/share/zoneinfo folder to the /etc/timezone or /etc/localtime location. The /usr/share/zoneinfo folder is divided into subfolders based on location. Each location folder may also be subdivided into more detailed location folders. Eventually, you'll see a time zone template file associated with your specific time zone, such as /usr/share/zoneinfo/US/Eastern.

Before you can copy the new time zone file, you'll need to remove the original `timezone` or `localtime` file:

```
$ sudo ln -s /usr/share/zoneinfo/America/Chicago /etc/localtime
$ date
Sat Dec  4 07:23:14 CST 2021
$
```

The new time zone appears in the output from the `date` command.

If you just need to change the time zone for a single session or program, instead of changing the system time zone you can set the time zone using the TZ environment variable. That overrides the system time zone for the current session.

Setting the Time and Date

Once you have the correct time zone for your Linux system, you can work on setting the correct time and date values. There are a few different commands available to do that.

Legacy Commands

There are two legacy commands that you should be able to find in all Linux distributions for working with time and date values:

- *hwclock* displays or sets the time as kept on the internal BIOS or UEFI clock on the workstation or server.

- *date* displays or sets the date as kept by the Linux system.

The `hwclock` command provides access to the hardware clock built into the physical workstation or server that the Linux system runs on. You can use the `hwclock` command to set the system time and date to the hardware clock on the physical workstation or server. Or, it also allows you to change the hardware clock to match the time and date on the Linux system.

The `date` command is the Swiss Army knife of time and date commands. It allows you to display the time and date in a multitude of formats in addition to setting the time and/or date. The + option allows you to specify the format used to display the time or date value by defining command sequences:

```
$ date +"%A, %B %d, %Y"
Saturday, December 04, 2021
$
```

Table 9.1 shows the different command sequences available in the `date` command.

TABLE 9.1   The date format command sequences

Sequence	Description
%a	Abbreviated weekday name
%A	Full weekday name
%b	Abbreviated month name
%B	Full month name
%c	Date and time
%C	Century (e.g., 20)
%d	Numeric day of month
%D	Full numeric date
%e	Day of month, space padded
%F	Full date in SQL format (YYYY-MM-dd)
%g	Last two digits of year of ISO week number
%G	Year of the ISO week number
%h	Alias for %b
%H	Hour in 24-hour format
%I	Hour in 12-hour format
%j	Numeric day of year
%k	Hour in 24-hour format, space padded
%l	Hour in 12-hour format, space padded
%m	Numeric month
%M	Minute
%n	A newline character
%N	Nanoseconds

TABLE 9.1   The date format command sequences *(continued)*

Sequence	Description
%p	AM or PM
%P	Lowercase am or pm
%r	Full 12-hour clock time
%R	Full 24-hour hour and minute
%s	Seconds since 1970-01-01 00:00:00 UTC
%S	Second
%t	A tab character
%T	Full time in hour:minute:second format
%u	Numeric day of week; 1 is Monday
%U	Numeric week number of year, starting on Sunday
%V	ISO week number
%w	Numeric day of week; 0 is Sunday
%W	Week number of year, starting on Monday
%x	Locale's date representation as month/day/year or day/month/year
%X	Locale's full time representation
%y	Last two digits of the year
%Y	Full year
%z	Time zone in +hhmm format
%:z	Time zone in +hh:mm format
%::z	Time zone in +hh:mm:ss format
%:::z	Numeric time zone with : to necessary precision
%Z	Alphabetic time zone abbreviation

As you can see from Table 9.1, the `date` command provides numerous ways for you to display the time and date in your programs and shell scripts.

You can also set the time and date using the `date` command by specifying the value in the following format:

`date MMDDhhmm[[CC]YY][.ss]`

The month, date, hour, and minute values are required, with the year and seconds assumed, or you can include the year and seconds as well if you prefer.

The *timedatectl* Command

If your Linux distribution uses the Systemd set of utilities (see Chapter 6), you can use the *timedatectl* command to manage the time and date settings on your system:

```
$ timedatectl
               Local time: Sat 2021-12-04 08:27:18 EST
           Universal time: Sat 2021-12-04 13:27:18 UTC
                 RTC time: Sat 2021-12-04 13:27:17
                Time zone: America/New_York (EST, -0500)
System clock synchronized: yes
              NTP service: active
           RTC in local TZ: no
$
```

The `timedatectl` command provides one-stop shopping to see all of the time information, including the hardware clock, called RTC, the date information, and the time zone information.

You can also use the `timedatectl` command to modify any of those settings as well by using the `set-time` option:

```
# timedatectl set-time "2021-12-04 08:30:00"
```

You can also use the `timedatectl` command to synchronize the workstation or server hardware clock and the Linux system time.

The Network Time Protocol

These days most Linux systems connected to the Internet utilize the Network Time Protocol (NTP) to keep the time and date synchronized with a centralized time server. If your Linux system does this, you won't be able to alter the time or date by using either the `date` or `timedatectl` command. Instead, you'll need to point your Linux server to an appropriate network time server.

There are three common NTP software implementations used in the Linux world:

- `ntpd`: Legacy software that uses the Simple Network Time Protocol (SNTP) to connect to a network time server

- chrony: An improved version of the ntpd software that utilizes security features
- timesyncd: Part of the Systemd startup utilities package that provides NTP services

The legacy ntpd software technically isn't supported anymore, but due to its simplicity a few Linux distributions still use it. Most Debian-based Linux distributions (including Ubuntu) use the Systemd startup utilities and thus utilize the timesyncd service to provide network time services. Although Red Hat–based systems also use Systemd, Red Hat has chosen to implement the more versatile chrony software to supply network time services.

> The timesyncd software stores its configuration settings in the /etc/systemd/timesyncd.conf file. If multiple configuration files are required, they are stored in the /etc/systemd/timesyncd.conf.d directory. The chrony software stores its configuration settings in the /etc/chrony/chrony.conf configuration file.

Watching System Time

The Linux+ exam also covers the *time* command, although it's not related to the time and date specifically. The time command displays the amount of time it takes for a program to run on the Linux system:

```
$ time timedatectl
Local time: Sat 2021-12-04 08:40:40 EST
Universal time: Sat 2021-12-04 13:40:40 UTC
RTC time: Sat 2021-12-04 13:40:38
Time zone: America/New_York (EST, -0500)
System clock synchronized: yes
NTP service: active
RTC in local TZ: no

real    0m0.037s
user    0m0.004s
sys     0m0.006s
$
```

After the normal command output, you'll see three additional lines of information:

- real: The elapsed amount of time between the start and end of the program
- user: The amount of user CPU time the program took
- sys: The amount of system CPU time the program took

This information can be invaluable when you're troubleshooting programs that seem to take additional system resources to process.

Exercise 9.1 walks through using the different locale, time, and date functions you have available in Linux.

EXERCISE 9.1

Experimenting with Time

This exercise will demonstrate how to check the current time, date, and time zone on your Linux system.

1. Log in as root, or acquire root privileges by using su or by using sudo with each of the following commands.

2. Type **locale** to display the current localization settings for your system. Write down the current character set assigned for your system.

3. Change the localization to another country, such as Great Britain, by setting the LANG environment variable. Type **export LANG=en_GB.UTF-8** to make the change.

4. Type **locale** to display the updated localization settings.

5. If your Linux distribution uses the Systemd utilities, type **localectl** to display the system localization defined on your system.

6. Change the localization by typing **localectl set-locale "LANG=en_GB_UTF-8"**.

7. Change the localization back to your normal locale by using either the **locale** or the **localectl** command.

8. Display the current date and time on your system by typing the **date** command.

9. Observe how long it takes to run the date command on your Linux system by typing **time date**. The output shows how long it took your Linux system to process the request.

Summary

The Linux system supports many different languages by incorporating different character sets. A character set defines how the Linux system displays and uses the characters contained in the language. While Linux supports many different character sets, the most common ones are ASCII, Unicode, UTF-8, and UTF-16. The ASCII character set is only useful for English language characters, whereas the UTF-8 and UTF-16 character sets are commonly used to support other languages.

The Linux system maintains the character set settings as a set of environment variables that begin with LC_. The locale command displays all the localization environment variables. Each individual LC_ environment variable represents a category of other environment variables that fine-tune the localization settings even further. You can display those environment variable settings by adding the -ck option to the locale command.

You change the individual LC_ environment variables by using the Linux export command. Instead of changing all the LC_ environment variables, you can set the special LANG or LC_ALL environment variable. Changing either of those variables will automatically change the other environment variables. Alternatively, if your Linux distribution supports the Systemd utilities, you can use the localectl command to display and change localization environment variable values.

You must define a time zone for your Linux system. Debian-based Linux distributions use the /etc/timezone file to determine the system time zone, while Red Hat–based Linux distributions use the /etc/localtime file. Both files utilize a binary format, so you can't edit them directly. Linux maintains a library of time zone files in the /usr/share/zoneinfo folder. Just copy or link the appropriate time zone file from the /usr/share/zoneinfo folder to the time zone file for your Linux system.

There are three commands that you can use in Linux to display or change the time and date. The hwclock command displays the time as kept on the hardware clock for your Linux system. You can set the Linux system time to that or set the hardware clock to your Linux system time. The date command allows you to display the Linux system time and date in a multitude of formats by using a command-line sequence. It also allows you to set the date and time for the Linux system from the command line. For systems that use the Systemd utilities, the timedatectl command provides a single location to display all the system time and date information.

The time command doesn't have anything to do with the current system time but instead provides information on the amount of time an individual application uses on the Linux system. You can use the time command to see how much real time elapsed between when the application started and when it finished as well as to display the amount of system or user CPU time it required.

Exam Essentials

Describe how Linux works with different languages.   Linux stores and displays language characters by using character sets. ASCII, Unicode, and UTF-8 are the most commonly used character sets for Linux.

Explain how to change the current character set on a Linux system.   You can use the export command to change the LANG or LC_ALL environment variable to define a new character set. If your Linux distribution uses the Systemd utilities, you can also use the localectl command to display or change the system character set.

Describe how the time zone is set on a Linux system.   Time zones are defined in Linux by individual files in the /usr/share/zoneinfo folder. Debian-based Linux distributions copy the appropriate time zone file to the /etc/timezone file, whereas Red Hat–based Linux distributions use the /etc/localtime file. To change the time zone for an individual script or program, use the TZ environment variable.

Summarize the tools you have available to work with the time and date on a Linux system. The hwclock command allows you to sync the Linux system time with the hardware clock on the system, or vice versa. The date command allows you to display the time and date in a multitude of formats or set the current time and date. The timedatectl command is from the Systemd utilities and allows you to display lots of different information about the system and hardware time and date in addition to allowing you to set them.

Describe how NTP works and how Linux systems use it. The Network Time Protocol (NTP) allows Linux systems to synchronize their time and date from a centralized server across the network. There are three common software packages that implement NTP in Linux: the ntpd package, the chrony package, and the timesyncd program from the Systemd utilities.

Explain how you can see the amount of time it takes for an application to run on the system. The time command allows you to place a timer on a specific application as it runs on the system. The output from the time command shows the actual elapsed time it took the program to run and how much user and system CPU time the application required.

Review Questions

1. Which character set uses 7 bits to store characters?

   A. UTF-8

   B. UTF-16

   C. ASCII

   D. Unicode

   E. UTF-32

2. What two character sets use a transformation code to store characters?

   A. UTF-8

   B. UTF-16

   C. ASCII

   D. Unicode

   E. locale

3. Which character set uses a 3-byte code and can represent characters from most languages used in the world?

   A. ASCII

   B. LC_ALL

   C. UTF-8

   D. UTF-16

   E. Unicode

4. What Linux command displays all the localization environment variables and their values?

   A. date

   B. time

   C. hwclock

   D. LANG

   E. locale

5. What two environment variables control all the localization settings?

   A. LC_MONETARY

   B. LC_NUMERIC

   C. LANG

   D. LC_CTYPE

   E. LC_ALL

6. _____ is the ability to adapt a Linux system to a specific language.
   A. `locale`
   B. Localization
   C. Character set
   D. Unicode
   E. ASCII

7. What Systemd utility allows you to change the localization on your Linux system?
   A. `timedatectl`
   B. `time`
   C. `date`
   D. `localectl`
   E. `locale`

8. Which Linux command changes the value of a localization environment variable?
   A. `time`
   B. `export`
   C. `locale`
   D. `date`
   E. `hwclock`

9. Which LC_ environment variable determines how Linux displays dollar and cents values?
   A. `LC_NUMERIC`
   B. `LC_MONETARY`
   C. `LC_CTYPE`
   D. `LC_TIME`
   E. `LC_COLLATE`

10. A _____ determines the time relative to the UTC time in a specific location.
    A. time zone
    B. localization
    C. character set
    D. locale
    E. hardware clock

11. Which Linux commands allow you to retrieve the time from the physical workstation or server? (Choose all that apply.)
    A. `date`
    B. `hwclock`
    C. `time`
    D. `locale`
    E. `timedatectl`

12. What file do Red Hat–based systems use to define the time zone for the Linux system?

    A. `/etc/localtime`

    B. `/etc/timezone`

    C. `/usr/share/zoneinfo`

    D. `/usr/share/timezone`

    E. `/usr/share/localtime`

13. Which folder contains template files for each time zone that Linux supports?

    A. `/etc/localtime`

    B. `/usr/share/zoneinfo`

    C. `/etc/timezone`

    D. `$HOME`

    E. `/usr/share/timezone`

14. Which command displays the current date, system time, hardware time, and time zone?

    A. `date`

    B. `timedatectl`

    C. `time`

    D. `hwclock`

    E. `localectl`

15. Which command do you use to display the current time and date using a specific output format?

    A. `date`

    B. `time`

    C. `timedatectl`

    D. `localectl`

    E. `hwclock`

16. Which commands allow you to set the Linux system time to the workstation BIOS clock time? (Choose all that apply.)

    A. `hwclock`

    B. `date`

    C. `time`

    D. `timedatectl`

    E. `localectl`

17. What network time package do Red Hat–based Linux systems use to synchronize the system time with a network time server?

    A. ntpd

    B. chrony

    C. localectl

    D. timedatectl

    E. timesyncd

18. Which environment variable can programmers use to temporarily change the time zone setting for just their environment?

    A. LANG

    B. LC_MONETARY

    C. LC_NUMBERIC

    D. LC_ALL

    E. TZ

19. Which character set has replaced ASCII as the default character set used in U.S. Linux installations?

    A. Unicode

    B. UTF-16

    C. UTF-8

    D. UTF-32

    E. locale

20. Which command lists all the localizations installed on your Linux system?

    A. timecatectl

    B. localectl

    C. locale

    D. LANG

    E. LC_ALL

Managing
Your System

PART

III

Chapter

10

Administering Users and Groups

✓ **Objective 2.2 Given a scenario, implement identity management.**

If you want to buy a famous and expensive piece of art, you should make sure it isn't a fake. In other words, you want to make sure it is authentic. The same is true for allowing users access to a computer system. You want to make sure they are authentic users who have been previously given authorization to access the system. This process, called *authentication*, is defined as determining whether a person or program is who they claim to be. This chapter covers administering the access controls Linux uses to check a user's credentials and permit or deny access to the system.

Besides user authentication, you need to know how to audit users, manage group memberships, configure user environments, and, if needed, set up disk space usage limits for the accounts. We'll cover those topics as well.

Managing User Accounts

Adding and modifying user account credentials, which includes usernames, account information, and passwords, is an important (but tedious) part of system administration. In addition, you need to know how to delete these credentials when warranted. Managing user accounts and looking at the underlying credential framework is covered in the following sections.

Adding Accounts

To add a new user account on the system, the useradd utility is typically used. However, the process actually involves several players besides the useradd command. A depiction of the process is illustrated in Figure 10.1.

You can see in Figure 10.1 that there are several team players involved in the account creation process. Notice that the /etc/skel directory is bolded. This is because, depending on the other configuration files, it may not be used in the process. The same goes for the /home/*userid* directory. It may not be created or it may have an alternative name, depending on the system's account creation configuration. You'll learn more about these directories shortly.

Before we jump into the useradd utility details, let's look at the two files and the directory involved in the creation side of the process.

FIGURE 10.1   Adding a user account

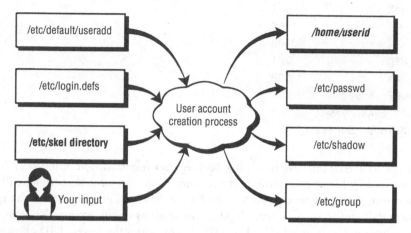

The */etc/login.defs* File

This configuration file is typically installed by default on most Linux distributions. It contains directives for use in various shadow password suite commands. *Shadow password suite* is an umbrella term for commands dealing with account credentials, such as the useradd, userdel, and passwd commands.

The directives in this configuration file control password length, how long until the user is required to change the account's password, whether or not a home directory is created by default, and so on. The file is typically filled with comments and commented-out directives (which make the directives inactive). Listing 10.1 shows only the active directives within the /etc/login.defs file, after stripping out blank and comment lines on a Rocky Linux distribution.

Listing 10.1: Active directives in the /etc/login.defs configuration file

```
$ grep -v ^$ /etc/login.defs | grep -v ^\#
MAIL_DIR      /var/spool/mail
UMASK      022
HOME_MODE      0700
PASS_MAX_DAYS  99999
PASS_MIN_DAYS  0
PASS_MIN_LEN  5
PASS_WARN_AGE  7
UID_MIN                1000
UID_MAX                60000
```

```
SYS_UID_MIN              201
SYS_UID_MAX              999
GID_MIN                 1000
GID_MAX                60000
SYS_GID_MIN              201
SYS_GID_MAX              999
CREATE_HOME      yes
USERGROUPS_ENAB  yes
ENCRYPT_METHOD   SHA512
$
```

Notice the UID_MIN directive in Listing 10.1. A *User Identification Number (UID)* is the number used by Linux to identify user accounts. A *user account,* sometimes called a *normal account,* is any account an authorized human has been given to access the system and perform daily tasks, such as open desktop applications or run scripts. While humans use account names, Linux uses UIDs. The UID_MIN indicates the lowest UID allowed for user accounts. On the system in Listing 10.1, UID_MIN is set to 1000. This is typical, though some systems set it at 500.

System accounts are accounts that provide services (daemons) or that perform special tasks, such as the root user account. A system account's minimum UID is set by the SYS_UID_MIN directive, and its maximum is set by the SYS_UID_MAX directive. The settings in this file are typical.

Keep in mind that these settings are for accounts created *after* the initial Linux distribution installation. For example, the root user account always has a UID of 0, which is below the SYS_UID_MIN, as shown snipped in Listing 10.2.

Listing 10.2: The root user account's UID

```
$ gawk -F: '{print $3, $1}' /etc/passwd | sort -n
0 root
1 bin
2 daemon
3 adm
[...]
```

Some additional directives critical to common user account creation are covered briefly in Table 10.1.

TABLE 10.1   A few vital /etc/login.defs directives

Name	Description
PASS_MAX_DAYS	Number of days until a password change is required. This is the password's expiration date.
PASS_MIN_DAYS	Number of days after a password is changed until the password may be changed again.

Name	Description
PASS_MIN_LENGTH	Minimum number of characters required in password.
PASS_WARN_AGE	Number of days a warning is issued to the user prior to a password's expiration.
CREATE_HOME	Default is no. If set to yes, a user account home directory is created.
ENCRYPT_METHOD	The method used to hash account passwords.

The /etc/login.defs file is only one of the configuration files used for the user account process's creation side. The other file is covered next.

The */etc/default/useradd* File

The /etc/default/useradd file is another configuration file that directs the process of creating accounts. It typically is a much shorter file than the /etc/login.defs file. An example from a Rocky Linux distribution is shown in Listing 10.3.

Listing 10.3: The /etc/default/useradd configuration file

```
$ cat /etc/default/useradd
# useradd defaults file
GROUP=100
HOME=/home
INACTIVE=-1
EXPIRE=
SHELL=/bin/bash
SKEL=/etc/skel
CREATE_MAIL_SPOOL=yes
$
$ useradd -D
GROUP=100
HOME=/home
INACTIVE=-1
EXPIRE=
SHELL=/bin/bash
SKEL=/etc/skel
CREATE_MAIL_SPOOL=yes
$
```

Notice in Listing 10.3 that there are two different ways to display the active directives in this file. You can use the cat command or invoke the useradd -D command. Both are equally simple to use. One cool fact about the useradd -D command is that you can use it to modify the directives within the /etc/default/useradd file.

In Listing 10.3, notice the HOME directive. It is currently set to /home, which means that any newly created user accounts will have their account directories located within the /home directory. Keep in mind that if CREATE_HOME is not set or set to no in the /etc/login .defs file, a home directory is *not* created by default.

Some additional directives critical to common user account creation are covered briefly in Table 10.2.

TABLE 10.2   A few vital /etc/default/useradd directives

Name	Description
HOME	Base directory for user account directories.
INACTIVE	Number of days after a password has expired and has not been changed until the account will be deactivated. See PASS_MAX_DAYS in Table 10.1.
SKEL	The skeleton directory.
SHELL	User account default shell program.

The SHELL directive needs a little more explanation. Typically it is set to /bin/bash, which means when you access the command line, your user process is running the /bin/bash shell program. This program provides you with the prompt at the command line and handles any commands you enter there.

 Be aware that some distributions, such as Ubuntu, set the SHELL directive by default to /bin/sh, which is a symbolic link to another shell. On Ubuntu this links to the Dash shell instead of the Bash shell.

The */etc/skel* Directory

The /etc/skel directory, or the *skeleton directory* (see Table 10.2) as it is commonly called, holds files. If a home directory is created for a user, these files are to be copied to the user account's home directory when the account is created. Listing 10.4 shows the files within the /etc/skel directory on a Fedora Workstation distribution.

Listing 10.4: Files in the /etc/skel directory

```
$ ls -a /etc/skel
.  ..  .bash_logout  .bash_profile  .bashrc  .mozilla
$
```

In Listing 10.4, the `ls` command was employed with the `-a` option so that hidden files (files starting with a dot) are displayed. Recall that hidden files do not normally display without the `-a` option on the `ls` command. These files are account environment files as well as a Mozilla Firefox web browser configuration file directory. We'll cover environment files later in this chapter. You can modify any of these files or add new files and directories, if needed.

 The /etc/skel files are copied to user account home directories only when the account is created. Therefore, if you make changes to the files later, you'll have to migrate those changed files to current user accounts either by hand or by shell scripts.

Now that we've covered the files in the creation side of the user account creation process, let's look at the files and directories that are built or modified as part of the process. Go back and look at Figure 10.1, if necessary, to refresh your memory of the various file and directory names.

The */etc/passwd* File

Account information is stored in the `/etc/passwd` file. Each account's data occupies a single line in the file. When an account is created, a new record for that account is added to the `/etc/passwd` file. A snipped example is shown in Listing 10.5.

Listing 10.5: Account records in the `/etc/passwd` file

```
$ cat /etc/passwd
root:x:0:0:root:/root:/bin/bash
bin:x:1:1:bin:/bin:/sbin/nologin
daemon:x:2:2:daemon:/sbin:/sbin/nologin
[...]
tcpdump:x:72:72::/:/sbin/nologin
user1:x:1000:1000:User One:/home/user1:/bin/bash
Christine:x:1001:1001:Christine B:/home/Christine:/bin/bash
[...]
$
```

The `/etc/passwd` file records contain several fields. Each field in a record is delimited by a colon (`:`). There are seven fields in total, as described in Table 10.3.

TABLE 10.3 The /etc/passwd file's record fields

Field No.	Description
1	User account's username.
2	Password field. Typically this file is no longer used to store passwords. An x in this field indicates passwords are stored in the /etc/shadow file.

TABLE 10.3   The /etc/passwd file's record fields *(continued)*

Field No.	Description
3	User account's user identification number (UID).
4	User account's group identification number (GID).
5	Comment field. This field is optional. Traditionally it contains the user's full name.
6	User account's home directory.
7	User account's default shell. If set to /sbin/nologin or /bin/false, then the user cannot interactively log into the system.

You would think that the password file would hold passwords, but due to its file permissions, the password file can be compromised. Therefore, passwords are stored in the more locked-down /etc/shadow file.

You may find yourself working for an organization that has passwords stored in the /etc/passwd file. If so, politely suggest that the passwords be migrated to the /etc/shadow file via the pwconv command. If the organization refuses, walk, or even better run, to the door and go find a job at a different company.

You may have noticed that in a /etc/password record, field #7 may contain either the /sbin/nologin or /bin/false default shell. This is to prevent an account from interactively logging into the system. The /sbin/nologin is typically set for system service account records. System services (daemons) do need to have system accounts, but they do *not* interactively log in. Instead, they run in the background under their own account name. If a malicious person attempted to interactively log in using the account (and they made it past other blockades, which you'll learn about shortly), they are politely kicked off the system. Basically, /sbin/nologin displays a brief message and logs you off before you reach a command prompt. If desired, you can modify the message shown by creating the file /etc/nologin.txt and adding the desired text.

The /bin/false shell is a little more brutal. If this is set as a user account's default shell, there are no messages shown, and the user is just logged out of the system.

The */etc/shadow* File

Another file that is updated when an account is created is the /etc/shadow file. It contains information regarding the account's password, even if you have not yet provided a password for the account. Like the /etc/passwd file, each account's data occupies a single file line. A snipped example is shown in Listing 10.6.

Listing 10.6: Account records in the /etc/shadow file

```
$ sudo cat /etc/shadow
root:!::0:99999:7:::
bin:*:17589:0:99999:7:::
daemon:*:17589:0:99999:7:::
[...]
user1:$6$bvqdqU[...]:17738:0:99999:7:::
Christine:Wb8I8Iw$6[...]:17751:0:99999:7:::
[...]
$
```

The /etc/shadow records contain several fields. Each field in a record is delimited by a colon (:). There are nine fields in total, described in Table 10.4.

TABLE 10.4   The /etc/shadow file's record fields

Field No.	Description
1	User account's username.
2	Password field. The password is a salted and hashed password. A !! or ! indicates a password has not been set for the account. A ! or * indicates the account cannot use a password to log in. A ! in front of a password indicates the account has been locked.
3	Date of last password change in Unix Epoch time (days) format.
4	Number of days after a password is changed until the password may be changed again.
5	Number of days until a password change is required. This is the password's expiration date.
6	Number of days a warning is issued to the user prior to a password's expiration. (See field #5).
7	Number of days after a password has expired (see field #5) and has not been changed until the account will be deactivated.
8	Date of account's expiration in Unix Epoch time (days) format.
9	Called the *special flag*. It is a field for a special future use, is currently not used, and is blank.

Notice that field #1 is the account's username. This is the only field shared with the /etc/passwd file.

 Unix Epoch time, which is also called *POSIX time*, is the number of seconds since January 1, 1970, although the /etc/shadow file expresses it in days. It has a long history with Unix and Linux systems and will potentially cause problems in the year 2038. You don't have to drag out your calculator to determine what a field's date is using the Epoch. Instead, the chage utility, covered later in this chapter, does that for you.

It's vital to understand the different possible expirations. When password expiration has occurred, there is a grace period. The user will have a certain number of days (designated in field #7) to log into the account using the old password but must change the password immediately. However, if password expiration has occurred and the user does *not* log in to the system in time, the user is effectively locked out of the system.

With account expiration, there is no grace period. After the account expires, the user cannot log into the account with its password.

You may have noticed that we have not yet covered the /etc/group file. It does get modified as part of the account creation process. However, that discussion is saved for the section "Managing Groups" later in this chapter.

The Account Creation Process

Distributions tend to vary greatly in their configuration when it comes to user accounts. Therefore, before you launch into creating accounts with the useradd utility, it's wise to review some directives within each distro's user account configuration files (see Tables 10.1 and 10.2). In Listing 10.7, the CREATE_HOME and SHELL directives are checked on a Rocky Linux distribution.

Listing 10.7: Checking user account directives on Fedora Workstation

```
$ grep CREATE_HOME /etc/login.defs
CREATE_HOME       yes
$
$ useradd -D | grep SHELL
SHELL=/bin/bash
$
```

You can see on this Rocky Linux distribution that the home directory will be created by default because CREATE_HOME is set to yes. The SHELL directive is pointing to the Bash shell, /bin/bash, which is the typical shell for most interactive user accounts.

The useradd command, as mentioned earlier, is the primary tool for creating user accounts on most distributions. Creating an account on a Rocky Linux distribution with the useradd utility is shown in Listing 10.8.

Listing 10.8: Creating a user account on a Rocky Linux Workstation

```
$ sudo useradd DAdams
[sudo] password for Christine:
$
$ grep ^DAdams /etc/passwd
DAdams:x:1002:1002::/home/DAdams:/bin/bash
$
$ sudo grep ^DAdams /etc/shadow
DAdams:!!:17806:0:99999:7:::
$
$ sudo ls -a /home/DAdams/
.  ..  .bash_logout  .bash_profile  .bashrc  .mozilla
$
```

Because the Rocky Linux distribution we are using in Listing 10.8 has the CREATE_HOME directive set to yes and SHELL set to /bin/bash, there is no need to employ any useradd command options. The only argument needed is the user account name, which is DAdams. After the utility is used to create the account in Listing 10.8, notice that records now exist for the new user account in both the /etc/passwd and /etc/shadow files. Also, a new directory was created, /home/DAdams, which contains files from the /etc/skel directory. Keep in mind at this point that no password has been added to the DAdams account yet, and thus its record in the /etc/shadow file shows !! in the password field.

Now let's take a look at creating an account on a different Linux distribution. The Ubuntu Desktop distro does things a little differently. In Listing 10.9, you can see that CREATE_HOME is *not* set, so it will default to no.

Listing 10.9: Checking user account directives on Ubuntu Desktop

```
$ grep CREATE_HOME /etc/login.defs
$
$ useradd -D | grep SHELL
SHELL=/bin/sh
$
```

Also in Listing 10.9, notice that the SHELL directive is set to /bin/sh instead of the Bash shell. This means that when you create an interactive user account, you will need to specify Bash shell, if desired.

Therefore, when creating a user account on this Ubuntu distribution, if you want the account to have a home directory and use the Bash shell, you will need to employ additional useradd command options. The useradd utility has many useful options for various needs, and the most typical ones are listed in Table 10.5.

TABLE 10.5 The useradd command's commonly used options

Short	Long	Description
-c	--comment	Comment field contents. Traditionally it contains the user's full name. Optional.
-d	--home or --home-dir	User's home directory specification. Default action is set by the HOME and CREATE_HOME directives.
-D	--defaults	Display /etc/default/useradd directives.
-e	--expiredate	Date of account's expiration in *YYYY-MM-DD* format. Default action is set by the EXPIRE directive.
-f	--inactive	Number of days after a password has expired and has not been changed until the account will be deactivated. A -1 indicates that the account will never be deactivated. Default action is set by the INACTIVE directive.
-g	--gid	Account's group membership, which is active when user logs into system (default group).
-G	--groups	Account's additional group memberships.
-m	--create-home	If it does not exist, create the user account's home directory. Default action is set by the CREATE_HOME directive.
-M	N/A or --no-create-home	Do *not* create the user account's home directory. Default action is set by the CREATE_HOME directive.
-s	--shell	Account's shell. Default action is set by the SHELL directive.
-u	--uid	Account's User Identification (UID) number.
-r	--system	Create a system account instead of a user account.

We need to employ a few of the options in Table 10.5 to create a user account on the Ubuntu Desktop distribution. An example is shown in Listing 10.10.

Listing 10.10: Creating a user account on Ubuntu Desktop

```
$ sudo useradd -md /home/JKirk -s /bin/bash JKirk
[sudo] password for Christine:
$
$ grep ^JKirk /etc/passwd
```

```
JKirk:x:1002:1002::/home/JKirk:/bin/bash
$
$ sudo grep ^JKirk /etc/shadow
JKirk:!:17806:0:99999:7:::
$
$ sudo ls -a /home/JKirk/
.  ..  .bash_logout  .bashrc  examples.desktop  .profile
$
$ sudo ls -a /etc/skel
.  ..  .bash_logout  .bashrc  examples.desktop  .profile
$
```

Notice in Listing 10.10 that three options are used along with the useradd command. Because this system does not have the CREATE_HOME directive set, the -m option is needed to force useradd to make a home directory for the account. The -d switch designates that the directory name should be /home/JKirk. Because the SHELL directive is set to /bin/sh on this system, the -s option is needed to set the account's default shell to /bin/bash.

After the utility is used to create the account in Listing 10.10, notice that records now exist for the new user account in the /etc/passwd and /etc/shadow files. Also, a new directory was created, /home/JKirk, which contains files from this distro's /etc/skel directory. Keep in mind at this point that no password has been added to the JKirk account yet, and thus its record in the /etc/shadow file shows ! in the password field.

> The Ubuntu and Debian distributions promote the use of the adduser program instead of the useradd utility. Their man pages refer to the useradd command as a "low-level utility." Some other distros include a symbolic link to useradd named adduser, which may help (or not). The adduser configuration information is typically stored in the /etc/adduser.conf file.

Another way to view account records in the /etc/passwd and /etc/shadow files is via the getent utility. For this program you pass only the filename followed by the account name whose record you wish to view. The command is employed in Listing 10.11 to view the account that was created in Listing 10.10.

Listing 10.11: Using getent to view a user account on Ubuntu Desktop

```
$ getent passwd JKirk
JKirk:x:1002:1002::/home/JKirk:/bin/bash
$
$ getent shadow JKirk
$
$ sudo getent shadow JKirk
JKirk:!:17806:0:99999:7:::
$
```

Notice in Listing 10.11 that when super user privileges are not used with getent for the shadow file, nothing is returned. This is because getent honors the security settings on the /etc/shadow file.

If you need to modify the /etc/default/useradd file's directive settings, instead of using a text editor, you can employ the useradd -D command. Just tack on the needed arguments. For example, to modify the SHELL directive to point to the Bash shell, use super user privileges and issue the useradd -D -s /bin/bash command.

When creating an account, you can create a password via the crypt utility and then add it when the account is created via the -p option on the useradd utility. However, that is not only cumbersome but considered a bad practice. In the next section, we'll cover creating and managing account passwords properly.

Maintaining Passwords

When you first create an interactive account, you should immediately afterward create a password for that account using the passwd utility. In Listing 10.12, a password is created for the new DAdams account on a Rocky Linux system.

Listing 10.12: Using passwd for a new account on Fedora Workstation

```
$ sudo passwd DAdams
Changing password for user DAdams.
New password:
Retype new password:
passwd: all authentication tokens updated successfully.
$
```

You can also update a password for a particular user using the passwd utility and pass the user's account name as an argument, similar to what is shown in Listing 10.12. If you need to update your own account's password, just enter passwd with no additional command arguments.

The passwd utility works hand in hand with pluggable authentication modules (PAMs). For example, when you set or change a password via the passwd utility, the pam-cracklib PAM checks the password to flag easily guessed passwords or passwords that use words found in the dictionary. PAM is covered in more detail in Chapter 16, "Looking at Access and Authentication Methods."

You can do more than set and modify passwords with the passwd utility. You can also lock or unlock accounts, set an account's password to expired, delete an account's password, and so on. Table 10.6 shows commonly used passwd switches; all of these options require super user privileges.

TABLE 10.6   The passwd command's commonly used options

Short	Long	Description
-d	--delete	Removes the account's password.
-e	--expire	Sets an account's password as expired. User is required to change account password at next login.
-i	--inactive	Sets the number of days after a password has expired and has not been changed until the account will be deactivated.
-l	--lock	Places an exclamation point (!) in front of the account's password within the /etc/shadow file, effectively preventing the user from logging into the system via using the account's password.
-n	--minimum	Sets the number of days after a password is changed until the password may be changed again.
-S	--status	Displays the account's password status.
-u	--unlock	Removes a placed exclamation point (!) from the account's password within the /etc/shadow file.
-w	--warning or --warndays	Sets the number of days a warning is issued to the user prior to a password's expiration.
-x	--maximum or --maxdays	Sets the number of days until a password change is required. This is the password's expiration date.

One option in Table 10.6 needs a little more explanation, and that is the -S option. An example is shown in Listing 10.13.

Listing 10.13: Using passwd -S to view an account's password status

```
$ sudo passwd -S DAdams
DAdams PS 2021-10-01 0 99999 7 -1 (Password set, SHA512 crypt.)
$
```

In Listing 10.13, the DAdams account's password status is displayed. The status contains the account password's state, which is either a usable password (P), no password (NP), or a locked password (L). After the password state, the last password change date is shown, followed by the password's minimum, maximum, warning, and inactive settings. Additional status is shown within the parentheses, which includes whether or not the password is set as well as the hash algorithm used to protect it.

You can also use the chage utility to display similar password information, but in a more human-readable format, as shown in Listing 10.14.

Listing 10.14: Using chage -l to view an account's password status

```
$ sudo chage -l DAdams
Last password change                               : Oct 02, 2021
Password expires                                   : never
Password inactive                                  : never
Account expires                                    : never
Minimum number of days between password change     : 0
Maximum number of days between password change     : 99999
Number of days of warning before password expires  : 7
$
```

The chage program can modify password settings as well. You can either employ various command options (see its man pages for details) or use the chage utility interactively, as shown in Listing 10.15.

Listing 10.15: Using chage to change an account password's settings

```
$ sudo chage DAdams
Changing the aging information for DAdams
Enter the new value, or press ENTER for the default

        Minimum Password Age [0]: 5
        Maximum Password Age [99999]: 30
        Last Password Change (YYYY-MM-DD) [2021-10-02]:
        Password Expiration Warning [7]: 15
        Password Inactive [-1]: 3
        Account Expiration Date (YYYY-MM-DD) [-1]:
$
```

Notice in Listing 10.15 that the password expiration warning is set to 15 days. This is a good setting if your company allows two-week vacations.

Modifying Accounts

The utility employed to modify accounts is the usermod program. Similar to the passwd command, you can lock and unlock accounts, as shown in Listing 10.16.

Listing 10.16: Using usermod to lock an account

```
$ sudo usermod -L  DAdams
$
$ sudo passwd -S DAdams
DAdams LK 2021-10-01 5 30 15 3 (Password locked.)
$
$ sudo getent shadow DAdams
DAdams: !$6$B/zCaNx[...]:17806:5:30:15:3::
```

```
$
$ sudo usermod -U  DAdams
$
$ sudo passwd -S DAdams
DAdams PS 2021-10-01 5 30 15 3 (Password set, SHA512 crypt.)
$
```

Notice in Listing 10.16 that the usermod -L command is used to lock the DAdams account. The passwd -S command shows that the password status is LK, indicating it is locked. In Listing 10.16, the snipped getent utility output shows that an exclamation point (!) was placed in front of the DAdams account's password, which is what is causing the account to be locked. The lock is then removed via the usermod -U command, and the status is rechecked.

You can make many modifications to user accounts via the usermod utility's switches. The commonly used options are shown in Table 10.7.

TABLE 10.7   The usermod command's commonly used options

Short	Long	Description
-c	--comment	Modify the comment field contents.
-d	--home	Set a new user home directory specification. Use with the -m option to move the current directory's files to the new location.
-e	--expiredate	Modify the account's expiration date. Use YYYY-MM-DD format.
-f	--inactive	Modify the number of days after a password has expired and has not been changed that the account will be deactivated. A -1 indicates that the account will never be deactivated.
-g	--gid	Change the account's default group membership.
-G	--groups	Update the account's additional group memberships. If only specifying new group membership, use the -a option to avoid removing the other group memberships.
-l	--login	Modify the account's username to the specified one. Does not modify the home directory.
-L	--lock	Lock the account by placing an exclamation point in front of the password within the account's /etc/shadow file record.
-s	--shell	Change the account's shell.
-u	--uid	Modify the account's User Identification (UID) number.
-U	--unlock	Unlock the account by removing the exclamation point from the front of the password within the account's /etc/shadow file record.

Notice that you can change an account's default group and provide memberships to additional groups. Account groups are covered in detail later in this chapter.

Where usermod comes in really handy is in a situation where you've created an account but forgot to check the distribution's account creation configuration settings. Listing 10.17 shows an example of this on an Ubuntu Desktop distribution.

Listing 10.17: Using usermod to modify an account

```
$ sudo useradd -md /home/DBowman DBowman
$
$ sudo getent passwd DBowman
DBowman:x:1003:1003::/home/DBowman:/bin/sh
$
$ sudo usermod -s /bin/bash DBowman
$
$ sudo getent passwd DBowman
DBowman:x:1003:1003::/home/DBowman:/bin/bash
$
```

In Listing 10.17, the user account DBowman is created, but when the account record is checked using the getent utility, it shows that the /bin/sh shell is being used instead of the Bash shell. To fix this problem, the usermod command is employed with the -s option, and the account's shell is modified to the /bin/bash shell instead.

Deleting Accounts

Deleting an account on Linux is fairly simple. The userdel utility is the key tool in this task. The most common option to use is the -r switch. This option will delete the account's home directory tree and any files within it. Listing 10.18 shows an example of deleting an account.

Listing 10.18: Using userdel to delete an account

```
$ sudo ls -a /home/DBowman
.  ..  .bash_logout  .bashrc  examples.desktop  .profile
$
$ sudo getent passwd DBowman
DBowman:x:1003:1003::/home/DBowman:/bin/bash
$
$ sudo userdel -r DBowman
userdel: DBowman mail spool (/var/mail/DBowman) not found
$
$ sudo ls -a /home/DBowman
ls: cannot access '/home/DBowman': No such file or directory
```

```
$
$ sudo getent passwd DBowman
$
```

The first two commands in Listing 10.18 show that the /home/DBowman directory exists and has files within it and that the account does have a record within the /etc/passwd file. The third command includes the userdel -r command to delete the account as well as the home directory. Notice that an error message is generated stating that the /var/mail/DBowman file could not be found. This is not a problem. It just means that this file was not created when the account was created. Finally, the last two commands show that both the /home/DBowman directory and its files were removed and that the /etc/passwd file no longer contains a record for the DBowman account.

Real World Scenario

Account Deletion Policies

Prior to deleting any accounts on a system, check with your employer's human resources staff and/or legal department or counsel. There may be policies in place concerning file retention for terminated or retired employees as well as those individuals who have left the company to change jobs. You may be required to back up files prior to deleting them from the system and/or perform some other types of documentation. If your employer has no such policy, it is a good idea to suggest that one be developed.

Managing Groups

Groups are organizational structures that are part of Linux's *discretionary access control (DAC)*. DAC is the traditional Linux security control, where access to a file, or any object, is based on the user's identity and current group membership. When a user account is created, it is given membership to a particular group, called the account's *default group*. Though a user account can have lots of group memberships, its process can have only one designated current group at a time. The default group is an account's current group, when the user first logs into the system.

Groups are identified by their name as well as their *group identification number (GID)*. This is similar to how users are identified by UIDs in that the GID is used by Linux to identify a particular group, whereas humans use group names.

If a default group is not designated when a user account is created, then a new group is created. This new group has the same name as the user account's name, and it is assigned a new GID. To see an account's default group, you can use the getent command to view the /etc/passwd record for that account. Recall that the fourth field in the record is the account's GID, which is the default group. Review Table 10.3 if you need a refresher on the various /etc/passwd record fields. Listing 10.19 shows an example of viewing an account's default group information for the DAdams account, which was created on a Rocky Linux distribution.

Listing 10.19: Viewing an account's group memberships

```
$ getent passwd DAdams
DAdams:x:1002:1002::/home/DAdams:/bin/bash
$
$ sudo groups DAdams
DAdams : DAdams
$
$ getent group DAdams
DAdams:x:1002:
$
$ grep 1002 /etc/group
DAdams:x:1002:
$
```

The first command in Listing 10.19 shows that the DAdams account's default group has a GID of 1002, but it does not provide a group name. The groups command does show the group name, which is the same as the user account name, DAdams. This is typical when no default group was designated at account creation time. The third command, another getent command, shows that the group DAdams does indeed map to the 1002 GID. The fourth command confirms this information.

To add a user to a new group or change the account's default group, the group must pre-exist. This task is accomplished via the groupadd utility. The group's GID will be automatically set by the system, but you can override this default behavior with the -g command option. An example of creating a new group is shown in Listing 10.20.

Listing 10.20: Using the groupadd utility to create a new group

```
$ sudo groupadd -g 1042 Project42
$
$ getent group Project42
Project42:x:1042:
$
$ grep Project42 /etc/group
Project42:x:1042:
$
```

Notice in Listing 10.20 that super user privileges are required to create a new group. The getent utility, as well as the grep command, is used to show the new group record in the

/etc/group file. The fields in the /etc/group file are delimited by a colon (:) and are as follows:

- Group name
- Group password: An x indicates that if a group password exists, it is stored in the /etc/gshadow file.
- GID
- Group members: User accounts that belong to the group, separated by a comma.

The Ubuntu and Debian distributions promote the use of the addgroup program instead of the groupadd program. They consider the groupadd command to be a low-level utility.

The new group created did not have a group password created for it. However, the x in the Project42 group record within the /etc/group file does not prove this. To make sure there is no group password, the /etc/gshadow file, where group passwords are stored, is checked in Listing 10.21.

Listing 10.21: Checking for a group password

```
$ sudo getent gshadow Project42
Project42:!::
$
```

The command in Listing 10.21 shows the Project42 group's record within the /etc/ gshadow file. The second field contains an exclamation point (!), which indicates that no password has been set for this group.

Group passwords, if set, allow user accounts access to groups to whom they do not belong. If a group password is used, this password is typically shared among the various users who need access to the group. This is a bad security practice. Passwords should never be shared. Each account needs to have its own password, and access to groups should only be allowed via group membership, not group passwords.

Once a new group is created, you can set group membership, which is simply adding user accounts to the group. Listing 10.22 shows an example of doing this with the usermod command.

Listing 10.22: Employing usermod to add an account to a group

```
$ sudo groups DAdams
DAdams : DAdams
$
```

```
$ sudo usermod -aG Project42 DAdams
$
$ sudo groups DAdams
DAdams : DAdams Project42
$
$ getent group Project42
Project42:x:1042:DAdams
$
```

Notice that the usermod command in Listing 10.22 uses two options, -aG. The -G adds the DAdams account as a member of the Project42 group, but the -a switch is important because it preserves any previous DAdams account group memberships. After the DAdams account is added as a Project42 group member, you can see in the last two command results that the /etc/group file record for Project42 was updated.

If you need to modify a particular group, the groupmod command is helpful. A group's GID is modified with the -g option, while a group's name is modified with the -n switch. In Listing 10.23, the Project42 group's GID is modified.

Listing 10.23: Using groupmod to modify a group

```
$ getent group Project42
Project42:x:1042:DAdams
$
$ sudo groupmod -g 1138 Project42
$
$ getent group Project42
Project42:x:1138:DAdams
$
```

Notice that in Listing 10.23, the Project42 group's GID is modified to 1138. The getent command confirms that the /etc/group file was updated. If the 1138 GID was already in use by another group, the groupmod command would have displayed an error message and not changed the group's GID.

To remove a group, the groupdel utility is employed. An example is shown in Listing 10.24.

Listing 10.24: Using groupdel to delete a group

```
$ sudo groupdel Project42
$
$ getent group Project42
$
```

```
$ sudo groups DAdams
DAdams : DAdams
$
$ sudo find / -gid 1138 2>/dev/null
$
```

Notice in Listing 10.24 after the Project42 group is deleted that the getent command shows that the Project42 group record has been removed from the /etc/group file. What is really nice is that any member of that deleted group has also had their group information updated, as shown in the third command.

Once you have removed a group, it is important to search through the virtual directory system for any files that may have access settings for that group. You can do this audit using the find command and the deleted group's GID. An example of this task is shown as the fourth command. If you need help remembering how to use the find utility, go back to Chapter 3, "Managing Files, Directories, and Text," where the command was originally covered.

Besides adding, modifying, and deleting user accounts and groups, there are a few other critical tasks involved with administering them. These topics are covered in the next few sections.

Setting Up the Environment

After a user authenticates with the Linux system and before reaching the Bash shell's command-line prompt, the user environment is configured. This environment consists of environment variables, command aliases, and various other settings. For example, the PATH environment variable, covered in Chapter 3, is often manipulated in configuring the user's environment.

The user environment configuration is accomplished via environment files. These files contain Bash shell commands to perform the necessary operations and are covered in the following sections along with a few environment variable highlights.

Perusing Bash Parameters

The Bash shell uses a feature called *environment variables* to store information about the shell session and the working environment (thus the name *environment variable*). You can view all the various environment variables set on your system by using the set, env, and printenv commands. However, for the user environment purposes, we're going to focus on only a *few* of these variables. These are listed in Table 10.8.

TABLE 10.8   A few environment variables associated with a user environment

Name	Description
HISTCONTROL	Governs how commands are saved within the history list
HISTSIZE	Controls the maximum number of commands saved within the history list
PATH	Sets the directories in which the shell searches for command programs
PS1	Configures the shell's primary prompt
SHELL	Sets the shell program's absolute directory reference
USER	Contains the current process's user account name

Typically environment variable names are all uppercase. However, you will sometimes see them written with a preceding dollar sign ($), such as $PS1. This is because you can use or display what is stored in the environment variable by adding the $. For example, echo $HISTSIZE will display the history list's maximum number of saved commands.

While you can modify these variables on the fly, the focus here is on how these parameters are persistently set or modified for user login processes. When you start a Bash shell by logging in to the Linux system, by default Bash checks several files for the configuration. These files are called *environment files*, which are sometimes called *startup files*. The environment files that Bash processes depend on the method you use to start the Bash shell. You can start a Bash shell in three ways:

- As a default login shell, such as when logging into the system at a tty# terminal
- As an interactive shell that is started by spawning a subshell, such as when opening a terminal emulator in a Linux GUI
- As a noninteractive shell (also called *non-login shell*) that is started, such as when running a shell script

The environment files are actually shell scripts. Shell scripting is covered more thoroughly in Chapter 25, "Deploying Bash Scripts." The following sections take you through the various available environment files.

Understanding User Entries

There are four potential files found in the user's home directory, $HOME, that are environment files. For a default login or interactive shell, the first file found in the following order is run, and the rest are ignored:

- .bash_profile

- .bash_login
- .profile

Typically, the fourth file, .bashrc, is run from the file found in the preceding list. However, any time a noninteractive shell is started, the .bashrc file is run.

In Listing 10.25, on a Rocky Linux distribution, the user's directory is checked for all four environment files. Notice that two of them are not found. Therefore, only the .bash_profile and .bashrc files are employed on this system.

Listing 10.25: Reviewing a user account's environment files

```
$ pwd
/home/Christine
$ ls .bash_profile .bash_login .profile .bashrc
ls: cannot access '.bash_login': No such file or directory
ls: cannot access '.profile': No such file or directory
.bash_profile   .bashrc
$
```

 When referring to a user account's environment files, often symbols for environment files denoting the user's home directory are employed. For example, you may see the .bashrc environment file referred to as the $HOME/.bashrc or the ~/.bashrc file.

If you want to modify your shell's primary prompt ($PS1) persistently, you can do so by adding the modification to one of your local environment configuration files. Listing 10.26 shows the PS1 variable's modification on a Fedora Workstation distribution.

Listing 10.26: Persistently setting a user account's shell prompt

```
$ grep PS1 .bash_profile
PS1="To infinity and beyond: "
$
```

Notice in Listing 10.26 that the user's prompt is still set to a $. The new prompt designated in the $HOME/.bash_profile file will not take effect until the file is run, which can be done manually or automatically when the user logs out and back into the shell.

These individual user environment files are typically populated from the /etc/skel directory, depending on your account creation configuration settings. For future accounts, you can make changes to the skeleton environment files. Just keep in mind that any individual user who can access the command line has the ability to modify their own files. Thus, for environment configurations that need to apply to all users, it is better to make a global entry in one of the global environment files, which are covered next.

Grasping Global Entries

Global configuration files modify the working environment and shell sessions for all users starting a Bash shell. As mentioned earlier, the global entries in these files can be modified by the account user by adding user entries to their $HOME environment files.

The global environment files consist of the following:

- The /etc/profile file
- Files within the /etc/profile.d/ directory
- The /etc/bashrc or the /etc/bash.bashrc file

Whether your Linux system has the /etc/bashrc or the /etc/bash.bashrc file depends on which distribution you are running. Either file is typically called from the user's $HOME/.bashrc file.

It is recommended that instead of changing the /etc/profile or other files for global environment needs, you create a custom environment file, give it an .sh file extension, and place it in the /etc/profile.d/ directory. All the .sh files within the /etc/profile.d/ directory are run via the /etc/profile environment file for logins to the Bash shell.

Now you know how to set up persistent changes to user environments both locally and globally. Next, we'll explore keeping an eye on those users.

Querying Users

Several utilities allow you to audit which users are currently accessing the system as well as users who have accessed it in the past. You can also verify the account name you are using at present and review various information concerning user accounts.

Exploring the *whoami* Utility

The whoami command will display what user account you are currently using. While this may seem silly, it is important to know what account you are currently using, especially if your organization has shared accounts or the distribution you're using allows interactive logins into the root account.

It is considered a bad security practice to share user accounts as well as log directly into the root user account. If you need super user account access, it is better to obtain sudo privileges. The sudo command is covered thoroughly in Chapter 15, "Applying Ownership and Permissions."

The whoami command is demonstrated in Listing 10.27. Notice that it only displays the current user account's name.

Listing 10.27: Employing the whoami utility

```
$ whoami
Christine
$
```

Understanding the *who* Utility

The who command provides a little more data than the whoami utility. You can view information concerning your own account or look at every current user on the system. Examples are shown in Listing 10.28.

Listing 10.28: Using the who command

```
$ who
user1     tty2          2018-10-03 13:12
Christine pts/0          2018-10-03 14:10 (192.168.0.102)
$
```

Notice in Listing 10.28, when the who command is used by itself, it shows all the current system users, the terminal they are using, the date and time they entered the system, and in cases of remote users, their remote IP address.

Though it is a very short command, w provides a great deal of useful information. An example is shown in Listing 10.29.

Listing 10.29: Employing the w command

```
$ w
 09:58:31 up 49 min,  5 users,  load average: 0.81, 0.37, 0.27
USER      TTY      LOGIN@   IDLE   JCPU    PCPU WHAT
user1     tty2     09:10    49:11  43.89s  0.30s /usr/libexe[...]
Christin  pts/1    09:14    2.00s  0.04s   0.01s w
Rich      tty3     09:56    1:35   0.85s   0.81s top
Kevin     tty4     09:57    1:03   16.17s  16.14s ls --color=[...]
Tim       tty5     09:57    38.00s 0.08s   0.03s nano data42[...]
$
```

Notice the w command's verbose output in Listing 10.29. The first displayed line shows the following information:

- The current time
- How long the system has been up
- How many users are currently accessing the system
- The CPU load averages for the last 1, 5, and 15 minutes

The next several lines concern current system user information. The columns are as follows:

- USER: The account's name
- TTY: The account's currently used terminal
- LOGIN@: When the user logged into the account
- IDLE: How long it has been since the user interacted with the system
- JCPU: How much total CPU time the account has used
- PCPU: How much CPU time the account's current command (process) has used
- WHAT: What command the account is currently running

The w utility pulls user information from the /var/run/utmp file. It also gathers additional data for display from the /proc/ directory files.

Identifying with the *id* Program

The id utility allows you to pull out various data about the current user process. It also displays information for any account whose identification you pass to id as an argument. The id command provides a nice one-line summary, as shown in Listing 10.30.

Listing 10.30: Employing the id command

```
$ id DAdams
uid=1002(DAdams) gid=1002(DAdams) groups=1002(DAdams)
$
$ id -un 1004
Kevin
$
```

If you don't want all that information the first command provides in Listing 10.30, you can filter the results by employing various id utility options, as shown in the second command in Listing 10.30. A few of the more common ones are shown in Table 10.9.

TABLE 10.9   The id command's commonly used options

Short	Long	Description
-g	--group	Displays the account's current group's GID, which is either the account's default group or a group reached by using the newgrp command
-G	--groups	Displays all the account's group memberships via each one's GIDs
-n	--name	Displays the account's name instead of UID or group name instead of GID by using this switch with the -g, -G, or -u options
-u	--user	Displays the account's UID

The id utility is very useful in shell scripts. In snipped Listing 10.31, you can see how it is used to set the USER environment variable in the /etc/profile file on a Rocky Linux system.

Listing 10.31: Using the id utility within an environment file

```
$ grep USER /etc/profile
    USER="`/usr/bin/id -un`"
[...]
$
```

Displaying Access History with the *last* Utility

The last command pulls information from the /var/log/wtmp file and displays a list of accounts showing the last time they logged in/out of the system or if they are still logged on. It also shows when system reboots occur and when the wtmp file was started. A snipped example is shown in Listing 10.32.

Listing 10.32: Using the last command

```
$ last
Tim       tty5                            Thu Oct  4 09:57    still logged in
Kevin     tty4                            Thu Oct  4 09:57    still logged in
Rich      tty3                            Thu Oct  4 09:56    still logged in
Christin  pts/1       192.168.0.102       Thu Oct  4 09:14    still logged in
user1     tty2        tty2                Thu Oct  4 09:10    still logged in
reboot    system boot 4.17.12-200.fc28    Thu Oct  4 09:09    still running
Christin  pts/0       192.168.0.102       Wed Oct  3 14:10 - 15:32  (01:22)
user1     tty2                            Wed Oct  3 13:12 - 15:33  (02:21)
[...]
wtmp begins Thu Jul 26 16:30:32 2018
$
```

Be aware that the /var/log/wtmp file typically gets automatically rotated via the cron utility, which is covered in Chapter 26, "Automating Jobs." If you need to gather information from old wtmp files, you can use the -f switch. For example, you could type **last -f /var/log/wtmp.1** to view data from the /var/log/wtmp.1 file.

The last command and the various other utilities covered in these sections are helpful for auditing current users and checking your own account's identity. They are more tools for your Linux administration tool belt.

Managing Disk Space Usage

One way to prevent a filesystem from filling up with files and causing program or entire system issues is to set limits on users' disk space usage. This is accomplished with quotas. Linux can put a cap on the number of files a user may create as well as restrict the total filesystem space consumed by a single user. Not only are these limits available for user accounts, but they also may be set for groups.

The Linux system implements file number quota limits via their inode numbers. Back in Chapter 3 we mentioned file inode (index) numbers. Typically there is one inode number per file, unless a file is hard-linked.

There are essentially four steps for enabling quotas on a particular filesystem. You will need to employ super user privileges to accomplish these steps. They are as follows:

1. Modify the /etc/fstab file to enable filesystem quota support.
2. If the filesystem is already mounted, unmount and remount it. If the filesystem was not previously mounted, then just mount it.
3. Create the quota files.
4. Establish user or group quota limits and grace periods.

The necessary /etc/fstab file modification is fairly simple. You just edit the file and add either usrquota or grpquota or both to the filesystem's mount options (fourth field). An example is shown in Listing 10.33.

Listing 10.33: Setting filesystem quotas in the /etc/fstab file

```
$ grep /dev/sdb1 /etc/fstab
/dev/sdb1 /home/user1/QuotaFSTest ext4 defaults,usrquota,grpquota 0 0
$
```

Once you have the /etc/fstab file modified, if the filesystem is already mounted, you will need to unmount it using the umount command. You then mount or remount the system, using the mount -a command, which will mount any unmounted filesystems listed in the /etc/fstab file. An example is shown in Listing 10.34.

Listing 10.34: Mounting or remounting a quota-enabled filesystem

```
# umount /dev/sdb1
# mount -a
# mount | grep /dev/sdb1
/dev/sdb1 on /home/user1/QuotaFSTest type ext4 (rw,relatime,seclabel,quota,usr
quota,grpquota,data=ordered)
#
```

Notice in Listing 10.34 that you can check if the mount was successful by using the `mount` command and the `grep` utility. Also note that the mounted filesystem has both `usrquota` (user quotas) and `grpquota` (group quotas) enabled.

Once the filesystem has been properly mounted with quota support enabled, you can create the quota files needed to enforce limits. This is done with the `quotacheck` utility. The `-c` switch creates the needed files through a scan of the filesystem, recording any current quota usage. The `-u` option creates the `aquota.user` file, and the `-g` option creates the `aquota.group` file. Therefore, if you are only implementing user and not group quotas, you could leave off the `-g` switch, and vice versa. An example of using `quotacheck` is shown in Listing 10.35.

Listing 10.35: Using `quotacheck` to create user and group quota files

```
# quotacheck -cug /home/user1/QuotaFSTest
#
# ls /home/user1/QuotaFSTest
aquota.group  aquota.user  lost+found
#
```

> If you are setting up quotas on more than one filesystem, you can issue the `quotacheck` command one time. Just employ the `-a` option along with the other command switches and it will create the desired quota files for any quota-enabled filesystems designated as currently mounted in the `/etc/mtab` file.

With the quota files created, you can start creating quota limits for user accounts and/or groups by employing the `edquota` utility. To edit user quotas, use the `-u` option (which is the default), and to edit group quotas, use the `-g` switch. A snipped example of editing a user account's quota is shown in Listing 10.36.

Listing 10.36: Employing `edquota` to create user and group quota files

```
# edquota -u user1
Disk quotas for user user1 (uid 1000):
Filesystem      blocks    soft    hard inodes    soft    hard
/dev/sdb1          212    4096    6144      2       0       0
~
[...]
```

When you enter the `edquota` command, you are put into the `vim` (`vi`) editor for the quota file, unless you have set the `$EDITOR` environment variable to point to another text editor. In the quota file, there are two preset items that you cannot permanently modify: `blocks` (blocks used) and `inodes` (number of current files). That is because this information was obtained when the `quotacheck` command was previously run and it is not set via the `edquota` utility.

You can, however, modify the soft and hard limits for both blocks and inodes. When you set a hard block limit, you are setting the maximum number of blocks the user can fill with data. When you set inode hard limits, you are setting the total number of files that the user can create. Once the user hits either of these limits, no more disk space or file creation is available for that account on this particular filesystem. Note that if set to 0, the limit is disabled. Notice in Listing 10.36 that inode limits are disabled.

Soft limits are a little nicer. Once the user hits a set soft limit, they can go for an extended period past this limit. It is called a *grace period*.

Once you have user (or group) quotas modified, you need to establish the grace period for any soft limits set. To do this, you use the edquota -t command. These grace periods are used for all users and groups. An example is shown in Listing 10.37.

Listing 10.37: Employing edquota -t to set soft limit grace periods

```
# edquota -t
Grace period before enforcing soft limits for users:
Time units may be: days, hours, minutes, or seconds
  Filesystem      Block grace period      Inode grace period
  /dev/sdb1             7days                   7days
~
```

When you issue the edquota -t command, you are again thrown into the vim editor, unless you have modified the $EDITOR environment variable. Grace periods can be set for both blocks and inodes and can be a matter of days, hours, minutes, or even seconds, which doesn't seem very graceful.

If you have some sort of odd problem when enabling filesystem quotas, you can quickly turn them off with the quotaoff command, using super user privileges. The –a option will allow you to turn them off for all the system's quota-enabled filesystems. You will need to specify user quotas (–u) and/or group quotas (–g) in the command. Once you have fixed the issues, turn filesystem quotas back on using the quotaon command.

When you have modified a user's quota limits and set grace periods, it's a good idea to double-check your modifications. The quota command can help here. An example is shown in Listing 10.38.

Listing 10.38: Using quota to check a user's quota limits

```
# quota -u user1
Disk quotas for user user1 (uid 1000):
Filesystem blocks quota limit grace  files quota limit grace
/dev/sdb1    212   4096  6144          2     0     0
#
```

Notice in Listing 10.38 that no information is listed for the user account in the grace column. This means that the user has *not* gone over a soft limit and is *not* currently in a grace period.

After all that work, you should do another check. You can audit all your filesystems employing quota limits with the repquota command. An example is shown in Listing 10.39.

Listing 10.39: Using repquota to check all the filesystems' quotas

```
# repquota -a
*** Report for user quotas on device /dev/sdb1
Block grace time: 7days; Inode grace time: 7days
                        Block limits              File limits
User          used    soft    hard  grace    used  soft  hard  grace
----------------------------------------------------------------------
root      --    12       0       0              1     0     0
user1     --   212    4096    6144              2     0     0
#
```

This should keep your filesystems humming along. However, be aware that it is a good idea to set up a periodic check of your filesystems' quotas using the quotacheck utility. You can automate this by setting up a cron job to do so, as covered in Chapter 26.

Summary

Managing the user account and group memberships for a Linux system involves many critical pieces. You need to understand the account creation process as well as the files used. You must grasp the entire mechanism for times when troubleshooting authentication issues for a particular user is necessary. In addition, being able to use various utilities for identifying various users can assist.

User accounts may be gathered together into various groups, which provide additional access. These group memberships are part of the authorization in which users can gain entry into various files and directories. Knowing the key areas of group administration is critical for proper Linux system management.

Besides protecting your system through properly authenticated and authorization user and group mechanisms, you can also shield your filesystems from overuse. In particular, setting up filesystem user and group quotas will provide an additional layer of protection.

Exam Essentials

Describe the players in managing user accounts.   The /etc/login.defs and /etc/default/useradd files configure various settings for the useradd command's default behavior. Because the directive settings within these files vary from distribution to distribution, it is wise to peruse them prior to employing the useradd utility to create accounts. When an account is created, the /etc/passwd, /etc/shadow, and /etc/group files are all modified. Depending on the user account creation configuration, a user home directory may be created and files copied to it from the /etc/skel directory.

Summarize managing groups.   The commands involved in creating, modifying, and deleting groups are the groupadd, groupmod, and groupdel commands. These commands cause modifications to the /etc/group file. If you need to add a user to a group, you need to employ the usermod utility. A user can easily switch from the account's default group to another group in which the account is a member by using the newgrp program. Account group membership can be audited via the groups and getent commands as well as by viewing the /etc/group file.

Outline the environment files.   The Bash shell uses environment variables to store information about the shell session and the working environment. These variables are set using environment files. Which environment files are run depends on how a user is logging into a system as well as the distribution the account is on. User environment files are hidden files in that they begin with a dot (.) and are potentially the .bash_profile, .bash_login, .profile, and .bashrc files. Global files may include /etc/bashrc, /etc/bash.bashrc, /etc/profile, and files within the /etc/profile.d/ directory.

Explain the various methods to query user account information.   There are several utilities you can employ to determine user account information for users who are currently logged into their accounts as well as those who are not. The "who" commands have three variations, which are the whoami, who, and w utilities. The id program is useful for matching UID and GID numbers to particular user accounts. The last command is helpful for viewing not only when a system has rebooted but also whether or not a user is currently logged into the system or when the last time the account was accessed.

Describe how to manage filesystem usage quotas.   Prior to setting user account or group quota limits on a system, you must enable quotas on the filesystem using the usrquota and grpquota options in the /etc/fstab file. Once the filesystem is unmounted and then remounted, you can create the needed user and/or group files with the quotacheck utility. After that is accomplished, user or group limits are set with the edquota command. You can also view and/or verify quotas using the repquota program.

Review Questions

1. Which of the following are fields within an /etc/passwd file record? (Choose all that apply.)
    A. User account's username
    B. Password
    C. Password change date
    D. Special flag
    E. UID

2. Which of the following are fields in an /etc/shadow file record? (Choose all that apply.)
    A. Password expiration date
    B. Account expiration date
    C. Password
    D. Comment
    E. Default shell

3. Which field contains the same data for both an /etc/passwd and an /etc/shadow file record?
    A. Password
    B. Account expiration date
    C. UID
    D. GID
    E. User account's username

4. Which of the following commands will allow you to view the NUhura account's record data in the /etc/passwd file? (Choose all that apply.)
    A. getent NUhura passwd
    B. cat /etc/passwd
    C. passwd NUhura
    D. grep NUhura /etc/passwd
    E. getent passwd NUhura

5. You use the useradd -D command to view account creation configuration directives. What file does this command pull its displayed information from?
    A. The /etc/passwd file
    B. The /etc/shadow file
    C. The /etc/group file
    D. The /etc/login.defs file
    E. The /etc/default/useradd file

6. You create an account using the appropriate utility, except for some reason the account's home directory was not created. Which of the following most likely caused this to occur?

   A. The HOME directive is set to no.

   B. You did not employ super user privileges.

   C. The CREATE_HOME directive is not set.

   D. The INACTIVE directive is set to −1.

   E. The EXPIRE date is set and it is before today.

7. Your boss has asked you to remove KSingh's account and all his home directory files from the system immediately. Which command should you use?

   A. usermod −r KSingh

   B. rm −r /home/KSingh

   C. userdel Ksingh

   D. userdel −r KSingh

   E. usermod −d KSingh

8. Which of the following will allow you to change an account's /etc/shadow file record data? (Choose all that apply.)

   A. The passwd command

   B. The usermod command

   C. The userdel command

   D. The getent command

   E. The chage command

9. Which of the following commands will allow you to switch temporarily from your account's default group to another group you are a member of?

   A. The usermod command

   B. The newgrp command

   C. The groups command

   D. The groupadd command

   E. The groupmod command

10. Which of the following commands is the best one to add JKirk as a member to a new group called the NCC-1701 group and not remove any of the account's previous group memberships?

   A. usermod −g NCC-1701 JKirk

   B. usermod −G NCC-1701 JKirk

   C. usermod −aG NCC-1701 JKirk

   D. groupadd NCC-1701

   E. groupmod NCC-1701 JKirk

11. Which of the following commands could be used to view the members of the NCC-1701 group? (Choose all that apply.)

    A. groups NCC-1701

    B. getent group NCC-1701

    C. getent groups NCC-1701

    D. grep NCC-1701 /etc/group

    E. grep NCC-1701 /etc/groups

12. User environment files typically come from where?

    A. /etc/skel

    B. /home/*userid*

    C. $HOME

    D. ~

    E. /etc/

13. A user has logged into the tty3 terminal. Which of the following user environment files is executed first if found in the user's home directory?

    A. The .bash_login file

    B. The .bashrc file

    C. The .profile file

    D. The .bash.bashrc file

    E. The .bash_profile file

14. Which of the following files and directories may be involved in setting up the environment for all system users? (Choose all that apply.)

    A. /etc/bash_profile/

    B. /etc/profile

    C. /etc/profile.d/

    D. /etc/bashrc

    E. /etc/bash.bashrc

15. Which of the following commands displays information about the account issuing the command? (Choose all that apply.)

    A. whoami

    B. who am i

    C. cat $HOME/.bashrc

    D. cat $HOME/.profile

    E. id

16. Which of the following commands will display CPU load data along with information concerning users who are currently logged into the system?

    A. The who command

    B. The id command

    C. The whoami command

    D. The w command

    E. The last command

17. The last command, by default, pulls its data from what file?

    A. The /var/run/utmp file

    B. The /var/log/wtmp file

    C. The /var/log/wtmp.1 file

    D. The /etc/shadow file

    E. The /etc/passwd file

18. Which of the following are options used in the /etc/fstab file to designate a filesystem as one that uses quotas? (Choose all that apply.)

    A. usrquota

    B. quotaon

    C. grpquota

    D. quotacheck

    E. aquota.user

19. A problem has occurred concerning group quotas on three filesystems. You need to quickly remove all filesystems' quota limits to temporarily resolve this issue. What is the best command to employ?

    A. vi /etc/fstab

    B. quotaoff -a

    C. quotacheck -cg

    D. quotacheck -cu

    E. umount

20. You need to edit quota grace periods. Which of the following commands should you use?

    A. edquota -u

    B. edquota -g

    C. edquota -t

    D. edquota -G

    E. edquota --grace

Chapter

11

Handling Storage

✓ **Objective 1.1: Summarize Linux fundamentals.**

✓ **Objective 1.3: Given a scenario, configure and manage storage using the appropriate tools.**

The world runs on data. Whether it's an employee database, a folder with all of your family pictures, or just your weekly bowling scores, the ability to save and retrieve data is a must for every application. Linux provides lots of different ways to store and manage files for applications. This chapter first discusses the basics of how Linux handles storage devices, and then it walks through how you use those methods to manage data in a Linux environment.

Storage Basics

The most common way to persistently store data on computer systems is to use a *hard disk drive (HDD)*. Hard disk drives are physical devices that store data using a set of disk platters that spin around, storing data magnetically on the platters with a movable read/write head that writes and retrieves magnetic images on the platters.

These days, another popular type of persistent storage is called a *solid-state drive (SSD)*. These drives use integrated circuits to store data electronically. There are no moving parts contained in SSDs, making them faster and more resilient than HDDs. Although currently SSDs are more expensive than HDDs, technology is quickly changing that, and it may not be long before HDDs are a thing of the past.

Linux handles both HDD and SSD storage devices the same way. It mostly depends on the connection method used to connect the drives to the Linux system. The following sections describe the different methods that Linux uses in connecting and using both HDD and SSD devices.

Drive Connections

While HDDs and SSDs differ in how they store data, they both interface with the Linux system using the same methods. There are four main types of drive connections that you'll run into with Linux systems:

- *Parallel Advanced Technology Attachment (PATA)* connects drives using a parallel interface, which requires a wide cable. PATA supports two devices per adapter.

- *Serial Advanced Technology Attachment (SATA)* connects drives using a serial interface, but at a much faster speed than PATA. SATA supports up to four devices per adapter.

- *Small Computer System Interface (SCSI)* connects drives using a parallel interface, but with the speed of SATA. SCSI supports up to eight devices per adapter.

- Nonvolatile Memory Express (NVMe) connects solid-state drives using a parallel interface for maximum data transfer speeds. The NVMe standard supports up to 12 devices per adapter.

When you connect a drive to a Linux system, the Linux kernel assigns the drive device a file in the /dev folder. That file is called a *raw device*, as it provides a path directly to the drive from the Linux system. Any data written to the file is written to the drive, and reading the file reads data directly from the drive.

For PATA devices, this file is named /dev/hd*x*, where *x* is a letter representing the individual drive, starting with a. For SATA and SCSI devices, Linux uses /dev/sd*x*, where *x* is a letter representing the individual drive, again starting with a. With NVMe devices, Linux uses /dev/nvme*x*, again where *x* is a letter representing the individual drive. Thus, to reference the first SATA device on the system, you'd use /dev/sda, then for the second device /dev/sdb, and so on.

Partitioning Drives

Most operating systems, including Linux, allow you to *partition* a drive into multiple sections. A partition is a self-contained section in the drive that the operating system treats as a separate storage space.

Partitioning drives can help you better organize your data, such as segmenting operating system data from user data. If a rogue user fills up the disk space with data, the operating system will still have room to operate on the separate partition.

Partitions must be tracked by some type of indexing system on the drive. Systems that use the old BIOS boot loader method (see Chapter 5, "Explaining the Boot Process") use the *Master Boot Record (MBR)* method for managing disk partitions. This method only supports up to four *primary partitions* on a drive. Each primary partition itself, however, can be split into multiple *extended partitions*.

Systems that use the UEFI boot loader method (see Chapter 5) use the more advanced *GUID Partition Table (GPT)* method for managing partitions, which supports up to 128 partitions on a drive. Linux assigns the partition numbers in the order that the partition appears on the drive, starting with number 1.

Linux creates /dev files for each separate disk partition. It attaches the partition number to the end of the device name and numbers the primary partitions starting at 1, so the first primary partition on the first SATA drive would be /dev/sda1. MBR extended partitions are numbered starting at 5, so the first extended partition is assigned the file /dev/sda5.

Automatic Drive Detection

Linux systems detect drives and partitions at boot time and assign each one a unique device filename. However, with the invention of removable USB drives (such as memory sticks), which can be added and removed at will while the system is running, that method needed to be modified.

Most Linux systems now use the *udev* application. The udev program runs in the background at all times and automatically detects new hardware connected to the running Linux system. As you connect new drives, USB devices, or optical drives (such as CD and DVD devices), udev will detect them and assign each one a unique device filename in the /dev folder.

Another feature of the udev application is that it also creates *persistent device files* for storage devices. When you add or remove a removable storage device, the /dev name assigned to it may change, depending on what devices are connected at any given time. That can make it difficult for applications to find the same storage device each time.

To solve that problem, the udev application uses the /dev/disk folder to create links to the /dev storage device files based on unique attributes of the drive. There are four separate folders udev creates for storing links:

- */dev/disk/by-id* links storage devices by their manufacturer make, model, and serial number.

- */dev/disk/by-label* links storage devices by the label assigned to them.

- */dev/disk/by-path* links storage devices by the physical hardware port they are connected to.

- */dev/disk/by-uuid* links storage devices by the 128-bit universally unique identifier (UUID) assigned to the device.

With the udev device links, you can specifically reference a storage device by a permanent identifier rather than where or when it was plugged into the Linux system.

Partitioning Tools

After you connect a drive to your Linux system, you'll need to create partitions on it (even if there's only one partition). Linux provides several tools for working with raw storage devices to create partitions. The following sections cover the most popular partitioning tools you'll run across in Linux.

Working with *fdisk*

The most common command-line partitioning tool is the *fdisk* utility. The fdisk program allows you to create, view, delete, and modify partitions on any drive that uses the MBR method of indexing partitions.

To use the fdisk program, you must specify the drive device name (not the partition name) of the device you want to work with:

```
$ sudo fdisk /dev/sda
[sudo] password for rich:
Welcome to fdisk (util-linux 2.23.2).
```

Changes will remain in memory only, until you decide to write them.
Be careful before using the write command.

Command (m for help):

The fdisk program uses its own command line that allows you to submit commands to work with the drive partitions. Table 11.1 shows the common commands you have available to work with.

TABLE 11.1   Common fdisk commands

Command	Description
a	Toggle a bootable flag.
b	Edit bsd disk label.
c	Toggle the DOS compatibility flag.
d	Delete a partition.
g	Create a new empty GPT partition table.
G	Create an IRIX (SGI) partition table.
l	List known partition types.
m	Print this menu.
n	Add a new partition.
o	Create a new empty DOS partition table.
p	Print the partition table.
q	Quit without saving changes.
s	Create a new empty Sun disk label.
t	Change a partition's system ID.
u	Change display/entry units.
v	Verify the partition table.
w	Write table to disk and exit.
x	Extra functionality (experts only).

The p command displays the current partition scheme on the drive:

```
Command (m for help): p

Disk /dev/sda: 10.7 GB, 10737418240 bytes, 20971520 sectors
Units = sectors of 1 * 512 = 512 bytes
Sector size (logical/physical): 512 bytes / 512 bytes
I/O size (minimum/optimal): 512 bytes / 512 bytes
Disk label type: dos
Disk identifier: 0x000528e6

   Device Boot      Start        End      Blocks   Id  System
/dev/sda1    *       2048    2099199     1048576   83  Linux
/dev/sda2         2099200   20971519     9436160   83  Linux

Command (m for help):
```

In this example, the /dev/sda drive is sectioned into two partitions, sda1 and sda2. The Id and System columns refer to the type of filesystem the partition is formatted to handle. We cover that in the section "Understanding Filesystems" later in this chapter. Both partitions are formatted to support a Linux filesystem. The first partition is allocated about 1 GB of space, whereas the second is allocated a little over 9 GB of space.

The fdisk command is somewhat rudimentary in that it doesn't allow you to alter the size of an existing partition; all you can do is delete the existing partition and rebuild it from scratch.

To be able to boot the system from a partition, you must set the boot flag for the partition. You do that with the a command. The bootable partitions are indicated in the output listing with an asterisk.

If you make any changes to the drive partitions, you must exit using the w command to write the changes to the drive.

Working with *gdisk*

If you're working with drives that use the GPT indexing method, you'll need to use the *gdisk* program:

```
$ sudo gdisk /dev/sda
[sudo] password for rich:
GPT fdisk (gdisk) version 1.0.3

Partition table scan:
  MBR: protective
  BSD: not present
  APM: not present
  GPT: present
```

```
Found valid GPT with protective MBR; using GPT.

Command (? for help):
```

The gdisk program identifies the type of formatting used on the drive. If the drive doesn't currently use the GPT method, gdisk offers you the option to convert it to a GPT drive.

WARNING   Be careful with converting the drive method specified for your drive. The method you select must be compatible with the system firmware (BIOS or UEFI). If not, your drive will not be able to boot.

The gdisk program also uses its own command prompt, allowing you to enter commands to manipulate the drive layout, as shown in Table 11.2.

TABLE 11.2   Common gdisk commands

Command	Description
b	Back up GPT data to a file.
c	Change a partition's name.
d	Delete a partition.
i	Show detailed information on a partition.
l	List known partition types.
n	Add a new partition.
o	Create a new empty GUID partition table (GPT).
p	Print the partition table.
q	Quit without saving changes.
r	Recovery and transformation options (experts only).
s	Sort partitions.
t	Change a partition's type code.
v	Verify disk.
w	Write table to disk and exit.
x	Extra functionality (experts only).
?	Print this menu.

You'll notice that many of the gdisk commands are similar to those in the fdisk program, making it easier to switch between the two programs. One of the added options that can come in handy is the i option, which displays more detailed information about a partition:

```
Command (? for help): i
Partition number (1-3): 2
Partition GUID code: 0FC63DAF-8483-4772-8E79-3D69D8477DE4 (Linux filesystem)
Partition unique GUID: 5E4213F9-9566-4898-8B4E-FB8888ADDE78
First sector: 1953792 (at 954.0 MiB)
Last sector: 26623999 (at 12.7 GiB)
Partition size: 24670208 sectors (11.8 GiB)
Attribute flags: 0000000000000000
Partition name: ''

Command (? for help):
```

The GNU *parted* Command

The GNU *parted* program provides yet another command-line interface for working with drive partitions:

```
$ sudo parted
GNU Parted 3.2
Using /dev/sda
Welcome to GNU Parted! Type 'help' to view a list of commands.
(parted) print
Model: ATA VBOX HARDDISK (scsi)
Disk /dev/sda: 15.6GB
Sector size (logical/physical): 512B/512B
Partition Table: gpt
Disk Flags:

Number  Start    End     Size    File system     Name  Flags
 1      1049kB   1000MB  999MB   fat32                  boot, esp
 2      1000MB   13.6GB  12.6GB  ext4
 3      13.6GB   15.6GB  2000MB  linux-swap(v1)

(parted)
```

One of the selling features of the parted program is that it allows you to modify existing partition sizes, so you can easily shrink or grow partitions on the drive.

The GNU parted package also contains the partprobe utility. The partprobe command triggers the Linux system to reread the partition table for a specific disk. While not necessary on a system with local hard drives, systems that share drives may need to use this if one system updates the partition table of a hard drive and the other system doesn't yet know about the update.

Graphical Tools

There are also some graphical tools available to use if you're working from a graphical desktop environment. The most common of these is the GNOME Partition Editor, called *GParted*. Figure 11.1 shows an example of running the gparted command in an Ubuntu desktop environment.

FIGURE 11.1   The GParted interface

Partition	File System	Mount Point	Size	Used	Unused	Flags
/dev/sda1	fat32	/boot/efi	953.00 MiB	7.96 MiB	945.04 MiB	boot, esp
/dev/sda2	ext4	/	11.76 GiB	5.07 GiB	6.70 GiB	
/dev/sda3	linux-swap		1.86 GiB	0.00 B	1.86 GiB	

The gparted window displays each of the drives on a system one at a time, showing all of the partitions contained in the drive in a graphical layout. You right-click a partition to select options for mounting or unmounting, formatting, deleting, or resizing the partition.

Although it's certainly possible to interact with a drive as a raw device, that's not usually how Linux applications work. There's a lot of work trying to read and write data to a raw device. Instead, Linux provides a method for handling all the dirty work for us, and we cover it in the next section.

Understanding Filesystems

Just like storing stuff in a closet, storing data in a Linux system requires some method of organization for it to be efficient. Linux utilizes *filesystems* to manage data stored on storage devices. A filesystem utilizes a method of maintaining a map to locate each file placed in the storage device. This and the following sections describe the Linux filesystem and show how you can locate files and folders contained in it.

The Linux filesystem can be one of the most confusing aspects of working with Linux. Locating files on drives, CDs, and USB memory sticks can be a challenge at first.

If you're familiar with how Windows manages files and folders, you know that Windows assigns *drive letters* to each storage device you connect to the system. For example, Windows uses C: for the main drive on the system or E: for a USB memory stick plugged into the system.

In Windows, you're used to seeing file paths such as

```
C:\Users\rich\Documents\test.docx
```

This path indicates that the file is located in the Documents folder for the rich user account, which is stored on the disk partition assigned the letter C (usually the first drive on the system).

The Windows path tells you exactly what physical device the file is stored on. However, Linux doesn't use this method to reference files. It uses a *virtual directory* structure. The virtual directory contains file paths from all the storage devices installed on the system consolidated into a single directory structure.

The Virtual Directory

The Linux virtual directory structure contains a single base directory, called the *root directory*. The root directory lists files and folders beneath it based on the folder path used to get to them, similar to the way Windows does it.

> **NOTE**
>
> Be careful with the terminology here. Although the main admin user account in Linux is called *root*, that's not related to the root of the virtual directory, usually called root, but denoted as just a single forward slash (/). In fact, the root user account uses a special Home directory /root, making things even more confusing!

For example, a Linux file path could look like this:

```
/home/rich/Documents/test.doc
```

First, note that the Linux path uses forward slashes instead of the backward slashes that Windows uses. That's an important difference that trips many novice Linux administrators. As for the path itself, also notice that there's no drive letter. The path only indicates that the file test.doc is stored in the Documents folder for the user rich; it doesn't give you any clues as to which physical device contains the file.

Linux places physical devices in the virtual directory using *mount points*. A mount point is a folder placeholder in the virtual directory that points to a specific physical device. Figure 11.2 demonstrates how this works.

In Figure 11.2, there are two drives used on the Linux system. The first drive on the left is associated with the root of the virtual directory. The second drive is mounted at the location /home, which is where the user folders are located. Once the second drive is mounted to the virtual directory, files and folders stored on the drive are available under the /home folder.

FIGURE 11.2   The Linux virtual directory structure divided between two drives

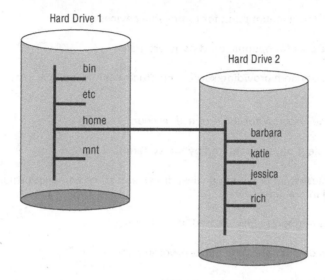

Since Linux stores everything in the virtual directory, it can get somewhat complicated. Fortunately, there's a standard format defined for the Linux virtual directory, called the Linux *filesystem hierarchy standard (FHS)*. The FHS defines core folder names and locations that should be present on every Linux system and what type of data they should contain. Table 11.3 shows just a few of the more common folders defined in the FHS.

TABLE 11.3   Common Linux FHS folders

Folder	Description
/bin	Executable programs necessary for the system to run in single-user mode
/boot	Contains bootloader files used to boot the system
/dev	Device files
/etc	System service configuration files
/home	Contains user data files
/lib	Library files required by executable programs

TABLE 11.3   Common Linux FHS folders *(continued)*

Folder	Description
/media	Used as a mount point for removable devices
/mnt	Also used as a mount point for removable devices
/opt	Contains data for optional third-party programs
/proc	Virtual filesystem providing kernel and process information as files, updated in real time
/root	The home directory for the root user account
/sbin	Executable programs required by the system
/sys	Virtual filesystem providing device, driver, and some kernel information as files, updated in real time
/tmp	Contains temporary files created by system users
/usr	Contains data for standard Linux programs
/usr/bin	Contains local user programs and data
/usr/local	Contains data for programs unique to the local installation
/usr/sbin	Contains data for system programs and data
/var	Files whose content is expected to change frequently, such as log files

WARNING   While the FHS helps standardize the Linux virtual filesystem, not all Linux distributions follow it completely. It's best to consult with your specific Linux distribution's documentation on how it manages files in the virtual directory structure.

Maneuvering around the Filesystem

Using the virtual directory makes it a breeze to move files from one physical device to another. You don't need to worry about drive letters, just the locations in the virtual directory:

```
$ cp /home/rich/Documents/myfile.txt /media/usb
```

In moving the file from the `Documents` folder to a USB memory stick, we used the full path in the virtual directory to both the file and the USB memory stick. This format is called an *absolute path*. The absolute path to a file always starts at the root folder (/) and includes every folder along the virtual directory tree to the file.

Alternatively, you can use a *relative path* to specify a file location. The relative path to a file denotes the location of a file relative to your current location in the virtual directory tree structure. If you were already in the `Documents` folder, you'd just need to type

```
$ cp myfile.txt /media/usb
```

When Linux sees that the path doesn't start with a forward slash, it assumes the path is relative to the current directory.

Formatting Filesystems

Before you can assign a drive partition to a mount point in the virtual directory, you must format it using a filesystem. Linux supports numerous filesystem types, with each having different features and capabilities. The following sections discuss the different filesystems that Linux supports and how to format a drive partition for the filesystems.

Common Filesystem Types

Each operating system utilizes its own filesystem type for storing data on drives. Linux not only supports several of its own filesystem types, it also supports filesystems of other operating systems. The following sections cover the most common Linux and non-Linux filesystems that you can use in your Linux partitions.

Linux Filesystems

When you create a filesystem specifically for use on a Linux system, there are six main filesystems that you can choose from:

- *btrfs*: A newer, high-performance filesystem that supports files up to 16 exbibytes (EiB) in size and a total filesystem size of 16EiB. It also can perform its own form of Redundant Array of Inexpensive Disks (RAID) as well as logical volume management (LVM).

It includes additional advanced features such as built-in snapshots for backup, improved fault tolerance, and data compression on the fly.

- *eCryptfs*: The Enterprise Cryptographic File System (eCryptfs) applies a POSIX-compliant encryption protocol to data before storing it on the device. This provides a layer of protection for data stored on the device. Only the operating system that created the filesystem can read data from it.

- *ext3*: Also called ext3fs, this is a descendant of the original Linux ext filesystem. It supports files up to 2 tebibytes (TiB), with a total filesystem size of 16 TiB. It supports journaling as well as faster startup and recovery.

- *ext4*: Also called ext4fs, it's the current version of the original Linux filesystem. It supports files up to 16 TiB, with a total filesystem size of 1 EiB. It also supports journaling and utilizes improved performance features.

- *XFS*: A 64-bit high-performance journaling filesystem created by Silicon Graphics in 1993 and ported to Linux in 2001. It supports filesystems up to 8 exbibytes.

- *swap*: The swap filesystem allows you to create virtual memory for your system using space on a physical drive. The system can then swap data out of normal memory into the swap space, providing a method of adding additional memory to your system. This is not intended for storing persistent data.

Most Linux distributions these days use the ext4fs filesystem as the default, although Red Hat has recently chosen the XFS filesystem as the default. Both filesystems provide *journaling*, which is a method of tracking data not yet written to the drive in a log file, called the journal. If the system fails before the data can be written to the drive, the journal data can be recovered and stored upon the next system boot.

Non-Linux Filesystems

One of the great features of Linux that makes it so versatile is its ability to read data stored on devices formatted for other operating systems, such as Apple and Microsoft. This feature makes it a breeze to share data between different systems running different operating systems.

Here's a list of common non-Linux filesystems that Linux can handle:

- *CIFS*: The Common Internet File System (CIFS) is a filesystem protocol created by Microsoft for reading and writing data across a network using a network storage device. It was released to the public for use on all operating systems.

- *HFS*: The Hierarchical File System (HFS) was developed by Apple for its macOS systems. Linux can also interact with the more advanced HFS+ filesystem.

- *ISO-9660*: The ISO-9660 standard is used for creating filesystems on CD-ROM devices.

- *NFS*: The Network File System (NFS) is an open source standard for reading and writing data across a network using a network storage device.

- *NTFS*: The New Technology File System (NTFS) is the filesystem used by the Microsoft NT operating system and subsequent versions of Windows. Linux can read and write data on an NTFS partition as of kernel 2.6.x.

- *SMB*: The Server Message Block (SMB) filesystem was created by Microsoft as a pro-prietary filesystem used for network storage and interacting with other network devices (such as printers). Support for SMB allows Linux clients and servers to interact with Microsoft clients and servers on a network.

- *UDF*: The Universal Disc Format (UDF) is commonly used on DVD-ROM devices for storing data. Linux can both read data from a DVD and write data to a DVD using this filesystem.

- *VFAT*: The Virtual File Allocation Table (VFAT) is an extension of the original Micro-soft File Allocation Table (FAT) filesystem. It's not commonly used on drives but is com-monly used for removable storage devices such as USB memory sticks.

- *ZFS*: The Zettabyte File System (ZFS) was created by Sun Microsystems (now part of Oracle) for its Unix workstations and servers. Another high-performance filesystem, it has features similar to the btrfs Linux filesystem.

It's generally not recommended to format a partition using a non-Linux filesystem if you plan on using the drive for only Linux systems. Linux supports these filesystems mainly as a method for sharing data with other operating systems.

Creating Filesystems

The Swiss Army knife for creating filesystems in Linux is the mkfs program. The *mkfs* program is actually a front end to several individual tools for creating specific filesystems, such as the mkfs.ext4 program for creating ext4 filesystems.

The beauty of the mkfs program is that you only need to remember one program name to create any type of filesystem on your Linux system. Just use the -t option to specify the filesystem type:

```
$ sudo mkfs -t ext4 /dev/sdb1
mke2fs 1.44.1 (24-Mar-2018)
Creating filesystem with 2621440 4k blocks and 655360 inodes
Filesystem UUID: f9137b26-0caf-4a8a-afd0-392002424ee8
Superblock backups stored on blocks:

32768, 98304, 163840, 229376, 294912, 819200, 884736, 1605632
Allocating group tables: done
Writing inode tables: done
Creating journal (16384 blocks): done
Writing superblocks and filesystem accounting information: done
$
```

After you specify the -t option, just specify the partition device filename for the partition you want to format on the command line. Notice that the mkfs program does a lot of things behind the scenes when formatting the filesystem. Each filesystem has its own method for indexing files and folders and tracking file access. The mkfs program creates all the index files and tables necessary for the specific filesystem.

WARNING   Be very careful when specifying the partition device filename. When you format a partition, any existing data on the partition is lost. If you specify the wrong partition name, you could lose important data or make your Linux system unable to boot.

Mounting Filesystems

Once you've formatted a drive partition with a filesystem, you can add it to the virtual directory on your Linux system. This process is called *mounting* the filesystem.

You can either manually mount the partition in the virtual directory structure from the command line or allow Linux to automatically mount the partition at boot time. The following sections walk through both of these methods.

Manually Mounting Devices

To temporarily mount a filesystem to the Linux virtual directory, use the mount command. The basic format for the mount command is

```
mount -t fstype device mountpoint
```

Use the -t command-line option to specify the filesystem type of the device:

```
$ sudo mount -t ext4 /dev/sdb1 /media/usb1
$
```

If you specify the mount command with no parameters, it displays all of the devices currently mounted on the Linux system. Be prepared for a long output, though, as most Linux distributions mount lots of virtual devices in the virtual directory to provide information about system resources. Listing 11.1 shows a partial output from a mount command.

Listing 11.1 Output from the mount command

```
$ mount
...
/dev/sda2 on / type ext4 (rw,relatime,errors=remount-ro,data=ordered)
/dev/sda1 on /boot/efi type vfat
 (rw,relatime,fmask=0077,dmask=0077,codepage=437,iocharset=iso8859
-1,shortname=mixed,errors=remount-ro)
...
/dev/sdb1 on /media/usb1 type ext4 (rw,relatime,data=ordered)
```

```
/dev/sdb2 on /media/usb2 type ext4 (rw,relatime,data=ordered)
rich@rich-TestBox2:~$
```

To save space, we trimmed down the output from the `mount` command to show only the physical devices on the system. The main hard drive device (`/dev/sda`) contains two partitions, and the USB memory stick device (`/dev/sdb`) also contains two partitions.

> The `mount` command uses the `-o` option to specify additional features of the filesystem, such as mounting it in read-only mode, user permissions assigned to the mount point, and how data is stored on the device. These options are shown in the output of the `mount` command. Usually you can omit the `-o` option to use the system defaults for the new mount point.

The downside to the `mount` command is that it only temporarily mounts the device in the virtual directory. When you reboot the system, you have to manually mount the devices again. This is usually fine for removable devices, such as USB memory sticks, but for more permanent devices it would be nice if Linux could mount them for us automatically. Fortunately for us, Linux can do just that.

To remove a mounted drive from the virtual directory, use the `umount` command (note the missing *n*). You can remove the mounted drive by specifying either the device filename or the mount point directory.

Automatically Mounting Devices

For permanent storage devices, Linux maintains the */etc/fstab* file to indicate which drive devices should be mounted to the virtual directory at boot time. The `/etc/fstab` file is a table that indicates the drive device file (either the raw file or one of its permanent udev filenames), the mount point location, the filesystem type, and any additional options required to mount the drive. Listing 11.2 shows the `/etc/fstab` file from an Ubuntu workstation.

Listing 11.2 The `/etc/fstab` file

```
$ cat /etc/fstab
# /etc/fstab: static file system information.
#
# Use 'blkid' to print the universally unique identifier for a
# device; this may be used with UUID= as a more robust way to name devices
# that works even if disks are added and removed. See fstab(5).
#
# <file system> <mount point>   <type>  <options>        <dump>  <pass>
# / was on /dev/sda2 during installation
UUID=46a8473c-8437-4d5f-a6a1-6596c492c3ce /               ext4
  errors=remount-ro 0        1
# /boot/efi was on /dev/sda1 during installation
```

```
UUID=864B-62F5  /boot/efi        vfat    umask=0077        0       1
# swap was on /dev/sda3 during installation
UUID=8673447a-0227-47d7-a67a-e6b837bd7188 none            swap    sw
0       0
$
```

This /etc/fstab file references the devices by their udev UUID value, ensuring that the correct drive partition is accessed no matter the order in which it appears in the raw device table. The first partition is mounted at the /boot/efi mount point in the virtual directory. The second partition is mounted at the root (/) of the virtual directory, and the third partition is mounted as a swap area for virtual memory.

You can manually add devices to the /etc/fstab file so that they are mounted automatically when the Linux system boots. However, if they don't exist at boot time, that will generate a boot error.

On Linux servers using systemd, if you only use the /etc/fstab file, systemd still manages these filesystems. The mount points listed in /etc/fstab are converted into native units when either the server is rebooted or systemd is reloaded. In fact, using /etc/fstab for persistent filesystems is the preferred method over manually creating a mount unit file. For more information on this process, type **man systemd-fstab-generator** at the command line.

If you use the encryptfs filesystem type on any partitions, they will appear in the /etc/crypttab file and will be mounted automatically at boot time. While the system is running, you can also view all of the currently mounted devices, whether they were mounted automatically by the system or manually by users, by viewing the /etc/mtab file.

Managing Filesystems

Once you've created a filesystem and mounted it to the virtual directory, you may have to manage and maintain it to keep things running smoothly. The following sections walk through some of the Linux utilities available for managing the filesystems on your Linux system.

Retrieving Filesystem Stats

As you use your Linux system, there's no doubt that at some point you'll need to monitor disk performance and usage. There are a few different tools available to help you do that:

- *df* displays disk usage by partition.
- *du* displays disk usage by directory, good for finding users or applications that are taking up the most disk space.
- *iostat* displays a real-time chart of disk statistics by partition.
- *lsblk* displays current partition sizes and mount points.

A quick way to get a snapshot of the disk space situation on your Linux system is to use the df and du commands:

```
$ df -t xfs -h
Filesystem            Size  Used Avail Use% Mounted on
/dev/mapper/rl-root    15G  6.6G  7.7G  47% /
/dev/sda1            1014M  351M  664M  35% /boot
$ sudo du -d 1
318632   ./boot
0        ./dev
0        ./proc
9448     ./run
0        ./sys
32400    ./etc
48       ./root
704712   ./var
5711056  ./usr
114656   ./home
369421   ./media
0        ./mnt
18856    ./opt
0        ./srv
12       ./tmp
7279241  .
$
```

The df command shows the overall disk space available on the system, and the du command helps show what directories have the most data in them.

In addition to these tools, the /proc and /sys folders are special filesystems that the kernel uses for recording system statistics. Two directories that can be useful when working with filesystems are the /proc/partitions and /proc/mounts folders, which provide information on system partitions and mount points, respectively. Additionally, the /sys/block folder contains separate folders for each mounted drive, showing partitions and kernel-level stats.

If your Linux system uses specialized storage devices, there are often additional command tools available other than the standard Linux tools. For example, if your Linux system uses SCSI controllers you can use the `lssci` command to display information about the hard drives connected to the SCSI controllers, or for systems that use fiber-channel networks to connect a storage area network (SAN) to your Linux system, the `fcstat` command is very useful.

Some filesystems, such as ext3 and ext4, allocate a specific number of inodes when created. An *inode* is an entry in the index table that tracks files stored on the filesystem. If the filesystem runs out of inode entries in the table, you can't create any more files, even if there's available space on the drive. Using the `-i` option with the `df` command will show you the percentage of inodes used on a filesystem and can be a lifesaver.

Filesystem Tools

Linux uses the `e2fsprogs` package of tools to provide utilities for working with ext filesystems (such as ext3 and ext4). The most popular tools in the `e2fsprogs` package are as follows:

- *blkid* displays information about block devices, such as storage drives.
- *chattr* changes file attributes on the filesystem.
- *debugfs* manually views and modifies the filesystem structure, such as undeleting a file or extracting a corrupted file.
- *dumpe2fs* displays block and superblock group information.
- *e2label* changes the label on the filesystem.
- *resize2fs* expands or shrinks a filesystem.
- *tune2fs* modifies filesystem parameters.

These tools help you fine-tune parameters on an ext filesystem, but if corruption occurs on the filesystem, you'll need the `fsck` program.

The XFS filesystem also has a set of tools available for tuning the filesystem. Here are the two that you'll most likely run across:

- *xfs_admin* displays or changes filesystem parameters such as the label or UUID assigned.
- *xfs_info* displays information about a mounted filesystem, including the block sizes and sector sizes as well as label and UUID information.

If you're using the btrfs filesystem, the `btrfs` command provides access to several utilities for managing the filesystem:

- *balance* balances filesystem chunks across multiple devices
- *check* performs an offline check of a btrfs filesystem

- *device* provides device management for btrfs filesystems by adding or deleting a physical device.

- *filesystem* provides filesystem management utilities for an existing btrfs filesystem, such as displaying information and resizing filesystems.

- *quota* allows you to set quotas on btrfs filesystems.

- *restore* allows you to restore files from a damaged btrfs filesystem.

While these ext, XFS, and btrfs tools are useful, they can't help fix things if the filesystem itself has errors. For that, the *fsck* program is the tool to use:

```
$ sudo fsck -f /dev/sdb1
fsck from util-linux 2.31.1
e2fsck 1.44.1 (24-Mar-2018)
Pass 1: Checking inodes, blocks, and sizes
Pass 2: Checking directory structure
Pass 3: Checking directory connectivity
Pass 4: Checking reference counts
Pass 5: Checking group summary information
/dev/sdb1: 11/655360 files (0.0% non-contiguous), 66753/2621440 blocks
$
```

 As of this writing the XFS module for `fsck` does not repair XFS filesystems. For now you'll need to use the `xfs_repair` tool.

The `fsck` program is a front end to several different programs that check the various filesystems to match the index against the actual files stored in the filesystem. If any discrepancies occur, run the `fsck` program in repair mode, and it will attempt to reconcile the discrepancies and fix the filesystem.

Storage Alternatives

Standard partition layouts on storage devices do have their limitations. Once you create and format a partition, it's not easy making it larger or smaller. Individual partitions are also susceptible to disk failures, in which case all of the data stored in the partition will be lost.

To accommodate more dynamic storage options, as well as fault-tolerance features, Linux has incorporated a few advanced storage management techniques. The following sections cover three popular techniques.

Multipath

The Linux kernel now supports Device Mapper Multipathing (DM-multipathing), which allows you to configure multiple paths between the Linux system and network storage devices. Multipathing aggregates the paths providing for increased throughout while all of the paths are active or for fault tolerance if one of the paths becomes inactive.

Linux DM-multipathing includes the following tools:

- *dm-multipath*: The kernel module that provides multipath support
- *multipath*: A command-line command for viewing multipath devices
- *multipathd*: A background process for monitoring paths and activating/ deactivating paths
- *kpartx*: A command-line tool for creating device entries for multipath storage devices

The DM-multipath feature uses the dynamic */dev/mapper* device file folder in Linux. Linux creates a /dev/mapper device file named mpath*N* for each new multipath storage device you add to the system, where *N* is the number of the multipath drive. That file acts as a normal device file to the Linux system, allowing you to create partitions and filesystems on the multipath device just as you would a normal drive partition.

Logical Volume Manager

The Linux *Logical Volume Manager (LMV)* also utilizes the /dev/mapper dynamic device folder to allow you to create virtual drive devices. You can aggregate multiple physical drive partitions into virtual volumes, which you then treat as a single partition on your system.

The benefit of LVM is that you can add and remove physical partitions as needed to a logical volume, expanding and shrinking the logical volume as needed.

Using LVM is somewhat complicated. Figure 11.3 demonstrates the layout for an LVM environment.

FIGURE 11.3   The Linux LVM layout

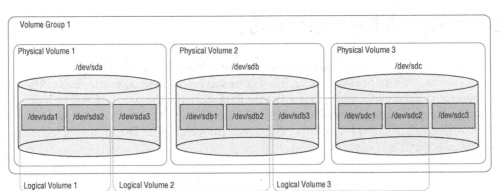

In the example shown in Figure 11.3, three physical drives each contain three partitions. The first logical volume consists of the first two partitions of the first drive. The second logical volume spans drives, combining the third partition of the first drive with the first and second partitions of the second drive to create one volume. The third logical volume consists of the third partition of the second drive and the first two partitions of the third drive. The third partition of the third drive is left unassigned and can be added later to any of the logical volumes when needed.

For each physical partition, you must mark the partition type as the Linux LVM filesystem type in `fdisk` or `gdisk`. Then, you must use several LVM tools to create and manage the logical volumes. Table 11.4 lists the LVM tools available in Linux.

TABLE 11.4   Linux LVM commands

Command	Description
lvchange	Modifies settings for a logical volume
lvconvert	Adds or removes a mirror to a non-mirrored logical volume
lvcreate	Creates a logical volume
lvdisplay	Displays information about a logical volume
lvextend	Adds to an existing logical volume
lvmdump	Creates a tarball of LVM settings
lvremove	Removes an existing logical volume
lvrename	Changes the name assigned to a logical volume
lvresize	Changes the size of the logical volume
lvs	Displays information about a logical volume
lvsscan	Scans the system for logical volumes
pvchange	Modifies settings for a physical volume
pvck	Checks the consistency of the LVM metadata on a physical volume
pvcreate	Creates a physical volume
pvdisplay	Displays information about the physical volumes
pvmove	Moves any used volumes from one device to another

TABLE 11.4   Linux LVM commands *(continued)*

Command	Description
pvremove	Removes a physical volume
pvs	Displays information about the physical volumes
pvscan	Scans disks for LVM and non-LVM volumes
vgcfbackup	Creates a text backup of the volume group metadata
vgcfrestore	Restores volume group metadata from a backup file
vgchange	Modifies settings for a volume group
vgck	Checks the integrity of a volume group
vgconvert	Changes the LVM metadata from one format to another
vgcreate	Combines physical volumes into a volume group
vgdisplay	Displays information about a volume group
vgexport	Exports a volume group
vgextend	Adds a physical volume to an existing volume group
vgimport	Imports a volume group
vgimportclone	Import and rename a duplicated volume group
vgmerge	Combines two volume groups into a single volume group
vmremove	Removes a physical volume from a volume group
vgrename	Changes the name of an existing volume group
vgs	Displays information about a volume group
vgscan	Scans disks for LVM volume groups

The logical volumes create entries in the /dev/mapper folder that represent the LVM device you can format with a filesystem and use like a normal partition. Listing 11.3 shows the steps you'd take to create a new LVM logical volume and mount it to your virtual directory.

Listing 11.3 Creating, formatting, and mounting a logical volume

```
$ sudo gdisk /dev/sdb

Command (? for help): n
Partition number (1-128, default 1): 1
First sector (34-10485726, default = 2048) or {+-}size{KMGTP}:
Last sector (2048-10485726, default = 10485726) or {+-}size{KMGTP}:
Current type is 'Linux filesystem'
Hex code or GUID (L to show codes, Enter = 8300): 8e00
Changed type of partition to 'Linux LVM'

Command (? for help): w

Final checks complete. About to write GPT data.
THIS WILL OVERWRITE EXISTING PARTITIONS!!

Do you want to proceed? (Y/N): Y
OK; writing new GUID partition table (GPT) to /dev/sdb.
The operation has completed successfully.

$ sudo pvcreate /dev/sdb1
  Physical volume "/dev/sdb1" successfully created.

$ sudo vgcreate newvol /dev/sdb1
  Volume group "newvol" successfully created

$ sudo lvcreate -l 100%FREE -n lvdisk newvol
  Logical volume "lvdisk" created.

$ sudo mkfs -t ext4 /dev/mapper/newvol-lvdisk
mke2fs 1.44.1 (24-Mar-2018)
Creating filesystem with 1309696 4k blocks and 327680 inodes
Filesystem UUID: 06c871bc-2eb6-4696-896f-240313e5d4fe
Superblock backups stored on blocks:
        32768, 98304, 163840, 229376, 294912, 819200, 884736

Allocating group tables: done
Writing inode tables: done
Creating journal (16384 blocks): done
Writing superblocks and filesystem accounting information: done
```

```
$ sudo mkdir /media/newdisk
$ sudo mount /dev/mapper/newvol-lvdisk /media/newdisk
$ cd /media/newdisk
$ ls -al
total 24
drwxr-xr-x 3 root root  4096 Jan 10 10:17 .
drwxr-xr-x 4 root root  4096 Jan 10 10:18 ..
drwx------ 2 root root 16384 Jan 10 10:17 lost+found
$
```

Although the initial setup of a LVM is complicated, it does provide great benefits. If you run out of space in a logical volume, just add a new disk partition to the volume.

Using RAID Technology

Redundant Array of Inexpensive Disks (RAID) technology has changed the data storage environment for most data centers. RAID technology allows you to improve data access performance and reliability as well as implement data redundancy for fault tolerance by combining multiple drives into one virtual drive. There are several versions of RAID commonly used:

- *RAID-0*: Disk striping, spreads data across multiple disks for faster access.

- *RAID-1*: Disk mirroring duplicates data across two drives.

- *RAID-10*: Disk mirroring and striping provides striping for performance and mirroring for fault tolerance.

- *RAID-4*: Disk striping with parity adds a parity bit stored on a separate disk so that data on a failed data disk can be recovered.

- *RAID-5*: Disk striping with distributed parity adds a parity bit to the data stripe so that it appears on all of the disks so that any failed disk can be recovered.

- *RAID-6*: Disk striping with double parity stripes both the data and the parity bit so two failed drives can be recovered.

The downside is that hardware RAID storage devices can be somewhat expensive (despite what the *I* stands for) and are often impractical for most home uses. Because of that, Linux has implemented a software RAID system that can implement RAID features on any disk system.

The *mdadm* utility allows you to specify multiple partitions to be used in any type of RAID environment. The RAID device appears as a single device in the /dev/mapper folder, which you can then partition and format to a specific filesystem. You can view the current status of the kernel's RAID state by displaying the contents of the /proc/mdstat file.

Encrypting Partitions

These days data security is a must in most business environments. With the popularity of portable laptops and external storage devices, often sensitive corporate (and sometimes personal) data is easily available for thieves to steal.

One line of defense to help protect data is encryption. Linux provides utilities to encrypt individual files, but that can get tedious. A better solution is to encrypt the entire partition where the data is stored. A popular tool for that is the *Linux Unified Key Setup (LUKS)*. The LUKS system was created in 2004 by Clemens Fruhwirth specifically for encrypting Linux partitions.

The core utility in LUKS is the `cryptsetup` utility. It allows you to create encrypted partitions, then open them to make them available for formatting and mounting in the Linux virtual directory.

The first step is to format a partition to use for encryption, using the `luksFormat` option:

```
$ sudo cryptsetup -y -v luksFormat /dev/sdb1

WARNING!
This will overwrite data on /dev/sdb1 irrevocably.

Are you sure? (Type 'yes' in capital letters): YES
Enter passphrase for /dev/sdb1:
Verify passphrase:
Key slot 0 created.
Command successful.
$
```

In this step you must specify the passphrase required to open the encrypted partition.

After you create the encrypted partition, you can make it available for use by using the `luksOpen` option:

```
$ sudo cryptsetup -v luksOpen /dev/sdb1 safedata
Enter passphrase for /dev/sdb1:
Key slot 0 unlocked.
Command successful.
$
```

The `luksOpen` option requires that you know the passphrase used to encrypt the partition. The first parameter after the `luksOpen` option specifies the physical partition, and the second parameter defines a name used to map the opened partition to a virtual device in the /dev/mapper directory:

```
$ ls /dev/mapper -l
total 0
```

```
crw-------. 1 root root 10,236 Dec 22 08:29 control
lrwxrwxrwx. 1 root root       7 Dec 22 08:29 rl-root -> ../dm-0
lrwxrwxrwx. 1 root root       7 Dec 22 08:29 rl-swap -> ../dm-1
lrwxrwxrwx. 1 root root       7 Dec 22 09:02 safedata -> ../dm-2
$
```

The `/dev/mapper/safedata` device file now references the opened encrypted partition and can be handled as a normal Linux partition:

```
$ sudo mkfs -t ext4 /dev/mapper/safedata
mke2fs 1.45.6 (20-Mar-2020)
Creating filesystem with 257792 4k blocks and 64512 inodes
Filesystem UUID: e2f03597-0108-48b3-a66b-d58fdd9c427f
Superblock backups stored on blocks:
        32768, 98304, 163840, 229376

Allocating group tables: done
Writing inode tables: done
Creating journal (4096 blocks): done
Writing superblocks and filesystem accounting information: done
$ sudo mount /dev/mapper/safedata /mnt/mydata
$
```

After you create the filesystem and mount the partition, you can create, modify, and delete files and directories in the `/mnt/mydata` directory just as you would any other Linux filesystem.

To close an encrypted partition so that it can't be accessed, use the `luksClose` command option:

```
$ sudo cryptsetup -v luksClose /dev/mapper/safedata
Command successful.
$ ls /dev/mapper -l
total 0
crw-------. 1 root root 10, 236 Dec 22 08:29 control
lrwxrwxrwx. 1 root root       7 Dec 22 08:29 rl-root -> ../dm-0
lrwxrwxrwx. 1 root root       7 Dec 22 08:29 rl-swap -> ../dm-1
$
```

When you close the encrypted partition, Linux removes it from the `/dev/mapper` directory, making it inaccessible. To mount the partition again, you would need to use the `luksOpen` option in the `cryptsetup` command and provide the passphrase.

EXERCISE 11.1

Experimenting with Filesystems

This exercise will demonstrate how to partition, format, and mount a drive for use on a Linux system using a USB memory stick. You'll need to have an empty USB memory stick available for this exercise. All data will be deleted from the USB memory stick.

1. Log into your Linux system and open a new command prompt.

2. Insert a USB memory stick into your system. If you're using a virtual machine (VM) environment, you may need to configure the VM to recognize the new USB device. For VirtualBox, click the Devices menu bar item, select USB, and then select the USB device name.

3. The Linux system should mount the device automatically. Type **dmesg | tail** to display the last few lines from the system console output. This should show whether the USB device was mounted and, if so, the device name assigned to it, such as /dev/sdb1.

4. Unmount the device using the command **sudo umount /dev/xxxx**, where *xxxx* is the device name shown from the dmesg output.

5. Type **fdisk /dev/xxx** to partition the disk, where *xxx* is the device name, without the partition number (such as /dev/sdb). At the command prompt, type **p** to display the current partitions.

6. Remove the existing partition by typing **d**.

7. Create a new partition. Type **n** to create a new partition. Type **p** to create a primary partition. Type **1** to assign it as the first partition. Press the Enter key to accept the default starting location and then press Enter again to accept the default ending location. Type **y** to remove the original VFAT signature if prompted.

8. Save the new partition layout. Type **w** to save the partition layout and exit the fdisk program.

9. Create a new filesystem on the new partition. Type **sudo mkfs -t ext4 /dev/xxx1**, where *xxx* is the device name for the USB memory stick.

10. Create a new mount point in your home folder. Type **mkdir mediatest1**.

11. Mount the new filesystem to the mount point. Type **sudo mount -t ext4 /dev/xxx1 mediatest1**, where *xxx* is the device name. Type **ls mediatest1** to list any files currently in the filesystem.

12. Remove the USB stick by typing **sudo umount /dev/xxx1**, where *xxx* is the device name.

13. If you want to return the USB memory stick to a Windows format, you can change the filesystem type of the USB memory stick to VFAT, or you can reformat it using the Windows format tool in File Manager.

Summary

The ability to permanently store data on a Linux system is a must. The Linux kernel supports both hard disk drive (HDD) and solid-state drive (SSD) technologies for persistently storing data. It also supports the three main types of drive connections—PATA, SATA, and SCSI. For each storage device you connect to the system, Linux creates a raw device file in the /dev folder. The raw device is hdx for PATA drives and sdx for SATA and SCSI drives, where x is the drive letter assigned to the drive.

Once you connect a drive to the Linux system, you'll need to create partitions on the drive. For MBR disks, you can use the fdisk or parted command-line tool or the gparted graphical tool. For GPT disks, you can use the gdisk or gparted tool. When you partition a drive, you must assign it a size and a filesystem type.

After you partition the storage device, you must format it using a filesystem that Linux recognizes. The mkfs program is a front-end utility that can format drives using most of the filesystems that Linux supports. The ext4 filesystem is currently the most popular Linux filesystem. It supports journaling and provides good performance. Linux also supports more advanced filesystems, such as btrfs, xfs, zfs, and of course, the Windows VFAT and NTFS filesystems.

After creating a filesystem on the partition, you'll need to mount the filesystem into the Linux virtual directory using a mount point and the mount command. The data contained in the partition's filesystem appears under the mount point folder in the virtual directory. To automatically mount partitions at boot time, make an entry for each partition in the /etc/ fstab file.

There are a host of tools available to help you manage and maintain filesystems. The df and du command-line commands are useful for checking disk space for partitions and the virtual directory, respectively. The fsck utility is a vital tool for repairing corrupted partitions and is run automatically at boot time against all partitions automatically mounted in the virtual directory.

Linux also supports alternative solutions for storage, such as multipath I/O for fault tolerance, logical volumes (in which you can add and remove physical partitions), software RAID technology, and the ability to create encrypted partitions.

Exam Essentials

Describe how Linux works with storage devices.   Linux creates raw device files in the /dev folder for each storage device you connect to the system. Linux also assigns a raw device file for each partition contained in the storage device.

Explain how to prepare a partition to be used in the Linux virtual directory.   To use a storage device partition in the virtual directory, it must be formatted with a filesystem that Linux recognizes. Use the mkfs command to format the partition. Linux recognizes several different filesystem types, including ext3, ext4, btrfs, xfs, and zfs.

Describe how Linux can implement a fault-tolerance storage configuration.   Linux supports two types of fault-tolerance storage methods. The multipath method uses the mdadm utility to create two paths to the same storage device. If both paths are active, Linux aggregates the path speed to increase performance to the storage device. If one path fails, Linux automatically routes traffic through the active path. Linux can also use standard RAID technology to support RAID levels 0, 1, 10, 4, 5, or 6 for fault tolerance and high-performance storage.

Describe how Linux uses virtual storage devices.   Linux uses the logical volume manager (LVM) to create a virtual storage device from one or more physical devices. The pvcreate command defines a volume from a physical partition, and the vgcreate command creates a volume group from one or more virtual volumes. The lvcreate command then creates a logical volume in the /dev/mapper folder from one or more partitions in the volume group. This method allows you to add or remove drives in a filesystem to grow or shrink the filesystem area as needed.

List some of the filesystem tools available in Linux.   The df tool allows you to analyze the available and used space in drive partitions, whereas the du tool allows you to analyze space in the virtual directory structure. The e2fsprogs package provides a wealth of tools for tuning ext filesystems, such as debugfs, dumpe2fs, tune2fs, and blkid. Linux also provides the xfs_admin and xfs_info tools for working with xfs filesystems. The fsck tool is available for repairing corrupted filesystems and can repair most cases of file corruption.

Review Questions

1. Which type of storage device uses integrated circuits to store data with no moving parts?
   - **A.** SSD
   - **B.** SATA
   - **C.** SCSI
   - **D.** HDD
   - **E.** PATA

2. What raw device file would Linux create for the second SCSI drive connected to the system?
   - **A.** /dev/hdb
   - **B.** /dev/sdb
   - **C.** /dev/sdb1
   - **D.** /dev/hdb1
   - **E.** /dev/sda

3. What program runs in the background to automatically detect and mount new storage devices?
   - **A.** mkfs
   - **B.** fsck
   - **C.** umount
   - **D.** mount
   - **E.** udev

4. What folder does the udev program use to create a permanent link to a storage device based on its serial number?
   - **A.** /dev/disk/by-path
   - **B.** /dev/sdb
   - **C.** /dev/disk/by-id
   - **D.** /dev/disk/by-uuid
   - **E.** /dev/mapper

5. Which partitioning tool provides a graphical interface?
   - **A.** gdisk
   - **B.** gparted
   - **C.** fdisk
   - **D.** parted
   - **E.** fsck

6. Linux uses _____ to add the filesystem on a new storage device to the virtual directory for users to access.
   - **A.** Mount points
   - **B.** Drive letters
   - **C.** /dev files
   - **D.** /proc folder
   - **E.** /sys folder

7. What filesystem is the latest version of the first Linux filesystem?
   - **A.** reiserFS
   - **B.** btrfs
   - **C.** ext3
   - **D.** ext4
   - **E.** nfs

8. What tool do you use to create a new filesystem on a partition?
   - **A.** fdisk
   - **B.** mkfs
   - **C.** fsck
   - **D.** gdisk
   - **E.** parted

9. What tool do you use to manually add a filesystem to the virtual directory?
   - **A.** fsck
   - **B.** mount
   - **C.** umount
   - **D.** fdisk
   - **E.** mkfs

10. The _____ program is a handy tool for repairing corrupted filesystems.
   - **A.** fsck
   - **B.** mount
   - **C.** umount
   - **D.** fdisk
   - **E.** mkfs

Chapter

12

Protecting Files

✓ **Objective 1.2: Given a scenario, manage files and directories**

Protecting data includes creating and managing *backups*. A backup, often called an *archive*, is a copy of data that can be restored sometime in the future should the data be destroyed or become corrupted.

Backing up your data is a critical activity, but even more important is planning your backups. These plans include choosing backup types, determining the right compression methods to employ, and identifying which utilities will serve your organization's data needs best. You may also need to transfer your backup files over the network. In this case, ensuring that the archive is secure during transit is critical as well as validating its integrity once it arrives at its destination. All of these various topics concerning protecting your data files are covered in this chapter.

Understanding Backup Types

There are different classifications for data backups. Understanding these various categories is vital for developing your backup plan. The following backup types are the most common types:

- System image
- Full
- Incremental
- Differential
- Snapshot
- Snapshot clone

Each of these backup types is explored in this section. Their advantages and disadvantages are included.

System Image A *system image* is a copy of the operating system binaries, configuration files, and anything else you need to boot the Linux system. Its purpose is to quickly restore your system to a bootable state. Sometimes called a *clone*, these backups are not normally used to recover individual files or directories, and in the case of some backup utilities, you cannot do so.

Full A *full backup* is a copy of all the data, ignoring its modification date. This backup type's primary advantage is that it takes a lot less time than other types to restore a system's data. However, not only does it take longer to create a full backup compared to the other types, it also requires more storage. It needs no other backup types to restore a system fully.

Incremental   An *incremental backup* only makes a copy of data that has been modified since the last backup operation (any backup operation type). Typically, a file's modified timestamp is compared to the last backup type's timestamp. It takes a lot less time to create this backup type than the other types, and it requires a lot less storage space. However, the data restoration time for this backup type can be significant. Imagine that you performed a full backup copy on Monday and incremental backups on Tuesday through Friday. On Saturday the disk crashes and must be replaced. After the disk is replaced, you will have to restore the data using Monday's backup and then continue to restore data using the incremental backups created on Tuesday through Friday. This is very time-consuming and will cause significant delays in getting your system back in operation. Therefore, for optimization purposes, it requires a full backup to be completed periodically.

Differential   A *differential backup* makes a copy of all data that has changed since the last full backup. It could be considered a good balance between full and incremental backups. This backup type takes less time than a full backup but potentially more time than an incremental backup. It requires less storage space than a full backup but more space than a plain incremental backup. Also, it takes a lot less time to restore using differential backups than incremental backups, because only the full backup and the latest differential backup are needed. For optimization purposes, it requires a full backup to be completed periodically.

Snapshot   A *snapshot backup* is considered a hybrid approach, and it is a slightly different flavor of backups. First a full (typically read-only) copy of the data is made to backup media. Then pointers, such as hard links, are employed to create a reference table linking the backup data with the original data. The next time a backup is made, instead of a full backup, an incremental backup is made (only modified or new files are copied to the backup media), and the pointer reference table is copied and updated. This saves space because only modified files and the updated pointer reference table need to be stored for each additional backup.

NOTE   The snapshot backup type described here is a copy-on-write snapshot. There is another snapshot flavor called a *split-mirror snapshot*, where the data is kept on a mirrored storage device. When a backup is run, a copy of all the data is created, not just new or modified data.

With a snapshot backup, you can go back to any point in time and do a full system restore from that point. It also uses a lot less space than the other backup types. In essence, snapshots simulate multiple full backups per day without taking up the same space or requiring the same processing power as a full backup type would. The `rsync` utility (described later in this chapter) uses this method.

Snapshot Clone   Another variation of a snapshot backup is a *snapshot clone*. Once a snapshot is created, such as an LVM snapshot, it is copied, or cloned. Snapshot clones are useful in high data I/O environments. When performing the cloning, you minimize any adverse performance impacts to production data I/O because the clone backup takes place on the snapshot and not on the original data.

While not all snapshots are writable, snapshot clones are typically modifiable. If you are using LVM, you can mount these snapshot clones on a different system. Thus, a snapshot clone is useful in disaster recovery scenarios.

Your particular server environment as well as data protection needs will dictate which backup method to employ. Most likely you need a combination of the preceding types to properly protect your data.

Looking at Compression Methods

Backing up data can potentially consume large amounts of additional disk or media space. Depending on the backup types you employ, you can reduce this consumption via data compression utilities. The following popular utilities are available on Linux:

- gzip
- bzip2
- xz
- zip

The advantages and disadvantages of each of these data compression methods are explored in this section.

gzip   The gzip utility was developed in 1992 as a replacement for the old compress program. Using the Lempel-Ziv (LZ77) algorithm to achieve text-based file compression rates of 60–70 percent, gzip has long been a popular data compression utility. To compress a file, simply type **gzip** followed by the file's name. The original file is replaced by a compressed version with a .gz file extension. To reverse the operation, type **gunzip** followed by the compressed file's name.

bzip2   Developed in 1996, the bzip2 utility offers higher compression rates than gzip but takes slightly longer to perform the data compression. The bzip2 utility employs multiple layers of compression techniques and algorithms. Until 2013, this data compression utility was used to compress the Linux kernel for distribution. To compress a file, simply type **bzip2** followed by the file's name. The original file is replaced by a compressed version with a .bz2 file extension. To reverse the operation, type **bunzip2** followed by the compressed file's name, which decompresses (inflates) the data.

 Originally there was a bzip utility program. However, in its layered approach, a patented data compression algorithm was employed. Thus, bzip2 was created to replace it and uses the Huffman coding algorithm instead, which is patent free.

xz   Developed in 2009, the xz data compression utility quickly became very popular among Linux administrators. It boasts a higher default compression rate than bzip2 and gzip via the LZMA2 compression algorithm. However, with certain xz command options, you can employ the legacy LZMA compression algorithm, if needed or desired. The xz compression utility in 2013 replaced bzip2 for compressing the Linux kernel for distribution. To compress a file, simply type **xz** followed by the file's name. The original file is replaced by a compressed version with an .xz file extension. To reverse the operation, type **unxz** followed by the compressed file's name.

zip   The zip utility has the ability to operate on multiple files. If you have ever created a zip file on a Windows operating system, then you've used this file format. Multiple files are packed together in a single file, often called a *folder* or an *archive file*, and then compressed. Another difference from the other Linux compression utilities is that zip does not replace the original file(s). Instead, it places a copy of the file(s) into the archive file.

To archive and compress files with zip, type **zip** followed by the final archive file's name, which traditionally ends in a .zip extension. After the archive file, type one or more files you desire to place into the compressed archive, separating them with a space. The original files remain intact, but a copy of them is placed into the compressed zip archive file. To reverse the operation, type **unzip** followed by the compressed archive file's name.

It's helpful to see a side-by-side comparison of the various compression utilities using their defaults. In Listing 12.1, an example on a Rocky Linux distribution is shown.

Listing 12.1 Comparing the various Linux compression utilities

```
# cp /var/log/wtmp wtmp
#
# cp wtmp wtmp1
# cp wtmp wtmp2
# cp wtmp wtmp3
# cp wtmp wtmp4
#
# ls -lh wtmp?
-rw-r--r--. 1 root root 210K Oct  9 19:54 wtmp1
-rw-r--r--. 1 root root 210K Oct  9 19:54 wtmp2
-rw-r--r--. 1 root root 210K Oct  9 19:54 wtmp3
-rw-r--r--. 1 root root 210K Oct  9 19:54 wtmp4
#
# gzip wtmp1
# bzip2 wtmp2
# xz wtmp3
# zip wtmp4.zip wtmp4
  adding: wtmp4 (deflated 96%)
```

```
#
# ls -lh wtmp?.*
-rw-r--r--. 1 root root 7.7K Oct  9 19:54 wtmp1.gz
-rw-r--r--. 1 root root 6.2K Oct  9 19:54 wtmp2.bz2
-rw-r--r--. 1 root root 5.2K Oct  9 19:54 wtmp3.xz
-rw-r--r--. 1 root root 7.9K Oct  9 19:55 wtmp4.zip
#
# ls wtmp?
wtmp4
#
```

In Listing 12.1, first the /var/log/wtmp file is copied to the local directory using super user privileges. Four copies of this file are then made. Using the ls -lh command, you can see in human-readable format that the wtmp files are 210K in size. Next, the various compression utilities are employed. Notice that when using the zip command, you must give it the name of the archive file, wtmp4.zip, and follow it with any file names. In this case, only wtmp4 is put into the zip archive. After the files are compressed with the various utilities, another ls -lh command is issued in Listing 12.1. Notice the various file extension names as well as the files' compressed sizes. You can see that the xz program produces the highest compression of this file, because its file is the smallest in size. The last command in Listing 12.1 shows that all the compression programs but zip removed the original file.

For the previous data compression utilities, you can specify the level of compression and control the speed via the -# option. The # is a number from 1 to 9, where 1 is the fastest but lowest compression and 9 is the slowest but highest compression method. The zip utility does not yet support these levels for compression, but it does for decompression. Typically, the utilities use -6 as the default compression level. It is a good idea to review these level specifications in each utility's man page, since useful but subtle differences exist.

There are many compression methods. However, when you use a compression utility along with an archive and restore program for data backups, it is vital that you use a lossless compression method. A lossless compression is just as it sounds: no data is lost. The gzip, bzip2, xz, and zip utilities provide lossless compression. Obviously it is important not to lose data when doing backups.

Comparing Archive and Restore Utilities

There are several programs you can employ for managing backups. Some of the more popular products are Amanda, Bacula, Bareos, Duplicity, and BackupPC. Yet often these GUI and/or web-based programs have command-line utilities at their core. Our focus here is on those command-line utilities:

- cpio
- dd
- rsync
- tar

Copying with *cpio*

The cpio utility's name stands for "copy in and out." It gathers together file copies and stores them in an archive file. The program has several useful options. The more commonly used ones are described in Table 12.1.

TABLE 12.1 The cpio command's commonly used options

Short	Long	Description
-I	N/A	Designates an archive file to use.
-i	--extract	Copies files from an archive or displays the files within the archive, depending on the other options employed. Called *copy-in mode*.
N/A	--no-absolute-filenames	Designates that only relative path names are to be used. (The default is to use absolute path names.)
-o	--create	Creates an archive by copying files into it. Called *copy-out mode*.
-t	--list	Displays a list of files within the archive. This list is called a *table of contents*.
-v	--verbose	Displays each file's name as each file is processed.

To create an archive using the cpio utility, you have to generate a list of files and then pipe them into the command. Listing 12.2 shows an example of doing this task.

Listing 12.2 Employing cpio to create an archive

```
$ ls Project4?.txt
Project42.txt   Project43.txt   Project44.txt
Project45.txt   Project46.txt
$
```

```
$ ls Project4?.txt | cpio -ov > Project4x.cpio
Project42.txt
Project43.txt
Project44.txt
Project45.txt
Project46.txt
59 blocks
$
$ ls Project4?.*
Project42.txt   Project44.txt   Project46.txt
Project43.txt   Project45.txt   Project4x.cpio
$
```

Using the ? wildcard and the ls command, various text files within the present working directory are displayed first in Listing 12.2. This command is then used, and its STDOUT is piped as STDIN to the cpio utility. (See Chapter 4, "Searching and Analyzing Text," if you need a refresher on STDOUT and STDIN.) The options used with the cpio command are -ov, which create an archive containing copies of the listed files. They also display the file's name as they are copied into the archive. The archive file used is named Project4x. cpio. Though not necessary, it is considered good form to use the .cpio extension on cpio archive files.

 You can back up data based on its metadata, and not its file location, via the cpio utility. For example, suppose you want to create a cpio archive for any files within the virtual directory system owned by the JKirk user account. You can use the find / -user JKirk command and pipe it into the cpio utility in order to create the archive file. This is a handy feature.

You can view the files stored within a cpio archive fairly easily. Just employ the cpio command again, and use its -itv options and the -I option to designate the archive file, as shown in Listing 12.3.

Listing 12.3 Using cpio to list an archive's contents

```
$ cpio -itvI Project4x.cpio
-rw-r--r--   1 Christin Christin 29900 Aug 19 17:37 Project42.txt
-rw-rw-r--   1 Christin Christin     0 Aug 19 18:07 Project43.txt
-rw-rw-r--   1 Christin Christin     0 Aug 19 18:07 Project44.txt
-rw-rw-r--   1 Christin Christin     0 Aug 19 18:07 Project45.txt
-rw-rw-r--   1 Christin Christin     0 Aug 19 18:07 Project46.txt
59 blocks
$
```

Though not displayed in Listing 12.3, the cpio utility maintains each file's absolute directory reference. Thus, it is often used to create system image and full backups.

To restore files from an archive, employ just the -ivI options. However, because cpio maintains the files' absolute paths, this can be tricky if you need to restore the files to another directory location. To do this, you need to use the --no-absolute-filenames option, as shown in Listing 12.4.

Listing 12.4 Using cpio to restore files to a different directory location

```
$ ls -dF Projects
Projects/
$
$ mv Project4x.cpio Projects/
$
$ cd Projects
$ pwd
/home/Christine/Answers/Projects
$
$ ls Project4?.*
Project4x.cpio
$
$ cpio -iv --no-absolute-filenames -I Project4x.cpio
Project42.txt
Project43.txt
Project44.txt
Project45.txt
Project46.txt
59 blocks
$
$ ls Project4?.*
Project42.txt   Project44.txt   Project46.txt
Project43.txt   Project45.txt   Project4x.cpio
$
```

In Listing 12.4 the Project4x.cpio archive file is moved into a preexisting subdirectory, Projects. By stripping the absolute path names from the archived files via the --no-absolute-filenames option, you restore the files to a new directory location. If you wanted to restore the files to their original location, simply leave that option off and just use the other cpio switches shown in Listing 12.4.

Archiving with *tar*

The tar utility's name stands for tape archiver, and it is popular for creating data backups. As with cpio, with the tar command, the selected files are copied and stored in a single file. This file is called a *tar archive file*. If this archive file is compressed using a data compression utility, the compressed archive file is called a *tarball*.

The tar program has several useful options. Commonly used ones for creating data backups are described in Table 12.2.

TABLE 12.2   The tar command's commonly used tarball creation options

Short	Long	Description
-c	--create	Creates a tar archive file. The backup can be a full or incremental backup, depending on the other selected options.
-u	--update	Appends files to an existing tar archive file, but only copies those files that were modified since the original archive file was created.
-g	--listed-incremental	Creates an incremental or full archive based on metadata stored in the provided file.
-z	--gzip	Compresses tar archive file into a tarball using gzip.
-j	--bzip2	Compresses tar archive file into a tarball using bzip2.
-J	--xz	Compresses tar archive file into a tarball using xz.
-v	--verbose	Displays each file's name as each file is processed.

To create an archive using the tar utility, you have to add a few arguments to the options and the command. Listing 12.5 shows an example of creating a tar archive.

Listing 12.5 Using tar to create an archive file

```
$ ls Project4?.txt
Project42.txt  Project43.txt  Project44.txt
Project45.txt  Project46.txt
$
$ tar -cvf Project4x.tar Project4?.txt
Project42.txt
```

```
Project43.txt
Project44.txt
Project45.txt
Project46.txt
$
```

In Listing 12.5, three options are used. The −c option creates the tar archive. The −v option displays the filenames as they are placed into the archive file. Finally, the −f option designates the archive filename, which is Project42x.tar. Though not required, it is considered good form to use the .tar extension on tar archive files. The command's last argument designates the files to copy into this archive.

 You can also use the old-style tar command options. For this style, you remove the single dash from the beginning of the tar option. For example, −c becomes c. Keep in mind that additional old-style tar command options must not have spaces between them. Thus, tar cvf is valid, but tar c v f is not.

If you are backing up lots of files or large amounts of data, it is a good idea to employ a compression utility. This is easily accomplished by adding an additional switch to your tar command options. An example is shown in Listing 12.6, which uses gzip compression to create a tarball.

Listing 12.6 Using tar to create a tarball

```
$ tar -zcvf Project4x.tar.gz Project4?.txt
Project42.txt
Project43.txt
Project44.txt
Project45.txt
Project46.txt
$
$ ls Project4x.tar.gz
Project4x.tar.gz
$
```

Notice in Listing 12.6 that the tarball filename has the .tar.gz file extension. It is considered good form to use the .tar extension and tack on an indicator showing the compression method that was used. However, you can shorten it to .tgz if desired.

There is a useful variation of this command to create both full and incremental backups. A simple example helps to explain this concept. The process for creating a full backup is shown in Listing 12.7.

Listing 12.7 Using `tar` to create a full backup

```
$ tar -g FullArchive.snar -Jcvf Project42.txz Project4?.txt
Project42.txt
Project43.txt
Project44.txt
Project45.txt
Project46.txt
$
$ ls FullArchive.snar Project42.txz
FullArchive.snar   Project42.txz
$
```

Notice the `-g` option in Listing 12.7. The `-g` option creates a file, called a *snapshot file*, `FullArchive.snar`. The `.snar` file extension indicates that the file is a tarball snapshot file. The snapshot file contains metadata used in association with `tar` commands for creating full and incremental backups. The snapshot file contains file timestamps, so the `tar` utility can determine if a file has been modified since it was last backed up. The snapshot file is also used to identify any files that are new or determine if files have been deleted since the last backup.

The previous example created a full backup of the designated files along with the metadata snapshot file, `FullArchive.snar`. Now the same snapshot file will be used to help determine if any files have been modified, are new, or have been deleted to create an incremental backup, as shown in Listing 12.8.

Listing 12.8 Using `tar` to create an incremental backup

```
$ echo "Answer to everything" >> Project42.txt
$
$ tar -g FullArchive.snar -Jcvf Project42_Inc.txz Project4?.txt
Project42.txt
$
$ ls Project42_Inc.txz
Project42_Inc.txz
$
```

In Listing 12.8, the file `Project42.txt` is modified. Again, the `tar` command uses the `-g` option and points to the previously created `FullArchive.snar` snapshot file. This time, the metadata within `FullArchive.snar` shows the `tar` command that the `Project42.txt` file has been modified since the previous backup. Therefore, the new tarball only contains the `Project42.txt` file, and it is effectively an incremental backup. You can continue to create additional incremental backups using the same snapshot file as needed.

The `tar` command views full and incremental backups in levels. A full backup is one that includes all the files indicated, and it is considered a level 0 backup. The first tar incremental backup after a full backup is considered a level 1 backup. The second tar incremental backup is considered a level 2 backup, and so on.

Whenever you create data backups, it is a good practice to verify them. Table 12.3 provides some `tar` command options for viewing and verifying data backups.

TABLE 12.3   The `tar` command's commonly used archive verification options

Short	Long	Description
-d	--compare --diff	Compares a tar archive file's members with external files and lists the differences.
-t	--list	Displays a tar archive file's contents.
-W	--verify	Verifies each file as the file is processed. This option cannot be used with the compression options.

Backup verification can take several different forms. You might ensure that the desired files (sometimes called *members*) are included in your backup by using the -v option on the `tar` command in order to watch the files being listed as they are included in the archive file. You can also verify that desired files are included in your backup after the fact. Use the -t option to list tarball or archive file contents. An example is shown in Listing 12.9.

Listing 12.9 Using `tar` to list a tarball's contents

```
$ tar -tf Project4x.tar.gz
Project42.txt
Project43.txt
Project44.txt
Project45.txt
Project46.txt
$
```

You can verify files within an archive file by comparing them against the current files. The option to accomplish this task is the -d option. An example is shown in Listing 12.10.

Listing 12.10 Using `tar` to compare tarball members to external files

```
$ tar -df Project4x.tar.gz
Project42.txt: Mod time differs
Project42.txt: Size differs
$
```

Another good practice is to verify your backup automatically immediately after the tar archive is created. This is easily accomplished by tacking on the –W option, as shown in Listing 12.11.

Listing 12.11 Using tar to verify backed-up files automatically

```
$ tar -Wcvf ProjectVerify.tar Project4?.txt
Project42.txt
Project43.txt
Project44.txt
Project45.txt
Project46.txt
Verify Project42.txt
Verify Project43.txt
Verify Project44.txt
Verify Project45.txt
Verify Project46.txt
$
```

You cannot use the –W option if you employ compression to create a tarball. However, you could create and verify the archive first and then compress it in a separate step. You can also use the –W option when you extract files from a tar archive. This is handy for instantly verifying files restored from archives.

Table 12.4 lists some of the options that you can use with the tar utility to restore data from a tar archive file or tarball. Be aware that several options used to create the backup, such as –g and –W, can also be used when restoring data.

TABLE 12.4   The tar command's commonly used file restore options

Short	Long	Description
-x	--extract --get	Extracts files from a tarball or archive file and places them in the current working directory
-z	--gunzip	Decompresses files in a tarball using gunzip
-j	--bunzip2	Decompresses files in a tarball using bunzip2
-J	--unxz	Decompresses files in a tarball using unxz

Extracting files from an archive or tarball is fairly simple using the tar utility. Listing 12.12 shows an example of extracting files from a previously created tarball.

Listing 12.12 Using `tar` to extract files from a tarball

```
$ mkdir Extract
$
$ mv Project4x.tar.gz Extract/
$
$ cd Extract
$
$ tar -zxvf Project4x.tar.gz
Project42.txt
Project43.txt
Project44.txt
Project45.txt
Project46.txt
$
$ ls
Project42.txt   Project44.txt   Project46.txt
Project43.txt   Project45.txt   Project4x.tar.gz
$
```

In Listing 12.12, a new subdirectory, `Extract`, is created. The tarball created back in Listing 12.6 is moved to the new subdirectory, and then the files are restored from the tarball. If you compare the `tar` command used in this listing to the one used in Listing 12.6, you'll notice that here the `-x` option was substituted for the `-c` option used in Listing 12.6. Also notice in Listing 12.12 that the tarball is not removed after a file extraction, so you can use it again and again, as needed.

> The `tar` command has many additional capabilities, such as using `tar` backup parameters and/or the ability to create backup and restore shell scripts. Take a look at the GNU `tar` website, www.gnu.org/software/tar/manual, to learn more about this popular command-line backup utility.

Since the `tar` utility is the tape archiver, you can also place your tarballs or archive files on tape, if desired. After mounting and properly positioning your tape, simply substitute your SCSI tape device filename, such as `/dev/st0` or `/dev/nst0`, in place of the archive or tarball filename within your `tar` command.

Duplicating with *dd*

The dd utility allows you to back up nearly everything on a disk, including the old Master Boot Record (MBR) partitions some older Linux distributions still employ. It's primarily used to create low-level copies of an entire hard drive or partition. It is often used in digital forensics for creating system images, for copying damaged disks, and for wiping partitions.

The command itself is fairly straightforward. The basic syntax structure for the dd utility is as follows:

```
dd  if=input-device of=output-device [OPERANDS]
```

The *output-device* is either an entire drive or a partition. The *input-device* is the same. Just make sure that you get the right device for out and the right one for in; otherwise you may unintentionally wipe data.

Besides the of and if, there are a few other arguments (called *operands*) that can assist in dd operations. Commonly used ones are described in Table 12.5.

TABLE 12.5 The dd command's commonly used operands

Operand	Description
bs=BYTES	Sets the maximum block size (number of BYTES) to read and write at a time. The default is 512 bytes.
count=N	Sets the number (N) of input blocks to copy.
status=LEVEL	Sets the amount (LEVEL) of information to display to STDERR.

The status=LEVEL operand needs a little more explanation. LEVEL can be set to one of the following:

- none only displays error messages.
- noxfer does not display final transfer statistics.
- progress displays periodic transfer statistics.

It is usually easier to understand the dd utility through examples. A snipped example of performing a bit-by-bit copy of one entire disk to another disk is shown in Listing 12.13.

Listing 12.13 Using dd to copy an entire disk

```
# lsblk
NAME          MAJ:MIN RM   SIZE RO TYPE MOUNTPOINT
[…]
sdb            8:16   0     4M  0 disk
└sdb1          8:17   0     4M  0 part
sdc            8:32   0     1G  0 disk
└sdc1          8:33   0 1023M  0 part
[…]
#
```

```
# dd if=/dev/sdb of=/dev/sdc status=progress
8192+0 records in
8192+0 records out
4194304 bytes (4.2 MB) copied, 0.232975 s, 18.0 MB/s
#
```

In Listing 12.13, the `lsblk` command is used first. When copying disks via the dd utility, make sure the drives are not mounted anywhere in the virtual directory structure. The two drives involved in this operation, /dev/sdb and /dev/sdc, are not mounted. With the dd command, the `if` operand is used to indicate the disk we wish to copy, which is the /dev/sdb drive. The `of` operand indicates that the /dev/sdc disk will hold the copied data. Also, `status=progress` will display period transfer statistics. You can see in Listing 12.13 from the transfer statistics that there is not much data on /dev/sdb, so the dd operation finished quickly.

You can also create a system image backup using a dd command similar to the one shown in Listing 12.13, with a few needed modifications. The basic steps are as follows:

1. Shut down your Linux system.

2. Attach the necessary spare drives. You'll need one drive the same size or larger for each system drive.

3. Boot the system using a live CD, DVD, or USB so that you can either keep the system's drives unmounted or unmount them prior to the backup operation.

4. For each system drive, issue a dd command, specifying the drive to back up with the `if` operand and the spare drive with the `of` operand.

5. Shut down the system, and remove the spare drives containing the system image.

6. Reboot your Linux system.

If you have a disk you are getting rid of, you can also use the dd command to zero out the disk. An example is shown in Listing 12.14.

Listing 12.14 Using dd to zero an entire disk

```
# dd if=/dev/zero of=/dev/sdc status=progress
1061724672 bytes (1.1 GB) copied, 33.196299 s, 32.0 MB/s
dd: writing to '/dev/sdc': No space left on device
2097153+0 records in
2097152+0 records out
1073741824 bytes (1.1 GB) copied, 34.6304 s, 31.0 MB/s
#
```

The `if=/dev/zero` uses the zero device file to write zeros to the disk. You need to perform this operation at least 10 times or more to thoroughly wipe the disk. You can also employ the /dev/random and/or the /dev/urandom device files to put random data onto the disk. This particular task can take a long time to run for large disks. It is still better to shred any disks that will no longer be used by your company.

Replicating with *rsync*

Originally covered in Chapter 3, "Managing Files, Directories, and Text," the rsync utility is known for speed. With this program, you can copy files locally or remotely, and it is wonderful for creating backups.

Before exploring the rsync program, it is a good idea to review a few of the commonly used options. Table 3.4 in Chapter 3 contains the more commonly used rsync options. Besides the options listed in Table 3.4, there are a few additional switches that help with secure data transfers via the rsync utility:

- The -e, or --rsh, option changes the program to use for communication between a local and remote connection. The default is OpenSSH.

- The -z, or --compress, option compresses the file data during the transfer.

Back in Chapter 3 we briefly mentioned the archive option, -a (or --archive), which directs rsync to perform a backup copy. However, it needs a little more explanation. This option is the equivalent of using the -rlptgoD options and does the following:

- Directs rsync to copy files from the directory's contents and for any subdirectory within the original directory tree, consecutively copying their contents as well (recursively).

- Preserves the following items:

  - Device files (only if run with super user privileges)
  - File group
  - File modification time
  - File ownership (only if run with super user privileges)
  - File permissions
  - Special files
  - Symbolic links

It's fairly simple to conduct rsync backup locally. The most popular options, -ahv, allow you to back up files to a local location quickly, as shown in Listing 12.15.

Listing 12.15 Using rsync to back up files locally

```
$ ls -sh *.tar
40K Project4x.tar  40K ProjectVerify.tar
$
$ mkdir TarStorage
$
$ rsync -avh *.tar TarStorage/
sending incremental file list
Project4x.tar
ProjectVerify.tar
```

```
sent 82.12K bytes  received 54 bytes  164.35K bytes/sec
total size is 81.92K  speedup is 1.00
$
$ ls TarStorage
Project4x.tar  ProjectVerify.tar
$
```

Where the rsync utility really shines is with protecting files as they are backed up over a network.

For a secure remote copy to work, you need the OpenSSH service up and running on the remote system. In addition, the rsync utility must be installed on both the local and remote machines. An example of using the rsync command to securely copy files over the network is shown in Listing 12.16.

Listing 12.16 Using rsync to back up files remotely

```
$ ls -sh *.tar
40K Project4x.tar  40K ProjectVerify.tar
$
$ rsync -avP -e ssh *.tar user1@192.168.0.104:~
user1@192.168.0.104's password:
sending incremental file list
Project4x.tar
      40,960 100%    7.81MB/s    0:00:00 (xfr#1, to-chk=1/2)
ProjectVerify.tar
      40,960 100%   39.06MB/s    0:00:00 (xfr#2, to-chk=0/2)

sent 82,121 bytes  received 54 bytes  18,261.11 bytes/sec
total size is 81,920  speedup is 1.00
$
```

Notice in Listing 12.16 that the -avP options are used with the rsync utility. These options not only set the copy mode to archive but will provide detailed information as the file transfers take place. The important switch to notice in this listing is the -e option. This option determines that OpenSSH is used for the transfer and effectively creates an encrypted tunnel so that anyone sniffing the network cannot see the data flowing by. The *.tar in the command simply selects what local files are to be copied to the remote machine. The last argument in the rsync command specifies the following:

- The user account (user1) located at the remote system to use for the transfer.
- The remote system's IPv4 address, but a hostname can be used instead.
- Where the files are to be placed. In this case, it is the home directory, indicated by the ~ symbol.

Notice also in that last argument that there is a needed colon (:) between the IPv4 address and the directory symbol. If you do not include this colon, you will copy the files to a new file named `user1@192.168.0.104~` in the local directory.

 The `rsync` utility uses OpenSSH by default. However, it's good practice to use the `-e` option. This is especially true if you are using any `ssh` command options, such as designating an OpenSSH key to employ or using a different port than the default port of 22. OpenSSH is covered in more detail in Chapter 16, "Looking at Access and Authentication Methods."

The `rsync` utility can be handy for copying large files to remote media. If you have a fast CPU but a slow network connection, you can speed things up even more by employing the `rsync -z` option to compress the data for transfer. This is not using `gzip` compression but instead applying compression via the `zlib` compression library. You can find more out about `zlib` at `https://zlib.net`.

Securing Offsite/Off-System Backups

In business, data is money. Thus it is critical not only to create data archives but also to protect them. There are a few additional ways to secure your backups when they are being transferred to remote locations.

Besides `rsync`, you can use the `scp` utility, which is based on the Secure Copy Protocol (SCP). Also, the `sftp` program, which is based on the SSH File Transfer Protocol (SFTP), is a means for securely transferring archives. We'll cover both utilities in the following sections.

Copying Securely via *scp*

The `scp` utility is geared for quickly transferring files in a noninteractive manner between two systems on a network. This program employs OpenSSH.

It is best used for small files that you need to securely copy on the fly, because if it gets interrupted during its operation, it cannot pick back up where it left off. For larger files or more extensive numbers of files, it is better to employ either the `rsync` or the `sftp` utility.

There are some rather useful `scp` options. A few commonly used switches are listed in Table 12.6.

TABLE 12.6   The scp command's commonly used copy options

Short	Description
-C	Compresses the file data during transfer
-p	Preserves file access and modification times as well as file permissions
-r	Copies files from the directory's contents, and for any subdirectory within the original directory tree, consecutively copies their contents as well (recursively)
-v	Displays verbose information concerning the command's execution

Performing a secure copy of files from a local system to a remote system is rather simple. You do need the OpenSSH service up and running on the remote system. An example is shown in Listing 12.17.

Listing 12.17 Using scp to copy files securely to a remote system

```
$ scp Project42.txt  user1@192.168.0.104:~
user1@192.168.0.104's password:
Project42.txt   100%   29KB  20.5MB/s   00:00
$
```

Notice that to accomplish this task, no scp command options are employed. The -v option gives a great deal of information that is not needed in this case.

WARNING The scp utility will overwrite any remote files with the same name as the one being transferred without asking or even displaying a message stating that fact. You need to be careful when copying files using scp that you don't tromp on any existing files.

A handy way to use scp is to copy files from one remote machine to another remote machine. An example is shown in Listing 12.18.

Listing 12.18 Using scp to copy files securely from/to a remote system

```
$ ip addr show | grep 192 | cut -d" " -f6
192.168.0.101/24
$
$ scp user1@192.168.0.104:Project42.txt user1@192.168.0.103:~
user1@192.168.0.104's password:
user1@192.168.0.103's password:
```

```
Project42.txt                   100%    29KB    4.8MB/s    00:00
Connection to 192.168.0.104 closed.
$
```

First in Listing 12.18, the current machine's IPv4 address is checked using the `ip addr show` command. Next the `scp` utility is employed to copy the `Project42.txt` file from one remote machine to another. Of course, you must have OpenSSH running on these machines and have a user account you can log into as well.

Transferring Securely via *sftp*

The `sftp` utility will also allow you to transfer files securely across the network. However, it is designed for a more interactive experience. With `sftp`, you can create directories as needed, immediately check on transferred files, determine the remote system's present working directory, and so on. In addition, this program employs OpenSSH.

To get a feel for how this interactive utility works, it's good to see a simple example. One is shown in Listing 12.19.

Listing 12.19 Using `sftp` to access a remote system

```
$ sftp Christine@192.168.0.104
Christine@192.168.0.104's password:
Connected to 192.168.0.104.
sftp>
sftp> bye
$
```

In Listing 12.19, the `sftp` utility is used with a username and a remote host's IPv4 address. Once the user account's correct password is entered, the `sftp` utility's prompt is shown. At this point, you are connected to the remote system. At the prompt you can enter any commands, including `help`, to see a display of all the possible commands and, as shown in the listing, `bye` to exit the utility. Once you have exited the utility, you are no longer connected to the remote system.

Before using the `sftp` interactive utility, it's helpful to know some of the more common commands. A few are listed in Table 12.7.

TABLE 12.7 The `sftp` command's commonly used commands

Command	Description
bye	Exits the remote system and quits the utility.
exit	Exits the remote system and quits the utility.
get	Gets a file (or files) from the remote system and stores it (them) on the local system. Called *downloading*.
reget	Resumes an interrupted `get` operation.

Command	Description
put	Sends a file (or files) from the local system and stores it (them) on the remote system. Called *uploading*.
reput	Resumes an interrupted put operation.
ls	Displays files in the remote system's present working directory.
lls	Displays files in the local system's present working directory.
mkdir	Creates a directory on the remote system.
lmkdir	Creates a directory on the local system.
progress	Toggles on/off the progress display. (Default is on.)

It can be a little tricky the first few times you use the sftp utility if you have never used an FTP interactive program in the past. An example of sending a local file to a remote system is shown in Listing 12.20.

Listing 12.20 Using sftp to copy a file to a remote system

```
$ sftp Christine@192.168.0.104
Christine@192.168.0.104's password:
Connected to 192.168.0.104.
sftp>
sftp> ls
Desktop     Documents    Downloads    Music    Pictures
Public      Templates
Videos
sftp>
sftp> lls
AccountAudit.txt  Grades.txt         Project43.txt   ProjectVerify.tar
err.txt           Life               Project44.txt   TarStorage
Everything        NologinAccts.txt   Project45.txt   Universe
Extract           Project42_Inc.txz  Project46.txt
FullArchive.snar  Project42.txt      Project4x.tar
Galaxy            Project42.txz      Projects
sftp>
sftp> put Project4x.tar
Uploading Project4x.tar to /home/Christine/Project4x.tar
Project4x.tar                100%   40KB  15.8MB/s   00:00
sftp>
```

```
sftp> ls
Desktop         Documents   Downloads   Music   Pictures
Project4x.tar   Public      Templates   Videos
sftp>
sftp> exit
$
```

In Listing 12.20, after the connection to the remote system is made, the `ls` command is used in the `sftp` utility to see the files in the remote user's directory. The `lls` command is used to see the files within the local user's directory. Next the `put` command is employed to send the `Project4x.tar` archive file to the remote system. There is no need to issue the `progress` command because by default progress reports are already turned on. Once the upload is completed, another `ls` command is used to see if the file is now on the remote system, and it is.

 Real World Scenario

Backup Rule of Three

Businesses need to have several archives in order to properly protect their data. The Backup Rule of Three is typically good for most organizations, and it dictates that you should have three archives of all your data. One archive is stored remotely to prevent natural disasters or other catastrophic occurrences from destroying all your backups. The other two archives are stored locally, but each is on a different media type. You hear about the various statistics concerning companies that go out of business after a significant data loss. A scarier statistic would be the number of system administrators who lose their jobs after such a data loss because they did not have proper archival and restoration procedures in place.

The `rsync`, `scp`, and `sftp` utilities all provide a means to securely copy files. However, when determining what utilities to employ for your various archival and retrieval plans, keep in mind that one utility will not work effectively in every backup case. For example, generally speaking, `rsync` is better to use than `scp` in backups because it provides more options. However, if you just have a few files that need secure copying, `scp` works well. The `sftp` utility works well for any interactive copying, yet `scp` is faster because `sftp` is designed to acknowledge every packet sent across the network. It's most likely you will need to employ all of these various utilities in some way throughout your company's backup plans.

Checking Backup Integrity

Securely transferring your archives is not enough. You need to consider the possibility that the archives could become corrupted during transfer.

Ensuring a backup file's integrity is fairly easy. A few simple utilities can help.

Digesting an MD5 Algorithm

The md5sum utility is based on the MD5 message digest algorithm. It was originally created to be used in cryptography. It is no longer used in such capacities due to various known vulnerabilities. However, it is still excellent for checking a file's integrity.

A simple example is shown in Listing 12.21 and Listing 12.22. Using the file that was uploaded using sftp earlier in the chapter, md5sum is used on the original and the uploaded file.

Listing 12.21 Using md5sum to check the original file

```
$ ip addr show | grep 192 | cut -d" " -f6
192.168.0.101/24
$
$ md5sum Project4x.tar
efbb0804083196e58613b6274c69d88c  Project4x.tar
$
```

Listing 12.22 Using md5sum to check the uploaded file

```
$ ip addr show | grep 192 | cut -d" " -f6
192.168.0.104/24
$
$ md5sum Project4x.tar
efbb0804083196e58613b6274c69d88c  Project4x.tar
$
```

md5sum produces a 128-bit hash value. You can see from the results in the two listings that the hash values match. This indicates no file corruption occurred during its transfer.

WARNING   A malicious attacker can create two files that have the same MD5 hash value. However, at this point in time, a file that is not under the attacker's control cannot have its MD5 hash value modified. Therefore, it is imperative that you have checks in place to ensure that your original backup file was not created by a third-party malicious user. An even better solution is to use a stronger hash algorithm.

Securing Hash Algorithms

The Secure Hash Algorithms (SHA) is a family of various hash functions. Though typically used for cryptography purposes, they can also be used to verify an archive file's integrity.

Several utilities implement these various algorithms on Linux. The quickest way to find them is using the method shown in Listing 12.23. Keep in mind that your particular distribution may store them in the /bin directory instead.

Listing 12.23 Looking at the SHA utility names

```
$ ls -1 /usr/bin/sha???sum
/usr/bin/sha224sum
/usr/bin/sha256sum
/usr/bin/sha384sum
/usr/bin/sha512sum
$
```

Each utility includes the SHA message digest it employs within its name. Therefore, sha384sum uses the SHA-384 algorithm. These utilities are used in a similar manner to the md5sum command. A few examples are shown in Listing 12.24.

Listing 12.24 Using sha512sum to check the original file

```
$ sha224sum Project4x.tar
c36f1632cd4966967a6daa787cdf1a2d6b4ee5592
4e3993c69d9e9d0  Project4x.tar
$
$ sha512sum Project4x.tar
6d2cf04ddb20c369c2bcc77db294eb60d401fb443
d3277d76a17b477000efe46c00478cdaf25ec6fc09
833d2f8c8d5ab910534ff4b0f5bccc63f88a992fa9
eb3  Project4x.tar
$
```

Notice in Listing 12.24 the different hash value lengths produced by the different commands. The sha512sum utility uses the SHA-512 algorithm, which is the best to use for security purposes and is typically employed to hash salted passwords in the /etc/shadow file on Linux.

You can use these SHA utilities, just like the md5sum program was used in Listings 12.21 and 12.22, to ensure archive files' integrity. That way, backup corruption is avoided as well as any malicious modifications to the file.

Summary

Providing appropriate archival and retrieval of files is critical. Understanding your business and data needs is part of the backup planning process. As you develop your plans, look at integrity issues, archive space availability, privacy needs, and so on. Once rigorous plans are in place, you can rest assured that your data is protected.

Exam Essentials

Describe the different backup types.   A system image backup takes a complete copy of files the operating system needs to operate. This allows a restore to take place, which will get the system back up and running. The full, incremental, and differential backups are tied together in how data is backed up and restored. Snapshots and snapshot clones are also closely related and provide the opportunity to achieve rigorous backups in high I/O environments.

Summarize compression methods.   The different utilities, `gzip`, `bzip2`, `xz`, and `zip`, provide different levels of lossless data compression. Each one's compression level is tied to how fast it operates. Reducing the size of archive data files is needed not only for backup storage but also for increasing transfer speeds across the network.

Compare the various archive/restore utilities.   The assorted command-line utilities each have their own strengths in creating data backups and restoring files. While `cpio` is one of the oldest, it allows for various files through the system to be gathered and put into an archive. The `tar` utility has long been used with tape media but provides rigorous and flexible archiving and restoring features, which make it still very useful in today's environment. The `dd` utility shines when it comes to making system images of an entire disk. Finally, not only is `rsync` very fast, but it also allows encrypted transfers of data across a network for remote backup storage.

Explain the needs when storing backups on other systems.   To move an archive across the network to another system, it is important to provide data security. Thus, often OpenSSH is employed. In addition, once an archive file arrives at its final destination, it is critical to ensure that no data corruption has occurred during the transfer. Therefore, tools such as `md5sum` and `sha512sum` are used.

Review Questions

1. Time and space to generate archives are not an issue, and your system's environment is not a high I/O one. You want to create full backups for your system only once per week and need to restore data as quickly as possible. Which backup type plan should you use?

   A. Full archive daily

   B. Incremental archive daily

   C. Differential archive daily

   D. Full archive weekly; incremental daily

   E. Full archive weekly; differential daily

2. The system admin took an archive file and applied a compression utility to it. The resulting file extension is `.gz`. Which compression utility was used?

   A. The `xz` utility

   B. The `gzip` utility

   C. The `bzip2` utility

   D. The `zip` utility

   E. The `dd` utility

3. You need to quickly create a special archive. This archive will be a single compressed file, which contains any files with the extension `.snar` across the virtual directory structure. Which archive utility should you use?

   A. The `tar` utility

   B. The `dd` utility

   C. The `rsync` utility

   D. The `cpio` utility

   E. The `zip` utility

4. An administrator needs to create a full backup using the `tar` utility, compress it as much as possible, and view the files as they are being copied into the archive. What `tar` options should the admin employ?

   A. `-xzvf`

   B. `-xJvf`

   C. `-czvf`

   D. `-cJf`

   E. `-cJvf`

5. You need to create a low-level backup of all the data on the /dev/sdc drive and want to use the /dev/sde drive to store it on. Which dd command should you use?

   A. dd of=/dev/sde if=/dev/sdc

   B. dd of=/dev/sdc if=/dev/sde

   C. dd of=/dev/sde if=/dev/sdc count=5

   D. dd if=/dev/sde of=/dev/sdc count=5

   E. dd if=/dev/zero of=/dev/sdc

6. You need to create a backup of a user directory tree. You want to ensure that all the file metadata is retained. Employing super user privileges, which of the following should you use with the rsync utility?

   A. The -r option

   B. The -z option

   C. The -a option

   D. The -e option

   E. The --rsh option

7. You decide to compress the archive you are creating with the rsync utility and employ the -z option. Which compression method are you using?

   A. compress

   B. gzip

   C. bzip2

   D. xz

   E. zlib

8. Which of the following is true concerning the scp utility? (Choose all that apply.)

   A. Well suited for quickly transferring files between two systems on a network

   B. Is faster than the sftp utility

   C. An interactive utility useful for quickly transferring large files

   D. Can be interrupted during file transfers with no ill effects

   E. Uses OpenSSH for file transfers

9. You are transferring files for a local backup using the sftp utility to a remote system and the process gets interrupted. What sftp utility command should you use next?

   A. The progress command

   B. The get command

   C. The reget command

   D. The put command

   E. The reput command

10. You have completed a full archive and sent it to a remote system using the `sftp` utility. You employ the `md5sum` program on both the local archive and its remote copy. The numbers don't match. What most likely is the cause of this?

   A.   The local archive was corrupted when it was created.

   B.   The archive was corrupted when it was transferred.

   C.   You used incorrect commands within the `sftp` utility.

   D.   The numbers only match if corruption occurred.

   E.   You used incorrect utility switches on `md5sum`.

Chapter

13

Governing Software

✓ **Objective 1.6 Given a scenario, build and install software**

A Linux system is only as good as the software you install on it. The Linux kernel by itself is pretty boring; you need applications such as web servers, database servers, browsers, and word processing tools to actually do anything useful with your Linux system. This chapter addresses the role of software on your Linux system and how you get and manage it. First we discuss just how software is created in the age of open source and how you retrieve and compile software code. Next, we explore the ways Linux makes things easier for us by bundling prebuilt software packages to make installation and removal of applications a breeze.

Working with Source Code

The "source" part of the open source world refers to the availability of the actual programming code used to create applications. While many commercial applications hide their source code from prying eyes, open source projects make their program code openly available for anyone to peruse and modify if needed. Most applications in the Linux environment are distributed as open source projects, so you're free to download, modify, compile, and run those applications on your Linux system.

While this may sound complicated, it really isn't. The following sections walk through the process of downloading, extracting, compiling, and running open source application code on your Linux system.

Downloading Source Code

Once developers are ready to release their open source applications to the world, they publish them on the Internet. Developers for most open source packages use a website to host their code and documentation, and many even provide user forums that allow customers to discuss issues and possible improvements.

While you can use a graphical browser to connect to a website and download source code, that's not always available, especially in Linux server environments. Linux provides a couple of command-line tools to help us download source code files directly from the command line.

The wget application is a command-line tool from the GNU Project that allows you to retrieve files from remote servers using FTP, FTPS, HTTP, or HTTPS. You specify the protocol, server name, and file to download using a standard URL format, where *remotehost* is the full hostname for the location hosting the files, and *filename* is the name of the source code file you wish to retrieve, including the folder path required:

```
wget http://remotehost/filename
```

The wget application supports lots of command-line options to help you customize the connection and download. These especially come in handy if you write scripts to automatically download files. Check out the manual pages for wget to see the different options available.

Yet another solution is the cURL application. It does the same thing as wget but supports many more protocols, such as DAP, DICT, FILE, Gopher, IMAP, LDAP, POP3, RTSP, SCP, SFTP, SMTP, and TFTP. It too uses the standard URL format for you to specify the protocol, server name, and file to download.

One nice feature of cURL is its ability to work with the secure HTTPS protocol. It will warn you if the remote website is using a self-signed certificate or if the certificate is signed by an untrusted certificate authority (CA).

A relatively recent advancement in software distribution is GitHub (https://github.com). It provides a centralized location on the Internet for projects that use the Git version control system (see Chapter 27, "Controlling Versions with Git"). The code for many open source projects is now posted in GitHub, even if there is already a dedicated website for the project. You can use both wget and cURL to download project code from GitHub.

Bundling Source Code Packages

Distributing the source code for applications can be a bit tricky. Source code projects often consist of many different files:

- Source code files
- Header files
- Library files
- Documentation files

Trying to distribute a large batch of files for a project can be a challenge. Linux provides somewhat of an odd solution for that.

The tar program was originally developed for archiving files and folders to tape drives for backups (the tar name originally stood for tape archiver). These days it also comes in handy for bundling project files to distribute on the Internet.

The tar command allows you to specify multiple files, or even multiple folders of files, to bundle together into a single output file. You can then transfer the entire project bundle as a single file and extract the files and folders on a remote system. It's so versatile in what it can do that there is a long list of command-line options available, which can become somewhat imposing.

For most bundling operations, three basic option groups are commonly used for the tar command:

- -cvf: Create a new tar file
- -tvf: Display the contents of a tar file
- -xvf: Extract the contents of a tar file

To create a new tar archive file, specify the output file name and then the list of files and folders to bundle, as shown in the example in Listing 13.1.

Listing 13.1: Using the tar command to bundle files

```
$ tar -cvf test.tar test1.txt test2.txt test3.txt
test1.txt
test2.txt
test3.txt
$ ls -al
total 32
drwxr-xr-x  2 rich rich  4096 Dec  5 08:33 .
drwxr-xr-x 19 rich rich  4096 Dec  5 08:28 ..
-rw-r--r--  1 rich rich   795 Dec  5 08:19 test1.txt
-rw-r--r--  1 rich rich  1020 Dec  5 08:19 test2.txt
-rw-r--r--  1 rich rich  2280 Dec  5 08:20 test3.txt
-rw-r--r--  1 rich rich 10240 Dec  5 08:33 test.tar
$
```

In Listing 13.1, test.tar is the name of the archive file you want to create. For the input files and folders, you can use wildcard characters to specify the names, or even redirect a listing of files to the tar command, making it very versatile in scripts. One of the advantages of bundling folders with tar is that it preserves the folder structure of your environment, including file and folder ownership, making it easier to extract the files and re-create the original environment.

Though not required, it's become somewhat of a de facto standard in Linux to use a .tar filename extension to identify a tar archive file. This is commonly called a *tarball* in Linux circles.

If you need to see what's in a tar archive file, use the -tvf option group:

```
$ tar -tvf test.tar
-rw-r--r-- rich/rich      795 2018-12-05 08:19 test1.txt
-rw-r--r-- rich/rich     1020 2018-12-05 08:19 test2.txt
-rw-r--r-- rich/rich     2280 2018-12-05 08:20 test3.txt
$
```

Notice that both the file ownerships and the file permissions are retained within the tar archive file. When you extract the files onto another system, they'll be assigned to the userid that matches the user number assigned to the original files.

Extracting the files and folders from a tar file is just a matter of using the −xvf option group:

```
$ tar -xvf test.tar
test1.txt
test2.txt
test3.txt
$ ls -al
total 32
drwxr-xr-x  2 rich rich  4096 Dec  5 08:38 .
drwxr-xr-x 20 rich rich  4096 Dec  5 08:38 ..
-rw-r--r--  1 rich rich   795 Dec  5 08:19 test1.txt
-rw-r--r--  1 rich rich  1020 Dec  5 08:19 test2.txt
-rw-r--r--  1 rich rich  2280 Dec  5 08:20 test3.txt
-rw-r--r--  1 rich rich 10240 Dec  5 08:38 test.tar
$
```

The tar archive method makes bundling files for distribution easy, but it does tend to create a very large file, which can be awkward to handle. Linux developers usually compress the final tar archive file using some type of file compression utility.

In Linux there is a plethora of ways to create compressed files. Table 13.1 lists the most popular methods you'll run into.

TABLE 13.1   Linux compression methods

Method	Filename extension	Description
bzip2	.bz2	Improvement to the gzip method that reduces file sizes
compress	.Z	The original Unix compress utility
gzip	.gz	Fast compression method that produces moderate-sized files
xz	.xz	Creates smaller compressed files but can be very slow

By far the most common zip utility used in Linux for tar archive files is the GNU gzip package. To compress a single file, use the gzip command with the filename, as shown in Listing 13.2.

Listing 13.2: Compressing a tar archive file

```
$ gzip test.tar
$ ls -al
total 24
drwxr-xr-x  2 rich rich 4096 Dec  5 08:53 .
drwxr-xr-x 20 rich rich 4096 Dec  5 08:39 ..
-rw-r--r--  1 rich rich  795 Dec  5 08:19 test1.txt
-rw-r--r--  1 rich rich 1020 Dec  5 08:19 test2.txt
-rw-r--r--  1 rich rich 2280 Dec  5 08:20 test3.txt
-rw-r--r--  1 rich rich  204 Dec  5 08:33 test.tar.gz
$
```

As seen in Listing 13.2, gzip adds a .gz filename extension to the end of the file that's compressed.

NOTE   Often with compressed tar archive files, you'll see developers shorten the .tar.gz filename extension pair to just .tgz.

To decompress a compressed tarball and extract the original files, you have a couple of options. One option is to use a two-step approach. First use the gunzip command directly on the compressed tar file:

```
$ gunzip test.tar.gz
```

This restores the original test.tar file. Then you extract the tar file using the standard -xvf options of the tar command.

The second option is to decompress and extract the tarball file in one step by just adding the -z option to the tar command line:

```
$ tar -zxvf test.tgz
test1.txt
test2.txt
test3.txt
$ ls -al
total 24
drwxr-xr-x 2 rich rich 4096 Dec  5 09:03 .
drwxr-xr-x 3 rich rich 4096 Dec  5 09:02 ..
-rw-r--r-- 1 rich rich  795 Dec  5 08:19 test1.txt
-rw-r--r-- 1 rich rich 1020 Dec  5 08:19 test2.txt
-rw-r--r-- 1 rich rich 2280 Dec  5 08:20 test3.txt
-rw-r--r-- 1 rich rich  204 Dec  5 09:02 test.tgz
$
```

One important thing to note is that when you use the gunzip program directly, it removes the compressed file and replaces it with the original file, but when you use the -z option with the tar command, it retains the compressed file along with decompressing and extracting the original files.

Compiling Source Code

Once you have the source code package files downloaded onto your Linux system, you'll need to compile them to create an executable file to run the application. Linux supports a wide variety of programming languages, so you'll need to know just what programming language the application was written in. Once you know that, you'll need to install a *compiler* for the program code. A compiler converts the source code into an executable file the Linux system can run.

The most common tool used for compiling programs in Linux is the *GNU Compiler Collection (gcc)*. While originally created to support only the C programming language, gcc now supports an amazing array of different programming languages, such as Ada, C++, Fortran, Go, Java, Objective-C, Objective-C++, and OpenMP.

Most Linux distributions don't include the gcc program by default, so most likely you'll need to install it on your Linux system. For Ubuntu, it's part of the build-essentials package, while for Rocky Linux you'll find it in the Development Tools package group.

To compile simple one-file programs, just run the gcc command-line command against the source code file to produce the executable file that you run on your system. The -o option allows you to specify the name of the compiled output file; otherwise it defaults to the ugly a.out filename:

```
$ cat hello.c
#include <stdio.h>
int main() {
    printf("Hello, this is my first C program!\n");
    return 0;
}
$ gcc -o hello hello.c
$ ./hello
Hello, this is my first C program!
$
```

As mentioned earlier, most larger applications require additional header and library files besides the source code files to build the final application file. Depending on just how many source code, header, and library files are required for an application, the gcc command process can get very long and complicated. Separate library files need to be compiled in the proper order before the main program file can be compiled, creating a difficult road map to follow to generate the application.

There's a simple solution available for you to help keep track of all that. The make utility allows developers to create scripts that guide the compiling and installation process of application source code packages so that even novices can compile and install an application from source code.

Usually there are three steps involved with installing an application that uses a make script:

1. Run the configure utility, which analyzes your Linux system and customizes the make script to build the application for your environment.

2. Run the make utility by itself to build the necessary library files and executable files for the application.

3. Run make install as the root user account to install the application files in the appropriate locations on your system.

What makes C language programs so complicated is that they often split the application functions into separate library files. Each library file contains one or more specialized functions used in the application code.

The benefit of splitting functions into separate library files is that multiple applications that use the same functions can share the same library files. These files, called *shared libraries*, make it easier to distribute applications but more complicated to keep track of what library files are installed with which applications.

While not necessary for compiling the application source code, the *ldd* utility can come in handy if you need to track down missing library files for an application. It displays a list of the library files required for the specified application file:

```
$ ldd hello
    linux-vdso.so.1 (0x00007fff7dff4000)
    libc.so.6 => /lib64/libc.so.6 (0x00007fe154e57000)
    /lib64/ld-linux-x86-64.so.2 (0x00007fe15521c000)
$
```

My simple hello application requires two external library files, the standard linux-vdso.so.1 and libc.so.6 files, which provide the ability for the printf() function to display the output. The ldd utility also shows where those files were found on the Linux system. That in itself can be helpful when troubleshooting issues with applications picking up the wrong library files.

Packaging Applications

While the tar, gcc, and make programs make it easier to distribute, compile, and install application source code, that's still somewhat of a messy process for installing new applications. For most Linux users, all they want to do is download an application and use it.

To help solve that problem, Linux distributions have created a system for bundling already compiled applications for distribution. This bundle is called a *package*, and it consists of all the files required to run a single application. You can then install, remove, and manage the entire application as a single package rather than as a group of disjointed files.

Tracking software packages on a Linux system is called *package management*. Linux implements package management by using a database to track the installed packages on the system. The package management database keeps track of not only what packages are installed but also the exact files and file locations required for each application. Determining what applications are installed on your system is as easy as querying the package management database.

As you would expect, different Linux distributions have created different package management systems for working with their package management databases. However, over the years, two main package management systems have risen to the top and have become standards:

- Debian package management
- Red Hat package management

Because of their popularity, these are the two package management methods covered by the Linux+ exam, so these are the two package management methods we'll cover in detail in this chapter.

Each package management system uses a different method of tracking application packages and files, but they both track similar information:

- Application files: The package database tracks each individual file as well as the folder where it's located.

- Library dependencies: The package database tracks what library files are required for each application and can warn you if a dependent library file is not present when you install a package.

- Application version: The package database tracks version numbers of applications so that you know when an updated version of the application is available.

The following sections discuss the tools for using each of these package management systems.

Installing and Managing Packages

Both the Debian and Red Hat package management systems have similar sets of tools for working with software packages in the package management system. We'll now take a look at both systems and the tools to use with them.

Debian Package Tools

As you can probably guess, the Debian package management system is mostly used on Debian-based Linux systems, such as Ubuntu. Debian bundles application files into a single DEB package file for distribution. The core tool to use for handling DEB files is the dpkg program.

The dpkg program is a command-line utility that has options to install, update, and remove DEB package files on your Linux system. The basic format for the dpkg command is as follows:

dpkg [*options*] *action package-file*

The action parameter defines the action to be taken on the file. Table 13.2 lists common actions you'll need to use.

TABLE 13.2   The dpkg command actions

Action	Description
-C	Searches for broken installed packages and suggests how to fix them
--configure	Reconfigures an installed package
--get-selections	Displays currently installed packages
-i	Installs the package
-I	Displays information about an uninstalled package file
-l	Lists all installed packages matching a specified pattern
-L	Lists the installed files associated with a package
-p	Displays information about an installed package
-P	Removes an installed package, including configuration files
-r	Removes an installed package but leaves the configuration files
-S	Locates the package that owns the specified files

Each action has a set of options that you can use to modify the basic behavior of the action, such as to force overwriting an already installed package or ignore any dependency errors.

To use the dpkg program, you must have the DEB software package available, either from an installation DVD or by downloading the package from the Internet. Often you can find DEB versions of application packages ready for distribution on the application website, or most distributions maintain a central location for packages to download.

The Debian distribution also provides a central clearinghouse for Debian packages at www.debian.org/distrib/packages.

When you download a DEB package for a precompiled application, be careful that you get the correct package for your workstation processor chip. Source code files are compiled for specific processors, and trying to run the wrong one on your system will not work. Usually the processor type is added as part of the package name.

Once you download the DEB package, use dpkg with the -i option to install it:

```
$ sudo dpkg -i zsh_5.3.1-4+b2_amd64.deb
Selecting previously unselected package zsh.
(Reading database ... 204322 files and directories currently installed.)
Preparing to unpack zsh_5.3.1-4+b2_amd64.deb ...
Unpacking zsh (5.3.1-4+b2) ...
dpkg: dependency problems prevent configuration of zsh:
 zsh depends on zsh-common (= 5.3.1-4); however:
  Package zsh-common is not installed.


dpkg: error processing package zsh (--install):
 dependency problems - leaving unconfigured
Processing triggers for man-db (2.8.3-2ubuntu0.1) ...
Errors were encountered while processing:
 zsh
$
```

You can see in this example that the package management software checks to ensure that any packages that are required for the application are installed and produces an error message if any of them are missing. This gives you a clue as to what other packages you need to install.

If you'd like to see all of the packages installed on your system, use the -l option:

```
$ dpkg -l
Desired=Unknown/Install/Remove/Purge/Hold
| Status=Not/Inst/Conf-files/Unpacked/halF-conf/Half-inst/trig-aWait/Trig
|/ Err?=(none)/Reinst-required (Status,Err: uppercase=bad)
||/ Name           Version      Architecture Description
+++-==============-============-============-===============================
ii  accountsservic 0.6.45-1ubun amd64        query and manipulate accounts
ii  acl            2.2.52-3buil amd64        Access control list utilities
ii  acpi-support   0.142        amd64        scripts for handling ACPI
ii  acpid          1:2.0.28-1ub amd64        Advanced Config and Power
ii  adduser        3.116ubuntu1 all          add and remove users
ii  adium-theme-ub 0.3.4-0ubunt all          Adium message style for Ubuntu
```

```
ii  adwaita-icon-t 3.28.0-1ubun all            default icon theme of GNOME
ii  aisleriot      1:3.22.5-1    amd64          GNOME solitaire card game
...
```

You can also provide a search term on the command line to limit the packages returned in the output:

```
$ dpkg -l openssh*
Desired=Unknown/Install/Remove/Purge/Hold
| Status=Not/Inst/Conf-files/Unpacked/halF-conf/Half-inst/trig-aWait/Trig
|/ Err?=(none)/Reinst-required (Status,Err: uppercase=bad)
||/ Name            Version        Architecture Description
+++-===============-=============-=============-===============================
ii  openssh-client 1:7.6p1-4ubu amd64          secure shell (SSH) client
un  openssh-server <none>        <none>         (no description available)
$
```

If you need to remove a package, you have two options. The -r action removes the package but keeps any configuration and data files associated with the package installed. This is useful if you're just trying to reinstall an existing package and don't want to have to reconfigure things. If you really do want to remove the entire package, use the -P action, which purges the entire package, including configuration files and data files from the system.

> Be very careful with the -p and -P options. They're easy to mix up. The -p option lists the packages, whereas the -P option purges the packages. Quite a difference!

The dpkg tool gives you direct access to the package management system, making it easier to install applications on your Debian-based system.

Red Hat Package Tools

The Red Hat Linux distribution, along with other Red Hat–based distributions such as Fedora, Rocky, and CentOS, use the RPM package file format. The main tool for working with RPM files is the rpm program.

Similar to the dpkg tool, the rpm program is also a command-line program to install, modify, and remove RPM software packages. The basic format for the rpm program is as follows:

```
rpm action [options] package-file
```

The actions for the rpm command are shown in Table 13.3.

To use the rpm command, you must have the RPM package file downloaded onto your system. While you can use the -i action to install packages, it's more common to use the -U action, which installs the new package or upgrades the package if it's already installed. Adding the -vh option is a popular combination that shows the progress of the update and what it's doing:

TABLE 13.3   The rpm command actions

Action	Description
-b	Builds a binary package from source files
-e	Uninstalls the specified package
-F	Upgrades a package only if an earlier version already exists
-i	Installs the specified package
-q	Queries if the specified package is installed
-U	Installs or upgrades the specified package
-V	Verifies if the package files are present

```
$ sudo rpm -Uvh zsh-5.0.2-31.el7.x86_64.rpm
Preparing...                    ############################### [100%]
Updating / installing...
  1:zsh-5.0.2-31.el7            ############################### [100%]
$
```

You use the -q action to query the package management database for installed packages:

```
$ rpm -q zsh
zsh-5.0.2-31.el7.x86_64
$
```

If you need to remove an installed package, just use the -e action:

```
$ sudo rpm -e zsh
$ sudo rpm -q zsh
package zsh is not installed
$
```

The -e action doesn't show if it was successful, but it will display an error message if something goes wrong with the removal.

Understanding Repositories

The dpkg and rpm commands are useful tools, but they both have their limitations. If you're looking for new software packages to install, it's up to you to find them. Also, if a package depends on other packages to be installed, it's up to you to install those packages first and in the correct order. That can become somewhat of a pain to keep up with.

To solve that problem, each Linux distribution has its own central clearinghouse of packages, called a *repository*. The repository contains software packages that have been tested and known to install and work correctly in the distribution environment. By placing all known packages into a single repository, the Linux distribution can create a one-stop shopping environment for installing all applications for the system.

Most Linux distributions create and maintain their own repositories of packages. There are also additional tools for working with package repositories. These tools can interface directly with the package repository to find new software and even automatically find and install any dependent packages the application requires to operate.

Besides the officially supported distribution package repositories, many third-party package repositories have sprung up on the Internet. Often specialized or custom software packages aren't distributed as part of the normal Linux distribution repository but are available in third-party repositories. The repository tools allow you to retrieve those packages as well.

The following sections walk through how to use the Debian and Red Hat repository tools.

Debian Repository Tools

The core tool used for working with Debian repositories is the `apt` suite of tools. This includes the `apt-cache` program, which provides information about the package database, and the `apt-get` program, which does the work of installing, updating, and removing packages. To make things easier, the `apt` program is a front-end script that can call either of the core programs as needed.

The `apt` suite of tools relies on the `/etc/apt/sources.list` file to identify the locations of where to look for repositories. By default, each Linux distribution enters its own repository location in that file, but you can add additional repository locations as well if you install third-party applications not supported by the distribution.

There are a few useful command options in the `apt-cache` program for displaying information about packages:

- `depends`: Displays the dependencies required for the package
- `pkgnames`: Displays all the packages installed on the system
- `showpkg`: Displays information about the specified package
- `stats`: Displays package statistics for the system
- `unmet`: Displays any unmet dependencies for installed packages

The workhorse of the `apt` suite of tools is the `apt` program. It's what you use to install and remove packages from a Debian package repository. Table 13.4 lists the `apt` commands.

TABLE 13.4 The apt program action commands

Action	Description
autoremove	Removes any unneeded packages automatically installed as a dependency of another installed package
full-upgrade	Works the same as upgrade but will remove any installed packages required to upgrade the entire system
install	Installs a new software package from the repository
list	Displays the currently installed packages
purge	Removes the specified application, along with any configuration or data files
reinstall	Attempts to reinstall an existing package from the repository
remove	Removes the specified application, but keeps any configuration or data files
satisfy	Attempts to resolve software dependencies in the installed packages
search	Searches for a specific package in the repository
show	Displays information about the specified package
update	Downloads package information from all configured repositories
upgrade	Installs available upgrades from all installed packages

Installing a new package from the repository is as simple as specifying the package name with the install action:

```
$ sudo apt install zsh
Reading package lists... Done
Building dependency tree
Reading state information... Done
Suggested packages:
  zsh-doc
The following NEW packages will be installed:
  zsh
0 upgraded, 1 newly installed, 0 to remove and 0 not upgraded.
Need to get 707 kB of archives.
After this operation, 2,390 kB of additional disk space will be used.
```

```
Get:1 http://us.archive.ubuntu.com/ubuntu focal/main amd64 zsh amd64
5.8-3ubuntu1 [707 kB]
Fetched 707 kB in 1s (731 kB/s)
Selecting previously unselected package zsh.
(Reading database ... 195185 files and directories currently installed.)
Preparing to unpack .../zsh_5.8-3ubuntu1_amd64.deb ...
Unpacking zsh (5.8-3ubuntu1) ...
Setting up zsh (5.8-3ubuntu1) ...
Processing triggers for man-db (2.9.1-1) ...
$
```

If any dependencies are required, the apt program retrieves those as well and installs them automatically.

 The upgrade action provides a great way to keep your entire Debian-based system up-to-date with both package and kernel updates released to the distribution repository. Running that command will ensure that your packages and the Linux kernel have all the security and bug fixes installed. However, that also means that you fully trust the distribution developers to put only tested packages in the repository. Occasionally a package may make its way into the repository before being fully tested and cause issues.

Red Hat Repository Tools

In the past, the core tool used for working with Red Hat repositories has been the yum tool (short for YellowDog Update Manager, originally developed for the YellowDog Linux distribution). This tool has recently been replaced by the dnf tool, which is an updated version of yum with additional features added. The dnf tool allows you to query, install, and remove software packages on your system directly from a Red Hat repository.

Both the yum and dnf commands use the /etc/yum.repos.d folder to hold files that list the different repositories it checks for packages. For a default Rocky Linux system, that folder contains several repository files:

```
$ cd /etc/yum.repos.d
$ ls -al
total 88
drwxr-xr-x.   2 root root 4096 Nov 30 09:15 .
drwxr-xr-x. 150 root root 8192 Dec 27 09:34 ..
-rw-r--r--.   1 root root 1485 Sep  4 13:28 epel-modular.repo
-rw-r--r--.   1 root root 1564 Sep  4 13:28 epel-playground.repo
-rw-r--r--.   1 root root 1422 Sep  4 13:28 epel.repo
-rw-r--r--.   1 root root 1584 Sep  4 13:28 epel-testing-modular.repo
-rw-r--r--.   1 root root 1521 Sep  4 13:28 epel-testing.repo
```

```
-rw-r--r--.  1 root root  700 Oct  8 19:29 Rocky-AppStream.repo
-rw-r--r--.  1 root root  685 Oct  8 19:29 Rocky-BaseOS.repo
-rw-r--r--.  1 root root 1753 Oct  8 19:29 Rocky-Debuginfo.repo
-rw-r--r--.  1 root root  350 Oct  8 19:29 Rocky-Devel.repo
-rw-r--r--.  1 root root  685 Oct  8 19:29 Rocky-Extras.repo
-rw-r--r--.  1 root root  721 Oct  8 19:29 Rocky-HighAvailability.repo
-rw-r--r--.  1 root root  680 Oct  8 19:29 Rocky-Media.repo
-rw-r--r--.  1 root root  670 Oct  8 19:29 Rocky-NFV.repo
-rw-r--r--.  1 root root  680 Oct  8 19:29 Rocky-Plus.repo
-rw-r--r--.  1 root root  705 Oct  8 19:29 Rocky-PowerTools.repo
-rw-r--r--.  1 root root  736 Oct  8 19:29 Rocky-ResilientStorage.repo
-rw-r--r--.  1 root root  671 Oct  8 19:29 Rocky-RT.repo
-rw-r--r--.  1 root root 2335 Oct  8 19:29 Rocky-Sources.repo
$
```

Each file in the yum.repos.d folder contains information on a repository, such as the URL address of the repository and the location of additional package files within the repository. The yum program checks each of these defined repositories for the package requested on the command line.

The dnf program is very versatile. Table 13.5 shows the commands you can use with it.

TABLE 13.5   The dnf action commands

Action	Description
alias	Defines an alias that points to a list of other dnf commands
autoremove	Removes any packages installed as a dependency that is no longer needed
check	Examines the local package database and reports any problems
check-update	Checks the repository for updates to a specified package
clean	Performs cleanup of temporary files kept for repositories
deplist	Deprecated alias for the repoquery command
distro-sync	Downgrades or installs packages to place the system in sync with the current repositories
downgrade	Downgrades the specified package to the version available in the repository
group	Manages a set of packages as a single entity
help	Displays help for the dnf command

TABLE 13.5 The dnf action commands *(continued)*

Action	Description
history	Displays previous dnf commands
info	Displays information about an installed and available package
install	Installs the current version of a package from the repository
list	Displays all installed and available packages
makecache	Downloads metadata for the repositories
mark	Marks a specified package as being installed
module	Manages module packages
provides	Displays the package that installed the specified file
reinstall	Attempts to reinstall the specified package
remove	Removes the specified package from the system, including any packages that depend on the specified package
repoinfo	Displays information about the configured repositories
repolist	Displays a list of the currently configured repositories
repoquery	Searches the configured repositories for the specified package
repository-packages	Runs commands on all packages in the repository
search	Searches package metadata for specified keywords
shell	Displays an interactive shell for entering multiple dnf commands
swap	Removes and reinstalls the specified package
updateinfo	Displays update advisory messages
upgrade	Installs the latest version of the specified packages, or all packages if none specified
upgrade-minimal	Installs only the latest package versions that provide a bugfix or security fix

Installing new applications is a breeze with dnf:

```
$ sudo dnf install zsh
Last metadata expiration check: 0:00:19 ago on Mon 27 Dec 2021 20:04:03 AM EST.
Dependencies resolved.
================================================================================
 Package        Architecture    Version                    Repository
Size
================================================================================
Installing:
 zsh            x86_64          5.5.1-6.el8_1.2            baseos         2.9 M

Transaction Summary
================================================================================
Install  1 Package

Total download size: 2.9 M
Installed size: 6.9 M
Is this ok [y/N]: y
Downloading Packages:
zsh-5.5.1-6.el8_1.2.x86_64.rpm                  1.1 MB/s | 2.9 MB     00:02
--------------------------------------------------------------------------------
Total                                           376 kB/s | 2.9 MB     00:07
Running transaction check
Transaction check succeeded.
Running transaction test
Transaction test succeeded.
Running transaction
  Preparing        :
1/1
  Installing       : zsh-5.5.1-6.el8_1.2.x86_64
1/1
  Running scriptlet: zsh-5.5.1-6.el8_1.2.x86_64
1/1
  Verifying        : zsh-5.5.1-6.el8_1.2.x86_64
1/1

Installed:
  zsh-5.5.1-6.el8_1.2.x86_64

Complete!
$
```

One nice feature of dnf is the ability to group packages for distribution. Instead of having to download all of the packages needed for a specific environment (such as for a web server that uses the Apache, MySQL, and PHP servers), you can download the package group that bundles the packages together. This makes for an even easier way to get packages installed on your system.

 The openSUSE Linux distribution uses the RPM package management system and distributes software in RPM files but doesn't use the yum or dnf tools. Instead, openSUSE has created its own package manager called ZYpp. The main tool in the ZYpp package is the zypper program.

Graphical Package Tools

Both the Debian-based and Red Hat–based package management systems have graphical tools for making it easier to install software in desktop environments. One tool that is available in both the Ubuntu and Rocky distributions is *gnome-software*.

The gnome-software program is a graphical front end to the *PackageKit* tool, which itself is a front end that standardizes the interface to multiple package management tools, including apt and yum. By including both PackageKit and gnome-software, Linux distributions can provide a standard graphical interface for users to manage their software packages. Figure 13.1 shows the gnome-software package as it appears in the Ubuntu 20.04 Linux distribution.

FIGURE 13.1   The Ubuntu Software package graphical tool

![Screenshot of the Ubuntu Software package graphical tool showing the Explore tab with a Spotify banner, Editor's Picks including powershell, ONLYOFFICE D..., Thunderbird, 1password, bitwarden, and konversation, and Categories such as Art and Design, Books and Reference, Development, Devices and IoT, Education, Entertainment, Finance, Games, Health and Fitness, Music and Audio, News and Weather, and Personalisation.]

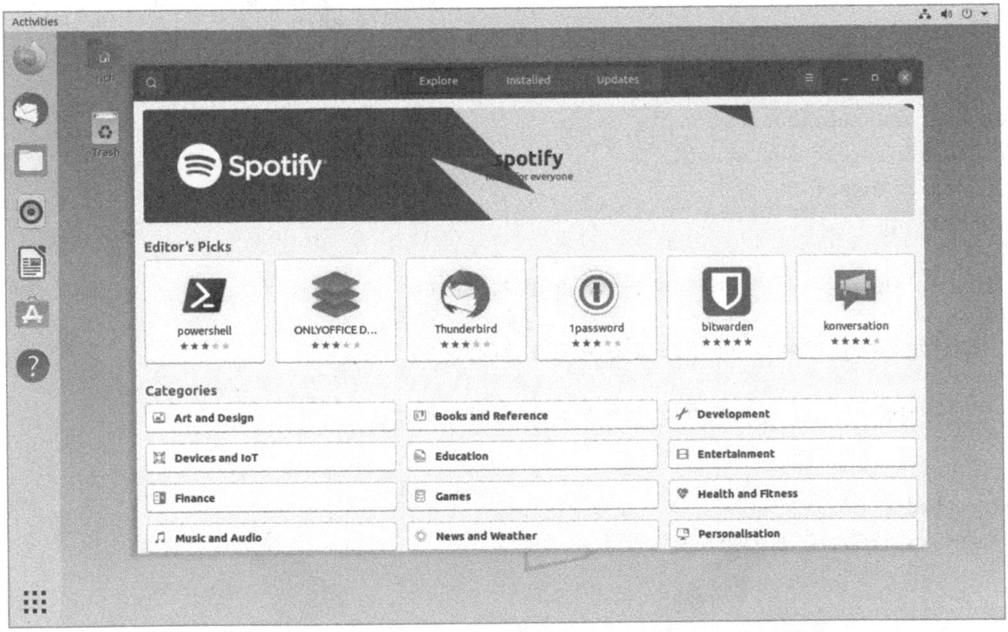

You can search for packages, view the installed packages, and even view the updated packages available in the repository. If you're using the Rocky Linux distribution, the gnome-software interface looks the same, as shown in Figure 13.2.

Finally, some standardization is happening across Linux distributions, at least where it comes to graphical software package management tools.

FIGURE 13.2   The Rocky Linux software package graphical tool

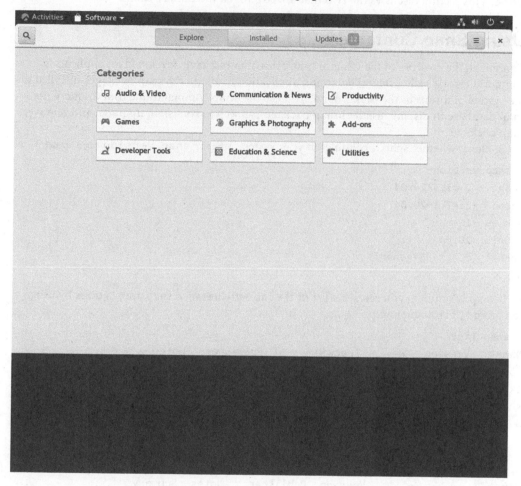

Using Application Containers

A relatively new feature in the Linux world is the use of *containers*. Containers allow you to bundle all of the files required for an application, including any dependencies, into one distribution package—the container. This ensures that you can install everything needed to run an application at once, and that all the files required to run an application are available, no matter what platform you install the container on.

The downside to this method, though, is that any dependencies shared among multiple applications are duplicated for each application. However, this method ensures that each application has exactly the correct dependencies (and versions) required to run properly, and it is quickly gaining in popularity, especially in environments where applications may need to switch servers frequently.

As expected, there are multiple application container formats available in the Linux world. This section discusses the two that are covered in the Linux+ exam.

Using Snap Containers

Canonical, the creators of the Ubuntu Linux distribution, have developed an application container format called *snap*. The snapd application manages the snap packages installed on the system and runs in the background. You use the snap command-line tool to query the snap database to display installed snap packages, as well as to install, upgrade, and remove snap packages.

To check whether snap is running on your system, use the snap version command:

```
$ snap version
snap    2.47.1+20.04
snapd   2.47.1+20.04
series  16
ubuntu  20.04
kernel  5.4.0-53-generic
$
```

If snap is running, you can see a list of the currently installed snap applications by using the snap list command:

```
$ snap list
Name     Version    Rev    Tracking        Publisher    Notes
core18   20200929   1932   latest/stable   canonical*   base
lxd      4.0.4      18150  4.0/stable/...  canonical*   -
snapd    2.47.1     9721   latest/stable   canonical*   snapd
$
```

To search the snap repository for new applications, use the snap find command:

```
$ snap find stress-ng
Name                     Version  Publisher        Notes  Summary
stress-ng  V0.11.24  cking-kernel-tools  -      A tool to load, stress
test and
 benchmark a computer system
$
```

To view more information about a snap application, use the snap info command:

```
$ snap info stress-ng
name:      stress-ng
summary:   A tool to load, stress test and benchmark a computer system
```

```
publisher: Colin King (cking-kernel-tools)
store-url: https://snapcraft.io/stress-ng
contact:   colin.king@canonical.com
license:   GPL-2.0
description: |
  stress-ng can stress various subsystems of a computer.  It can stress load
  CPU, cache, disk, memory, socket and pipe I/O, scheduling and much more.
  stress-ng is a re-write of the original stress tool by Amos Waterland but
  has many additional features such as specifying the number of bogo
  operations to run, execution metrics, a stress verification on memory and
  compute operations and considerably more stress mechanisms.
snap-id: YMJsyW4vySPdys8BCA7jx8UiOVSVhUT6
channels:
  latest/stable:    V0.11.24                        2020-11-13 (5273) 3MB -
  latest/candidate: V0.11.24                        2020-11-13 (5273) 3MB -
  latest/beta:      V0.11.24                        2020-11-13 (5273) 3MB -
  latest/edge:      V0.11.24-44-20201121-7613-g2627a 2020-11-21 (5298) 3MB -
$
```

To install a new snap, use the snap `install` command.

```
$ sudo snap install stress-ng
[sudo] password for rich:
stress-ng V0.11.24 from Colin King (cking-kernel-tools) installed
$
```

You can check that the software container was installed by using the `list` command:

```
$ snap list
Name       Version    Rev    Tracking        Publisher          Notes
core18     20200929   1932   latest/stable   canonical*         base
lxd        4.0.4      18150  4.0/stable/...  canonical*         -
snapd      2.47.1     9721   latest/stable   canonical*         snapd
stress-ng  V0.11.24   5273   latest/stable   cking-kernel-tools -
$
```

Finally, you can remove an installed application container by using the `remove` command:

```
$ sudo snap remove stress-ng
stress-ng removed
$
```

As the snap is removed, you'll see some messages about the progress of the removal. Instead of removing a snap, if you prefer you can just disable it without removing it. Just use the snap `disable` command. To reenable the snap, use the snap `enable` command.

Using Flatpak Containers

The *flatpak* application container format was created as an independent open source project with no direct ties to any specific Linux distribution. That said, battle lines have already been drawn, with Red Hat–based Linux distributions oriented toward using flatpak instead of Canonical's snap container format.

WARNING   While Red Hat desktop distributions install flatpak by default, the server distributions don't. However, you can easily install flatpak as a package using the standard dnf or rpm method.

To display the current flatpak containers installed on the system, use the list command:

```
$ flatpak list
$
```

Not too exciting. When you first install flatpak there won't be any containers installed, but now you know that flatpak is installed.

By default Red Hat–based Linux distributions don't configure any repositories for flatpak (repositories in flatpak are called *remotes*). The most popular flatpak remote is Flathub. Currently, to set flatpak to point to the Flathub remote you use the following:

```
$ sudo flatpak remote-add --if-not-exists flathub
https://flathub.org/repo/flathub.flatpakrepo
[sudo] password for rich:
$
```

To find an application in the flatpak repository, you use the flatpak search command:

```
$ sudo flatpak search mosh
Name      Description        Application ID     Version    Branch     Remotes
Mosh      The Mobile Shell   org.mosh.mosh      1.3.2      stable     flathub
$
```

When working with a container, you must use its Application ID value and not its name. To install the application, use the flatpak install command:

```
$ sudo flatpak install org.mosh.mosh
Looking for matches...
Found similar ref(s) for 'org.mosh.mosh' in remote 'flathub' (system).
Use this remote? [Y/n]: Y
Required runtime for org.mosh.mosh/x86_64/stable
(runtime/org.freedesktop.Platform/x86_64/21.08) found in remote flathub
Do you want to install it? [Y/n]: Y

org.mosh.mosh permissions:
    network    ssh-auth
```

```
        ID                                   Branch Op Remote   Download
1. org.freedesktop.Platform.GL.default 21.08  i   flathub 130.9 MB / 131.2 MB
2. org.freedesktop.Platform.Locale     21.08  i   flathub  17.7 kB / 325.0 MB
3. org.freedesktop.Platform.openh264   2.0    i   flathub   1.5 MB / 1.5 MB
4. org.freedesktop.Platform           21.08  i   flathub 153.7 MB / 198.9 MB
5. org.mosh.mosh                       stable i   flathub  10.5 MB / 12.7 MB


Installation complete.
$
```

To check if the installation went well, use the flatpak list command again:

```
$ flatpak list
Name              Application ID                        Version Branch Installation
Freedesktop Plat... org.freedesktop.Platform            21.08.7 21.08  system
Mesa              ...freedesktop.Platform.GL.default   21.3.1  21.08  system
openh264          ...g.freedesktop.Platform.openh264   2.1.0   2.0    system
Mosh              org.mosh.mosh                         1.3.2   stable system
$
```

And finally, to remove an application container, use the flatpak uninstall command:

```
$ sudo flatpak uninstall org.mosh.mosh


        ID            Branch      Op
1. [-] org.mosh.mosh    stable       r


Uninstall complete.
$
```

Working with flatpak containers is a bit different from using package management systems, but once you get comfortable with the format of things, it's not all that different from the standard package management system.

 AppImage is yet another format for distributing software in the Linux world. AppImage is a bit different in that standard users don't need root privileges to install an AppImage package on the system. Instead of installing the software in the standard Linux system directories, AppImage distributes applications as a compressed disk image that standard users can mount in their Home directories and run. Of course, this means each individual user on the system who wants to run the application has to download a separate AppImage file to run the application.

EXERCISE 13.1

Working with Packages

This exercise demonstrates how to work with a package management system to install software.

1. Log into your Linux system and open a new command prompt.

2. Display the packages currently installed on your system. For Debian-based systems such as Ubuntu, use the command **sudo apt-cache pkgnames**. For Red Hat–based systems such as Rocky, use the command **sudo dnf list**.

3. If it's not already installed on your system, install the zsh shell package. For Debian-based systems, use the command **sudo apt install zsh**. For Red Hat–based systems, use the command **sudo dnf install zsh**. If the zsh package is already installed, try installing the tcsh package, which is an open source version of the C shell found in many Unix systems.

4. Display the installed packages on your system again to see if the newly installed package appears.

5. Now remove the package from your system. For Debian-based systems, use the command **sudo apt remove zsh**. For Red Hat–based systems, use the command **sudo dnf remove zsh**.

6. Display the installed packages yet again to see if the package was properly removed.

Summary

The ability to easily install and remove applications is a must for every Linux system. In the open source world, developers release their applications as source code bundles using the tar and gzip utilities to create a tarball file. After you download a tarball file, you must decompress and extract the files it contains to be able to compile the application. The gcc program is the most common program for compiling many open source applications. You use the configure and make utilities to create and run installation scripts to make it easier to install applications from source code.

Most Linux distributions help simplify application installation by precompiling the source code and bundling the necessary application files into a package. Package management software makes it easier to track what applications are installed on your Linux system and where their files are located. Debian-based Linux distributions use the DEB package management format, with the dpkg tool, while Red Hat–based Linux distributions use the RPM package management format, with the rpm tool.

While package management systems make it easier to install and remove packages, it's still somewhat of a hassle finding packages. Most Linux distributions now maintain their own repository of packages and provide additional tools, making it easier to retrieve and install packages from the repository. For Debian-based systems, the `apt` suite of tools, including `apt-cache` and `apt-get`, and `apt` are used to retrieve packages from the repository and maintain the package management database. For Red Hat–based systems, either `yum` or `dnf` is the package tool to use.

Application containers are now becoming somewhat popular in the Linux world. An application container bundles all software required to run an application, including dependency applications and all libraries, into a single installation package. The two most popular application container formats are snap and flatpak.

Exam Essentials

Describe how developers bundle their open source applications for distribution.   Linux developers bundle source code files, headers, libraries, and documentation files into a single file for distribution. They use the `tar` utility to archive multiple files and folders into a single archive file and then often compress the archive file using the `gzip` utility. You can use the `wget` or `cURL` program to download the source code distribution files and then use the `gzip` and `tar` utilities to decompress and extract the source code files.

Explain how to generate an executable program from a source code tarball.   After you decompress and extract the source code files from a distribution tarball file, you must compile the source code to create an executable file for the application. First, you must use the `configure` utility. This examines your Linux system to ensure that it has the correct dependencies required for the application and configures the installation script to find the dependencies. Next, you run the `make` utility. The `make` utility runs a script that uses the `gcc` compiler to compile the necessary library and source code files to generate the executable file for your system. Once that script completes, use the `make` script with the `install` option to install the executable file on your Linux system.

Describe how Linux packages applications for distribution.   Linux uses a package management system to track what applications are installed on your system. The distribution bundles precompiled application files into a package, which you can easily download and install. The package management database keeps track of which packages are installed and the location of all the files contained within the package. You can also query the package management database to determine what packages are installed and remove packages from the system using the package management tools. Debian-based Linux systems use the `dpkg` tool to interact with the package management database, whereas Red Hat–based Linux systems use the `rpm` tool.

Describe how Linux distributions use repositories.   While using packages makes installing, tracking, and removing software applications easier, you still must be able to find the latest packages for your applications. Most Linux distributions help with that by creating a centralized repository of current application packages, along with tools to work with the repository. For Debian-based systems, the `apt` suite of tools allows you to query the repository for package information and download any new or updated packages. Red Hat–based systems use the `yum` or `dnf` tool to interact with their repositories. All three tools allow you to query the remote repository for packages, query the local package management database, and install or remove packages as you need.

Explain how application containers differ from package management systems. Application containers such as snap and flatpak bundle all of the files required to run an application, including any dependency applications, into a single package. While this can create duplicate copies of dependent applications, it ensures that each application has exactly the correct version of libraries and dependent applications installed to work, making it a breeze to move applications from one system to another.

Review Questions

1. Which two programs should you use to download tarballs from an application's website? (Choose two.)

   A. wget

   B. cURL

   C. dpkg

   D. rpm

   E. yum

2. Fred received an application in source code format. What script should he run to create the executable application program?

   A. dpkg

   B. rpm

   C. yum

   D. make

   E. wget

3. Sherri is trying to compile an application from source code. Before she can create the application executable file, what script should she run to create the make script?

   A. make

   B. make install

   C. configure

   D. gcc

   E. dpkg

4. What is the most common compiler used for open source Linux applications?

   A. gcc

   B. make

   C. configure

   D. dpkg

   E. rpm

5. Harry has finished writing his application source code but needs to package it for distribution. What tool should he use so that it can be extracted in any Linux distribution?

   A. dpkg

   B. rpm

   C. yum

   D. apt-get

   E. tar

6. What `tar` command-line options are commonly used together to extract and decompress files from a tarball file?

   A. -Uvh

   B. -zxvf

   C. -xvf

   D. -zcvf

   E. -cvf

7. What filename extension does the Rocky Linux distribution use for packages?

   A. .deb

   B. .rpm

   C. .tgz

   D. .tar

   E. .gz

8. Sally needs to install a new package on her Ubuntu Linux system. The package was distributed as a DEB file. What tool should she use?

   A. rpm

   B. yum

   C. dnf

   D. dpkg

   E. tar

9. What tools do you use to install packages from a Red Hat–based repository? (Choose two.)

   A. dpkg

   B. tar

   C. yum

   D. apt-get

   E. dnf

10. What application container format do Red Hat–based Linux distributions utilize for installing applications?

    A. flatpak

    B. rpm

    C. dpkg

    D. snap

    E. gcc

Chapter

14

Tending
Kernel Modules

✓ **Objective 1.7: Given a scenario, manage software configurations.**

A *module* (also called a kernel module) is a self-contained driver library file. The advantage of using modules, instead of compiling all their features into the kernel, is that they keep the Linux kernel lighter and more agile. We can add certain kernel functionality as needed or on demand because modules can be loaded and unloaded into the kernel dynamically. They extend the functionality of the kernel without the need to reboot the system.

We'll take a look at the various kernel module types, where their files are stored, and module configuration file locations. We'll also explore in this chapter how to dynamically link and unlink the modules, view module information, and remove modules.

Exploring Kernel Modules

Kernel modules come in different flavors. They are as follows:

- Device driver: Facilitates communication with a hardware device.

- Filesystem driver: Required for filesystem I/O.

- Network driver: Used to implement network protocols.

- System calls: Provides additional functions for adding/modifying system services.

- Executable loader: Allows additional executable formats to load.

There are a few different files and directories you should be familiar with when working with modules. Modules required to support a kernel are stored in the /lib/modules/ directory tree. Each Linux kernel version available on your system has its own subdirectory within the /lib/modules/ directory. An example of this directory and its kernel version subdirectories on an Ubuntu 20.04 distribution is shown in Listing 14.1.

Listing 14.1: Viewing a /lib/modules directory

```
$ ls -F /lib/modules
5.11.0-40-generic/   5.4.0-31-generic/   5.4.0-47-generic/
5.4.0-26-generic/    5.4.0-42-generic/   5.4.0-48-generic/

$
```

Be aware that distributions may implement this directory a little differently. For instance, Red Hat–based distributions have the /lib/modules/ directory hard-linked to the /usr/lib/modules/ directory. Thus, they are the same directory, but with two different names. An example on a Rocky Linux 8.5 system is shown snipped in Listing 14.2.

Listing 14.2: Viewing a /lib/modules and a /usr/lib/modules directory

```
$ ls -F /lib/modules
4.18.0-305.19.1.el8_4.x86_64/    4.18.0-348.2.1.el8_5.x86_64/
4.18.0-305.3.1.el8_4.x86_64/     4.18.0-348.el8.x86_64/
$ ls -F /usr/lib/modules
4.18.0-305.19.1.el8_4.x86_64/    4.18.0-348.2.1.el8_5.x86_64/
4.18.0-305.3.1.el8_4.x86_64/     4.18.0-348.el8.x86_64/
$ ls -id /lib/modules
16808755 /lib/modules
$ ls -id /usr/lib/modules
16808755 /usr/lib/modules
$
```

Notice in Listing 14.2 that the two directories share the same inode number. Hard links were originally covered in Chapter 3, "Managing Files, Directories, and Text."

If needed, you can customize a module to define any unique parameters required, such as hardware settings essential for the device to operate. On some older Linux distributions there is a single configuration file, /etc/modules.conf, and on more modern distributions there are configuration directories:

- /etc/modprobe.d/ or /etc/modules-load.d/ contains configuration files generated at system installation or created by an administrator.

- /lib/modprobe.d/ stores configuration files generated by third-party software packages.

- /usr/lib/modprobe.d/, if it exists, is typically hard-linked to the /lib/modprobe.d/directory.

- /run/modprobe.d/ stores configuration files generated at runtime.

Within each configuration directory are multiple configuration files that have a .conf filename extension. An example on a Rocky Linux 8.5 distribution is shown in Listing 14.3.

Listing 14.3: Viewing /etc/modprobe directories

```
$ ls /etc/modprobe.d
firewalld-sysctls.conf   lockd.conf   nvdimm-security.conf   tuned.conf
kvm.conf                 mlx4.conf    truescale.conf         vhost.conf
```

```
$ ls /lib/modprobe.d
dist-alsa.conf  dist-blacklist.conf  libmlx4.conf  systemd.conf
$
```

In the Linux virtual directory system are many potential locations for kernel modules as well as module configuration files. Therefore, it is wise to take a look around your own Linux server and note their locations.

 For systemd systems, the systemd-modules-load.service handles loading kernel modules at boot time. You can find the various directories it may load modules from by using grep on the service unit file and searching for the ConditionDirectoryNotEmpty directive.

Many device driver kernel modules are loaded either at system boot time or dynamically when hardware devices are attached to the system. If problems occur, you need to know what utilities to use to help you diagnose the issue. There are three handy programs that can help with modules:

- dmesg displays the current kernel ring buffer.
- lsmod shows brief module information.
- modinfo provides detailed module data.

When it comes to modules, a module failure sometimes triggers a kernel message. The dmesg command is handy in that you can view kernel messages related to current events. At boot time, your distribution may take a snapshot of the kernel ring buffer and store the data in a file (typically the /var/log/dmesg file). Both of these ring buffer information sources can help you track down kernel module problems.

 A ring buffer is a fixed-size data structure in memory. It is not shaped in a ring but instead more like a tube. In the kernel ring buffer, as new messages enter the tube, the older messages are moved toward the structure's end and the oldest messages "drop out" of the tube's end (are deleted).

The dmesg utility will simply dump the current kernel ring buffer to STDOUT. It is helpful to employ the grep command to dig through the messages. A snipped example of this is shown in Listing 14.4.

Listing 14.4: Using dmesg with grep to display module messages

```
$ dmesg | grep -i driver
[…]
[    1.674321] e1000: Intel(R) PRO/1000 Network Driver - version 7.3.21-k8-
NAPI
[    3.614747] cdrom: Uniform CD-ROM driver Revision: 3.20
[…]
```

```
[    48.828793] tun: Universal TUN/TAP device driver, 1.6
[ 8760.969714] usbcore: registered new interface driver usb-storage
[…]
$
```

You can employ different search terms to filter the dmesg utility's output. For example, if you want to find information only on a USB device issue, you could pipe the dmesg output to the grep -i usb command.

The lsmod utility displays the status of modules currently within the Linux kernel. Listing 14.5 shows a snipped example of this on an openSUSE distribution.

Listing 14.5: Employing lsmod to display module status

```
$ lsmod
Module               Size  Used by
af_packet           49152  4
[…]
bridge             172032  1 ebtable_broute
stp                 16384  1 bridge
btrfs             1327104  1
[…]
scsi_dh_alua        20480  0
$
```

In the lsmod output, each module is listed on a separate line. The first column is the module's name.

Notice in Listing 14.5 the Used by column. The digit in this column indicates the number of processes or other modules currently using the module. If it is another kernel module using it, the other's module's name is displayed.

You can get the same information that the lsmod utility displays by looking at the /proc/modules file's contents. However, it is not as nicely formatted.

You can find out more detailed information concerning a particular kernel module via the modinfo utility. It may require super user privileges, as shown snipped in Listing 14.6.

Listing 14.6: Using modinfo to display detailed module information

```
$ sudo modinfo bridge
filename:       /lib/modules/[…]/kernel/net/bridge/bridge.ko
alias:          rtnl-link-bridge
version:        2.3
license:        GPL
suserelease:    openSUSE Leap 15.0
```

```
srcversion:      D39BA7E56E769F636E31A8C
depends:         stp,llc
retpoline:       Y
intree:          Y
vermagic:        [...]SMP mod_unload modversions retpoline
$
```

Notice the kernel module's filename in Listing 14.6. Kernel module files typically have a .ko file extension. Also notice that the module's version number is displayed. This is helpful if you need to track down known bugs related to a particular module.

It is possible to configure the kernel to not allow kernel modules to be installed at runtime. While this is not common, you may run into this situation, so it's good to know it exists. You can check the current kernel option settings using the sysctl command, with the –a option:

```
$ sysctl -a
[...]
kernel.module_disable = 0
[...]
$
```

If the kernel.module_disable option is set to a value of 1, you won't be able to install modules. Most Linux distributions store kernel settings that are applied at boot time in the /etc/sysctl.conf file, or as separate configuration files in the /etc/sysctl.d directory. Check those files to see if the option is set, and edit the file if you need to add modules.

Installing Kernel Modules

Linux typically automatically loads modules as they are needed on the system. Often, though, you may want to test a new module or try new module configurations. To do so, you may need to manually install modules into the kernel. This is also called *inserting* or *loading* a module. In this section, we'll look at a few utilities that can help you load modules into the kernel. They are as follows:

- insmod
- modprobe
- depmod

The `insmod` utility allows you to insert a single module into the Linux kernel. Unfortunately, because it is so basic, you have to provide an absolute directory reference to the module file. Also, the command does not load any needed module dependencies. A snipped example on an openSUSE distribution is shown in Listing 14.7.

Listing 14.7: Using `insmod` to insert a single module into the kernel

```
$ lsmod | grep -i joydev
$
$ sudo insmod  /lib/modules/[…]/kernel/drivers/input/joydev.ko
$
$ lsmod | grep -i joydev
joydev                  24576  0
$
```

In Listing 14.7, the system is checked for a loaded module that has a module name of `joydev` using the `lsmod` command. It is not found. Thus, the `insmod` command inserts it into the kernel using its full filename and directory location. The `lsmod` command is employed again to show that the module is now indeed loaded into the kernel.

The `modprobe` command is easier to use than the `insmod` utility because you can denote modules by their module name. It also loads any additional modules that the inserted module needs to operate (dependencies). A snipped example is shown in Listing 14.8, which employs the `-v` switch on the `modprobe` command to display more information while it inserts a module and all of its currently unloaded dependencies.

Listing 14.8: Using `modprobe` to insert a module and its dependencies

```
$ sudo modprobe -v dm_mirror
insmod /lib/modules/[…]/kernel/drivers/md/dm-log.ko
insmod /lib/modules/[…]/kernel/drivers/md/dm-region-hash.ko
insmod /lib/modules/[…]/kernel/drivers/md/dm-mirror.ko
$
$ lsmod | grep -i  dm_mirror
dm_mirror               28672  0
dm_region_hash          16384  1 dm_mirror
dm_log                  16384  2 dm_mirror,dm_region_hash
dm_mod                 139264  3 dm_mirror,dm_log,dm_multipath
$
$ sudo modinfo dm_mirror
filename:       /lib/modules/[…]/kernel/drivers/md/dm-mirror.ko
license:        GPL
```

```
author:           Joe Thornber
description:      device-mapper mirror target
suserelease:      openSUSE Leap 15.0
srcversion:       A784B0C071D49F47F94E83B
depends:          dm-region-hash,dm-mod,dm-log
retpoline:        Y
intree:           Y
vermagic:         […]SMP mod_unload modversions retpoline
parm:             raid1_resync_throttle:A percentage […]
$
```

The dm_mirror module allows volume managers to mirror logical volumes. In Listing 14.8, when the modprobe command is used to load this module, it loads two other modules as well, which the dm_mirror module needs to work properly. Notice that the modprobe utility is calling the insmod utility to perform the insertion work. Also notice that the dm_mirror module has a slightly different filename, dm-mirror.ko, shown in the modinfo utility's output.

The modprobe program uses the modules.dep file to determine any module dependencies. This file is typically located in the /lib/modules/ subdirectory, as shown snipped in Listing 14.9.

Listing 14.9: Viewing the modules.dep dependencies file

```
$ ls /lib/modules/[…]/modules.dep
/lib/modules/[…]/modules.dep
$
$ grep -i mirror /lib/modules/[…]/modules.dep
kernel/drivers/md/dm-mirror.ko:
kernel/drivers/md/dm-region-hash.ko
kernel/drivers/md/dm-log.ko
kernel/drivers/md/dm-mod.ko
$
```

In Listing 14.9, the modules.dep file is searched for the word mirror using the grep utility. To see a particular module's dependencies, you locate the module's filename within the file. After the colon (:), the module's dependencies are listed by their full module filename. So for the dm_mirror modules (dm-mirror.ko), the module dependencies are the dm-region-hash, dm-log, and dm-mod modules. This corresponds with what was shown in the modinfo utility's output in Listing 14.8.

You can employ the depmod command to scan through the system looking for any hardware that was not automatically detected. This is useful for troubleshooting problems with new devices. A snipped example is shown in Listing 14.10.

Listing 14.10: Using the depmod utility to update the `modules.dep` file

```
$ sudo depmod -v
[…]
/lib/modules/[…]/kernel/sound/soc/intel/
atom/snd-soc-sst-atom-hifi2-platform.ko needs
"snd_pcm_lib_preallocate_pages_for_all":
/lib/modules/[…]/kernel/sound/core/snd-pcm.ko
[…]
$
```

In Listing 14.10, the depmod utility scans the system, determines any needed modules, reviews the modules' dependencies, and updates the appropriate `modules.dep` file. Notice that it also displays its activity to STDOUT.

Removing Kernel Modules

It's a good idea to remove any kernel modules you are no longer using on your Linux system. If you just need to remove (unload) a module with no dependencies, you can employ the rmmod command. An example is shown in Listing 14.11.

Listing 14.11: Using the rmmod utility to remove a module

```
$ lsmod | grep joydev
joydev                 24576  0
$
$ sudo rmmod -v joydev
$
$ lsmod | grep joydev
$
```

Notice in Listing 14.11 that the rmmod utility understands module names, so you don't have to provide an absolute directory reference to the module file. Once the module is unloaded, the lsmod utility no longer displays the module's name in its output.

The modprobe utility is useful for removing modules that have one or more dependencies. You just need to add the -r switch, and if you desire detailed information, include the -v switch, as shown snipped in Listing 14.12.

Listing 14.12: Using the modprobe utility to remove a module and its dependencies

```
$ sudo modprobe -rv dm_mirror
rmmod dm_mirror
rmmod dm_region_hash
rmmod dm_log
$
```

In Listing 14.12, the module dm_mirror is unloaded along with its two dependencies. Note that if the module was not loaded, you would not see any messages and just get a command-line prompt back.

Summary

When kernel modules fail or when you need to test a new module, it is vital to understand where module files as well as their configuration files are located. Equally important is the ability to diagnose problems using the various command-line utilities available for this purpose. Because modules can be dynamically linked and unlinked with the kernel, you should understand how to perform these tasks using the correct tools. These additional tools in your Linux tool belt will allow you to quickly resolve issues concerning kernel modules.

Exam Essentials

Describe the locations of kernel module files.   Kernel module files have a .ko file extension and are typically located in a subdirectory of the /lib/modules/ directory. There is a subdirectory for each particular Linux kernel version. Some distributions have additional directories, such as /usr/lib/modules/, which are hard-linked to the /lib/modules/ directory.

Distinguish the locations of module configuration files.   Older Linux distributions use a single file, /etc/modules.conf, as their kernel modules configuration file. More modern distributions use configuration directories, which can be the /etc/modprobe.d/, /etc/modules-load.d/, /lib/modprobe.d/, /usr/lib/modprobe.d/, and/or /run/modprobe.d/ directory. Within configuration directories, module configuration files have a .conf file extension.

Summarize the utilities used to troubleshoot modules.   Because when kernel modules fail they often issue a kernel message, you can employ the dmesg utility to view recent kernel messages or peruse the /var/log/dmesg file, if available, for boot time kernel problems. The lsmod utility displays all the currently loaded modules, the number of processes and other modules using them, and the other modules' names. The modinfo program is very helpful because it displays detailed information concerning a module, including its dependencies.

Compare the utilities used to install kernel modules.   The low-level insmod utility requires a full module filename in order to insert a module into the kernel, which can be cumbersome. In addition, it does not load any module dependencies. On the other hand, the modprobe utility only requires the module's name. Also, it searches the modules.dep file to determine and load any module dependencies.

Explain the utilities used to remove kernel modules.   The `rmmod` utility is a low-level utility. Though it does not require a full module filename in order to unlink a module from the kernel, it does not unload any module dependencies. So you could end up with unneeded modules, still linked to the kernel. The `modprobe` utility, using the `-r` option, will unload the module and unlink any module dependencies.

Review Questions

1.   Which of the following is true concerning a kernel module? (Choose all that apply.)
     A.   It is a self-contained driver library file.
     B.   It is compiled into the Linux kernel.
     C.   It allows the addition of functionality when required.
     D.   It can be loaded when needed.
     E.   It keeps the Linux kernel lighter and more agile.

2.   Where are module files stored? (Choose all that apply.)
     A.   A /lib/modules/kernel/ subdirectory
     B.   A /lib/modules/*KernelVersion*/ subdirectory
     C.   A /usr/lib/modules/kernel/ subdirectory
     D.   A /usr/lib/modules/*KernelVersion*/ subdirectory
     E.   A /lib/kernel/modules subdirectory

3.   Where can a module's configuration information be stored? (Choose all that apply.)
     A.   The /etc/modules.conf file
     B.   The /etc/modprobe.d/*.conf files
     C.   The /etc/modules.d/*.conf files
     D.   The /lib/modprobe.d/*.conf files
     E.   The /usr/lib/modprobe.d/*.conf files

4.   You need to determine the dependencies of the unloaded xyz module. Which is the best utility to employ to accomplish this task?
     A.   dmesg
     B.   insmod
     C.   lsmod
     D.   modprobe
     E.   modinfo

5.   You need to install the xyz module, including all its needed dependencies. Which of the following utilities should you use?
     A.   insmod
     B.   modinfo
     C.   modprobe
     D.   lsmod
     E.   depmod

6. When you install a USB device on a Linux system, it appears that the device is not being detected. Which of the following is the best command to troubleshoot this particular situation?

    A. lsmod

    B. modinfo

    C. dmesg

    D. depmod

    E. insmod

7. The modprobe utility uses the _____ file to determine any module dependencies.

    A. modules.dep

    B. /lib/modules

    C. /usr/lib/modules

    D. /etc/modprobe.d

    E. /lib/modprobe.d

8. You need to insert the abc module into the Linux kernel. This module does not have any dependencies. What is the best utility to use?

    A. lsmod

    B. modinfo

    C. dmesg

    D. depmod

    E. insmod

9. You need to unload the abc module from the Linux kernel. This module does not have any dependencies. What is the best utility to use?

    A. insmod

    B. unload

    C. rmmod

    D. modprobe

    E. rm -f

10. You need to remove the xyz module and all of its dependencies. Which is the best command to employ?

    A. dmesg

    B. modprobe -r

    C. lsmod

    D. paste

    E. groupdel

Securing
Your System

Chapter

15

Applying Ownership and Permissions

✓ **Objective 2.5: Given a scenario, apply the appropriate access controls.**

Preventing unauthorized access to files and directories is a major part of any Linux administrator's job. Linux provides a few different methods for protecting files, which can make security a little bit complicated. This chapter dives into Linux file and directory security and demonstrates how to implement it on your Linux system. First, you'll see how Linux assigns ownership to files and directories. Then, the chapter discusses the basic file and directory security features that have been available since the dawn of Linux. Following that is an examination of a couple of newer methods for adding more protection to files and applications on your system. A brief overview describes how Linux handles administrator privileges when required to do work on the system.

Looking at File and Directory Permissions

The core security feature of Linux is file and directory permissions. Linux accomplishes that by assigning each file and directory an owner and allowing that owner to set the basic security settings to control access to the file or directory. The following sections walk through how Linux handles ownership of files and directories as well as the basic permission settings that you can assign to any file or directory on your Linux system.

Understanding Ownership

Linux uses a three-tiered approach to protecting files and directories:

Owner: In the Linux system, each file and directory is assigned to a single owner. The Linux system administrator can assign the owner specific privileges to the file or directory.

Group: The Linux system also assigns each file and directory to a single group of users. The administrator can then assign that group privileges that are specific to the file or directory and that differ from the owner privileges.

Others: This category of permissions is assigned to any user account that is not the owner or in the assigned user group.

You can view the assigned owner and group for a file or directory by adding the -l option to the ls command, as shown in Listing 15.1.

Listing 15.1: Viewing file owner and group settings

```
$ ls -l
total 12
-rw-rw-r--  1 Rich sales 1521 Jan 19 15:38 customers.txt
-rw-r--r--  1 Christine sales  479 Jan 19 15:37 research.txt
-rw-r--r--  1 Christine sales  696 Jan 19 15:37 salesdata.txt
$
```

In Listing 15.1, the first column, -rw-rw-r--, defines the access permissions assigned to the owner, group, and others. That will be discussed later in the chapter in the section "Controlling Access Permissions." The third column in Listing 15.1, the Rich or Christine value, shows the user account assigned as the owner of the file. The fourth column, sales, shows the group assigned to the file.

WARNING   Many Linux distributions (such as both Ubuntu and Rocky Linux) assign each user account to a separate group with the same name as the user account. This helps prevent accidental sharing of files. However, it can also make things a little confusing when you're working with owner and group permissions and you see the same name appear in both columns. Be careful when working in this type of environment.

When a user creates a file or directory, by default the Linux system automatically assigns that user as the owner and uses the primary group the user belongs to as the group for the file or directory. You can change the default owner and group assigned to files and directories by using Linux commands. The following sections show how to do that.

Changing File or Directory Ownership

The root user account can change the owner assigned to a file or directory by using the chown command. The chown command format looks like this:

```
chown [options] newowner filenames
```

The *newowner* parameter is the username of the new owner to assign to the file or directory, and *filenames* is the name of the file or directory to change. You can specify more than one file or directory by placing a space between each file or directory name:

```
$ sudo chown Christine customers.txt
$ ls -l
total 12
-rw-rw-r-- 1 Christine sales 1521 Jan 19 15:38 customers.txt
-rw-r--r-- 1 Christine sales  479 Jan 19 15:37 research.txt
-rw-r--r-- 1 Christine sales  696 Jan 19 15:37 salesdata.txt
$
```

There are a few command-line options available for the chown command, but they are mostly obscure and not used much. One that may be helpful for you is the -R option, which recursively changes the owner of all files under the specified directory.

Changing the File or Directory Group

The file or directory owner, or the root user account, can change the group assigned to the file or directory by using the chgrp command. The chgrp command uses this format:

chgrp [*options*] *newgroup filenames*

The *newgroup* parameter is the name of the new user group assigned to the file or directory, and the *filenames* parameter is the name of the file or directory to change. If you're the owner of the file, you can only change the group to a group that you belong to. The root user account can change the group to any group on the system:

```
$ sudo chgrp marketing customers.txt
$ ls -l
total 12
-rw-rw-r-- 1 Christine marketing 1521 Jan 19 15:38 customers.txt
-rw-r--r-- 1 Christine sales       479 Jan 19 15:37 research.txt
-rw-r--r-- 1 Christine sales       696 Jan 19 15:37 salesdata.txt
$
```

The chown command allows you to change both the owner and the group assigned to a file or directory at the same time using this format:

chown *newowner:newgroup filenames*

This is often preferred over using the separate chgrp command.

Controlling Access Permissions

After you've established the file or directory owner and group, you can assign specific permissions to each. Linux uses three types of permission controls:

Read: The ability to access the data stored in the file or directory

Write: The ability to modify the data stored in the file or directory

Execute: The ability to run the file on the system, or the ability to list the files contained in the directory

You can assign each tier of protection (owner, group, and others) different read, write, and execute permissions. This creates a set of nine different permissions that are assigned to each file and directory on the Linux system. The nine permissions appear in the `ls` output as the first column of information when you use the `-l` option, as shown in Listing 15.1. Figure 15.1 shows the order in which the permissions are displayed in the `ls` output.

FIGURE 15.1   File and directory permissions as displayed in the `ls` output

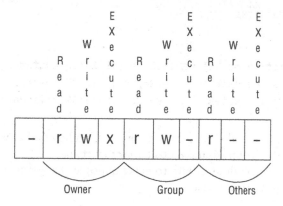

In Figure 15.1, the first character denotes the object type. A dash indicates a file, and a d indicates a directory.

The next three characters denote the owner permissions in the order of read, write, and execute. A dash indicates the permission is not set, whereas the r, w, or x indicates the read, write, or execute permission is set. In the example in Listing 15.1, all three files use rw- for the owner permissions, which means the owner has permissions to read and write to the file but cannot execute, or run, the file. This is common with data files.

The second set of three characters denotes the group permissions for the file or directory. Again, this uses the read, write, and execute order, with a dash indicating the permission is not set. After making the change to the `customers.txt` file for the marketing group, the `sales` group can only read the `research.txt` and `salesdata.txt` files, but the `marketing` group can both read and write the `customers.txt` file.

Finally, the third set of three characters denotes the permissions assigned to user accounts that are not the owner or a member of the group assigned to the file or directory. The same order of read, write, and execute is used. In the Listing 15.1 examples, other user accounts on the system can read the files but not write or execute them.

Either the root user account or the owner of the file or directory can change the assigned permissions by using the `chmod` command.

The format of the `chmod` command can be somewhat confusing. It uses two different modes for denoting the read, write, and execute permission settings for the owner, group, and others. Both modes allow you to define the same sets of permissions, so there's no reason to use one mode over the other.

In *symbolic mode*, you denote permissions by using a letter code for the owner (u), group (g), others (o), or all (a) and another letter code for the read (r), write (w), or execute (x)

permission. The two codes are separated with a plus sign (+) if you want to add the permission, a minus sign (−) to remove the permission, or an equal sign (=) to set the permission as the only permission. Listing 15.2 shows an example of this.

Listing 15.2: Changing file permissions

```
$ chmod g-w customers.txt
$ ls -al
total 12
-rw-r--r--  1 Christine marketing 1521 Jan 19 15:38 customers.txt
-rw-r--r--  1 Christine sales       479 Jan 19 15:37 research.txt
-rw-r--r--  1 Christine sales       696 Jan 19 15:37 salesdata.txt
$
```

In Listing 15.2, the g−w code in the chmod command indicates that we are removing the write permission for the group from the customers.txt file.

You can combine letter codes for both to make multiple changes in a single chmod command, as shown in Listing 15.3.

Listing 15.3: Combining permission changes

```
$ chmod ug=rwx salesdata.txt
$ ls -l
total 12
-rw-rw-r-- 1 Christine marketing 1521 Jan 19 15:38 customers.txt
-rw-r--r-- 1 Christine sales       479 Jan 19 15:37 research.txt
-rwxrwxr-- 1 Christine sales       696 Jan 19 15:37 salesdata.txt
$
```

The ug code assigns the change to both the owner and the group, whereas the rwx code assigns the read, write, and execute permissions. We use the equal sign to set those permissions.

The second mode available in chmod is called *octal mode*. With octal mode, the nine permission bits are represented as three octal numbers, one each for the owner, group, and other permissions. Table 15.1 shows how the octal number matches the three symbolic mode permissions.

TABLE 15.1   Octal mode permissions

Octal value	Permission	Meaning
0	---	No permissions
1	--x	Execute only
2	-w-	Write only

Octal value	Permission	Meaning
3	-wx	Write and execute
4	r--	Read only
5	r-x	Read and execute
6	rw-	Read and write
7	rwx	Read, write, and execute

You must specify the three octal values in the owner, group, and others in the correct order, as shown in Listing 15.4.

Listing 15.4: Using octal mode to assign permissions

```
$ chmod 664 research.txt
$ ls -l
total 12
-rw-r--r-- 1 Christine marketing 1521 Jan 19 15:38 customers.txt
-rw-rw-r-- 1 Christine sales       479 Jan 19 15:37 research.txt
-rwxrwxr-- 1 Christine sales       696 Jan 19 15:37 salesdata.txt
$
```

The 664 octal mode set the owner and group permissions to read and write (6) but the others permission to read only (4). You can see the results from the ls output. This is a handy way to set all the permissions for a file or directory in a single command.

Exploring Special Permissions

There are three special permission bits that Linux uses for controlling the advanced behavior of files and directories.

The *Set User ID (SUID)* bit is used with executable files. It tells the Linux kernel to run the program with the permissions of the file owner and not the user account actually running the file. This feature is most commonly used in server applications that must run as the root user account to have access to all files on the system, even if the user launching the process is a standard user.

The SUID bit is indicated by an s in place of the execute permission letter for the file owner: rwsr-xr-x. The execute permission is assumed for the system to run the file. If the SUID bit is set on a file that doesn't have execute permission for the owner, it's indicated by an uppercase S.

To set the SUID bit for a file, in symbolic mode add s to the owner permissions, or in octal mode include a 4 at the start of the octal mode setting:

```
# chmod u+s myapp
# chmod 4750 myapp
```

The *Set Group ID (SGID*, also called *GUID)* bit works differently in files and directories. For files, it tells Linux to run the program file with the file's group permissions. It's indicated by an s in the group execute position: rwxrwsr--.

For directories, the SGID bit helps us create an environment where multiple users can share files. When a directory has the SGID bit set, any files users create in the directory are assigned the group of the directory and not that of the user. That way, all users in that group can have the same permissions as all the files in the shared directory.

To set the SGID bit, in symbolic mode add s to the group permissions, or in octal mode include a 2 at the start of the octal mode setting:

```
# chmod g+s /sales
# chmod 2660 /sales
```

Finally, the *sticky bit* is used to protect a file from being deleted by those who don't own it, even if they belong to the group that has write permissions to the file. The sticky bit is denoted by a t in the execute bit position for others: rwxrw-r-t.

The sticky bit is often used on directories shared by groups. The group members have read and write access to the data files contained in the directory, but only the file owners can remove files from the shared directory.

To set the sticky bit, in symbolic mode add t to the owner permissions, or in octal mode include a 1 at the start of the octal mode setting:

```
# chmod o+t /sales
# chmod 1777 /sales
```

Managing Default Permissions

When a user creates a new file or directory, the Linux system assigns it a default owner, group, and permissions. The default owner, as expected, is the user who created the file. The default group is the owner's primary group.

The *user mask* feature defines the default permissions Linux assigns to the file or directory. The user mask is an octal value that represents the bits to be removed from the octal mode 666 permissions for files or the octal mode 777 permissions for directories.

The user mask value is set with the umask command. You can view your current umask setting by simply entering the command by itself on the command line:

```
$ umask
0022
$
```

The output of the umask command shows four octal values. The first octal value represents the mask for the SUID (4), GUID (2), and sticky (1) bits assigned to files and directories you create. The next three octal values mask the owner, group, and others permission settings.

The mask is a bitwise mask applied to the permission bits on the file or directory. Any bit that's set in the mask is removed from the permissions for the file or directory. If a bit isn't set, the mask doesn't change the setting. Table 15.2 demonstrates how the umask values work in practice when creating files and directories on your Linux system.

TABLE 15.2   Results from common umask values for files and directories

umask	Created files	Created directories
000	666 (rw-rw-rw-)	777 (rwxrwxrwx)
002	664 (rw-rw-r--)	775 (rwxrwxr-x)
022	644 (rw-r--r--)	755 (rwxr-xr-x)
027	640 (rw-r-----)	750 (rwxr-x---)
077	600 (rw-------)	700 (rwx------)
277	400 (r--------)	500 (r-x------)

You can test this by creating a new file and directory on your Linux system:

```
$ mkdir test1
$ touch test2
$ ls -l
total 4
drwxr-xr-x 2 rich rich 4096 Jan 19 17:08 test1
-rw-r--r-- 1 rich rich    0 Jan 19 17:08 test2
$
```

The umask value of 0022 created the default file permissions of rw-r--r--, or octal 644, on the test2 file, and rwx-r-xr-x, or octal 755, on the test1 directory, as expected (note that the directory entry starts with a d in the permissions list).

You can change the default umask setting for your user account by using the umask command from the command line:

```
$ umask 027
$ touch test3
$ ls -l test3
-rw-r----- rich rich 0 Jan 19 17:12 test3
$
```

The default permissions for the new file have changed to match the umask setting.

> The umask value is normally set in a script that the Linux system runs at login time, such as in the /etc/profile file. If you override the setting from the command line, that will only apply for the duration of your session. You can override the system default umask setting by adding it to the .bash_profile file in your $HOME directory.

Access Control Lists

The basic Linux method of permissions has one drawback in that it's somewhat limited. You can only assign permissions for a file or directory to a single group or user account. In a complex business environment with different groups of people needing different permissions to files and directories, that approach doesn't work.

Linux developers have devised a more advanced method of file and directory security called an *access control list (ACL)*. The ACL allows you to specify a list of multiple users or groups and the permissions that are assigned to them. Just like the basic security method, ACL permissions use the same read, write, and execute permission bits, but now they can be assigned to multiple users and groups.

To use the ACL feature in Linux, you use the setfacl and getfacl commands. The getfacl command allows you to view the ACLs assigned to a file or directory, as shown in Listing 15.5.

Listing 15.5: Viewing ACLs for a file

```
$ touch test
$ ls -l
total 0
-rw-r----- 1 rich rich 0 Jan 19 17:33 test
$ getfacl test
# file: test
# owner: rich
# group: rich
user::rw-
group::r--
other::---
$
```

If you've only assigned basic security permissions to the file, those still appear in the getfacl output, as shown in Listing 15.5.

To assign permissions for additional users or groups, you use the setfacl command:

```
setfacl [options] rule filenames
```

The `setfacl` command allows you to modify the permissions assigned to a file or directory by using the -m option or to remove specific permissions using the -x option. You define the *rule* with three formats:

```
u[ser]:uid:perms
g[roup]:gid:perms
o[ther]::perms
```

To assign permissions for additional user accounts, use the user format; for additional groups, use the group format; and for others, use the other format. For the `uid` or `gid` value, you can use either the numerical user identification number or group identification number or the names. Here's an example:

```
$ setfacl -m g:sales:rw test
$ ls -l
total 0
-rw-rw----+ 1 rich rich 0 Jan 19 17:33 test
$
```

This example adds read and write permissions for the `sales` group to the `test` file. Notice that there's no output from the `setfacl` command. When you list the file, only the standard owner, group, and others permissions are shown, but a plus sign (+) is added to the permissions list. This indicates that the file has additional ACLs applied to it. To view the additional ACLs, use the `getfacl` command again:

```
$ getfacl test
# file: test
# owner: rich
# group: rich
user::rw-
group::r--
group:sales:rw-
mask::rw-
other::---
$
```

The `getfacl` output now shows that there are permissions assigned to two groups. The default file group (`rich`) is assigned read permissions, but now the `sales` group has read and write permissions to the file. To remove the permissions, use the -x option:

```
$ setfacl -x g:sales test
$ getfacl test
# file: test
# owner: rich
# group: rich
```

```
user::rw-
group::r--
mask::r--
other::---
```

```
$
```

Linux also allows you to set a default ACL on a directory that is automatically inherited by any file created in the directory. This feature is called *inheritance*.

To create a default ACL on a directory, start the rule with a d: followed by the normal rule definition. That looks like this:

```
$ sudo setfacl -m d:g:sales:rw /shared/sales
```

This example assigns the read and write permissions to the sales group for the /shared/sales directory. Now all files created in that folder will automatically be assigned read and write permissions for the sales group.

Context-Based Permissions

Both the original permissions method and the advanced ACL method of assigning permissions to files and directories are called *discretionary access control (DAC)* methods. The permission is set at the discretion of the file or directory owner. There's nothing an administrator can do to prevent users from granting full permission to others on all the files in their directories.

To provide complete protection of your Linux system, it helps to utilize some type of *mandatory access control (MAC)* method. MAC methods allow the system administrator to define security based on the context of an object in the Linux system to override permissions set by file and directory owners. MAC methods provide rules for administrators to restrict access to files and directories not only to users but also to applications running on the system.

 You may also see the term *role-based access control (RBAC)* used in security literature. The RBAC method is a subcategory of MAC, basing security permissions on the roles users and processes play in the Linux system.

There are currently two popular MAC implementations in Linux:

- SELinux for Red Hat–based systems
- AppArmor for the Ubuntu system

The following sections provide more detail on using SELinux and AppArmor in your Linux environment.

Using SELinux

The *Security-Enhanced Linux (SELinux)* application is a project of the U.S. National Security Agency (NSA) and has been integrated into the Linux kernel since version 2.6.x. It is now a standard part of Red Hat–based Linux distributions, such as Fedora, Rocky, and CentOS, and an optional installation for Debian-based distributions.

SELinux implements MAC security by allowing you to set policy rules for controlling access between various types of objects on the Linux system, including users, files, directories, memory, network ports, and processes. Each time a user or process attempts to access an object on the Linux system, SELinux intercepts the attempt and evaluates it against the defined policy rules.

Enabling SELinux

The `/etc/selinux/config` file controls the basic operation of SELinux. There are two primary settings that you need to specify:

SELINUX: This setting determines the operation of SELinux. Set it to `enforcing` to enable the policy rules on the system and to block any unauthorized access. When you set it to `permissive`, SELinux monitors policy rules and logs any policy violations but doesn't enforce them. The `disabled` setting value completely disables SELinux from monitoring actions on the system.

SELINUXTYPE: This setting determines which policy rules are enforced. The `targeted` setting is the default and only enforces network daemon policy rules. The `minimum` setting only enforces policy rules on specified processes. The `mls` setting uses multilayer security, providing advanced policies following the Bell–LaPadula model of security control, which is mandated by most U.S. government and military environments that require high security. It uses security classifications such as top secret, unclassified, and public. The `strict` setting enforces policy rules for all daemons but is not recommended for use anymore.

To change the state of SELinux, you can also use the `setenforce` utility from the command line. However, you can only use the utility to change SELinux between enforcing and permissive modes. To disable SELinux, you must make the change in the SELinux configuration file. To see the current mode of SELinux, use the `getenforce` utility:

```
$ sudo getenforce
Enforcing
$
```

For a more detailed listing of the SELinux status, use the `sestatus` utility:

```
$ sudo sestatus
SELinux status:                 enabled
SELinuxfs mount:                /sys/fs/selinux
SELinux root directory:         /etc/selinux
```

```
Loaded policy name:              targeted
Current mode:                    enforcing
Mode from config file:           enforcing
Policy MLS status:               enabled
Policy deny_unknown status:      allowed
Memory protection checking       actual (secure)
Max kernel policy version:       33
$
```

After you've enabled SELinux, it starts enforcing access rules on the objects defined in a set of policies. The next sections explain how SELinux policies work.

Understanding Security Context

SELinux labels each object on the system with a *security context.* The security context defines what policies SELinux applies to the object. The security context format is as follows:

user:role:type:level

The *user* and *role* attributes are used only in the multilayer security mode and can get quite complex. Systems running in the default targeted security mode only use the *type* attribute to set the object security type and control access based on that. The *level* attribute sets the security sensitivity level and clearance level. It is optional under the targeted security mode and is mostly used in highly secure environments.

To view the security context assigned to objects, add the -Z option to common Linux commands such as id, ls, ps, and netstat. For example, to view your user security context, use the following command:

```
$ id -Z
unconfined_u:unconfined_r:unconfined_t:s0-s0:c0.c1023
$
```

The unconfined_u user security context means the user account is not assigned to a specific security policy; likewise, the unconfined_r for the role and the unconfined_t for the type. The level security context of s0-s0:c0.c1023 means the security and clearance levels for the object are also not set.

To view the security context for a file, use this:

```
$ ls -Z test1.txt
unconfined_u:object_r:user_home_t:s0 test1.txt
$
```

Again, the user attribute is unconfined_u, but now the type attribute is set to user_home_t. You can use this attribute in a security policy to set the access for files in each user account's $HOME directory.

To examine the security context assigned to a process, use the following command:

```
$ ps -axZ | grep sshd
```

```
system_u:system_r:sshd_t:s0-s0:c0.c1023 1029 ? Ss 0:00
 /usr/sbin/sshd [...]
$
```

The process required for the sshd application is set to the system_u user security context and system_r role security context. These indicate that the process is system related. The type security context for the process is different, which means it can be controlled with separate policies.

You'll often see the security context referred to as a label in SELinux documentation and literature. SELinux must assign the label to each object on the system when it's first enabled, which can be a long process.

The semanage utility allows you to view and set the security context for user accounts on the system. For files and directories, the Linux system sets their security context when they are created, based on the security context of the parent directory. You can change the default security context assigned to a file by using the chcon or the restorecon utility.

The chcon format is as follows:

```
chcon -u newuser -r newrole -t newtype filename
```

The newuser, newrole, and newtype values define the new user, role, and type security contexts you want assigned to the specified file.

The restorecon utility restores the security context of a file or directory back to the default settings as defined in the policies. You can use the -R option to recursively restore the security context on all files under a specified directory.

The runcon utility allows you to start an application with a specified security context, but be careful. If an application starts without having access to any required configuration or logging files, strange things can, and usually will, happen.

Using Policies

SELinux controls access to system objects based on policies. In the targeted security mode, each policy defines what objects in a specific type security context can access objects in another type security context. This is called *type enforcement*.

For example, an application labeled with the type security context sshd_t is only allowed to access files labeled with the type security context sshd_t. This restricts access from the application to only certain files on the system.

SELinux maintains policies as text files in the /etc/selinux directory structure. For example, all policies for the targeted security mode are under the /etc/selinux/targeted directory.

Creating your own policies can be somewhat complicated. Fortunately, SELinux includes policy groups, called *modules*, that you can install as standard RPM packages. Use the semodule utility to list, install, and remove policy modules in your system.

To make things even easier, SELinux uses a method of enabling and disabling individual policies without having to modify a policy file. A *Boolean* is a switch that allows you to enable or disable a policy rule from the command line based on its policy name. To view the current setting of a policy, use the getsebool command:

```
$ getsebool antivirus_can_scan_system
antivirus_can_scan_system --> off
$
```

To view all of the policies for the system, include the -a option, as shown in Listing 15.6.

Listing 15.6: Using the -a option with the getsebool command

```
$ sudo getsebool -a
abrt_anon_write --> off
abrt_handle_event --> off
abrt_upload_watch_anon_write --> on
antivirus_can_scan_system --> off
antivirus_use_jit --> off
auditadm_exec_content --> on
authlogin_nsswitch_use_ldap --> off
authlogin_radius --> off
authlogin_yubikey --> off
awstats_purge_apache_log_files --> off
boinc_execmem --> on
cdrecord_read_content --> off
cluster_can_network_connect --> off
cluster_manage_all_files --> off
cluster_use_execmem --> off
cobbler_anon_write --> off
cobbler_can_network_connect --> off
cobbler_use_cifs --> off
cobbler_use_nfs --> off
collectd_tcp_network_connect --> off
condor_tcp_network_connect --> off
conman_can_network --> off
conman_use_nfs --> off
...
```

Listing 15.6 just shows a partial output from the getsebool command; there are lots of different policies installed by default in most Red Hat Linux environments.

To change the Boolean setting, use the setsebool command:

```
$ sudo setsebool antivirus_can_scan_system on
```

```
$ getsebool antivirus_can_scan_system
antivirus_can_scan_system --> on
$
```

This setting only applies to your current session. To make the change permanent, you must add the -P option to the command. Doing so gives you full control over the policy settings defined for SELinux.

 Each time SELinux denies an event due to a security policy, it logs the action in the /var/log/audit/audit.log file. You can view this file to see what events security policies are blocking on your system. The audit2allow utility is a handy tool that can read an audit log entry and generate a policy rule that would allow the denied event. However, be careful with this tool, as there may have been a valid reason why the event was denied.

Using AppArmor

Debian-based Linux distributions commonly use the *AppArmor* MAC system. AppArmor isn't as complex or versatile as SELinux; it only controls the files and network ports that applications have access to.

 As of Ubuntu 18.04LTS, AppArmor is installed by default, but the utilities and profile packages aren't. Use apt to install the apparmor-utils and apparmor-profiles packages.

AppArmor also defines access based on policies but calls them *profiles*. Profiles are defined for each application in the /etc/apparmor.d directory structure. Normally, each application package installs its own profiles.

Each profile is a text file that defines the files and network ports the application is allowed to communicate with and the access permissions allowed for each. The name of the profile usually references the path to the application executable file, replacing the slashes with periods. For example, the profile name for the mysqld application program is called usr.sbin.mysqld.

 AppArmor profiles can use variables, called *tunables*, in the profile definition. The variables are then defined in files contained in the /etc/apparmor.d/tunables directory. This allows you to easily make changes to the variables to alter the behavior of a profile without having to modify the profile itself.

To determine the status of AppArmor on your Linux system, use the aa-status command, as shown in Listing 15.7.

Listing 15.7: The aa-status command output

```
$ sudo aa-status
apparmor module is loaded.
63 profiles are loaded.
42 profiles are in enforce mode.
   /snap/snapd/14066/usr/lib/snapd/snap-confine
   /snap/snapd/14066/usr/lib/snapd/snap-confine//mount-namespace-
capture-helper
   /snap/snapd/14295/usr/lib/snapd/snap-confine
   /snap/snapd/14295/usr/lib/snapd/snap-confine//mount-namespace-
capture-helper
   /usr/bin/evince
   /usr/bin/evince-previewer
   /usr/bin/evince-previewer//sanitized_helper
...
21 profiles are in complain mode.
   /usr/sbin/dnsmasq
   /usr/sbin/dnsmasq//libvirt_leaseshelper
   avahi-daemon
   chromium_browser
   chromium_browser//chromium_browser_sandbox
   chromium_browser//lsb:release
   chromium_browser//xdgsettings
   identd
...
3 processes have profiles defined.
3 processes are in enforce mode.
   /usr/sbin/cups-browsed (687)
   /usr/sbin/cupsd (679)
   /snap/snap-store/558/usr/bin/snap-store (1795) snap.snap-
store.ubuntu-software
0 processes are in complain mode.
0 processes are unconfined but have a profile defined.
$
```

The output from the aa-status command in Listing 15.7 shows all of the profiles in enforce, complain, or disabled status. After you've installed the apparmor-utils package, you have a few different useful commands for working with AppArmor at your disposal. You can view a listing of active network ports on your system that don't have a profile defined by using the aa-unconfined command:

```
$ sudo aa-unconfined
```

```
465 /lib/systemd/systemd-resolved not confined
747 /usr/sbin/avahi-daemon not confined
748 /usr/sbin/cupsd confined by '/usr/sbin/cupsd (enforce)'
804 /usr/sbin/cups-browsed confined by '/usr/sbin/cups-browsed (enforce)'
885 /usr/sbin/xrdp-sesman not confined
912 /sbin/dhclient confined by '/sbin/dhclient (enforce)'
935 /usr/sbin/xrdp not confined
982 /sbin/dhclient confined by '/sbin/dhclient (enforce)'
992 /usr/sbin/apache2 not confined
993 /usr/sbin/apache2 not confined
994 /usr/sbin/apache2 not confined
1094 /usr/sbin/mysqld confined by '/usr/sbin/mysqld (enforce)'
$
```

To turn off a specific profile, use the `aa-complain` command, which places the profile in complain mode:

```
$ sudo aa-complain /usr/sbin/tcpdump
Setting /usr/sbin/tcpdump to complain mode.
$
```

In complain mode, any violations of the profile will be logged but not blocked. If you want to completely disable an individual profile, use the `aa-disable` command:

```
$ sudo aa-disable /usr/sbin/tcpdump
Disabling /usr/sbin/tcpdump.
$
```

To turn a profile back on, use the `aa-enforce` command:

```
$ sudo aa-enforce /usr/sbin/tcpdump
Setting /usr/sbin/tcpdump to enforce mode.
$
```

Though not quite as versatile as SELinux, the AppArmor system provides a basic level of security protection against compromised applications on your Linux system.

Understanding Linux User Types

One of the more confusing topics in Linux is the issue of user types. In Linux, not all users are created equal, with some user accounts having different purposes, and therefore different permissions, than others. The following sections discuss the different types of Linux user accounts and how to change between them.

Types of User Accounts

While in Linux all user accounts are created the same way using the useradd utility (see Chapter 10, "Administering Users and Groups"), not all user accounts behave the same way. There are three basic types of user accounts in Linux:

Root: The root user account is the main administrator user account on the system. It is identified by being assigned the special user ID value of 0. The root user account has permission to access all files and directories on the system, regardless of any permission settings assigned.

Standard: Standard Linux user accounts are used to log into the system and perform standard tasks, such as running desktop applications or shell commands. Standard Linux users normally are assigned a $HOME directory, with permissions to store files and create subdirectories. Standard Linux users cannot access files outside their $HOME directory unless given permission by the file or directory owner. Most Linux distributions assign standard user account user IDs over 1000.

Service: Service Linux user accounts are used for applications that start in the background, such as network services like the Apache web server or MySQL database server. By setting the password value in the shadow file to an asterisk, these user accounts are restricted so that they cannot be used to log into the system. Also, the login shell defined in the /etc/passwd file is set to the nologin value to prevent access to a command shell. Service accounts normally have a user ID less than 1000.

Some Linux distributions, such as Ubuntu, don't allow you to log in directly as the root user account. Instead they rely on escalating privileges (discussed in the next section) to allow standard user accounts to perform administrative tasks.

Escalating Privileges

While the root user account has full access to the entire Linux system, it's generally considered a bad practice to log in as the root user account to perform system-related activities. There's no accountability for who logs in with the root user account, and providing the root user account password to multiple people in an organization can be dangerous.

Instead, most Linux administrators use privilege escalation to allow their standard Linux user account to run programs with the root administrator privileges. This is done using three different programs:

- *su*: The su command is short for *substitute user*. It allows a standard user account to run commands as another user account, including the root user account. To run the su command, the standard user must provide the password for the substitute user account. While this solves the problem of knowing who is performing the administrator task, it doesn't solve the problem of multiple people knowing the root user account password.

- *sudo*: The sudo command is short for *substitute user do*. It allows a standard user account to run any command as another user account, including the root user account. The sudo command prompts the user for their own password to validate who they are.

- *sudoedit*: The sudoedit command allows a standard user to open a file in a text editor with privileges of another user account, including the root user account. The sudoedit command also prompts the user for their own password to validate who they are.

Although the su command is somewhat self-explanatory, the sudo and sudoedit commands can be a bit confusing. Running a command with administrator privileges by supplying your own user password seems a bit odd.

Each Linux system uses a file that defines which users are allowed to run the sudo command, usually located at /etc/sudoers. The sudoers file contains a list of not only user accounts but also groups whose users are allowed administrator privileges. There are two common user groups that are used for these privileges. Debian-based distributions use the sudo group, and Red Hat–based distributions use the wheel group (short for *big wheel*).

WARNING   Never open the sudoers file using a standard editor. If multiple users open the sudoers file at the same time, odd things can happen and corrupt the file. The visudo command securely opens the file in an editor so that you can make changes.

Restricting Users and Files

Finally, there are two commands that you should know about that don't really have anything to do with file ownership or permissions but instead are related to user and file restrictions.

The ulimit command helps you restrict access to system resources for each user account. Listing 15.8 shows the output from running the ulimit command with the -a option, which displays the settings for the user account.

Listing 15.8: The ulimit command output

```
$ ulimit -a
core file size          (blocks, -c) 0
data seg size           (kbytes, -d) unlimited
scheduling priority             (-e) 0
file size               (blocks, -f) unlimited
pending signals                 (-i) 19567
max locked memory       (kbytes, -l) 16384
max memory size         (kbytes, -m) unlimited
open files                      (-n) 1024
pipe size            (512 bytes, -p) 8
```

```
POSIX message queues      (bytes, -q) 819200
real-time priority                (-r) 0
stack size                (kbytes, -s) 8192
cpu time                 (seconds, -t) unlimited
max user processes                (-u) 19567
virtual memory            (kbytes, -v) unlimited
file locks                        (-x) unlimited
$
```

As a user account consumes system resources, it places a load on the system, but in CPU time and memory. If you're working in a multiuser Linux environment, you may need to place restrictions on how many resources each user account can consume. That's where the ulimit command comes in. Table 15.3 shows the command-line options you can use to restrict specific resources for the user account.

TABLE 15.3   The ulimit command options

Option	Description
-a	Lists the limits for the current user account
-b	Sets the maximum socket buffer size
-c	Sets the maximum core file size
-d	Sets the maximum data segment size for processes
-e	Sets the maximum allowed scheduling priority
-f	Sets the maximum file size allowed to be written
-i	Sets the maximum number of pending signals
-k	Sets the maximum number of kqueues that can be allocated
-l	Sets the maximum size of memory that can be locked
-m	Sets the maximum resident set size
-n	Sets the maximum number of open file descriptors
-p	Sets the maximum pipe size in 512k blocks
-r	Sets the maximum real-time scheduling priority value
-s	Sets the maximum stack size

Option	Description
-t	Sets the maximum amount of CPU time the user account is allowed
-u	Sets the maximum number of processes the user can run simultaneously
-v	Sets the maximum amount of virtual memory available to the user
-x	Sets the maximum number of file locks
-P	Sets the maximum number of pseudo-terminals the user account can log into
-T	Sets the maximum number of threads the user can have

As you can tell from Table 15.3, with the ulimit command the Linux administrator can place some pretty severe restrictions on just what an individual user account can do on the system.

You can also set restrictions on what users can or can't do with files and directories. File and directory *attributes* define actions that the filesystem can allow or block on the file or directory.

The chattr command modifies the attributes assigned to a file or directory. The format of the chattr command is:

chattr [*mode*] *files*...

The *mode* option defines what attributes to set or unset. Table 15.4 defines the different attributes available in Linux.

TABLE 15.4   Linux file and directory attributes

Attribute	Description
a	Can only open in append mode when writing.
A	The access time for the file is not modified when the file is open.
c	Automatically compress the file on the disk.
C	The file is not automatically copied on write for journaling filesystems.
d	Do not back up the file with the dump program.
D	All changes are synchronously written to disk without caching (applies to directories only).

TABLE 15.4 Linux file and directory attributes *(continued)*

Attribute	Description
e	Linux is using extents for mapping blocks on the disk.
E	The file is encrypted by the filesystem.
F	When applied to a directory, all path lookups in the directory are case-insensitive.
i	The file can't be modified or deleted.
I	Index the directory using a hash tree.
j	If the filesystem supports journaling, data written to the file is written to the journal before being written to the file.
N	The file contains data stored in the inode table itself.
P	When applied to a directory, files in the directory inherit the project ID of the directory.
s	If the file is deleted, its blocks are zeroed and written back to the disk.
S	Changes to the file are written synchronously to the disk and not stored in a buffer.
t	If the file contains a partial block fragment at the end, it will not be merged with other files.
T	The directory is deemed the top of a directory hierarchy for storage purposes.
U	Save the contents of the file when deleted, allowing for the undelete feature.
V	Apply file authentication to the file.

To assign an attribute to a file or directory you precede the attribute with a plus sign:

```
$ sudo chattr +i test1.txt
$ rm test1.txt
rm: cannot remove 'test1.txt': Operation not permitted
$
```

This example sets the immutable attribute (i) to a file, making it impossible to delete the file. This particular attribute can only be set by the root user account, thus the need to use the sudo command. After setting the attribute, the file can no longer be deleted.

To display the current attributes applied to a file or directory, use the `lsattr` command:

```
$ lsattr test1.txt
----i-------------- test1.txt
$
```

To remove the attribute, use the minus sign with the `chattr` command:

```
$ sudo chattr -i test1.txt
$ lsattr test1.txt
------------------- test1.txt
$ rm test1.txt
$
```

WARNING   Not all filesystems support all the file and directory attributes. You'll need to consult the documentation for your specific filesystem to determine what file and directory attributes are available for you to use.

Exercise 15.1 walks through how to set up a simple shared directory where multiple user accounts can have read/write access to files.

EXERCISE 15.1

Creating a Shared Directory

This exercise demonstrates how to use the GUID bit to create a directory where multiple users can both read and write to files.

1. Log into your Linux system and open a new command prompt.

2. Create the first test user account by using the command **sudo useradd -m test1**. Assign the test account a password by using the command **sudo passwd test1**.

3. Create a second test user account by using the command **sudo useradd -m test2**. Assign that test account a password by using the command **sudo passwd test2**.

4. Create a new group named sales by using the command **sudo groupadd sales**.

5. Add both test user accounts to the sales group by using the commands **sudo usermod -G sales test1** and **sudo usermod -G sales test2**. You can check your work by examining the group file using the command **cat /etc/group | grep sales**. You should see both the test1 and test2 user accounts listed as members of the group.

6. Create a new shared directory by using the command **sudo mkdir /sales**. Change the default group assigned to the directory by using the command **sudo chgrp sales /sales**. Grant members of the sales group write privileges to the /sales directory by using the command **sudo chmod g+w /sales**. Set the GUID bit for the /sales directory by using the command **sudo chmod g+s /sales**. This ensures that any files created in the /sales directory are assigned to the sales group.

7. Log out from the Linux system; then log in using the test1 user account and open a new command prompt.

8. Change to the /sales directory using the command **cd /sales**.

9. Create a new text file using the command **echo "This is a test" > testfile.txt**. You can view the contents of the file using the command **cat testfile.txt**.

10. Log out from the Linux system; then log in using the test2 user account and open a new command prompt.

11. Change to the /sales directory using the command **cd /sales**.

12. View the test file using the command **cat testfile.txt**.

13. Add to the test file using the command **echo "This was added by the test2 user account" >> testfile.txt**. View the contents of the file using the command **cat testfile.txt** to ensure that the test2 user account also has write access to the file.

14. Log out from the Linux system; then log in using your normal user account.

15. Change to the /sales directory and see if you can view the contents of the test file by using the command **cat testfile.txt**.

16. Attempt to add text to the file by using the command **echo "This was added by me" >> testfile.txt**. This command should fail, as you're not a member of the sales group nor the owner of the file.

Summary

File and directory security is a major responsibility of all Linux administrators. The Linux system provides several layers of security that you can apply to files and directories to help keep them safe.

Linux assigns a set of read, write, and execute permissions to all files and directories on the system. You can define separate access settings for the file or directory owner, for a specific group defined for the Linux system, and for all other users on the system. The grouping of three access level settings and permissions provides for nine possible security settings applied to each file and directory. You can set those using the chmod command, using either symbolic mode or octal mode.

A more advanced method of file and directory security involves setting an access control list (ACL) for each file and directory. The ACL can define read, write, and execute permissions for multiple users or groups. The setfacl command allows you to set these permissions, and you use the getfacl command to view the current permissions.

The next level of security involves setting context-based permissions. Red Hat–based Linux distributions use the SELinux program to allow you to set policy rules that control access to files, directories, applications, and network ports based on the context of their use. For Debian-based Linux distributions, the AppArmor program provides advanced security for applications accessing files.

Linux handles security based on the user type. The root user account has full administrator privileges on the Linux system and can access any file, directory, or network port regardless of any security settings. Service user accounts are used to start and run applications that require access to a limited set of files and directories. Service user accounts usually can't log into the system from a terminal, nor can they open any type of command-line shell. The last type of user accounts is the standard user account. These accounts are for normal system users who need to log into a terminal and run applications.

Exam Essentials

Describe the basic level of file and directory security available in Linux.   Linux provides basic file and directory security by utilizing three categories of read, write, and execute permissions. The file or directory owner is assigned one set of permissions, the primary group is assigned another set of permissions, and everyone else on the Linux system is assigned a third set of permissions. You can set the permissions in the three categories separately to control the amount of access the group members and others on the Linux system have.

Explain how to modify the permissions assigned to a file or directory.   Linux uses the chmod command to assign permissions to files and directories. The chmod command uses two separate modes to assign permissions: symbolic mode and octal mode. Symbolic mode uses a single letter to identify the category for the owner (u), group (g), everyone else (o), and all (a). Following that, a plus sign, minus sign, or equal sign is used to indicate to add, remove, or set the permissions. The permissions are also indicated by a single letter for read (r), write (w), or execute (x) permissions. In octal mode an octal value is used to represent the three permissions for each category. The three octal values define the full set of permissions assigned to the file or directory.

Describe how Linux uses an access control list (ACL) to provide additional protection to files and directories.   Linux allows you to set additional permissions for multiple users and groups to each file and directory. The setfacl command provides an interface for you to define read, write, and execute permissions for users or additional groups outside the owner and primary group assigned to the file or directory. The getfacl command allows you to view the additional permissions.

Describe how Linux uses context-based permissions for further file and directory security.   Packages such as SELinux (for Red Hat–based distributions) and AppArmor (for Debian-based distributions) provide role-based mandatory access control (RBMAC) to enforce security permissions that override what the file or directory owner sets. The system administrator can define policies (or profiles in AppArmor) that are evaluated by the Linux kernel after any standard permissions or ACL rules are applied. You can fine-tune these permissions to control exactly what type of access the system allows to each individual file or directory.

Review Questions

1. What permissions can be applied to a file or directory? (Choose three.)
   - A. Read
   - B. Write
   - C. Delete
   - D. Modify
   - E. Execute

2. What user categories can be assigned permissions in Linux? (Choose three.)
   - A. Root
   - B. Owner
   - C. Group
   - D. Others
   - E. Department

3. Sam needs to allow standard users to run an application with root privileges. What special permissions bit should she apply to the application file?
   - A. The sticky bit
   - B. The SUID bit
   - C. The GUID bit
   - D. Execute
   - E. Write

4. What are the equivalent symbolic mode permissions for the octal mode value of 644?
   - A. `rwxrw-r--`
   - B. `-w--w--w-`
   - C. `-w-r--r--`
   - D. `rwxrw-rw-`
   - E. `rw-r-r--`

5. Fred was assigned the task of creating a new group on the company Linux server and now needs to assign permissions for that group to files and directories. What Linux utility should he use to change the group assigned to the files and directories? (Choose all that apply.)
   - A. `chgrp`
   - B. `chown`
   - C. `chmod`
   - D. `chage`
   - E. `ulimit`

6. Sally needs to view the ACL permissions assigned to a file on her Linux server. What command should she use?

    A. `ls -Z`

    B. `ls -l`

    C. `getfacl`

    D. `chmod`

    E. `setfacl`

7. What SELinux mode tracks policy violations but doesn't enforce them?

    A. Disabled

    B. Enforcing

    C. Targeted

    D. Permissive

    E. MLS

8. Ted is tasked with documenting the SELinux security context assigned to a group of files in a directory. What command should he use?

    A. `getsebool`

    B. `setsebool`

    C. `ls -Z`

    D. `getenforce`

    E. `ls -l`

9. Mary is required to log into her Linux system as a standard user but needs to run an application with administrator privileges. What commands can she use to do that? (Choose all that apply.)

    A. `su`

    B. `wheel`

    C. `visudo`

    D. `sudo`

    E. `adm`

10. What user groups are commonly used to assign privileges for group members to run applications as the administrator? (Choose two.)

    A. `lp`

    B. `adm`

    C. `wheel`

    D. `sudo`

    E. `su`

Chapter

16

Looking at Access and Authentication Methods

✓ **Objective 2.1: Summarize the purpose and use of security best practices in a Linux environment.**

✓ **Objective 2.2: Given a scenario, implement identity management.**

✓ **Objective 2.4: Given a scenario, configure and execute remote connectivity for system management.**

Part of properly securing a system and its data involves providing appropriate access and authentication methods. There are many tools available to provide these services. However, it is crucial to understand how they work and how to configure them appropriately.

We'll take a look at the various authentication and access methods, where their configuration files are stored, and how to properly configure them. We'll cover some important encryption and authentication topics as well.

Getting to Know PAM

Pluggable authentication modules (PAMs) provide centralized authentication services for Linux and applications. Sun Microsystems started the Linux-PAM project in 1997 to explore using pluggable authentication in a Linux environment. Today, PAM is typically used on all Linux distributions.

PAM provides authentication libraries that compile into the application, becoming an interface the application requiring authentication and an authentication method. It supports lots of different underlying authentication libraries (called modules), including:

- Password: PAM supports using both the /etc/passwd and /etc/shadow password files to authenticate using a text password.

- Certificate: PAM can use public key infrastructure (PKI) certificate stores to authenticate users.

- Lightweight Directory Access Protocol (LDAP): PAM can connect to a centralized LDAP server in an organization to support network logins.

- Kerberos: PAM supports the Kerberos authentication system, which issues a token to clients when they log into the system. These tokens can then be used for authentication on multiple network resources. This process is often referred to as single sign-on (SSO), where you need to log in just once to access multiple resources on the network.

- Multifactor authentication (MFA): PAM supports several types of MFA environments, such as biometrics, tokens, PKI, and onetime passwords emailed to users.

The beauty of PAM is that programs don't need to change anything to utilize different authentication methods—PAM controls that all with configuration files. Programs that use PAM services are compiled with the PAM library, libpam.so, and have an associated PAM configuration file. Applications that use PAM are called "PAM-aware." You can quickly determine if a program is PAM-aware by using the ldd command. A snipped example is shown in Listing 16.1.

Listing 16.1: Using `ldd` to determine if application is PAM-aware

```
# ldd /bin/login | grep libpam.so
        libpam.so.0 => /lib64/libpam.so.0 (0x00007fbf2ce71000)
#
```

In Listing 16.1, the `ldd` utility is employed to display all the program's shared library dependencies. The display output is piped into `grep` to search for only the PAM `libpam.so` library. In this case, the application is compiled with the PAM library. Besides being compiled with the PAM `libpam.so` library, the application needs to have a configuration file to use PAM.

Exploring PAM Configuration Files

PAM configuration files are located in the `/etc/pam.d/` directory. Listing 16.2 shows this directory's files on a Rocky Linux distribution.

Listing 16.2: Viewing the `/etc/pam.d/` directory's contents

```
$ ls /etc/pam.d/
atd                   gdm-fingerprint           pluto              su
chfn                  gdm-launch-environment    polkit-1           sudo
chsh                  gdm-password              postlogin          sudo-i
cockpit               gdm-pin                   remote             su-l
config-util           gdm-smartcard             runuser            system-auth
crond                 login                     runuser-l          systemd-user
cups                  other                     smartcard-auth     vlock
fingerprint-auth      passwd                    sshd               vmtoolsd
gdm-autologin         password-auth             sssd-shadowutils   xserver
$
```

Notice in Listing 16.2 that there is a `login` configuration file. This file is displayed snipped in Listing 16.3.

Listing 16.3: Viewing the `/etc/pam.d/login` file's contents

```
$ cat /etc/pam.d/login
#%PAM-1.0
[…]
auth       include    postlogin
account    required   pam_nologin.so
account    include    system-auth
password   include    system-auth
[…]
session    optional   pam_keyinit.so force revoke
[…]
$
```

The records in a PAM configuration file have a specific syntax:

type control-flag pam-module [module-options]

The type (*TYPE*), sometimes called a *context* or *module interface*, designates a particular PAM service type. The four PAM service types are shown in Table 16.1.

TABLE 16.1   *TYPE* in /etc/pam.d/ configuration file records

Interface	Service description
account	Implements account validation services, such as enforcing time-of-day restrictions as well as determining if the account has expired
auth	Provides account authentication management services, such as asking for a password and verifying that the password is correct
password	Manages account passwords, such as enforcing minimum password lengths and limiting incorrect password entry attempts
session	Provides authenticated account session management for session start and session end—such as logging when the session began and ended—as well as mounting the account's home directory, if needed

The *PAM-MODULE* portion of the /etc/pam.d/ configuration file record is simply the filename of the module that will be doing the work. For example, pam_nologin.so is shown in the /etc/pam.d/login configuration file in Listing 16.3. Additional module options can be included after the module's filename.

A designated *PAM-MODULE* is called in the order in which it is listed within the PAM configuration file. This is called the *module stack*. Each *PAM-MODULE* returns a status code, which is handled via the record's *CONTROL-FLAG* setting. Together these status codes and settings create a final status, which is sent to the application. Table 16.2 lists the various control flags and their responses or actions.

TABLE 16.2   The *CONTROL-FLAG* settings for /etc/pam.d/ configuration file records

Control flag	Description
include	Adds status codes and response ratings from the designated PAM configuration files into the final status.
optional	Conditionally adds the module's status code to the final status. If this is the only record for the PAM service type, it is included. If not, the status code is ignored.
requisite	If the module returns a fail status code, a final fail status is immediately returned to the application without running the rest of the modules within the configuration file.

Control flag	Description
required	If the module returns a fail status code, a final fail status will be returned to the application, but only after the rest of the modules within the configuration file run.
substack	Forces the included configuration files of a particular `type` to act together returning a single status code to the main module stack.
sufficient	If the module returns a success status code and no preceding stack modules have returned a fail status code, a final success status is immediately returned to the application without running the rest of the modules in the configuration file. If the module returns a fail status code, it is ignored.

The `/etc/pam.d/` configuration files' module stack process of providing a final status is a little confusing. A simplification to help you understand the progression is depicted in Figure 16.1.

FIGURE 16.1   The PAM module stack process

Using Figure 16.1 as a guide, imagine that the application subject (user) needs authentication to access the system. The appropriate `/etc/pam.d/` configuration file is employed. Going through the authentication module stack, the user passes through the various security checkpoints. At each checkpoint, a guard (PAM module) checks a different requirement, determines whether or not the user has the required authentication, and issues a fail or success card. The final guard reviews the status cards along with their control flags listed on a clipboard. This guard determines whether or not the subject may proceed through the "System Access" doorway. Of course, keep in mind that if any of the checkpoints are listed as `requisite`, and the user fails that checkpoint, they would be immediately tossed out.

Enforcing Strong Passwords

When a password is modified via the passwd command, PAM is employed. These various PAM modules can help to enforce strong passwords:

- pam_unix.so
- pam_pwhistory.so
- pam_pwquality.so

 Typically you'll find the pam_pwquality.so module installed by default. However, for Ubuntu, you will need to manually install it. Use an account with super user privileges and type **sudo apt-get install libpam-pwquality** at the command line.

The pam_unix.so module performs authentication using account and password data stored in the /etc/passwd and /etc/shadow files.

The pam_pwhistory.so module checks a user's newly entered password against a history database to prevent a user from reusing an old password. The password history file, /etc/security/opasswd, is locked down. Passwords are also stored salted and hashed, using the same hashing algorithm employed for passwords stored in the /etc/shadow file.

To use the pam_pwhistory.so module, you must modify one of the /etc/pam.d configuration files. Along with specifying the password type and the module name, you can set one or more of the *MODULE-OPTIONS* listed in Table 16.3.

TABLE 16.3   The *MODULE-OPTIONS* for password reuse prevention

Module option	Description
enforce_for_root	If this option is used, the root account must have its password checked for reuse when resetting its password.
remember=N	Designates that N passwords will be remembered. The default is 10, and the maximum is 400.
retry=N	Limits the number of reused password entries to N before returning with an error. The default is 1.

For Ubuntu, you need to put this configuration information in the /etc/pam.d/common-password and /etc/pam.d/common-auth files. For other distributions, you put this configuration in the system's default /etc/pam.d/ files password-auth and system-auth.

> If you directly modify the /etc/pam.d/password-auth and system-auth files, they can be overwritten by the authconfig utility. You can avoid this by creating a local file instead, such as password-auth-local. Red Hat has an excellent description of how to accomplish this task. Just use your favorite search engine and type **Hardening Your System with Tools and Services Red Hat** to find this information.

A snipped example of the newly modified Rocky Linux /etc/pam.d/password-auth file is shown in Listing 16.4.

Listing 16.4: Viewing the modified /etc/pam.d/password-auth file

```
# grep password /etc/pam.d/password-auth
[…]
password    required      pam_pwhistory.so
password    sufficient    pam_unix.so […] use_authtok
[…]
#
```

In Listing 16.4, the grep command is employed to search for PAM password type records. The newly added pam_pwhistory.so module record uses a required control flag and no options. Note that the next record is for the pam_unix.so module and it uses the use_authtok option, which tells the module to use the password already entered instead of prompting for it again. Typically, it is best to place the password history record directly above this pam_unix.so record.

> The pam_pwhistory.so module is not compatible with Kerberos and LDAP. Before employing it, be sure to review its man pages.

Now that password history is being enforced, you can test it by trying to reset your password to the current password. A snipped example is shown in Listing 16.5.

Listing 16.5: Trying to reuse an old password after password history is enforced

```
$ passwd
Changing password for user Christine.
Changing password for Christine.
(current) UNIX password:
New password:
BAD PASSWORD: The password is the same as the old one
[…]
passwd: Have exhausted maximum number of retries for service
$
```

Using `pam_pwquality.so`, you can enforce rules for new passwords, such as setting a minimum password length. You can configure needed directives in the `/etc/security/pwquality.conf` file or pass them as module options. A snipped example of the file is shown in Listing 16.6.

Listing 16.6: Viewing the `/etc/security/pwquality.conf` file's contents

```
$ cat /etc/security/pwquality.conf
# Configuration for systemwide password quality limits
[…]
# difok = 5
[…]
# minlen = 9
[…]
# dcredit = 1
[…]
$
```

 The `pam_pwquality.so` module replaces the older, deprecated `pam_cracklib.so` module. The modules act similarly. So if you are familiar with the deprecated `pam_cracklib.so`, then you'll recognize the `pam_pwquality.so` configuration.

There are several password quality directives you can set in the `pwquality.conf` file. Table 16.4 describes some common ones.

TABLE 16.4   Common password quality directives in the `pwquality.conf` file

Directive	Description
`minlen` = N	Enforces the minimum number N of characters for a new password. (Default is 9 and minimum allowed is 6.) The `*credit` settings affect this directive as well.
`dcredit` = N	If N is positive, adds N credits to password's `minlen` setting for any included digits. If N is negative, N digits must be in the password. (Default is 1.)
`ucredit` = N	If N is positive, adds N credits to password's `minlen` setting for any included uppercase characters. If N is negative, N uppercase characters must be in the password. (Default is 1.)
`lcredit` = N	If N is positive, adds N credits to password's `minlen` setting for any included lowercase characters. If N is negative, N lowercase characters must be in the password. (Default is 1.)

Directive	Description
ocredit = N	If N is positive, adds N credits to password's minlen setting for any included other characters (not letters or numbers). If N is negative, N other characters must be in the password. (Default is 1.)
difok = N	Enforces the number N of characters that must be different in new password.

To help you understand Table 16.4's credit directives, let's focus on the dcredit setting. If you set dcredit = -3, this means that three digits must be in the new password. If you set dcredit = 3, this means that if there are three digits in the new password, the password required length minlen has now been reduced by three.

Once you have the pwquality.conf file directives completed, you'll need to enable the pam_pwquality.so module in the proper /etc/pam.d/ configuration file. This is similar to how the pwhistory.so module is handled.

Locking Out Accounts

A *brute-force attack* occurs when a malicious user attempts to gain system access via trying different passwords over and over again for a particular system account. To prevent these attacks, you can lock out a user account after a certain number of failed attempts.

> **WARNING**   Be very careful when modifying PAM configuration files for user account lockout. If they are configured incorrectly, you could lock out all accounts, including your own and/or the root account.

The pam_tally2.so and pam_faillock.so modules allow you to implement account lockout. Which one you choose depends on your distribution (for example, pam_faillock is not installed by default on Ubuntu) as well as the various module options you wish to employ.

The two modules share three key module options. They are as described in Table 16.5.

TABLE 16.5   Key pam_tally2.so and pam_faillock.so module options

Module option	Description
deny = N	Locks account after N failed password entries. (Default is 3.)
silent	Displays no informational messages to user.
unlock_time = N	Unlocks a locked account after being locked for N seconds. If this option is not set, an administrator must manually unlock the account.

On a current Ubuntu distribution, it is typically better to use the `pam_tally2.so` module. Keep in mind that on a current CentOS distro, it may not work well. In Listing 16.7 a snipped display of a modified /etc/pam.d/common-auth file includes this module.

Listing 16.7: Viewing an Ubuntu /etc/pam.d/common-auth file's contents

```
$ cat /etc/pam.d/common-auth
auth     required      pam_tally2.so  deny=2 silent
[…]
auth     […]           pam_unix.so nullok_secure
[…]
$
```

The `pam_tally2.so` configuration in Listing 16.7 allows only two failed login attempts prior to locking the account. Also, it does not automatically unlock the account after a certain time period.

 On Ubuntu systems, the pam-auth-update utility is involved in managing PAM modules. Before you modify PAM configuration files on an Ubuntu system, it is a good idea to understand how this utility works. Review its man pages for details.

The `pam_tally2` command allows you to view failed login attempts. Listing 16.8 shows an example of this on an Ubuntu distribution.

Listing 16.8: Employing the `pam_tally2` utility to view login failures

```
$ sudo pam_tally2
Login   Failures Latest failure    From
user1      4     11/08/19 16:28:14 /dev/pts/1
$
```

In Listing 16.8, the user1 account has four login attempt failures. Since the `pam_tally2.so` module option is set to deny=2, the account is now locked. You cannot unlock an account that has been locked by PAM via the usermod or passwd utility. Instead, you have to employ the `pam_tally2` command and add the -r (or --reset) and -u (or --user) options as shown in Listing 16.9. This wipes out the login failure tally so that the account is no longer locked out.

Listing 16.9: Using the `pam_tally2` utility to reset login failure tallies

```
$ sudo pam_tally2 -r -u user1
Login          Failures Latest failure     From
user1             4     11/08/19 16:28:14  /dev/pts/1
$
$ sudo pam_tally2
$
```

The pam_tally2.so module has useful module options in addition to those shown in Table 16.5. Also, the pam_tally2 command has some further helpful switches. These items share a man page. You can review it by typing **man pam_tally2** at the command line.

On a current Red Hat–based distribution, it is typically better to use the pam_faillock.so module. Listing 16.10 shows a snipped display of a modified /etc/pam.d/system-auth file that includes this module.

Listing 16.10: Viewing a Rocky Linux /etc/pam.d/system-auth file's contents

```
# cat /etc/pam.d/system-auth
[…]
auth        required      pam_env.so
auth        required      pam_faillock.so preauth silent audit deny=2
auth        required      pam_faildelay.so delay=2000000
auth        sufficient    pam_unix.so nullok try_first_pass
auth        [default=die] pam_faillock.so authfail audit deny=2
auth        sufficient    pam_faillock.so authsucc audit deny=2
[…]
account     required      pam_faillock.so
account     required      pam_unix.so
[…]
#
```

Notice in Listing 16.10 that there are four pam_faillock.so module records. In these records are a few options and one control flag that have not yet been covered:

- preauth: If there have been a large number of failed consecutive authentication attempts, block the user's access.

- audit: If a nonexistent user account is entered, log the attempted account name.

- [default=die]: Returned code treated as a failure. Return to the application immediately.

- authfail: Record authentication failure into the appropriate user tally file.

- authsucc: Identify failed authentication attempts as consecutive or nonconsecutive.

To have pam_faillock.so work correctly, you need to modify the password-auth file as well and add the exact same records as were added to the Listing 16.10 file. It is also located in the /etc/pam.d/ directory.

The faillock command allows you to view failed login attempts. Listing 16.11 shows an example of this on a Rocky Linux distribution.

Listing 16.11: Using the `faillock` utility to view and reset login failure tallies

```
# faillock
user1:
When                   Type  Source   Valid
2018-11-08 17:47:23 TTY    tty2          V
2018-11-08 17:47:31 TTY    tty2          V
#
# ls -F /var/run/faillock
user1
#
# faillock --reset --user user1
#
# faillock
user1:
When                   Type  Source   Valid
#
```

Notice in Listing 16.11 that the `faillock` utility displays records for each failed login attempt. In this case, since deny=2 is set, the `user1` account is locked out. To unlock the account, the `faillock` command is used again with the appropriate options. Another item to note in Listing 16.11 is the `/var/run/faillock` directory. When the `pam_faillock .so` module is configured, each user receives a failed login attempt tally file in this directory. However, the file is not created until a login failure first occurs.

 Real World Scenario

PAM Integration with LDAP

To allow multiple servers to share the same authentication database, many companies use a network authentication system. Microsoft Active Directory is the most popular one used today. However, in the open source world, Lightweight Directory Access Protocol (LDAP) provides this service, with the favored implementation being the OpenLDAP package. Most Linux distributions include both client and server packages for implementing LDAP in a Linux network environment.

If you are using LDAP on your system, you can integrate it with PAM. The `pam_ldap.so` module is the primary module for this purpose. It provides authentication and authorization services as well as managing password changes for LDAP. The `pam_ldap.so` module's fundamental configuration file is the `/etc/ldap.conf` file.

You will need to modify the appropriate PAM configuration file(s). This may include manually editing the /etc/pam.d/system-auth file on a Red Hat–based system or using the pam-auth-update utility on a Debian-based distribution to modify the /etc/pam.d/ common-* files. Depending on the system's distribution, there may be additional configuration activities for integrating PAM with LDAP. See your distribution-specific documentation and/or man pages for more details.

Limiting Root Access

It is best to employ the sudo command (see Chapter 15, "Applying Ownership and Permissions") to gain super user privileges as opposed to logging into the root user account. Even better is to have the root account disabled for login via its /etc/shadow file record. However, if you absolutely must log in to the root account, you can limit the locations where this is done.

If properly configured, the pam_securetty.so PAM module and the /etc/securetty file are used to restrict root account logins. They do so by limiting root logins only to devices listed in the secure TTY file. A snipped listing of this file on an Ubuntu distro is shown in Listing 16.12.

Listing 16.12: Viewing the /etc/securetty file

```
$ cat /etc/securetty
# /etc/securetty: list of terminals on which root is allowed to login.
# See securetty(5) and login(1).
[…]
console

# Local X displays […]
:0
:0.0
:0.1
[…]
# Virtual consoles
tty1
tty2
tty3
tty4
[…]
$
```

To understand the /etc/securetty file records, you need to know how TTY terminals are represented. When you log into a virtual console, typically reached by pressing a
Ctrl+Alt+Fn key sequence, you are logging into a terminal that is represented by a /dev/
tty* file. For example, if you press Ctrl+Alt+F2 and log into the tty2 terminal, that terminal
is represented by the /dev/tty2 file. Notice that the /etc/securetty file records in Listing 16.12 only show the virtual console terminal name (e.g., tty4) and not its device file.

> If you are in a terminal emulator or logged into a console terminal, you
> can view your own process's current terminal by entering **tty** at the
> command line.

When you log into the system via its graphical interface, a who or w command's output
will show something similar to :0 in your process's TTY column. In Listing 16.12, you can
find records for those logins as well.

If you then open a terminal emulator program, you are opening a TTY terminal, called a
pseudo-TTY, that is represented by a /dev/pts/* file, such /dev/pts/0. These TTY terminals are *not* listed in the /etc/securetty file because the user has already logged into
the graphical environment.

> If your system employs the pam_securetty.so module but there is no
> /etc/securetty file, the root user can access the system via any device,
> such as a console terminal or network interface. This is considered an
> insecure environment.

The pam_securetty.so module is typically placed in either the /etc/pam.d/login
and/or the /etc/pam.d/remote configuration files. An example of this is shown snipped on
an Ubuntu distribution in Listing 16.13.

Listing 16.13: Finding the files that use the pam_securetty.so module

```
$ grep pam_securetty /etc/pam.d/*
/etc/pam.d/login:auth […] pam_securetty.so
$
```

> While this configuration will disable root account logins at tty* and :0
> devices, it does not disable all root logins. The root account can still be
> accessed via SSH utilities, such as ssh and scp. (SSH is covered later
> in this chapter.) In addition, the su and sudo commands (covered in
> Chapter 15) are not hampered from accessing the root account by this
> PAM configuration.

On this Ubuntu distribution, only the login PAM configuration file includes the
pam_securetty.so module. Notice in Listing 16.13 that the PAM service *type* used for
this module is auth.

Exploring PKI Concepts

The primary purpose of cryptography is to encode data in order to hide it or keep it private. In cryptography, *plaintext* (text that can be read by humans or machines) is turned into *ciphertext* (text that cannot be read by humans or machines) via cryptographic algorithms. Turning plaintext into ciphertext is called *encryption*. Converting text from ciphertext back into plaintext is called *decryption*.

Cryptographic algorithms use special data called *keys* for encrypting and decrypting; they are also called *cipher keys*. When encrypted data is shared with others, some of these keys must also be shared. Problems ensue if a key from a trustworthy source is snatched and replaced with a key from a nefarious source. The *public key infrastructure (PKI)* helps to protect key integrity. The PKI is a structure built from a team of components that work together to prove authenticity and validation of keys as well as the people or devices that use them.

Getting Certificates

A few members of the PKI team are the *certificate authority (CA)* structure and CA-issued *digital certificates*. After verifying a person's identity, a CA issues a digital certificate to the requesting person. The digital certificate provides identification proof along with an embedded key, which now belongs to the requester. The certificate holder can now use the certificate's key to encrypt data and sign it using the certificate. This provides authenticity and validation for those that will decrypt the data, especially if it is transmitted over a network.

Digital certificates issued from a commercial CA take effort to obtain as well as money, although progress is being made with open source CA sites, such as `letsencrypt.org`, that offer free digital certificates. If you are simply developing a new application, are in its testing phase, or are practicing for a certification exam, you can generate and sign your own certificate. This type of certificate is called a *self-signed digital certificate*. While self-signed certificates are useful in certain situations, they should never be used in an Internet production environment (although some organizations allow their use in Intranet applications).

Discovering Key Concepts

It is critical to understand cipher keys and their role in the encryption/decryption process. Cipher keys come in two flavors:

Private Keys   *Symmetric keys*, also called private or secret keys, encrypt data using a cryptographic algorithm and a *single* key. Plaintext is both encrypted and decrypted using the same key, and it is typically protected by a password called a passphrase. Symmetric key cryptography is very fast. Unfortunately, if you need others to decrypt the data, you have to share the private key, which is its primary disadvantage.

Public/Private Key Pairs   *Asymmetric keys*, also called public/private key pairs, encrypt data using a cryptographic algorithm and *two* keys. Typically the public key is used to encrypt the data and the private key decrypts the data. The private key can be protected with a passphrase and is kept secret. The public key of the pair is meant to be shared.

Asymmetric keys are used by system users as well as many applications, such as SSH. Figure 16.2 provides a scenario of using a public/private key pair between two people.

FIGURE 16.2   Asymmetric encryption example

Notice in Figure 16.2 that in order for Bob to encrypt data (a message in this case) for Helen, he must use her public key. Helen in turn uses her private key to decrypt the data. However, problems occur if Bob is not sure that he is really getting Helen's public key. He may be getting a public key from a nefarious user named Evelyn and accidentally send his encrypted message to her. This is an on-path attack. Digital signatures, which are covered later, help in this situation.

Securing Data

An important concept in PKI and cryptography is hashing. *Hashing* uses a one-way mathematical algorithm that turns plaintext into a fixed-length ciphertext. Because it is one way, you cannot "de-hash" a hashed ciphertext. The ciphertext created by hashing is called a *message digest*, hash, hash value, fingerprint, or signature.

The beauty of a cryptographic message digest is that it can be used in data comparison. For example, if hashing produces the exact same message digest for plaintext `FileA` and for plaintext `FileB`, then both files contain the exact same data. This type of hash is often used in cyberforensics.

 Hashing is useful for things like making sure a large downloaded file was not corrupted when it was being transferred. However, cryptographic hashing must use an algorithm that is collision free. In other words, the hashing algorithm cannot create the same message digest for two different inputs. Some older hash algorithms, such as MD5, are not collision free.

Be aware that simple message digests, called *non-salted* and *non-keyed message digests*, are created only using the plaintext file as input. This hash can be strengthened by adding *salt*, which is random data added along with the input file to protect the hash from certain malicious attacks. A *salted hash* is used in the `/etc/shadow` file to protect passwords.

A *keyed message digest* is created using the plaintext file along with a private key. This cryptographic hash type is strong against multiple malicious attacks and often employed in Linux applications, such as SSH.

Signing Transmissions

Another practical implementation of hashing is in *digital signatures*. A digital signature is a cryptographic token that provides authentication and data verification. It is simply a message digest of the original plaintext data, which is then encrypted with a user's private key and sent along with the ciphertext.

The ciphertext receiver decrypts the digital signature with the sender's public key so that the original message digest is available. The receiver also decrypts the ciphertext and then hashes its plaintext data. Once the new message digest is created, the data receiver can compare the new message digest to the sent message digest. If they match, the digital signature is authenticated, which means the encrypted data did come from the sender. Also, it indicates that the data was not modified in transmission.

 A malicious individual can intercept a signed transmission, replace the ciphertext with new ciphertext, and add a new digital signature for that data. Signing transmissions alone does not protect from an on-path attack. It is best to employ this method along with digital certificates and other security layers.

Using SSH

When you connect over a network to a remote server, if it is not via an encrypted method, network sniffers can view the data being sent and received. Secure Shell (SSH) has resolved this problem by providing an encrypted means for communication. It is the de facto standard software used by those wishing to send data securely to/from remote systems.

SSH employs public/private key pairs (asymmetric) for its encryption. When an SSH connection is being established between two systems, each sends its public key to the other.

Exploring Basic SSH Concepts

You'll typically find OpenSSH (www.openSSH.com) installed by default on most distributions. However, if for some reason you are unable to use basic SSH services, you may want to check if the needed OpenSSH packages are installed (managing packages was covered in Chapter 13, "Governing Software"). Table 16.6 shows the distributions used by this book and their basic OpenSSH service package names.

TABLE 16.6   Various distros' OpenSSH package names

Distribution	OpenSSH package names
Rocky	openssh, openssh-clients, openssh-server
Fedora	openssh, openssh-clients, openssh-server
openSUSE	openssh
Ubuntu	openssh-server, openssh-client

To create a secure OpenSSH connection between two systems, use the ssh command. The basic syntax is as follows:

ssh [*options*] *username@hostname*

 If you attempt to use the ssh command and get a no route to host message, first check if the sshd daemon is running. On a systemd system, the command to use with super user privileges is **systemctl status sshd**. If the daemon is running, check your firewall settings, which are covered in Chapter 18, "Overseeing Linux Firewalls."

For a successful encrypted connection, both systems (client and remote) must have the OpenSSH software installed and the sshd daemon running. A snipped example is shown in Listing 16.14 connecting from a Rocky Linux system to a remote openSUSE Linux server.

Listing 16.14: Using ssh to connect to a remote system

```
$ ssh Christine@192.168.0.105
The authenticity of host '192.168.0.105 (192.168.0.105)' can't be established.
ECDSA key fingerprint is SHA256:BnaCbm+ensyrkflKk1rRSVwxHi4NrBWOOSOdU+14m7w.
ECDSA key fingerprint is MD5:25:36:60:b7:99:44:d7:74:1c:95:d5:84:55:6a:62:3c.
Are you sure you want to continue connecting (yes/no)? yes
Warning: Permanently added '192.168.0.105' (ECDSA) to the list of known hosts.
Password:
[…]
Have a lot of fun...
Christine@linux-1yd3:~> ip addr show | grep 192.168.0.105
    inet 192.168.0.105/24 […] dynamic eth1
Christine@linux-1yd3:~>
Christine@linux-1yd3:~> exit
logout
Connection to 192.168.0.105 closed.
$
$ ls .ssh
known_hosts
$
```

In Listing 16.14, the ssh command uses no options, includes the remote system account username, and uses the remote system's IPv4 address instead of its hostname. Note that you do *not* have to use the remote system account username if the local account name is identical. However, in this case, you do have to enter the remote account's password to gain access to the remote system.

The OpenSSH application keeps track of any previously connected hosts in the ~/.ssh/ known_hosts file. This data contains the remote servers' public keys.

The ~/ symbol combination represents a user's home directory. You may also see in documentation $HOME as the representation. Therefore, to generically represent any user's home directory that contains a hidden subdirectory .ssh/ and the known_hosts file, it is written as ~/.ssh/ known_hosts or $HOME/.ssh/known_hosts.

If you have not used ssh to log in to a particular remote host in the past, you'll get a scary-looking message like the one shown in Listing 16.14. The message just lets you know that this particular remote host is not in the known_hosts file. When you type **yes** at the message's prompt, it is added to the collective.

If you have previously connected to the remote server and you get a warning message that says WARNING: REMOTE HOST IDENTIFICATION HAS CHANGED, pay attention. It's possible that the remote server's public key has changed. However, it may also indicate that the remote system is being spoofed or has been compromised by a malicious user.

The rsync utility, which was covered in Chapter 3, "Managing Files, Directories, and Text," can employ SSH to quickly copy files to a remote system over an encrypted tunnel. To use OpenSSH with the rsync command, add the *username@hostname* before the destination file's location. An example is shown in Listing 16.15.

Listing 16.15: Using rsync to securely transfer a file over SSH

```
$ ls -sh Project4x.tar
40K Project4x.tar
$
$ rsync Project4x.tar Christine@192.168.0.105:~
Password:
$
```

In Listing 16.15, the Project4x.tar file is sent to a remote system using the rsync command and OpenSSH. Notice that the remote system's username and IP address has an added colon (:). This is to designate that the file is being transferred to a remote system. If you did not add the colon, the rsync command would not transfer the file. It would simply rename the file to a name with Christine@ and tack on the IP address too.

After the colon, the file's directory destination is designated. The ~ symbol indicates to place the file in the user's home directory. You could also give the file a new name, if desired.

You can also use the ssh command to send commands to a remote system. Just add the command, between quotation marks, to the ssh command's end. An example is shown in Listing 16.16.

Listing 16.16: Using ssh to send a command to a remote system

```
$ ssh Christine@192.168.0.105 "ls -sh Project4x.tar"
Password:
40K Project4x.tar
$
```

In Listing 16.16, the command checks if our file was properly transferred to the remote system. The Project4x.tar file was successfully moved.

Configuring SSH

It's a good idea to review the various OpenSSH configuration files and their directives. Ensuring that your encrypted connection is properly configured is critical for securing remote system communications. Table 16.7 lists the primary OpenSSH configuration files.

TABLE 16.7   Primary OpenSSH configuration files

Configuration file	Description
~/.ssh/config	Contains OpenSSH client configurations. May be overridden by ssh command options.
/etc/ssh/ssh_config	Contains OpenSSH client configurations. May be overridden by ssh command options or settings in the ~/.ssh/config file.
/etc/ssh/sshd_config	Contains the OpenSSH daemon (sshd) configurations.

If you need to make SSH configuration changes, it is essential to know which configuration file(s) to modify. The following guidelines can help:

- For an individual user's connections to a remote system, create and/or modify the client side's ~/.ssh/config file.

- For every user's connection to a remote system, create and modify the client side's /etc/ssh/ssh_config file.

- For incoming SSH connection requests, modify the /etc/ssh/sshd_config file on the server side.

Keep in mind that in order for an SSH client connection to be successful, besides proper authentication, the client and remote server's SSH configuration must be compatible.

There are several OpenSSH configuration directives. You can peruse them all via the man pages for the ssh_config and sshd_config files. However, there are a few vital directives for the sshd_config file:

- AllowTcpForwarding: Permits SSH port forwarding. (See Chapter 8, "Comparing GUIs.")

- ForwardX11: Permits X11 forwarding. (See Chapter 8.)

- PermitRootLogin: Permits the root user to log in through an SSH connection. Typically, should be set to no.

- Port: Sets the port number the OpenSSH daemon (sshd) listens on for incoming connection requests. (Default is 22.)

An example of why you might change the client's ssh_config or ~/.ssh/config file is when the remote system's SSH port is modified in the sshd_config file. In this case, if the client-side configuration files were not changed to match this new port, the remote user would have to modify their ssh command's options. An example of this is shown snipped in Listing 16.17. In this listing, the remote Ubuntu server has OpenSSH listening on port 1138, instead of the default port 22, and the user must use the -p option with the ssh command to reach the remote server.

Listing 16.17: Using ssh to connect to a nondefault port on a remote system

```
$ ssh -p 1138 192.168.0.104
[…]
Christine@192.168.0.104's password:
Welcome to Ubuntu 18.04.1 LTS (GNU/Linux 4.15.0-36-generic x86_64)
[…]
Christine@Ubuntu1804:~$
Christine@Ubuntu1804:~$ ip addr show | grep 192.168.0.104
    inet 192.168.0.104/24 […]
Christine@Ubuntu1804:~$
Christine@Ubuntu1804:~$ exit
logout
Connection to 192.168.0.104 closed.
$
```

To relieve the OpenSSH client users of this trouble, create or modify the ~/.ssh/config file for individual users, or for all client users, modify the /etc/ssh/ssh_config file. Set Port to 1138 in the configuration file. This makes it easier on both the remote users and the system administrator.

> **NOTE** Often system admins will change the OpenSSH default port from port 22 to another port. On public-facing servers, this port is often targeted by malicious attackers. However, if you change the OpenSSH port on a system using SELinux, you'll need to let SELinux know about the change. The needed change is often documented in the top of the /etc/ssh/ sshd_config file on SELinux systems.

Generating SSH Keys

Typically, OpenSSH will search for its system's public/private key pairs. If they are not found, OpenSSH automatically generates them. These key pairs, also called *host keys*, are stored in the /etc/ssh/ directory in files. Listing 16.18 shows key files on a Fedora distribution.

Listing 16.18: Looking at OpenSSH key files on a Fedora system

```
$ ls -1 /etc/ssh/*key*
/etc/ssh/ssh_host_ecdsa_key
/etc/ssh/ssh_host_ecdsa_key.pub
/etc/ssh/ssh_host_ed25519_key
/etc/ssh/ssh_host_ed25519_key.pub
/etc/ssh/ssh_host_rsa_key
/etc/ssh/ssh_host_rsa_key.pub
$
```

In Listing 16.18, both private and public key files are shown. The public key files end in the .pub filename extension, whereas the private keys have no filename extension. The filenames follow this standard:

ssh_host_*KeyType*_key

The key filename's *KeyType* corresponds to the digital signature algorithm used in the key's creation. The different types you may see on your system are as follows:

- dsa

- rsa

- ecdsa

- ed25519

> It is critical that the private key files be properly protected. Private key files should have a 0640 or 0600 (octal) permission setting and be root owned. However, public key files need to be world readable. File permissions were covered in Chapter 15, "Applying Ownership and Permissions."

There may be times you need to manually generate these keys or create new ones. In order to do so, the ssh-keygen utility is employed. In Listing 16.19, a snipped example of using this utility is shown on a Fedora system.

Listing 16.19: Using ssh-keygen to create a new public/private key pair

```
$ sudo ssh-keygen -t rsa -f /etc/ssh/ssh_host_rsa_key
Generating public/private rsa key pair.
/etc/ssh/ssh_host_rsa_key already exists.
Overwrite (y/n)? y
Enter passphrase (empty for no passphrase):
Enter same passphrase again:
```

```
Your identification has been saved in /etc/ssh/ssh_host_rsa_key.
Your public key has been saved in /etc/ssh/ssh_host_rsa_key.pub.
The key fingerprint is:
[...]
$
```

The ssh-keygen has several options. For the commands in Listing 16.19, only two are employed. The -t option sets *KeyType*, which is rsa in this example. The -f switch designates the private key file to store the key. The public key is stored in a file with the same name, but the .pub file extension is added. Notice that this command asks for a passphrase, which is associated with the private key.

Authenticating with SSH Keys

Entering the password for every command employing SSH can be tiresome. However, you can use keys instead of a password to authenticate. A few steps are needed to set up this authentication method:

1. Log into the SSH client system.
2. Generate an SSH ID key pair.
3. Securely transfer the public SSH ID key to the SSH server computer.
4. Log into the SSH server system.
5. Add the public SSH ID key to the ~/.ssh/authorized_keys file on the server system.

Let's look at these steps in a little more detail. First, you should log into the client system via the account you will be using as the SSH client. On that system, generate the SSH ID key pair via the ssh-keygen utility. You must designate the correct key pair filename, which is id_*TYPE*, where *TYPE* is dsa, rsa, or ecdsa. An example of creating an SSH ID key pair on a client system is shown snipped in Listing 16.20.

Listing 16.20: Using ssh-keygen to create an SSH ID key pair

```
$ ssh-keygen -t rsa -f ~/.ssh/id_rsa
Generating public/private rsa key pair.
Enter passphrase (empty for no passphrase):
Enter same passphrase again:
Your identification has been saved in /home/Christine/.ssh/id_rsa.
Your public key has been saved in /home/Christine/.ssh/id_rsa.pub.
[...]
$
$ ls .ssh/
id_rsa  id_rsa.pub  known_hosts
$
```

Notice in Listing 16.20 the key file's name. The ssh-keygen command in this case generates a private key, stored in the ~/.ssh/id_rsa file, and a public key, stored in the ~/.ssh/id_rsa.pub file. You may enter a passphrase if desired. In this case, no passphrase was entered.

Once these keys are generated on the client system, the public key must be copied to the server system. Using a secure method is best, and the ssh-copy-id utility allows you to do this. Not only does it copy over your public key, it also stores it in the server system's ~/.ssh/authorized_keys file for you. In essence, it completes steps 3 through 5 in a single command. A snipped example of using this utility is shown in Listing 16.21.

Listing 16.21: Using ssh-copy-id to copy the SSH public ID key

```
$ ssh-copy-id -n Christine@192.168.0.104
[…]
Would have added the following key(s):

ssh-rsa AAAAB3NzaC1yc2EAAAADAQABAAAABAQCsP[…]
8WJVE5RWAXN[…]
=-=-=-=-=-=-=-=
$ ssh-copy-id  Christine@192.168.0.104
[…]Source of key(s) to be installed: "/home/Christine/.ssh/id_rsa.pub"
[…]
Christine@192.168.0.104's password:

Number of key(s) added: 1
[…]
$
```

Notice in Listing 16.21 that the ssh-copy-id -n command is employed first. The -n option allows you to see what keys would be copied and installed on the remote system without actually doing the work (a dry run).

The next time the command is issued in Listing 16.21, the -n switch is removed. Thus, the id_rsa.pub key file is securely copied to the server system, and the key is installed in the ~/.ssh/authorized_keys file. Notice that when using the ssh-copy-id command, the user must enter their password to allow the public ID key to be copied over to the server.

Now that the public ID key has been copied over to the SSH server system, the ssh command can be used to connect from the client system to the server system with no need to enter a password. This is shown along with using the scp command in Listing 16.22. Note that at the IP address's end, you must add a colon (:) when using the scp command to copy over files.

Listing 16.22: Testing out password-less SSH connections

```
$ ssh Christine@192.168.0.104
Welcome to Ubuntu 18.04.1 LTS (GNU/Linux 4.15.0-36-generic x86_64)
[…]
Christine@Ubuntu1804:~$ ls .ssh
authorized_keys  known_hosts
Christine@Ubuntu1804:~$
Christine@Ubuntu1804:~$ exit
logout
Connection to 192.168.0.104 closed.
$
$ scp Project4x.tar Christine@192.168.0.104:~
Project4x.tar        100%    40KB   6.3MB/s   00:00
$
$ ssh Christine@192.168.0.104
Welcome to Ubuntu 18.04.1 LTS (GNU/Linux 4.15.0-36-generic x86_64)
[…]
Christine@Ubuntu1804:~$ ls
Desktop    Downloads         Music      Project4x.tar  Templates
Documents  examples.desktop  Pictures   Public         Videos
Christine@Ubuntu1804:~$ exit
logout
Connection to 192.168.0.104 closed.
$
```

> If your Linux distribution does not have the ssh-copy-id command, you can employ the scp command to copy over the public ID key. In this case you would have to manually add the key to the bottom of the ~/.ssh/ authorized_keys file. To do this you can use the cat command and the >> symbols to redirect and append the public ID key's standard output to the authorized keys file.

Authenticating with the Authentication Agent

Another method to connect to a remote system with SSH is via the authentication agent. Using the agent, you only need to enter your password to initiate the connection. After that, the agent remembers the password during the agent session. A few steps are needed to set up this authentication method:

1. Log into the SSH client system.

2. Generate an SSH ID key pair and set up a passphrase.

3. Securely transfer the public SSH ID key to the SSH server computer.

4. Log into the SSH server system.

5. Add the public SSH ID key to the ~/.ssh/authorized_keys file on the server system.

6. Start an agent session.

7. Add the SSH ID key to the agent session.

Steps 1 through 5 are nearly the same steps performed for setting up authenticating with SSH ID keys instead of a password. One exception to note is that a passphrase *must* be created when generating the SSH ID key pair for use with an agent. An example of setting up an ECDSA key to use with an SSH agent is shown snipped in Listing 16.23.

Listing 16.23: Generating and setting up an ID key to use with the SSH agent

```
$ ssh-keygen -t ecdsa -f ~/.ssh/id_ecdsa
Generating public/private ecdsa key pair.
Enter passphrase (empty for no passphrase):
Enter same passphrase again:
Your identification has been saved in /home/Christine/.ssh/id_ecdsa.
[…]
$ ssh-copy-id  -i ~/.ssh/id_ecdsa Christine@192.168.0.104
[…]
Number of key(s) added: 1
[…]
$
```

Once you have the key pair properly created with a passphrase on the remote system, securely transmitted, and installed on the server's authorized key file, you can employ the ssh-agent utility to start an SSH agent session. After the session is started, add the private ID key to the session via the ssh-add command. A snipped example of this is shown in Listing 16.24.

Listing 16.24: Starting an SSH agent session and adding an ID key

```
$ ssh-agent /bin/bash
[Christine@localhost ~]$
[Christine@localhost ~]$ ssh-add ~/.ssh/id_ecdsa
Enter passphrase for /home/Christine/.ssh/id_ecdsa:
Identity added: /home/Christine/.ssh/id_ecdsa (/home/Christine/.ssh/id_ecdsa)
[Christine@localhost ~]$
[Christine@localhost ~]$ ssh Christine@192.168.0.104
Welcome to Ubuntu 18.04.1 LTS (GNU/Linux 4.15.0-36-generic x86_64)
[…]
Christine@Ubuntu1804:~$ exit
```

```
logout
Connection to 192.168.0.104 closed.
[Christine@localhost ~]$
[Christine@localhost ~]$ exit
exit
$
```

Notice in Listing 16.24 that the ssh-agent command is followed by /bin/bash, which is the Bash shell. This command starts a new session, an agent session, with the Bash shell running. Once the private SSH ID key is added using the ssh-add command and entering the private passphrase, you can connect to remote systems without entering a password or passphrase again. However, if you exit the agent session and start it up again, you must re-add the key and reenter the passphrase.

WARNING   The ssh-add command allows you to remove ID in an agent session, if so desired. Include the –d option to do so.

An SSH agent session allows you to enter the session one time and add the key, then connect as often as needed to remote systems via encrypted SSH methods without entering a password or passphrase over and over again. Not only does this provide security, it provides convenience, which is a rare combination.

Using SSH Securely

There are a few things you can do to enhance SSH's security on your systems:

▪ Use a different port for SSH than the default port 22.

▪ Disable root logins via SSH.

▪ Manage TCP Wrappers.

One item touched upon earlier in this chapter is not using port 22 as the SSH port for any public-facing systems. You change this by modifying the Port directive in the /etc/ssh/sshd_config file to another port number. Keep in mind that there are advantages and disadvantages to doing this. It may be a better alternative to beef up your firewall as opposed to changing the default SSH port.

Another critical item is disabling root login via SSH. By default, any system that allows the root account to log in and has OpenSSH enabled permits root logins via SSH. Because root is a standard username, malicious attackers can use it in brute-force attacks. Since root is a super user account, it needs extra protection.

To disable root login via SSH, edit the /etc/ssh/sshd_config file. Set the PermitRootLogin directive to no, and either restart the OpenSSH service or reload its configuration file.

TCP Wrappers are an older method for controlling access to network-based services. If a service can employ TCP Wrappers, it will have the libwrap library compiled with it.

You can check for support by using the `ldd` command as shown snipped in Listing 16.25. In this listing on an Ubuntu system, you can see that TCP Wrappers can be used by the SSH service.

Listing 16.25: Using the `ldd` command to check for TCP Wrappers support

```
$ which sshd
/usr/sbin/sshd
$
$ ldd /usr/sbin/sshd | grep libwrap
        libwrap.so.0 […]
$
```

TCP Wrappers employ two files to determine who can access a particular service. These files are `/etc/hosts.allow` and `/etc/hosts.deny`. As you can tell by their names, the `hosts.allow` file typically allows access to the designated service, while the `hosts.deny` file commonly blocks access. These files have simple record syntax:

service: IPaddress…

The search order of these files is critical. For an incoming service request, the following takes place:

- The `hosts.allow` file is checked for the remote IP address.
  - If found, access is allowed, and no further checks are made.
- The `hosts.deny` file is checked for the remote IP address.
  - If found, access is denied.
  - If not found, access is allowed.

Because access is allowed if the remote system's address is not found in either file, it is best to employ the `ALL` wildcard in the `/etc/hosts.deny` file:

`ALL: ALL`

This disables all access to all services for any IP address not listed in the `/etc/hosts.allow` file. Be aware that some distributions use `PARANOID` instead of `ALL` for the address wildcard.

The record's *IPaddress* can be either IPv4 or IPv6. To list individual IP addresses in the `hosts.allow` file, you specify them separated by commas as such:

`sshd: 172.243.24.15, 172.243.24.16, 172.243.24.17`

Typing in every single IP address that is allowed to access the OpenSSH service is not necessary. You can specify entire subnets. For example, if you need to allow all the IPv4 addresses in a Class C network access on a server, you specify only the first three address octets followed by a trailing dot as such:

`sshd: 172.243.24.`

TCP Wrappers were created prior to the time administrators used fire-walls. While they are still used by some, their usefulness is limited, and they are considered deprecated by many distributions. It is best to move this protection to your firewall.

Using VPN as a Client

While SSH is great for securely connecting from a client to a server on the same local network, it is not as useful for accessing a remote system over a public network. Fortunately, *virtual private networks (VPNs)* work well in this situation. A VPN establishes a secure encrypted connection between two systems on separate networks with a public network between them. The encrypted connection acts as a separate private network, allowing you to pass any type of data between the two systems securely. There are many different VPN packages available on Linux, such as OpenVPN.

When choosing software that will provide VPN as a client, it is vital to understand what security methods a package employs. Making good VPN choices is critical for keeping your virtual network private. In addition, you should consider the data packet transportation method. When using a VPN, often UDP-based systems offer better performance over TCP-based systems.

SSL/TLS   SSL/TLS is actually the same secure communication protocol. Originally it was called SSL (Secure Sockets Layer). As the protocol advanced and improved through time, the name was changed to TLS (Transport Layer Security). As long as you are using a current version, this protocol provides secure data encryption over a network between systems. Your VPN client application should use TLS 1.2 at a minimum. Earlier versions of the protocol have known problems.

TLS is a stream-oriented protocol that prevents on-path attacks. It employs symmetric encryption for the data and a public key for confirming the system's identity. Data includes a message authentication code to prevent alteration during transmission. In addition, TLS has restrictions that curb captured data from being replayed at a later time, called a *replay attack*.

Point-to-Point Tunneling Protocol (PPTP) is an older protocol that has many documented weaknesses. It is vulnerable to on-path attacks, and therefore any VPN client using this protocol should not be implemented on your system.

DTLS   Datagram Transport Layer Security (DTLS) is also a secure communication protocol, but it is designed to employ only UDP packets. Thus, it is sometimes known as the UDP TLS. With TPC, which is a connection-based protocol, additional communication takes place to establish the connection. Because UDP is a connectionless protocol,

DTLS is faster, and it does not suffer the performance problems of other stream-based protocols.

DTLS is based upon SSL/TLS, and it provides similar security protections. Thus, it is favorable to use for VPN software.

IPSec   Internet Protocol Security (IPSec) is not a cryptographic protocol but a framework that operates at the Network layer. By itself, it does not enforce a particular key method or encryption algorithm. It is typically at a VPN application's core.

It employs the Authentication Header (AH) protocol for authentication. IPSec also uses the Encapsulating Security Payload (ESP) for authentication, data encryption, data integrity, and so on. For key management, typically the Internet Security Association and Key Management Protocol (ISAKMP) is employed, but it's not required.

IPSec has two modes: tunnel mode and transport mode. In tunnel mode, all the data and its associated headers added for transportation purposes (called a *datagram*) are protected. Thus, no one can see any data or routing information because the entire connection is secured. In transport mode, only the data is protected, and it is secured by ESP.

The OpenVPN package uses a custom protocol, sometimes called the OpenVPN protocol. It does, however, use SSL/TLS for its key exchange. This software product is multiplatform and does not have problems with establishing VPNs through firewalls and NATs, like IPSec has known to suffer. Therefore, the OpenVPN package is very popular.

There are many good choices for secure VPN clients. Creating a checklist of your environment's required features is a good place to start.

Summary

Assessing your system's and users' needs for appropriate access and authentication methods is vital for securing your system. Using the correct products and configuring them correctly not only helps to keep systems secure, it provides less frustration for your users. It makes your job easier as well.

Exam Essentials

Summarize various PAM modules and features.   PAM is a one-stop shop for various applications to implement authentication services. For an application to use PAM, it must be compiled with the `libpam.so` module and have an associated PAM configuration file. The configuration files are located in the `/etc/pam.d/` directory. Applications can enforce strong passwords employing any of the three PAM modules—`pam_unix.so`, `pam_pwhistory.so`, and `pam_pwquality.so` (the latter of which was formerly called `pam_cracklib.so`). PAM can also provide account lockouts to protect against brute-force attacks. This is accomplished via the `pam_tally.so` or `pam_faillock.so` module, depending on the system's distribution. If your environment incorporates LDAP, it also can be integrated with PAM. The PAM module to do so is the `pam_ldap.so` module.

Describe PKI and its components.   PKI protects cipher key integrity. This framework includes the CA structure, which validates a person's or device's identity and provides a signed digital certificate. The certificate includes a public key and can be sent to others so they can verify that the public key is valid and does truly come from the certificate holder. Self-signed certificates are available but should only be used for testing purposes. Symmetric key encryption uses only a private key for both encrypting and decrypting data. Asymmetric key encryption uses a public/private key pair, where commonly the public key is used for encryption and the private key is used for decryption. Hashing data prior to encryption and then encrypting the produced message digest allows you to add a digital signature to your transmitted encrypted data. It provides a means of data integrity.

Explain the various SSH features and utilities.   The OpenSSH application provides SSH services via the `ssh` command and `sshd` daemon. To configure SSH client connections, you can either use `ssh` command-line options or employ the `~/.ssh/config` or `/etc/ssh/ssh_config` file. For the server side, the configuration file is `/etc/ssh/sshd_config`. When you initially establish an SSH connection from a client to a remote SSH server, the server's key information is stored in the `~/.ssh/known_hosts` file. If keys need to be regenerated or you are setting up a password-less login, you can employ the `ssh-keygen` utility to create the needed keys. When you are setting up a password-less login, two files should be created, which are located in the `~/.ssh/` directory and named `id_rsa` and `id_rsa.pub`. The public key is copied to the SSH server system and placed in the `~/.ssh/authorized_keys` file via the `ssh-copy-id` command. An alternative is to use the `ssh-agent` and add the needed key via the `ssh-add` command.

Compare the various VPN client security implementations.   Typically used when needed to traverse a public network, VPN software establishes a secure encrypted connection between two systems. The protocols involved may be SLS/TLS, DTLS, and IPSec. The SLS/TLS protocol is stream-oriented and protects against on-path attacks. DTLS only uses UDP packets, which makes it faster than TCP packet-only protocols. IPSec operates at the Network layer. It provides two modes—tunnel mode and transport mode. OpenVPN is the most popular VPN software; it uses its own proprietary protocol but employs SLS/TLS for the key exchange.

Review Questions

1. For an application to use PAM, it needs to be compiled with which PAM library?

    A. `ldd`

    B. `pam_nologin.so`

    C. `pam_unix.so`

    D. `libpam`

    E. `pam_cracklib`

2. Which of the following are PAM control flags? (Choose all that apply.)

    A. `requisite`

    B. `required`

    C. `allowed`

    D. `sufficient`

    E. `optional`

3. Which of the following will display failed login attempts? (Choose all that apply.)

    A. `tally2`

    B. `pam_tally2`

    C. `pam_tally2.so`

    D. `pam_faillock`

    E. `faillock`

4. Leigh encrypts a message with Luke's public key and then sends the message to Luke. After receiving the message, Luke decrypts the message with his private key. What does this describe? (Choose all that apply.)

    A. Symmetric key encryption

    B. Asymmetric key encryption

    C. Public/private key encryption

    D. Secret key encryption

    E. Private key encryption

5. Which of the following best describes a digital signature?

    A. Plaintext that has been turned into ciphertext

    B. Ciphertext that has been turned into plaintext

    C. A framework that proves authenticity and validation of keys as well as the people or devices that use them

    D. A digital certificate that is not signed by a CA but by an end user

    E. An original plaintext hash, which is encrypted with a private key and sent along with the ciphertext

6. The OpenSSH application keeps track of any previously connected hosts and their public keys in what file?

   A. `~/.ssh/known_hosts`

   B. `~/.ssh/authorized_keys`

   C. `/etc/ssh/known_hosts`

   D. `/etc/ssh/authorized_keys`

   E. `/etc/ssh/ssh_host_rsa_key.pub`

7. Which of the following are OpenSSH configuration files? (Choose all that apply.)

   A. `~./ssh/config`

   B. `/etc/ssh/ssh_config`

   C. `/etc/ssh/sshd_config`

   D. `/etc/sshd/ssh_config`

   E. `/etc/sshd/sshd_config`

8. Which of the following files may be involved in authenticating with SSH keys?

   A. `/etc/ssh/ssh_host_rsa_key`

   B. `/etc/ssh/ssh_host_rsa_key.pub`

   C. `~/.ssh/id_rsa_key`

   D. `~/.ssh/id_rsa_key.pub`

   E. `~/.ssh/id_rsa`

9. Which of the following is true concerning TCP wrappers? (Choose all that apply.)

   A. The `/etc/hosts.allow` file is consulted first.

   B. The `/etc/hosts.allow` file should contain `ALL: ALL` to provide the best security.

   C. If an application is compiled with the `libwrap` library, it can employ TCP Wrappers.

   D. IP addresses of remote systems can be listed individually or as entire subnets.

   E. TCP Wrappers are considered to be deprecated by many distributions, and firewalls should be used instead.

10. Which of the following protocols or frameworks might be involved in using VPN software as a client? (Choose all that apply.)

    A. Tunnel

    B. SSL/TLS

    C. Transport

    D. IPSec

    E. DTLS

Chapter 17

Implementing Logging Services

✓ Objective 1.7: Given a scenario, manage software configurations

Lots of things happen on a Linux system while it's running. Part of your job as a Linux administrator is knowing just what is happening and watching for when things go wrong. The primary tool for accomplishing that task is the logging service. All Linux distributions implement some type of logging service that tracks system events and stores them in log files. This chapter explores the two most popular logging methods used in Linux distributions: `rsyslog` and `systemd-journald`. First, the chapter explains Linux logging principles to help give you an idea of what logging is all about. Then the chapter discusses both the `rsyslogd` and the `systemd-journald` methods of generating logs.

Understanding the Importance of Logging

All Linux distributions implement some method of *logging*. Logging directs short messages that indicate what events happen, and when they happen, to users, files, or even remote hosts for storage. If something goes wrong, the Linux administrator can review the log entries to help determine the cause of the problem.

The following sections discuss the basics of how logging has been implemented in Linux and show the main logging packages that you'll most likely run into while working with various Linux distributions.

The syslog Protocol

In the early days of Unix, myriad logging methods were used to track system and application events. Applications used different logging methods, making it difficult for system administrators to troubleshoot issues.

In the mid-1980s, Eric Allman defined a protocol called *syslog* for logging events from his Sendmail mail application. The syslog protocol quickly became a standard for logging both system and application events in Unix and made its way to the Linux world.

What made the syslog protocol so popular is that it defines a standard message format that specifies the timestamp, type, severity, and details of an event. That standard can be used by the operating system, applications, and even devices that generate errors.

The type of event is defined as a *facility* value. The facility defines what is generating the event message, such as a system resource or an application. Table 17.1 lists the facility values defined in the syslog protocol.

TABLE 17.1   The syslog protocol facility values

Code	Keyword	Description
0	kern	Messages generated by the system kernel
1	user	Messages generated by user events
2	mail	Messages from a mail application
3	daemon	Messages from system applications running in background
4	auth	Security or authentication messages
5	syslog	Messages generated by the logging application itself
6	lpr	Printer messages
7	news	Messages from the news application
8	uucp	Messages from the Unix-to-Unix copy program
9	cron	Messages generated from the cron job scheduler
10	authpriv	Security or authentication messages
11	ftp	File Transfer Protocol application messages
12	ntp	Network Time Protocol application messages
13	security	Log audit messages
14	console	Log alert messages
15	solaris-cron	Another scheduling daemon message type
16-23	local0-local7	Locally defined messages

As you can tell from Table 17.1, the syslog protocol covers many different types of events that can appear on a Linux system.

Each event is also marked with a *severity*. The severity value defines how important the message is to the health of the system. Table 17.2 shows the severity values as defined in the syslog protocol.

TABLE 17.2 The syslog protocol severity values

Code	Keyword	Description
0	emerg	An event that causes the system to be unusable
1	alert	An event that requires immediate attention
2	crit	An event that is critical but doesn't require immediate attention
3	err	An error condition that allows the system or application to continue
4	warning	A non-normal warning condition in the system or application
5	notice	A normal but significant condition message
6	info	An informational message from the system
7	debug	Debugging messages for developers

Combining the facility and severity codes with a short informational message provides enough logging information to troubleshoot almost any problem in Linux.

The History of Linux Logging

Over the years there have been many open source logging projects for Linux systems. The following have been the most prominent:

- *Sysklogd*: The original syslog application, this program includes two programs: the syslogd program to monitor the system and applications for events and the klogd program to monitor the Linux kernel for events.

- *Syslogd-ng*: This program added advanced features, such as message filtering and the ability to send messages to remote hosts.

- *Rsyslog*: The project claims the *r* stands for *rocket fast*. Speed is the focus of the rsyslog project, and the rsyslog application quickly became the standard logging package for many Linux distributions.

- *Systemd-journald*: This is part of the Systemd application for system startup and initialization (see Chapter 6, "Maintaining System Startup and Services"). Many Linux distributions are now using it for logging. It does not follow the syslog protocol but uses a completely different way of reporting and storing system and application events.

The following sections dive into the details of the two most popular logging applications: rsyslog and systemd-journald.

Basic Logging Using *rsyslog*

The `rsyslog` application utilizes all of the features of the original syslog protocol, including the configuration format and logging actions. The following sections walk you through how to configure the `rsyslog` logging application and where to find the common log files it generates.

Configuration

The `rsyslog` package uses the `rsyslogd` program to monitor events and log them as directed, using the `/etc/rsyslog.conf` configuration file to define what events to listen for and how to handle them. Many Linux distributions also use the `/etc/rsyslog.d` directory to store individual configuration files that are included as part of the `rsyslog.conf` configuration. This allows separate applications to define their own log settings.

The configuration file contains rules that define how the program handles syslog events received from the system, kernel, or applications. The format of an `rsyslogd` rule is as follows:

facility.priority action

The *facility* entry uses one of the standard syslog protocol facility keywords. The *priority* entry uses the severity keyword as defined in the syslog protocol, but with a twist. When you define a severity, `syslogd` will log all events with that severity or higher (lower severity code). Thus, the entry

`kern.crit`

logs all kernel event messages with a severity of critical, alert, or emergency. To log only messages with a specific severity, use an equal sign before the priority keyword:

`kern.=crit`

You can also use wildcard characters for either the facility or priority. The entry

`*.emerg`

logs all events with an emergency severity level.

The *action* entry defines what `rsyslogd` should do with the received syslog message. The six action options you have available are as follows:

- Forward to a regular file
- Pipe the message to an application
- Display the message on a terminal or the system console
- Send the message to a remote host
- Send the message to a list of users
- Send the message to all logged-in users

Listing 17.1 shows the entries in the configuration file for an Ubuntu 20.04 system.

Listing 17.1: The `rsyslog.conf` configuration entries for Ubuntu 20.04

```
auth,authpriv.*          /var/log/auth.log
*.*;auth,authpriv.none   -/var/log/syslog
kern.*                   -/var/log/kern.log
mail.*                   -/var/log/mail.log
mail.err                 /var/log/mail.err
*.emerg                  :omusrmsg:*
```

The first entry shown in Listing 17.1 defines a rule to handle all `auth` and `authpriv` facility type messages. This shows that you can specify multiple facility types by separating them with commas. The rule also uses a wildcard character for the priority, so all severity levels will be logged. This rule indicates that all security event messages will be logged to the `/var/log/auth.log` file.

The second entry defines a rule to handle all events (`*.*`) except security events (the `.none` priority). The event messages are sent to the `/var/log/syslog` file. The minus sign in front of the filename tells `rsyslogd` not to sync the file after each write, increasing the performance. The downside to this is if the system crashes before the next normal system sync, you may lose the event message.

The `kern.*` entry defines a rule to store all kernel event messages in a separate log file, located in the `/var/log/kern.log` file. This has become somewhat of a standard in Linux distributions.

The `*.emerg` entry defines a rule to handle all emergency events. The `omusrmsg` command indicates to send the event message to a user account on the system. By specifying the wildcard character, this rule sends all emergency event messages to all users on the system.

For comparison, Listing 17.2 shows the entries in the `rsyslogd` configuration file for a Rocky Linux 8.5 system.

Listing 17.2: The `rsyslog.conf` configuration file for Rocky Linux 8.5

```
*.info;mail.none;authpriv.none;cron.none    /var/log/messages
authpriv.*                                  /var/log/secure
mail.*                                      -/var/log/maillog
cron.*                                      /var/log/cron
*.emerg                                     :omusrmsg:*
uucp,news.crit                              /var/log/spooler
local7.*                                    /var/log/boot.log
```

Notice that Red Hat–based systems use the `/var/log/messages` file for informational messages and the `/var/log/secure` file for security messages.

As you can guess, for busy Linux systems it doesn't take long to generate large log files. To help combat that, many Linux distributions install the `logrotate` utility. It automatically splits `rsyslogd` log files into archive files based on a time or the size of the file. You can usually identify archived log files by the numerical extension added to the log filename.

Making Log Entries

If you create and run scripts on your Linux system (see Chapter 25, "Deploying Bash Scripts"), you may want to log your own application events. You can do that with the `logger` command-line tool:

```
logger [-isd] [-f file] [-p priority] [-t tag] [-u socket] [message]
```

The `-i` option specifies the process ID (PID) of the program that created the log entry as part of the event message. The `-p` option allows you to specify the event priority. The `-t` option allows you to specify a tag to add to the event message to help make finding the message in the log file easier. You can specify the message either as text in the command line or as a file using the `-f` option. The `-d` and `-u` options are advanced options for sending the event message to the network. The `-s` option sends the event message to the standard error output.

An example of using `logger` in a script would look like this:

```
$ logger This is a test message from rich
```

On an Ubuntu system, you can look at the end of the `/var/log/syslog` file to see the log entry:

```
$ tail /var/log/syslog
...
Feb  8 20:21:02 myhost rich: This is a test message from rich
```

Notice that `rsyslogd` added the timestamp, host, and user account for the message. This is a great troubleshooting tool!

Finding Event Messages

Generally, most Linux distributions create log files in the `/var/log` directory. Depending on the security of the Linux system, many log files are readable by everyone, but some may not be.

As seen in Listing 17.1 and Listing 17.2, most Linux distributions create separate log files for different event message types, although they don't always agree on the log filenames.

It's also common for individual applications to have a separate directory under the `/var/log` directory for their own application event messages, such as `/var/log/apache2` for the Apache web server.

The easiest way to find the log files for your system is to examine the /etc/rsyslog.conf configuration file. Just remember to also look for additional configuration files in the /etc/rsyslog.d directory.

Since rsyslogd log files are text files, you can use any of the standard text tools available in Linux, such as cat, head, tail, and, of course, vi to view them. One common trick for administrators is to use the -f option with the tail command. That displays the last few lines in the log file but then monitors the file for any new entries and displays those too.

While not part of rsyslogd, some Linux distributions also include the lastb tool. It displays the event messages from the /var/log/wtmp log file, used by many Linux distributions to log user logins.

Journaling with *systemd-journald*

The Systemd system services package includes the systemd-journald journal utility for logging. Notice that we called it a journal utility instead of a logging utility. The systemd-journald program uses its own method of storing event messages, completely different from how the syslog protocol specifies.

The following sections discuss how to use the systemd-journald program to track event messages on your Linux system.

Configuration

The systemd-journald service reads its configuration from the /etc/systemd/journald.conf configuration file. When you examine this file, you'll notice that there aren't any rules defined, only settings that control how the application works:

- The Storage setting determines how systemd-journald stores event messages. When the setting is set to auto, it will look for the /var/log/journal directory and store event messages there. If that directory doesn't exist, it stores the event messages in the temporary /run/log/journal directory, which is deleted when the system shuts down. You must manually create the /var/log/journal directory for the event messages to be stored permanently. If you set the Storage setting to persistent, systemd-journald will create the directory automatically. When set to volatile, it only stores event messages in the temporary directory.

- The Compress setting determines whether to compress the journal files.

- There are several file maintenance settings that control how much space the journal is allowed to use as well as how often to split journal files for archive, based on either time or file size.

- The ForwardToSyslog setting determines if systemd-journald should forward any received messages to a separate syslog program, such as rsyslogd, running on the system. This provides two layers of logging capabilities.

There are quite a few settings that allow you to customize exactly how systemd-journald works in your system. For a full list and explanation of all the settings, type **man journald.conf** at the command prompt.

Viewing Logs

The systemd-journald program doesn't store journal entries in text files. Instead it uses its own binary file format that works like a database. While this makes it a little harder to view journal entries, it does provide for quick searching for specific event entries.

The journalctl program is our interface to the journal files. The basic format for the journalctl command is as follows:

journalctl [*options*] [*matches*]

The *options* control data returned by the matches is displayed. Table 17.3 lists the options available.

TABLE 17.3   The journalctl command options

Option	Description
-a	Displays all data fields
-e	Jumps to the end of the journal and uses the pager utility to display the entries
-l	Displays all printable data fields
-n *number*	Shows the most recent *number* of journal entries
-r	Reverses the order of the journal entries in the output

The *matches* parameter defines what type of journal entries to display. Table 17.4 lists the matches available.

TABLE 17.4 The journalctl matches parameter

Match	Description
Fields	Matches specific fields in the journal
Kernel	Only displays kernel journal entries
PRIORITY=*value*	Matches only entries with the specified priority
_UID=*userid*	Matches only entries made by the specified user ID
_HOSTNAME=*host*	Matches only entries from the specified host
_TRANSPORT=*trans*	Matches only entries received by the specified transport method
_UDEV_SYSNAME=*dev*	Matches only entries received from the specified device
OBJECT_PID=*pid*	Matches only entries made by the specified application process ID

The journalctl command is great for when you are looking for specific event entries in the journal; it allows you to filter out events using the matches and determine how to display them using the options, as shown in Listing 17.3.

Listing 17.3: Output from the journalctl command

```
[rich@localhost ~]$ journalctl -r _TRANSPORT=kernel
-- Logs begin at Fri 2019-02-08 12:47:04 EST, end at...
Feb 08 12:48:36 localhost.localdomain kernel: TCP: lp registered
Feb 08 12:48:17 localhost.localdomain kernel: fuse init (API version 7.22)
Feb 08 12:47:43 localhost.localdomain kernel: virbr0: port 1(virbr0-nic)
Feb 08 12:47:43 localhost.localdomain kernel: IPv6: ADDRCONF(NETDEV_UP)
Feb 08 12:47:43 localhost.localdomain kernel: virbr0: port 1(virbr0-nic)
Feb 08 12:47:35 localhost.localdomain kernel: e1000: enp0s8 NIC Link is Up
Feb 08 12:47:32 localhost.localdomain kernel: IPv6: ADDRCONF(NETDEV_CHANGE)
Feb 08 12:47:32 localhost.localdomain kernel: ip_set: protocol 6
Feb 08 12:47:32 localhost.localdomain kernel: IPv6: ADDRCONF(NETDEV_UP)
...
```

That makes digging through journal files much easier!

Exercise 17.1 walks you through monitoring the system logs in real time and watching as you send a message to the logging facility on your Linux system.

EXERCISE 17.1

Creating a Log or Journal Entry

This exercise demonstrates how to create a log or journal entry and view that entry in both `rsyslogd` logs and `systemd-journald` journals.

1. Log into your Linux graphical desktop and open two new command prompt windows. If you're using virtual terminals, open two separate virtual terminal sessions.

2. Start monitoring the standard log file in one command prompt window or virtual terminal session. On Ubuntu systems, use **sudo tail -f /var/log/syslog**. For Red Hat–based systems such as Fedora, Rocky, and CentOS, use **sudo tail -f /var/log/messages**.

3. In the second command prompt window or virtual terminal session, create a log event by using the command **logger This is a test log entry**.

4. Observe the output in the first window or virtual terminal session. You should see the new log entry appear at the end of the log file appropriate for your system.

5. Display the end of the journal by using the command **journalctl -r**. You should see your log event message appear in the journal as well. Both Debian and Red Hat–based systems use `systemd-journald` but also forward event messages to the `rsyslogd` application, so you can often see events in both systems.

Summary

Logging events that occur on your Linux system or applications is crucial to being able to troubleshoot problems. The Linux system has adopted the syslog protocol method for handling event messages. The syslog protocol defines an event type, called the facility, and an event severity. This helps you determine which events are important to act on and which ones are just informational.

The `rsyslogd` logging application utilizes the syslog protocol to log system and application events. The `/etc/rsyslogd.conf` configuration file controls what events are logged and how they are logged. The `rsyslogd` application can log events to files, applications, remote hosts, terminals, and even directly to users.

The Linux Systemd services package also includes its own method for logging events called journaling. The `systemd-journald` application monitors the system and applications for all events and sends them to a special journal file. The operation of `systemd-journald` is controlled by the `/etc/systemd/journald` configuration file. You must use the `journalctl` application to read events stored in the journal file.

Exam Essentials

Describe the logging protocol used by most Linux logging applications.   The syslog protocol has become the de facto standard for most Linux logging applications. It identifies events using a facility code, which defines the event type, and a severity, which defines how important the event message is. The `sysklogd`, `syslogd-ng`, and `rsyslogd` applications all use the syslog protocol for managing system and application events in Linux.

Describe how the `rsyslogd` application directs events to specific locations.   The `rsyslogd` application uses the `/etc/rsyslogd.conf` configuration file to define rules for handling events. Each rule specifies a syslog facility and severity along with an action to take. Events that match the facility and have a priority equal to or higher than the severity defined are sent to the defined action. The action can be sending the event message to a log file, piping the message to an application, or sending the event message to a remote host or to a user on the system.

Explain how the Systemd service uses a different method for logging events.   The Systemd service package uses the `systemd-journald` application, which doesn't use the syslog protocol for logging events. Instead, `systemd-journald` creates its own binary journal files for storing event messages. The binary journal file is indexed to provide faster searching for events. The `journalctl` application provides the interface for sending search queries to the journal files and displaying the search results.

Review Questions

1. What protocol became a de facto standard in Linux for tracking system event messages?
    A. SMTP
    B. FTP
    C. NTP
    D. syslog
    E. `journalctl`

2. Nancy wants to write a `rsyslogd` rule that separates event messages coming from the system job scheduler to a separate log file. Which syslog facility keyword should she use?
    A. `cron`
    B. `user`
    C. `kern`
    D. `console`
    E. `local0`

3. What syslog severity level has the highest priority ranking in `rsyslogd`?
    A. `crit`
    B. `alert`
    C. `emerg`
    D. `notice`
    E. `err`

4. What syslog severity level represents normal but significant condition messages?
    A. `crit`
    B. `notice`
    C. `info`
    D. `alert`
    E. `local0`

5. What syslog application is known for its rocket-fast speed?
    A. `syslogd`
    B. `syslog-ng`
    C. `systemd-journald`
    D. `klogd`
    E. `rsyslogd`

6. What configuration file does the `rsyslogd` application use by default?

   A. `rsyslog.conf`

   B. `journald.conf`

   C. `syslogd.conf`

   D. `rsyslog.d`

   E. `syslog.d`

7. James needs to log all kernel messages that have a severity level of warning or higher to a separate log file. What facility and priority setting should he use?

   A. `kern.=warn`

   B. `kern.*`

   C. `*.info`

   D. `kern.warn`

   E. `kern.alert`

8. Barbara wants to ensure that the journal log files will be saved after the next reboot of her Linux system. What `systemd-journald` configuration setting should she use?

   A. `Storage=auto`

   B. `Storage=persistent`

   C. `ForwardToSyslog=on`

   D. `Storage=volatile`

   E. `ForwardToSyslog=off`

9. Katie wants to display the most recent entries in the journal log on her Linux system. What `journalctl` option should she use?

   A. `-a`

   B. `-l`

   C. `-r`

   D. `-e`

   E. `-n`

10. Tony is trying to troubleshoot errors produced by an application on his Linux system but has to dig through lots of entries in the journal log file to find them. What `journalctl` match option would help him by only displaying journal entries related to the specific application?

    A. `OBJECT_PID`

    B. `Kernel`

    C. `_TRANSPORT`

    D. `_UID`

    E. `_UDEV`

Chapter
18

Overseeing
Linux Firewalls

✓ **Objective 2.3: Given a scenario, implement and
configure firewalls**

A firewall in a building is a fireproof wall that helps to prevent fire from spreading throughout the structure. In computer security, *firewalls* prevent the spread of unwanted, unauthorized, or malicious network traffic.

Firewalls are implemented in different forms. You can provide layered security by using multiple firewall structures. A firewall is either a hardware device or a software application, network-based or host-based, and a network-layer or application-layer filter. In this chapter, we'll take a look at software application firewalls that are host-based and that operate at the Network layer.

Providing Access Control

Firewalls provide access control to your system or network. An *access control list (ACL)* implemented within a firewall identifies which network packets are allowed in or out. This is often referred to as *packet filtering*.

Don't confuse a firewall ACL with Linux file and directory ACLs, which were covered in Chapter 15, "Applying Ownership and Permissions." Commands such as setfacl and getfacl are *not* associated with firewalls.

A firewall ACL identifies a network packet by reviewing its control information along with other network data. This may include the following information:

- Source address
- Destination address
- Network protocol
- Inbound port
- Outbound port
- Network state

Once a network packet is identified, the firewall's ACL rules also determine what happens to that packet. The rules typically include the following actions:

- Accept
- Reject

- Drop
- Log

It's important to distinguish between reject and drop. A reject action typically includes a message sent back to the application sending the packet, whereas a drop action does not. By dropping the network packet, the Linux system does not provide any information to a potentially malicious outside attacker.

 Real World Scenario

Firewall Logs

Logging firewall traffic is critical. Your organization's requirements dictate the amount of data to track. If your company must comply with regulations, such as the Health Insurance Portability and Accountability Act (HIPAA) or the Payment Card Industry Data Security Standard (PCI DSS), the log data volume increases.

Besides compliance issues, firewall logs can be monitored, provide alerts, and/or take needed actions to protect a system. These logs help determine if an attack is taking place. Software utilities, such as Graylog's open source product (www.graylog.com), allow you to process firewall logs in real time.

Managing your firewall logs is a complex issue. The *NIST Special Publication 800-92, Guide to Computer Security Log Management*, is a helpful publication that can guide your organization's analysis requirements and determine what appropriate steps to take.

On Linux, the /etc/services file documents the different standard application services names and their corresponding port numbers and protocols as well as any aliases. This information is standardized by the Internet Assigned Numbers Authority (IANA). This service catalog is used by various utilities such as the netstat network tool, and firewall applications, such as UFW, to determine the appropriate port and protocol information for a particular service.

Each non-comment record in the /etc/services file uses the following syntax:

ServiceName PortNumber/ProtocolName [Aliases]

By default port numbers 1 through 1023 are *privileged ports*. Only a super user can run a service on a privileged port. Therefore, these designated ports help prevent malicious users from setting up fake services on them.

> The /etc/services file is not a configuration file. Most services have configuration files, which allow you to change their default port if desired. For example, the OpenSSH configuration file, /etc/ssh/sshd_config, contains the Port directive, which is set to 22 by default, and you can modify it, if needed.

Firewalls can operate in either a stateful or stateless manner. There are pros and cons to both technologies:

Stateless   This technology is the older of the two. In this mode, the firewall focuses only on individual packets. The firewall views each packet's control information and decides what to do with the packet based on the defined ACL rules. This simplicity makes stateless firewalls fast.

However, because a stateless firewall does not track information such as active network connections, network status, data flows, and traffic patterns, it is vulnerable to certain malicious activity. This includes network attacks that spread themselves among multiple packets. In addition, a stateless firewall's ACL rules are static. If an administrator changes them, the firewall software typically must be restarted.

Stateful   This technology is the younger of the two. While it also employs packet filtering, it does not treat packets as individuals, but instead as a team. It tracks active network connections, such as TCP and UDP, and keeps an eye on network status. A stateful firewall determines if packets have fragmented. Thus, it is not vulnerable to attacks that spread themselves among multiple packets.

Stateful firewalls keep network information in memory. For example, when a TCP connection's first packet comes into a stateful firewall's view, the firewall monitors the connection process and tracks its states, such as SYN-SENT, SYN-RECEIVED, and ESTABLISHED. Once the connection is made, the firewall creates a record in its memory-based connection table. It uses this record for tracking the network connection. Thus, instead of just using ACL rules for that connection's packets, it employs the connection table as well. This allows it to make faster decisions for established connections' individual packets.

While the memory table allows faster access for established connections, building the table's record for new connections is slower. In addition, this makes the stateful firewall more vulnerable to DDoS attacks than stateless ones.

Looking at Firewall Technologies

Embedded in the Linux kernel is netfilter. This software provides code hooks into the kernel, which allow other packages to implement firewall technologies. From a functionality standpoint, think of netfilter as a network sniffer that is planted in the Linux kernel and offers up packet filtering services.

The organization that maintains `netfilter` provides an informational website at `https://netfilter.org`. They also manage the `iptables` firewall software, which employs `netfilter`.

Another firewall technology that uses `netfilter` is `firewalld`. The newer `firewalld` service allows modified filter rules to be updated dynamically with no need to restart the service. For Red Hat–based distributions, if you configure your network environment during the installation it will install the `firewalld` service by default.

Debian-based distributions use yet another firewall service that utilizes `netfilter`: the Uncomplicated Firewall (UFW). This firewall configuration tool is an interface to the `netfilter` firewall that provides easier rule management.

Although `firewalld` and UFW services provide easy-to-use interfaces to the `netfilter` firewall, they have an additional layer that can slow down the packet filtering process. While this is fine for most server environments, if you're using Linux as a dedicated network firewall, speed is of the essence. The nftable service provides low-level access to the `netfilter` firewall similar to `iptables` but is not quite as complicated as `iptables`.

The following sections discuss each of these four firewall services.

Familiarizing Yourself with *firewalld*

The `firewalld` service provides packet filtering and user interfaces for the GUI environment and the command line. It offers support for IPv4 as well as IPv6, and much more. You can find additional details from the `firewalld` official website at `www.firewalld.org`.

This firewall service is called the dynamic firewall daemon because you can change an ACL rule without needing to restart the service. The rules are loaded instantaneously via its D-Bus interface.

 D-Bus is the message bus daemon. It provides communication services between any two applications on a systemwide or per-session basis. It can also register to be notified of events, making it a powerful communication tool. The `firewalld` service employs a dbus Python library module to integrate D-Bus services.

A central part of `firewalld` is *zones*. Network traffic is grouped into a predefined rule set, or zone. Each zone has a configuration file that defines this rule set, also called a *trust level*. The traffic grouping can be a system's network interface or a source address range, which identifies traffic from other systems. Each network connection can be a member of only one zone at a time.

By default, `firewalld` zone configuration files are stored in the `/usr/lib/firewalld/zones/` directory. Customized or user-created zone configuration files are stored in the `/etc/firewalld/zones/` directory. Table 18.1 shows the predefined zones on a system employing `firewalld`. The zones are listed in the order of the least trusted to the most trusted network connections.

TABLE 18.1 The predefined firewalld zones

Name	Description
drop	Drops all incoming network packets. Allows only outbound network connections.
block	Accepts only network connections that originated on the system. Rejects incoming network packets and sends an icmp-host-prohibited or icmp6-adm-prohibited message back.
public	Accepts only selected incoming network connections. Typically used in a public setting, where other systems on the network are not trusted.
external	Performs similar to public but is typically used on external networks, when masquerading is enabled for the local systems.
dmz	Performs similar to public but is used in a location's demilitarized zone, which is publicly accessible and has limited access to the internal network.
work	Accepts only selected incoming network connections. Typically used in a work setting, where other systems on the network are mostly trusted.
home	Performs similar to work but is used in a home setting, where other systems on the network are mostly trusted.
internal	Performs similar to work but is typically used on internal networks, where other systems on the network are mostly trusted.
trusted	Accepts all network connections.

The firewall-cmd utility allows you to view and interact with various firewalld configuration settings. For example, to see all the predefined zones on a system, use the --get-zones option, as shown on a Rocky Linux distribution in Listing 18.1.

Listing 18.1: Viewing the predefined zones with the firewall-cmd command

```
$ firewall-cmd --get-zones
block dmz drop external home internal public trusted work
$
$ ls /usr/lib/firewalld/zones
block.xml   drop.xml       home.xml       public.xml   work.xml
dmz.xml     external.xml   internal.xml   trusted.xml
$
```

The firewalld configuration files use Extensible Markup Language (XML). Though you may be tempted to edit these files directly, it is better to employ the firewalld utilities to modify and manage the firewall configuration.

NetworkManager is also integrated with firewalld. Thus, when a new network device is added via NetworkManager, firewalld automatically assigns it to the *default zone*. The default zone is typically preset to the public zone, but it can be customized using the firewall-cmd utility. You can view the system's current default zone as shown in Listing 18.2.

Listing 18.2: Viewing the default zone with the firewall-cmd command

```
$ firewall-cmd --get-default-zone
public
$
```

If you need a different default zone, you can alter it. Just use super user privileges and employ the --set-default-zone=zone option.

You can also view all the currently active zones as well as their traffic grouping. Just employ the --get-active-zones switch as shown in Listing 18.3.

Listing 18.3: Viewing the active zones with the firewall-cmd command

```
$ firewall-cmd --get-active-zones
public
  interfaces: enp0s8
$
```

If desired, you can use the graphical firewalld configuration utility, firewall-config, instead of using the command-line utility. Typically it is easy to find this utility on firewalld systems by typing **firewall** into the GUI's search box.

Besides zones, firewalld also employs *services*. A service is a predefined configuration set for a particular offered system service, such as DNS. The configuration information may contain items such as a list of ports, protocols, and so on. For example, the DNS service configuration set denotes that DNS uses both the TCP and UDP protocols on port number 53. Listing 18.4 shows a snipped listing of the various predefined services on a Rocky Linux distro.

Listing 18.4: Viewing the predefined services with the `firewall-cmd` command

```
$ firewall-cmd --get-services
[...]
amanda-client amanda-k5-client bacula bacula-client
[...]
dhcp dhcpv6 dhcpv6-client dns docker-registry
[...]
$
$ ls -1 /usr/lib/firewalld/services
amanda-client.xml
amanda-k5-client.xml
bacula-client.xml
bacula.xml
[...]
dhcp.xml
dns.xml
[...]
$
```

Using a `firewalld` service allows easier firewall configurations for a particular offered system service, because you can simply assign them to a zone. An example is shown in Listing 18.5.

Listing 18.5: Assigning the DNS service to the dmz zone

```
# firewall-cmd --add-service=dns --zone=dmz
success
#
# firewall-cmd --list-services --zone=dmz
ssh dns
#
```

> In an emergency situation, you can quickly disable all network traffic via `firewalld`. Use super user privileges and issue the command **firewall-cmd --panic-on** at the command line. Once things have calmed down, you can re-enable network traffic by typing **firewall-cmd --panic-off**.

When you modify the `firewalld` configuration, by default you modify the *runtime* environment. The runtime environment is the configuration actively employed by the `firewalld` service.

The other `firewalld` environment is the *permanent* environment. This environment is the firewall configuration stored within the configuration files. It is loaded when the system boots (or when `firewalld` is restarted or reloaded) and becomes the active runtime environment.

Both of these `firewalld` environments have their place. The permanent environment is useful for production, whereas the runtime configuration is useful for testing firewall setting changes.

If you have tested firewall configuration changes in the runtime environment and wish to make them permanent, it is easily done. Just issue the `firewall-cmd --runtime-to-permanent` command using super user privileges. If you feel confident that your runtime environment configuration modifications are correct, you can tack on the `--permanent` option to the `firewall-cmd` command. This adds the changes to both the runtime and permanent environment at the same time. See the man pages for the `firewall-cmd` command for more information.

> The `iptables` service should not run alongside `firewalld`. This is easily shown on a systemd system. Use super user privileges and type the **`systemctl show --property=Conflicts firewalld`** command. You will see `iptables.service` listed in the output as a conflict. Also, while the `iptables` command is still available on many `firewalld` systems, it should not be employed. Instead of the `iptables` command, use either the `firewall-cmd` or `firewall-config` utility for setting up and managing your firewall configuration. If you just cannot give up the past, use the `firewall-cmd` command with its `--direct` switch. This allows you to employ the `firewalld` direct interface and use commands similar to `iptables` commands. Documentation notes that the direct interface should be used only as a last resort.

Investigating *iptables*

The `iptables` firewall service uses a series process called *chains* to handle network packets that enter the system. The chains determine the path each packet takes as it enters the Linux system to reach the appropriate application. As an application sends packets back out to the network to remote clients, these chains are also involved. Figure 18.1 shows different chains involved with processing network packets on a Linux system.

Notice in Figure 18.1 that there are five separate chains to process packets:

FIGURE 18.1   The packet processing chain

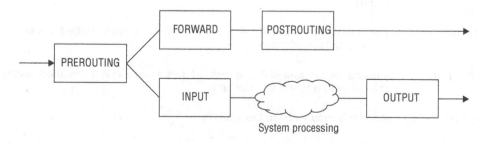

- PREROUTING handles packets before the routing decision process.
- INPUT handles packets destined for the local system.
- FORWARD handles packets being forwarded to a remote system.
- POSTROUTING handles packets being sent to remote systems, after the forward filter.
- OUTPUT handles packets output from the local system.

Each chain contains *tables* that define rules for handling the packets. There are five table types:

- filter applies rules to allow or block packets from exiting the chain.
- mangle applies rules to change features of the packets before they exit the chain.
- nat applies rules to change the addresses of the packets before they exit the chain.
- raw applies a NOTRACK setting on packets that are not to be tracked.
- security applies mandatory access control rules.

Implementing network address translation (NAT) requires using the nat table to alter the packets' address in the OUTPUT chain. Implementing a firewall is a little trickier, as you apply filter tables to the INPUT, OUTPUT, and FORWARD chains in the process. This provides multiple locations in the process to block packets.

Each chain also has a *policy* value. The policy entry defines how a packet is handled by default for the chain, when no rules apply to the packet. There are two different policy values:

- ACCEPT: Pass the packet along to the next chain.
- DROP: Don't pass the packet to the next chain.

The tool you use to view and alter the chains and filters in the iptables service is the iptables command. Table 18.2 shows the commonly used iptables command-line options.

TABLE 18.2 The iptables command's commonly used options

Option	Description
-L [*chain*]	Lists the rules in this *chain*. If *chain* is not specified, list all rules in all chains.
-S [*chain*]	Lists the rules' details in this *chain*. If *chain* is not specified, list all rules' details in all chains.
[-t *table*]	Applies the command to this *table*. If -t *table* is not specified, apply the command to the filter table.
-A *chain rule*	Adds this new *rule* to this *chain*.

Option	Description
-I *chain index rule*	Inserts this new *rule* to this *chain* at this *index* location.
-D *chain rule*	Deletes this *rule* from this *chain*.
-R *chain index rule*	Removes this *rule* from this *chain* at this *index* location.
-F [*chain*]	Removes (flush) all rules from this *chain*. If *chain* is not specified, remove all rules from all chains.
-P *chain policy*	Defines this default *policy* for this *chain*.

To quickly view the filter table's chains and rules, use super user privileges and the -L option on the iptables command. A snipped example on a Fedora system is shown in Listing 18.6.

Listing 18.6: Viewing the filter table's chains and rules

```
$ sudo iptables -L
Chain INPUT (policy ACCEPT)
target     prot opt source               destination
ACCEPT     udp  --  anywhere             anywhere             udp dpt:domain
[...]
Chain OUTPUT (policy ACCEPT)
target     prot opt source               destination
ACCEPT     udp  --  anywhere             anywhere             udp dpt:bootpc
OUTPUT_direct  all  --  anywhere         anywhere
$
```

Notice that the -t filter option is not needed in this case. This is because the iptables command applies commands to the filter table by default.

> Keep in mind that you may see many more chains than the basic five listed in Figure 18.1. This is especially true on a firewalld system. However, on a firewalld system, it is best to employ the firewall-cmd command instead for accurate and detailed information.

If you want to block all packets leaving your Linux system, you would just change the default OUTPUT chain to a DROP policy. Be careful here, because if you are using ssh to enter your system, this will cause your connection packets to be dropped as well! Listing 18.7

shows a snipped example of blocking all outbound packets on a Fedora system. Notice how the ping command operation is no longer permitted after this modification.

Listing 18.7 Employing the iptables command to drop all outbound packets

```
$ sudo iptables -P OUTPUT DROP
$
$ ping -c 3 192.168.0.105
PING 192.168.0.105 (192.168.0.105) 56(84) bytes of data.
ping: sendmsg: Operation not permitted
[...]
$ sudo iptables -P OUTPUT ACCEPT
$
$ ping -c 3 192.168.0.105
PING 192.168.0.105 (192.168.0.105) 56(84) bytes of data.
64 bytes from 192.168.0.105: icmp_seq=1 ttl=64 time=0.062 ms
[...]
$
```

In Listing 18.7, after the default OUTPUT chain is changed back to an ACCEPT policy, the ping packets are permitted.

> The iptables service firewall is managed by the iptables command only for IPv4 packets. If you have IPv6 packets traversing your network, you also have to employ the ip6tables command.

To change chain rules, you need to use some additional command-line options in the iptables command. These rule options are shown in Table 18.3.

TABLE 18.3   The iptables command's commonly used chain options

Option	Description
-d *address*	Applies rule only to packets with this destination *address*
-s *address*	Applies rule only to packets with this source *address*
-i *name*	Applies rule only to packets coming in through the *name* network interface
-o *name*	Applies rule only to packets going out through the *name* network interface
-p *protocol*	Applies rule only to packets using this *protocol*, such as tcp, udp, or icmp
-j *target*	Applies this *target* action (the rule) to the selected packets

The -j option in Table 18.3 needs a little more explanation. This is the actual rule applied to the identified packets. The most commonly used different *target* values are as follows:

- ACCEPT: Pass the packet along to the next chain.
- DROP: Don't pass the packet to the next chain.
- REJECT: Don't pass the packet, and send a reject notice to the sender.

Putting a rule together and adding it to a chain is a little tricky, so an example will help. In snipped Listing 18.8, an Ubuntu system at IP address 192.168.0.104 is shown successfully sending a ping to a remote Fedora system, whose IP address is 192.168.0.105.

Listing 18.8: Sending a ping to a remote system successfully

```
$ ip addr show | grep 192.168.0.104
    inet 192.168.0.104/24 brd 192.168.0.255 [...] enp0s8
$
$ ping -c 1 192.168.0.105
PING 192.168.0.105 (192.168.0.105) 56(84) bytes of data.
64 bytes from 192.168.0.105: icmp_seq=1 ttl=64 time=0.305 ms

--- 192.168.0.105 ping statistics ---
1 packets transmitted, 1 received, 0% packet loss, time 0ms
rtt min/avg/max/mdev = 0.305/0.305/0.305/0.000 ms
$
```

Now on the Fedora system, using super user privileges, the following command is issued:

```
sudo iptables -I INPUT 1 -s 192.168.0.104 -j REJECT
```

This new rule will be inserted (-I) into the INPUT chain's filter table at index 1 (first rule in the chain). Any packets coming from the source (-s) address of 192.168.0.104 (the Ubuntu system) will be rejected (REJECT). Now that this rule is in place, when the Ubuntu system tries to ping the Fedora system, it will fail, as shown in snipped Listing 18.9.

Listing 18.9: Blocking a ping to a remote system that blocks the packets

```
$ ping -c 1 192.168.0.105
PING 192.168.0.105 (192.168.0.105) 56(84) bytes of data.
From 192.168.0.105 icmp_seq=1 Destination Port Unreachable

--- 192.168.0.105 ping statistics ---
1 packets transmitted, 0 received, +1 errors, 100% packet loss, time 0ms

$
```

You aren't stuck with the iptables' default chains—you can actually create your own. This is especially helpful if you'd like to employ the LOG target to create log files of particular packets. Look in the man pages for iptables as well as iptables-extensions for more details.

Although you don't need to reload the iptables service to have new or modified rules take effect, these rules have no *persistency*. In other words, if the system was rebooted or the iptables service restarted, you would lose all those new or modified ACL rules.

As long as the iptables service is enabled to start at system boot, Red Hat and Red Hat–based distributions, such as Fedora and Rocky Linux, will automatically load iptables rules stored in these files:

- IPv4 rules: /etc/sysconfig/iptables
- IPv6 rules: /etc/sysconfig/ip6tables

Debian and Debian-based distributions, such as Ubuntu, need an additional software package, iptables-persistent, installed and enabled. The files this package uses to load persistent rules are as follows:

- IPv4 rules: /etc/iptables/rules.v4
- IPv6 rules: /etc/iptables/rules.v6

You won't find these rule files for iptables service on the distribution versions recommended for this book because they use newer firewall technologies. If desired, you can use Fedora version 20 or older to play with these iptables' files.

If you need to save the current iptables rules, employ the iptables-save command. This utility needs its output redirected to a file because by default, it sends the rules to STDOUT.

To restore saved iptables rules, employ the iptables-restore command. This utility needs its input redirected from a file. So, if you were testing an ACL change that was not working well, you could quickly restore the iptables' original rules. On an older Fedora distribution, you use super user privileges and issue the iptables-restore < /etc/sysconfig/iptables command to restore all the original IPv4 rules.

Exploring *nftables*

You may have noticed that the format to create rules in iptables can often get somewhat complicated, especially compared to tools like firewalld. A good compromise is the nftables service.

The nftables service provides low-level access to the netfilter chains similar to iptables, making it extremely efficient and fast. However, the command syntax for building rules in nftables has been simplified, making it easier to work with.

The nftables service utilizes the same concept of tables, chains, policies, and rules as iptables. You can list the existing tables defined by using the list option of the nft command, as shown in Listing 18.10.

Listing 18.10: Listing tables in nftables

```
$ sudo nft list tables
table ip filter
table ip6 filter
table bridge filter
table ip security
table ip raw
table ip mangle
table ip nat
table ip6 security
table ip6 raw
table ip6 mangle
table ip6 nat
table bridge nat
table inet firewalld
table ip firewalld
table ip6 firewalld
$
```

Notice in Listing 18.10 that in a Red Hat system the firewalld service creates its own tables in netfilter, which nftables detects. To create a new table, use the add table option in nft, as shown in Listing 18.11.

Listing 18.11: Creating a new table using nftables

```
$ sudo nft add table ip rich
$ sudo nft list tables ip
table ip filter
table ip security
table ip raw
table ip mangle
table ip nat
table ip firewalld
table ip rich
$ sudo nft list table ip rich
table ip rich {
}
$
```

The add command created the table rich, but as Listing 18.11 shows, the table is empty by default.

After you create a table, the next step is to create chains, which will contain the rules you define for the firewall definitions. As you would expect, the add chain option does this. The basic format for the add chain option looks like this:

nft add chain [*family*] *table_name* *chain_name* { type *type* hook
 hook priority *value* \; [policy *policy* \;] [comment \"*text
comment*\" \;] }

The type value can be filter, router, or nat (the same as in iptables), and the hook value can be prerouting, input, forward, output, or postrouting (again the same as in iptables). The priority value determines the order in which the chain is processed; lower priority values are processed first. The policy value can be either accept or drop. Listing 18.12 shows an example of creating a chain.

Listing 18.12: Creating a new chain using nftables

```
$ sudo nft 'add chain ip rich test { type filter hook input
 priority 0; policy drop; }'
$ sudo nft list table ip rich
table ip rich {
    chain test {
        type filter hook input priority filter; policy drop;
    }
}
$
```

As seen in Listing 18.12, you must place single quotes around the add chain command. The default policy for this chain is set to drop, so all incoming packets will be dropped, unless they match a rule that says otherwise.

Once you have a chain created, you can define rules to apply to the chain using the add rule option. The format for rules is one of the selling points of nftables. The format uses simple syntax, similar to that used by the popular tcpdump monitoring program. Listing 18.13 shows an example of adding a rule for allowing SSH traffic.

Listing 18.13: Adding a new rule using nftables

```
$ sudo nft 'add rule ip rich test tcp dport ssh accept'
$ sudo nft list table ip rich
table ip rich {
    chain test {
        type filter hook input priority filter; policy drop;
        tcp dport 22 accept
    }
}
$
```

Listing 18.13 shows that the rule has been added to the test chain. You can then create additional rules in the same chain, or create additional chains with different priorities to contain additional rules.

To remove a rule from a table, use the flush table option:

```
$ sudo nft flush table rich
$ sudo nft list table ip rich
table ip rich {
    chain test {
        type filter hook input priority filter; policy drop;
    }
}
$
```

To remove a chain from a table use the delete chain option. To remove an entire table, use the delete table option:

```
$ sudo nft delete table ip rich
$ sudo nft list tables ip
table ip filter
table ip security
table ip raw
table ip mangle
table ip nat
table ip firewalld
$
```

WARNING If you decide to use nftables for your firewall, it's advisable to disable any other firewall software, such as iptables, firewalld, or ufw. Since they all use the same netfilter service, the rules in each firewall configuration could conflict—or at least make things extremely complicated when trying to sort out why things are being blocked or allowed.

Understanding UFW

The Uncomplicated Firewall (UFW) is the default firewall service on Ubuntu distributions. It is configured with the ufw command-line utility or Gufw for the GUI.

By default, the UFW service is disabled. You start the service and set it to start at boot time by using the `sudo ufw enable` command, but do not use a system initialization tool, such as `systemctl`. This is because the firewall services covered here are not traditional SysV or systemd services but instead are interface services for the `netfilter` firewall. Thus, if you choose to start UFW, be aware that neither the `iptables` nor the `firewalld` service can be running.

There are several UFW commands that let you control the firewall's state as well as view its status. These commands are shown in Table 18.4. Each one requires super user privileges.

TABLE 18.4   The `ufw` commands to control state and view status

Command	Description
`ufw enable`	Starts the UFW firewall and enables it to start at system boot
`ufw disable`	Stops the UFW firewall and disables it from starting at system boot
`ufw reset`	Disables the UFW firewall and resets it to installation defaults
`ufw reload`	Reloads the UFW firewall
`ufw status`	Displays the UFW firewall's current state

To view the current state of the UFW service, use `sudo ufw status verbose` if you need more information than just `status` provides. Enabling the UFW firewall service and viewing its current state is shown snipped in Listing 18.14.

Listing 18.14 Enabling UFW and viewing its status

```
$ sudo ufw enable
[...]
Firewall is active and enabled on system startup
$
$ sudo ufw status verbose
Status: active
Logging: on (low)
Default: deny (incoming), allow (outgoing), disabled (routed)
New profiles: skip
$
```

Viewing the verbose status of the UFW firewall provides information that helps to explain its configuration:

- `Status`: UFW service is running and will start on system boot (`active`), or the services stopped and a system boot does not change this (`disabled`).

- `Logging`: The service's logging feature can be set to `off`; log all blocked packets (`low`), which is the default; log all blocked, invalid, no-policy-match, and new connection packets (`medium`) with rate limiting; log medium-log-level packets and all other packets (`high`) with rate limiting; and log everything with no rate limits (`full`).

- `Default`: Shows the default policy for `incoming`, `outgoing`, and `routed` packets, which can be set to either `allow` the packet, drop (`deny`) the packet, or `reject` the packet and send a rejection message back.

- `New profiles`: Shows the default policy for automatically loading new profiles into the firewall, which can be set to ACCEPT, DROP, REJECT, or SKIP, where ACCEPT is considered a security risk.

The various default UFW policies are stored in the `/etc/default/ufw` configuration file. When first installed, these settings allow all outgoing connections and block all incoming connections. You can make modifications to the firewall as needed using the `ufw` command and its various arguments. A few common arguments are shown in Table 18.5.

TABLE 18.5 The `ufw` command's commonly used arguments

Argument	Description
`allow` *Identifiers*	Sets the rule identified by *Identifiers* to `allow` packets
`deny` *Identifiers*	Sets the rule identified by *Identifiers* to deny (drop) packets
`reject` *Identifiers*	Sets the rule identified by *Identifiers* to `reject` packets
`delete` *RULE* | *NUM*	Deletes the rule identified by *RULE* or *NUM*
`insert` *NUM RULE*	Inserts the *RULE* at index *NUM*
`default` *POLICY DIRECTION*	Modifies the default *DIRECTION* policy, where *POLICY* is `allow`, `deny`, or `reject`, and *direction* is `incoming`, `outgoing`, or `routed`
`logging` *LEVEL*	Sets the logging level, where *LEVEL* is on, `off`, low (default), `medium`, `high`, or `full`

When creating new UFW rules, you can use either *simple* or *full syntax*. Simple syntax involves designating the rule using only the port number or its service name. You can also add the protocol to the port number, as shown in Listing 18.15.

Listing 18.15: Using ufw simple syntax to add an ACL rule

```
$ sudo ufw allow 22/tcp
Rule added
Rule added (v6)
$
$ sudo ufw status
Status: active

To                      Action      From
--                      ------      ----
22/tcp                  ALLOW       Anywhere
22/tcp (v6)             ALLOW       Anywhere (v6)

$
```

Notice that when the rule is added, that two rules were applied—one for IPv4 and one for IPv6 packets. With full syntax, there are many options. For example, you can employ settings such as those listed in Table 18.6.

TABLE 18.6 The ufw command's full syntax common settings

Setting	Description
comment "*string*"	Displays this comment for rejected traffic
in	Applies rule only to incoming traffic
out	Applies rule only to outgoing traffic
proto *protocol*	Applies rule to this *protocol*
port *port#*	Applies rule to this *port#*
from *source*	Applies rule to traffic from this *source*, which may be a single IP address, subnet, or any traffic
on *interface*	Applies rule to traffic on this network *interface*
to *destination*	Applies rule to traffic going to this *destination*, which may be a single IP address, subnet, or any traffic

You *do not* need to issue the **ufw reload** command after you add, delete, or modify a rule. The change automatically takes effect.

You can specify a rule via a service name (e.g., telnet) with the ufw command. When doing this, ufw checks the /etc/services file to determine the appropriate port and protocol information for that service.

An example of using the UFW full syntax is shown in Listing 18.16. In this case, network packets coming from any systems in the 192.168.0.0 class C subnet will be denied access to port 80 on this system.

Listing 18.16: Using ufw full syntax to add an ACL rule

```
$ sudo ufw deny from 192.168.0.0/24 to any port 80
Rule added
$
$ sudo ufw show added
Added user rules (see 'ufw status' for running firewall):
ufw allow 22/tcp
ufw deny from 192.168.0.0/24 to any port 80
$$
```

View any user-added rules using the ufw show added command as shown in Listing 18.16. The UFW rules are stored in the /etc/ufw/ directory, and user-added rules are placed into the user.rules file within that directory, as shown in Listing 18.17.

Listing 18.17: Displaying the /etc/ufw/ directory's contents

```
$ ls /etc/ufw/
after6.rules    applications.d    before.rules    user6.rules
after.init      before6.rules     sysctl.conf     user.rules
after.rules     before.init       ufw.conf
$
```

If you need to delete a rule, it's easiest to do so by the rule number. First view the rules via their numbers and then employ the ufw delete command, as shown in Listing 18.18.

Listing 18.18: Deleting a rule via its number

```
$ sudo ufw status numbered
Status: active

     To                        Action      From
     --                        ------      ----
[ 1] 22/tcp                    ALLOW IN    Anywhere
[ 2] 80                        DENY IN     192.168.0.0/24
```

```
[ 3] 22/tcp (v6)                   ALLOW IN    Anywhere (v6)

$
$ sudo ufw delete 2
Deleting:
 deny from 192.168.0.0/24 to any port 80
Proceed with operation (y|n)? y
Rule deleted
$
```

UFW uses *profiles* for common applications and daemons. These profiles are stored in the /etc/ufw/applications.d/ directory. Use the ufw app list command to see the currently available UFW application profiles. An example is shown snipped in Listing 18.19.

Listing 18.19: Viewing the available UFW application profiles

```
$ sudo ufw app list
Available applications:
  CUPS
  OpenSSH
$
$ sudo ufw app info OpenSSH
Profile: OpenSSH
Title: Secure shell server, an rshd replacement
Description: OpenSSH is a free implementation[...]

Port:
  22/tcp
$
```

You can also view detailed information on these profiles, as you can also see in Listing 18.19. The profiles not only provide application documentation but also allow you to modify the ports and protocols used by the applications as well as create nontypical application profiles for your system's needs.

> **WARNING** Do not modify the profiles in the /etc/ufw/applications.d/ directory. Instead, create a subdirectory there and name it *custom.d*. This will prevent your custom profiles from being overwritten during UFW software package updates. See the ufw man pages for more details on profile specifications.

Once you have created a new profile or updated an old one, use the ufw app update all command to update UFW on the profile changes. Also, when using a profile to specify a rule's ports and protocols, you must employ app instead of port in your syntax for creating new rules.

Forwarding IP Packets

There is a packet-forwarding feature in Linux. This feature is used for various purposes, such as allowing Linux to forward packets to a remote host or for IP masquerading. You must enable packet forwarding in the kernel prior to employing it. To enable that feature, just set the `ip_forward` entry for IPv4 or the `forwarding` entry for IPv6. You can do that with the `sysctl` command:

```
sudo sysctl -w net.ipv4.ip_forward=1
sudo sysctl -w net.ipv6.conf.all.forwarding=1
```

You can check the current kernel values by using the `cat` command in the `/proc` file-system entries. If the files contain the number 1, the feature is enabled, as shown in Listing 18.20, and if it is disabled, the files will contain the number 0.

Listing 18.20: Viewing the packet forwarding files

```
$ cat /proc/sys/net/ipv4/ip_forward
1
$ cat /proc/sys/net/ipv6/conf/all/forwarding
1
$
```

Once those kernel values are set, your Linux system is able to forward traffic from one network interface to another network interface. If there are multiple network interfaces on the Linux system, it knows which interface to use to send traffic to remote hosts via the routing table. Routing tables were covered in Chapter 7, "Configuring Network Connections."

Dynamically Setting Rules

In protecting your system, it helps to have software that monitors the network and applications running on the system, looking for suspicious behavior. These applications are called *intrusion detection systems (IDSs)*. Some IDS applications allow you to dynamically change rules so that these attacks are blocked. Two of those IDS programs are DenyHosts and Fail2Ban.

Another helpful utility in your firewall toolbelt is one that allows you to quickly change rules without having to type out long IP addresses or MAC addresses over and over again. An IPset can help with this issue.

DenyHosts

The DenyHosts application is a Python script, which helps protect against brute-force attacks coming through OpenSSH. The script can be run as a service or as a `cron` job.

It monitors sshd log messages in the distribution's authentication log files, such as /var/log/secure and /var/log/auth.log. If it sees repeated failed authentication attempts from the same host, it blocks the IP address via the /etc/hosts.deny file.

To configure DenyHosts you modify its /etc/denyhosts.conf file. You also need to have the TCP Wrappers files, /etc/hosts.allow and /etc/hosts.deny, ready to go.

DenyHosts works only with IPv4 OpenSSH traffic. For all others, you'll have to employ a different utility. Also, be aware that some distro repositories claim DenyHosts is no longer being developed. Therefore, install and use with caution.

Fail2Ban

The Fail2Ban service also monitors system logs, looking for repeated failures from the same host. If it detects a problem, Fail2Ban can block the IP address of the offending host from accessing your system. While DenyHosts works only with TCP Wrappers, Fail2Ban can work with TCP Wrappers, iptables, firewalld, and so on.

The fail2ban-client program monitors both system and application logs, looking for problems. It monitors common system log files such as the /var/log/pwdfail and /var/log/auth.log log files, looking for multiple failed login attempts. When it detects a user account that has too many failed login attempts, it blocks access from the host the user account was attempting to log in from.

A great feature of Fail2Ban is that it can also monitor individual application log files, such as the /var/log/apache/error.log log file for the Apache web server. Just as with the system log files, if Fail2Ban detects too many connection attempts or errors coming from the same remote host, it will block access from that host.

The /etc/fail2ban/jail.conf file contains the Fail2Ban configuration. It defines the applications to monitor, where their log files are located, and what actions to take if it detects a problem.

The downside to using Fail2Ban is that it can have false positives that detect a problem when there really isn't one. This can cause it to block a valid client from accessing the system. Fortunately, Fail2Ban is robust enough that you can configure it to release the block after a set time to allow the client to reconnect correctly.

IPset

An *IPset* is a named set of IP addresses, network interfaces, ports, MAC addresses, or subnets. By creating these sets, you can easily manage the groupings through your firewall and any other application that supports IPsets.

The `ipset` utility is used to manage IPsets and requires super user privileges. When you create an IPset, you need to first determine what name you will give it. After that, decide how you want the IPset to be stored. Your storage choices are `bitmap`, `hash`, or `list`. There are two ways to create an IPset via the `ipset` command:

```
ipset create IPset-Name  storage-method:set-type
ipset -N IPset-Name  storage-method:set-type
```

An example of creating a subnet IPset and adding members to it on a Rocky Linux distribution is shown in Listing 18.21.

Listing 18.21: Creating and populating a subnet IPset

```
# ipset create BadGuyNets hash:net
#
# ipset add BadGuyNets 1.1.1.0/24
# ipset -A BadGuyNets 2.2.0.0/15
#
```

Once you have completed your IPset population, you can review your handiwork. Just employ the `ipset list` command as shown snipped in Listing 18.22.

Listing 18.22: Viewing a subnet IPset

```
# ipset list
Name: BadGuyNets
Type: hash:net
[...]
Members:
1.1.1.0/24
2.2.0.0/15
```

Once it's created and populated, block the IPset in either your `iptables` or `firewalld` ACL rules. To make the IPset persistent, you save it via the `ipset save` command and redirect its STDOUT to the `/etc/ipset.conf` file or use the `-f` option.

After you create an IPset, you need to start the `ipset` service. However, you may not find a service file to start or enable on systemd systems. Therefore, if your distribution uses systemd, you will need to either create an `ipset.service` file or obtain one from a reliable source.

You can delete a single item from your named IPset by using the `ipset del` command. To remove the entire IPset, you'll need to destroy it, as shown in Listing 18.23.

Listing 18.23: Deleting a subnet IPset

```
# ipset destroy BadGuyNets
#
# ipset list
#
```

> Only the `firewalld` and *iptables* service commands directly support IPset. However, you can use IPset with UFW, but it takes a little more work. You must modify the before.init and after.init scripts within the /etc/ufw/ directory. Find out more information about these scripts in the man pages for ufw-framework.

Summary

Properly managing your system's firewall application and its packet filtering ACL is vital for securing your system. To do this, you must understand the underlying framework of the firewall software, how to modify its ACL rules, and what additional applications can be used alongside it to block malicious network traffic. Using the correct products and properly configuring them not only helps to keep systems secure but makes your job easier as well.

Exam Essentials

Summarize various firewall features.   A firewall ACL identifies which network packets are allowed in or out. A stateless firewall views each packet's control information and decides what to do with the packet based on the defined ACL rules. A stateful firewall tracks active network connections, such as TCP and UDP; keeps an eye on network status; and can determine if packets have fragmented. Firewalls employ the /etc/services file, which documents the different standard application services names and their corresponding port numbers, protocols, and aliases.

Describe firewalld and its commands.   For the `firewalld` service, network traffic is grouped into a zone, which is a predefined rule set. Each zone has a configuration file that defines this rule set, also called trust levels. The `firewalld` zone configuration files are stored in the /usr/lib/firewalld/zones/ directory. Customized or user-created zone configuration files are stored in the /etc/firewalld/zones/ directory. For `firewalld`, a service is a predefined configuration set for a particular service, such as DNS. When you modify the `firewalld` configuration, by default you modify the runtime environment, which is the active situation. The permanent environment is the firewall settings within the configuration files. The `firewall-cmd` utility allows you to view and interact with `firewalld`.

Describe iptables and its commands.   The `iptables` firewall service uses a series process called chains to handle network packets that enter the system. The chains determine the path each packet takes to the appropriate application as it enters the Linux system. Each chain has a policy value and contains tables that define rules for handling the packets. ACL rules in `iptables` have target values for identified packets, which determine the action taken on them. The `iptables` command allows you to view and interact with various `iptables` configuration settings.

Describe UFW and its commands.   The Uncomplicated Firewall (UFW) is the default firewall service on Ubuntu distributions. It is configured with the `ufw` command-line utility or the `Gufw` for the GUI. Default UFW policies are stored in the `/etc/default/ufw` configuration file. When creating new UFW rules, you can use either simple or full syntax. User-added UFW rules are stored in the `/etc/ufw/user.rules` file. UFW uses profiles for common applications and daemons, and they are stored in the `/etc/ufw/applications.d/` directory.

Explain how to dynamically change packet filtering.   The DenyHosts application is a Python script, which helps protect against brute-force attacks coming through OpenSSH. It monitors `sshd` log messages and modifies the `/etc/hosts.deny` file to block an identified attack. The Fail2Ban service also monitors system logs, looking for repeated failures from the same host. If it detects a problem, Fail2Ban blocks the IP address of the offending host. An IPset is a named set of IP addresses, network interfaces, ports, MAC addresses, or subnets. By creating these sets, you can easily block the groupings through a firewall.

Review Questions

1. Which of the following is true concerning firewalls on Linux that were covered in this chapter? (Choose all that apply.)

    A. They use ACLs for allowing packets.

    B. They detect malicious behavior.

    C. They inspect network packet control information.

    D. They use `iptables` embedded in the Linux kernel.

    E. They employ configuration files for persistency.

2. Which of the following options best describes packet filtering?

    A. Identifying network packets via their control information and allowing them into the system

    B. Identifying network packets via their control information and determining what to do based on ACL rules

    C. Identifying network packets via their payload and determining what to do based on ACL rules

    D. Identifying network packets by their source address and determining what to do based on ACL rules

    E. Identifying network packets by their payload and determining what to do based on their source address

3. Which of the following are benefits of a stateful firewall over a stateless firewall? (Choose all that apply.)

    A. It operates faster.

    B. It is not as vulnerable to DDoS attacks.

    C. It determines if packets are fragmented.

    D. It operates faster for established connections.

    E. It is vulnerable to DDoS attacks.

4. The `firewalld` service uses _____, which is a predefined rule set.

    A. `netfilter`

    B. `firewall-cmd`

    C. Services

    D. `reject`

    E. Zones

5. Peter, a Linux system administrator, has been testing a new `firewalld` configuration. The test was successful. What should Peter do next?

    A. Using super user privileges, issue the `reboot` command.

    B. Using super user privileges, issue the `firewall-cmd --panic-on` command.

    C. Nothing. If the test was successful, the runtime environment is the permanent environment.

    D. Issue the `firewall-cmd --runtime-to-permanent` command using super user privileges.

    E. Issue another `firewall-cmd` command, but add the `--permanent` option to it.

6. Peter is a Linux system administrator of a system using the iptables service. He wants to add a rule to block only incoming `ping` packets and not send a rejection message to the source. What command should he employ?

    A. `sudo iptables -P INPUT DROP`

    B. `sudo iptables -A INPUT -p icmp -j REJECT`

    C. `sudo iptables -A INPUT -p icmp -j DROP`

    D. `sudo iptables -D INPUT -p icmp -j DROP`

    E. `sudo iptables -A OUTPUT -p icmp -j REJECT`

7. Which of the following commands will allow you to view the various rules in a UFW firewall with their associated numbers?

    A. `sudo ufw show numeric`

    B. `sudo ufw status`

    C. `sudo ufw status verbose`

    D. `sudo ufw status numbered`

    E. `sudo ufw enable`

8. Which of the following is an example of UFW simple syntax for blocking all incoming and outgoing OpenSSH connections without providing a blocking message?

    A. `sudo ufw deny 22/tcp`

    B. `sudo ufw drop 22/tcp`

    C. `sudo ufw reject 22/tcp`

    D. `sudo ufw accept 22/tcp`

    E. `sudo ufw block 22/tcp`

9. Which of the following are true concerning both DenyHosts and Fail2Ban? (Choose all that apply.)

    A. It is an intrusion detection system (IDS).

    B. It modifies the `/etc/hosts.deny` file.

    C. It only handles OpenSSH traffic.

    D. Its configuration file is named `jail.conf`.

    E. It can work with TCP Wrappers, `iptables`, and `firewalld`.

10. Virginia is administering a Linux system with a firewall. She has already set up an IPset and named it BlockThem. A new attack has begun to occur from the 72.32.138.96 address. Along with super user privileges, what command should she issue to add this IPv4 address to the IPset?

    A. `ipset create BlockThem hash:net`

    B. `ipset -n BlockThem hash:net`

    C. `ipset save -f /etc/ipset.conf`

    D. `ipset -A BlockThem 72.32.138.0/24`

    E. `ipset add BlockThem 72.32.138.96`

Chapter

19

Embracing Best Security Practices

✓ Objective 2.1: Summarize the purpose and use of security best practices in a Linux environment

In this chapter we'll explore some of the common practices used to make your Linux system more secure. Fortunately, many knowledgeable Linux administrators have blazed a trail for us to follow to implement good security practices on our Linux systems. This chapter divides these practices into three categories: user security, system security, and network security.

User Security

While a great deal of work is spent in trying to keep unauthorized users out of Linux systems, as the Linux administrator you need to worry about the authorized users as well. The following sections discuss techniques you can use on your Linux system to help identify authorized users, know what they are doing, and provide easier access to network resources after a user authenticates on a server.

Authentication Methods

The standard user ID/password combination has been used for decades in server environments. However, there are limitations to the user ID/password authentication method:

- Users might share their user ID and password with others.
- Passwords generated by users can often be easy to guess.
- Each server has its own database of user IDs and passwords. Users who need to log into multiple servers must present their user ID and password multiple times.

Because of some of these limitations, Linux administrators have been using other authentication methods. We'll examine those you'll come across on the Linux+ exam.

Kerberos

Students at MIT developed the Kerberos project to support the single sign-on (SSO) concept on networks. With SSO, you need to log into the network only once to access any server on the network. Three pieces are involved with the Kerberos authentication process:

- *Authentication server (AS)*: Users log into the AS to initiate the authentication process. The AS acts as the traffic cop, directing the login process through the multiple Kerberos servers involved.

- *Key distribution center (KDC)*: The AS passes the login request to the KDC, which issues the user a ticket-granting ticket (TGT) and maintains it on the server. The TGT has a timestamp and time limit for how long the ticket is valid. The KDC encrypts the ticket to make it harder to duplicate or impersonate valid tickets.

- *Ticket-granting service (TGS)*: After the KDC issues the user a ticket, the user can log into servers on the network that support the Kerberos system. When the user attempts to log into a server, that server contacts the TGS to determine if the user's ticket is valid. If the ticket is valid, the server uses the `kinit` utility to store the ticket in a credentials cache, which maintains any tickets used to log into the server. To view the tickets contained in the server's credentials cache, use the `klist` command.

Kerberos centralizes the authentication process but still requires individual servers to maintain their own database of the objects on the server that the user account has access to. That itself can become complicated when working with multiple servers on a network.

LDAP

This is where the *Lightweight Directory Access Protocol (LDAP)* comes into play. LDAP utilizes a hierarchical tree database structure to store information about both network users and resources. Network administrators can enter permissions for various network resources into the LDAP database structure. When a user account requests access to a resource on a server, the server accesses the centralized LDAP database to determine if it should grant the user access to the resource. This provides a centralized authorization database for all of the servers in a network.

One nice feature of LDAP is that you can distribute the LDAP database among multiple servers on the network. Each server can contain either a part of the LDAP database tree or a copy of the entire tree. This can help speed up the lookup process, especially for networks that are geographically separated.

 While you can use LDAP for user authentication, many network administrators implement a combination of Kerberos for authentication and LDAP for resource authorization. This utilizes the strengths of both packages and is the model on which Microsoft's Active Directory is built.

RADIUS

As its name suggests, the *Remote Authentication Dial-In User Service (RADIUS)* protocol is somewhat of an old authentication technology. It was originally created to provide centralized authentication services for dial-up bulletin board servers. However, its simplicity and ease of implementation make it a popular option for modern authentication applications requiring a simple authentication approach. You'll commonly find RADIUS authentication servers in network environments for authenticating network access, such as the IEEE 802.1x authentication protection on network switches.

The RADIUS protocol allows an authentication server to authenticate not only the user account but also other information about the user, such as a network address, phone number, and access privileges. Though not as versatile as LDAP, it can provide some basic database features for authentication to multiple devices on the network.

TACACS+

The *Terminal Access Controller Access-Control System (TACACS)* defines a family of protocols that provide remote authentication in a server environment. The original TACACS authentication protocol was popular in the early days of Unix systems.

The original TACACS protocol uses a centralized authentication server to authenticate user accounts from a single database server. Each server on a network submits the authentication request individually to the centralized server, requiring users to log into each server separately, even though there's a common authentication database.

 Cisco Systems updated the original TACACS protocol and called the update *TACACS+*. The TACACS+ protocol incorporates full authentication, authorization, and accounting features and also encrypts all data as it traverses the network.

Multifactor Authentication

The user ID/password method of authenticating user accounts has been around for a long time and is ripe with problems. There's nothing to prevent a user from sharing their user ID and password with others, allowing them to log into the system and perform actions.

Over the years other login methods have been developed to help provide a more secure login environment. The idea of two-factor authentication requires a user to have two pieces of information to log into a system: something they know (such as a password) and something they possess. There are a few different types of possessions that two-factor authentication utilizes:

- *Biometrics*: The most basic form of two-factor authentication is biometrics. Biometrics uses a physical feature that you have to authenticate you. This includes features such as fingerprints, iris scanning, and even facial recognition.

- *Tokens*: Digital tokens store a digital ID as an encrypted file. You must present the file to the server to gain authorization to access the server. Tokens can be *hardware tokens*, which are often stored on USB devices, such as thumb drives, or they can be *software tokens*, files that reside on the network device.

- *Public key infrastructure (PKI)*: PKI adds a level of complexity and security to tokens by incorporating an asynchronous key environment. In an asynchronous key system, two token keys are used together: a private key and a public key. The private key uniquely matches its public key, and no other key will match. The user maintains control over their private key but can share the public key with any server that requires it for login.

The user then presents the private key to the server for login. The server matches the private key presented to the public key stored on the server.

- *One-time password*: With the one-time password setup, you log into a server using your standard user ID and password, but then the server sends an additional password to the email address or text message that's on file for your user account. You must have access to that account to receive the additional password and apply it to the login. This ensures that the login attempt is being performed by the person who has control over the account.

Unique User Accounts

The key to any type of security plan is to know what your authorized users are doing. This helps in detecting rogue users purposely doing harm to the system, and it can help in detecting novice users who accidentally do wrong things.

The main goal of monitoring users is *nonrepudiation*. Nonrepudiation means that every action a user takes can be tracked back to that exact user. So that every action on the system can be attributed to a specific user, every user must log in with a unique user account. The various Linux system logs will track the actions that user account takes and when they're taken.

Don't allow users to share their user accounts with others, and under no circumstances should you assign the same user account to more than one person. This ensures that you know what user to question when you see inappropriate actions tagged to a specific user account appear in the system log files. That may not end the problem, but at least it gives you a starting point in troubleshooting the issue.

Enforce Strong Passwords

Password-based authentication is only as good as the passwords your system users use. Good security practices mandate that user passwords should be complex and change at a regular interval. Unfortunately, on their own most users prefer to not use complex passwords, nor change them at any regular interval. Fortunately, Linux provides a few ways for you to force your system users to follow good security practices with their passwords.

Chapter 10, "Administering Users and Groups," introduced the /etc/login.defs configuration file, which defines how the system handles user passwords. Using this file, you can define some basic security settings for passwords with the following settings:

- PASS_MAX_DAYS: The number of days until a password change is required
- PASS_MIN_DAYS: The number of days after a password is changed until the password may be changed again
- PASS_MIN_LENGTH: The minimum number of characters required in a password
- PASS_WARN_AGE: The number of days a warning is issued to the user prior to a password's expiration

These settings apply to the length and age of a password but not to the complexity level. For that, you need to use features in the pluggable authentication modules (PAM) authentication services (see Chapter 16, "Looking at Access and Authentication Methods").

As mentioned in Chapter 16, the PAM system provides libraries that control how the Linux system authenticates user accounts for access. Each library uses settings that customize the method and process used to authenticate users. Defining password complexity rules is one of those library settings.

The pwquality.so library defines password rules that apply to the system user accounts. By adding this library to the PAM rules, you can set additional password rules above what the standard /etc/login.defs settings define.

The pwquality.so library is installed by default in Red Hat–based distributions, but you must install it in Debian-based distributions. For Debian-based distributions, such as Ubuntu, install the libpam-pwquality software package.

In Red Hat–based distributions, you define the password quality settings in the /etc/pam.d/system-auth configuration file. For Debian-based distributions, you define them in the /etc/pam.d/common-password file. In both files the quality settings are defined on this line:

```
password     requisite     pam_pwquality.so
```

The settings are added at the end of the line, in this format:

directive=value

Table 19.1 shows the standard password directives available in the pwquality .so library.

TABLE 19.1   PAM password standard directives

Directive	Description
difok	Specifies the number of character changes in a new password from the old password
enforce_for_root	Specifies if the password enforcement rules apply to the root user account
maxrepeat	Specifies the maximum number of characters that can repeat
minlen	Specifies the minimum password length
reject_username	Rejects a password if it contains the username spelled either forward or in reverse
retry	Specifies the number of password attempts that are allowed

You'll notice in Table 19.1 that these directives don't include any password complexity directives. The complexity setting directives work a bit differently, using a concept called *credits*.

With credits you define one or more types of password requirements, such as uppercase letters, lowercase letters, numbers, or special characters, and then define how many of each type the user passwords must contain (for example, one uppercase letter, two lowercase letters, and one number). This system allows passwords to be any length, as long as the mandated types and quantities are present, and in any order. Table 19.2 shows the pwquality.so complexity directives.

TABLE 19.2   The PAM password complexity directives

Directive	Description
dcredit	Number of numeric characters
lcredit	Number of lowercase characters
ocredit	Number of special characters
ucredit	Number of uppercase characters

The credit directives are somewhat odd in that you specify the values as negative numbers. For example, to specify a complexity rule that requires at least one numeric character, two lowercase characters, and one uppercase character, you'd use the rule

```
password   requisite   pwquality.so dcredit=-1 lcredit=-2
ucredit=-1
```

The required characters can appear anywhere in the password, and there can be more than the specified minimum present in the password value.

Restricting the Root Account

The root user account is important in that it has complete privileges over all aspects of the Linux system. It's imperative that you protect who can use the root user account and where they can use it from.

There are several security best practices for helping restrict just how the root user account is used on your Linux system. The following sections discuss some basic security ideas you should think about.

Completely Blocking Root Access

The su and sudo commands allow any user account to perform administrative jobs without actually logging in as the root user account. This is better because they provide a way of logging who is performing those administrative tasks. With the su and sudo commands, there may not even be a reason to allow the root user account to log in at all.

To prevent anyone from logging into the Linux system as the root user account, you can use a trick that involves the /etc/passwd file. The /etc/passwd file maintains several pieces of information about user accounts, including the shell that Linux runs when the user account logs into the system. The trick of locking out a user account is to replace the default Bash shell assigned to the root user account with the /usr/sbin/nologin shell, like this:

```
root:x:0:0:root:/root:/usr/sbin/nologin
```

The nologin shell doesn't produce a usable shell; it just displays a message on the console:

```
$ /usr/sbin/nologin
This account is currently not available.
$
```

When you assign that as a user's shell, the account can't log into the system but just sees the output message. Setting this for the root user account prevents it from being able to log in, but the su command will still work just fine.

> The /usr/sbin/nologin utility is also handy for securing service accounts. Applications that need to continually run in background mode, such as web and database servers, need to log into the system but not to a Bash shell. Best security practices mandate that individual applications each use their own login account (called a service account) rather than log in as the root user account, thus limiting the damage that an attacker can do if an application is compromised. The best way to restrict service accounts is to assign the /usr/sbin/nologin shell as their default login shell in the /etc/passwd file.

Blocking Root Access from Specific Devices

For Linux systems that use a console physically attached to the system, you may want to block anyone from walking up to the system and logging in as the root user account.

To do this, create an /etc/securetty file on the system. The /etc/securetty file lists all the devices the root user account is permitted to log in from. If this file is empty, the root user account will not be able to log in from any physical console, although this does not block the root user account from logging in via the network.

Blocking Root Access from SSH

To block the root user account from logging in from the network, you'll need to modify the OpenSSH program, which provides secure connections to your Linux system. You accomplish this by a setting in the OpenSSH configuration file.

The OpenSSH configuration file is located at `/etc/ssh/sshd_config`. Open the file in a text editor, and look for this line:

```
#PermitRootLogin yes
```

Remove the pound sign to make the setting active, and change the `yes` to `no` to block the root user account from logging in via SSH.

System Security

As the Linux administrator, it's your job to ensure that the system keeps running and stays secure under all conditions. The following sections describe a few techniques that can help you with that task.

Separation of Data

When you install most Linux distributions, by default they create a single partition for the root of the virtual directory (see Chapter 11, "Handling Storage"), using all of the available disk space on the system. Creating just a single partition on the entire disk provides for maximum flexibility in using the disk space; both the Linux system and the users have access to the entire disk. However, this can cause issues.

The Linux system continually writes data to the virtual directory. The kernel logs each kernel event to a log file. As each user logs into the system, that event is logged to a log file. On an active Linux system, the system writes lots of data to the disk.

But with all that logging there's a catch. If the Linux system attempts to write to the disk but there's no room in the virtual directory filesystem to store any more data, the system halts. This can be a crucial problem in a multiuser Linux system.

If all disk space is allocated to the single partition, the same disk space is used to manage system files and user files. If a user decides to store their entire music library onto the Linux system, that may fill up the disk space and not leave any room for the system logging. If the system logging stops, no one can log into the Linux system!

In a multiuser environment, it's always a good practice to separate the user data storage from the system storage. When you use two separate partitions, if users fill up their storage partition, the system can still operate in its own storage partition.

The most common way to do this is to create two partitions on the disk and then assign one to the root (/) folder and the other to the `/home` directory in the virtual directory.

Disk Encryption

Data finding its way into the wrong hands has become a major issue in today's world. There are plenty of stories of important data being compromised from stolen laptops, systems being compromised, and rogue applications uploading data to remote websites.

One method to help protect your data is to encrypt it, which makes the data significantly harder for an attacker to use should it become compromised.

However, encrypting individual files is somewhat of a hassle. You need to decrypt the files each time you need to access the data in them and then re-encrypt the files when you're done. Also, while you're using the files in their decrypted state, you're vulnerable to an attack that can read the data.

Instead of encrypting individual files, the solution is to use *disk encryption*. Disk encryption works at the kernel level and encrypts every file that's stored on the disk partition. You don't need to do anything special from your applications. As you read data from files on the encrypted disk, the kernel automatically decrypts it, and as you write data to files on the encrypted disk, the kernel automatically encrypts them.

The *Linux Unified Key Setup (LUKS)* application acts as the co-between when working with files on a filesystem. It uses two components to interface between the kernel and applications:

- *dm-crypt*: This module plugs into the kernel and provides the interface between a virtual mapped drive and the actual physical drive. It does this using the /dev/mapper area.

- *cryptmount*: The cryptmount command creates the virtual mapped drive and interfaces it with the physical drive via the dm-crypt module. This ensures that all data passed to the virtual drive is encrypted before being stored on the physical drive.

Restricting Applications

Much like a busy freeway, if your Linux system supports multiple users running multiple applications, sometimes collisions can occur. A rogue application can attempt to access data intended for another application (either by accident or on purpose), causing problems for the other applications.

One method of protecting applications from each other is incorporating a *chroot jail*. The chroot utility runs a command in a new root directory structure, within the standard Linux virtual filesystem. All disk access performed by the command is restricted to the new root directory structure.

The format of the chroot utility is

```
chroot starting_directory command
```

The first parameter specifies the location to start the new root directory structure. The second parameter defines the command to run within the new structure. As the command runs, it references files and directories relative to the new root directory structure, not the system root directory structure. You can create a chroot jail in any location within the virtual filesystem on the Linux system.

> Since the application running in the chroot jail thinks the new root directory is the real directory structure, you must copy any Linux utilities or libraries that it requires into the new root directory structure using the same paths.

Preventing Unauthorized Rebooting

If your Linux server is located in a publicly accessible area, you may need to take precautions to prevent an attacker from rebooting the server and taking control. There are three common practices that you can follow to prevent that.

Preventing Access to the BIOS/UEFI

When you start a computer system, it uses either the Basic Input/Output System (BIOS) or the newer Unified Extensible Firmware Interface (UEFI) to control how the system boots. Access to either of these utilities can allow an attacker to redirect the system to boot from a DVD disc or other portable medium.

To restrict this, it's always a good idea to enable the password feature in the BIOS or UEFI software. When a password is assigned, you must enter it to gain access to the BIOS or UEFI menu system to make changes.

Preventing Access to the GRUB Bootloader

During the boot process, when Linux starts to boot, it uses the GRUB bootloader to load the appropriate operating system image from a hard drive. The GRUB system also provides a way for you to break out of the boot process and access the GRUB menu, where you can alter where or how the Linux system boots.

To protect your Linux system from physical attack, you should also place a password on the GRUB bootloader system to prevent unauthorized users from accessing the GRUB menu. Since the GRUB configuration files are plaintext, for best security you should encrypt the password value before storing it in the configuration file.

To do this on a Debian-based system, use the `grub-mkpasswd-pbkdf2` utility:

```
$ grub-mkpasswd-pbkdf2
Enter password:
Reenter password:
PBKDF2 hash of your password is
grub.pbkdf2.sha512.10000.FE548777A9E101604D00DB
610E6BBB8E2269D4E98E17C1533C3B64EE3305B21D4F8AE089EE900668C78FCA4BE429D906
ED104
9A8EF5C80A7621E5E17866DC556.250AAB4CD88CB2FB80D29D04DF3C381946A76AC9E1059
B2C109
015217A63422C748A4E6E642517E15659FB69C4EAE55D953A4484C9C0D88DE37C099EAD79C27B
$
```

After you've created the encrypted password, you can add it to the password setting in the GRUB configuration file. On the Ubuntu system, the file is /etc/grub.d/ 40_custom. Add the lines

```
set superuser "userid"
password_pbkdf2 userid password
```

where userid is the user account you want to use to log into the GRUB boot menu and password is the value provided from the grub-mkpasswd-pbkdf2 utility.

For Red Hat–based systems, the utility to generate the password is grub-md5-crypt. The line to add to the GRUB menu file is

```
password -md5 password
```

Now when you reboot your Linux system, it will prompt you for the user account and password before allowing you to enter the GRUB menu.

Disabling the Ctrl+Alt+Del Key Combination

The Windows operating system has used the Ctrl+Alt+Del key combination, commonly called the *three-finger salute*, to reboot the entire system since the early days of Windows. This action has carried over to the Linux world and is commonly supported by most Linux distributions that run on IBM-compatible hardware.

If your Linux system has a physical console that is open to others, it's a good idea to disable the Ctrl+Alt+Del key combination from rebooting your system. How to disable the key combination depends on what startup method your Linux system uses.

For systems that use the SystV init method, the Ctrl+Alt+Del action is defined in the /etc/inittab file:

```
ca::ctrlaltdel:/sbin/shutdown -t3 -r now
```

The key combination triggers the /sbin/shutdown program, which initiates the shutdown of the Linux system. To prevent that, you just need to modify what program the key combination runs. For example, to just log the event, use the logger application:

```
ca::ctrlaltdel:/bin/logger -p authpriv.warning -t init "Ctrl+Alt+Del
was ignored"
```

Now if anyone attempts the Ctrl+Alt+Del key combination, the event will just trigger an entry in the standard log file for the system and not reboot the system.

For systems that use the systemd startup method, you'll need to disable the ctrl-alt-del.target target using the systemctl command:

```
$ sudo systemctl mask ctrl-alt-del.target
```

Now systemd will ignore the Ctrl+Alt+Del key combination as well.

Restricting Unapproved Jobs

The at and cron utilities allow users to schedule jobs when they're not logged into the system. In some environments, that may be a security issue and needs to be prevented.

Both the at and cron utilities provide deny list and allow list files for either denying or allowing user accounts to schedule jobs. These files are as follows:

- /etc/at.allow
- /etc/at.deny
- /etc/cron.allow
- /etc/cron.deny

As the filenames suggest, the .allow files contain lists of user accounts allowed to schedule jobs, whereas the .deny files contain lists of user accounts prevented from scheduling jobs. The order in which Linux checks these can get a little complicated:

1. If a user is found in the .allow file, they are allowed to schedule a job, and no further checks are performed.
2. If the user is not found in the .allow file, the system checks the .deny file.
3. If the user is found in the .deny file, they are not allowed to schedule a job.
4. If the user is not found in the .deny file, they are allowed to schedule a job.

So by default, if both the .allow and .deny files are empty or don't exist, all user accounts are allowed to schedule jobs on the Linux system.

Banners and Messages

Providing information to users is yet another vital job of the Linux system administrator. Linux provides two ways for you to present canned messages to your system users as they log into the system:

- */etc/login.warn*: The system displays the contents of the login.warn file before the login prompt at console logins. This is often used to display legal disclaimers and warnings to attackers on your system.

- */etc/motd*: The system displays the contents of the motd file (short for *message of the day*) immediately after the user logs into the console or terminal session. This is often used for informational messages, such as if there are any hardware failures on the system or any scheduled downtime coming up.

Restricting USB Devices

USB devices have made life much easier for us, but they've also created some security concerns. The ability to easily plug in a portable storage device and copy files can be a nightmare for administrators responsible for protecting the data on the system.

For systems that require a high level of data protection, it's a good idea to prevent users from plugging in USB storage devices to copy data. While there's no one command to help with that task, you can implement a workaround by exploiting how the modprobe utility works.

When a user plugs in a USB storage device, the kernel automatically looks for a module to support the device. If none is installed, it calls the modprobe utility to automatically load the appropriate kernel module to support the device. The modprobe utility uses configuration files to define how it operates and where it looks for module files. The configuration file is stored in the /etc/modprobe.d directory.

Besides the configuration file, within the modprobe.d directory is also the blacklist.conf file. The blacklist.conf file defines modules that are blocked from loading into the kernel. So one workaround is to block the module required to interface with USB storage devices from loading.

When you install a USB storage device, the kernel loads two modules: uas and usb:storage. To prevent that from happening, open the blacklist.conf text file and add these lines:

```
blacklist uas
blacklist usb:storage
```

Save the file and then reboot the Linux system. Now if a user plugs in a USB storage device, the system should ignore the kernel request to load the module necessary to interface with the device. However, it will still allow other types of USB devices, such as keyboards and mice, to operate just fine.

Looking for Trouble

With all the viruses, malware, and spyware floating around the Internet, these days it's hard to keep track of what applications can cause problems on your system. While it's true that fewer viruses have been written for Linux systems compared to Windows systems, they still exist, and you still must be vigilant to protect your system.

As a Linux administrator, it's your job to keep up-to-date on what attacks can be made against your Linux system. The U.S. Department of Homeland Security has contracted with the MITRE Corporation, a nonprofit organization, to publicly publish information system security alerts, called *Common Vulnerabilities and Exposures (CVE)*.

MITRE maintains a database of published CVE events and assigns each entry with a unique CVE Identifier. You can view the current CVE events posted on the cve.mitre.org website.

Each CVE event describes the risk involved with an event and the steps you should take as a Linux administrator to mitigate the risk. It's important to monitor the CVE database for new attacks against Linux systems.

Auditing

The standard system logs available on your Linux system provide a wealth of information about what's going on in your Linux system, but they don't quite cover everything. Events occur that aren't logged, such as when standard user accounts access files they shouldn't or outside attackers probe your system from the network.

Tracking this type of information requires a more robust security auditing system above the standard `rsyslog` log events. The *auditd* package provides this extra level of logging for us.

The `auditd` package allows you to define your own set of security rules to monitor and log lots of different types of system events, such as the following events:

- File and directory access by users

- System calls made by applications

- Specific commands run by users

- Network access by users

- Network connection attempts made by external hosts

You define events to monitor by creating rules. There are three types of rules you can create:

- System rules: Log system calls made by applications

- File system rules: Log access to files and directories

- Control rules: Rules that modify the `auditd` behavior

You can define the rules either in the `/etc/audit/audit.rules` file or on the fly by using the `auditctl` utility. Rules defined using the `auditctl` utility are valid only until the system reboots. Rules added to the `audit.rules` file are persistent.

Network Security

Placing your Linux system on a network is like having the front door to your house open to the public. Any device on the network can attempt to access your Linux system from the network. The following sections describe some basic security measures you can take to help protect your Linux system when it's connected to a network.

Denying Hosts

The most basic network security feature you can implement is to use the `/etc/hosts.deny` file. The `/etc/hosts.deny` file creates a deny list of hosts you don't want to allow to connect to network resources on your Linux system. The TCP Wrappers program on the Linux system (discussed in Chapter 16) reads the `hosts.deny` file and blocks any attempts from those hosts to access your system. You can list hosts by name or IP address in the `hosts.deny` file.

If you want to take a more extreme approach to network security, you can use the `/etc/hosts.allow` file. As you can probably guess, when the `hosts.allow` file exists, only hosts found in it are allowed access to network resources on the Linux system. The TCP Wrappers application handles the `hosts.allow` and `hosts.deny` files in the same way the `at.allow` and `at.deny` files work. If both files are empty or missing, all hosts are allowed to access the network resources on the system.

Disabling Unused Services

There are many legacy network applications that have still hung around on Linux systems. Unfortunately, many of those legacy network applications use unsecure methods of transferring user data as well as application data. Also unfortunately, many Linux distributions may still activate these legacy network applications by default, providing a backdoor to your Linux system that you may not even know exists.

Some of the more common legacy network services that may still be operational are listed here:

- *FTP*: The original File Transfer Protocol (FTP) sends user account and application data across the network in plaintext using TCP ports 21 and 22.

- *Telnet*: The original remote terminal application also sends all user and application data across the network in plaintext using TCP port 23.

- *Finger*: An old legacy application that provides remote lookup services to find users on a Linux system. This utility has been compromised and is not typically installed anymore, but you can look for it on TCP port 79.

- *Mail services*: If your Linux system doesn't need to send and receive email, it's a good idea to uninstall any mail applications that may be installed and silently running in the background. The two most common Linux email packages are sendmail and Postfix. Both use TCP port 25 to receive email messages from remote hosts.

Changing Default Ports

For an application to communicate on the network, it must use a network port. The port is a unique number assigned to the application so that when a remote client communicates with the server, the server knows which application to send the connection to.

There are three categories of network ports:

- *Well-known ports*: Ports between 0 and 1023 that have been formally assigned to specific applications by the Internet Assigned Numbers Authority (IANA)

- *Registered ports*: Ports between 1024 and 49151, which are registered with IANA but not officially assigned

- *Private ports*: Ports greater than 49151, which can be used by any application

Most of the popular network applications have been allocated well-known ports by IANA and are expected to be using those ports. These ports are listed in the /etc/services file on the Linux system.

As an additional level of security, some Linux administrators prefer to move applications that normally use a well-known port to a private port. This may temporarily thwart attackers trying to exploit the application, as the application is not listening for connections on the port it normally should be. However, many advanced hackers use port scanning tools to look for applications on nonstandard ports. If you do move an application to a private port, you must ensure that any clients intending to use the application know that the assigned port has been changed.

> Most network applications define the default network port in their configuration file. Usually you can just edit the configuration file to change the default port and restart the application. However, make sure any clients that connect to the application also have the ability to change the port they try to connect with to access the application.

Using Encryption on the Network

These days it's never a good idea to send any type of data across the network in plaintext. Instead of using the legacy FTP application to transfer data and telnet to use a remote terminal, these tasks can be done using newer applications that employ encryption.

The Secure Sockets Layer (SSL) protocol, along with the newer Transport Layer Security (TLS) protocol, is commonly used to encrypt data as it traverses the network. To implement these protocols on a Linux system, you'll need to install the OpenSSL package (discussed in Chapter 2, "Introduction to Services").

The OpenSSL package doesn't provide the actual network applications but is a library that provides the framework required to send and receive encrypted data on the network. Both SSL and TSL require the use of certificates that are used to encrypt the data. They use PKI, which requires a private key for the server and a public key that can be sent to individual clients to authenticate and encrypt the network traffic.

In Exercise 19.1 you'll get some practice creating an encrypted partition on a removable USB stick. This helps protect your data in a mobile environment.

EXERCISE 19.1

Creating an Encrypted Disk

This exercise demonstrates how to use LUKS to encrypt a removable USB storage device so that any data stored on the device can be read only from your Linux system.

1.   Log into your Linux graphical desktop.

2.   Insert a blank USB storage device (or one with data you don't mind losing) into a USB port on your workstation.

3. Open the Disks application from your graphical desktop menu.

4. Select the icon for the USB storage device from the left-side list of storage devices.

5. Click the minus button under the disk partition layout on the right side of the window. Click the Delete button in the dialog box that appears (if the partition is a Linux partition and is currently mounted, you will have to unmount it first).

6. When the partition is deleted, a plus button will appear under the partition. Click the plus sign button to create a new partition.

7. Click the Next button to partition the entire USB drive.

8. In the Volume Name text box, type **Test Drive**.

9. In the Test section, select the radio button "Internal disk for use with Linux systems only (ext4)."

10. Under that option, select the Password Protect Volume (LUKS) check box. Click Next.

11. Enter a password for the encrypted volume, and confirm it. Don't forget the password you choose, as you'll need it to mount the new drive.

12. Click Create to start building the encrypted drive.

13. When the process completes, view the drive from your File Manager program.

14. Remove the USB drive and plug it into a non-Linux workstation. If the workstation prompts you to reformat the drive, select Cancel.

15. Plug the drive back into your Linux workstation. At the password prompt, enter the password you assigned in step 11. Linux will mount the drive and allow you to read and write to the drive.

16. If you wish to convert the USB drive back for normal use, plug it into your workstation and follow the prompts to reformat the drive.

Summary

There are many aspects to protecting a Linux system for use in today's world. Most security practices break down into user security, system security, and network security. For user security, there are many different methods for authenticating users and authorizing them to access resources. The Kerberos package provides a centralized login system for multiple network servers. The LDAP package creates a distributed database for defining resources and users and granting users access to the network resources. The RADIUS package is a simpler authentication package that's commonly used for network devices, such as switches and routers. The TACACS+ protocol was developed by Cisco Systems to provide advanced network authentication processes.

System security involves securing the Linux system environment itself. One step for system security is to utilize separate partitions for the OS files and user data files. That way, if an overzealous user fills up the disk space, it won't stop the OS. Disk encryption has also become an important tool these days, especially when storing data on removable devices. Protecting applications from one another is yet another system security feature. With the chroot jail process, you can create separate filesystem areas within the main filesystem so that applications can't trounce on each other's files.

Network security has become a popular topic these days, and Linux provides several tools that you can use to help out. The `hosts.deny` and `hosts.allow` files allow you to either block specific hosts or allow only specific hosts when communicating via the network. If your Linux system contains packages for some of the legacy network tools, such as FTP, Telnet, and Finger, it's a good idea to ensure that those software packages are disabled and that users can't run them. If you want to attempt to confuse potential attackers, you can move the default TCP or UDP ports used by standard applications to alternative port numbers. Finally, the chapter discussed using the OpenSSL package to provide SSL- and TLS-level encryption for network traffic.

Exam Essentials

Describe the different authentication methods available in Linux.   For network servers, the four most popular user authentication methods are Kerberos, which uses a single sign-on method of authenticating users; LDAP, which incorporates authorization as well as authentication; RADIUS, which provides a simple authentication process; and TACACS+, which is commonly used for network devices. Linux also supports several two-factor authentication methods, including using biometric data such as fingerprints, iris scans, and facial recognition; both software and hardware tokens, which provide a digital certificate identifying the user; and PKI, which allows users to create public and private keys so that they can keep their private key secret and only disclose their public key to servers.

Describe the different types of system security that you should consider on Linux systems.   The separation of system data and user data is a relatively simple security feature that you can implement. By creating a separate partition for user data, you will prevent a user from filling up the entire disk space on the system and stopping the server. Using encrypted storage is useful in environments where the storage device may leave the physical area, such as in laptops or external storage devices. Restricting applications using chroot is also helpful in preventing accidental or malicious applications from gaining data used by other applications. Likewise, disabling USB storage devices is a good option for systems that require control over data leaving the server. If your Linux system is in a vulnerable physical location, it's also a good idea to prevent unauthorized rebooting of the server by disabling the Ctrl+Alt+Del key combination along with implementing a BIOS/UEFI password as well as a GRUB boot menu password.

Explain the different methods of protecting your Linux system on the network.   For protecting your Linux system on the network, you can create a hosts deny list or allow list. The hosts.deny file allows you to block suspicious hosts from accessing network resources on your system. If you prefer, you can instead use the hosts.allow file to allow only specific hosts to connect to applications on your system. It's also a good idea to disable any unused network applications, especially those that send and receive user accounts and data in plaintext, such as FTP, Telnet, and Finger. It may also help to change the default ports used by network applications to help deter attackers from finding them on your system. Finally, it's a good idea to incorporate encryption on any network application on your Linux system. The OpenSSL package provides both SSL and TLS encryption services for any application.

Review Questions

1. Which authentication method issues tickets to users and helps with implementing the single sign-on feature in a network of servers?

    A. LDAP

    B. Kerberos

    C. RADIUS

    D. TACACS+

    E. Biometrics

2. Mary wants to implement two-factor authentication using fingerprint readers for her users to authenticate with the Linux system. Which method of authentication should she look into implementing?

    A. LDAP

    B. Tokens

    C. Biometrics

    D. PKI

    E. Kerberos

3. Jaime is interested in using a distributed database method for authorizing users to access resources located on multiple network servers. Which authentication method would be best for her to use?

    A. LDAP

    B. Kerberos

    C. Tokens

    D. RADIUS

    E. PKI

4. Fred wants to block users from logging in directly with the root user account from any console or terminal session. What is the best way he can do that?

    A. Implement biometric authentication.

    B. Implement tokens.

    C. Use Kerberos authentication.

    D. Remove root user entry from the `/etc/passwd` file.

    E. Set the default login shell for the root user to `/usr/sbin/nologin`.

5. Which directory should you place on a separate partition to separate user data from system data?

   A. /usr

   B. /home

   C. /etc

   D. /sbin

   E. /bin

6. Sally is concerned about an application that allows guests to connect to her Linux system and access a database. What can she do to limit the application to a specific directory structure on the Linux server so it can't access system data?

   A. Block the application network port.

   B. Move the application port to a private port number.

   C. Place the application in an encrypted partition.

   D. Run the application with `chroot`.

   E. Place the application in a separate partition.

7. Ted wants to provide encryption at the disk level so that users don't need to encrypt individual files as they store them. What Linux feature should he use?

   A. LUKS

   B. `chroot`

   C. `auditd`

   D. PKI

   E. Kerberos

8. Ned notices in the logs that a user account schedules a job every day at noon that uses all of the system resources. How can he prevent that user account from doing that?

   A. Use `chroot` for the user account.

   B. Use `nologin` as the user's default shell.

   C. Add the user account to the `/etc/cron.deny` file.

   D. Add the user account to the `/etc/hosts.deny` file.

   E. Create a `/etc/motd` message telling users to not schedule large jobs.

9. Tom sees an attacker continually attempt to break into a user account on his Linux system from a specific IP address. What can he do to quickly mitigate this issue?

   A. Place the application in a chroot jail.

   B. Add the `nologin` shell to the user account.

   C. Implement two-factor authentication.

   D. Add the attacker's IP address to the `/etc/hosts.deny` file.

   E. Add the user account to the `/etc/cron.deny` file.

10. Despite his warnings, Fred continues to see users transfer files to his Linux server using unsecure FTP. How can he stop this?

    A. Place a message in the `/etc/motd` file telling users to stop.

    B. Move the FTP application to a different network port.

    C. Place the user accounts in the `/etc/hosts.deny` file.

    D. Place the user accounts in the `/etc/cron.deny` file.

    E. Disable the FTP application ports.

Troubleshooting Your System

Chapter

20

Analyzing System Properties and Remediation

✓ **Objective 1.5: Given a scenario, use the appropriate networking tools or configuration files.**

✓ **Objective 4.1: Given a scenario, analyze and troubleshoot storage issues.**

✓ **Objective 4.2: Given a scenario, analyze and troubleshoot network resource issues.**

✓ **Objective 4.3: Given a scenario, analyze and troubleshoot central processing unit (CPU) and memory issues.**

Even well-maintained Linux systems run into problems. New or modified applications introduce different performance variables, unforeseen incidents cause outages, and aging hardware components may fail. Minimizing their effects requires understanding troubleshooting techniques and tools as well as the interactions between various system components.

Troubleshooting the Network

When network problems occur (and they will), devise a troubleshooting plan. First, identify symptoms, review recent network configuration changes, and formulate potential problem cause theories. Next, using the Open Systems Interconnection (OSI) model as a guide, look at hardware items (for example, cables), proceed to the Data Link layer (for example, network card drivers), continue to the Network layer (for example, routers), and so on.

Exploring Network Issues

In order to properly create a troubleshooting plan, you need to understand various network configuration and performance components. Understanding these elements assists in creating theories about problem causes and helps your exploration process through the OSI model.

Speeding Things Up

Familiarity with a few network terms and technologies will help in troubleshooting network problems and improving your network's performance.

Bandwidth *Bandwidth* is a measurement of the maximum data amount that can be transferred between two network points over a period of time. This measurement is typically represented by the number of bytes per second.

As an example, think about road design. Some roads are designed to handle cars traveling at 65 mph (~105 kph) safely. Other roads can only deal with traffic moving at around 35 mph (~56 kph).

Throughput *Throughput* is a measurement of the actual data amount that is transferred between two network points over a period of time. It is different from bandwidth in that bandwidth is the maximum rate and throughput is the actual rate.

Throughput may not reach the maximum bandwidth rate due to items such as a failing NIC or simply the protocol in use. Returning to the roadway analogy, though some roads can handle cars traveling at 65 mph safely, some cars may travel slower due to potholes on the road.

Saturation Network *saturation*, also called *bandwidth saturation*, occurs when network traffic exceeds capacity. In this case, a towel analogy is helpful. Imagine you have a towel that has absorbed as much water as it can. Once it can no longer absorb any more water, it has become saturated.

Saturation is also sometimes called *congestion*. Using our traffic analogy, when too many cars are on a particular roadway, congestion occurs and traffic slows.

Latency *Latency* is the time between a source sending a packet and the packet's destination receiving it. Thus, *high latency* is slow, which is typically a problem, and *low latency* is fast, which is often desired.

High latency is often caused by low bandwidth or saturation. In addition, routers overloaded by network traffic may cause high network latency.

Jitter is a term used to indicate high deviations from a network's average latency. For streaming services such as video, jitter can have a serious negative impact.

Routing Because a network is broken up into segments, you need routing to get packets from point A to point B through the network's various segments. Routers connect these network segments and forward IP packets to the appropriate network segment toward their ultimate destination.

Routers contain buffers that allow them to hold on to network packets when their outbound queues become too long. However, if the router cannot forward its IP packets in a reasonable time frame, it will drop packets located in its buffer. This condition often transpires when network bandwidth saturation is occurring.

Some router manufacturers attempt to avoid packet loss by increasing their routers' buffer size. This leads to a condition called *bufferbloat*, which increases network latency in congested segments due to packets staying too long in the router's buffer. You can find out more information about bufferbloat, how to test your routers for it, and resolutions at www.bufferbloat.net.

Dealing with Timeouts and Losses

A *packet drop*, also called *packet loss*, occurs when a network packet fails to reach its destination. Unreliable network cables, failing adapters, network traffic congestion, and under-performing devices are the main culprits of packet drop.

UDP does not guarantee packet delivery. Therefore, in services like VoIP that employ UDP, minor packet loss does not cause any problems. Most VoIP software compensates for these packet drops. You may hear what sounds like choppiness in a person's voice as you speak over a VoIP connection when it is experiencing minor packet drops.

TCP guarantees packet delivery and will retransmit any lost packets. Thus, if network packet loss occurs for services employing TCP, it will experience delays. If the packet drops are due to network traffic congestion, in some cases, the TCP packet retransmission only makes matters worse. Keep in mind that IP allows routers to drop packets if their buffer is full and they cannot send out their buffered packets fast enough. This will also cause TCP to retransmit packets.

 Packet drops on a router can also be caused by a denial-of-service (DoS) attack, called a *packet drop* or *black hole attack*. A malicious user manually or through software gains unauthorized access to a router. The router is then configured to drop packets instead of forwarding them.

In network communication, *timeouts* are typically preset time periods for handling unplanned events. For example, you open a web browser and proceed to enter the address to a site you wish to visit. The website is down, but still the browser attempts a connection. After a predetermined amount of time (the designated timeout period), the browser stops trying to connect and issues an error message.

You may experience network communication timeouts for a number of reasons:

- A system is down.
- An incorrect IP address was used.
- A service is not running or not offered on that system.
- A firewall is blocking the traffic.
- Network traffic is congested, causing packet loss.

Each of these items is worth exploring, if you or your system's processes are experiencing timeouts related to network communications.

Resolving the Names

The process of translating between a system's fully qualified domain name (FQDN) and its IP address is called *name resolution*. The Domain Name System (DNS) is a network protocol that uses a distributed database to provide the needed name resolutions.

Most systems simply use client-side DNS, which means they ask other servers for name resolution information. Using the /etc/resolv.conf and /etc/hosts files for configuring client-side DNS was covered in Chapter 7, "Configuring Network Connections." However, there are a few additional items concerning name resolution problems and performance that you need to know:

Name Server Location   With client-side DNS, when it comes to name server selection, location matters. If the name server you have chosen to set in the /etc/resolv.conf file is halfway around the world, your system's name resolutions are slower than if you chose a physically closer name server.

Consider Cache   A caching-only name server holds recent name resolution query results in its memory. If you are only employing client-side DNS, consider configuring your system to be a caching-only server, using software such as `dnsmasq`. By caching name resolutions, resolving speeds can improve significantly.

Secondary Server   If you are managing a DNS server for your company, besides a primary server, consider configuring a secondary server. This name server receives its information from the primary server and can increase name resolution performance by offloading the primary server's burden.

Configuring It Right

Network configuration was covered in Chapter 7. However, there are a few additional special topics that may help you with troubleshooting.

Interface Configurations   Being able to view a NIC's configuration and status is important in the troubleshooting process. You may need to view its IP address, its MAC address, subnet configuration, error rates, and so on. In addition, understanding configuration items such as whether or not a NIC has a static or DHCP-provided IP address is part of this process.

Be aware that if you use NetworkManager on a system with `firewalld` as its firewall service, when a new network device is added, it will automatically be added to the `firewalld` default zone. If the default zone is set to `public`, the network device will only accept selected incoming network connections. See Chapter 18, "Overseeing Linux Firewalls," for more details on `firewalld`.

Ports and Sockets   Ports and sockets are important structures in Linux networking. Understanding the difference between the two will help in the troubleshooting process.

A *port* is a number used by protocols, such as TCP and UDP, to identify which service or application is transmitting data. For example, port 22 is a well-known port designated for OpenSSH, and DNS listens on port 53. TCP and UDP packets contain both the packet's source and destination ports in their headers.

A program connection to a port is a *socket*. A *network socket* is a single endpoint of a network connection's two endpoints. That single endpoint is on the local system and bound to a particular port. Thus, a network socket uses a combination of an IP address (the local system) and a port number.

Localhost vs. a Unix Socket   The localhost designation and a Unix socket are often used for services, such as SQL. Being able to differentiate between the two is helpful.

Localhost is the hostname for the *local loopback interface*, which was first described in Chapter 7. Localhost uses the IPv4 address of 127.0.0.1 and the IPv6 address of ::1. Basically, it allows programs on the current system to test or implement networking services via TCP without needing to employ external networking structures.

Unix sockets, also called Unix domain sockets, are endpoints similar to network sockets. Instead of between systems over a network, these endpoint sockets are between processes on your local system. Your system's Unix domain sockets perform interprocess communications (IPC), which operate in a manner similar to a TCP/IP network. Thus, these sockets are also called *IPC sockets*.

If you have a service configuration choice between the two, typically a Unix socket will provide better performance than the localhost. This is due to the system employing normal networking behavior that consumes resources, such as performing data checksums and TCP handshakes when using localhost. In addition, due to special Unix socket files and the fact that Unix sockets understand file permissions, you can easily employ access control by setting access rights to these files.

Adapters   *Network adapters* are system hardware that allows network communications. These communications can be wired or wireless. Adapters also come in USB form factors but are not typically used in enterprise server environments.

Common problems that arise with network adapters are faulty or failing hardware and incorrect or inefficient drivers. In regard to faulty hardware, error rates on adapters generally should not exceed 0.01 percent of the adapter's bits per second (bps) throughput rate.

Though a network interface card (NIC) is an adapter, an adapter is not always a NIC. For example, a USB network adapter is not a NIC.

RDMA (Remote Direct Memory Access)   A technology to consider, if your system's network needs low latency, is *RDMA*. It allows direct access between a client's and server's memory. The results are significantly reduced network latency, higher bandwidth, and the side benefit of reducing the server's CPU overhead.

Unfortunately, this technology requires special hardware. To use it on a standard Linux system Ethernet NIC, you'll need to employ *soft-RoCE*. This software provides RDMA features over converged Ethernet (RoCE). What is really nice about soft-RoCE is that its driver is part of the Linux kernel, starting at v4.8.

Viewing Network Performance

Starting the troubleshooting process requires knowledge of the various tools to use. Here we provide a few tables to assist in your tool selection.

Since high latency (slowness) and network saturation tend to occur together, Table 20.1 shows tools you should use to tackle or monitor for these problems. Keep in mind that you should already know the bandwidth of the network segment(s) you are troubleshooting prior to using these tools.

TABLE 20.1   Commands to check for high latency, saturation

Command	Description
iperf, iperf3	Perform network throughput tests. The iperf command is version 2 of the utility, and iperf3 is version 3.
iftop -i *adapter*	Displays network bandwidth usage (throughput) for *adapter* in a continuous graph format.
mtr	Displays approximate travel times and packet loss percentages between the first 10 routers in the path from the source to the destination in a continuous graph or report format.
nc	Performs network throughput tests. (Called netcat)
netstat -s	Displays summary statistics that are broken down by protocol and contain packet rates, but not throughput. This command is deprecated.
ping, ping6	Perform simple ICMP packet throughput tests and display statistics on items such as round-trip times.
ss -s	Displays summary statistics that are broken down by socket type and contain packet rates but not throughput.
tracepath, tracepath6	Display approximate travel times between each router from the source to the destination, discovering the maximum transmission unit (MTU) along the way.
traceroute, traceroute6	Display approximate travel times between each router from the source to the destination.

Some of these tools are not installed by default. Also, they may not be in a distribution's standard repositories. See Chapter 13, "Governing Software," for details on how to install software packages.

To employ the iperf utility for testing throughput, you'll need two systems—one to act as the server and the other as a client. The utility must be installed on both systems, and you'll need to allow access to its default port 5001 (port 5201 for iperf3) through their firewalls. A snipped example of setting up and starting the iperf server on an Ubuntu system is shown in Listing 20.1.

Listing 20.1: Setting up the `iperf` server

```
$ sudo ufw allow 5001
Rule added
Rule added (v6)
$
$ iperf -s -t 120
------------------------------------------------------------
Server listening on TCP port 5001
[...]
```

The `iperf` command's `-s` option tells it to run as a server. The `-t` option is handy, because the service will stop after the designated number of seconds. This helps you avoid using Ctrl+C to stop the server.

Once you have the server side ready, configure the client side and perform a throughput test. A snipped example of setting up and starting an `iperf` client on a Fedora system is shown in Listing 20.2. Though the last output summary lists a `Bandwidth` column header, it is really showing you the achieved throughput.

Listing 20.2: Setting up the `iperf` client and conducting a throughput test

```
$ sudo firewall-cmd --add-port=5001/udp
success
$ sudo firewall-cmd --add-port=5001/tcp
success
$
$ iperf -c 192.168.0.104 -b 90Kb -d -P 5 -e -i 10
------------------------------------------------------------
Server listening on TCP port 5001 with pid 3857
[...]
Client connecting to 192.168.0.104, TCP port 5001 with pid 3857
[...]
[ ID] Interval        Transfer     Bandwidth        Write/Err  Rtry      Cwnd/RTT
[...]
[SUM] 0.00-10.04 sec   640 KBytes   522 Kbits/sec  5/0         2
[..]
[SUM] 0.00-11.40 sec  1.19 MBytes   873 Kbits/sec  850        5:5:0:0:0:0:0:835
$
```

Notice that a firewall rule was added for UDP traffic as well as TCP. This is necessary because of the use of the `-b` switch on the `iperf` client, which requires UDP. There are many options available with the `iperf` and `iperf3` utilities. The ones used in Listing 20.2 are described in Table 20.2.

TABLE 20.2   Basic `iperf` client-side options

Option	Description
-c *server-address*	Creates a client that connects to the server located at *server-address*.
-b *size*	Sets target bandwidth to *size* bits/sec (default is 1 Mb).
-d	Performs a bidirectional test between client and server.
-P *n*	Creates and runs *n* parallel client threads.
-e	Provides enhanced output. Not available on older utility versions.
-i *n*	Pauses between periodic bandwidth reports for *n* seconds.

Another handy utility to test throughput is the `netcat` utility, whose command name is `nc`. As with `iperf`, you need to set up both a server and a client to perform a test. Listing 20.3 shows an example of setting up a `netcat` server on an Ubuntu system. Notice how the firewall is modified to allow traffic to the port selected (8001) for the `netcat` server.

Listing 20.3: Setting up the nc server

```
$ sudo ufw allow 8001
Rule added
Rule added (v6)
$
$ nc -l 8001 > /dev/null
```

The `-l` option on the nc command tells it to go into listening mode and act as a server. The 8001 argument tells `netcat` to listen on port 8001. Because `netcat` is being used to test throughput, there is no need to display any received data. Thus, the data received is thrown into the black hole file (`/dev/null`).

To conduct a test with `netcat`, employ a utility that will send packets to the server and allow you to see the throughput rate. The dd command (covered in Chapter 12, "Protecting Files") works well, and an example of conducting a test on a Fedora system is shown in Listing 20.4.

Listing 20.4: Setting up the nc client and conducting a throughput test

```
$ dd if=/dev/zero bs=1M count=2 | nc 192.168.0.104 8001 -i 2
2+0 records in
2+0 records out
2097152 bytes (2.1 MB, 2.0 MiB) copied, 0.10808 s, 19.4 MB/s
Ncat: Idle timeout expired (2000 ms).
$
```

Notice for the dd command, no output file (of) switch is used. This forces the command's output to go to STDOUT, which is then redirected via the pipe (|) into the nc command. The nc command sends the output as packets through the network to the netcat server's IP address (192.168.0.104) at port 8001, where the listening server receives the packets. The -i 2 option tells netcat to quit and return to the command line after 2 seconds of idle time.

The throughput rate is displayed when dd completes its operation. You can increase the test traffic sent by increasing the data amount designated by the dd command's bs option and the number of times it is sent via the count switch. In the Listing 20.4 example, only 1 Mb was sent two times.

> **NOTE**   On some distributions, you will find a netcat command. This command is simply a softlink to the nc utility and provided for convenience.

High latency is sometimes caused by overloaded routers. Faulty hardware or improper configurations, such as the router's MTU being set too low, also contribute to the problem. The tracepath and traceroute utilities not only display what path a packet takes through the network's routers but can provide throughput information as well, allowing you to pinpoint potential problem areas.

The mtr utility can provide a nice graphical display or a simple report showing a packet's path, travel times, and items such as jitter. Listing 20.5 shows an example of using mtr to produce a static report.

Listing 20.5: Producing router performance reports with the mtr utility

```
$ mtr -o "L D A J" -c 20 -r 96.120.112.205
Start: 2018-12-21T13:47:39-0500
HOST: localhost.localdomain      Loss%  Drop    Avg   Jttr
  1.|-- _gateway                  0.0%     0     0.8    0.1
  2.|-- _gateway                  0.0%     0     3.8    7.1
  3.|-- 96.120.112.205            0.0%     0    15.5    1.8
$
```

The mtr command's -o option allows you to specify what statistics to view. In this example, packet loss (L), drop (D), travel time average (A), and jitter (J) are chosen. The -c switch lets you set the number of times a packet is sent through the routers, and the -r option designates that you want a static report. To show a continuous graphical display, leave off the -c and -r options. The last mtr argument is the destination IP address.

A faulty or failing adapter also can contribute to high latency. If you suspect that errors, packet drops, or timeouts are causing network problems, try employing the utilities in Table 20.3 to display these statistics.

TABLE 20.3   Commands to find failing/faulty network adapters

Command	Description
`ethtool -S` *adapter*	Shows *adapter* summary statistics.
`ifconfig` *adapter*	Shows *adapter* summary statistics. This command is deprecated.
`ip -s link show` *adapter*	Shows *adapter* summary statistics.
`netstat -i` *adapter*	Shows *adapter* summary statistics. To view over time, add the `-c #` switch, where # is the number of seconds between displays. This command is deprecated.

Using the `ip` utility is shown snipped in Listing 20.6. Notice that even though no packets have been dropped, it does show error rates hovering around 0.05 percent (RX or TX packets / RX or TX errors). Any rate over 0.01 percent is enough to consider the adapter faulty.

Listing 20.6: Viewing network adapter statistics with the `ip` utility

```
$ ip -s link show enp0s8
3: enp0s8: <BROADCAST,MULTICAST,UP,LOWER_UP> mtu 1500 [...]
[...]
    RX: bytes  packets  errors  dropped overrun mcast
    201885893  3023900  1510    0       0       318
    TX: bytes  packets  errors  dropped carrier collsns
    24443239380 15852137 7922   0       0       0
$
```

NOTE The `ping` and `ping6` utilities, covered earlier in Table 20.1, are helpful in discovering packet loss and timeout issues. In fact, they are often the first tools employed when such problems are occurring.

If you have a rather tricky network problem, it may be worth your while to directly look at the packets traveling over it. The tools to do so go by a variety of names, such as network sniffers and packet analyzers. Three popular ones are Wireshark, `tshark`, and `tcpdump`.

Wireshark (a GUI program) and `tshark` (also called terminal-based Wireshark) are closely linked, and that causes confusion when it comes to their installation. Table 20.4 lists the package names needed to obtain the correct tool for each distribution covered by this book.

TABLE 20.4   Listing Wireshark GUI and `tshark` package names

Distribution	Wireshark GUI package	`tshark` package
Rocky Linux 8	`wireshark-gnome`	`wireshark-cli`
Fedora 35	`wireshark`	`wireshark`
OpenSUSE Leap 15	`wireshark`	`wireshark`
Ubuntu 20.04 LTS	`wireshark`	`tshark`

Once you have the proper package installed, you can employ the tool to analyze packets. A simple snipped example of using `tshark` on an Ubuntu system is shown in Listing 20.7. The `tshark` command's `-i` option allows you to specify the interface from which to sniff packets. The `-c` switch lets you specify the number of packets to capture.

Listing 20.7: Using `tshark` to view packets

```
$ sudo tshark -i enp0s8 -c 10
[...]
Capturing on 'enp0s8'
    1 0.000000000 192.168.0.100 → 239.255.255.250 [...]
    2 0.493150205 fe80::597e:c86f:d3ec:8901 → ff02[...]
    3 0.683985479 192.168.0.104 → 192.168.0.101 SSH[...]
    4 0.684261795 192.168.0.104 → 192.168.0.101 SSH[...]
    5 0.684586349 192.168.0.101 → 192.168.0.104 TCP[...]
[...]
   10 1.198757076 192.168.0.104 → 192.168.0.101 SSH[...]
198 Server: Encrypted packet (len=144)
10 packets captured
$
```

Both `tshark` and `tcpdump` allow you to store the sniffed data into a file. Later the packet information can be viewed using the Wireshark utility, if you prefer viewing data via a GUI application.

Reviewing the Network's Configuration

In the network troubleshooting process, you might want to check your various network configurations. Network adapter configurations were covered in Chapter 7. You can use the tools listed earlier in Table 20.3 as well as the `nmcli` utility to review adapter settings.

Within a local network segment, routers do not use an IP address to locate systems. Instead they use the system's network adapter's media access control (MAC) address. MACs are mapped to their server's IPv4 address via the Address Resolution Protocol (ARP) table or IPv6 address Neighborhood Discovery (NDisc) table. An incorrect mapping or duplicate MAC address can wreak havoc in your network. Table 20.5 has the commands you can use to investigate this issue.

TABLE 20.5 Commands to check for incorrect MAC mappings or duplicates

Command	Description
arp	Displays the ARP table for the network's neighborhood. Checks for incorrect or duplicate MAC addresses.
ip neigh	Displays the ARP and NDISC tables for the network's neighborhood. Checks for incorrect or duplicate MAC addresses.

A misconfigured routing table can also cause problems. Double-check your system's routing table via the route command (deprecated) or the ip route show command.

Incorrect DNS information for your own servers is troublesome. Also, if you are considering changing your client-side DNS configuration, there are some utilities that can help you investigate slow query responses. The commands in Table 20.6 are good utilities to guide your investigations.

TABLE 20.6 Commands to research name server responses

Command	Description
host *FQDN*	Queries the DNS server for the *FQDN* and displays its IP address. Check the returned IP address for correctness.
dig *FQDN*	Performs queries on the DNS server for the *FQDN* and displays all DNS records associated with it. Check the returned information for correctness.
nslookup	Executes various DNS queries in an interactive or noninteractive mode. Check the returned information for correctness.
whois	Performs queries of Whois servers and displays *FQDN* information stored there. Check the returned information for correctness.

The nslookup utility is very handy for testing DNS lookup speeds. You follow the command with the FQDN to look up and then the DNS server you desire to test. Use it along with the time command to gather lookup time estimates, as shown snipped in Listing 20.8.

Listing 20.8: Testing DNS lookup speeds with the nslookup utility and the time command

```
$ time nslookup www.linux.org 8.8.8.8
[...]
Name:    www.linux.org
Address: 104.27.166.219
[...]
real    0m0.099s
[...]
$ time nslookup www.linux.org 9.9.9.9
[...]
Name:    www.linux.org
Address: 104.27.167.219
[...]
real    0m0.173s
[...]
$
```

 If your system employs IPsets in its firewall or other configurations, you may want to review those as well. Use super user privileges and type in **ipset list** to see the various IPsets and then review their use within configuration files.

The Network Mapper (nmap) utility is often used for penetration testing. However, it is also very useful for network troubleshooting. Though it's typically not installed by default, most distros have the nmap package in their standard repositories.

There are a number of different scans you can run with nmap. The snipped example in Listing 20.9 shows using nmap inside the system's firewall to see what ports are offering which services via the -sT options.

Listing 20.9: Viewing TCP ports and services using the nmap utility

```
$ nmap -sT 127.0.0.1
[...]
PORT     STATE SERVICE
22/tcp   open  ssh
631/tcp open  ipp
[...]
$
```

You can use nmap to scan entire network segments and ask for the mapper to fingerprint each system in order to identify the operating system running there via the -O option. To perform this scan, you need super user privileges, as shown in snipped Listing 20.10.

Listing 20.10: Viewing network segment systems' OSs using the nmap utility

```
$ sudo nmap -O 192.168.0.*
[...]
Nmap scan report for 192.168.0.102
[...]
Running: Linux 3.X|4.X
[...]
Nmap scan report for Ubuntu1804 (192.168.0.104)
[...]
Running: Linux 3.X|4.X
[...]
```

 Do not run the network mapper utility outside your home network without permission. For more information, read the nmap utility's legal issue guide at https://nmap.org/book/legal-issues.html.

Troubleshooting Storage Issues

Data storage is one of the areas where your systems can encounter problems. Trouble with storage tends to focus on failing hardware, disk I/O latency, and exhausted disk space. We'll focus on those three issues in the following sections.

Running Out of Filesystem Space

Nothing can ruin system uptime statistics like application crashes due to drained disk space. Two utilities that assist in troubleshooting and monitoring filesystem space are the du and df commands, which were covered in Chapter 11, "Handling Storage."

The df utility allows you to view overall space usage. In the example in Listing 20.11, only the ext4 filesystems are viewed via the -t option, and the results are displayed in human-readable format (-h), providing a succinct display.

Listing 20.11: Viewing filesystem space totals using the df utility

```
$ df -ht ext4
Filesystem      Size  Used Avail Use% Mounted on
/dev/sda1       9.8G  7.3G  2.0G  79% /
$
```

If you see a filesystem whose usage is above desired percentages, locate potential problem areas on the filesystem via the du command. First, obtain a summary by viewing the filesystem's mount point directory and only display space used by first-level subdirectories via the -d 1 option. An example is shown snipped in Listing 20.12 for a filesystem whose mount point is the / directory.

Listing 20.12: Viewing subdirectory space summaries using the du utility

```
$ sudo du -d 1 /
[...]
2150868 /var
[...]
48840   /home
{...}
```

After you find potential problem subdirectories, start digging down into them via du to find potential space hogs, as shown snipped in Listing 20.13.

Listing 20.13: Finding potential space hogs using the du utility

```
$ sudo du /var/log
[...]
499876  /var/log/journal/e9af6ca5a8fb4a70b2ddec4b1894014d
[...]
```

If you find that the filesystem actually needs the disk space it is using, the only choice is to add more space. If you set up the original filesystem on a logical volume, adding space via LVM tools is fairly simple (creating a logical volume was covered in Chapter 11).

If you don't have an extra physical volume in your volume group to add to the filesystem volume needing disk space, do the following:

1. Add a spare drive to the system, if needed.

2. Create a physical volume with the pvcreate command.

3. Add the new physical volume to the group with vgextend.

4. Increase the logical volume size by using the lvextend command.

Waiting on Disk I/O

If a disk is experiencing I/O beyond what it can reasonably handle, it can slow down the entire system. You can troubleshoot this issue by using a utility that displays *I/O wait* times, such as the iostat command. I/O wait is a performance statistic that shows the amount of time a processor must wait on disk I/O.

If you find that the `iostat` utility is not installed on your system, install the `sysstat` package to obtain it. Package installation was covered in Chapter 13.

The syntax for the `iostat` command is as follows:

iostat [*OPTION*] [*INTERVAL*] [*COUNT*]

If you simply enter **iostat** at the command line and press Enter, you'll see a static summary of CPU, filesystem, and partition statistics since the system booted. However, in troubleshooting situations, this is not worthwhile. There are a few useful `iostat` options to use for troubleshooting:

-y: Do not include the initial "since system booted" statistics.

-N: Display registered device mapper names for logical volumes.

-z: Do not show devices experiencing no activity.

-p *device*: Only show information regarding this *device*.

The `iostat` command's two arguments allow viewing of the statistics over time. The [*INTERVAL*] argument specifies how many seconds between each display, and [*COUNT*] sets the number of times to display. Keep in mind that if you use the -y option, you will not see the first statistics until after the set interval.

An example using `iostat` with appropriate options for a troubleshooting situation is shown snipped in Listing 20.14. In this case, only two statistics are shown 5 seconds apart. You can see that there is a rather high I/O wait (%iowait column) percentage, indicating a potential problem.

Listing 20.14: Troubleshooting I/O wait using the `iostat` utility

```
$ iostat -yNz 5 2
[...]
avg-cpu:   %user    %nice %system %iowait   %steal   %idle
           26.80     0.00   42.27   30.93     0.00    0.00

Device:              tps    kB_read/s   kB_wrtn/s   kB_read    kB_wrtn
sda               409.90         3.30     9720.72        16      47145
[...]
avg-cpu:   %user    %nice %system %iowait   %steal   %idle
           22.67     0.00   65.79   11.54     0.00    0.00

Device:              tps    kB_read/s   kB_wrtn/s   kB_read    kB_wrtn
sda               535.83         0.00     9772.77         0      48277
[...]
```

NOTE   To locate the application or process causing high I/O, employ the `iotop` utility. It is typically not installed by default but is available in the `iotop` package.

For problems with high I/O, besides employing different disk technologies, you will want to review the Linux kernel's defined *I/O scheduling*. I/O scheduling is a series of kernel actions that handle I/O requests and their associated activities. How these various operations proceed is guided by selecting a particular I/O scheduler, shown in Table 20.7, within a configuration file.

TABLE 20.7   I/O schedulers

Name	Description
cfq	Creates queues for each process and handles the various queues in a loop while providing read request priority over write requests. This scheduler is good for situations where more balance I/O handling is needed and/or the system has a multiprocessor.
deadline	Batches disk I/O requests and attempts to handle each request by a specified time. This scheduler is good for situations where increased database I/O and overall reduced I/O latency are needed, and/or an SSD is employed, and/or a real-time application is in use.
noop	Places all I/O requests into a single FIFO queue and handles them in order. This scheduler is good for situations where less CPU usage is needed and/or an SSD is employed.

The configuration file used for determining which I/O scheduler to use is in a directory associated with each disk. Listing 20.15 shows how to find the various disk directories and their associated scheduler file on a Rocky Linux distribution.

Listing 20.15: Locating a disk's scheduler file

```
# ls /sys/block
dm-0  dm-1  sda  sdb  sdc  sdd  sr0
#
# cat /sys/block/sda/queue/scheduler
[mq-deadline] kyber bfq none

#
```

The scheduler used for the sda disk, `mq-deadline`, is in brackets. To change the current I/O scheduler, you simply employ super user privileges and the `echo` command, as shown in Listing 20.16.

Listing 20.16: Changing a disk's scheduler file temporarily

```
# echo "bfq" > /sys/block/sda/queue/scheduler
#
# cat /sys/block/sda/queue/scheduler
mq-deadline kyber [bfq] none

#
```

If you determine that due to hardware limitations, a new and different hard drive is needed to handle the required I/O levels, the ioping utility can help you in the testing process. The ioping utility is typically not installed by default, but it is commonly available in a distribution's standard repositories.

 The ioping utility can destroy data on your disk! Be sure to thoroughly understand the command's options before employing it. If you desire a safer alternative, take a look at the stress-ng tool. This utility allows you to conduct stress tests for disks, your network, a system's CPUs, and so on.

Using the ioping command, you can test disk I/O latency, seek rates, and sequential speeds. You can also try out asynchronous, cache, and direct I/O rates.

A snipped example in Listing 20.17 shows a simple test that reads random data chunks (noncached) from a temporary file using the ioping command.

Listing 20.17: Conducting a noncached read test using the ioping utility

```
# ioping -c 3 /dev/sda
4 KiB <<< /dev/sda [...]: request=1 time=20.7 ms (warmup)
4 KiB <<< /dev/sda [...]: request=2 time=32.9 ms
4 KiB <<< /dev/sda [...]: request=3 time=25.5 ms

--- /dev/sda (block device 15 GiB) ioping statistics ---
2 requests completed in 58.4 ms, 8 KiB read, 34 iops, 137.0 KiB/s
generated 3 requests in 2.03 s, 12 KiB, 1 iops, 5.92 KiB/s
min/avg/max/mdev = 25.5 ms / 29.2 ms / 32.9 ms / 3.72 ms
#
```

The added -c 3 option specifies three tests. More thorough ioping tests help determine if a disk will work for a particular application's needs.

Measuring Disk Performance

One benchmark that's helpful in determining the overall I/O performance for disk drives is the input/output operations per second (IOPS) value. This value is the number of input or output operations a storage device can perform in a second. The IOPS values provide a way to not only evaluate disk drive performance but compare different types of storage, such as a single SATA or SSD drive versus a RAID or LVM setup.

A popular tool in the Linux environment for determining IOPS values is the flexible I/O tool called `fio`. The tool is available as the `fio` package in both the Debian-based and Red Hat–based software repositories, and it must be installed manually.

The `fio` tool performs multiple read/write operations on a file and directory you specify, with a file size and block size that you specify. The larger the file, the more accurate the IOPS reading you'll obtain. Listing 20.18 shows an example of performing an `fio` test on a disk.

Listing 20.18: Using the `fio` tool to determin disk I/O

```
# fio --randrepeat=1 --ioengine=libaio --direct=1
--gtod_reduce=1 --name=fiotest --filename=fiotest --bs=4k
--iodepth=64 -size=1G -readwrite=randrw -rwmixread=75

fiotest: (g=0): rw=randrw, bs=(R) 4096B-4096B, (W) 4096B-4096B, (T)
4096B-4096B, ioengine=libaio, iodepth=64
fio-3.19
Starting 1 process
fiotest: Laying out IO file (1 file / 1024MiB)
[...]
  read: IOPS=23.4k, BW=91.4MiB/s (95.9MB/s)(768MiB/8396msec)
   bw (  KiB/s): min=63425, max=101451, per=99.97%, avg=93588.81,
stdev=9628.66, samples=16
    iops        : min=15856, max=25362, avg=23396.88, stdev=2407.19, samples=16
  write: IOPS=7818, BW=30.5MiB/s (32.0MB/s)(256MiB/8396msec); 0 zone resets
   bw (  KiB/s): min=22658, max=33712, per=99.91%, avg=31245.31,
stdev=2927.74, samples=16
    iops        : min= 5664, max= 8428, avg=7811.06, stdev=732.05, samples=16
  cpu           : usr=2.80%, sys=34.02%, ctx=3045, majf=0, minf=7
  IO depths     : 1=0.1%, 2=0.1%, 4=0.1%, 8=0.1%, 16=0.1%, 32=0.1%,
>=64=100.0%
     submit     : 0=0.0%, 4=100.0%, 8=0.0%, 16=0.0%, 32=0.0%, 64=0.0%,
>=64=0.0%
     complete   : 0=0.0%, 4=100.0%, 8=0.0%, 16=0.0%, 32=0.0%, 64=0.1%,
>=64=0.0%
     issued rwts: total=196498,65646,0,0 short=0,0,0,0 dropped=0,0,0,0
     latency    : target=0, window=0, percentile=100.00%, depth=64
[...]
#
```

As you can see, the `fio` tool provides lots of detailed information about the read/write test. You can consult the `fio` man pages to learn about all the details. In Listing 20.18, the main IOPS information we're interested in here appears in these two lines:

```
read: IOPS=23.4k, BW=91.4MiB/s
write: IOPS=7818, BW=30.5MiB/s
```

For this disk drive, the read IOPS value was 23400, and the write IOPS was 7818. It's normal for the write IOPS value to be significantly lower than the read IOPS value because it takes longer to write data to the disk than to read it. Now you can use these values to compare against other storage devices on your system.

> Solid-state drives (SSDs) handle reads and writes a bit differently than standard SATA or SCSI drives. When a file is deleted in the filesystem stored on an SSD device, the `fstrim` application needs to run to determine which memory locations can be recovered (called SSD trimming). Maintaining unnecessary memory locations can slow down the read and write access to the SSD device. Most Linux distributions run the `fstrim` utility at periodic intervals automatically for internal SSD devices, but if you add an external SSD device to your Linux system, you may need to manually run the `fstrim` utility yourself to help increase performance on the device.

Failing Disks

If a small chunk of an HDD or SSD will not respond to I/O requests, the disk controller marks it as a bad sector. When a bad sector is marked, typically the controller's firmware will attempt to move the data from the marked sector to a new location and remap the logical sector to the new sector. Thus, the data is safe.

A random bad sector does not indicate a drive is failing. However, if you are seeing bad sectors more and more on your disk, then it needs to be replaced. Thus, you should monitor this situation.

> If the drive has self-monitoring analysis and reporting technology (SMART), you can employ the `smartctl` utility to check on its health.

Occasionally a file on the drive loses its matching inode number, called a mismatch (covered in Chapter 3, "Managing Files, Directories, and Text"), or some other type of disk corruption occurs. This leaves the data in place but nothing can access it, and the problem must be repaired manually.

One utility that will allow you to check and repair an ext2, ext3, or ext4 filesystem is the `fsck` command (covered in Chapter 11). The disk partition must be unmounted before you can run the utility on it.

For a btrfs filesystem, use the btrfs check command to check and/or repair an unmounted btrfs drive. If you have an XFS filesystem, use the xfs_check utility to check the disk and xfs_repair to check and repair the drive.

Physical damage or wear can sometimes cause unusual sounds from a drive. You may hear clicking, grinding, or scratching noises. These indicate a drive is failing and should be replaced as soon as possible.

In the cases where you do need to replace a drive and rebuild your partition(s), keep in mind that you can use the partprobe command. This nice utility allows your system to reread a disk's partition table without rebooting the system. You do need to use super user privileges to invoke it.

Troubleshooting the CPU

You need to correctly size your CPU(s) for your server application needs. An undersized processor will force you to obtain a new one, and an oversized processor will not be used to its full potential. Both waste money.

For troubleshooting, you need to understand your CPU(s)' hardware—the number of cores, whether or not hyperthreading is used, cache sizes, and so on. You can easily view your system's current processors' information. Use the less utility and pass it the /proc/cpuinfo filename. The first processor listed in this file is shown as processor 0.

To look at CPU usage, you can employ the uptime command. It shows how long the system has been up and running, but even more important, it displays CPU *load averages*. Load averages are the average amount of processes waiting for or using the CPU. For example, if you have a single core processor, then a load average of 2 would mean that typically a process is using the CPU while another process waits.

The uptime utility displays three load average numbers—a 1-, 5-, and 15-minute average. An example is shown in Listing 20.19.

Listing 20.19: Displaying load averages with the uptime utility

```
$ uptime
 15:12:41 up 54 min,  2 users,  load average: 0.95, 0.93, 0.90
$
```

This single-core CPU system has rather high load averages, which indicates a potential serious problem. First, check for a runaway process. If there is not one, you will want to investigate items such as interrupts from network and disks. The top utility can help here.

For a single-core CPU, a consistent load average above 0.70 indicates a problem. Consistent load averages of 1.00 are at emergency levels.

If you need to view CPU performance over time, the `sar` (system activity reporter) utility is useful. It's typically installed by default on most distributions, but if you need to install it, use the `sysstat` package.

The `sar` utility uses data stored by the `sadc` program in the `/var/log/sa/` directory, which contains up to a month's worth of data. By default, it displays data from the current file. Used without any options or arguments, `sar` will display today's stored CPU usage information in 10-minute intervals, as shown snipped in Listing 20.20.

Listing 20.20: Displaying CPU usage with the `sar` utility

```
$ sar -u
[...]
03:20:28 PM    CPU     %user    %nice    %system    %iowait    %steal    %idle
03:30:18 PM    all     32.15    0.00     67.85      0.00       0.00      0.00
03:40:01 PM    all     19.07    0.00     26.88      0.00       0.00      54.05
[...]
Average:       all     20.85    0.00     24.51      0.01       0.00      54.64
[...]
```

If your server is running multiple virtual machines, the `%steal` column of the `sar` utility output is handy. This column shows how much CPU is being utilized by virtual machines on the system.

 You may be able to improve CPU performance by modifying certain kernel parameters via the `sysctl` utility. For example, if your server has multiple processors, they may experience jitter (similar to network jitter), causing spikes in their performance and resulting in application slowness (high latency). If set to 1, the `skew_tick` parameter can reduce this jitter.

Troubleshooting Memory

Processes use RAM to temporarily store data because it is faster to access than data stored on a disk. One form of this is *disk buffering*, which improves disk read performance. Data is read from the disk and stored for a period of time in a memory location called a *buffer cache*. Subsequent accesses of that data are read from memory rather than disk, which significantly improves performance.

The speed that memory provides to processes is so valuable that the Linux kernel maintains and administers shared memory areas. These shared segments allow multiple running programs to read/write from/to a common shared memory data area, which considerably speeds up process interactions.

You can see detailed information concerning your system's RAM by viewing the /proc/meminfo file. To view shared memory segments, use the ipcs -m command. You can view memory statistics on a system using command-line tools such as free, sar, and vmstat.

Be aware that RAM bottlenecks often keep CPU usage artificially low. If you increase the RAM on your system, your processor loads may also increase.

Swapping

Memory is divided up into chunks called *pages*. When the system needs more memory, using a memory management scheme, it takes an idle process's memory pages and copies them to disk. This disk location is a special partition called *swap space* or *swap* or *virtual memory*. If the idle process is no longer idle, its memory pages are copied back into memory. This process of copying memory pages to/from the disk swap space is called *swapping*.

If your system does not have properly sized memory, you should see high RAM usage via the free command. In addition, the system will increase swapping, which results in increased disk I/O. The vmstat tool is handy in this case because it will allow you to view disk I/O specific to swapping as well as total blocks in and blocks out to the device. An example of using the vmstat utility is shown in Listing 20.21.

Listing 20.21: Displaying virtual memory statistics with the vmstat utility

```
$ vmstat
procs -----------memory---------- ---swap-- -----io---- -system-- ------cpu-----
 r  b   swpd   free   buff  cache   si   so    bi    bo   in   cs us sy id wa st
 2  0      0 3149092   3220 355180    0    0  1978    43  812  783 27 17 26 29  0
$
```

On a Linux system, swap space is either a disk partition or a file. A swap partition is a special disk partition that acts as the system's swap space.

It is generally recommended that you do not store your swap partitions/files on SSDs. This is due to their limited life span and wear-leveling. Heavy swapping could cause an early SSD death.

A useful utility for viewing memory and determining if swap is a file or a partition is the swapon -s command. If it's available, you can obtain the same information from the /proc/swaps file. An example of using the swapon -s command on a Rocky Linux distribution is shown in Listing 20.22.

Listing 20.22: Displaying a swap partition with the `swapon` utility

```
$ swapon -s
Filename        Type        Size      Used    Priority
/dev/dm-1       partition   1769468   0       -2

$
```

Notice that on this Rocky Linux distro, the swap space is a partition. The priority column within the preceding example's swap space statistics is shown as a negative 2 (-2). If there are multiple swap spaces, this priority number determines which swap is used first.

Another `swapon -s` example is enacted on an Ubuntu distribution and shown in Listing 20.23. Notice that in this case, the swap space is a file.

Listing 20.23: Displaying a swap file with the `swapon` utility

```
$ swapon -s
Filename        Type        Size      Used    Priority
/swapfile       file        483800    0       -2
$
```

During the Linux OS installation, typically a swap partition or file is created and added to the `/etc/fstab` configuration file. However, you may need to create additional swap partitions/files—for example, if you increase your system's RAM.

> If your swap partition is on a logical volume, add additional space via the LVM tools. Simply follow the steps covered in the section "Troubleshooting Storage Issues" earlier in this chapter as well as the following section. However, you can have more than one system swap space. In fact, in many cases it is desirable to do so for performance reasons.

For a new partition swap space, once you've created a new disk partition, use the `mkswap` command to "format" the partition into a swap partition. You use the same command for a new swap file and a logical volume. An example on a Rocky Linux system, using super user privileges, is shown in Listing 20.24.

Listing 20.24: Making a swap partition with the `mkswap` command

```
# mkswap /dev/sde1
Setting up swapspace version 1, size = 1048572 KiB
no label, UUID=e5bd150a-2f06-42ed-a0a9-a7372abd9dee
#

# blkid /dev/sde1
/dev/sde1: UUID="e5bd150a-2f06-42ed-a0a9-a7372abd9dee" TYPE="swap"
#
```

Now that the swap partition or file has been properly prepared, activate it using the swapon command. The free command is very useful here because it provides a simple view of your current free and used memory. An example of these two commands is shown in Listing 20.25.

Listing 20.25: Activating a swap partition with the swapon command

```
# free -h
              total        used        free      shared  buff/cache   available
Mem:           3.7G        359M        3.0G        9.3M        352M        3.1G
Swap:          1.5G          0B        1.5G
#
# swapon /dev/sde1
#
# swapon -s
Filename              Type            Size      Used   Priority
/dev/dm-1             partition       1572860   0      -1
/dev/sde1             partition       1048572   0      -2
#
# free -h
              total        used        free      shared  buff/cache   available
Mem:           3.7G        366M        3.0G        9.3M        352M        3.1G
Swap:          2.5G          0B        2.5G
#
```

You can see that the swap space size has increased 1 GB by adding a second swap partition. The -h option on the free command displays memory information in a more human-readable format.

> The free command's buffer cache output is displayed in the buff/cache column. Older versions of this command would show two columns for this data—buffers and cache. Linux divides up its buffer cache into distinct categories. Buffers are memory used by kernel buffers, while cache is memory used by process page caches and slabs (contiguous memory pages set aside for individual caches). The buff/cache column in the modern free command's output is simply a summation of these two memory use categories.

If desired, change the new swap partition's priority from its current negative 2 (-2) to a higher priority, using the swapon command, as shown in Listing 20.26. A higher number designates that the swap partition is used before other partitions for swap.

Listing 20.26: Changing a swap priority with the swapon command

```
# swapoff /dev/sde1
#
# swapon -p 0 /dev/sde1
#
# swapon -s
Filename          Type          Size      Used   Priority
/dev/dm-1         partition     1572860   0      -1
/dev/sde1         partition     1048572   0      0
#
```

You must first use the swapoff command on the swap partition to disengage it from swap space. After that, the swapon -p *priority* is used to change the preference priority. You can set *priority* to any number between 0 and 32767.

 WARNING If you want to move your system to a new swap partition or file, do not use the swapoff command on a current swap partition/file until your new swap partition is added to swap space. Otherwise, you may end up with a hung system.

If all is well with the new swap partition, add it to the /etc/fstab file so that it is persistent through system reboots. You can closely mimic the current swap file record's settings, but be sure to change the name to your new swap partition/file.

Running Out of Memory

By default, the Linux kernel allows itself to overcommit memory to various processes. This is done for efficiency and performance. However, due to this allowance, the system can become very low on free memory. In a critical low-memory situation, Linux first reclaims old memory pages. If it doesn't reclaim enough RAM to come out of a critical status, it employs the *out of memory killer* (also called the *OOM killer*).

When triggered, the OOM killer scans through the various processes using memory and creates a score. The score is based on the total memory a process (and its child processes) is using and the smallest number of processes that can be killed to come out of a critical low-memory status. The kernel, root, and crucial system processes are automatically given low scores. If a process has a high score, it is killed off. The OOM killer scans and kills off high-scoring processes until the system is back to normal memory status.

If you want to modify the behavior of the OOM killer, you can do so via the following kernel parameters with the `sysctl` command: `vm.panic_on_oom` and `kernel.panic`.

You can force the kernel to prevent memory overcommit via the `sysctl` command, changing the `vm.overcommit_memory` kernel parameter from its default of 0 to 1. However, this may not be the best solution. In many systems, it is better to fine-tune the memory overcommit by setting `vm.overcommit_memory` to 2. This allows you to allocate as much memory as defined in another kernel parameter, the `overcommit_ratio`. In this case, when a process requests memory that causes the system to exceed the set overcommit ratio, the allocation fails.

While you can modify kernel parameters with the `sysctl` command, the settings are not persistent. To make the settings persistent, make the appropriate edits to /etc/sysctl.conf or your distribution's applicable `sysctl` configuration file.

Surviving a Lost Root Password

Forgetting the root account's password is troublesome for many reasons. The quick fix is to reset it via the `passwd` command using your own account's super user privileges. However, if you were using the root account to gain super user privileges (which is a bad practice) or your privileges do not allow you to change the root password, you are in trouble. But all hope is not lost.

On older Linux distros and a few modern ones (Ubuntu), booting the system into single user mode will allow you to access the root account and change its password via the `passwd` command. To do so, follow these steps:

1. Boot (or reboot) the system. When the boot process reaches the boot menu, press the **E** key on the boot menu line you wish to edit (the kernel version the system typically runs).

2. Find the line that contains `linux` or `linux16` via an arrow key.

3. Go to the line's end, press the spacebar once, and type **1**.

4. Press Ctrl+X to boot the system.

5. Once the system is booted, press the Enter key if it states you are in Emergency or Rescue mode.

6. Change the root account's password using the `passwd` command.

7. Reboot the system using the `reboot` command.

On some modern Linux systems, such as Rocky Linux and Fedora distros, you'll need a slightly different approach. Follow these steps:

1. Boot (or reboot) the system. When the boot process reaches the boot menu, press the E key on the boot menu line you wish to edit (the kernel version the system typically runs).

2. Find the line that contains `linux` or `linux16` via an arrow key.

3. On that line, find `ro`. This is somewhere in the line's middle.

4. Replace `ro` with **rw init=/sysroot/bin/sh**. Don't replace anything else in that line but `ro`.

5. Press Ctrl+X to boot the system.

6. Once the system is booted, press the Enter key if it states you are in Emergency or Rescue mode.

7. Type **chroot /sysroot** to set up a jailed root environment.

8. Change the root account's password using the `passwd` command.

9. If the system uses SELinux (Rocky Linux and Fedora typically do), force SELinux to automatically relabel the system on the next boot by typing the **touch /.autorelabel** command.

10. Reboot the system with the `reboot` command. (Note: You may need to type **exit** and press Enter before trying to reboot your system.)

You'll have to wait a while for the system to go through its SELinux relabel process.

Summary

Troubleshooting Linux performance issues requires planning ahead for adverse incidents. In addition, you must understand the interactions between the various system properties, such as processors, disks, networks, and memory. Properly sizing system components and configuring Linux will provide a more trouble-free environment.

Exam Essentials

Describe network troubleshooting tools.   If your network is experiencing high latency, the tools to help troubleshoot this are `iperf`, `iperf3`, `iftop`, `mtr`, `nc` (netcat), `ping`, `ping6`, `ss`, `tracepath`, `tracepath6`, `traceroute`, and `traceroute6`. These utilities also assist in detecting network saturation problems. If failing or faulty adapters are a problem, the tools to diagnose this issue are `ethtool`, `ifconfig`, `ip`, and `netstat`. These utilities along with `nmcli` also help with NIC configuration problems. For incorrect or duplicate MAC addresses in a router, employ the arp or ip neigh command. To research slow or incorrect name server responses, the host, dig, nslookup, and whois utilities help.

Summarize potential disk problems and solutions.   The du and df utilities help in preventing the system from running out of filesystem space and with troubleshooting when it does. If it is a logical volume, employ the LVM tools to add additional space when needed. I/O wait times, which may slow overall system performance, are seen with the iostat command. Changing a system's I/O scheduler may help relieve this problem. The ioping utility tests a disk to determine if it is usable for a particular application. To repair an ext* filesystem, use the fsck command. The partprobe command works well for newly created partitions in that it forces a reread of a disk's partition table without rebooting the system.

Clarify CPU troubleshooting procedures.   It is important to understand your system's current processors' information, which you can find in the /proc/cpuinfo file. To view CPU usage, employ the uptime and/or the sar commands. If needed and appropriate, you can tweak kernel parameters related to processor handling using the sysctl utility.

Explain memory problems and solutions.   To view detailed system RAM information, look at the /proc/meminfo file's contents. If your system does not have properly sized memory, you can see high RAM usage via the free command. In addition, the vmstat tool allows you to view disk I/O specific to swapping, which increases when RAM is improperly sized. If you need to add additional swap space, the mkswap utility will "format" a partition/file into swap, and the swapon command will put it into swap space. If you need to uncouple a partition/file from swap space, use the swapoff utility. If memory use hits critical levels, the kernel releases the OOM killer, which kills off particular processes to bring memory usage back to reasonable levels. Memory management can be modified using certain kernel parameters and the sysctl tool.

Review Questions

1. Which of the following is true concerning network sockets? (Choose all that apply.)

   A. Numbers used to identify which service is transmitting data

   B. A single endpoint of a network connection's two endpoints

   C. Uses a combination of an IP address and a port number

   D. Endpoints between processes on a local system

   E. Provides better IPC than localhost

2. The system administrator, Preston, has noticed that the IPv4 network seems sluggish. He decides to run some tests to check for high latency. Which of the following utilities should he use? (Choose all that apply.)

   A. `iperf`

   B. `ping`

   C. `ip neigh`

   D. `dig`

   E. `traceroute`

3. Scott has formulated a problem cause theory that routers are saturated with traffic and dropping TCP packets from their queues. Which of the following tools should he employ to test this theory? (Choose all that apply.)

   A. `mtr`

   B. `ifconfig`

   C. `ethtool -s`

   D. `tracepath`

   E. `traceroute`

4. The network engineer, Keenser, believes the choices of name servers in the system's `/etc/resolv.conf` file are inefficient. Which of the following tools can he employ to test new server choices?

   A. `dnsmasq`

   B. `whois`

   C. `nmap`

   D. `nslookup`

   E. `ipset list`

5. Mera, a Linux system admin, believes a new application on her system is producing too much I/O for a particular partition, causing the system's processor to appear sluggish. Which tool should she use to test her problem cause theory?

    A. iostat

    B. ioping

    C. du

    D. df

    E. iotop

6. From analysis, Arthur believes the system's I/O throughput will improve by changing the I/O scheduler. On his system is a real-time application, which uses a database located on a solid-state drive. Which I/O scheduler should Arthur choose?

    A. scheduler

    B. deadline

    C. queue

    D. cfq

    E. noop

7. Using the uptime command, you will see CPU load averages in what increments? (Choose all that apply.)

    A. 1 minute

    B. 5 minutes

    C. 10 minutes

    D. 15 minutes

    E. 20 minutes

8. Mary wants to view her system's processor performance over time. Which is the best utility for her to employ?

    A. uptime

    B. sysstat

    C. sar

    D. cat /proc/cpuinfo

    E. sysctl

9. Gertie needs to determine a swap space element's type, name, and priority. Which command should she use?

    A. vmstat

    B. free

    C. fstab

    D. swapoff

    E. swapon -s

10. Elliot is administering a Linux system that has multiple swap spaces. One is on a logical volume, but it needs more space to accommodate additional RAM that is to be installed in the near future. What is the best way for Elliot to add swap space?

A. Add a partition and format it with the `mkswap` command.

B. Add a file and format it with the `mkswap` command.

C. Add a partition using the `swapon` utility.

D. Add a file using the `swapon` utility.

E. Use LVM tools to increase the logical volume.

Optimizing Performance

✓ Objective 1.4: Given a scenario, configure and use the appropriate processes and services.

✓ Objective 4.3: Given a scenario, analyze and troubleshoot central processing unit (CPU) and memory issues.

This chapter discusses how Linux handles applications running on the system. Linux must keep track of lots of different programs, all running at the same time. Your goal as the Linux administrator is to make sure everything runs smoothly. This chapter shows just how Linux keeps track of all the active programs and how you can peek at that information. You'll also see how to use command-line tools to manage the programs running on your Linux system.

Looking at Processes

At any given time a large number of active programs are running on the Linux system. Linux calls each running program a *process*. A process can run in the foreground, displaying output on a console display or graphical desktop window, or it can run in the background, working on data behind the scenes. The Linux system assigns each process a *process ID (PID)* and manages how the process uses memory and CPU time based on that PID.

When a Linux system first boots, it starts a special process called the *init process*. The init process is the core of the Linux system; it runs scripts that start all the other processes running on the system, including the processes that start the text consoles and graphical windows you use to log in (see Chapter 6, "Maintaining System Startup and Services").

You can watch just which processes are currently running on your Linux system by using the ps command. The default output of the ps command looks like this:

```
$ ps
PID    TTY       TIME      CMD
 2797  pts/0    00:00:00 bash
 2884  pts/0    00:00:00 ps
$
```

By default, the ps command only shows the processes that are running in the current user shell. In this example, we only had the command prompt shell running (Bash) and, of course, the ps command itself.

The basic output of the ps command shows the PID assigned to each process, the terminal (TTY) that they were started from, and the CPU time that the process has used.

The tricky feature of the ps command (and what makes it so complicated) is that at one time there were two versions of it in Linux. Each version had its own set of command-line parameters controlling the information it displayed. That made switching between systems somewhat complicated.

Recently, the GNU developers decided to merge the two versions into a single ps program, and of course, they added some additional parameters of their own. The current ps program used in Linux supports three different styles of command-line parameters:

- Unix-style parameters, which are preceded by a dash
- BSD-style parameters, which are not preceded by a dash
- GNU long parameters, which are preceded by a double dash

This makes for lots of possible parameters and options to use with the ps command. You can consult the ps man page to see all the possible parameters that are available. Most Linux administrators have their own set of commonly used parameters that they remember for extracting pertinent information. For example, if you need to see every process running on the system, use the Unix-style -ef parameter combination, like this:

```
$ ps -ef
UID        PID  PPID  C STIME TTY      TIME CMD
root         1     0  0 09:02 ?        00:00:02 /sbin/init
root         2     0  0 09:02 ?        00:00:00 [kthreadd]
root         3     2  0 09:02 ?        00:00:00 [ksoftirqd/0]
root         4     2  0 09:02 ?        00:00:00 [kworker/0:0]
root         5     2  0 09:02 ?        00:00:00 [kworker/0:0H]
root         6     2  0 09:02 ?        00:00:00 [kworker/u2:0]
root         7     2  0 09:02 ?        00:00:02 [rcu_sched]
root         8     2  0 09:02 ?        00:00:01 [rcuos/0]
root         9     2  0 09:02 ?        00:00:00 [rcu_bh]
root        10     2  0 09:02 ?        00:00:00 [rcuob/0
...
$
```

This format provides some useful information about the processes running:

UID: The user responsible for running the process

PID: The process ID of the process

PPID: The process ID of the parent process (if the process was started by another process)

C: The processor utilization over the lifetime of the process

STIME: The system time when the process was started

TTY: The terminal device from which the process was started

TIME: The cumulative CPU time required to run the process

CMD: The name of the program that was started in the process

Also notice in the -ef output that some process command names are shown in brackets. That indicates processes that are currently swapped out from physical memory into virtual memory on the hard drive. Processes that are swapped into virtual memory are called *sleep-ing*. Often the Linux kernel places a process into sleep mode while the process is waiting for an event.

When the event triggers, the kernel sends the process a signal. If the process is in *interruptible sleep* mode, it will receive the signal immediately and wake up. If the process is in *uninterruptible sleep* mode, it only wakes up based on an external event, such as hardware becoming available. It will save any other signals sent while it was sleeping and act on them once it wakes up.

If a process has ended but its parent process hasn't acknowledged the termination signal because it's sleeping, the process is considered a *zombie*. It's stuck in a limbo state between running and terminating until the parent process acknowledges the termination signal.

Monitoring Processes in Real Time

The ps command is a great way to get a snapshot of the processes running on the system, but sometimes you need to see more information to get an idea of just what's going on in your Linux system. If you're trying to find trends about processes that are frequently swapped in and out of memory, it's hard to do that with the ps command.

Instead, the *top* command can solve this problem. The top command displays process information similar to the ps command, but it does it in real-time mode. Figure 21.1 shows a snapshot of the top command in action.

FIGURE 21.1   The output of the top command

```
                              rich@localhost:~                                    ×

File  Edit  View  Search  Terminal  Help

top - 13:59:00 up 44 min,  1 user,  load average: 0.07, 0.09, 0.04
Tasks: 208 total,   2 running, 205 sleeping,   0 stopped,   1 zombie
%Cpu(s):  2.7 us,  0.7 sy,  0.0 ni, 96.0 id,  0.0 wa,  0.7 hi,  0.0 si,  0.0 st
MiB Mem : 10821.8 total,   8485.6 free,   1123.0 used,   1213.1 buff/cache
MiB Swap:  1728.0 total,   1728.0 free,      0.0 used.   9413.0 avail Mem

  PID USER      PR  NI    VIRT    RES    SHR S  %CPU  %MEM     TIME+ COMMAND
 2345 rich      20   0 3283072 380116 118852 S   2.7   3.4   0:27.93 gnome-s+
  595 root      20   0       0      0      0 S   0.3   0.0   0:00.10 xfsaild+
 4155 rich      20   0  729036  41524  28500 S   0.3   0.4   0:00.88 gnome-t+
 4320 rich      20   0  275188   5260   4404 R   0.3   0.0   0:00.04 top
    1 root      20   0  175604  13804   8804 S   0.0   0.1   0:01.24 systemd
    2 root      20   0       0      0      0 S   0.0   0.0   0:00.00 kthreadd
    3 root       0 -20       0      0      0 I   0.0   0.0   0:00.00 rcu_gp
    4 root       0 -20       0      0      0 I   0.0   0.0   0:00.00 rcu_par+
    6 root       0 -20       0      0      0 I   0.0   0.0   0:00.00 kworker+
    9 root       0 -20       0      0      0 I   0.0   0.0   0:00.00 mm_perc+
   10 root      20   0       0      0      0 S   0.0   0.0   0:00.19 ksoftir+
   11 root      20   0       0      0      0 R   0.0   0.0   0:00.13 rcu_sch+
   12 root      rt   0       0      0      0 S   0.0   0.0   0:00.00 migrati+
   13 root      rt   0       0      0      0 S   0.0   0.0   0:00.00 watchdo+
   14 root      20   0       0      0      0 S   0.0   0.0   0:00.00 cpuhp/0
   16 root      20   0       0      0      0 S   0.0   0.0   0:00.00 kdevtmp+
   17 root       0 -20       0      0      0 I   0.0   0.0   0:00.00 netns
```

The first section of the top output shows general system information. The first line shows the current time, how long the system has been up, the number of users logged in, and the load average on the system.

The load average appears as three numbers: the 1-minute, 5-minute, and 15-minute load averages. The higher the values, the more load the system is experiencing. It's not uncommon for the 1-minute load value to be high for short bursts of activity. If the 15-minute load value is high, your system may be in trouble.

The second line shows general process information (called tasks in top): how many processes are running, sleeping, stopped, or in a zombie state.

The next line shows general CPU information. The top display breaks down the CPU utilization into several categories depending on the owner of the process (user versus system processes) and the state of the processes (running, idle, or waiting). Table 21.1 describes these categories of time.

TABLE 21.1   The top CPU categories

Category	Symbol	Description
User	us	The amount of time the CPU spends running application code
System	sy	The amount of time the CPU spends working with system resources
Nice	ni	The amount of time the CPU spends running low-priority processes
Idle	id	The amount of time the CPU was not busy
Waiting	wa	The amount of time the CPU spends waiting for disk or network operations to complete (also called iowait)
Hardware Interrupt	hi	The amount of time the CPU spends processing hardware interrupts
Software Interrupt	si	The amount of time the CPU spends processing software interrupts

Following that, there are two lines that detail the status of the system memory. The first line shows the status of the physical memory in the system, how much total memory there is, how much is currently being used, and how much is free. The second memory line shows the status of the swap memory area in the system (if any is installed), with the same information.

Finally, the next section shows a detailed list of the currently running processes, with some information columns that should look familiar from the ps command output:

PID: The process ID of the process

USER: The username of the owner of the process

PR: The priority of the process

NI: The nice value of the process

VIRT: The total amount of virtual memory used by the process

RES: The amount of physical memory the process is using

SHR: The amount of memory the process is sharing with other processes

S: The process status (D = interruptible sleep, R = running, S = sleeping, T = traced or stopped, and Z = zombie)

%CPU: The share of CPU time that the process is using

%MEM: The share of available physical memory the process is using

TIME+: The total CPU time the process has used since starting

COMMAND: The command-line name of the process (program started)

By default, when you start top it sorts the processes based on the %CPU value. You can change the sort order by using one of several interactive commands. Each interactive command is a single character you can press while top is running and changes the behavior of the program. These commands are shown in Table 21.2.

TABLE 21.2 The top interactive commands

Command	Description
1	Toggles the single CPU and Symmetric Multiprocessor (SMP) state
b	Toggles the bolding of important numbers in the tables
I	Toggles Irix/Solaris mode
z	Configures color for the table
l	Toggles display of the load average information line
t	Toggles display of the CPU information line
m	Toggles display of the MEM and SWAP information lines
f	Adds or removes different information columns
o	Changes the display order of information columns
F or O	Selects a field on which to sort the processes (%CPU by default)

Command	Description
< or >	Moves the sort field one column left (<) or right (>)
r	Toggles normal or reverse sort order
h	Toggles showing of threads
c	Toggles showing of the command name or the full command line (including parameters) of processes
i	Toggles showing of idle processes
S	Toggles showing of the cumulative CPU time or relative CPU time
x	Toggles highlighting of the sort field
y	Toggles highlighting of running tasks
z	Toggles color and mono mode
u	Shows processes for a specific user
n or #	Sets the number of processes to display
k	Kills a specific process (only if process owner or if root user)
r	Changes the priority (renice) of a specific process (only if process owner or if root user)
d or s	Changes the update interval (default 3 seconds)
W	Writes current settings to a configuration file
q	Exits the top command

You have lots of control over the output of the top command. Use the F or O command to toggle which field the sort order is based on. You can also use the r interactive command to reverse the current sorting. Using this tool, you can often find offending processes that have taken over your system. A relatively new utility, the htop program is an improved version of the top utility, available in most Linux distributions as an additional software package that you can install. Figure 21.2 shows an example of the htop output display.

FIGURE 21.2 The output from the htop command tree view

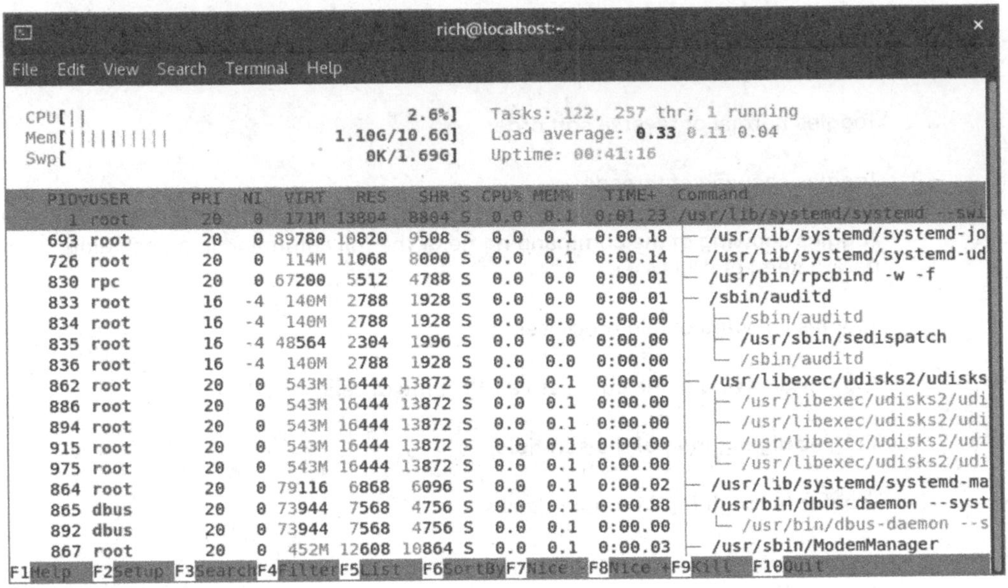

```
                                              rich@localhost:~                                    ×

 File   Edit   View   Search   Terminal   Help

    CPU[||                           2.6%]   Tasks: 122, 257 thr; 1 running
    Mem[|||||||||||                1.10G/10.6G]  Load average: 0.33 0.11 0.04
    Swp[                            0K/1.69G]   Uptime: 00:41:16

      PID USER      PRI  NI  VIRT   RES   SHR S CPU% MEM%   TIME+  Command
        1 root       20   0  171M 13804  8804 S  0.0  0.1  0:01.23 /usr/lib/systemd/systemd --swi
      693 root       20   0 89780 10820  9508 S  0.0  0.1  0:00.18 ├─ /usr/lib/systemd/systemd-jo
      726 root       20   0  114M 11068  8000 S  0.0  0.1  0:00.14 ├─ /usr/lib/systemd/systemd-ud
      830 rpc        20   0 67200  5512  4788 S  0.0  0.0  0:00.01 ├─ /usr/bin/rpcbind -w -f
      833 root       16  -4  140M  2788  1928 S  0.0  0.0  0:00.01 ├─ /sbin/auditd
      834 root       16  -4  140M  2788  1928 S  0.0  0.0  0:00.00 │  ├─ /sbin/auditd
      835 root       16  -4 48564  2304  1996 S  0.0  0.0  0:00.00 │  ├─ /usr/sbin/sedispatch
      836 root       16  -4  140M  2788  1928 S  0.0  0.0  0:00.00 │  └─ /sbin/auditd
      862 root       20   0  543M 16444 13872 S  0.0  0.1  0:00.06 ├─ /usr/libexec/udisks2/udisks
      886 root       20   0  543M 16444 13872 S  0.0  0.1  0:00.00 │  ├─ /usr/libexec/udisks2/udi
      894 root       20   0  543M 16444 13872 S  0.0  0.1  0:00.00 │  ├─ /usr/libexec/udisks2/udi
      915 root       20   0  543M 16444 13872 S  0.0  0.1  0:00.00 │  ├─ /usr/libexec/udisks2/udi
      975 root       20   0  543M 16444 13872 S  0.0  0.1  0:00.00 │  └─ /usr/libexec/udisks2/udi
      864 root       20   0 79116  6868  6096 S  0.0  0.1  0:00.02 ├─ /usr/lib/systemd/systemd-ma
      865 dbus       20   0 73944  7568  4756 S  0.0  0.1  0:00.88 ├─ /usr/bin/dbus-daemon --syst
      892 dbus       20   0 73944  7568  4756 S  0.0  0.1  0:00.00 │  └─ /usr/bin/dbus-daemon --s
      867 root       20   0  452M 12608 10864 S  0.0  0.1  0:00.03 ├─ /usr/sbin/ModemManager
 F1Help  F2Setup F3Search F4Filter F5List  F6SortBy F7Nice  F8Nice + F9Kill   F10Quit
```

The htop output uses color-coding to make things easier to read, along with use of the mouse to select items. Instead of cryptic letters for actions, it uses function keys to easily perform display functions, such as sorting or filtering the output, searching the output, or arranging the output in a tree to easily view parent and child processes. Perhaps one of its more popular features that makes it improved over top is the ability to customize the output display so that you only see the process information columns you're interested in monitoring.

Managing Processes

One of the jobs of a Linux system administrator is to be on the watch for runaway processes that can take down the Linux system. You've already seen how to use the ps and top commands to monitor how processes are doing on the system; the next step is to see how to stop a runaway process.

Setting Priorities

By default, all processes running on the Linux system are created equal; that is, they all have the same priority to obtain CPU time and memory resources. However, you may run some applications that either don't need to have the same level of priority or may need a higher level of priority.

The nice and renice commands allow you to set and change the priority level assigned to an application process. The nice command allows you to start an application with a non-default priority setting. The format looks like this:

```
nice -n value command
```

The kernel is the final judge in determining whether it can start an application with a different priority level, even if you tell it to. If the Linux system is heavily loaded, the kernel can choose to ignore any nice or renice commands.

The value parameter is a numeric value from –20 to 19. The lower the number, the higher priority the process receives. The default priority is 0. The command parameter indicates the program you want to start at the specified priority:

```
$ nice -n 10 ./myscript.sh
$
```

To change the priority of a process that's already running, use the renice command:

```
renice priority [-p pids] [-u users] [-g groups]
```

The renice command allows you to change the priority of multiple running processes based on a list of PID values, all of the processes started by one or more users, or all of the processes started by one or more groups.

```
$ renice 15 -p 3178
$
```

Only the root user account can set a priority value less than 0 or decrease the priority value (increase the priority) of a running process.

Stopping Processes

Sometimes a process gets hung up and just needs a gentle nudge to either get going again or stop. Other times, a process runs away with the CPU and refuses to give it up. In both cases, you need a command that will allow you to control a process. To do that, Linux follows the Unix method of interprocess communication.

In Linux, processes communicate with each other using process signals. A process signal is a predefined message that processes recognize and may choose to ignore or act on. The developers program how a process handles signals. Most well-written applications have the ability to receive and act on the standard Unix process signals. These signals are shown in Table 21.3.

TABLE 21.3 Linux process signals

Number	Name	Description
1	SIGHUP	Hangs up
2	SIGINT	Interrupts
3	SIGQUIT	Stops running
9	SIGKILL	Unconditionally terminates
11	SIGSEGV	Segments violation
15	SIGTERM	Terminates if possible
17	SIGSTOP	Stops unconditionally but doesn't terminate
18	SIGTSTP	Stops or pauses but continues to run in the background
19	SIGCONT	Resumes execution after STOP or TSTP

While a process can send a signal to another process, there are two commands available in Linux that allow you to send process signals to running processes.

The *kill* Command

The *kill* command allows you to send signals to processes based on their process ID (PID). By default, the kill command sends a SIGTERM signal to all the PIDs listed on the command line. Unfortunately, you can only use the process PID instead of its command name, making the kill command difficult to use sometimes.

To send a process signal, you must either be the owner of the process or be logged in as the root user.

```
$ kill 3940
-bash: kill: (3940) - Operation not permitted
$
```

The SIGTERM signal only asks the process to kindly stop running. Unfortunately, if you have a runaway process, most likely it will ignore the request. When you need to get forceful, the -s parameter allows you to specify other signals (either using their name or using their signal number).

The generally accepted procedure is to first try the TERM signal. If the process ignores that, try the SIGINT or SIGHUP signal. If the program recognizes these signals, it will try to gracefully stop doing what it was doing before shutting down. The most forceful signal is the SIGKILL signal. When a process receives this signal, it immediately stops running. Use this as a last resort, as it can lead to corrupted files.

One of the scary things about the `kill` command is that there's no output from it:

```
$ sudo kill -s SIGHUP 3940
$
```

To see if the command was effective, you'll have to perform another `ps` or `top` command to see if the offending process stopped.

 WARNING   Be careful of killing processes that may have open files. Files can be damaged and unrepairable if the process is abruptly stopped. It's usually a good idea to run the `lsof` command first to see a list of the open files and their processes.

The *pkill* Command

The *pkill* command is a powerful way to stop processes by using their names rather than the PID numbers. The `pkill` command allows you to use wildcard characters as well, making it a very useful tool when you've got a system that's gone awry:

```
$ sudo pkill http*
$
```

This example will `kill` all of the processes that start with `http`, such as the `httpd` services for the Apache web server.

 WARNING   Be careful with the search capability of the `pkill` command. It's usually a good idea to check the search term against the currently running processes to make sure you don't accidentally kill any other processes that match the search. The `pgrep` command allows you to display all processes that match the search term. You can also use the `pidof` command to view the PID of a specified program to ensure you have the correct PID and application.

The following exercise demonstrates how to monitor the running processes on your Linux system and how to remove a process you no longer want running.

EXERCISE 21.1

Managing a Running Process

1. Log into your Linux graphical desktop and open two new command prompt windows. If you're using virtual terminals, open two separate virtual terminal sessions.

2. In the first command prompt, enter a command to run the sleep program for 1000 seconds by typing **sleep 1000**.

3.   In the second command prompt window or virtual terminal session, look for the PID of the sleep program by typing **pgrep sleep**.

4.   Once you know the PID, use the kill command to stop it prematurely by typing **sudo kill -SIGHUP** *pid*, where *pid* is the PID of the sleep program you found in step 3.

5.   Observe the command prompt in the first window. It should return, indicating that the sleep program is no longer running.

6.   Check the running processes to ensure that the command is no longer running by typing **pgrep sleep**.

Summary

Managing applications running on Linux systems is a crucial job for administrators. The Linux system allocates CPU time and memory for each process, and knowing how each process consumes those resources is helpful. You can view the running applications and the resources they consume by using the ps command. There are many different ways to view process information using the ps command, allowing you to customize the display exactly how you like.

For real-time monitoring of applications, use the top command. With the top command, you can view a real-time display of applications, their system state, and the resources they consume. The top command allows you to sort the display based on many different features, such as CPU usage or memory usage.

For managing applications as they run on the system, you can use the nice and renice commands. The nice command allows you to start an application at a different priority level than the applications that are already running. This allows users to run applications in the background at a lower priority or allows the system administrator to start applications with a higher priority. With the renice command, you can change the priority of an application that's already running.

If an application causes problems and needs to be stopped, you can use the standard Linux kill command, but you need to know the process ID assigned to the application by the system. The pkill command is customized for stopping applications by their name instead of process ID. You can also use wildcard characters to stop multiple applications, but doing so can be dangerous. To test which applications would be stopped, use the pgrep command to search for running applications using the wildcard search.

Exam Essentials

Explain how to view the status of applications running on the Linux system.   The ps and top commands display the status of applications running on the system. Both commands display the status of each application, whether it's running, sleeping, or waiting for resources.

Explain how you would find what applications are using the most resources on your system.   The top command allows you to monitor the applications running on the Linux system in real time. It displays the amount of CPU and memory each application is consuming and allows you to sort the display on any of the displayed data fields. This allows you to easily monitor which applications are using the most CPU time or the most memory at any given moment.

Describe how you can stop an application that's causing problems on the Linux system.   Linux applications are programmed to respond to Linux signals. The kill command allows you to send Linux signals to running applications. If you send a KILL signal to an application, it will stop running on the system. Alternatively, you can send an INT signal to interrupt the application, allowing you to close it down gracefully if the application responds. The pkill application allows you to send Linux signals to applications based on their process name and lets you specify the process name using wildcard characters. This combination can come in handy if you need to stop multiple applications spawned from a single parent application.

Review Questions

1. What are the three types of option styles available for the `ps` command? (Choose three.)
    - **A.** BSD style
    - **B.** Linux style
    - **C.** Unix style
    - **D.** GNU style
    - **E.** Numeric style

2. How do you identify the legacy Unix style options for the `ps` command?
    - **A.** Use a double dash in front of the option.
    - **B.** Use a single dash in front of the option.
    - **C.** Do not place a dash in front of the option.
    - **D.** Unix-style options are numerical.
    - **E.** Unix-style options use hexadecimal numbers.

3. By default, if you specify no command-line options, what does the `ps` command display?
    - **A.** All processes running on the terminal
    - **B.** All active processes
    - **C.** All sleeping processes
    - **D.** All processes run by the current shell
    - **E.** All processes run by the current user

4. Charles noticed that his Linux system is running slow and needs to find out what application is causing the problem. What tool should he use to show the current CPU utilization of all the processes running on his system?
    - **A.** `top`
    - **B.** `ps`
    - **C.** `lsof`
    - **D.** `pkill`
    - **E.** `kill`

5. What `top` command displays cumulative CPU time instead of relative CPU time?
    - **A.** `l`
    - **B.** `F`
    - **C.** `r`
    - **D.** `y`
    - **E.** `S`

6. Shelly thinks that one of the applications on her Linux system is taking up too much physical memory and may have a problem. What column of data from the top display should she focus on?

   A. VIRT

   B. RES

   C. SHR

   D. S

   E. %MEM

7. Jessica has an application that crunches lots of numbers and uses a lot of system resources. She wants to run the application with a lower priority so that it doesn't interfere with other applications on the system. What tool should she use to start the application program?

   A. renice

   B. pkill

   C. nice

   D. kill

   E. pgrep

8. Jimmy noticed his Linux system was running slow. He ran the top command and found out that a data-intensive application was consuming most of the CPU time. He doesn't want to kill the application but wants to give it a lower priority so that it doesn't take up too much CPU time. What tool should he use to change the priority of the running application?

   A. renice

   B. pkill

   C. nice

   D. kill

   E. pgrep

9. Hank needs to stop an application from running on his Linux system. He knows the name of the application file but not the process ID assigned to it. What tool can he use to stop the application?

   A. renice

   B. pkill

   C. nice

   D. kill

   E. pgrep

10. Frankie used the ps command to find the process ID of an application that he needs to stop. What command-line tool should he use to stop the application based on its process ID?

   A. renice

   B. pkill

   C. nice

   D. kill

   E. pgrep

Chapter

22

Investigating User Issues

✓ **Objective 4.4: Given a scenario, analyze and troubleshoot user access and file permissions**

An old troubleshooting technique is to break a problem in half: if the cause is not in the first half, it's in the second half. Break the second part in half and continue to analyze. In this chapter, we're splitting user issues into system access and file difficulties. We further divide these problem categories while stepping you through various items to consider as you move toward a solution.

Troubleshooting Access

If a user is having trouble accessing their desired applications, a mixed bag of authentication issues can be the cause. We'll take a look at local and remote access as well as authentication scenarios.

Local

Local access refers to those users who are using a directly connected interface to the server. These are typically server administrators but may be application users as well. Begin troubleshooting by gathering some basic information:

- Is this a newly created user account?
- What is the username being entered for the account?
- Has the user ever logged into the account?
- Is the user attempting to log in via the GUI or a text-based (virtual) terminal (for example, tty2)?

Checking a Newly Created User Account

If the account is a newly created account, confirm that it was properly built. New system administrators often create user accounts with the useradd command (see Chapter 10, "Administering Users and Groups") but forget to add its password with the passwd utility. Use either the grep or the getent command to check the /etc/passwd and /etc/shadow file records. An example is shown in Listing 22.1 for a new user account, JKirk, on an Ubuntu Desktop distribution.

Listing 22.1: Viewing a user account record with the `getent` command

```
$ sudo getent passwd JKirk
JKirk:x:1002:1002::/home/JKirk:/bin/bash
$
$ sudo getent shadow JKirk
JKirk:!:17806:0:99999:7:::
$
```

Notice that in the password field for the `JKirk` shadow record, there is an exclamation mark (`!`). This indicates a password was not created for the account.

 Make sure your system users know that usernames are case sensitive on Linux. Other operating systems, such as Windows, have usernames that are case insensitive, and this can cause confusion.

Checking Account Accesses

Look at the last time the account was successfully accessed. The `lastlog` utility searches through the `/var/log/lastlog` file for users who have logged into the system, but it only maintains the most recent login. The `last` command searches the `/var/log/wtmp` file for users who have logged in/out and keeps records for the most recent logins and beyond. This file is typically rotated with earlier versions and given a numeric extension. Thus, the next oldest version of `wtmp` is `wtmp.1`. The `last` command's `-f` option will help you search through the various files, as shown in Listing 22.2.

Listing 22.2: Viewing successful logins with the `last` command

```
$ sudo last -f /var/log/wtmp -f /var/log/wtmp.* | grep JPicard
JPicard  tty3                       Wed Jan  4 13:14 - 13:14  (00:00)
$
$ sudo lastlog -u JPicard
Username        Port     From          Latest
JPicard         tty3                   Wed Jan  4 13:14:11 -0500 2023
$
```

Notice the `last` command shows that the `JPicard` account was logged into on January 4 at the tty3 terminal, and this is confirmed via the `lastlog` command.

You can also employ the `lastb` command. This command allows you to search for unsuccessful login attempts, as shown in Listing 22.3. Notice that the `JPicard` account had two failed login attempts at the tty4 terminal.

Listing 22.3: Viewing unsuccessful login attempts with the `lastb` command

```
$ sudo lastb -f /var/log/btmp -f /var/log/btmp.* | grep JPicard
JPicard   tty4                      Wed Jan  4 13:29 - 13:29   (00:00)
JPicard   tty4                      Wed Jan  4 13:29 - 13:29   (00:00)
```

Checking Privilege Elevation Issues

Most Linux distributions allow use of the `sudo` command to let users perform administrative tasks as the root user account, which is called privilege elevation. If there's a user account that's not allowed to use the `sudo` command, you need to check a few things.

First, take a look at the `/etc/sudoers` file to see what users and groups are allowed to elevate their privileges. If the user account isn't specified directly in the `/etc/suoders` file, there may be some groups that are specified. Those would have entries that look like this:

```
# Members of the admin group may gain root privileges
%admin ALL=(ALL) ALL


# Allow members of group sudo to execute any command
%sudo ALL=(ALL:ALL) ALL
```

In this configuration from an Ubuntu system, users in the `admin` group are allowed to use the `sudo` command for root privilege elevation, and members of the `sudo` group can gain privileges to execute any command as any user account.

The next step is to see what groups the user account belongs to. The easiest way to do that is by using the `id` command:

```
$ id rich
uid=1000(rich) gid=1000(rich) groups=1000(rich),4(adm),24(cdrom),27(sudo),
30(dip),46(plugdev),
120(lpadmin),131(lxd),132(sambashare)
$
```

The output from the `id` command shows all of the groups the user account belongs to. In this example, the `rich` user account does belong to the `sudo` group, so it should have access to use the `sudo` command for privilege elevation as any user account on the system.

Checking GUI Issues

If you find that the account successfully logged into the system in the past and has no recent failed attempts, find out the user's local access method. If using the GUI, have the user attempt to log into a text-based terminal, such as the tty2 terminal. If the user cannot successfully log into a terminal, then something else is amiss. The next few chapter sections after this one will help.

If the user can successfully log into a text-based terminal but not the GUI, you've narrowed down the problem. Determine what services are running. For older SysVinit systems, the `runlevel` command will show whether the graphical environment is current (see Chapter 6, "Maintaining System Startup and Services"). For systemd systems, use the command shown in the snipped example in Listing 22.4.

Listing 22.4: Viewing the current systemd target using the `systemctl` command

```
$ sudo systemctl status graphical.target
  graphical.target - Graphical Interface
[...]
   Active: active since Wed [...]
[...]
```

The `graphical.target` is active, which indicates GUI services are available. Thus, providing GUI services is not the problem. Begin investigating other potential GUI issues, starting with the display manager (Chapter 8, "Comparing GUIs").

> If your system does not use a graphical environment, check to see whether multiple users are allowed to log into the system. For systemd systems, check if the `multi-user.target` is active. See Chapter 6 for SysVinit systems.

Checking Terminal Issues

If the user typically logs into a text-based terminal but can't, have them log into a different terminal, either at a different virtual terminal or a graphical desktop. If the login is successful, then look at the original terminal's device file to determine if it is corrupted by using the `ls -l` command. An example is shown snipped in Listing 22.5.

Listing 22.5: Viewing terminal device files with the `ls -l` command

```
$ ls -l /dev/tty?
crw--w---- 1 root   tty 4, 0 Jan  4 09:38 /dev/tty0
crw--w---- 1 gdm    tty 4, 1 Jan  4 09:38 /dev/tty1
[...]
crw--w---- 1 root   tty 4, 9 Jan  4 09:38 /dev/tty9
$
```

Notice the `c` at the beginning of each terminal's device file record. This indicates the device file is a character file. If you see a dash (–) instead, the file is corrupted. Rebuild it using super user privileges and the `mknod` command.

> If you are attempting to log into the root account or your own system administrator account and have forgotten the password, follow the guidelines in Chapter 20, "Analyzing System Properties and Remediation," in the "Surviving a Lost Root Password" section.

If the user attempts to log into a different text-based terminal and can't, check to see if getty services are running. These services provide the login prompts for the text-based terminals. An example of checking for getty services on a systemd system is shown snipped in Listing 22.6.

Listing 22.6: Checking for getty services with the `systemctl` command

```
$ sudo systemctl status getty.target
  getty.target - Login Prompts
[...]
    Active: active since Wed 2023-01-04 09:38:13 EST; 6h ago
[...]
```

The `getty.target` is active, so getty services are available. If a user still cannot log into the system, you'll need to explore additional issues.

> Check the /etc/security/access.conf file. This file is scanned when a user attempts to log into the system. Its configuration accepts or blocks users/groups from accessing the system. It can also prohibit certain logins to the text-based terminals, as well as logins originating over the network.

Checking Additional Local Issues

Determine if the account is locked. You can employ the `passwd -S` or the `getent` command to check this, as shown snipped in Listing 22.7.

Listing 22.7: Checking if an account is locked with the `passwd` and `getent` commands

```
$ sudo passwd -S KJaneway
KJaneway L 01/02/2019 0 99999 7 -1
$
$ sudo getent shadow KJaneway
KJaneway:!$6$[...]0:17898:0:99999:7:::
$
```

The `L` after the user `KJaneway` account's name indicates the account is locked. However, that code is also shown for accounts that have no password set. Thus, the `getent` command is also employed. The exclamation point (`!`) at the front of the account password's field verifies that the account is indeed locked. To unlock the account, if desired, use super user privileges and the `usermod -U` or the `passwd -u` command.

> Check the user's keyboard. Sometimes incorrect keyboard mappings or corrupted hardware can cause wrong characters to be sent to authentication programs.

The account may have expired. Account expiration dates are typically set up for temporary account users, such as contractors or interns. You can view this information using the chage command, as shown snipped in Listing 22.8.

Listing 22.8: Checking if an account is expired with the chage command

```
$ date
Wed Jan  4 16:17:48 EST 2023
$
$ sudo chage -l JArcher
[...]
Account expires          : Jan 01, 2023
[...]
```

Notice that this account's expiration date has passed. Therefore, the JArcher account is now expired and the user cannot log into it. If this was a mistake or you need to modify it, use super user privileges and the chage -E command to set a new expiration date for the account.

Confirm that the user is using the correct password, and check if the account's password is expired. Employ the chage -l command to view this as well.

Remote

For remote access problems, first check that the system is accessible over the network (network troubleshooting was covered in Chapter 20). If the system is accessible, determine how the user is attempting to access the system.

If the user is employing OpenSSH, first confirm that the OpenSSH server is running on the system and that the firewall is properly configured to allow access (firewalls were covered in Chapter 18, "Overseeing Linux Firewalls"). Next review the sshd_config configuration file. The AllowUsers and AllowGroups directives restrict access. Ensure that these are correctly set. In addition, verify that there are no specific override settings for this particular user at the file's bottom. Be sure to review any configuration files on the client side as well, such as ~/.ssh/config and /etc/ssh/ssh_config (OpenSSH was covered in Chapter 16, "Looking at Access and Authentication Methods").

Have the user tack the -vvv option onto their ssh command. This provides a great deal of verbose information, which may help in the troubleshooting process.

Determine whether authentication through OpenSSH is via a username and password or via a token. If it is a username/password, check that the sshd_config directive PasswordAuthentication is set to yes. If all is well with the configuration file, troubleshooting topics in the next section may help.

If the OpenSSH authentication is token based, ensure that the private key was properly copied over to the server from the remote system. Also, confirm that the public key is stored in the `~/.ssh/authorized_keys` file on the client side.

 If the user's X11 GUI is transferred over the network, make sure the `ForwardX11` directive is set and that the user is employing the -X option with the `ssh` command. See Chapter 8 for additional details.

If your users are employing a remote desktop application, such as VNC, xrdp, NX, or SPICE, review their configurations. More information can be found on these topics in Chapter 8.

Authentication

Layered authentication software could be at the problem's heart. One place to check is PAM (covered in Chapter 16). Look through the PAM configuration files, such as `/etc/pam.d/sshd`, to ensure that directives are properly set. Also employ the `pam_tally2` or `faillock` utility to check if the user's account is locked due to too many failed login attempts.

Does your system employ other authentication products, such as LDAP (covered in Chapter 16) or Kerberos (covered in Chapter 19, "Embracing Best Security Practices")? You'll want to check their configuration files. Also take a look through their log files to ensure that a policy violation has not locked out the user's account.

Don't forget to check your Linux kernel security module, such as SELinux or AppArmor (covered in Chapter 15, "Applying Ownership and Permissions"). While the purpose of these modules is to protect the system from attackers, sometimes policy violations can lock out legitimate users. For AppArmor, policy violations are stored in either `audit.log` (produced by `auditd`) or `messages.log`, depending on its configuration. If using the `auditd` service, you can search for AppArmor policy violations in the `audit.log` file using the `ausearch` command.

For SELinux, check the audit log file using the `sealert` command, as shown in Listing 22.9. Notice that no SELinux policy violations were logged.

Listing 22.9: Checking SELinux policy violations with the `sealert` command

```
# sealert -a /var/log/audit/audit.log
100% done
found 0 alerts in /var/log/audit/audit.log
#
```

 For SELinux, use the `id -Z` command to view a user's SELinux context. See Chapter 15 for additional helpful SELinux and AppArmor commands.

For authentication issues, peruse through these various log files as well:

- `/var/log/auth.log` (Debian-based distros)
- `/var/log/secure` (Red Hat–based distros)

These log files typically contain information such as authentication failures and can provide you with a great deal of information. Use `grep` to search for a particular username, if desired.

Examining File Obstacles

Various problems may ensue when managing files. Understanding the typical problems will help in your file troubleshooting efforts.

File Permissions

You're editing a configuration file using the `vim` editor, but when you try to save the file, you get a "Can't open file for writing" error message. That's frustrating. Problems like this are directly related to file permissions.

When encountering these issues, first use the `ls -l` command to view a file's permission settings and ownerships (covered in Chapter 15). Note the file's owner and group. Then determine the permissions of the owner, group, and everyone else (world or other). An example is shown in Listing 22.10.

Listing 22.10: Determining file permissions with the `ls -l` command

```
$ ls -l HelloWorld.sh
-rwxr-xr--. 1 root wheel 72 Jan  4 09:29 HelloWorld.sh
$
```

In this case, the file is owned by `root`, who has permission to read, write to, and execute the file. The file's group is `wheel`. Those members can read and execute the file. Finally, everyone else who is not the file's owner or does not belong to the file's group can only read the file.

If a problem occurs trying to access this file, determine the user's username and group memberships using the `id` command. Match their identity against the file's permissions to find the problem. An example is shown in Listing 22.11.

Listing 22.11: Troubleshooting file access with the `id` command

```
$ whoami
Christine
$
$ ./HelloWorld.sh
```

```
-bash: ./HelloWorld.sh: Permission denied
$
$ id Christine
uid=1001(Christine) gid=1001(Christine) groups=1001(Christine)
```

Christine cannot execute this file because she is not the file's owner, nor is she in the file's group (see Listing 22.10). The third permission set applies to her and only allows her to read the file. To let her run the file, add her to the wheel group, set her as the file's owner, or modify the file's world permissions.

Directory Permissions

While the directory permission settings look very similar to file permissions, their effect is different. Table 22.1 shows permission effects on actions (covered in Chapter 15) associated with the entity to whom the permission applies (owner, group, or other).

TABLE 22.1   Directory permission effects

Permission	Effect
r	Allows user to display directory's files
w	Allows user to create, move (rename), modify attributes, and delete files within the directory
x	Allows user to change their present working directory to this directory (via the cd command) as long as this permission is set in all parent directories as well

A few examples will help you to understand these permissions. For example, the user Christine can list the /etc directory's contents, due to the directory's read permission for other (world), as shown snipped in Listing 22.12.

Listing 22.12: Understanding directory permission effects of the read privilege

```
$ whoami
Christine
$ ls -ld /etc
drwxr-xr-x. 143 root root 12288 Jan  4 09:22 /etc
$
$ ls /etc
abrt                    gshadow-                profile
adjtime                 gss                     profile.d
[...]
```

The next example, Listing 22.13, shows that the parent directory (/home) does allow a user to use cd to change their present working directory to it. However, a subdirectory (Samantha) blocks it by not granting the execute (x) privilege.

Listing 22.13: Understanding directory permission effects of the execute privilege

```
$ whoami
Christine
$ ls -ld /home/
drwxr-xr-x. 5 root root 52 Nov  8 14:31 /home/
$ cd /home
$ pwd
/home
$
$ ls -ld /home/Samantha
drwx------. 5 Samantha Samantha 128 Nov  8 14:38 /home/Samantha
$
$ cd /home/Samantha
-bash: cd: /home/Samantha: Permission denied
$
```

> If a subdirectory does grant execute permission but one of its parent directories does not, a user will *not* be able to use cd to get to that subdirectory. All directories in that path must have the execute permission set on them for that user.

If you have a directory shared among users and they are able to delete each other's files but that is not desired, employ the sticky bit on the directory. This permission (covered in Chapter 15) will solve the problem.

Working with Advanced Permissions

Besides the standard Linux file and directory permissions, you may run into a system that utilizes one of the more advanced Linux permission features.

Access control lists (ACLs) allow you to specify permissions for multiple users or groups besides the standard owner, group, and others set. If your Linux system utilizes ACLs, always check the getfacl utility for additional ACL permissions applied to a file or directory:

```
$ getfacl test.txt
# file: test.txt
# owner: rich
# group: rich
user::rw-
```

```
group::r--
group:sales:rw-
mask::rw-
other::---
$
```

In this example the owner has assigned `sales` group read permissions to the file using ACLs. To change ACL settings, use the `setfacl` utility.

Besides ACL permissions, Linux systems may also employ context-based permissions using either SELinux (most common in Red Hat–based Linux distributions) or AppArmor (most common in Debian-based Linux distributions).

To determine if SELinux is active on your Linux system, use the `sestatus` command:

```
$ sudo sestatus
SELinux status:              enabled
SELinuxfs mount:             /sys/fs/selinux
SELinux root directory:      /etc/selinux
Loaded policy name:          targeted
Current mode:                enforcing
Mode from config file:       enforcing
Policy MLS status:           enabled
Policy deny_unknown status:  allowed
Memory protection checking   actual (secure)
Max kernel policy version:   331
$
```

If SELinux is enabled, use the `-Z` command-line option for the `ls` command to view additional context permissions for files and directories:

```
$ ls -Z test1.txt
unconfined_u:object_r:user_home_t:s0 test1.txt
$
```

You can change the security context for a file by using the `chcon` command:

```
chcon -u newuser -r newrole -t newtype filename
```

SELinux controls access to objects using policies. The `getsebool` command allows you to list the policies and determine if they're active or disabled, and use the `setsebool` command to activate or deactivate them.

To determine if AppArmor is active on your system, use the `aa-status` utility:

```
$ sudo aa-status
apparmor module is loaded.
...
$
```

AppArmor uses profiles to set context permissions. While this output has been truncated, in the actual `aa-status` output you'll see lots of information about the profiles loaded in the enforce, complain, and disable modes. Use the `aa-enforce`, `aa-complain`, or `aa-disable` command to change profile settings to accommodate your permission requirements.

File Creation

A user goes to create a file and permission is denied. First check the directory permissions. If all is well there, consider the following items:

Are quotas enforced on this partition?   The user may have hit a quota limit. Check the partition's `/etc/fstab` record for either `usrquota` or `grpquota` to see if quotas are enabled on this filesystem (covered in Chapter 10) or use the `repquota` utility. If quotas are enabled, check the user's (or group's) quota usage using the `quota` command. If the user has exceeded quota limits and the grace period has passed, turn off quotas with `quotaoff`, extend the user's quotas, or have the user delete unneeded files.

Has the disk run out of space?   The `df` command (covered in Chapter 20) can help you quickly determine if the partition on which the user is attempting to create a file has run out of space. If you are out of space, take the appropriate action (also covered in Chapter 20).

Has the partition run out of inodes?   *Inode exhaustion* is an unusual situation, but it does happen. An inode number (covered in Chapter 3, "Managing Files, Directories, and Text") is a file's associated index number. If a filesystem runs out of inodes, no additional files can be created on it. Check if this is the problem by employing the `df -i` command, which shows each filesystem's inode use.

If inodes are exhausted, you cannot extend them after filesystem creation. Instead, look for directories that have a large amount of small unnecessary files, such as a temporary directory, and remove what you can. A good practice is to put applications that create many small files on their own large partitions formatted to provide higher amounts of inode numbers. At filesystem creation, increase inode counts above their defaults by using utility options like the `mke2fs -i` command.

What is the user's umask setting?   The umask setting (covered in Chapter 15) subtracts permissions from the default file and directory permission settings. Thus, when a user is creating files and/or directories, the permissions set on them are affected by this setting. Have the user enter **umask** at the command line (or check the user's environment file) to determine its setting. If it is set too high (for example, removing needed write permissions for created subdirectories), you have found the cause of the problem.

If a file cannot be deleted or renamed, check the file's attributes using the `lsattr` *filename* command. If you see an `i` among the dashes preceding the filename, the file has the immutable bit set. This bit prevents even users with super user privileges from deleting the file. To remove the file's immutable bit, use super user privileges and issue the **chattr -i** *filename* command.

Just as with access issues, check your Linux kernel security module (SELinux or AppArmor) in situations where a user cannot create or delete files. Peruse the appropriate policy violation log files (`/var/log/messages` or `/var/log/audit/audit.log`) using the appropriate tools.

If your system uses SELinux but does not employ `auditd`, the SELinux policy violation messages are stored in the `/var/log/messages` file.

After you have found the policy violation concerning the file or directory in question, determine if the file/directory was mislabeled, the policy is incorrect, or possibly the wrong security context was used. Take appropriate actions to remedy the situation.

Exploring Environment and Shell Issues

When dealing with user problems, a potential issue is the user account's default shell. Check it using the `getent` command, as shown on an Ubuntu distribution in Listing 22.14.

Listing 22.14: Determining an account's default shell with the `getent` command

```
$ getent passwd BSisko
BSisko:x:1007:1007::/home/BSisko:/bin/sh
$
$ readlink -f /bin/sh
/bin/dash
$
```

Notice that instead of the `/bin/bash` shell as the default shell, the `/bin/sh` shell is used. On this system, the `/bin/sh` file is linked to the `/bin/dash` shell. If this is not desired, you can change the user's default shell via the `usermod` command (see Chapter 10).

If a user cannot log into the system, check to see that their default shell is set to /sbin/false, /sbin/nologin, or something similar. These shells are typically for daemons and prevent the daemon from logging into the system.

Incorrect or improperly set environment variables can cause various user difficulties. Review a user's environment files (covered in Chapter 10), such as the ~/.profile file. While you're at it, check the system's global environment variable settings using the set, env, or printenv command.

Ensure that environment variables are exported so that they are available in subshells (a subshell may occur when a shell script is executed.) An example of this problem is shown in Listing 22.15.

Listing 22.15: Demonstrating what happens when variables are not exported

```
$ EDITOR='nano'
$ echo $EDITOR
nano
$
$ bash
$
$ echo $EDITOR
$
$ exit
exit
$
```

The user sets the environment variable EDITOR so that their default text editor is now nano. However, when a new subshell is created via the bash command, the setting is lost. To keep the setting persistent, it needs to be exported as well as stored in a user's environment file. An example of exporting the variable is shown in Listing 22.16.

Listing 22.16: Demonstrating the export command

```
$ export EDITOR='nano'
$
$ echo $EDITOR
nano
$
$ bash
$
$ echo $EDITOR
nano
$
```

It is also important to make sure you have environment variables in the correct file, global or per user. Also, you must understand what type of login the user conducts in order to set these variables in the right file (see Chapter 10).

Summary

User issue troubleshooting is tricky. Many components are involved in access, authentication, file management, and the user's shell and environment. Understanding common problems will assist in fixing an issue.

Exam Essentials

Summarize user access problems/solutions.   For impeded local access, research corrupted terminal files, improperly configured GUI components, and expired passwords/accounts. Remote access problems are often caused by misconfigured OpenSSH components or remote desktop applications. Other issues can involve layered authentication software such as PAM or a system's kernel security module, such as SELinux or AppArmor.

Describe various file problems/solutions.   File access and management requires understanding of basic file and directory permissions as well as ownership and group membership. Additional system items to review include filesystem quotas, disk space, inode use, and umask settings. Check the kernel security module log files for policy violations as well. If a user cannot delete a file, look for the immutable bit set on the file.

Explain user environment and shell issues.   Improperly configured environment variables or ones that are not exported will cause user problems. Examine the various environment files, both global and user, for issues. Difficulties may also arise from the user account's default shell setting.

Review Questions

1. Lamar, a contractor, claims he cannot log into his account locally. He was able to do so yesterday. No one else seems to be having problems accessing the system. What should you check first?

    A. Check if GUI services are running using the `systemctl` command.

    B. Look at the OpenSSH server configuration files.

    C. Determine if his account has expired by using the `chage` command.

    D. See if the account is locked using the `faillock` utility.

    E. Check for policy violations in the SELinux log files.

2. Irene normally logs into the system locally via the tty4 terminal but cannot today. She tries her authentication at the tty3 terminal and logs in successfully. What should you check first?

    A. Determine if getty services are running using the `systemctl` command.

    B. Review access rules in the `/etc/security/access.conf` file.

    C. See if the account is locked using the `passwd -S` command.

    D. Use the `last` command to see when she last logged in.

    E. Check if the tty4 device file is corrupted using the `ls -l` command.

3. Vincent is attempting to remotely log into the system using OpenSSH without success. He asks you what he can do to help troubleshoot this problem. What should you recommend first?

    A. Check the `/etc/ssh/sshd_config` configuration file.

    B. Add the `-vvv` option on to Vincent's `ssh` command.

    C. Add the `-X` option onto Vincent's `ssh` command.

    D. Confirm that Vincent's public key is stored in the `~/.ssh/authorized_keys` file.

    E. Check the `~/.ssh/config` configuration file.

4. Anton is struggling to determine why a particular user cannot log into a Rocky Linux system, where SELinux is disabled and `auditd` is not used. Which of the following are the best log files to peruse? (Choose two.)

    A. `/var/log/audit/audit.log`

    B. `/var/log/messages`

    C. `/var/log/auth`

    D. `/var/log/secure`

    E. `/var/log/lastlog`

5. Tarissa needs to run a shell script, which has the permissions of `rwxr--r--`, is owned by `root`, and belongs to the `wheel` group. Tarissa's user account is `T2T1000`, and she is a member of the `admin` group. What can be done to allow her to run this script? (Choose all that apply.)

   A. Add Tarissa to the `wheel` group.

   B. Create a new account for Tarissa named `wheel`.

   C. Add `w` to the script file's group permissions.

   D. Add `x` to the script file's group permissions.

   E. Nothing. Tarissa can run the script now.

6. Miles needs to change his present working directory to the `/home/miles` directory. He does not own the directory, nor is he a member of its group. Assuming needed parent directory permissions are set, what needs to take place for this to successfully occur?

   A. Nothing. The `/home/miles` directory is Miles's home directory, so he can access it by default.

   B. The execute (`x`) permission needs to be added.

   C. The write (`w`) permission needs to be added.

   D. The read (`r`) permission needs to be added.

   E. The dash (`-`) permission needs to be added.

7. Sarah, a system administrator, attempts to create a file and receives an error message indicating the file cannot be created. Which of the following might be the problem? (Choose all that apply.)

   A. The filesystem on which she is attempting to create the file has quotas set, and she is past her quota and grace period.

   B. The filesystem on which she is attempting to create the file has run out of space.

   C. The file that she is attempting to create has the immutable bit set and therefore cannot be created.

   D. The action is triggering either a SELinux or an AppArmor policy violation.

   E. The filesystem is experiencing inode exhaustion and therefore cannot accommodate any new files.

8. A user cannot delete one of their files but is able to delete other files in their directory. John, a system administrator, is attempting to troubleshoot this issue. What command should he use first on the file?

   A. `chown`

   B. `chattr`

   C. `chmod`

   D. `umask`

   E. `lsattr`

9. Melissa wants to set her default editor to the `vim` editor and wants this to stay set when she enters a subshell. What should she do?

  A. Put `EDITOR='vim'` in the `/etc/profile` file.

  B. Put `export EDITOR='vim'` in the `/etc/profile` file.

  C. Put `EDITOR='vim'` in her `~/.profile` file.

  D. Put `export EDITOR='vim'` in her `~/.profile` file.

  E. Put `export EDITOR='vim'` in her `~/. bash.bashrc` file.

10. Mark Watney, a system administrator, has his account, `MW2015`, modified by a new system administrator intern. When Mark logs into the system and tries to group a list of commands by using braces, it no longer works. No one else is having this problem. He suspects his account's default shell has been changed from `/bin/bash` to `/bin/tcsh`. Which of the following will help determine if his suspicion is correct? (Choose all that apply.)

  A. `cat /etc/profile`

  B. `echo $SHELL`

  C. `sudo grep tcsh$ /etc/passwd`

  D. `sudo getent shadow MW2015`

  E. `sudo getent passwd MW2015`

Chapter

23

Dealing
with Linux Devices

✓ **Objective 1.1: Summarize Linux fundamentals**

The typical Linux system has lots of different hardware devices connected to it. The list can include hard drives, monitors, keyboards, printers, audio cards, and network cards. Part of your job as a Linux administrator is to make sure all of those devices are working, and working properly. This chapter walks you through how to install and troubleshoot the different types of hardware devices that can be connected to your Linux system. First, the chapter discusses the different types of device interfaces you may need to work with on your Linux system and how they communicate with the operating system. Following that, the chapter discusses the Linux utilities available for you to monitor and troubleshoot how those devices on your system are working. Finally, the chapter dives into the topic of hot-pluggable devices, a topic that has become extremely important with the popularity of USB devices.

Communicating with Linux Devices

For any device to work on your Linux system, the Linux kernel must recognize it and know how to talk to it. The kernel uses installed modules (see Chapter 14, "Tending Kernel Modules") to know how to communicate with each type of hardware device on the system. If the module for a particular hardware device isn't loaded, then the kernel won't be able to communicate with the device.

After the kernel module is installed, the kernel must know how to communicate with the device. Linux supports several different types of hardware interfaces and methods for communicating with devices.

Device Interfaces

Each device you connect to your Linux system uses some type of standard protocol to communicate with the system hardware. The kernel module software must know how to send data to and receive data from the hardware device using those protocols. There are currently three popular standards used to connect devices.

PCI Boards

The *Peripheral Component Interconnect* (PCI) standard was developed in 1993 as a method for connecting hardware boards to PC motherboards. The standard has been updated a few times to accommodate faster interface speeds as well as increase data bus sizes on motherboards. The *PCI Express (PCIe)* standard is currently used on most server and desktop workstations to provide a common interface for external hardware cards.

Lots of different client devices use PCI boards to connect to a server or desktop workstation:

Internal Hard Drives   Hard drives using the *Serial Advanced Technology Attachment (SATA)* and the *Small Computer System Interface (SCSI)* connectors often use PCI boards to connect with workstations or servers. The Linux kernel automatically recognizes both SATA and SCSI hard drives connected to PCI boards.

External Hard Drives   Network hard drives using the Fibre Channel standard provide a high-speed shared drive environment for server environments. To communicate on a Fibre Channel network, the server usually uses PCI boards that support the *Host Bus Adapter (HBA)* standard.

Network Interface Cards   Hard-wired network cards allow you to connect the workstation or server to a local area network using the common RJ-45 cable standard. These types of connections are mostly found in high-speed network environments that require high throughput to the network.

Wireless Cards   There are PCI boards available that support the IEEE 802.11 standard for wireless connections to local area networks. Although not commonly used in server environments, they are popular in workstation environments.

Bluetooth Devices   The Bluetooth technology allows for short-distance wireless communication with other Bluetooth devices in a peer-to-peer network setup. They are most commonly found in workstation environments.

Video Accelerators   Applications that require advanced graphics often use video accelerator cards, which offload the video processing requirements from the CPU to provide faster graphics. While these are popular in gaming environments, you'll also find video accelerator cards used in video processing applications for editing and processing movies, and in applications that require advanced mathematical operations, such as block chain generation.

Audio Cards   Similarly, applications that require high-quality sound often use specialty audio cards to provide advanced audio processing and play, such as handling Dolby surround sound to enhance the audio quality of movies.

The USB Interface

The *Universal Serial Bus (USB)* interface has become increasingly popular due to its ease of use and its increasing support for high-speed data communication. Since the USB interface uses serial communications, it requires fewer connectors with the motherboard, allowing for smaller interface plugs.

The USB standard has evolved over the years. The original version 1.0 only supported data transfer speeds up to 12 Mbps. The 2.0 standard increased the data transfer speed to 480 Mbps. The current USB standard, 4.0, allows for data transfer speeds up to 40 Gbps, making it useful for high-speed connections to external storage devices.

A myriad of devices can connect to systems using the USB interface. You can find hard drives, printers, digital cameras and camcorders, keyboards, mice, and network cards that have versions that connect using the USB interface.

Linux and USB devices

There are two steps to get Linux to interact with USB devices. The first step is that the Linux kernel must have the proper module installed to recognize the USB controller installed on your server, workstation, or laptops. The controller provides communication between the Linux kernel and the USB bus on the system. When the Linux kernel can communicate with the USB bus, any device you plug into a USB port on the system will be recognized by the kernel but is not necessarily usable. The second step is that the Linux system must have a kernel module installed for the individual device type plugged into the USB bus. Linux distributions have a wide assortment of modules installed by default. Should you run into a USB device that doesn't work on your Linux system, refer to Chapter 14 for information on installing kernel modules.

The GPIO Interface

The *general-purpose input/output (GPIO)* interface has become popular with small utility Linux systems designed for controlling external devices for automation projects. This includes popular hobbyist Linux systems such as the Raspberry Pi and BeagleBone kits.

The GPIO interface provides multiple digital input and output lines that you can control individually, down to the single-bit level. The GPIO function is normally handled by a specialty integrated circuit (IC) chip, which is mapped into memory on the Linux system.

The GPIO interface is ideal for supporting communications to external devices such as relays, lights, sensors, and motors. Applications can read individual GPIO lines to determine the status of switches, turn relays on or off, or read digital values returned from any type of analog-to-digital sensors such as temperature or pressure sensors.

With the GPIO interface, you have a wealth of possibilities for using Linux to control objects and environments. You can write programs that control the temperature in a room, sense when doors or windows are opened or closed, sense motion in a room, or even control the operation of a robot.

The */dev* Directory

Once the Linux kernel can communicate with a device on an interface, it must be able to transfer data to and from the device. For many devices, this is done using *device files*. Device files are files that the Linux kernel creates in the special /dev directory to interface with hardware devices.

To retrieve data from a specific device, a program just needs to read the Linux device file associated with that device. The Linux operating system handles all the unsightliness of interfacing with the actual hardware. Likewise, to send data to the device, the program just needs to write to the Linux device file.

As you add hardware devices such as USB drives, network cards, or hard drives to your system, Linux creates a file in the /dev directory representing that hardware device. Application programs can then interact directly with that file to store and retrieve data on the device. This is much easier than requiring each application to know how to directly interact with a device.

There are two types of device files in Linux, based on how Linux transfers data to the device:

- **Character device files:** Transfer data one character at a time. This method is often used for serial devices such as terminals and USB devices.

- **Block device files:** Transfer large blocks of data. This method is often used for high-speed data transfer devices such as hard drives and network cards.

The type of device file is denoted by the first letter in the permissions list, as shown in Listing 23.1.

Listing 23.1: Partial output from the /dev directory

```
$ ls -al sd* tty*
brw-rw---- 1 root disk    8,  0 Feb 16 17:49 sda
brw-rw---- 1 root disk    8,  1 Feb 16 17:49 sda1
crw-rw-rw- 1 root tty     5,  0 Feb 16 17:49 tty
crw--w---- 1 root tty     4,  0 Feb 16 17:49 tty0
crw--w---- 1 gdm  tty     4,  1 Feb 16 17:49 tty1
```

The hard drive devices, sda and sda1, show the letter b, indicating that they are block device files. The tty terminal files show the letter c, indicating that they are character device files.

There are also a few special character device files that provide useful features for the shell. Ones of note are as follows:

- /dev/null: When data is redirected to this device, the data is discarded. This is handy for redirecting program messages that you don't want displayed.

- /dev/random and /dev/urandom: These devices files provide access to the kernel's random number generator. The /dev/random device blocks requests until enough random data has been generated to calculate a true random number.

The /dev/urandom device doesn't block but just returns a random number using the random data currently available. Though less accurate, it's usually fine for most random number uses.

▪ /dev/zero: When data is read from this device, it returns a NULL character (0x00). This is an excellent resource for creating null files, or erasing previously stored data on a disk partition.

Besides device files, Linux also provides a system called the *device mapper*. The device mapper function is performed by the Linux kernel. It maps physical block devices to virtual block devices. These virtual block devices allow the system to intercept the data written to or read from the physical device and perform some type of operation on them. Mapped devices are used by the Logical Volume Manager (LVM) for creating logical drives and by the Linux Unified Key Setup (LUKS) for encrypting data on hard drives.

The device mapper creates virtual devices in the /dev/mapper directory. These files are links to the physical block device files in the /dev directory.

The */proc* Directory

The /proc directory is one of the most important tools you can use when troubleshooting hardware issues on a Linux system. It's not a physical directory on the filesystem but instead a virtual directory that the kernel dynamically populates to provide access to information about the system hardware settings and status.

The Linux kernel changes the files and data in the /proc directory as it monitors the status of hardware on the system. To view the status of the hardware devices and settings, you just need to read the contents of the virtual files using standard Linux text commands.

There are different /proc files available for different system features, including the IRQs, I/O ports, and DMA channels in use on the system by hardware devices. The following sections discuss the files used to monitor these features and how you can access them.

Interrupt Requests

Interrupt requests (called IRQs) allow hardware devices to indicate when they have data to send to the CPU. The PnP system must assign each hardware device installed on the system a unique IRQ address. You can view the current IRQs in use on your Linux system by looking at the /proc/interrupts file using the Linux cat command, as shown in Listing 23.2.

Listing 23.2: Listing system interrupts from the /proc directory

```
$ cat /proc/interrupts
          CPU0
    0:       36   IO-APIC   2-edge      timer
    1:      297   IO-APIC   1-edge      i8042
```

```
    8:          0    IO-APIC    8-edge       rtc0
    9:          0    IO-APIC    9-fasteoi    acpi
   12:        396    IO-APIC   12-edge       i8042
   14:          0    IO-APIC   14-edge       ata_piix
   15:        914    IO-APIC   15-edge       ata_piix
   18:          2    IO-APIC   18-fasteoi    vboxvideo
   19:       4337    IO-APIC   19-fasteoi    enp0s3
...
$
```

In Listing 23.2, the first column indicates the IRQ assigned to the device. Some IRQs are reserved by the system for specific hardware devices, such as 0 for the system timer and 1 for the system keyboard. Other IRQs are assigned by the system as devices are detected at boot time.

I/O Ports

The system I/O ports are locations in memory where the CPU can send data to and receive data from the hardware device. As with IRQs, the system must assign each device a unique I/O port. This is yet another feature handled by the PnP system.

You can monitor the I/O ports assigned to the hardware devices on your system by looking at the /proc/ioports file, as shown in Listing 23.3.

Listing 23.3: Displaying the I/O ports on a system

```
$ cat /proc/ioports
0000-0cf7 : PCI Bus 0000:00
  0000-001f : dma1
  0020-0021 : pic1
  0040-0043 : timer0
  0050-0053 : timer1
  0060-0060 : keyboard
  0064-0064 : keyboard
  0070-0071 : rtc_cmos
    0070-0071 : rtc0
  0080-008f : dma page reg
  00a0-00a1 : pic2
  00c0-00df : dma2
  00f0-00ff : fpu
  0170-0177 : 0000:00:01.1
    0170-0177 : ata_piix
  01f0-01f7 : 0000:00:01.1
    01f0-01f7 : ata_piix
```

```
0376-0376 : 0000:00:01.1
  0376-0376 : ata_piix
03c0-03df : vga+
03f6-03f6 : 0000:00:01.1
  03f6-03f6 : ata_piix
0cf8-0cff : PCI conf1
0d00-ffff : PCI Bus 0000:00
...
$
```

There are lots of different I/O ports in use on the Linux system at any time, so your output will most likely differ from this example. With PnP, I/O port conflicts aren't very common, but it is possible that two devices are assigned the same I/O port. In that case, you can manually override the settings automatically assigned by using the `setpci` command.

Direct Memory Access

Using I/O ports to send data to the CPU can be somewhat slow. To speed things up, many devices use direct memory access (DMA) channels. DMA channels do what the name implies; they send data from a hardware device directly to memory on the system, without having to wait for the CPU. The CPU can then read those memory locations to access the data when it's ready.

As with I/O ports, each hardware device that uses DMA must be assigned a unique channel number. To view the DMA channels currently in use on the system, just display the `/proc/dma` file:

```
$ cat /proc/dma
 4: cascade
$
```

This output indicates that only DMA channel 4 is in use on the Linux system.

The */sys* Directory

Yet another tool available for working with devices is the /sys directory. The /sys directory is another virtual directory, similar to the /proc directory. It provides additional information about hardware devices that any user on the system can access.

A number of information files are available within the /sys directory. They are broken down into subdirectories based on the device and function in the system. You can take a look at the subdirectories and files available within the /sys directory on your system by using the `ls` command-line command, as shown in Listing 23.4.

Listing 23.4: The contents of the /sys directory

```
$ ls -al /sys
total 4
```

```
dr-xr-xr-x  13 root root    0 Feb 16 18:06 .
drwxr-xr-x  25 root root 4096 Feb  4 06:54 ..
drwxr-xr-x   2 root root    0 Feb 16 17:48 block
drwxr-xr-x  41 root root    0 Feb 16 17:48 bus
drwxr-xr-x  62 root root    0 Feb 16 17:48 class
drwxr-xr-x   4 root root    0 Feb 16 17:48 dev
drwxr-xr-x  14 root root    0 Feb 16 17:48 devices
drwxr-xr-x   5 root root    0 Feb 16 17:49 firmware
drwxr-xr-x   8 root root    0 Feb 16 17:48 fs
drwxr-xr-x   2 root root    0 Feb 16 18:06 hypervisor
drwxr-xr-x  13 root root    0 Feb 16 17:48 kernel
drwxr-xr-x 143 root root    0 Feb 16 17:48 module
drwxr-xr-x   2 root root    0 Feb 16 17:48 power
$
```

Notice the different categories of information available. You can obtain information about the system bus, devices, kernel, and even kernel modules installed.

Working with Devices

Linux provides a wealth of command-line tools for using the devices connected to your system as well as monitoring and troubleshooting the devices if there are problems. The following sections walk through some of the popular tools you'll want to know about when working with Linux devices.

Finding Devices

One of the first tasks for a new Linux administrator is to find the different devices installed on the Linux system. Fortunately there are a few command-line tools to help out with that.

The *lsdev* command

The lsdev command-line command displays information about the hardware devices installed on the Linux system. It retrieves information from the /proc/interrupts, /proc/ioports, and /proc/dma virtual files and combines them in one output, as shown in Listing 23.5.

Listing 23.5: Output from the lsdev command

```
$ lsdev
Device          DMA   IRQ  I/O Ports
...
acpi                   9
```

```
ACPI                          4000-4003 4004-4005 4008-400b 4020-4021
ahci                          d240-d247 d248-d24b d250-d257 d258-d25b
ata_piix          14 15       0170-0177 01f0-01f7 0376-0376 03f6-03f6
cascade           4
dma                           0080-008f
dma1                          0000-001f
dma2                          00c0-00df
e1000                          d010-d017
enp0s3               19
fpu                           00f0-00ff
i8042             1 12
Intel                          d100-d1ff        d200-d23f
keyboard                      0060-0060    0064-0064
ohci_hcd:usb1        22
PCI                         0000-0cf7 0cf8-0cff 0d00-ffff
pic1                          0020-0021
pic2                          00a0-00a1
piix4_smbus                    4100-4108
rtc0                  8        0070-0071
rtc_cmos                      0070-0071
snd_intel8x0         21
timer                 0
timer0                        0040-0043
timer1                        0050-0053
vboxguest            20
vboxvideo            18
vga+                          03c0-03df
$
```

This provides you with one place to view all the important information about the devices running on the system, making it easy to pick out any conflicts that can be causing problems.

The lsdev tool is part of the procinfo package. You may need to manually install that package in some Linux distributions.

The *lsblk* command

The lsblk command-line command displays information about the block devices installed on the Linux system. By default, the lsblk command displays all of the block devices, as shown in Listing 23.6.

Listing 23.6: The output from the `lsblk` command

```
$ lsblk
NAME                 MAJ:MIN RM    SIZE RO TYPE MOUNTPOINT
loop0                    7:0   0  34.6M  1 loop /snap/gtk-common-themes/818
loop1                    7:1   0   2.2M  1 loop /snap/gnome-calculator/222
...
sda                      8:0   0    10G  0 disk
  sda1                   8:1   0    10G  0 part
    ubuntu--vg-root    253:0   0     9G  0 lvm  /
    ubuntu--vg-swap_1  253:1   0   976M  0 lvm  [SWAP]
sr0                     11:0   1  1024M  0 rom
$
```

If you notice at the end of Listing 23.6, the `lsblk` command also indicates blocks that are related, as with the device-mapped LVM volumes and the associated physical hard drive. You can modify the `lsblk` output to see additional information about the blocks by adding command-line options. The `-S` option displays only information about SCSI block devices on the system:

```
$ lsblk -S
NAME HCTL       TYPE VENDOR   MODEL          REV TRAN
sda  2:0:0:0    disk ATA      VBOX HARDDISK  1.0 sata
sr0  1:0:0:0    rom  VBOX     CD-ROM         1.0 ata
$
```

This is a quick way to view the different SCSI drives installed on the system.

The *dmesg* command

The kernel ring buffer records kernel-level events as they occur. Since it's a ring buffer, the event messages overwrite after the buffer area fills up. You can view the current messages in the kernel ring buffer by using the `dmesg` command. It helps to monitor it whenever you install a new device, as shown in Listing 23.7.

Listing 23.7: Partial output from the `dmesg` command

```
[ 2525.499216] usb 1-2: new full-speed USB device number 3 using ohci-pci
[ 2525.791093] usb 1-2: config 1 interface 0 altsetting 0 endpoint 0x1 has
 invalid maxpacket 512, setting to 64
[ 2525.791107] usb 1-2: config 1 interface 0 altsetting 0 endpoint 0x81 has
 invalid maxpacket 512, setting to 64
[ 2525.821079] usb 1-2: New USB device found, idVendor=abcd, idProduct=1234
[ 2525.821088] usb 1-2: New USB device strings: Mfr=1, Product=2,
 SerialNumber=3
```

```
[ 2525.821094] usb 1-2: Product: UDisk
[ 2525.821099] usb 1-2: Manufacturer: General
⬚
[ 2525.821104] usb 1-2: SerialNumber: [ 2525.927096] usb-storage 1-2:1.0: USB
Mass Storage device detected
[ 2525.927096] usb-storage 1-2:1.0: USB Mass Storage device detected
[ 2525.927950] scsi host3: usb-storage 1-2:1.0
[ 2525.928033] usbcore: registered new interface driver usb-storage
[ 2525.940376] usbcore: registered new interface driver uas
[ 2526.961754] scsi 3:0:0:0: Direct-Access     General  UDisk
 5.00 PQ: 0 ANSI: 2
[ 2526.966646] sd 3:0:0:0: Attached scsi generic sg2 type 0
[ 2526.992707] sd 3:0:0:0: [sdb] 31336448 512-byte logical blocks: (16.0
 GB/14.9 GiB)
[ 2527.009197] sd 3:0:0:0: [sdb] Write Protect is off
[ 2527.009200] sd 3:0:0:0: [sdb] Mode Sense: 0b 00 00 08
[ 2527.026764] sd 3:0:0:0: [sdb] No Caching mode page found
[ 2527.026770] sd 3:0:0:0: [sdb] Assuming drive cache: write through
[ 2527.127613]  sdb: sdb1
[ 2527.229943] sd 3:0:0:0: [sdb] Attached SCSI removable disk
```

The output from the dmesg command shows the steps the kernel took to recognize the new USB device that was plugged into the system.

Since the kernel is responsible for detecting devices and installing the correct modules, the dmesg command is a great troubleshooting tool to use when a device isn't working correctly. It can help you determine if a hardware device module didn't load correctly.

Working with PCI Devices

The lspci command allows you to view the currently installed and recognized PCI and PCIe devices on the Linux system. There are lots of command-line options you can include with the lspci command to display information about the PCI and PCIe cards installed on the system. Table 23.1 shows some common ones that come in handy.

TABLE 23.1 The lspci command-line options

Option	Description
-A	Defines the method to access the PCI information
-b	Displays connection information from the card point of view
-k	Displays the kernel driver modules for each installed PCI card
-m	Displays information in machine-readable format

Option	Description
-n	Displays vendor and device information as numbers instead of text
-q	Queries the centralized PCI database for information about the installed PCI cards
-t	Displays a tree diagram that shows the connections between cards and buses
-v	Displays additional information (verbose) about the cards
-x	Displays a hexadecimal output dump of the card information

The output from the `lspci` command without any options shows all devices connected to the system, as shown in Listing 23.8.

Listing 23.8: Using the `lspci` command

```
$ lspci
00:00.0 Host bridge: Intel Corporation 440FX - 82441FX PMC [Natoma] (rev 02)
00:01.0 ISA bridge: Intel Corporation 82371SB PIIX3 ISA [Natoma/Triton II]
00:01.1 IDE interface: Intel Corporation 82371AB/EB/MB PIIX4 IDE (rev 01)
00:02.0 VGA compatible controller: InnoTek Systemberatung GmbH VirtualBox
 Graphics Adapter
00:03.0 Ethernet controller: Intel Corporation 82540EM Gigabit Ethernet
 Controller (rev 02)
00:04.0 System peripheral: InnoTek Systemberatung GmbH VirtualBox Guest
Service
00:05.0 Multimedia audio controller: Intel Corporation 82801AA AC'97 Audio
 Controller (rev 01)
00:06.0 USB controller: Apple Inc. KeyLargo/Intrepid USB
00:07.0 Bridge: Intel Corporation 82371AB/EB/MB PIIX4 ACPI (rev 08)
00:0d.0 SATA controller: Intel Corporation 82801HM/HEM (ICH8M/ICH8M-E) SATA
Controller [AHCI mode] (rev 02)
$
```

You can use the output from the `lspci` command to troubleshoot PCI card issues, such as if a card isn't recognized by the Linux system.

Working with USB Devices

You can view the basic information about USB devices connected to your Linux system by using the `lsusb` command. Table 23.2 shows the options that are available with that command.

TABLE 23.2   The lsusb command options

Option	Description
-d	Displays only devices from the specified vendor ID
-D	Displays information only from devices with the specified device file
-s	Displays information only from devices using the specified bus
-t	Displays information in a tree format, showing related devices
-v	Displays additional information about the devices (verbose mode)
-V	Displays the version of the lsusb program

The basic lsusb program output is shown in Listing 23.9.

Listing 23.9: The lsusb output

```
$ lsusb
Bus 001 Device 003: ID abcd:1234 Unknown
Bus 001 Device 002: ID 80ee:0021 VirtualBox USB Tablet
Bus 001 Device 001: ID 1d6b:0001 Linux Foundation 1.1 root hub
$
```

Most systems incorporate a standard USB hub for connecting multiple USB devices to the USB controller. Fortunately, there are only a handful of USB hubs on the market, so all Linux distributions include the device drivers necessary to communicate with each of these USB hubs. That guarantees that your Linux system will at least detect when a USB device is connected.

Supporting Monitors

Two basic elements control the video environment on your Linux system: the video card and the monitor. To display any type of text or graphics, your Linux system must know how to interact with both of them. This is where the X Window System software comes in.

The *X Window System* was developed at the Massachusetts Institute of Technology (MIT) to provide a standard protocol for interacting with displays. The X Window System is most commonly referred to as just X, or X11, since the last version defined is version 11.

The X11 system operates beneath the graphical desktop environment on your Linux system, as shown in Figure 23.1.

FIGURE 23.1   The standard Linux graphics environment

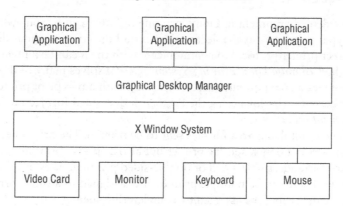

The job of X11 is to interact with the hardware level of your system's video environment—the video card, monitor, keyboard, and mouse—and provide a standard interface that any desktop management software (such as KDE or GNOME) can use. Because of this, the X11 software must be able to interact with all of those hardware devices.

The original X11 software for Linux was the XFree86 package. This was notorious for being difficult to configure and get working with different types of video hardware. Because of that, newer X11 packages have surfaced and have become more common:

- **X.org:** A user-friendly X11 software package for Linux, developed as a direct replacement for XFree86, but using simple text-based configuration files. It stores configuration files in a common /etc/X11 directory.

- **Wayland:** A simpler, more secure graphical software package, developed by Red Hat, and released as open source software. Wayland is becoming more popular with Linux distributions, quickly replacing even X.org. It stores separate configuration files for each user in the ~/.config/weston.ini file in each user's home directory.

Both the X.org and Wayland systems attempt to automatically detect the video card, monitor, keyboard, and mouse installed on the system at each boot time and dynamically change the configuration files accordingly. If you make any changes to the video card or monitor, they will automatically detect the new equipment and alter the configuration accordingly, making it a breeze to swap out new video equipment.

The X.org and Wayland packages include several different drivers that support common video cards and monitors. For both packages, however, if they don't recognize the specific video card or monitor on your system, they default to using generic drivers that may not produce the best-quality video experience. If your Linux system uses a specialty graphics card or monitor, it's best to obtain the Linux drivers for them and follow the documentation to manually install the updated drivers.

Using Printers

Just as with the video environment in Linux, printing in Linux can be somewhat complex. With different types of printers available, trying to install the correct printer drivers as well as using the correct printer protocol to communicate with them can be a nightmare.

Fortunately, the *Common Unix Printing System (CUPS)* solves many of those problems for us. CUPS provides a common interface for working with any type of printer on your Linux system. It accepts print jobs using the PostScript document format and sends them to printers using a *print queue* system.

The print queue is a holding area for files sent to be printed. The print queue is normally configured to support not only a specific printer but also a specific printing format, such as landscape or portrait mode, single-sided or double-sided printing, or even color or black-and-white printing. There can be multiple print queues assigned to a single printer or multiple printers that can accept jobs assigned to a single print queue.

The CUPS software uses the Ghostscript program to convert the PostScript document into a format understood by the different printers. The Ghostscript program requires different drivers for the different printer types to know how to convert the document to make it printable on a certain type of printer. This is done using configuration files and drivers. Fortunately, CUPS installs many different drivers for common printers on the market and automatically sets the configuration requirements to use them. The configuration files are stored in the `/etc/cups` directory.

To define a new printer on your Linux system you can use the CUPS web interface. Open your browser and navigate to the URL `http://localhost:631`. Figure 23.2 shows the web interface used by CUPS.

FIGURE 23.2   The CUPS main web page

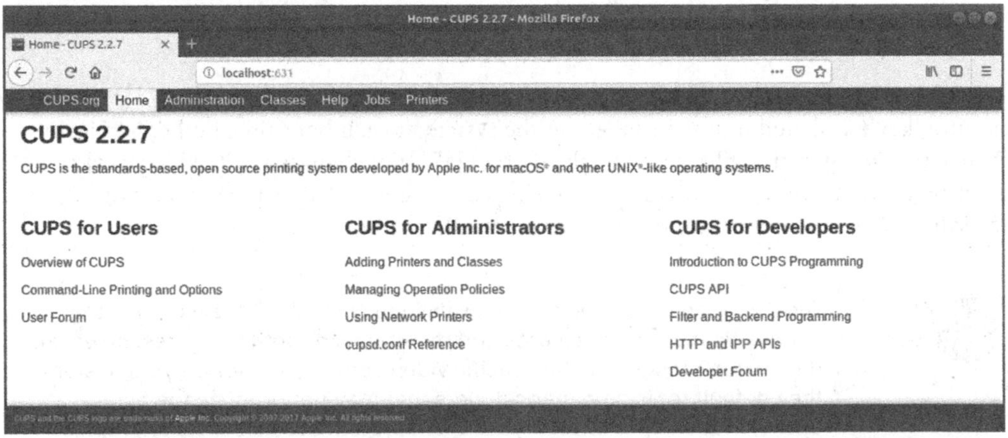

The CUPS web interface allows you to define new printers, modify existing printers, and check on the status of print jobs sent to each printer. Not only does CUPS recognize directly connected printers, but you can also configure network printers using several standard network printing protocols, such as the Internet Printing Protocol (IPP) or the Microsoft Server Message Block (SMB) protocol.

Aside from the CUPS web interface, there are a few command-line tools you can use for interacting with the print queues:

- lpc: Start, stop, or pause the print queue.

- lpq: Display the print queue status, along with any print jobs waiting in the queue.

- lpr: Submit a new print job to a print queue.

- lprm: Remove a specific print job from the print queue.

If you're working from the command line, you can check the status of any print queue as well as submit print jobs. For each of the commands, to specify the printer use the -P command-line option along with the printer name, as shown in Listing 23.10.

Listing 23.10: Printing from the command line in Linux

```
$ lpq -P EPSON_ET_3750_Series
EPSON_ET_3750_Series is ready
no entries
$ lpr -P EPSON_ET_3750_Series test.txt
$ lpq -P EPSON_ET_3750_Series
EPSON_ET_3750_Series is ready and printing
Rank     Owner   Job     File(s)                    Total Size
active   rich    1       test.txt                   1024 bytes
$
```

The first line in Listing 23.10 uses the lpq command to check the status of the print queue, which shows that the printer is ready to accept new jobs and doesn't currently have any jobs in the print queue. The lpr command submits a new print job to print a file. After the new print job is submitted, the lpq command shows that the printer is currently printing and shows the print job that's being printed.

Red Hat–based systems use the Automatic Bug Reporting Tool (abrt) to create a report if any kernel-level hardware errors are detected. Red Hat Linux customers can send the report to tech support to help troubleshoot the hardware issue.

Using Hot-Pluggable Devices

Computer hardware is generally categorized into two types:

- Cold-pluggable devices
- Hot-pluggable devices

Cold-pluggable devices are hardware that can be connected to the system only when the system is completely powered down. These usually include things commonly found inside the computer case, such as memory, PCI cards, and hard drives. You can't remove any of these things while the system is running.

Conversely, you can usually add and remove hot-pluggable devices at any time. They are often external components, such as network connections, monitors, and USB devices. The trick with hot-pluggable devices is that somehow the Linux kernel needs to know when the device is connected and automatically load the correct device driver module to support the device.

Linux provides an entire subsystem that interacts with hot-pluggable devices, making them accessible to users. This subsystem is described in the following sections.

Detecting Dynamic Devices

The *udev device manager* is a program that is automatically started at boot time by the `init` process (usually at run level 5 via the `/etc/rc5.d/udev` script) or the systemd systems and runs in the background at all times. It listens to kernel notifications about hardware devices. As new hardware devices are plugged into the running system, or existing hardware devices removed, the kernel sends out notification event messages.

The udev program listens to these notification messages and compares the messages against rules defined in a set of configuration files, normally stored under the `/etc/udev/rules.d` directory. If a device matches a defined rule, udev acts on the event notification as defined by the rule.

Each Linux distribution defines a standard set of rules for udev to follow. Rules define actions such as mounting USB memory sticks under the `/media` folder when they're installed or disabling network access when a USB network card is removed. You can modify the rules defined, but it's usually not necessary.

Working with Dynamic Devices

While the udev program runs in the background on your Linux system, you can still interact with it using the udevadm command-line tool. The udevadm command allows you to send commands to the udev program. The format of the udevadm command is as follows:

udevadm *command* [*options*]

Table 23.3 shows the commands available to send to the udevadm program.

TABLE 23.3 The udevadm commands

Command	Description
control	Modifies the internal state of udev
info	Queries the udev database for device information

Command	Description
monitor	Listens for kernel events and displays them
settle	Watches the udev event queue
test	Simulates a udev event
test-builtin	Runs a built-in device command for debugging
trigger	Requests device events from the kernel

The control command allows you to change the currently running udev program. For example, by adding the -R option, you can force udev to reload the rules defined in the /etc/udev/rules.d directory.

Exercise 23.1 walks you through how to view the kernel messages and device entries that occur when you connect a USB storage device to the Linux system.

EXERCISE 23.1

Adding a USB Storage Device to the Linux System

1. Log into your Linux graphical desktop and open a command prompt window.

2. At the command prompt, enter the **lsusb** command to view any USB controllers and devices connected to your system.

3. Plug a USB storage device, such as a memory stick, into a USB port; then wait a minute or so for the kernel to detect it.

4. Type the command **dmesg**, and observe the kernel ring buffer entries entered when the kernel detected the new USB device. Note the device name assigned to the new device (such as sdb1).

5. Type the **lsusb** command again and see if the new device appears in the output.

6. Type the command **lsblk** to view the device and partition in the block table and to note where the partition is mounted in the virtual directory.

7. Type the command **ls /dev/sd**∗ to view the SCSI devices on the system. You should see the USB device name that appeared in the dmesg output appear as a device file in the /dev folder.

8. Use the graphical desktop interface to safely eject the USB storage device.

9. Type the command **dmesg** to view the kernel entries when the device was removed.

10. Type the command **ls /dev/sd**∗ to see if the device file has been removed.

Summary

There are lots of ways to connect hardware devices to Linux systems. Both PCI and USB interfaces provide a standard way for connecting devices to the main motherboard so they can communicate. The newer GPIO interface provides a way to interact with smaller devices that use a single line for inputs and outputs that control sensors, switches, relays, and motors.

Besides the physical interfaces, Linux also uses files to communicate with devices. When you connect a device to the system, Linux automatically creates a file in the /dev directory that's used for applications to send data to and receive data from the devices. The kernel uses the /proc directory to create virtual files that contain information about the devices and system status. The /sys directory is also used by the kernel to create files useful for trouble-shooting device issues.

Linux provides a handful of command-line tools that you'll find useful when trying to troubleshoot device problems. The lsdev command allows you to view the status and settings for all devices on the system. The lsblk command provides information about block devices, such as hard drives and network cards, that are connected. The dmesg command lets you peek at the kernel ring buffer to view kernel event messages as it detects and works with devices. The lspci and lsusb commands allow you to view the PCI and USB devices that are connected to the Linux system.

Linux also provides software to help with monitors and printers. The X11 protocol, used by the XFree86 and X.org software packages, detects and interfaces with the video card, monitor, keyboard, and mouse connected to the system, providing a standard interface for applications to use. The CUPS software provides a standard method for applications to send documents to both local and network printers.

Finally, the chapter discussed how Linux handles hot-pluggable devices. The udev application monitors the kernel events for information about new hardware detected on USB ports. If a new device is detected, udev handles the device as defined in the rules set. The udevadm application allows you to control how udev works on your system.

Exam Essentials

Describe how Linux systems communicate with devices.   Linux systems create files in the /dev folder that applications use to send data to devices and retrieve data from devices. Device files can be either character files, which send and receive data one character at a time, or block files, which send and receive data in blocks.

Explain how you would find the hardware settings for a PCI board plugged into the Linux system.   The lspci command displays the PCI devices currently connected to the system. You can use that information with the lsdev command, which displays the interrupts, I/O ports, and DMA channels used by each device. You can also find that information in the /proc/interrupts, /proc/ioports, and /proc/dma files.

Explain how Linux can detect hot-pluggable devices.   The udev application runs in the background, monitoring the kernel ring buffer for new devices. When a new device is added, the udev application detects it from the kernel ring buffer messages and follows instructions defined in rules contained in the `/etc/udev/rules.d` directory.

Review Questions

1. What type of hardware interface uses interrupts, I/O ports, and DMA channels to communicate with the PC motherboard?

    A. USB

    B. GPIO

    C. PCI

    D. Monitors

    E. Printers

2. What filesystem does the Linux system use to track ports used to communicate with PCI boards?

    A. /proc/ioports

    B. /proc/interrupts

    C. /sys

    D. /dev

    E. /proc/dma

3. Where does Linux create files to send data to and receive data from directly with devices?

    A. /sys

    B. /proc

    C. /etc

    D. /dev

    E. /dev/mapper

4. Katie Jane created a new LVM volume on her Linux system. Where in the virtual directory should she look to find the virtual file related to the new volume?

    A. /dev

    B. /dev/mapper

    C. /proc

    D. /sys

    E. /etc

5. Joel installed a new PCI card in his Linux system but is now getting a conflict with another device on the system. What command can he use to display the interrupts, I/O ports, and DMA channels in use by all the existing devices?

    A. lsdev

    B. lsblk

    C. lspci

    D. lsusb

    E. dmesg

6. Which Linux command displays the contents of the kernel ring buffer?

    A. `lsdev`

    B. `lsblk`

    C. `lspci`

    D. `lsusb`

    E. `dmesg`

7. Which software packages implement the X Windows graphical system in Linux? (Choose two.)

    A. `X.org`

    B. CUPS

    C. Wayland

    D. X11

    E. `udev`

8. Sophia needs to connect her Linux system to a new network printer on the office network. What software package does she need to ensure is installed so she can configure the new network printer?

    A. `X.org`

    B. CUPS

    C. Wayland

    D. X11

    E. `udev`

9. Which program runs in the background monitoring the kernel ring buffer messages for new devices?

    A. `X.org`

    B. CUPS

    C. Wayland

    D. X11

    E. `udev`

10. Which program allows you to reload the defined rules for detecting and installing new devices?

    A. `udevadm`

    B. `udev`

    C. `lsusb`

    D. `lspci`

    E. `lsdev`

Chapter

24

Troubleshooting Application and Hardware Issues

✓ **Objective 4.1: Given a scenario, analyze and troubleshoot storage issues**

✓ **Objective 4.3: Given a scenario, analyze and troubleshoot central processing unit (CPU) and memory issues**

A Linux system's primary purpose is to serve. However, if one of its applications or the hardware it uses is not functioning properly, the system cannot fulfill its duty. Understanding common and a few uncommon problems with both applications and hardware will help you quickly resolve any issues.

Dealing with Storage Problems

Troubleshooting storage issues ranges from the easy-to-check items all the way to the strange and obscure. For example, if you just installed a drive, test connections to ensure they are tight. Disks that were previously working fine may suffer from degrading storage. These issues and more are covered in the following sections.

Exploring Common Issues

If you are fairly new to Linux system administration, most likely you are unaware of common storage problems. The following can help you prepare:

Degraded Storage/Mode *Degraded storage* refers to the storage medium's gradual decay due to time or improper use, which causes data degeneration or loss. For example, an SSD has limited endurance due to its finite number of program/erase (PE) cycles. Thus, employing an SSD in your swap space is unwise.

Degraded mode refers to a situation in which one or more disks in a RAID array have failed. In this case, troubleshooting efforts require you to employ the mdadm -D command to view a particular array's detailed status. If the status contains the word degraded, add another partition to the array so that it can recover.

Missing Devices Storage devices can go "missing" on Linux, but the cause varies. If it is network attached storage (NAS), check your network first (see Chapter 20, "Analyzing System Properties and Remediation").

If it is a locally attached device and other utilities, such as lsblk, are not displaying it, use super user privileges and try the lspci -M command. This command will perform a thorough scan of all PCI-attached devices.

The conduit to Linux devices is through the device files, such as /dev/sdb. Ensure that the particular partition's device file is available and not corrupted. If needed, rebuild it using the mknod command.

Check that you (or the utility configuration) are using the correct device file name. A whole disk is referred to by the device filename with no numbers, such as /dev/sdc. A disk partition is specified by the device filename and its number, like /dev/sdc2. When using an NvME SSD, the device filename, such as /dev/nvme0n1p1, has extra items, including the namespace.

Missing Volumes   Another form of a lost device is a missing volume. If you perform a pvscan on the physical devices that make up a logical volume and get a "Couldn't find device" message, you've got a missing volume. Typically, the cause is a failed or unintentionally removed disk.

If a disk that was part of a logical volume's group has failed, the missing disk's UUID will display in the pvscan message. You can replace the failed volume (pvcreate), restore the group's metadata (vgcfgrestore), recover the group (vgscan), and then activate it (vgchange) using LVM tools.

Missing Mount Points   A "Mount point does not exist" error message implies the obvious—the directory on which you are attempting to mount the filesystem does not exist. It was either deleted or never created in the first place. Simply make it with appropriate privileges using the mkdir command.

However, this error message can also be generated for a not-so-obvious problem. It centers on employing the bind option, either at the command line via the mount command or in the /etc/fstab file. This option moves a filesystem from its current mount point to a new mount point. If it is not already mounted somewhere, you'll get a "Mount point does not exist" error message.

Before removing a directory, check if it is a mount point. You can do that quickly by employing the mountpoint *directory-name* command.

Storage Integrity   A *bad block* (also called a bad sector) is a small chunk of a disk drive that will not respond to I/O requests due to corruption or physical damage. A random bad block does not indicate a drive is failing, but these storage devices need monitoring, because increasing bad sectors indicate it needs replacing.

Besides using the fsck command (covered in Chapter 11, "Handling Storage"), you can employ the badblocks utility to monitor a drive. It is different from fsck in that it focuses on a particular partition and does not perform any repairs. It is wise to back up and unmount a partition before checking for bad sectors. Use the nondestructive test by issuing the **badblocks -nsv** *partition-device-file* command. The utility provides progress as it runs, and when the tests are complete, it issues a final bad blocks status.

In addition, a disk's manufacturer often provides its own set of testing programs. Typically these programs let you know whether or not to replace the drive but do not provide detailed data on bad sectors.

The dmesg command displays the kernel ring buffer, which can contain messages such as disk I/O errors. These are indicators of potential problems.

Performance Issues   Poor storage performance adversely affects applications. Besides using utilities such as iostat, ioping, iotop, and sar (covered in Chapter 20) to monitor storage performance problems, you can also employ hdparm to determine a drive's read speeds. This utility is useful for PATA or SATA drives. SCSI drives that have SCSI/ATA command translation are also supported.

The dstat utility is similar to iostat but provides additional helpful data for troubleshooting storage performance problems. For example, this tool displays throughput statistics associated with network use or per individual LV drives.

Another handy utility that works specifically with logical volumes is the dmstats utility. This tool allows the setup and management of statistics for any devices charted by the device mapper. You can determine device mapper filenames associated with logical volumes using the lsblk -p utility.

A GUI tool that gauges disk performance is the gnome-disks utility. However, back up any of the disk's data before performing a write benchmark.

Resource Exhaustion   *Resource exhaustion* is a situation in which a system's finite resources are committed and unavailable to others. Running out of inode numbers or disk space (covered in Chapter 20) are two examples.

Threat agents can engage in a storage resource exhaustion attack via file descriptor leaks. A file descriptor is commonly used in programming languages to access a file, pipe, or network socket. You can prevent this attack type by setting the PAM nofile limit in the /etc/security/limits.conf file. (PAM was covered in Chapter 16, "Looking at Access and Authentication Methods.")

Dealing with Specialized Issues

One of the first things you should check for an older storage device experiencing problems is whether or not the device's manufacturer has a new driver or firmware available. Often this can resolve a tricky issue.

Another item to check is the device's Linux module (driver). If it is not loaded or built into the Linux kernel, your device will not function. Start with the dmesg utility to gain some clues. A snipped example is shown in Listing 24.1.

Listing 24.1: Looking up disk information via the dmesg command

```
# dmesg | grep sde
[…]
[    5.566479] sd 6:0:0:0: [sde] Attached SCSI disk
```

The dmesg utility's output is searched using grep to find information concerning the sde disk (/dev/sde). The important clue here is that the disk is an attached SCSI disk.

The available SCSI disk driver information is stored within a /sys/ directory, as shown in Listing 24.2.

Listing 24.2: Determining the driver via the ls and udevadm commands

```
# ls /sys/bus/scsi/drivers
sd  sr
#
# udevadm info -an /dev/sde | grep DRIVERS | grep sd
    DRIVERS=="sd"
```

Notice that the sd and sr drivers are used for SCSI devices. The udevadm command confirms which one is employed for the /dev/sde disk.

After the driver (module) is determined, use the lsmod command to see if it is currently loaded into the kernel. A snipped example is shown in Listing 24.3.

Listing 24.3: Determining if the module is loaded using the lsmod command

```
# lsmod | grep sd
sd_mod                  46322  5
[…]
# modinfo sd_mod
filename:       /lib/modules/3.10.0-
862.11.6.el7.x86_64/kernel/drivers/scsi/sd_mod.ko.xz
[…]
description:    SCSI disk (sd) driver
[…]
```

If the module is not loaded, it may be built into the kernel. You can check this by looking at the modules.builtin file, as shown snipped in Listing 24.4.

Listing 24.4: Determining if the module is built in using the cat command

```
$ cat /lib/modules/$(uname -r)/modules.builtin | grep sd_mod
kernel/drivers/scsi/sd_mod.ko
```

If the module is not loaded or built into the kernel, dynamically load it using super user privileges and the modprobe command (Chapter 14, "Tending Kernel Modules").

Seeking SATA

An adapter is a piece of hardware that may have one or more software interfaces. The various storage interfaces, such as SATA drives, can have unique problems. On Linux, SATA drives are self-configuring. They are typically connected to the SCSI bus and are denoted by the /dev/sd* device files.

 If you are using a Linux distro with a kernel version prior to 2.6.16 (released March 2006), be aware that SATA suspend and resume is not supported. The system will hang when the device is accessed after a resume operation. Fix this problem by adding SATA power management support via a kernel patch.

On Linux, some SATA devices may fail earlier than others due to frequent head loads and unloads. Often this is due to aggressive power management.

You can check for this situation on a SATA drive, if it uses self-monitoring analysis and reporting technology (SMART), via the smartctl -a command. Look at the Start_Stop_Count, which is the number of loads and unloads. For a particular disk, a high count compared to other drives is indicative of this problem. Double-check it using the hdparm -B command on the drive. If the command returns a low number, such as 1, then aggressive power management is confirmed. You can modify this by using super user privileges and typing **hdparm -B 127** *device-filename*, which will not only remove the aggressive power management but also typically improves performance and extends the drive's life.

 If you are using a virtual machine, the smartctl command will fail. This is due to virtualized disks not supporting SMART.

Comprehending SCSI

On Linux, the SCSI framework consists of three integral parts:

- Upper: The device driver (for example, disk driver) layer
- Middle: The SCSI routing layer
- Lower: The host bus adapter (HBA) driver layer

The upper layer is closest to the application or user command, whereas the lower SCSI layer is right next to the actual hardware. The HBA is either a circuit board or an integrated circuit adapter, which connects to the disk drive. Just like device drivers, the HBA driver is either loaded or built into the kernel.

Problems can occur if either the HBA or device driver is not loaded or built into the kernel. Earlier, in Listing 24.3 and Listing 24.4, a check was done for a SCSI upper-layer driver. In Listing 24.5, a snipped example shows looking for the HBA driver (module) and checking whether or not it is loaded or built in.

Listing 24.5: Determining a module name and if it is loaded

```
# udevadm info -an /dev/sda | grep -i drivers
    DRIVERS=="sd"
[…]
    DRIVERS=="ahci"
[…]
#
# lsmod | grep ahci
ahci                    34056   3
[…]
#
# modinfo ahci
[…]
description:    AHCI SATA low-level driver
[…]
```

Notice that the HBA driver is the Advanced Host Controller Interface (ACHI) driver, and it is loaded into the kernel. This particular driver allows you to hot-plug SATA drives, which are treated as SCSI devices. In other words, the SATA drives are attached to the SCSI framework.

When you attach a SATA drive as a hot-plugged SCSI device, you will need to enable it. This is accomplished by either rebooting the system or modifying the /sys/class/ scsi_host/host#/scan file. The # is the drive's SCSI host number. An example of determining the appropriate host number and modifying the file is shown snipped in Listing 24.6.

Listing 24.6: Enabling a hot-plugged SATA drive

```
# lsblk -S
NAME HCTL        TYPE VENDOR   MODEL          REV TRAN
[…]
sde  6:0:0:0     disk ATA      VBOX HARDDISK  1.0 sata
[…]
#
# echo '- - -' > /sys/class/scsi_host/host6/scan
```

In this example, the lsblk -S command only shows attached SCSI framework devices, and the SATA drive is sde (/dev/sde). The HTCL column in the output shows the device's host number (the first number prior to the first colon). In this case, the host number is 6. After the disk's host number is determined, the characters '- - -' are echoed into the appropriate file (note the required spaces between each dash). This action forces the system to scan the device attached to the SCSI framework at that host number, which enables the drive.

Moderating RAID

A Linux system can employ software and hardware RAID. Software RAID arrays are implemented through the Multiple Devices (md) driver. Check the status of your software RAID array by viewing the /proc/mdstat file.

If it is SATA based and a drive goes offline, a software RAID array can hang. This occurs if the HBA does not handle hot-plug action. Thus, it is wise to check if your lower SCSI framework layer's driver supports hot-plugging. If your HBA uses the AHCI module (driver), hot-plugging is allowed.

Hardware-based RAID arrays are managed via a hardware device connected to the Linux SCSI framework. A hardware RAID controller's data, such as the manufacturer and model number, are obtained using super user privileges and entering **lspci -knn | grep "RAID bus controller"** at the command line. This is useful if you inherited a Linux system and need to obtain manufacturer utilities to troubleshoot and monitor a hardware-based RAID array.

Uncovering Application Permission Issues

A user notifies you that an application has issued an I/O error when they attempt to run it. The problem is possibly a permission issue. You will need to gather some information before starting your troubleshooting:

1. Determine which account runs the application and the account's name.

2. Discover the specific program action that raised the error.

3. Obtain a full directory reference for any files on which the application was attempting to perform reads/writes or for any files it was attempting to create.

4. Record, if applicable, any additional applications it was trying to launch.

5. Document, if applicable, any local or remote services the application is attempting to employ, such as NTP or a file server (Chapter 2, "Introduction to Services").

> If the application uses services, such as OpenSSH and/or an authentication server, it is important to know what service accounts are involved. Record this information as well.

When you have these details, you are ready to proceed in your troubleshooting process.

Ownership Look at the various application files involved using the ls -l command. Determine what username owns the files and the permissions granted to those owners.

Don't forget to look at the directory permissions as well. You'll need to know the entire directory tree's owners and permissions.

If the application is not run under a username that owns the file or the directory tree, you'll need to go on to group memberships and possibly other permissions. File and directory permission troubleshooting was covered in Chapter 22, "Investigating User Issues," if you need a refresher.

Group Memberships   Uncover the groups to which the end user running the application belongs. If the application is run under a different account, check that account's group memberships.

When you have that information, you can check the application files involved. Identify the group permissions of those files as well as the directory tree to uncover any potential problems.

Executables   If the application cannot be run by a particular account, check the execute privileges. Keep in mind that if the application kicks off additional programs, you will need to check the privileges for those as well.

If you are using a script that changes its present working directory and it fails, then check the directory tree it is trying to access. The execute privilege must be granted on every single directory within the tree in order for an account to change its present working directory to that particular location.

Inheritance   If the application is creating files in a particular directory and can no longer access those files, check for forced inheritance via ACLs (covered in Chapter 15, "Applying Ownership and Permissions"). If the directory has a default ACL, any files created within that directory that do not have ACLs set specifically for them will inherit their ACL from the directory. You can view default directory ACLs using the `getfacl` `-d` or the `--default` command.

If you find that a directory's default ACL is behind the problem, consider removing the default ACL and defining the needed ACL on the directory. Another alternative is to explicitly set the application file's ACL, which will override the inherited directory default ACL. Employ the `setfacl` utility to enact these changes.

You can try out basic application permission problem troubleshooting using Exercise 24.1.

EXERCISE 24.1

Troubleshooting Application Permission Issues

1. Log into your Linux system via a tty terminal, using a non-root account that can access super user privileges via the sudo command.

2. At the command-line prompt, type **touch /tmp/fileA.txt** and press the Enter key. The touch command was covered in Chapter 3, "Managing Files, Directories, and Text."

3. Change the newly created file's owner and group to root by typing **sudo chown root:root /tmp/fileA.txt** and pressing Enter. If requested, enter the account's sudo password. The sudo and chown commands were covered in Chapter 15.

4. Next, you will create a small application using the nano text editor (covered in Chapter 4, "Searching and Analyzing Text"). Type **nano application.sh** and press Enter. This will put you into the nano text editor.

5. Type in the following, pressing the Enter key as needed:

```
#!/bin/bash
echo "Creating file /tmp/Activity.txt…"
echo "Hello World" > /tmp/Activity.txt
echo "Removing file…"
rm -ir /tmp/*.*
exit
```

6. Press Ctrl+O and then the Enter key to write out the text editor's buffer to the activity.sh file.

7. Press Ctrl+X to leave the text editor.

8. Run the application by typing **bash activity.sh** and pressing Enter.

9. When asked a question, type **y** at the prompt and press Enter. You should receive at least one error message relating to the attempt to delete the /tmp/fileA.txt file, but you may receive more error messages depending on what files and directories are currently located in the /tmp/ directory.

10. Now you can begin the troubleshooting process. Since you ran the application, record your user account's name.

11. Document the action that causes the error to occur. (Hint: It was associated with the /tmp/fileA.txt file.)

12. Record the problem file's full directory reference. (Hint: Look at the previous step.)

13. Document that the application is not trying to launch any additional applications or employing local or remote services.

14. Display the problem file's directory's ownership, group membership, and various permissions by typing **ls -ld /tmp** and pressing Enter.

15. Record the directory's owner and its associated permissions.

16. Document the directory's group and its associated permissions.

17. Record the directory's other permissions. Note that if you see a t in the permissions, this refers to the sticky bit (covered in Chapter 15).

18. Determine which of the three directory permission sets (owner, group, or other) would apply to your user account and record it.

19. Using Table 22.1 in Chapter 22 and the information you uncovered in the last several steps, discover the cause of this application problem. Record your theory.

20. The application's problem was caused by using the `/tmp/*.*` file wildcard designation as the `rm -ir` command's argument. If the sticky bit is set on the `/tmp/` directory, your account can only delete files from that directory, which you own. Therefore, to fix the problem, if desired, change the `rm -ir /tmp/*.*` line in the `activity.sh` application to `rm -i /tmp/activity.txt` instead.

Analyzing Application Dependencies

In Chapter 13, "Governing Software," we covered using package management commands, such as `apt-cache depends` and `yum deplist`, to display a repository-managed application's dependencies. There are some special problems you can run into with programs and their various dependencies. The more common ones associated with the certification exam are examined here.

Versioning

Typically, application software programs and operating systems are continually updated. These updates may improve performance or add additional functionality. To keep track of the various application updates, a technique called *versioning* is employed. Versioning is the management of multiple application software updates through a numbering process. Different versions (releases) of an application have different numbers, which typically increase for newer application updates.

For example, the Linux kernel version 2.6.0 was released in December 2003. Current kernel versions can be found at www.kernel.org and have numerically higher numbers compared to the 2.6.0 version. These higher numbers indicate newer releases.

You can use versioning to determine if application updates or patches have been released. This is helpful when troubleshooting application software issues.

Updating Issues

If an application is experiencing problems, check for a new software update. If the application is available through a repository, use your distro's particular package management to check for a new version (see Chapter 13).

Consider setting up a test system with the application environment and apply application updates to it. You can conduct thorough planned tests prior to updating production applications. Before applying any production application updates, ensure that you have an excellent backup. These two items should protect you from most bad situations.

If an application begins experiencing problems after a recent update, review the distro's package management history information. For example, on a system using RPM, using super user privileges you can issue the command rpm -q *package-name* --last to see the latest update history for the *package-name* package. On a Debian system, check the /var/log/apt/history.log file. You'll need to uninstall any installed packages or libraries causing the problem using the appropriate package management utility (see Chapter 13).

> On modern Ubuntu distro versions, unattended upgrades are configured. This allows automatic security upgrades to software and requires no human intervention. If you desire to turn this off, change the APT::Periodic::Update-Package-Lists directive in the /etc/apt/apt.conf.d/10periodic file from 1 to 0. Find out more about this feature by typing **man unattended-upgrade** at the command line.

When one software package depends on another package or library to operate properly, it is called a *dependency*. A *broken dependency* (also called an *unmet dependency*) is an undesirable situation, where a software package has been installed but one or more of its needed packages or libraries are not installed. Sometimes a package upgrade can break dependencies, resulting in what is called a *broken package*.

To check for broken dependencies, on a Debian package management system, use the apt-get check command. The YUM package manager will not update programs that cause a broken dependency, but if you installed a program using the rpm utility that caused problems, you can issue the **rpm -aV** command on any Red Hat package managed system to see damaged software packages.

Patching

A *patch* refers to program changes or configuration file updates for a particular application or system service. Patches may correct serious problems or fix security vulnerabilities and are often issued out of the normal software update cycle. *Patching* is the act of applying a patch. It does not necessarily involve updating all your system's software. There are many conflicting theories on patch management, but at the heart of the issue is keeping your applications and Linux system running smoothly, safely, and effectively for your users.

A kernel patch release is a little different. It is a special source code package that only contains the changes applied to the major kernel source code release. You just download the patch source code package, use the Linux patch command to apply the patch updates to the existing kernel source code files on your system, and then recompile the kernel. Typically, your package manager handles this for you when you update packages (software) on the system.

Dealing with Libraries

Application functions are often split into separate library files (shared libraries) so that multiple applications that use the same functions can share these library files. Libraries were first covered in Chapter 13.

If an application begins experiencing problems after a software upgrade, it may be related to a recently upgraded shared library the application employs. You can check which libraries a program uses by typing **ldd** *program-name* at the command line. It is helpful to redirect this command's output into another file. Use the grep command to search package management log files to determine if one of the application's libraries was recently updated. An example is shown snipped in Listing 24.7.

Listing 24.7: Using ldd and grep to discover a recently upgraded library

```
$ which ssh
/usr/bin/ssh
$
$ ldd /usr/bin/ssh > lib.txt
$
$ cat lib.txt
[…]
        libk5crypto.so.3 […]
[…]
$
$ grep -B 2 -A 2 libk5crypto /var/log/apt/history.log
Start-Date: 2019-01-22  13:37:45
Commandline: /usr/bin/unattended-upgrade
Upgrade: libk5crypto3:amd64 (1.16-2build1, 1.16-2ubuntu0.1)
End-Date: 2019-01-22  13:37:49

$
```

The application used in this example is the OpenSSH ssh program. Notice one of its libraries was recently upgraded. (The -B and -A options on the grep command allow you to pull additional lines below and above the found content.) If it began experiencing problems shortly after this library upgrade, you have a probable cause. Check to see if a new upgrade or patch is available for this library. If not, you may have to uninstall it and install an earlier version.

Exploring Environment Variable Issues

If you have a newly installed application that is not executing, check the PATH environment variable. This variable determines what directories are searched for a program that the Bash shell does not directly handle. An example of displaying the variable's contents is shown in Listing 24.8.

Listing 24.8: Viewing the PATH environment variable

```
$ echo $PATH
/usr/local/sbin:/usr/local/bin:/usr/sbin:/usr/bin:
/sbin:/bin:/usr/games:/usr/local/games:/snap/bin
$
```

If you need to modify this parameter for everyone, create a Bash script file (Bash scripts are covered in Chapter 25, "Deploying Bash Scripts") in the /etc/profile.d/ directory. Be sure to use the .sh file extension. The file must be owned by root and belong to the root group. Set the file's other (world) permissions to r so that all users can read the file. The script is read by the /etc/profile or /etc/bashrc file, depending on your distribution, when a user logs into the system or starts a new shell.

If only certain users need this particular PATH modification, make it in their ~/.profile, ~/.bash_profile, or ~./bash_login file. Environment files were discussed in Chapter 10, "Administering Users and Groups."

Gaining GCC Compatibility

The most common tool used for compiling programs in Linux is the GNU Compiler Collection (GCC). If you have problems compiling an application on Linux with GCC, there are several potential causes. They are as follows:

- GCC uses the system C library, which might not be compliant with the ISO C standard.

- There are several notable incompatibilities between GNU C and non-ISO versions of C.

- GCC uses corrected versions of system header files, which can cause issues.

Note that besides these issues, you might be using an older version of gcc and need to update it. For example, if your system distro is CentOS 7 and you are using gcc v4.4.*, you need to upgrade the GCC package.

You can find detailed documentation on the GCC compiler at its website—https://gcc.gnu.org. This site includes FAQs and other useful information.

Perusing Repository Problems

The very first thing to check when you get an odd error message concerning a package that cannot be found, updated, or installed is your network connection. Often a system that is not network-connected causes this problem. However, various package repositories (also called *repos*) can become corrupted.

On a system using a Debian package manager, such as Ubuntu, if you get a message saying it cannot download repository information or something similar, use the apt-get clean command. This command cleans up the database and any temporary download files. After that, try to update the local repository with apt-get update, which attempts to retrieve updated information about packages in the repository.

On a Debian package management system, consider using the apt-get dist-upgrade command instead of apt-get upgrade to update all the system's packages. dist-upgrade prevents any software from being upgraded that will break a dependent package.

On a system using a Red Hat package manager, such as Rocky Linux, you can employ the yum clean all or zypper clean -a command, depending on your distro. Next, update the local repository with the yum check-update or zypper refresh command.

If you are attempting to install or update packages from a nonstandard repository, you may need to enable that repo on your system. To see a list of the enabled repositories on your system, use the yum repolist or zypper repos command on Red Hat package systems. For Debian package systems, you'll need to issue the grep -v "#" /etc/apt/sources.list command to see the enabled repositories.

Before you add any additional nonstandard repositories, back up the repository file(s), such as these:

- /etc/apt/sources.list
- /etc/yum.repos.d/*.*
- /etc/zypp/repos.d/*.*

You have to manually edit the sources.list file to add and enable a new repository. To add and enable a new repo with YUM, use the yum-config-manager --add-repo *repository-url* command. The zypper command is similar but also requires a repository name alias—zypper addrepo *repository-url alias*.

Keep in mind that we have only touched on a few of the more common problems you can run into with programs and their various dependencies. Be sure to employ your distribution's man pages for additional help.

Looking at SELinux Context Violations

Application issues can be caused by your system's Linux kernel security module, such as SELinux (covered in Chapter 15). An incorrect policy configuration, which triggers a violation, can prevent applications from serving their purpose. Check the audit log file using the sealert command first. If this tool is not available, you can install it via the setroubleshoot package.

A mislabeled file can cause problems, such as access being denied to applications. Use the ls -Z command to view a file's SELinux context. If it or its parent directory needs to have their context changed, use the chcon utility to modify it, the semanage command to make it permanent, and restorecon to fix the labels. Don't forget to employ all three of those commands or you won't resolve the problem.

You can change the mode for SELinux temporarily from enforcing to permissive via the `setenforce permissive` command with super user privileges. This allows you to make context changes and see if it triggers any violations without actually blocking access. Once you've got the correct SELinux policies in place, put it back into enforcing mode using the `setenforce enforcing` command.

An application that is confined by SELinux needs the proper Booleans set to allow appropriate access. The `getsebool` command will allow you to review the application's Booleans. If you need to change them, employ super user privileges and the `setsebool` command.

If you are seeing a great deal of SELinux context violations in your log or journal files and have not had application problems in the past, it is possible that your system has an intruder. Use an intrusion detection tool to confirm.

Exploring Firewall Blockages

If an application is experiencing problems over the network and there are no network issues, you may want to check the local and remote systems' firewalls. Any application updates or firewall modifications can trigger this problem. Firewalls were covered in Chapter 18, "Overseeing Linux Firewalls."

Unrestricting ACLs

A firewall ACL identifies a network packet by reviewing its control information along with other network data. Therefore, when troubleshooting an application issue related to a firewall, you'll need to gather the following information for the application packets traveling back and forth:

- Source address or hostname
- Destination address or hostname
- Network protocol(s) used
- Inbound port(s) used
- Outbound port(s) used

You also need to know both your source and destination systems' firewall application in use. When you've gathered this information, you can review the firewall settings on both sides to determine if the ACLs are overly restrictive.

For example, if you are using `firewalld` on your application's host system, you can quickly check the current default zone, as shown in Listing 24.9.

Listing 24.9: Viewing the `default` zone with the `firewall-cmd` command

```
$ firewall-cmd --get-default-zone
drop
$
```

Notice that this system has its `firewalld` default set to the `drop` zone. This means all incoming network packets are dropped and only outbound network connections are allowed. If the application receives data or connections from other systems, then this firewall ACL setting is overly restrictive.

Unblocking Ports

If your application relies on another system service (daemon), you'll want to check rules related to the service port. Blocking a port needed by the external service would adversely affect the application. If your application is designed to use a port that is not dedicated to a well-known service, check it as well.

For example, if you are providing public web services on your system, you need to allow incoming and outbound packets associated with the HTTPS protocol port 443. If your system is using the `iptables` firewall software, you can view the current ACL rules via the `iptables -L` command. If the packet filter is blocking port 443 via a particular rule or policy, you can modify the chain using a command similar to the one in Listing 24.10, which opens up port 443.

Listing 24.10: Modifying the firewall with the `iptables` command

```
$ iptables -A INPUT -p tcp --dport 443 -j ACCEPT
$
```

Keep in mind you also need to modify the `OUTPUT` chain rules to allow your web server to establish connections. In addition, if your application allows HTTP traffic, you must modify rules for port 80 as well.

 View firewall log file entries as you investigate application problems. If needed, you can often increase the amount of information that is logged. For example, the UFW firewall has a `full` setting, which logs everything.

Unblocking Protocols

Besides ports, be aware of the various protocols, such as UDP, TCP, and ICMP, that your application employs. If it uses another system service, you must know the protocols it uses as well. The `/etc/services` file can help.

For example, say an application is working with a DNS caching server on the local network. DNS protocol uses port 53. Check the `/etc/services` (well-known ports) file to find the transport protocols it employs, as shown snipped in Listing 24.11.

Listing 24.11: Checking DNS's protocols in the /etc/services file

```
$ grep 53 /etc/services
domain          53/tcp                    # Domain Name Server
domain          53/udp
[...]
$
```

Unblock port 53 on the DNS server system for both TCP and UDP, since DNS listens for requests using those two transport protocols. Also, unblock them for both inbound and outbound packets.

Troubleshooting Additional Hardware Issues

Linux requires hardware to operate. When hardware stops working correctly, Linux does not function properly. Thus, understanding how to troubleshoot all hardware is an essential skill for a Linux system administrator.

Looking at Helpful Hardware Commands

When you are troubleshooting hardware problems, there are many Linux command-line tools that can help. The lspci, lsusb, and lsdev commands are a few, which were introduced in Chapter 23, "Dealing with Linux Devices." We'll cover a couple more great utilities, dmidecode and lshw, here.

Understanding the *dmidecode* Utility

Before looking at the dmidecode command, you need to know about the Distributed Management Task Force (DMTF) and its standards. The DMTF is a nonprofit organization whose goal is to simplify the management of network-accessible technologies, like servers, through standards. In essence, it helps to make system administration easier.

DMTF created the Desktop Management Interface (DMI) and System Management BIOS (SMBIOS) standards. The DMI specification consists of four components, which provide information about the hardware being used on a computer as well as some additional helpful data. The SMBIOS standard consists of items, such as data structures, used to read management information produced by a computer's BIOS. These two standards interact with each other and are widely adopted by hardware manufacturers.

To use these standards, you need two things—a DMI/SMBIOS-compliant computer and a software interface to their data structures. The software interface on a Linux system is the dmidecode utility.

The dmidecode utility pulls its information, by default, from the sysfs filesystem and specifically from tables in the /sys/firmware/dmi/tables/ directory. You can check if those tables exist on your system by using the command in Listing 24.12. Notice on this system that the tables exist.

Listing 24.12: Checking for tables in the sysfs filesystem

```
# ls /sys/firmware/dmi/tables
DMI  smbios_entry_point
#
```

The -h option on the dmidecode command describes the various options you can use to uncover information in your hardware troubleshooting process. While you must use super user privileges with the command for extracting table information, you don't have to do so for getting help. An example is shown in Listing 24.13.

Listing 24.13: Looking at the dmidecode help facility

```
$ dmidecode -h
Usage: dmidecode [OPTIONS]
Options are:
 -d, --dev-mem FILE      Read memory from device FILE (default: /dev/mem)
 -h, --help              Display this help text and exit
 -q, --quiet             Less verbose output
 -s, --string KEYWORD    Only display the value of the given DMI string
 -t, --type TYPE         Only display the entries of given type
 -u, --dump              Do not decode the entries
     --dump-bin FILE     Dump the DMI data to a binary file
     --from-dump FILE    Read the DMI data from a binary file
     --no-sysfs          Do not attempt to read DMI data from sysfs files
 -V, --version           Display the version and exit
$
```

Of the various options, the most useful for troubleshooting is the -t, or --type, switch. This allows you to pull specified information from the DMI/SMBIOS tables by providing an argument, which is either a number or a keyword. The keyword argument can be one of the following:

- baseboard
- bios
- cache
- chassis
- connector
- memory
- processor

- slot
- system

If the tables do not contain the needed information, you will only receive a message about where the utility attempted to extract data and possibly DMI and/or SMBIOS standard versions supported. Two examples are shown in Listing 24.14. Notice that there is no memory information available in the tables but that some system data is displayed.

Listing 24.14: Looking at dmidecode table data

```
# dmidecode -t memory
# dmidecode 3.0
Getting SMBIOS data from sysfs.
SMBIOS 2.5 present.

#
# dmidecode -t system
# dmidecode 3.0
Getting SMBIOS data from sysfs.
SMBIOS 2.5 present.

Handle 0x0001, DMI type 1, 27 bytes
System Information
        Manufacturer: innotek GmbH
        Product Name: VirtualBox
        Version: 1.2
        Serial Number: 0
        UUID: 3909BE96-5CA6-4801-8236-D6113BB5D2CF
        Wake-up Type: Power Switch
        SKU Number: Not Specified
        Family: Virtual Machine
```

If you are using a virtualized Linux system, the information from the dmidecode utility is suspect. Also, do not rely on this utility alone for hardware information. Its man page even states, "More often than not, information contained in the DMI tables is inaccurate, incomplete, or simply wrong."

Understanding the *lshw* Utility

Hardware information is stored in various /proc/ directory files on your system. While you could go rooting around and dig it out yourself, the lshw utility does it for you. It provides data on your system's processor(s), memory, NIC(s), USB controller(s), disk(s), and so on. It is typically installed by default on most distributions or available in a standard repository (Chapter 13 covered installing software packages).

Two helpful options are -short, which produces a nice table-formatted hardware data display, and -businfo, which shows information associated with SCSI, USB, IDE, and PCI devices. An example of using the -short option is shown snipped in Listing 24.15.

Listing 24.15: Using the -short option with the lshw command

```
# lshw -short
H/W path              Device      Class       Description
======================================================
                                  system      VirtualBox
/0                                bus         VirtualBox
/0/0                              memory      128KiB BIOS
/0/1                              memory      4GiB System memory
/0/2                              processor   Intel(R) Core(TM) […]
/0/100                            bridge      440FX - 82441FX PMC [Natoma]
/0/100/1                          bridge      82371SB PIIX3 ISA [Natoma/Triton II]
/0/100/1.1            scsi1       storage     82371AB/EB/MB PIIX4 IDE
/0/100/1.1/0.0.0      /dev/cdrom  disk        CD-ROM
/0/100/2                          display     VirtualBox Graphics Adapter
/0/100/3             enp0s3       network     82540EM Gigabit Ethernet Controller
/0/100/4                          generic     VirtualBox Guest Service
/0/100/5                          multimedia  82801AA AC'97 Audio Controller
/0/100/6                          bus         KeyLargo/Intrepid USB
/0/100/6/1           usb1         bus         OHCI PCI host controller
/0/100/7                          bridge      82371AB/EB/MB PIIX4 ACPI
/0/100/8             enp0s8       network     82540EM Gigabit Ethernet Controller
/0/100/d             scsi2        storage     82801HM/HEM (ICH8M/ICH8M-E) SATA […]
/0/100/d/0           /dev/sda     disk        16GB VBOX HARDDISK
/0/100/d/0/1                      volume      1GiB Linux filesystem partition
/0/100/d/0/2         /dev/sda2    volume      13GiB Linux LVM Physical Volume
partition
[…]
/0/4                              input       PnP device PNP0f03
/1                   virbr0-nic   network     Ethernet interface
[…]
#
```

You can also employ the -class option with the lshw utility. This option provides detailed information about a particular hardware component. The different classes available are displayed in the lshw -short command's output. A snipped example of using the -class option is shown in Listing 24.16.

Listing 24.16: Using the -class option with the lshw command

```
$ sudo lshw -class display
  *-display
       description: VGA compatible controller
       product: VirtualBox Graphics Adapter
       vendor: InnoTek Systemberatung GmbH
[…]

       configuration: driver=vboxvideo latency=0
[…]
$
```

 Another nice utility that can provide hardware information is the hwinfo command. It provides additional data for your troubleshooting process. If it is not installed by default on your distro, consider manually installing it.

Investigating Other Hardware Problems

Occasionally you have a hardware problem that is uncommon. Being able to quickly address these unique issues will make you stand out from your peers.

Memory   Physical problems with RAM are tricky to diagnose. Some symptoms of this issue include a system's performance slows over time, the system appears to hang when a memory-intensive application is running or at boot, kernel panics or segmentation faults occur intermittently, files are sporadically corrupted, and/or program installations fail.

First, make sure it is not a memory capacity issue, which often shows symptoms similar to hardware problems. Check using the free and vmstat utilities.

You can quickly determine hardware information about your RAM using the lshw utility. Just issue the **lshw -class memory** command.

If you recently added new memory, most likely you obtained a faulty component. Damage can also be done to RAM by power spikes or outages. In any case, you'll want to conduct a test on the memory. Typically you can conduct such a test via a system reboot and accessing the memtest or memtest86+ option in the server's boot menu. If this option is not available, you can employ the memtester utility. This command-line utility is typically not installed by default, but it is available either in your distribution's repository or as an RPM or dpkg file (see Chapter 13). When using this utility, you'll need to shut down any production applications and test the memory in chunks.

Printers   External hardware devices are typically plug-and-play for Linux, but odd problems do arise. When dealing with printers, the issue typically comes down to either an outdated/incorrect driver (PPD) or a bad connection. Start by checking the kernel ring buffer with dmesg and taking a look at the printer error log files, such as `/var/log/cups/error_log`.

Don't buy a doorstop. Make sure the printer your company is interested in purchasing is already supported by Linux. There are several websites that can help, such as www.openprinting.org/printers and tldp.org/HOWTO/Printing-HOWTO/printers.html. In addition, use your favorite search engine and enter **Linux Compatible Printers** to find more.

If the printer was recently installed, check its configuration. You can do this via a web browser, if available, on the system by entering **127.0.0.1:631** in the address bar. If your system does not have a GUI, you can look through the `/etc/cups/printers.conf` file to review the printer's configuration.

Determine how the printer connects to the system. Is it a network printer? Does it attach via a USB cable? Is the printer directly connected into a parallel port? If it is a network-connected printer, first check that the network is operational. If the printer is attached with a USB cable, start by troubleshooting the USB connections (covered later in this chapter). If it uses a parallel port on your system, it may be a bad adapter. If possible, consider switching it to a different connection type, such as USB, or obtaining a new printer with a more modern configuration.

Check if the printer's PostScript Printer Definition (PPD) file or driver needs updating. Go to the manufacturer or open source driver website to determine if an update is available. You can view all the currently available printer drivers on your system using the lpinfo -m command. Keep in mind the problem may involve a needed printer firmware update, so check for those as well.

Some manufacturers provide their own Linux tools to assist in printer troubleshooting. For example, Hewlett Packard offers the hp-info and hp-toolset utilities to help in managing and problem-solving their printers' issues.

Video   Hardware issues with video show up in sluggish displays, audio lag, glitches on the screen, and so on. You may even see a black screen or receive no audio output. Some problems can even cause the system to crash or hang.

As with many other hardware problems, first check the kernel ring buffer (dmesg) and video log files. If your system is still using X11, check the journal file or the `/var/log/Xorg.0.log` file. If you are employing Wayland, check the journal file via the journalctl command.

A graphics processing unit (GPU) exists on either a graphics card or on a motherboard. It is an assembly that performs some simple processing in order to relieve the CPU of such duties. Often a graphics card is called a GPU or GPU card.

To find out what graphics card driver your system is using, just type **lspci -vnn** at the command line and redirect STDOUT to a file. Peruse the file for the word VGA. This will show your graphics card driver data. You can also employ lshw -class display (or video) and look for the driver information there. When you have the driver's name, find out additional details through the modinfo *driver-name* command.

Check the manufacturer's or open source site to see if there is an updated graphics card driver available. If not, try testing the card on another system to see if you need to replace it.

 Some manufacturers provide their own utilities to manage their GPU cards. For example, Nvidia provides the nvidia-smi and nvidia-settings commands for their graphics cards.

Communications Ports   A *communications port* is a serial communications port. Though a rarity nowadays, it is often used to connect hardware such as point-of-sale devices. The device files that represent these serial ports are /dev/ttyS#.

When experiencing problems with a serial communications device, start the troubleshooting process by issuing **dmesg | grep ttyS** to find the device filename in use. When you have the full device filename, employ the setserial utility. This will provide detailed information on the serial device. Use super user privileges, and type **setserial -a** *device-file-name* at the command line. Look for the interrupt request (IRQ) number in the output.

When you know the IRQ of the serial device, you can check the interrupts file. If you do not find the IRQ number in the /proc/interrupts file, this indicates that the appropriate driver for the serial device is not loaded.

If the driver is loaded, check the manufacturer's website for a newly updated driver. Also, check the serial device's recommended configuration and make any modifications needed using the setserial utility.

USB   If you have a USB device, such as a printer, directly attached to your system and problems occur, there are some simple troubleshooting techniques you can employ. First, ensure that the USB module (driver) is loaded into the kernel by using super user privileges and typing **lsmod | grep usb** at the command line. If you get a response, it is loaded. If you just get a prompt back, then employ the modprobe command to load the module (Chapter 14).

If the driver is already loaded, try detaching the device's USB cable from the system. Watch the journal file via the journalctl -f command. If you are on an older Linux system, use the tail -f command on the appropriate log file, such as /var/log/

`syslog` or `/var/log/rsyslog`. After the watch is in place, plug the USB device's cable back in and see what log messages are generated. If the USB device is a printer, also check the `/var/log/cups/error_log` for any pertinent information. You may uncover some important details here.

When you have completed that activity, employ the `lsusb -v` command to see if the device is showing up on the USB bus. If you see the device's manufacturer and product information, then Linux can see the device. If the `lsusb` utility is not installed on your system, look through the kernel ring buffer using `dmesg`.

Check the USB's device files for corruption. This topic was covered earlier in the chapter in the Missing Devices list item in the section "Exploring Common Issues."

If your USB device is still not working, try attaching it to a different USB port. However, before doing so, put another watch on the appropriate journal or log files. You may also want to try switching out your USB cable to see if that resolves the issue(s).

Keyboard Mapping   If you press a key on your keyboard and a different letter appears on the screen, most likely you have a keyboard mapping issue. The fix depends on the particular distribution you are using.

For Red Hat–based distros, type **localectl** with no options and your current key map will display. To see the list of available key maps, enter **localectl list-keymaps** and a list of available key mappings will display. This list can be rather large, so you might want to redirect STDOUT to the `less` utility for your perusal. When you find the appropriate key mapping name, permanently set it by typing **localectl set-keymap** *keymap-name* at the command line.

TIP   You may wonder how you will enter these commands if your keyboard is not properly mapped. Write the commands down, and then try the various keyboard keys until you find each key that corresponds with every command letter or symbol and record it. Now use the recorded keyboard keys to enter the commands. Ta-da!

For Debian-based distros, use super user privileges and enter the **dpkg-reconfigure keyboard-configuration** command. This will take you into a text-based menu system where you can select the appropriate keyboard mapping.

Hardware or Software Compatibility Issues   Before you purchase any new hardware (or software for that matter), make sure it will work with your Linux distribution. Keep in mind that while Linux is the number-one operating system kernel for super computers and a strong contender in the server world, it does not always get the attention it deserves from hardware manufacturers. Therefore, often drivers are not available for brand-new devices, or you may end up with a manufacturer's poorly written device driver. Check with the Linux community to find well-developed drivers and hardware device recommendations. You'll save yourself a lot of trouble and headaches.

Summary

From application directory and file permissions to overly restrictive firewall ACLs and incorrect SELinux contexts, there are many issues that can cause an application to not function properly. In addition, hardware problems such as bad disk sectors, memory module corruption, flaky USB cables, and device drivers that need updating all require a knowledgeable troubleshooter. Having a firm grasp on this chapter's concepts will help you achieve that distinction.

Exam Essentials

Summarize application permission issues.   When an application throws an error relating to either I/O or an attempt to launch another executable, it can be due to an incorrect file or directory permission. Determine what user account the application is running under as well any files it is attempting to access and their residing directories. With that information in hand, gather file ownership and group membership. Looking at the various permissions associated with each of the three permission classifications (owner, group, other) will begin to uncover the core problem. Include directory permissions and default ACLs as well in the investigation.

Describe storage problems.   Common storage issues involve degraded storage, missing devices and/or volumes, absent mount points, and performance issues. They also may include storage integrity problems and/or resource exhaustion. The `dmesg` utility is essential for its use in uncovering root causes of problems with SATA and SCSI drives as well as the HBA. Uncovering and fixing RAID issues also requires the use of the Multiple Devices (`md`) utility and the `/proc/mdstat` file.

Explain application dependencies.   Using the appropriate utility and checking an application's version as well as available package versions will allow you to uncover whether or not a poor performing application's software has an upgrade available for it. Updating software packages, however, is not without problems. A software update may not properly update a package's dependencies or libraries, resulting in a broken application. If the new update needs to be compiled, issues with the GCC can cause complications. The system's package repository can have uncovered troubles, which prevent a software update from occurring.

Detail restrictive firewall ACLs. Applications that communicate with data, services, or end users over a network may run into problems with overly restrictive firewall settings. Gather together the source address (or host), destination address, and network protocols employed as well as the inbound and outbound ports used on both the client and the server side. Using this basic information, review the firewall's various ACLs. If a firewall setting is blocking this needed access, review the potential needed changes prior to enacting them.

Summarize uncommon hardware issues. RAM, printers, video apparatus, serial ports, USB devices, and keyboards can provide interesting problems to troubleshoot. Employing the `dmidecode` and `lshw` utilities as well as the `dmesg`, `lspci`, `lsusb`, and `lsdev` commands provides assistance in uncovering the root causes. Missing or outdated modules (drivers), faulty cables, corrupted device files, and incorrect key maps are some of the problem sources. You can save yourself some time and avoid issues in the first place if you ensure that your hardware and software are compatible prior to installing them.

Review Questions

1. Peter's system has a memory-intensive application running on it continually. To help improve performance, he has replaced the old hard drives with solid-state drives instead of increasing RAM. Which of the following is most likely true about this situation?

   A. The SSD for application data will enter a degraded mode.

   B. The SSD for swap will become degraded storage.

   C. The SSD will need a namespace in its device filename.

   D. The SSD will end up a missing volume.

   E. The SSD will experience resource exhaustion.

2. Mary adds the first SCSI disk to a Linux system that currently has only IDE drives. The system is not recognizing the new disk. Which of the following commands should she employ to troubleshoot the problem? (Choose all that apply.)

   A. `ls /sys/bus/scsi/drivers`

   B. `pvscan /dev/vg00/lvol0`

   C. `lsmod | grep` *module-name*

   D. `hdparm -B 127` *device-filename*

   E. `smartctl -a`

3. The system administrator, Norman, runs a Python program and receives an `IO Error: [Error 13] Permission denied` message. What information should he gather (or know) to start troubleshooting this issue? (Choose all that apply.)

   A. The disk type, where the program resides

   B. His user account name

   C. The program action that raised the error

   D. Filename and directory location of the program's I/O files

   E. The program's name

4. Harry has modified an application to create a file in a directory and then write data to it. The program creates the file with no problems but cannot write data to it and receives a permission error. Which of the following is most likely the issue?

   A. Directory ownership

   B. File ownership

   C. File group membership

   D. Permission inheritance

   E. Executable privileges

5. Ben updates his Ubuntu system's packages using the `sudo apt-get upgrade` command, and now the Apache Web service is not working properly. What command should he run?

    A. `sudo apt-get clean`

    B. `sudo zypper clean -a`

    C. `sudo ldd /usr/sbin/apache2`

    D. `sudo rpm -aV`

    E. `sudo apt-get check`

6. Peter writes a new C++ application to use for managing his older Linux server. The new app contains no programming or logic errors. However, when he tries to compile it, it does not work. Which of the following is most likely the issue?

    A. An incorrect application permission

    B. An incorrect file permission

    C. A missing or outdated GCC

    D. A missing or outdated device

    E. A repository problem

7. Mary confirms via the `sealert` utility that her application cannot access the file `flash .txt`. What command should she use next?

    A. `ls -l flash.txt`

    B. `ls -Z flash.txt`

    C. `ls -l flash.txt-directory`

    D. `setroubleshoot`

    E. `restorecon`

8. A clock-in/out application, which uses an NTP server on the local network, is throwing an error concerning reaching the server. There are currently no network problems. Which of the following are steps in the troubleshooting process for this issue? (Choose all that apply.)

    A. Check the firewall ACLs on the NTP server.

    B. Check the firewall ACLs on the application server.

    C. Use the `firewall-cmd --get-default-zone` command.

    D. Check the `/etc/services` file for NTP ports and transport protocols.

    E. View firewall log entries.

9. Your system administrator team member Norman tells you the device located at the communications port is not working. What command should you issue to start the troubleshooting process?

    A. `dmesg | grep -i COM`

    B. `dmesg | grep -i ttys`

    C. `sudo setserial -a /dev/COM1`

    D. `sudo setserial -a /dev/ttyS0`

    E. `cat /proc/interrupts`

10. Harry's newly installed USB printer is not working. The system employs CUPS. Which of the following are steps that may be included in the troubleshooting process? (Choose all that apply.)

A. Issue the `less /etc/printcap` command.

B. Use the `lpinfo -m` command to view available USB ports.

C. Put a watch on the appropriate log file and plug in the USB cable.

D. Use the `dmesg` and `grep` utilities to find printer information.

E. Use the `lsusb -v` command to see if the device is on the USB bus.

Automating
Your System

Chapter

25

Deploying Bash Scripts

✓ Objective 3.1: Given a scenario, create simple shell scripts to automate common tasks

Linux system administrators often need to perform the same tasks over and over, such as checking available disk space on the system or creating user accounts. Instead of entering multiple commands every time, you can write scripts that run in the shell to do these tasks automatically for you. This chapter explores how Bash shell scripts work and demonstrates how you can write your own scripts to automate everyday activities on your Linux system.

The Basics of Shell Scripting

Shell scripting allows you to write small programs that automate activities on your Linux system. Shell scripts can save you time by giving you the flexibility to quickly process data and generate reports that would be cumbersome to do by manually entering multiple commands at the command prompt. You can automate just about anything you do at the command prompt using shell scripts.

The following sections walk through the basics of what shell scripts are and how to get started writing them.

Running Multiple Commands

So far in this book we've been entering a single command at the command prompt and viewing the results. One exciting feature of the Linux command line is that you can enter multiple commands on the same command line and Linux will process them all. Just place a semicolon between each command you enter:

```
$ date ; who
Thu Feb 24 19:20:06 EST 2022
rich     :0          2022-02-24 19:15 (:0)
$
```

The Linux Bash shell runs the first command (date) and displays the output; then it runs the second command (who) and displays the output from that command immediately following the output from the first command. Although this may seem trivial, this is the basis of how shell scripts work.

Redirecting Output

Another building block of shell scripting is the ability to store command output. Often, when you run a command, you'd like to save the output for future reference. To help with this, the Bash shell provides output redirection.

Output redirection allows us to redirect the output of a command from the monitor to another device, such as a file. This feature comes in handy when you need to log data from a shell script that runs after business hours, so you can see what the shell script did when it ran.

To redirect the output from a command, you use the greater-than symbol (>) after the command and then specify the name of the file that you want to use to capture the redirected output. This is demonstrated in Listing 25.1.

Listing 25.1: Redirecting output to a file

```
$ date > today.txt
$ cat today.txt
Thu Feb 24 19:21:12 EST 2022
$
```

The example shown in Listing 25.1 redirects the output of the date command to the file named today.txt. Notice that when you redirect the output of a command, nothing displays on the monitor output. All of the text from the output is now in the file, as shown by using the cat command to display the file contents.

The greater-than output redirection operator automatically creates a new file for the output, even if the file already exists. If you prefer, you can append the output to an existing file by using the double greater-than symbol (>>), as shown in Listing 25.2.

Listing 25.2: Appending command output to a file

```
$ who >> today.txt
$ cat today.txt
Thu Feb 24 19:21:12 EST 2022
rich      :0           2022-02-24 19:15 (:0)
$
```

The today.txt file now contains the output from the original date command in Listing 25.1 and the output from the who command ran in Listing 25.2.

In Linux, everything is a file, including the input and output processes of a command. Linux identifies files with a file descriptor, which is a non-negative integer. The Bash shell reserves the first three file descriptors for input and output. File descriptor 0 is called STDIN and points to the standard input for the shell, which is normally the keyboard. File descriptor 1 is called STDOUT, which points to the standard output for the shell, typically the monitor. This is where the standard output messages go. File descriptor 2 is called STDERR, which is where the shell sends messages identified as errors. By default, this points to the same device as the STDOUT file descriptor, the monitor. You can redirect only the errors from your shell script to a separate file from the normal output by using 2> instead of the standard > output redirection character. This allows you to specify a separate file for monitoring error messages from commands.

Output redirection is a crucial feature in shell scripts. With it, we can generate log files from our scripts, giving us a chance to keep track of things as the script runs in background mode on the Linux system.

Piping Data

While output redirection allows us to redirect command output to a file, *piping* allows us to redirect the output to another command. The second command uses the redirected output from the first command as input data. This feature comes in handy when using commands that process data, such as the sort command.

The piping symbol is the bar (|) symbol, which usually appears above the backslash key on U.S. keyboards. Listing 25.3 shows an example of using piping.

Listing 25.3: Piping command output to another command

```
$ ls | sort
Desktop
Documents
Downloads
Music
Pictures
Public
Templates
test.txt
today.txt
Videos
$
```

The output from the `ls` command is sent directly to the `sort` command as input, but behind the scenes. You don't see the output from the `ls` command displayed on the monitor; you only see the output from the last command in the pipe line, which in this case is the `sort` command. There's no limit on how many commands you can link together with piping.

> The >, >>, and | symbols are part of a group of characters often referred to as *metacharacters*. Metacharacters are characters that have special meaning when used in the Linux shell. If you need to use a metacharacter as a standard character (such as using the > character as a greater-than symbol in your output instead of as a redirect symbol), you must identify the metacharacter by either placing a backslash in front of it or enclosing the metacharacter in single or double quotes. This method is called *escaping*.

The Shell Script Format

Placing multiple commands on a single line, by using either the semicolon or piping, is a great way to process data but can still get rather tedious. Each time you want to run the set of commands, you need to type them all at the command prompt.

However, Linux allows us to place multiple commands in a text file and then run the text file as a program from the command line. This is called a *shell script* because we're scripting out commands for the Linux shell to run.

Shell script files are plain-text files. To create a shell script file, you just need to use any text editor that you're comfortable with. If you're working from a KDE-based graphical desktop, you can use the KWrite program, or if you're working from a GNOME-based graphical desktop, you can use the GEdit program.

If you're working directly in a command-line environment, you still have some options. Many Linux distributions include either the `pico` or the `nano` editor to provide a graphical editor environment by using ASCII control characters to create a full-screen editing window.

If your Linux distribution doesn't include either the `pico` or the `nano` editor, there is still one last resort: the `vi` editor. The `vi` editor is a text-based editor that uses simple single-letter commands. It's the oldest text editor in the Linux environment, dating back to the early days of Unix, which may be one reason it's not overly elegant or user-friendly.

Once you've chosen your text editor, you're ready to create your shell scripts. First, for your shell script to work you'll need to follow a specific format for the shell script file. The first line in the file usually specifies the Linux shell required to run the script. This is written in somewhat of an odd format:

`#!/bin/bash`

The Linux world calls the combination of the pound sign and the exclamation symbol (`#!`) the *shebang*. It signals to the operating system which shell to use to run the shell script. Most Linux distributions support multiple Linux shells, but the most common is the Bash shell. You can run shell scripts written for other shells as long as those shells are installed on the Linux distribution.

> If you don't specify the shebang line in your shell script, Linux will run the script using the default shell defined for your user account in the /etc/passwd file. It's usually recommended to specify a shell, even if it is your default shell, to avoid any confusion or mistakes.

After you specify the shell, you're ready to start listing the commands in your script. You don't need to enter all of the commands on a single line; Linux allows you to place them on separate lines. Also, the Linux shell assumes each line is a new command in the shell script, so you don't need to use semicolons to separate the commands. Listing 25.4 shows an example of a simple shell script file.

Listing 25.4: A simple shell script file

```
$ cat test1.sh
#!/bin/bash
# This script displays the date and who's logged in
date
who
$
```

The test1.sh script file shown in Listing 25.4 starts out with the shebang line identifying the Bash shell, the standard shell in Linux. The second line in the code shown in Listing 25.4 demonstrates another feature in shell scripts. Lines that start with a pound sign are called *comment lines*. They allow you to embed comments into the shell script program to help you remember what the code is doing. The shell skips comment lines when processing the shell script. You can place comment lines anywhere in your shell script file after the opening shebang line.

> Notice in Listing 25.4 we used the .sh filename extension on the shell script file. While this is not required in Linux, it's become somewhat of a de facto standard among programmers. This helps identify that the text file is a shell script that can be run at the command line.

Running the Shell Script

If you just enter a shell script file at the command prompt to run it, you may be a bit disappointed:

```
$ test1.sh
test1.sh: command not found
$
```

Unfortunately, the shell doesn't know where to find the `test1.sh` command in the virtual directory. The reason for this is the shell uses a special environment variable called PATH to list directories where it looks for commands. If your local HOME folder is not included in the PATH environment variable list of directories, you can't run the shell script file directly. Instead, you need to use either a relative or an absolute path name to point to the shell script file. The easiest way to do that is by adding the `./` relative path shortcut to the file:

```
$ ./test1.sh
bash: ./test1.sh: Permission denied
$
```

Now the shell can find the program file, but there's still an error message. This time the error is telling us that we don't have permissions to run the shell script file. A quick look at the shell script file using the `ls` command with the `-l` option shows the permissions set for the file:

```
$ ls -l test1.sh
-rw-r--r-- 1 rich rich 73 Feb 24 19:37 test1.sh
$
```

By default, the Linux system didn't give anyone execute permissions to run the file. You can use the `chmod` command to add that permission for the file owner:

```
$ chmod u+x test1.sh
$ ls -l test1.sh
-rwxr--r-- 1 rich rich 73 Feb 24 19:37 test1.sh
$
```

The u+x option adds execute privileges to the owner of the file. You should now be able to run the shell script file and see the output:

```
$ ./test1.sh
Thu Feb 24 19:48:27 EST 2022
rich       :0              2022-02-24 19:15 (:0)
$
```

Now that you've seen the basics for creating and running shell scripts, the next sections dive into some more advanced features you can add to make fancier shell scripts.

Advanced Shell Scripting

The previous section walked you through the basics of how to group normal command-line commands together in a shell script file to run in the Linux shell. We'll add to that by showing more features available in shell scripts to make them look and act more like real programs.

Displaying Messages

When you string commands together in a shell script file, the output may be somewhat confusing to look at. It would help to be able to customize the output by separating it and adding our own text between the output from each listed command.

The echo command allows you to display text messages from the command line. When used at the command line, it's not too exciting:

```
$ echo This is a test
This is a test
$
```

But now you have the ability to insert messages anywhere in the output from the shell script file. Listing 25.5 demonstrates how this is done.

Listing 25.5: Using the echo statement in a script

```
$ cat test1.sh
#!/bin/bash
# This script displays the date and who's logged in
echo The current date and time is:
date
echo
echo "Let's see who's logged into the system:"
who
$ ./test1.sh
The current date and time is:
Thu Feb 24 19:55:44 EST 2022

Let's see who's logged into the system:
rich     :0              2022-02-24 19:15 (:0)
$
```

The shell script shown in Listing 25.5 adds three echo commands to the test1.sh script. Notice that the first echo command doesn't use any quotes, but the third one does. The reason for that is the text output from the third echo command contains single quotes. The single quote is also a metacharacter in the shell, which will confuse the echo command, so you need to place double quotes around the text. Also notice that the second echo command doesn't have any text on the line. That outputs a blank line, which is useful when you want to separate output from multiple commands.

Using Variables

Part of programming is the ability to temporarily store data to use later in the program. You do that by using *variables*.

Variables allow you to set aside locations in memory to temporarily store information and then recall that information later in the script by referencing the variable name.

There are two types of variables available in the Linux shell. The following sections explain how to use both types in your shell scripts.

Environment Variables

Environment variables track specific system information, such as the name of the system, the name of the user logged into the shell, the user's user ID (UID), the default home directory for the user, and the search path the shell uses to find executable programs. You can display a complete list of active environment variables available in your shell by using the set command, as shown in Listing 25.6.

Listing 25.6: Using the set command

```
$ set
BASH=/bin/bash
BASHOPTS=checkwinsize:cmdhist:complete_fullquote:expand_aliases:extglob:extquote
:force_fignore:histappend:interactive_comments:progcomp:promptvars:sourcepath
BASH_ALIASES=()
BASH_ARGC=()
BASH_ARGV=()
BASH_CMDS=()
BASH_COMPLETION_VERSINFO=([0]="2" [1]="8")
BASH_LINENO=()
BASH_SOURCE=()
BASH_VERSINFO=([0]="4" [1]="4" [2]="19" [3]="1" [4]="release" [5]="x86_64-pc-lin
ux-gnu")
BASH_VERSION='4.4.19(1)-release'
CLUTTER_IM_MODULE=xim
COLORTERM=truecolor
COLUMNS=80
DBUS_SESSION_BUS_ADDRESS=unix:path=/run/user/1000/bus
DESKTOP_SESSION=ubuntu
DIRSTACK=()
DISPLAY=:0
EUID=1000
GDMSESSION=ubuntu
...
```

There are environment variables that track just about every feature of the command-line shell. You can tap into these environment variables from within your scripts by using the environment variable name preceded by a dollar sign, as shown in Listing 25.7.

Listing 25.7: The test2.sh shell script file to display environment variables

```
$ cat test2.sh
#!/bin/bash
# display user information from the system.
echo User info for userid: $USER
echo UID: $UID
echo HOME: $HOME
$
```

The $USER, $UID, and $HOME environment variables are commonly used to display information about the logged-in user. If you run the test2.sh shell script shown in Listing 25.7, the output should look like this:

```
$ chmod u+x test2.sh
$ ./test2.sh
User info for userid: rich
UID: 1000
HOME: /home/rich
$
```

The values you see should be related to your user account. This allows you to dynamically retrieve information about the user account running your shell script to customize the output.

 If you write shell scripts to distribute for other Linux administrators to use, two additional helpful environment variables are the $SHELL variable, which returns the current shell program the script is running in, and the $PATH variable, which returns a list of directories the shell will look in to find commands. It's usually a good idea to check these two environment variables to make sure your script will run correctly in any Linux environment.

User Variables

User variables allow you to store your own data within your shell scripts. You assign values to user variables using the equal sign. Spaces must not appear between the variable name, the equal sign, and the value. Here are a few examples:

```
var1=10
var2=23.45
var3=testing
var4="Still more testing"
```

The shell script automatically determines the data type used for the variable value. Variables defined within the shell script are called *local variables* and are accessible only from within the shell script. *Global variables* are defined outside the shell script at the main shell level and are inherited by the script shell environment.

> The set command displays all of the global variables set. If you need to see the local variables set for your session, use the printenv command. The export command allows you to mark a variable as exportable, which means any child processes spawned from your shell will see it. Finally, the env command allows you to run a script and modify environment variables internal to the script without affecting the system environment variables.

Just as with environment variables, you can reference user variables using the dollar sign. Listing 25.8 shows an example of writing a shell script that uses user variables.

Listing 25.8: Using user variables in a shell script

```
$ cat test3.sh
#!/bin/bash
# testing variables
days=10
guest=Katie
echo $guest checked in $days days ago
$
```

Running the test3.sh script from Listing 25.8 produces the following output:

```
$ chmod u+x test3.sh
$ ./test3.sh
Katie checked in 10 days ago
$
```

After you store the data in a user variable, you can reference it anywhere in your shell script!

Command-Line Arguments

One of the most versatile features of shell scripts is the ability to pass data into the script when you run it. This allows you to customize the script with new data each time you run it.

One method of passing data into a shell script is to use *command-line arguments*. Command-line arguments are data you include on the command line when you run the command. Just start listing them after the command, separating each data value with a space, in this format:

```
command argument1 argument2 ...
```

You retrieve the values in your shell script code using special numeric *positional variables*. Use the variable $1 to retrieve the first command-line argument, $2 the second argument, and so on. Listing 25.9 shows how to use positional variables in your shell script.

Listing 25.9: Using command-line arguments in a shell script

```
$ cat test4.sh
#!/bin/bash
# Testing command line arguments
echo $1 checked in $2 days ago
$ chmod u+x test4.sh
$ ./test4.sh Barbara 4
Barbara checked in 4 days ago
$ ./test4.sh Jessica 5
Jessica checked in 5 days ago
$
```

The `test4.sh` shell script uses two command-line arguments. The `$1` variable holds the name of the person, and the `$2` variable holds the number of days ago they checked in. When you run the `test4.sh` shell script, be sure to include both data values in the command line. The shell won't produce an error message if a positional variable doesn't exist; you just won't get the results you expected:

```
$ ./test4.sh rich
rich checked in  days ago
$
```

It's up to you to check if the positional variable exists within your program code. We'll explore how to do that later when we discuss logic statements.

The Exit Status

When a shell script ends, it returns an *exit status* to the parent shell that launched it. The exit status tells us whether or not the shell script completed successfully.

Linux provides us with the special `$?` variable, which holds the exit status value from the last command that executed. To check the exit status of a command, you must view the `$?` variable immediately after the command ends. It changes values according to the exit status of the last command executed by the shell:

```
$ who
rich     :0              2019-02-20 23:16 (:0)
$ echo $?
0
$
```

By convention, the exit status of a command that successfully completes is 0. If a command completes with an error, then a positive integer value appears as the exit status.

You can change the exit status of your shell scripts by using the `exit` command. Just specify the exit status value you want in the `exit` command:

```
$ /bin/bash
$ exit 120
exit
$ echo $?
120
$
```

In this example we started a new child shell with the `/bin/bash` command and then used the `exit` command to exit the child shell with an exit status code of 120. Back in the parent shell, we then displayed the `$?` variable value to see if it matched what we had set in the `exit` command. As you write more complicated scripts, you can indicate errors by changing the exit status value. That way, by checking the exit status, you can easily debug your shell scripts.

Writing Script Programs

So far we've explored how to combine regular command-line commands within a shell script to automate common tasks that you may perform as the system administrator. But shell scripts allow us to do much more than just that. The Bash shell provides more programming-like commands that allow us to write full-fledged programs within our shell scripts, such as capturing command output, performing mathematical operations, checking variable and file conditions, and looping through commands. The following sections walk you through some of the advanced programming features available to you from the Bash shell.

Command Substitution

Quite possibly one of the most useful features of shell scripts is the ability to store and process data. So far we've discussed how to use output redirection to store output from a command to a file and piping to redirect the output of a command to another command. There's another technique, however, that can give you more flexibility in storing and using data in your scripts.

Command substitution allows you to assign the output of a command to a user variable in the shell script. After the output is stored in a variable, you can use standard Linux string manipulation commands (such as `sort` or `grep`) to manipulate the data before displaying it.

To redirect the output of a command to a variable, you need to use one of two command substitution formats:

- Placing backticks (`) around the command
- Using the command within the `$()` function

Both methods produce the same result—redirecting the output from the command into a user variable. Listing 25.10 demonstrates using both methods.

Listing 25.10: Demonstrating command substitution

```
$ var1=`date`
$ echo $var1
Fri Feb 18 18:05:38 EST 2022
$ var2=$(who)
$ echo $var2
rich :0 2022-02-18 17:56 (:0)
$
```

The output from the command substitutions is stored in the appropriate variables. You can then use those variables anywhere in your script program as a standard string value.

WARNING   The backtick character is not the same as a single quote. It's the character usually found on the same key as the tilde character (~) on U.S. keyboards. Because of the confusion between backticks and single quotes, it's become more popular in the Linux world to use the $() function format.

Performing Math

Eventually you'll want to do more than just manipulate text strings in your shell scripts. The world revolves around numbers, and at some point you'll probably need to do some mathematical operations with your data. Unfortunately, this is one place where the Bash shell shows its age. The mathematical features in the Bash shell aren't quite as fancy as the features found in newer shells, such as the Z shell. However, there are a couple of ways to use simple mathematical functions in Bash shell scripts.

To include mathematical expressions in your shell scripts, you use a special format. This format places the equation within the $[] characters:

```
result=$[ 25 * 5 ]
```

You can perform lots of different mathematical operations on data using this method, but there is a limitation. The $[] format allows you to use only integers; it doesn't support floating-point values.

If you need to do floating-point calculations, things get considerably more complicated in the Bash shell. One solution is to use the bc command-line calculator program. The bc calculator is a tool in Linux that can perform floating-point arithmetic:

```
$ bc
bc 1.07.1
Copyright 1991-1994, 1997, 1998, 2000, 2004, 2006, 2008, 2012-2017 Free
```

```
Software Foundation, Inc.
This is free software with ABSOLUTELY NO WARRANTY.
For details type 'warranty'.
12 * 5.4
64.8
3.156 * (3 + 5)
25.248
quit
$
```

Unfortunately, the bc calculator has some limitations of its own. The floating-point arithmetic is controlled by a built-in variable called scale. You must set this variable to the desired number of decimal places you want in your answers or you won't get what you were looking for:

```
$ bc -q
3.44 / 5
0
scale=4
3.44 / 5
.6880
quit
$
```

To embed a bc calculation into your script, things get a bit complicated. You must use command substitution to capture the output of the calculation into a variable, but there's a twist. The basic format you need to use is as follows:

variable=$(echo "*options*; *expression*" | bc)

The first parameter, options, allows us to set the bc variables, such as the scale variable. The *expression* parameter defines the mathematical expression to evaluate using bc. While this looks pretty odd, it works:

```
$ var1=$(echo "scale=4; 3.44 / 5" | bc)
$ echo $var1
.6880
$
```

This is not ideal, but it works for small projects. If you have a larger programming project that requires lots of calculations, we'd suggest looking into the Z shell. It supports lots of advanced mathematical functions and features.

Logic Statements

So far all of the shell scripts presented process commands in a linear fashion—one command after another. However, not all programming is linear. There are times when you'd like your program to test for certain conditions, such as if a file exists or if a mathematical expression is 0, and perform different commands based on the results of the test. For that, the Bash shell provides *logic statements*.

Logic statements allow us to test for a specific condition and then branch to different sections of code based on whether the condition evaluates to a True or a False logical value. Because of this, logic statements are also commonly referred to as *conditionals*. There are a couple of different ways to implement logic statements in Bash scripts.

The *if* Statement

The most basic logic statement is the *if condition statement*. The format for the if condition statement is as follows:

```
if [ condition ]
then
    commands
fi
```

If the `condition` you specify evaluates to a True logical value, the shell runs the commands in the then section of code. If the `condition` evaluates to a False logical value, the shell script skips the commands in the then section of code.

The condition expression is often referred to as a *comparison*, as it compares two values. Comparisons have quite a few different formats in Bash shell programming. There are built-in tests for numerical values, string values, Boolean logic values, and even files and directories. Table 25.1 lists the different built-in tests that are available.

TABLE 25.1   Condition tests

Test	Type	Description
n1 -eq *n2*	Numeric	Checks if *n1* is equal to *n2*
n1 -ge *n2*	Numeric	Checks if *n1* is greater than or equal to *n2*
n1 -gt *n2*	Numeric	Checks if *n1* is greater than *n2*
n1 -le *n2*	Numeric	Checks if *n1* is less than or equal to *n2*
n1 -lt *n2*	Numeric	Checks if *n1* is less than *n2*
n1 -ne *n2*	Numeric	Checks if *n1* is not equal to *n2*

Test	Type	Description
str1 = *str2*	String	Checks if *str1* is the same as *str2*
str1 != str2	String	Checks if *str1* is not the same as *str2*
str1 < str2	String	Checks if *str1* is less than *str2*
str1 > str2	String	Checks if *str1* is greater than *str2*
-n *str1*	String	Checks if *str1* has a length greater than zero
-z *str1*	String	Checks if *str1* has a length of zero
-d *file*	File	Checks if *file* exists and is a directory
-e *file*	File	Checks if *file* exists
-f *file*	File	Checks if *file* exists and is a file
-r *file*	File	Checks if *file* exists and is readable
-s *file*	File	Checks if *file* exists and is not empty
-w *file*	File	Checks if *file* exists and is writable
-x *file*	File	Checks if *file* exists and is executable
-O *file*	File	Checks if *file* exists and is owned by the current user
-G *file*	File	Checks if *file* exists and the default group is the same as the current user
file1 -nt *file2*	File	Checks if *file1* is newer than *file2*
file1 -ot *file2*	File	Checks if *file1* is older than *file2*

Listing 25.11 shows an example of using if-then condition statements in a shell script.

Listing 25.11: if condition statements

```
$ cat test5.sh
#!/bin/bash
# testing the if condition
```

```
if [ $1 -eq $2 ]
then
   echo "Both values are equal!"
   exit
fi

if [ $1 -gt $2 ]
then
   echo "The first value is greater than the second"
   exit
fi

if [ $1 -lt $2 ]
then
   echo "The first value is less than the second"
   exit
fi
$
```

The test5.sh script shown in Listing 25.11 evaluates two values entered as parameters on the command line:

```
$ chmod u+x test5.sh
$ ./test5.sh 10 5
The first value is greater than the second
$
```

Only the command from the if statement that evaluated to a True logical value was processed by the shell script.

The *case* Statement

Often you'll find yourself trying to evaluate the value of a variable, looking for a specific value within a set of possible values, similar to what we demonstrated in Listing 25.11. Instead of having to write multiple if statements testing for all of the possible conditions, you can use a case statement.

The case statement allows you to check multiple values of a single variable in a list-oriented format:

```
case variable in
pattern1) commands1;;
pattern2 | pattern3) commands2;;
*) default commands;;
esac
```

The `case` statement compares the variable specified against the different patterns. If the variable matches the pattern, the shell executes the commands specified for the pattern. You can list more than one pattern on a line, using the bar operator to separate each pattern. The asterisk symbol is the catchall for values that don't match any of the listed patterns. Listing 25.12 shows an example of using the `case` statement.

Listing 25.12: The case statement

```
$ cat test6.sh
#!/bin/bash
# using the case statement

case $USER in
rich | barbara)
    echo "Welcome, $USER"
    echo "Please enjoy your visit";;
testing)
    echo "Special testing account";;
jessica)
    echo "Don't forget to log off when you're done";;
*)
    echo "Sorry, you're not allowed here";;
esac
$ chmod u+x test6.sh
$ ./test6.sh
Welcome, rich
Please enjoy your visit
$
```

The `case` statement provides a much cleaner way of specifying the various options for each possible variable value. In the example shown in Listing 25.12, it checks for specific user accounts to output specific messages. If the user running the script is not one of those user accounts, it displays yet another message.

Loops

When you're writing scripts, you'll often find yourself in a situation where it would come in handy to repeat the same commands multiple times, such as applying a command against all the files in a directory. The Bash shell provides some basic looping commands to accommodate that.

The *for* Loop

The for statement iterates through every element in a series, such as files in a directory or lines in a text document. The format of the for command is as follows:

```
for variable in series ; do
    commands
done
```

The variable becomes a placeholder, taking on the value of each element in the series in each iteration. The commands can use the variable just like any other variable that you define in the script. Listing 25.13 shows how to use a for loop to iterate through all the files in a directory.

Listing 25.13: Using the for loop

```
$ cat test7.sh
#!/bin/bash
# iterate through the files in the Home folder
for file in $(ls | sort) ; do
    if [ -d $file ]
    then
        echo "$file is a directory"
    fi
    if [ -f $file ]
    then
        echo "$file is a file"
    fi
done
$
```

If you run the test7.sh shell script, you should see a listing of the files and directories in your home directory:

```
$ ./test7.sh
Desktop is a directory
Documents is a directory
Downloads is a directory
Music is a directory
Pictures is a directory
Public is a directory
Templates is a directory
test1.sh is a file
test2.sh is a file
test3.sh is a file
```

```
test4.sh is a file
test5.sh is a file
test6.sh is a file
test7.sh is a file
today.txt is a file
Videos is a directory
$
```

That saves a lot of coding from having to check each file manually in a bunch of if or case statements.

> When working with files in a directory, it's common to use wildcard characters to specify a range of files. There are three methods you can choose from:
>
> - A question mark (?) represents one character. Thus, c?t would match cat, cot, and cut.
> - An asterisk (*) represents any character, multiple characters, or even no characters. Thus, c*t would match cat, caveat, and ct.
> - A bracketed set of characters matches only the characters in the brackets. Thus, c[au]t would match cat and cut, but not cot.
>
> This method of using wildcard characters for filenames is also called *file globbing* and can be used in any situation where you iterate through multiple files.

The *while* Loop

Another useful loop statement is the while command. This is its format:

```
while [ condition ] ; do
    commands
done
```

The while loop keeps looping as long as the condition specified evaluates to a True logical value. When the condition evaluates to a False logical value, the looping stops. The condition used in the while loop is the same as that for the if statement, so you can test numbers, strings, and files. Listing 25.14 demonstrates using the while loop to calculate the factorial of a number.

Listing 25.14: Calculating the factorial of a number

```
$ cat test8.sh
#!/bin/bash
number=$1
```

```
factorial=1
while [ $number -gt 0 ] ; do
    factorial=$[ $factorial * $number ]
    number=$[ $number - 1 ]
done
echo The factorial of $1 is $factorial
```

The shell script retrieves the first parameter passed to the script and uses it in the while loop. The while loop continues looping as long as the value stored in the $number variable is greater than 0. In each loop iteration that value is decreased by 1, so at some point the while condition becomes False. When that occurs the $factorial variable contains the final calculation. When you run the test8.sh program, you should get the following results:

```
$ ./test8.sh 5
The factorial of 5 is 120
$ ./test8.sh 6
The factorial of 6 is 720
$
```

The while loop took all the hard work of iterating through the series of numbers. Now you can plug any number as the command-line parameter and calculate the factorial value!

The opposite of the while command is the until command. It iterates through a block of commands until the test condition evaluates to a True logical value.

Text Manipulation

Perhaps one of the most powerful uses of shell scripts is quickly and easily manipulating large amounts of data. Chapter 4, "Searching and Analyzing Text," introduced many useful command-line utilities for finding and manipulating text in text files; however, using these utilities in shell scripts puts them on steroids.

Shell scripts allow you to process large quantities of data files line by line, searching for specific data, or even replacing specific data with just a few simple commands. Here are some common command-line features you have at your fingertips:

- **globbing:** Globbing allows you to use wildcard characters to search for multiple files and directories in your scripts.

- **parameter expansion:** By placing braces around a variable name, such as ${test}, you can utilize parameter expansion, which allows you to specify a substring value from the variable based on an offset and length.

- **read:** The read utility allows you to read text files line by line to process using standard text manipulation tools.

- **regular expressions:** The use of regular expressions allows you to find and replace specific strings within files.

Exercise 25.1 walks you through how to write a Bash script to view the password information for all user accounts configured on your Linux system.

 For a thorough presentation of how to use shell scripts, check out *Linux Command Line and Shell Scripting Bible, 4th edition*, by Christine Bresnahan and Richard Blum (Wiley, 2021).

EXERCISE 25.1

Writing a Bash Script to View the Password Information for System Users

1. Log into your Linux graphical desktop and open a command prompt window.

2. At the command prompt, open a text editor of your choice and create the text file pwinfo.sh by typing **nano pwinfo.sh**, **pico pwinfo.sh**, or **vi pwinfo.sh**.

3. Enter the following code into the new text file:

    ```
    #!/bin/bash
    # pwinfo.sh - display password information for all users
    list=$(cut -d : -f 1 /etc/passwd)
    for user in $list ; do
        echo Password information for $user
        sudo chage -l $user
        echo "----------"
    done
    ```

4. Save the file using the appropriate save command for your editor.

5. Give yourself execute permissions to the file by typing **chmod u+x pwinfo.sh**.

6. Run the shell script by typing **./pwinfo.sh**.

7. Enter your password at the sudo command prompt.

    You should see the chage password information listed for all of the user accounts configured on the system.

Summary

Basic shell scripting allows us to combine multiple commands to run them as a single command. You can use output redirection to redirect the output of a command to a file that you can read later, or you can use piping to redirect the output of one command to use as input data for another command.

When you add multiple commands to a text file to run, you must start the text file with the shebang line (#!), which identifies the Linux shell you want to use. You'll also need to give yourself execute permissions to run the file by using the chmod command with the u+x option. You may also need to either specify the full path to the file when you run it from the command prompt or modify the PATH environment variable on your system so that the shell can find your shell script files.

The Bash shell provides additional features that you can add to your shell script files to make them look more like real programs. The echo statement allows you to interject text output between the command outputs in the script to help modify the output your script produces. The shell also provides both environment and user variables that you can access from within your shell script. Environment variables allow you to retrieve information about the shell environment your script is running in, such as what user account started the shell and information about that user account. User variables allow you to store and retrieve data from within your script, making it act like a real program.

The Bash shell also provides advanced programming features that you can use in your shell scripts. Command substitution allows you to capture the output from a command into a variable so that you can extract information from the command output within your shell script. The Bash shell supports rudimentary integer math operations but is not overly adept with handling floating-point numbers. You'll need help from other programs such as the bc calculator to do that.

Finally, the Bash shell supports some standard programming features such as if and case logic statements, allowing you to test numbers, strings, and files for specific conditions and run commands based on the outcome of those conditions. It also supports both for and while loops, which allow you to iterate through groups of data, processing each element within a set of commands. These features can help make your Bash shell scripts perform just like a real program.

Exam Essentials

Describe how to link multiple command-line commands together in a shell script.   The Bash shell allows you to place multiple commands sequentially in a file and will then process each command when you run the file from the command line. The output from each command will appear in the command-line output.

Explain how you can handle data within a Bash shell script.   The Bash shell provides two ways to handle data within commands. Output redirection allows you to redirect the output of a command to a text file, which you, or another command, can read later. Piping allows you to redirect the output of one command to use as the input data for another command. The output never displays on the monitor when you run the shell script; the data transfer happens behind the scenes.

Explain the type of data you can access from within a shell script. The Bash shell provides access to environment variables, which contain information about the shell environment the script is running in. You can obtain information about the system as well as the user account that's running the shell script. The shell script also has access to positional variables, which allow you to pass data to the shell script from the command line when you run the shell script.

Describe how you can manipulate output data from a command before you use it in another command within a shell script. Command substitution allows you to redirect the output of a command to a user variable in your shell script. You can then use standard Linux text processing commands to manipulate the data, such as sort it or extract data records from it, before redirecting the variable data to another command.

Describe how the Bash shell performs mathematical operations. The Bash shell uses the $[] symbol to define mathematical equations to process. The Bash shell can only perform integer math, so this capability is somewhat limited.

Explain the different methods for implementing logic within a Bash shell script. The Bash shell supports both if statements and the case statement. They both allow you to perform a test on a numerical value, a string value, or a file and then run a block of commands based on the outcome of the test.

Review Questions

1. What character or characters make up the shebang used in Linux to define the shell used for a shell script?

   A. >>

   B. #!

   C. |

   D. >

   E. 2>

2. Henry needs to store the output from his script into a new log file that he can read later. What character or characters should he use to do that?

   A. >>

   B. #!

   C. |

   D. >

   E. 2>

3. Jasmine has created a new Bash shell script and wants to run it from the command line. What chmod permissions should she assign to the file to run it as a shell script?

   A. 644

   B. u+r

   C. u+x

   D. u+w

   E. u=wr

4. What environment variable contains the username of the user who started the shell?

   A. $USER

   B. $UID

   C. $HOME

   D. $BASH

   E. $1

5. Zuri is writing a Bash shell script and needs to assign a number to a variable. How should he do that?

   A. var1=$(10)

   B. var1 = 10

   C. var1=10

   D. var1="10"

   E. var1=`10`

6. Cameron is writing a Bash shell script and needs to test if a file exists and that it's a file. What line of code should he write to do that?

   A. `if [ -e file ]`

   B. `if [ -f file ]`

   C. `if [ -d file ]`

   D. `if [ -x file ]`

   E. `if [ -w file ]`

7. What character or combination of characters do you use to redirect the output of one command to another command?

   A. `>>`

   B. `#!`

   C. `|`

   D. `>`

   E. `2>`

8. Christina is creating a Bash shell script and wants to make the script return a value of 2 if it fails. What statement should she add to do that?

   A. `#!`

   B. `$?`

   C. `$1`

   D. `exit`

   E. `while`

9. What command should you use to perform a command substitution to assign the output of a command to a variable in your shell script?

   A. `>`

   B. `>>`

   C. `$[]`

   D. `|`

   E. `$()`

10. What command should you use to perform a mathematical operation in your shell script?

   A. `>`

   B. `>>`

   C. `$[]`

   D. `|`

   E. `$()`

Chapter

26

Automating Jobs

✓ Objective 1.4: Given a scenario, configure and use the appropriate processes and services.

As you begin building shell scripts, you'll probably start to wonder how to run and control them on your Linux system. So far in this book, we've only run commands and scripts directly from the command-line interface in real-time mode. This isn't the only way to run scripts in Linux. There are quite a few other options available for running your shell scripts on Linux systems. This chapter examines different ways you can use to get your scripts started. Also, sometimes you might run into the problem of a script that gets stuck in a loop and you need to figure out how to get it to stop without having to turn off your Linux system. This chapter also examines the different ways you can control how and when your shell script runs on your system.

Running Scripts in Background Mode

There are times when running a shell script directly from the command-line interface is inconvenient. Some scripts can take a long time to process, and you may not want to tie up the command-line interface waiting. While the script is running, you can't do anything else in your terminal session. Fortunately, there's a simple solution to that problem. The following sections describe how to run your scripts in background mode on your Linux system.

Running in the Background

Running a shell script in background mode is a fairly easy thing to do. To run a shell script in background mode from the command-line interface, just place an ampersand symbol after the command:

```
$ ./test1.sh &
[1] 19555
$ This is a test program
Loop #1
Loop #2

$ ls -l
total 8
-rwxr--r--    1 rich     rich          219 Feb  26 19:27 test1.sh
$ Loop #3
```

When you place the ampersand symbol after a command, it separates the command from the Bash shell and runs it as a separate background process on the system. The first thing that displays is the line

```
[1] 19555
```

The number in the square brackets is the *job number* the shell assigns to the background process. The shell assigns each process started a unique job number. The next number is the process ID (PID) the Linux system itself assigns to the process. So every process running in a shell has a unique job number, and every process running on the Linux system has a unique PID.

As soon as the system displays these items, a new command-line interface prompt appears. You are returned to the shell, and the command you executed runs safely in background mode.

At this point, you can enter new commands at the prompt (as shown in the example). However, while the background process is still running, it still uses your terminal monitor for output messages. You'll notice from the example that the output from the `test1` `.sh` script appears in the output intermixed with any other commands that are run from the shell.

When the background process finishes, it displays a message on the terminal:

```
[1]+  Done                    ./test1.sh
```

This shows the job number and the status of the job (Done), along with the command used to start the job.

Running Multiple Background Jobs

You can start any number of background jobs at the same time from the command-line prompt:

```
$ ./test1.sh &
[1] 19582
$ This is the test1 program output
Test 1 Loop #1 output
$ ./test2.sh &
[2] 19597
$ This is the test2 program output
Test 2 Loop #1 output
$ ./test3.sh &
[3] 19612
$ This is the test3 program output
Test 3 Loop #1 output
Test 1 Loop #2 output
Test 2 Loop #2 output
Test 3 Loop #2 output
```

Each time you start a new job, the shell assigns it a new job number, and the Linux system assigns it a new PID. You can see that all of the scripts are running by using the ps command:

```
$ ps au
USER       PID %CPU %MEM  VSZ  RSS TTY        STAT START   TIME COMMAND
rich 19498 0.0 1.2 2688 1628 pts/0 S 11:38 0:00 -bash
rich 19582 0.0 0.9 2276 1180 pts/0 S 11:55 0:00 /bin/bash ./test3.sh
rich 9597  0.1 0.9 2276 1180 pts/0 S 11:55 0:00 /bin/bash ./test2.sh
rich 19612 0.1 0.9 2276 1180 pts/0 S 11:55 0:00 /bin/bash ./test1.sh
rich 19639 0.0 0.4 1564 552  pts/0 S 11:56 0:00 sleep 10
rich 19640 0.0 0.4 1564 552  pts/0 S 11:56 0:00 sleep 10
rich 19641 0.0 0.4 1564 552  pts/0 S 11:56 0:00 sleep 10
rich 19642 0.0 0.5 2588 744  pts/0 R 11:56 0:00 ps au
$
```

Each of the background processes you start appears in the ps command output listing of running processes. If all of the processes display output in your terminal session, things can get pretty messy pretty quickly. Fortunately, there's a simple way to solve that problem, which we'll discuss in the next section.

WARNING   You need to be careful when using background processes from a terminal session. Notice in the output from the ps command that each of the background processes is tied to the terminal session (pts/0) terminal. If the terminal session exits, the background process also exits. Some terminal emulators warn you if you have any running background processes associated with the terminal, while others don't. If you want your script to continue running in background mode after you've logged off the console, there's something else you need to do. The next section discusses that process.

Running Scripts without a Console

There will be times when you want to start a shell script from a terminal session and then let the script run in background mode until it finishes, even if you exit the terminal session. You can do this by using the nohup command.

The nohup command runs another command blocking any SIGHUP signals that are sent to the process. This prevents the process from exiting when you exit your terminal session (nohup is short for "no hangup").

You can combine the nohup command with the ampersand to run a script in the background and not allow it to be interrupted:

```
$ nohup ./test1.sh &
[1] 19831
$ nohup: appending output to  'nohup.out'
$
```

Just as with a normal background process, the shell assigns the command a job number, and the Linux system assigns a PID number. The difference is that when you use the nohup command, the script ignores any SIGHUP signals sent by the terminal session if you close the session.

Because the nohup command disassociates the process from the terminal, the process loses the output link to your monitor. To accommodate any output generated by the command, the nohup command automatically redirects output messages to a file, called nohup.out, in the current working directory.

The nohup.out file contains all of the output that would normally be sent to the terminal monitor. After the process finishes running, you can view the nohup.out file for the output results:

```
$ cat nohup.out
This is a test program
Loop #1
Loop #2
Loop #3
Loop #4
Loop #5
Loop #6
Loop #7
Loop #8  .
Loop #9
Loop #10
This is the end of the test program
$
```

The output appears in the nohup.out file just as if the process ran on the command line!

WARNING   If you run another command using nohup, the output is appended to the existing nohup.out file. Be careful when running multiple commands from the same directory, as all of the output will be sent to the same nohup.out file, which can get confusing.

Sending Signals

As discussed in Chapter 21, "Optimizing Performance," the Bash shell can send signals to processes running on the system. This allows you to stop or interrupt a runaway application process if necessary. While the kill and pkill commands discussed in Chapter 21 are good for stopping background processes, applications running in the foreground on the console are harder to control. Fortunately, there are two basic Linux signals you can generate using key combinations on the keyboard to interrupt or stop a foreground process.

Interrupting a Process

The Ctrl+C key combination generates a signal interrupt (SIGINT) signal and sends it to any processes currently running in the shell. You can test this by running a command that normally takes a long time to finish and pressing the Ctrl+C key combination:

```
$ sleep 100

$
```

The Ctrl+C key combination doesn't produce any output on the monitor; it just stops the current process running in the shell.

Pausing a Process

Instead of terminating a process, you can pause it in the middle of whatever it's doing. Sometimes this can be a dangerous thing (for example, if a script has a file lock open on a crucial system file), but often it allows you to peek inside what a script is doing without actually terminating the process.

The Ctrl+Z key combination generates a signal terminal stop (SIGTSTP) signal, stopping any processes running in the shell. Stopping a process is different than terminating the process, as stopping the process leaves the program still in memory and able to continue running from where it left off. In the following section, "Job Control," you'll learn how to restart a process that's been stopped.

When you use the Ctrl+Z key combination, the shell informs you that the process has been stopped:

```
$ sleep 100

[1]+  Stopped                 sleep 100
$
```

The number in the square brackets indicates the job number for the process in the shell. If you have a stopped job assigned to your shell session, Bash will warn you if you try to exit the shell:

```
$ exit
logout
There are stopped jobs.
$
```

You can view the stopped job by using the ps command:

```
$ ps au
USER PID    %CPU %MEM   VSZ  RSS TTY   STAT  START   TIME COMMAND
rich 20560  0.0  1.2   2688 1624 pts/0  S    05:15   0:00 -bash
rich 20605  0.2  0.4   1564  552 pts/0  T    05:22   0:00 sleep 100
rich 20606  0.0  0.5   2584  740 pts/0  R    05:22   0:00 ps au
$
```

The ps command shows the status of the stopped job as T, which indicates the command either is being traced or is stopped. The original Bash shell is shown as S, indicating that it's sleeping, waiting for the script to end. The ps command itself is shown with an R status, indicating that it's the currently running job.

If you really want to exit the shell with the stopped job still active, just type the exit command again. The shell will exit, terminating the stopped job. Alternately, now that you know the PID of the stopped job, you can use the kill command to send a signal kill (SIGKILL) signal to terminate it:

```
$ kill -9 20605
$
[1]+  Killed                sleep 100
$
```

When you kill the job, initially you won't get any response. However, the next time you do something that produces a shell prompt, you'll see a message indicating that the job was killed. Each time the shell produces a prompt, it also displays the status of any jobs that have changed states in the shell.

Another popular key combination is Ctrl+D. Instead of sending a signal, the Ctrl+D key combination sends an end-of-file (EOF) character to the standard input of the shell. This can come in handy when entering a data stream, indicating when the data is complete. However, if you send the Ctrl+D key combination without any data, it causes the shell to terminate. If the shell is your login shell, you will be automatically logged out of the system.

Job Control

In the previous section you saw how to use the Ctrl+Z key combination to stop a job running in the shell. After you stop a job, the Linux system lets you either kill or restart it. Restarting a stopped process requires sending it a signal continue (SIGCONT) signal.

The function of starting, stopping, killing, and resuming jobs is called *job control*. With job control, you have full control over how processes run in your shell environment.

The following sections describe the commands you can use to view and control jobs running in your shell.

Viewing Jobs

The key command for job control is the jobs command. The jobs command allows you to view the current jobs being handled by the shell. Listing 26.1 uses a shell script to demonstrate viewing a stopped job.

Listing 26.1: Stopping a running job

```
$ cat test2.sh
#!/bin/bash
# testing job control

echo "This is a test program $$"
count=1
while [ $count -le 10 ] ; do
   echo "Loop #$count"
   sleep 10
   count=$[ $count + 1 ]
done
echo "This is the end of the test program"
$ ./test2.sh
This is a test program 29011
Loop #1

[1]+  Stopped                 ./test2.sh
$ ./test2.sh > test2.sh.out &
[2] 28861
$
$ jobs
[1]+  Stopped                 ./test2.sh
[2]-  Running                 ./test2/sh >test2.shout &
$
```

The script shown in Listing 26.1 uses the $$ variable to display the PID that the Linux system assigns to the script; then it goes into a loop, sleeping for 10 seconds at a time for each iteration. In the example, we start the first script from the command-line interface and then stop it using the Ctrl+Z key combination. Next, another job is started as a background process, using the ampersand symbol. To make life a little easier, we redirected the output of that script to a file so that it wouldn't appear on the monitor.

After the two jobs were started, we used the jobs command to view the jobs assigned to the shell. The jobs command shows both the stopped and the running jobs along with their job numbers and the commands used in the jobs.

The jobs command uses a few different command-line parameters, shown in Table 26.1.

TABLE 26.1   The jobs command parameters

Parameter	Description
-l	Lists the PID of the process along with the job number
-n	Lists only jobs that have changed their status since the last notification from the shell
-p	Lists only the PIDs of the jobs
-r	Lists only running jobs
-s	Lists only stopped jobs

You probably noticed the plus and minus signs in the output in Listing 26.1. The job with the plus sign is considered the *default job*. It would be the job referenced by any job control commands if a job number wasn't specified in the command line. The job with the minus sign is the job that would become the default job when the current default job finishes processing. There will only be one job with the plus sign and one job with the minus sign at any time, no matter how many jobs are running in the shell.

Listing 26.2 shows an example of how the next job in line takes over the default status when the default job is removed.

Listing 26.2: Demonstrating job control

```
$ ./test2.sh
This is a test program 29075
Loop #1

[1]+  Stopped                 ./test2.sh
$ ./test2.sh
```

```
This is a test program 29090
Loop #1

[2]+  Stopped                 ./test2.sh
$ ./test2.sh
This is a test program 29105
Loop #1

[3]+  Stopped                 ./test2.sh
$ jobs -l
[1]   29075 Stopped           ./test2.sh
[2]- 29090 Stopped            ./test2.sh
[3]+ 29105 Stopped            ./test2.sh
$ kill -9 29105
$ jobs -l
[1]- 29075 Stopped            ./test2.sh
[2]+ 29090 Stopped            ./test2.sh
$
```

In Listing 26.2 we started, then stopped, three separate processes. The jobs command listing shows the three processes and their status. Note by the PID numbers that the default process (the one listed with the plus sign) is 29105, the last process started.

We then used the kill command to send a SIGHUP signal to the default process. In the next jobs listing, the job that previously had the minus sign, 29090, is now the default job.

Restarting Stopped Jobs

Under Bash job control, you can restart any stopped job as either a background process or a foreground process. A foreground process takes over control of the terminal you're working on, so be careful about using that feature.

To restart a job in background mode, use the bg command along with the job number:

```
$ bg 2
[2]+ ./test2.sh &
Test 2 Loop #2 output
$ Test 2 Loop #3 output
Test 2  Loop #4 output

$ jobs
[1]+  Stopped                 ./test2.sh
[2]-  Running                 ./test2.sh &
$ Test 2 Loop #6 output
```

```
Test 2 Loop #7 output
Test 2 Loop #8 output
Test 2 Loop #9 output
Test 2 Loop #10 output
This is the end of the test2 program

[2]-  Done                     ./test2.sh
$
```

Since we restarted the job in background mode, the command-line interface prompt appears, allowing us to continue with other commands. The output from the jobs command now shows that the job is indeed running (as you can tell from the output now appearing on the monitor).

To restart a job in foreground mode, use the fg command along with the job number:

```
$ jobs
[1]+  Stopped                  ./test2.sh
$ fg 1
./test4
Loop #2
Loop #3
```

Since the job is running in foreground mode, we don't get a new command-line interface prompt until the job finishes.

Running Like Clockwork

We're sure that, as you start working with scripts, there will be a situation in which you'll want to run a script at a preset time, usually at a time when you're not there. There are two common ways of running a script at a preselected time:

- The at command
- The cron table

Each method uses a different technique for scheduling when and how often to run scripts. The following sections describe each of these methods.

Scheduling a Job Using the *at* Command

The at command allows you to specify a time when the Linux system will run a script. It submits a job to a queue with directions on when the shell should run the job. Another command, atd, runs in the background and checks the job queue for jobs to run. Most Linux distributions start this automatically at boot time.

The `atd` command checks a special directory on the system (usually `/var/spool/at`) for jobs submitted using the `at` command. By default, the `atd` command checks this directory every 60 seconds. When a job is present, the `atd` command checks the time the job is set to be run. If the time matches the current time, the `atd` command runs the job.

The following sections describe how to use the `at` command to submit jobs to run and how to manage jobs.

The *at* Command Format

The basic `at` command format is pretty simple:

```
at [-f filename] time
```

By default, the `at` command submits input from STDIN to the queue. You can specify a filename used to read commands (your script file) using the `-f` parameter.

The `time` parameter specifies when you want the Linux system to run the job. You can get pretty creative with how you specify the time. The `at` command recognizes lots of different time formats. For example:

- A standard hour and minute, such as 10:15
- An AM/PM indicator, such as 10:15 p.m.
- A specific named time, such as now, noon, midnight, or teatime (4 p.m.)

If you specify a time that's already past, the `at` command runs the job at that time on the next day.

Besides specifying the time to run the job, you can also include a specific date, using a few different date formats:

- A standard date format, such as MMDDYY, MM/DD/YY, or DD.MM.YY
- A text date, such as Jul 4 or Dec 25, with or without the year
- You can also specify a time increment in different formats:
  - Now + 25 minutes
  - 10:15 p.m. tomorrow
  - 22:15 tomorrow
  - 10:15 + 7 days

When you use the `at` command, the job is submitted to a *job queue*. The job queue holds the jobs submitted by the `at` command for processing. There are 26 different job queues available for different priority levels. Job queues are referenced using lowercase letters, a through z.

By default all `at` jobs are submitted to job queue a, the highest-priority queue. If you want to run a job at a lower priority, you can specify the letter using the `-q` parameter.

Retrieving Job Output

When the job runs on the Linux system, there's no monitor associated with the job. Instead, the Linux system uses the email address of the user who submitted the job. Any output destined to STDOUT or STDERR is mailed to the user via the mail system.

Listing 26.3 shows a simple example of using the at command to schedule a job to run.

Listing 26.3: Using the at command to start a job

```
$ date
Thu Feb 24 18:48:20 EST 2022
$ at -f test3.sh 18:49
job 2 at Thu Feb 24 18:49:00 2022
$ mail
Heirloom Mail version 12.5 7/5/10.  Type ? for help.
"/var/spool/mail/rich": 1 message 1 new
>N  1 Rich                 Thu Feb 24 18:49  15/568   "Output from your job "
&
Message  1:
From rich@localhost.localdomain  Thu Feb 24 18:49:00 2022
Return-Path: <rich@localhost.localdomain>
X-Original-To: rich
Delivered-To: rich@localhost.localdomain
Subject: Output from your job         2
To: rich@localhost.localdomain
Date: Thu, 24 Feb 2022 18:49:00 -0500 (EST)
From: rich@localhost.localdomain (Rich)
Status: R

"This script ran at 18:49:00"
"This is the end of the script"


&
```

As shown in Listing 26.3, when we ran the at command, it produced a warning message, indicating what shell the system uses to run the script (the default shell assigned to /bin/sh, which for Linux is the Bash shell) along with the job number assigned to the job and the time the job is scheduled to run.

When the job completes, nothing appears on the monitor, but the system generates an email message. The email message shows the output generated by the script. If the script doesn't produce any output, it won't generate an email message, by default. You can change that by using the -m option in the at command. This generates an email message, indicating that the job completed, even if the script doesn't generate any output.

Listing Pending Jobs

The atq command allows you to view what jobs are pending on the system:

```
$ at -f test3.sh 10:15
warning: commands will be executed using /bin/sh
job 7 at 2022-03-04 10:15
$ at -f test5 4PM
warning: commands will be executed using /bin/sh
job 8 at 2022-03-03 16:00
$ at -f test5 1PM tomorrow
warning: commands will be executed using /bin/sh
job 9 at 2022-03-04 13:00
$ atq
7       2022-03-04 10:15 a
8       2022-03-03 16:00 a
9       2022-03-04 13:00 a
$
```

The job listing shows the job number, the date and time the system will run the job, and the job queue the job is stored in.

Removing Jobs

After you know the information about what jobs are pending in the job queues, you can use the atrm command to remove a pending job:

```
$ atrm 8
$ atq
7       2022-03-04 10:15 a
9       2022-03-04 13:00 a
$
```

Just specify the number of the job you want to remove. You can only remove jobs that you submit for execution. You can't remove jobs submitted by others.

Scheduling Regular Scripts

Using the at command to schedule a script to run at a preset time is great, but what if you need that script to run at the same time every day or once a week or once a month? Instead of having to continually submit at jobs, you can use another feature of the Linux system.

The Linux system uses the *cron* program to allow you to schedule jobs that need to run on a regular basis. The cron program runs in the background and checks special tables, called *cron tables*, for jobs that are scheduled to run.

The Cron Table

The cron table uses a special format for allowing you to specify when a job should be run. The format for the cron table entry is as follows:

```
min hour dayofmonth month dayofweek command
```

The cron table allows you to specify entries as specific values, ranges of values (such as 1–5) or as a wildcard character (the asterisk). For example, if you want to run a command at 10:15 a.m. every day, you would use the cron table entry of

```
15 10 * * * command
```

Because you can't indicate a.m. or p.m. in the cron table, you'll need to use the 24-hour clock format for p.m. times. The wildcard character used in the *dayofmonth*, *month*, and *dayofweek* fields indicates that cron will execute the command every day of every month at 10:15 a.m. To specify a command to run at 4:15 p.m. every Monday, you would use

```
15 16 * * 1 command
```

You can specify the *dayofweek* entry either as a three-character text value (mon, tue, wed, thu, fri, sat, sun) or as a numeric value, with 0 being Sunday and 6 being Saturday.

Here's another example: to execute a command at 12 noon on the first day of every month, you'd use the format

```
00 12 1 * * command
```

The *dayofmonth* entry specifies a date value (1–31) for the month.

When specifying the command or shell to run, you must use its full pathname. You can add any command-line parameters or redirection symbols you like, as a regular command line:

```
15 10 * * * /home/rich/test4.sh > test4out
```

The cron program runs the script using the user account that submitted the job. Thus, you must have the proper permissions to access the command and output files specified in the command listing.

Building the Cron Table

All system users can have their own cron table (including the root user) for running scheduled jobs. Linux provides the crontab command for handling the cron table. To list an existing cron table, use the -l parameter:

```
$ crontab -l
no crontab for rich
$
```

To add entries to your cron table, use the -e parameter. When you do that, the crontab command automatically starts the vi editor with the existing cron table or an empty file if it doesn't yet exist.

Working with Systemd Timers

Systems that utilize the systemd startup method (see Chapter 6, "Maintaining System Startup and Services") can also use the Systemd timer feature to automatically start programs. The timer unit files allow you to define events that occur at specific dates or times, similar to how the cron program works. The timer unit files, though, allow you to fine-tune exactly when a program starts.

Timer unit files are designated by a .timer file extension and include a [Timer] section that defines the directives required to determine when to start the event. Table 26.2 describes these directives.

As you can see in Table 26.2, timer units provide several options for how to set the timer that aren't available in the cron program, such as the amount of time since the program last completed. This allows you to choose exactly when a program should start on the system.

The following exercise walks you through working with jobs on your Linux system.

TABLE 26.2   Commonly used timer unit file [Timer] section directives

Directive	Description
AccuracySec	Specifies the accuracy of the timer. The default is one minute accuracy.
OnActiveSec	Defines the timer relative to the moment the timer is activated.
OnBootSec	Defines the timer relative to when the system was booted.
OnCalendar	Defines the timer as a specific date/time value.
OnStartupSec	Defines the timer relative to when the systemd program started.
OnUnitActiveSec	Defines the timer relative to when the timer unit was last activated.
OnUnitInactiveSec	Defines the timer relative to when the timer unit was last deactivated.
Persistent	When set, the time the timer unit was last triggered is stored on disk.
RandomizedDelaySec	Delays the timer activation by a random amount of time.
RemainAfterElapse	When set, the expired timer unit remains loaded, allowing you to query its status using systemctl.
Unit	Defines the unit file to start when the timer elapses.
WakeSystem	When set, the timer unit will cause the system to resume from being in a suspended state.

EXERCISE 26.1

Manipulating Jobs from the Command Line

This exercise walks you through how to run, pause, stop, and view jobs running within the Bash shell.

1. Log into your Linux graphical desktop and open a command prompt window.

2. At the command prompt, open a text editor of your choice and create the text file jobtest.sh by typing **nano jobtest.sh**, **pico jobtest.sh**, or **vi jobtest.sh**.

3. Enter the following code in the new text file:

```
#!/bin/bash
# jobtest.sh - run the sleep command in a loop for job testing
echo "This is a test program $$"
count=1
while [ $count -le 10 ] ; do
    echo "Program: $$ Loop #$count"
    sleep 10
    count=$[ $count + 1 ]
done
echo "This is the end of the test program"
```

4. Save the file using the appropriate save command for your editor.

5. Give yourself execute permissions to the file by typing **chmod u+x jobtest.sh**.

6. Run the shell script by typing **./jobtest.sh**.

7. Pause the job by pressing Ctrl+Z.

8. Start another copy of the job in background mode by typing **./jobtest.sh &**.

9. List the current shell jobs by typing **jobs**.

10. Restart the paused job in background mode by typing **bg _n_**, where _n_ is the job number assigned to the paused job.

11. List the current shell jobs by typing **jobs**. Note the status of the job that was previously paused.

12. Stop the running background jobs by using the **kill -9** command along with the appropriate PID values assigned to each job.

13. Type **jobs** to view the currently running jobs.

Summary

By default, when you run a script in a terminal session shell, the interactive shell is suspended until the script completes. You can cause a script or command to run in background mode by adding an ampersand sign (&) after the command name. When you run a script or command in background mode, the interactive shell returns, allowing you to continue entering more commands. Any background processes run using this method are still tied to the terminal session. If you exit the terminal session, the background processes also exit.

To prevent this from happening, use the nohup command. This command intercepts any signals intended for the command that would stop it, such as, for example, when you exit the terminal session. This allows scripts to continue running in background mode even if you exit the terminal session.

When you move a process to background mode, you can still control what happens to it. The jobs command allows you to view processes started from the shell session. Once you know the job ID of a background process, you can use the kill command to send Linux signals to the process or use the fg command to bring the process back to the foreground in the shell session. You can suspend a running foreground process by using the Ctrl+Z key combination and then place it back in background mode using the bg command.

Besides controlling processes while they're running, you can also determine when a process starts on the system. Instead of running a script directly from the command-line interface prompt, you can schedule the process to run at an alternative time. There are several different ways to accomplish this. The at command allows you to run a script once at a preset time. The cron program provides an interface that can run scripts at a regularly scheduled interval.

Exam Essentials

Describe how to run a shell script in background mode from your console or terminal session. To run a shell script in background mode, include the ampersand sign (&) after the shell script command on the command line. The shell will run the script in background mode and produce another command prompt for you to continue within the shell.

Explain how to disconnect a shell script from the console or terminal session so that it continues running if the session closes. The nohup command disconnects the shell script from the shell session and runs it as a separate process. If the console or terminal session exits, the shell script will continue running.

Explain how to stop or pause a shell script running in the foreground on a console or terminal session. To stop a shell script running in the foreground of a console or terminal session, press the Ctrl+C key combination. To pause a running shell script, press Ctrl+Z.

Describe how to list shell scripts running in background mode within a console or terminal session. The `jobs` command allows you to list the commands that are running within the console or terminal session. The output from the `jobs` command displays both the job number assigned by the shell and the process ID assigned by the Linux system.

Describe how to run a shell script at a specific time. The `at` command allows you to schedule a job to run at a specific time. You can specify the time by using an exact value, such as 10:00 p.m., or by using common date and time references, such as 10:00 a.m. tomorrow.

Explain how to run a shell script automatically at a set time every day. The `cron` process runs every minute and checks for jobs that are scheduled to run. You must define the jobs to run in the cron table by using the `crontab` command.

Review Questions

1. Frank wants to run his large number-crunching application in background mode on his console session. What command does he need to use to do that?

   A. >

   B. &

   C. |

   D. >>

   E. nohup

2. What command do you use to disconnect a shell script from the current console so that it can continue to run after the console exits?

   A. >

   B. &

   C. |

   D. >>

   E. nohup

3. When Melanie runs a shell script, she notices that it takes up all of the memory on her Linux system and she needs to stop it. How can she do that?

   A. Start it with the nohup command.

   B. Start it with the ampersand (&) command.

   C. Press Ctrl+C while the script is running.

   D. Redirect the output using the pipe symbol.

   E. Use the kill command to stop it.

4. How can you temporarily pause a shell script from running in foreground mode in a console session?

   A. Press the Ctrl+Z key combination.

   B. Press the Ctrl+C key combination.

   C. Start the command with the nohup command.

   D. Start the command with the ampersand (&) command.

   E. Start the command with the fg command.

5. How do you determine the default job running in a console session?

   A. By the PID number

   B. By the job number

   C. By a plus sign next to the job number in the jobs output

   D. By a minus sign next to the job number in the jobs output

   E. By using the ps command

6. Barbara has an application running in background mode in her console session and needs to bring it to foreground mode. What command should she use to do that?
   A. bg
   B. fg
   C. nohup
   D. &
   E. at

7. What command allows you to run a shell script at a specific time?
   A. nohup
   B. &
   C. at
   D. |
   E. >

8. Nick needs to run a report at midnight every day on his Linux system. How should he do that?
   A. Use the at command to schedule the job.
   B. Run the job using the nohup command.
   C. Run the job using the ampersand (&) symbol.
   D. Schedule the job using cron.
   E. Run the job using the atq command.

9. When will the cron table entry 10 5 * * * myscript run the specified shell script?
   A. At 10:05 a.m. every day
   B. On May 10th every year
   C. On October 5th every year
   D. At 5:10 p.m. every day
   E. At 5:10 a.m. every day

10. Jane needs to check on what jobs are scheduled to run automatically for her user account. What command should she use to list the cron table entries for her user account?
    A. cron
    B. at
    C. crontab
    D. jobs
    E. nohup

Chapter

27

Controlling Versions with Git

✓ **Objective 3.3: Given a scenario, perform basic version control using Git**

Linux is a popular development platform. If you are administering a system for programmers, it is important to understand the various tools they employ. In addition, you may find yourself writing complex shell scripts that require similar tools. In this chapter, we take you through the concepts of version control and the popular Git utility, which implements it.

Understanding Version Control

Two software developers, Natasha and Bruce, are working furiously on a new project called StoneTracker. The project is broken up into several program files that now have names such as `UI-3.2.A-73.py` due to all the modifications and revisions. Natasha and Bruce are constantly telling each other what file they are working on so that the other one doesn't accidentally overwrite it. In addition, they have created several directory trees to store the various project file amendments. The project has become bogged down with these complications and the extra communication it requires. These developers need version control. *Version control* (also known as *source control* or *revision control*) is a method or system that organizes various project files and protects modifications to them.

Version control methods or systems can control more than program files. They can typically handle plaintext files, executable files, graphics, word processing documents, compressed files, and more.

A version control system (VCS) provides a common central place to store and merge project files so that you can access the latest project version. A VCS protects a file so that it is not overwritten by another developer and eliminates any extra communications concerning who is currently modifying it.

Additional benefits include situations around new developers entering the project. For example, if Tony is a new team member, he can copy the latest StoneTracker project files via the version control system and begin work.

Distributed version control systems make projects even easier. The developers can perform their work offline, without any concerns as to whether or not they are connected to a network. The development work takes place locally on their own systems until they send a copy of their modified files and VCS metadata to the remote central system. Only at that time is a network connection required. A side benefit is that now the work is backed up to a central location.

A new version control system for Linux projects was created by Linus Torvalds in 2005. He desired a distributed VCS that could quickly merge files as well as provide other features that the Linux developers needed. The result was Git, which is a popular high-performance distributed VCS.

Git is a distributed VCS, which is often employed in agile and continuous software development environments. Figure 27.1 shows a conceptual depiction of the Git environment. To understand Git's underlying principles, you need to know a few terms about its configuration:

FIGURE 27.1   Conceptual depiction of the Git environment

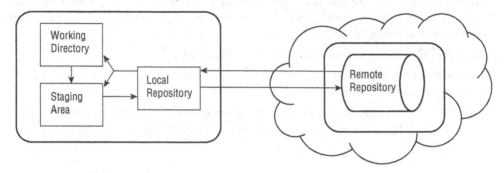

Working Directory   The working directory is where all the program files are created, modified, and reviewed. It is typically a subdirectory within the developer's home directory tree. The developer's computer system can be a local server or laptop, depending on workplace requirements.

Staging Area   A staging area is also called the *index*. This area is located on the same system as the working directory. Program files in the working directory are registered into the staging area via a Git command (`git add`). The staging area employs a hidden subdirectory named `.git`, which is created with the `git init` command.

When files are cataloged into the staging area, Git creates or updates information in the index file, `.git/index`, concerning those files. The data includes checksums, time-stamps, and associated filenames.

Besides updating the `index` file, Git compresses the program file(s) and stores the compressed file as an object(s), also called a *blob*, in a `.git/objects/` directory. If a program file has been modified, it is compressed and stored as a *new* object in the `.git/objects/` directory. Git does not just store file modifications; it keeps a compressed copy of *each* modified file.

Local Repository   The local repository contains each project file's history. It also employs the `.git` subdirectory. Project tree and commit information is stored as objects in the `.git/objects/` directory via a Git command (`git commit`). This data is called a *snapshot*. Every commit creates a new snapshot. Old snapshots can be viewed, and you can revert to previous ones if desired.

Remote Repository   The remote repository is typically a cloud-based location. However, it could also be another server on your local network, depending on your project's needs. Prominent remote repositories include GitHub, GitLab, BitBucket, and Launchpad. However, by far, GitHub is the most popular.

Using Git as your VCS includes the following benefits:

- **Performance:** Except for sending/retrieving files to/from the remote repository, Git uses only local files to operate, making it faster to employ.

- **History:** Git captures all the files' contents at the moment the file is registered with the index. When a `commit` is completed to the local repository, Git creates and stores a reference to that snapshot in time.

- **Accuracy:** Git employs checksums to protect file integrity.

- **Decentralization:** Developers can work on the same project, but they don't have to be on the same network or system.

Older VCSs required developers to be on the same network, which didn't provide a great deal of flexibility. They were also slower in operation, which is one reason Linus Torvalds decided to create Git.

Setting Up Your Git Environment

The Git utility typically is not installed by default. Thus, you'll need to install the `git` package prior to setting up your Git environment. See Chapter 13, "Governing Software," for details on package installation.

After you have the `git` package installed on your system, there are four basic steps to setting up your Git environment for a new project:

1. Create a working directory.
2. Initialize the `.git/` directory.
3. Set up local repository options.
4. Establish your remote repository.

To begin the process for a new project, create a working directory. A subdirectory in your local home folder will suffice. An example is shown in Listing 27.1.

Listing 27.1: Creating a working directory using the `mkdir` command

```
$ mkdir MWGuard
$
$ cd MWGuard
```

```
$ pwd
/home/Christine/MWGuard
$
```

In Listing 27.1 you create a simple subdirectory, MWGuard, for the project. After the working directory is created, you use the cd command to move your present working directory into it.

Within the working directory, initialize the .git/ directory. This task employs the git init command. An example is shown in Listing 27.2.

Listing 27.2: Initializing the .git/ directory via the git init command

```
$ git init
Initialized empty Git repository in /home/Christine/MWGuard/.git/
$
$ ls -ld .git
drwxrwxr-x. 7 Christine Christine 119 Feb  6 15:07 .git
$
```

The git init command creates the .git/ subdirectory. Because the directory name is preceded with a dot (.), it is hidden from regular ls commands. Use the ls -a command or add the directory name as an argument to the ls command, as was done in Listing 27.2, in order to view its metadata.

You can have multiple .git/ directories. Just create a separate working directory for each one.

If this is the first time you have built a .git/ subdirectory on your system, modify the global Git repository's configuration file to include your username and email address. This information assists in tracking file changes. The git config command lets you perform this task, as shown in Listing 27.3.

Listing 27.3: Modifying a local Git repository's config file using the git config command

```
$ git config --global user.name "Christine Bresnahan"
$
$ git config --global user.email "cbresn377@ivytech.edu"
$
$ git config --get user.name
Christine Bresnahan
$
$ git config --get user.email
cbresn377@ivytech.edu
$
```

By including the --global option on the git config command within Listing 27.3, you store the user.name and user.email data in the global Git configuration file. Notice that you can view this information by using the --get option and passing it the data's name as an argument.

Git configuration information is stored in the global ~/.gitconfig file and the local repository, which is the *working-directory*/.git/config configuration file. (Some systems have a system-level configuration file, /etc/gitconfig.) To view all the various configurations, use the git config --list command, as shown in Listing 27.4.

Listing 27.4: Viewing Git configuration settings using the git config --list command

```
$ git config --list
user.name=Christine Bresnahan
user.email=cbresn377@ivytech.edu
core.repositoryformatversion=0
core.filemode=true
core.bare=false
core.logallrefupdates=true
$
$ cat /home/Christine/.gitconfig
[user]
        name = Christine Bresnahan
        email = cbresn377@ivytech.edu
$
$ cat /home/Christine/MWGuard/.git/config
[core]
        repositoryformatversion = 0
        filemode = true
        bare = false
        logallrefupdates = true
$
```

The settings that are displayed via the --list option use a *file-section.name* format. Notice that when the two Git configuration files (global and project's local repository) are displayed to STDOUT via the cat command in Listing 27.4, the section names are shown along with the data they hold.

When your local Git environment is configured, it is time to establish your project's remote repository. For demonstration purposes, we chose the cloud-based remote repository GitHub. If you want to follow along, you can set up a free remote repository at github.com/join.

Though Git can work with any file type, its tools are aimed at plaintext files. Therefore, you will not be able to use all the git utilities on non-text files.

After you have your project's remote repository established, you'll need to record the URL it provides. This web address is used for sending your project files to the remote repository, which is covered later in this chapter.

Committing with Git

When you have your Git environment established, you can begin using version control. There are four steps:

1. Create or modify the program file(s).
2. Add the file(s) to the staging area (index).
3. Commit the file(s) to the local repository.
4. Push the file(s) to the remote repository.

Depending on your team's workflow, you may repeat certain steps before progressing to the next one. For example, in a single day, a programmer adds files as they are completed to the staging area. At the end of the day, the developer commits the project to the local repository and then pushes the project work to the remote repository for nonlocal team members to access.

In Listing 27.5, a simple shell script was created called MyScript.sh to use as a Git VCS example.

Listing 27.5: Viewing a simple shell script named MyScript.sh

```
$ cat MyScript.sh
#!/bin/bash
#
echo "Hello World"
#
exit
$
```

After the program is created (or modified), it is added to the staging area (index). This is accomplished through the git add command, as shown in Listing 27.6. The file is in the working directory, and you perform the git add command while located in that directory.

Listing 27.6: Adding a program to the staging area via the `git add` command

```
$ pwd
/home/Christine/MWGuard
$
$ git add MyScript.sh
$
$ git status
# On branch master
#
# Initial commit
#
# Changes to be committed:
#   (use "git rm --cached <file>..." to unstage)
#
#       new file:   MyScript.sh
#
$
```

The `git add` command does not provide any responses when it is executed. Thus, to see if it worked as desired, use the `git status` command, as shown in Listing 27.6. The `git status` command shows that a new file, MyScript.sh, was added to the index. Notice also the name `branch master`. Git branches are covered later in this chapter.

You can add all the files in the current working directory to the staging area's index at the same time. To accomplish this, issue the `git add .` command. Note the period (`.`) at the end of the command. It is effectively a wildcard, telling Git to add all the working directory's files to the index.

> If you have files in your working directory that you do not want added to the staging area index, create a .gitignore file in the working directory. Add the names of files and directories you do not want included in the index. The `git add .` command will now ignore those files.

The staging area's index filename is `.git/index`, and when the `file` command is used on it, in Listing 27.7, the file type is shown as a Git index. Git uses this file to track changes to the file.

Listing 27.7: Looking at the staging area index file with the `file` command

```
$ file .git/index
.git/index: Git index, version 2, 1 entries
$
```

The next step in the process is to commit the project to the local repository. This will create a project snapshot, which contains information such as the project's current tree structure and commit data. Git stores this data in the `.git/` directory. The commit is accomplished using the `git commit` command, as shown in Listing 27.8. The `-m` option adds a comment line to the `COMMIT_EDITMSG` file, which is used to help track changes. When you make commits later in the project's life, it is useful to include additional information to the `-m` option arguments, such as `-m "Presentation Layer Commit"`.

Listing 27.8: Committing a file with the `git commit` command

```
$ git commit -m "Initial Commit"
[master (root-commit) 6d2370d] Initial Commit
 1 file changed, 5 insertions(+)
 create mode 100644 MyScript.sh
$
$ cat .git/COMMIT_EDITMSG
Initial Commit
$
$ git status
# On branch master
nothing to commit, working directory clean
$
```

When you have committed the project to the local repository, the `git status` command will display the message shown in Listing 27.8 indicating that all the files have been committed.

> **NOTE** If you do not add the `-m` option and its argument to the `git commit` command, you are placed into the `vim` editor to edit the `.git/COMMIT_EDITMSG` file by hand. The `vim` editor was covered in Chapter 4, "Searching and Analyzing Text."

Now that the project is committed to the local repository, you can share it with other development team members by pushing it to the remote repository. If the project is complete, you can also share with others or the whole world.

If this is a new project, after you have set up your remote repository account, create a Markdown file called `README.md`. The file's content displays on the remote repository's web page and describes the repository. It uses what is called the *Markdown* language. An example of creating this file, adding it to the staging area index, and committing it to the local repository is shown in Listing 27.9.

Listing 27.9: Creating, adding, and committing a `README.md` file

```
$ pwd
/home/Christine/MWGuard
$
```

```
$ ls
MyScript.sh
$
$ echo "# Milky Way Guardian" > README.md
$ echo "## Programming Project" >> README.md
$
$ cat README.md
# Milky Way Guardian
## Programming Project
$
$ git add README.md
$
$ git status
# On branch master
# Changes to be committed:
#   (use "git reset HEAD <file>..." to unstage)
#
#       new file:   README.md
#
$ git commit -m "README.md commit"
[master 4541578] README.md commit
 1 file changed, 2 insertions(+)
 create mode 100644 README.md
$
```

You can get fancy with your README.md file by using various features
of the Markdown language. Find out more about Markdown at http://
guides.github.com/features/mastering-markdown.

At any time you can review the Git log, but it's always a good idea to do so before pushing the project to a remote repository. An example of how to view the log is shown in Listing 27.10. Each commit is given a hash number to identify it, which is shown in the log. Also, notice the different comment lines along with dates as well as author information.

Listing 27.10: Viewing the Git log via the `git log` command

```
$ git log
commit 45415785c17c213bac9c47ce815b91b6a9ac9f86
Author: Christine Bresnahan <cbresn377@ivytech.edu>
Date:   Fri Feb 11 13:49:49 2022 -0500
```

```
    README.md commit

commit 6d2370d2907345671123aeaaa71e147bd3f08f36
Author: Christine Bresnahan <cbresn377@ivytech.edu>
Date:   Wed Feb 9 15:23:11 2022 -0500

    Initial Commit
$
```

Before you can push your project to the remote repository, you need to configure its address on your system. This is done via the `remote add origin` *URL* command, where *URL* is the remote repository's address. An example is shown in Listing 27.11.

Listing 27.11: Configuring the remote repository with the `git remote` command

```
$ git remote add origin https://github.com/C-Bresnahan/MWGuard.git
$
$ git remote -v
origin  https://github.com/C-Bresnahan/MWGuard.git (fetch)
origin  https://github.com/C-Bresnahan/MWGuard.git (push)
$
```

Notice in Listing 27.11 that you can check the status of the remote address using the `git remote -v` command. It's a good idea to check the address before pushing a project.

> **TIP**
>
> If you make a mistake, such as a typographical error, in the URL, you can remove the remote repository's address by using the `git remote rm origin` command. After it is removed, set up the remote address again using the correct URL.

After the remote repository URL is configured, push your project up to its location. An example is shown in Listing 27.12.

Listing 27.12: Pushing the project to the remote repository with `git push`

```
$ git push -u origin master
Username for 'https://github.com': C-Bresnahan
Password for 'https://C-Bresnahan@github.com':
Counting objects: 6, done.
Compressing objects: 100% (3/3), done.
Writing objects: 100% (6/6), 561 bytes | 0 bytes/s, done.
Total 6 (delta 0), reused 0 (delta 0)
To https://github.com/C-Bresnahan/MWGuard.git
 * [new branch]      master -> master
Branch master set up to track remote branch master from origin.
$
```

Typically the remote repository will demand a username and a password, unless you have set it up to use SSH keys (OpenSSH was covered in Chapter 16, "Looking at Access and Authentication Methods"). When the project is pushed to the remote repository, you should be able to view it. If it is a private repository, you'll have to log into the remote repository in order to see your work. Figure 27.2 shows the remote repository for this project. Keep in mind that different providers will have different user interfaces for your projects.

FIGURE 27.2   MWGuard remote repository

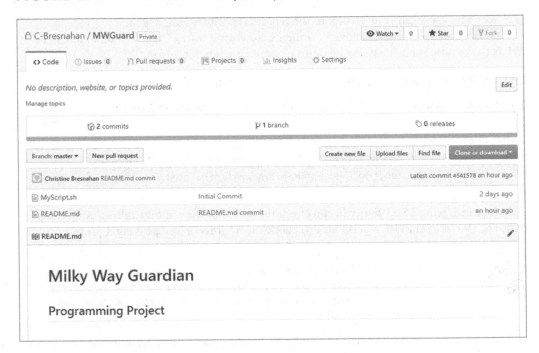

What is really nice about the remote repository is that your project team can pull down the latest files for the project using the `git pull` command. You'll need to either set up access for them to the remote repository or make it public. A snipped example of pulling files is shown in Listing 27.13.

Listing 27.13: Pulling the latest project files from the remote repository with `git pull`

```
$ whoami
Rich
$
$ git remote add origin https://github.com/C-Bresnahan/MWGuard.git
$
$ git pull -u origin master
```

```
[...]
Auto-merging MyScript.sh
[...]
$
```

 If the individual pulling down the project files already has a modified version of a particular file in their local repository that was not uploaded to the remote repository, the `git pull` command will fail. However, the error message will instruct how to rectify this problem.

A new development team member can copy the *entire* project, including the `.git/` files, to their local system from the remote repository using the `git clone` command. A snipped example is shown in Listing 27.14.

Listing 27.14: Cloning a project from remote repository via `git clone`

```
$ whoami
Samantha
$
$ ls
$
$ git clone https://github.com/C-Bresnahan/MWGuard.git
Cloning into 'MWGuard'...
[...]
remote: Total 6 (delta 0), reused 6 (delta 0), pack-reused 0
Unpacking objects: 100% (6/6), done.
$
$ ls
MWGuard
$ cd MWGuard
$ ls -a
.  ..  .git  MyScript.sh  README.md
$
$ git log
commit 45415785c17c213bac9c47ce815b91b6a9ac9f86
Author: Christine Bresnahan <cbresn377@ivytech.edu>
Date:    Fri Feb 11 13:49:49 2022 -0500

     README.md commit

commit 6d2370d2907345671123aeaaa71e147bd3f08f36
Author: Christine Bresnahan <cbresn377@ivytech.edu>
```

```
Date:   Wed Feb 9 15:23:11 2022 -0500

    Initial Commit
$
```

When the project is cloned from the remote repository, the working directory is automatically created, along with the `.git/` directory, the Git staging area (index), and the local repository. The `git log` command shows the project's history. This is an easy way for a new team member to grab everything needed to begin working on the project.

Tags

As you start committing newer versions of files to your project and the project history becomes longer, things can quickly get confusing. To help maintain some organization, the Git software provides *tagging*.

Tagging allows you to mark specific commit versions with additional information, such as a release number. You can then easily reference specific versions in the repository based on the tags you assigned.

There are two tag formats available in Git:

- **Lightweight**: Only includes a tag name
- **Annotated**: Includes the tag name, plus additional metadata that can provide additional information to help identify the version

To create a lightweight tag, just use the `git tag` command, along with the tag name:

```
$ git tag v2.0
$
```

The command doesn't return any information, but you can verify that the tag was created by using the `git tag` command without any parameters, which lists the existing tag names:

```
$ git tag
v0.1
v1.0
v1.5
v2.0
$
```

To create an annotated tag, include the -a parameter, along with the -m parameter to specify the descriptive text you want to add:

```
$ git tag -a v2.1 -m "development code for 2.0 branch"
$
```

Tags can help you identify production versus development versions, making it easier to identify where in the commit history release changes occur.

Merging Versions

A helpful concept in Git is branches. A *branch* is an area within a local repository for a particular project section. By default, Git stores your work in the `master` branch, as shown in Listing 27.15.

Listing 27.15: Viewing the branch in use with the `git status` command

```
$ git status
# On branch master
nothing to commit, working directory clean
$
```

You can have multiple branches within a project. A simple example is having a branch for production software (`master`), a branch for software in development (`develop`), and a branch for testing development changes (`test`). You can designate the branch you wish to work on to protect files in another branch from being changed. Using the example, you certainly would not want your development code files going into the production branch (`master`). Instead, you want them maintained in the `develop` branch until they are tested in the `test` branch and ready for production.

Let's take a look at a project that needs to use branches. The StoneTracker project is in production, and its files are managed via the `master` branch, as shown in Listing 27.16.

Listing 27.16: Viewing the current branch in use via the `git branch` command

```
$ git branch
* master
$
```

Notice the `* master` line in Listing 27.16. The asterisk (`*`) indicates that the current branch is `master` and that it is the only branch. If there were more branches, they would also be displayed. The current branch always has the asterisk next to it.

You can view the filenames within a particular branch by using the `git ls-tree` command. The StoneTracker project's committed files are shown in Listing 27.17.

Listing 27.17: Viewing the file names in the `master` branch

```
$ git ls-tree --name-only -r master
README.md
ST-Data.py
ST-Main.py
$
```

In the `master` branch (production), the StoneTracker project currently uses a text-based user interface via its business tier, `ST-Main.py`. The development team needs to add a presentation layer, which will provide a GUI. To create this new program without affecting production, they create a new branch to the project using the `git branch` command shown in Listing 27.18.

Listing 27.18: Creating a new branch with the `git branch branch-name` command

```
$ git branch develop
$
$ git branch
  develop
* master
$
```

Notice in Listing 27.18 that when the new branch, `develop`, is created, it is not set as the current branch. To change branches, the `git checkout` command is needed, as shown in Listing 27.19.

Listing 27.19: Switching to a branch via the `git checkout branch-name` command

```
$ git checkout develop
Switched to branch 'develop'
$
$ git branch
* develop
  master
$
```

Now that the branch is switched, development on the new user interface (`ST-UI.py`) can occur without affecting the `master` branch. However, Git VCS is still employed, as shown in Listing 27.20.

Listing 27.20: Using GIT VCS on the `develop` branch

```
$ ls
README.md  ST-Data.py  ST-Main.py  ST-UI.py
$
$ git add .
$
$ git status
# On branch develop
# Changes to be committed:
#   (use "git reset HEAD <file>..." to unstage)
#
#       new file:  ST-UI.py
#
$
```

```
$ git commit -m "New User Interface"
[develop 1a91bc3] New User Interface
 1 file changed, 47 insertions(+)
 create mode 100644 ST-UI.py
$
```

When development (and testing) on the new user interface is completed, the develop branch is merged with the master branch (production). To merge branches, use the git merge *branch-name-to-merge* command. Merges must be performed from the target branch. Therefore, in this case you must go back to the master branch prior to issuing the command, as shown snipped in Listing 27.21.

Listing 27.21: Merging a branch via the git merge command

```
$ git checkout master
Switched to branch 'master'
$ git branch
  develop
* master
$
$ git merge develop
Updating 0e08e81..1a91bc3
Fast-forward
 ST-UI.py | 47 [...]
 1 file changed, 47 insertions(+)
 create mode 100644 ST-UI.py
$
$ git ls-tree --name-only -r master
README.md
ST-Data.py
ST-Main.py
ST-UI.py
$
$ git log
commit 1a91bc30050ef1c0595894915295cc458b2539b7
Author: Christine Bresnahan <cbresn377@ivytech.edu>
Date:   Fri Feb 11 18:03:18 2022 -0500

    New User Interface

commit 0e08e810dd767acd64e09e45fff614288144da45
Author: Christine Bresnahan <cbresn377@ivytech.edu>
```

```
Date:   Fri Feb 11 16:50:10 2022 -0500

    Initial Production Commit
$
```

Notice in Listing 27.21 that now within the master branch, the new production tier program, ST-UI.py, is managed. Also notice that the Git logs between the two branches were also merged, as shown by the git log command.

 There is another flavor of merging called *rebasing*. Instead of simply merging the commits and history logs into a single branch, rebasing performs new commits for all the files, which simplifies the history logs. To rebase a project, replace git merge with the git rebase command. Which one you employ is dependent on your organization's development workflow as well as team member preferences.

Summary

The distributed VCS utility Git is useful in many ways beyond the needs of developers. Understanding how to set up working directories, staging areas, and local and remote repositories is a wonderful skill set. Not only will you be able to use the appropriate lingo with your programmers, you can implement Git for various other useful things to manage your Linux systems.

Exam Essentials

Describe version control.   Version control is a method or system that organizes various project files and protects modifications to them. A distributed VCS allows developers to work offline and independently. The Git VCS provides a working directory, staging area (index), and local repository and uses a remote repository provided by a third party. It is popular due to high performance, maintained modification history, file protection, and decentralization.

Explain how to set up your Git environment.   The git package provides the various Git tools used for VCSs. Create a working directory for each project using the mkdir command. The .git/ directory, used by both the staging area and the local repository, is initialized via the git init command. Finally, a third party, such as GitHub, can provide the remote repository to use with the various Git tools.

Detail committing with Git.   As needed, files are moved from the working directory to the staging area (index) via the `git add` utility. The project's workflow dictates when the programs are moved to the local directory via the `git commit` command and then on to the remote repository via the `git push` utility. If a remote developer needs the latest project files, the `git pull` command is used. For new team members who need all the project files, including modification history, the `git clone` command is used.

Summarize Git branches.   A Git branch is a local repository area employed for a particular project section, such as development or project testing. By default, the main branch is called the `master` branch. New branches are created using the `git branch` *branch-name* command. You can view the various branches available using the `git branch` utility, which uses an asterisk to denote the current branch. To switch to another project branch, `git checkout` *branch-name* is employed. After work on the branch is completed, its VCS files and project files can be merged with another branch via the `git merge` *branch-name-to-merge* command.

Review Questions

1. Which of the following is true concerning version control? (Choose all that apply.)
   - **A.** Provides a common place to merge and store files
   - **B.** Requires filenames to contain version numbers
   - **C.** May be distributed or nondistributed
   - **D.** Helps to protect files from being overwritten
   - **E.** Can deal with files other than programs

2. Conceptually Git is broken up into distinct areas. Which of the following is one of those areas? (Choose all that apply.)
   - **A.** Blob
   - **B.** Local repository
   - **C.** Remote repository
   - **D.** Index
   - **E.** Working directory

3. Which of the following are steps needed to set up a Git environment for the first time? (Choose all that apply.)
   - **A.** Create a working directory.
   - **B.** Initialize the `.git/` directory in the working directory.
   - **C.** Set up the local repository options.
   - **D.** Add files to the staging area when ready.
   - **E.** Establish the remote repository.

4. Natasha has created her working directory for a new project. What should she do next to set up her Git project environment?
   - **A.** Issue the `mkdir` command.
   - **B.** Enter the `git config --list` command.
   - **C.** Set up her GitHub repository.
   - **D.** Enter the `git init` command.
   - **E.** Start creating her program files.

5. When setting his Git configuration options, Bruce employs the `--global` option on his commands. What does this mean?
   - **A.** The configuration information is stored on GitHub.
   - **B.** The configuration information is stored in `~/.gitconfig`.
   - **C.** The configuration information is stored in the working directory's `.git/config` file.
   - **D.** The configuration information is stored in the working directory's `.git/index` file.
   - **E.** The configuration information is stored in the working directory's `.git/objects` directory.

6. Bruce has set up his Git environment and finished working on his new `GreenMass.sh` script. What should he do next?

   A. Add the script to the staging area.

   B. Issue the `git init` command.

   C. Commit the script to the local repository.

   D. Issue the `git log` command.

   E. Commit the script to the remote repository.

7. There are 25 files in Natasha's working directory and she only wants to add 22 of them to the index. She plans on using the `git add  .` command to be efficient. What should she do?

   A. Move the three files out of her working directory.

   B. Add the 22 files individually via the `git add` command.

   C. Create a new working directory for the three files.

   D. Add the three files' names to a `.gitignore` file.

   E. Temporarily delete the three files.

8. Natasha has completed her open source project, which is set to be released to the public today. She has moved the files to the staging area, committed her work to the local repository, and configured the remote repository's address. What is her next step?

   A. Go home and relax. She deserves it.

   B. Clone the remote repository to her local system.

   C. Push her project to the remote repository.

   D. Pull her project from the remote repository.

   E. Use the `remote add origin` *URL* command.

9. Which of the following commands allows you to switch to a new Git branch called `testing`?

   A. `git branch testing`

   B. `git ls-tree --name-only -r testing`

   C. `git branch`

   D. `git commit -m "testing"`

   E. `git checkout testing`

10. Tony created a new branch of the StoneTracker project called `report`. He has completed and tested his work. He now needs to merge it with the StoneTracker project's `master` branch. After switching branches to the `master` branch, what command should he employ?

    A. `git merge master`

    B. `git merge report`

    C. `git rebase master`

    D. `git rebase report`

    E. `git checkout master`

Realizing Virtual and Cloud Environments

Chapter

28

Understanding Cloud and Virtualization Concepts

✓ **Objective 3.2: Given a scenario, perform basic container operations.**

✓ **Objective 3.5: Summarize container, cloud, and orchestration concepts.**

Cloud technology has greatly changed the landscape of the computer world. Moving computer resources and applications into a shared network environment changes how many companies do business and provide services to customers. This chapter introduces the main concepts of just what a cloud is and the role that Linux plays in cloud computing. The chapter starts out by defining what cloud computing is and what the different types of cloud computing environments are. Next is a discussion of how virtualization plays an important role in cloud computing and how that is implemented in Linux. Finally, you'll learn how containers fit into cloud computing and how they have changed the way developers do their jobs.

Considering Cloud Services

Before diving into how Linux participates in cloud computing, it's a good idea to define just what a cloud is and what type of resources it provides.

What Is Cloud Computing?

The first mention of the term *cloud* came in documentation for the original ARPAnet network environment in 1977, the precursor to the modern-day Internet. In that documentation, the cloud symbol was commonly used to represent the large network of interconnected servers geographically dispersed. However, in this environment each server was self-contained and self-sufficient; there was no distributed computing.

The term *cloud computing* is related to distributed computing. In distributed computing, resources are shared among two or more servers to accomplish a single task, such as run an application. This environment became the precursor to what we know today as cloud computing, popularized by companies such as Amazon Web Services (AWS), Google Cloud Platform, and Microsoft Azure.

With cloud computing, you can deliver computing resources across the Internet. Now customers can purchase both hardware and software resources as needed from cloud computing vendors. This includes servers, storage space, databases, networks, operating systems, and even individual applications.

Figure 28.1 demonstrates the three different methods for providing cloud computing services.

FIGURE 28.1   Cloud computing methods

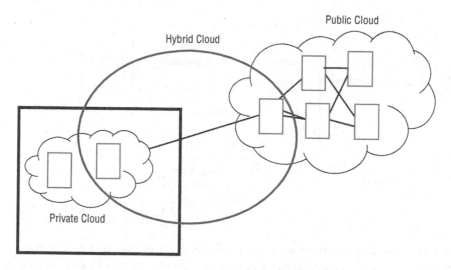

As shown in Figure 28.1, there are three primary methods for providing cloud computing environments:

- *Public*: In public cloud computing environments, a third party provides all of the computing resources outside the organization. This pool of resources is usually shared between multiple organizations that also have access to the platform.

- *Private*: In private cloud computing environments, each individual organization builds its own cloud computing resources to provide resources internally.

- *Hybrid*: In hybrid cloud computing environments, computing resources are provided internally within the organization but also connected to an external public cloud to help supplement resources when needed.

What Are the Cloud Services?

Cloud computing environments can customize the level of resources provided to customers, depending on each customer's needs. The following sections describe the three most popular models for providing resource levels that you'll find from cloud computing vendors.

Infrastructure as a Service (IaaS)

In the infrastructure-as-a-service (IaaS) model, the cloud computing vendor provides low-level server resources to host applications for organizations. These low-level resources include all of the physical components you'd need for a physical server, including CPU time, memory space, storage space, and network resources, as shown in Figure 28.2.

FIGURE 28.2   The IaaS cloud model

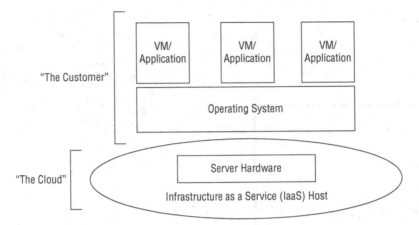

The server resources provided may be on a single server, or they may be distributed among several servers. In a distributed environment, the servers may be co-located in a single facility, or they may be separated into multiple facilities located in separate cities. This helps provide for increased availability.

As shown in Figure 28.2, in an IaaS model the customer supplies the operating system and any applications that it needs to run. Most IaaS environments support either the Linux or Windows operating system. The customer is responsible for any system administration work required for the operating system as well as any application administration. The cloud computing vendor takes responsibility for maintaining the physical infrastructure environment.

Platform as a Service (PaaS)

In the platform-as-a-service (PaaS) model, the cloud computing vendor provides the physical server environment as well as the operating system environment to the customer, as shown in Figure 28.3.

With the PaaS model, the cloud computing vendor takes responsibility for the physical components as well as the operating system administration. It provides system administration support to ensure that the operating system is properly patched and updated to keep up with current releases and security features. This allows the customer to focus on developing the applications running within the PaaS environment.

Software as a Service (SaaS)

In the software-as-a-service (SaaS) model, the cloud computing vendor provides a complete application environment, such as a mail server, database server, or web server. The vendor provides the physical server environment, the operating system, and the application software necessary to perform the function. This is shown in Figure 28.4.

FIGURE 28.3   The PaaS cloud model

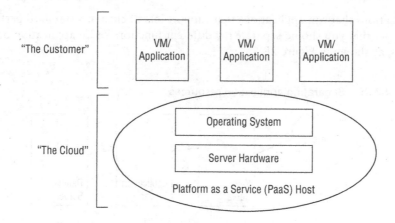

FIGURE 28.4   The SaaS cloud model

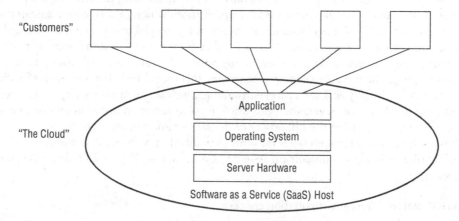

Understanding Virtualization

The downside to cloud computing environments is that they're very computing intensive. A lot of computer power is required to run a cloud computing environment, and that can become costly.

The technology that made cloud computing possible is virtualization, and this is also what has made Linux a popular choice for cloud computing vendors. The following sections describe what virtualization is, the different types of virtualization available, and how to implement virtualization in a Linux environment.

Hypervisors

For organizations that run applications that support lots of clients, a standard performance model dictates that you should separate the different functions of an application onto separate servers, as shown in Figure 28.5.

FIGURE 28.5   Separating application resources

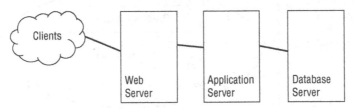

As shown in Figure 28.5, the web server, the application server, and the database server are located on separate servers. Customers only communicate with the front-end web server. The web server passes the connections to the application, which in turn communicates with the database server. From a performance standpoint, this model makes sense as you dedicate separate computing resources to each element. Also, from a security standpoint this helps compartmentalize access, making the job of any potential attackers a little more difficult.

However, with the increased capacity of servers, this model becomes somewhat inefficient. Dedicating an entire physical server to just running a web server, another physical server to just running the database server, and yet a third physical server to just running the application software doesn't utilize the full power of the servers and becomes costly.

This is where virtualization comes in. With virtualization, you can run multiple virtual smaller server environments on a single physical server. Figure 28.6 demonstrates this concept.

FIGURE 28.6   Server virtualization concept

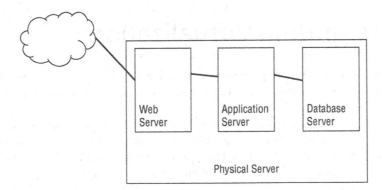

Each virtual server operates as a stand-alone server running on the physical server hardware. This is called a *virtual machine (VM)*. None of the virtual servers interacts with each other, so they act just as if they were located on separate physical servers. However, there needs to be a way for each virtual server to share the physical resources on the server fairly so that they don't conflict with one another.

This is where the *hypervisor* comes into play. The hypervisor, also called a *virtual machine monitor (VMM)*, acts as the traffic cop for the physical server resources shared between the virtual machines. It provides a virtual environment of CPU time, memory space, and storage space to each virtual machine running on the server. As far as each virtual machine is concerned, it has direct access to the server resources, and it has no idea that the hypervisor is in the middle controlling access to resources.

Since each virtual machine is a separate entity on the server, you can run different operating systems within the different virtual machines. This allows you to easily experiment with running applications in different operating systems, or just different versions of the same operating system—all without having to purchase additional servers.

Types of Hypervisors

There are two different methods for implementing hypervisors. The following sections discuss what they are and how they differ.

Type I Hypervisors

Type I hypervisors are commonly called bare-metal hypervisors. The hypervisor system runs directly on the server hardware, with no go-between. The hypervisor software interacts directly with the CPU, memory, and storage on the system, allocating them to each virtual machine as needed. Figure 28.7 illustrates this setup.

FIGURE 28.7 Type I hypervisors

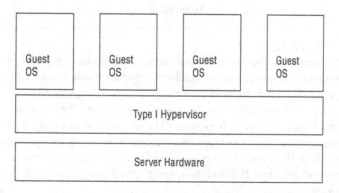

In the Linux world, two popular Type I hypervisor packages are used:

- **KVM:** The Linux Kernel–based Virtual Machine (KVM) utilizes a standard Linux kernel along with a special hypervisor module, depending on the CPU used (Intel or AMD). Once installed, it can host any type of guest operating systems.

- **XEN:** The XEN Project is an open source standard for hardware virtualization. Not only does it support Intel and AMD CPUs, but there's also a version for ARM CPUs. The XEN Project includes additional software besides the hypervisor software, such as an API stack for managing the hypervisor from a guest operating system.

Type II Hypervisors

Type II hypervisors are commonly called *hosted hypervisors* because they run on top of an existing operating system installation. The hypervisor software runs like any other application on the host operating system. Figure 28.8 shows how a Type II hypervisor works.

FIGURE 28.8   Type II hypervisors

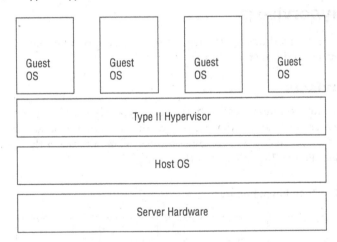

The Type II hypervisor software runs guest virtual machines as separate processes on the host operating system. The guest virtual machines support guest operating systems, which are completely separated from the host operating system. Thus, you can use a Linux host operating system and still run Windows or macOS guest operating systems.

The attraction of using a Type II hypervisor is that you can run it on an already installed operating system. You don't need to create a new server environment to run virtual machines. With the Type I hypervisors, you must dedicate a server to hosting virtual machines, whereas with a Type II hypervisor, your server can perform other functions while it hosts virtual machines.

There are many different popular Windows and macOS Type II hypervisors, such as VMware Workstation and QEMU, but for Linux the one commonly used is Oracle VirtualBox.

Hypervisor Templates

The virtual machines that you create to run in the hypervisor must be configured to determine the resources they need and how they interact with the hardware. You can save these configuration settings to template files so that you can easily duplicate a virtual machine environment either on the same hypervisor or on a separate hypervisor server.

The open source standard for virtual machine configurations is called the *Open Virtualization Format (OVF)*. The OVF format creates a distribution package consisting of multiple files. The package uses a single XML configuration file to define the virtual machine hardware environment requirements. Along with that file are additional files that define the virtual machine requirements for network access, virtual drive requirements, and any operating system requirements.

The downside to OVF templates is that they are cumbersome to distribute. The solution to that is the *Open Virtualization Appliance (OVA)* format. The OVA template bundles all of the OVF files into a single `tar` archive file for easy distribution.

Exploring Containers

While utilizing virtual machines is a great way to spin up multiple servers in a server environment, they're still somewhat clunky for working with and distributing applications. There's no need to duplicate an entire operating system environment to distribute an application. The solution to this problem is containers. The following sections explore what containers are and how they are changing the way developers manage and distribute applications in the cloud environment.

What Are Containers?

Developing applications requires lots of files. The application runtime files are usually co-located in a single directory, but often additional library files are required for interfacing the application to databases, desktop management software, or built-in operating system functions. These files are usually located in various hard-to-find places scattered around the Linux virtual directory.

Because of all the ancillary files required to run an application, all too often an application will work just fine in development and then come crashing down when deployed to a production environment that doesn't accurately reproduce the development environment. In the Windows world, this is commonly referred to as DLL hell, as different applications overwrite common DLL library files, breaking other applications. However, this isn't limited to the Windows world; it can also apply to the Linux world.

Containers are designed to solve this problem. A container gathers all of the files necessary to run an application—the runtime files, library files, database files, and any operating system–specific files. The container becomes self-sufficient for the application to run; everything the application needs is stored within the container.

If you run multiple applications on a server, you can install multiple containers. Each container is still a self-contained environment for each particular application, as shown in Figure 28.9.

The application containers are portable. You can run the same container in any host environment and expect the same behavior for the application. This is ideal for application developers. The developer can develop the application container in one environment, copy it to a test environment, and then deploy the application container to a production environment, all without worrying about missing files.

FIGURE 28.9   Running an application in a container

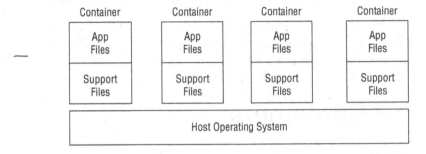

By packaging and distributing an application as a container, the developer ensures that the application will work for customers the same way it worked in the development environment.

Since containers don't contain the entire operating system, they're more lightweight than a full virtual machine, making them easier to distribute. The following sections describe two of the most common container packaging systems used in Linux.

 Chapter 19, "Embracing Best Security Practices," discussed the use of chroot jails as a method for separating applications running on a Linux system. The first containers utilized this same method to separate applications. Today's container packages use the chroot jail to separate applications but also incorporate advanced Linux features such as AppArmor and SELinux, kernel namespaces, control groups (cgroups), and additional kernel capabilities.

Container Software

Linux has been in the forefront of container development, making it a popular choice for developers. Two main container packages are commonly used in Linux:

- **LXC:** The *LXC* package was developed as an open source standard for creating containers. Each container in LXC is a little more involved than just a standard lightweight application container but not quite as heavy as a full virtual machine, placing it somewhere in the middle. LXC containers include their own bare-bones operating system that interfaces with the host system hardware directly, without requiring a host operating system to handle that part. Because the LXC containers contain their own mini–operating system, they are sometimes referred to as *virtual machines*, although that term isn't quite correct as the LXC containers still require a host operating system to operate.

- **Docker:** The *Docker* package was developed by Docker Inc. and released as an open source project. Docker is extremely lightweight, allowing several containers to run on the same host Linux system. Docker uses a separate daemon that runs on the host Linux system that manages the Docker images installed. The daemon listens for requests from the individual containers as well as from a Docker command-line interface that allows you to control the container environments.

Container Templates

Just like virtual machines, containers allow you to create templates to easily duplicate container environments. The different types of Linux containers use different methods for distributing templates.

The LXC package uses a separate utility called LXD to manage containers. In recent versions, LXD has become so popular that it is now packaged itself as container software, although it still uses the LXC system images of the container.

Docker uses Docker *container image* files to store container configurations. The container image file is a read-only container image that can store and distribute application containers.

Working with Docker

The Docker container software package provides an easy platform to run OS containers in your Linux environment. However, because Docker shares the host OS kernel with the containers, you can only run Linux containers on a Linux Docker host.

You use the `docker` command-line tool to easily interact with the Docker system, starting, stopping, and interacting with containers. Table 28.1 shows the commands available for you to use with the `docker` command.

You can either build a new container image from a Docker configuration file or download a preconfigured container image directly from a container repository, where other admins have posted their containers. Docker itself maintains a container repository at `http://hub.docker.com`.

The following exercise walks you through the steps to install and use Docker on your Linux system to start hosting Linux containers.

TABLE 28.1   The docker utility commands

Command	Description
attach	Connects the host STDIN, STDOUT, and STDERR to the container
build	Creates a new container image from a Docker configuration file
commit	Creates a new image of an edited container on the local system
cp	Copies files and directories between the local system and a container
exec	Connects to a running container and executes a command
images	Lists locally stored container images
inspect	Displays detailed information about containers
kill	Immediately stops a running container
login	Logs into the Docker hub repository
logs	Retrieves logs from a running container
ps	Lists running containers
pull	Retrieves a container from the Docker repository
push	Commits a container image to the Docker repository
rm	Deletes a stopped container
rmi	Deletes a container image from local storage
run	Starts a container image
stop	Stops a running container
start	Starts a stopped container

EXERCISE 28.1

Working with Containers

1. Install the Docker software from your distribution's software repository (see Chapter 13, "Governing Software"). For Ubuntu, type the command **sudo apt install docker**. For Red Hat–based distributions, such as Rocky Linux, the command is **sudo dnf install docker**.

2. After installing the Docker software, you communicate with it by using the docker command. Check to make sure Docker is running by typing **sudo docker ps** at the command line:

```
$ sudo docker ps
Emulate Docker CLI using podman. Create /etc/containers/nodocker to quiet msg.
CONTAINER ID  IMAGE        COMMAND     CREATED     STATUS      PORTS       NAMES
$
```

The output shows that Docker is running and lists any containers that are currently running (currently none).

3. Retrieve the Docker customized container image for a generic Apache web server by typing the command **sudo docker pull docker.io/library/httpd:latest**. This causes Docker to query the Docker repository at `http://hub.docker.com` and retrieve the latest version of a customized Apache web server running on a generic Linux OS platform. If you need to use a specific version of Apache, you can specify it after the container image name, such as **httpd:2.4**.

4. Deploy the httpd container image to your Docker environment by typing **sudo docker run -d -t -p 8088:80 --name myApache httpd**. This command starts the container in background mode (the –d option), connects a terminal to the container (the –t option), exposes TCP 80 port on the container to port 8088 on the host (the –p option), and gives the container a simple name to use for the docker commands. It's important to remember that containers are self-contained, so to connect to a port on the container you must instruct Docker to expose the port to the host system. When you run this command, Docker will display the ID assigned to the container. Verify that the container is running by typing **sudo docker ps**.

```
$ sudo docker run -d -t -p 8088:80 --name myApache httpd
Emulate Docker CLI using podman. Create /etc/containers/nodocker to quiet msg.
43ee094b028d7b3c9a168cf29284428b156624f8bfc3fcf5cbb5c644c56548cc
$ sudo docker ps
Emulate Docker CLI using podman. Create /etc/containers/nodocker to quiet msg.
CONTAINER ID  IMAGE                          COMMAND           CREATED
STATUS            PORTS                NAMES
43ee094b028d  docker.io/library/httpd:latest  httpd-foreground  4 seconds ago
Up 5 seconds ago  0.0.0.0:8088->80/tcp  myApache
$
```

The output shows that indeed the httpd container is running and that it has exposed the TCP 80 port on the container to TCP port 8088 on the host system.

5. Connect to the Apache web server running in the container by opening the browser in your host Linux desktop and typing **http://localhost:8088**. You will see the generic "It works!" message produced by the Apache web server.

6. Open an interactive Bash shell in the running container by typing **sudo docker exec -i -t myApache bash**. This connects to the container named myApache as an interactive terminal (the -i and -t options) and runs the bash command-line command, producing a shell prompt. You should see something like this:

```
$ sudo docker exec -it myApache bash
Emulate Docker CLI using podman. Create /etc/containers/nodocker to quiet msg.
root@43ee094b028d:/usr/local/apache2#
```

7. The Bash shell command prompt indicates that you are logged into the container OS as the root user account and that it is in the /usr/local/apache2 directory. From there you can view and modify the Apache web server configuration files or create new web pages in the /usr/local/apache2/htdocs directory. To return to the host system command line, type **exit**.

```
root@43ee094b028d:/usr/local/apache2# exit
exit
[rich@localhost ~]$
```

8. Stop the running container by typing **sudo docker stop myApache**. You can verify that the container has stopped by typing **sudo docker ps**.

9. Delete the container from your Docker system by typing **sudo docker rm myApache**.

10. If you don't want the httpd container image on your workstation anymore, type **sudo docker rmi httpd**.

Summary

Cloud computing provides an easy way to expand the computing resources for a company without having to purchase and administer your own hardware. There are three levels of cloud computing that each provide different services. Infrastructure as a service (IaaS) provides hardware resources such as servers, storage, and network. Platform as a service (PaaS) provides development environments that consist of an operating system and any libraries required to develop, test, and deliver application software. Software as a service (SaaS) runs applications from the cloud servers across the Internet.

Cloud computing environments use virtualization to implement many servers without lots of physical hardware. With virtualization, one large server can host multiple smaller guest systems. The hypervisor software manages the resources allocated to each guest system and manages how those resources are used.

There are two types of hypervisor environments used. Type I hypervisors interact directly with the system hardware. Guest systems receive system resources directly from the hypervisor software. Type II hypervisors run on top of a host operating system. The host operating system interacts with the system hardware and provides resources to the Type II hypervisor, which in turn allocates the resources to the guest systems.

Containers are a different type of virtualization. Containers provide a consistent runtime environment for a single application. When you deploy an application into a container, the application container is guaranteed to run the same way no matter what server it runs on. By deploying applications using containers, you're guaranteed the application will run the same way in the development, test, and production environments. Containers don't contain as much overhead as virtual machines, making them easier to distribute.

Exam Essentials

Describe the three primary methods of providing a cloud computing environment.   Public clouds are hosted on servers owned and operated by a third party. The company doesn't own or operate any of the server hardware; it just utilizes space on those servers. Other companies can rent space in the same public cloud. Private clouds are hosted on servers located within the corporate network. All of the application files as well as data files reside within the corporate network. Hybrid clouds utilize private cloud servers but also interface them with public cloud servers. With the hybrid cloud, data could be located either externally in the public cloud or internally on the private cloud.

Explain the three types of cloud services.   Infrastructure as a service (IaaS) provides hardware-level services to customers. This includes servers, storage space, and the network resources to connect them. Platform as a service (PaaS) provides on-demand environments for developing software. In the PaaS cloud service, the server hardware, operating system, and runtime libraries are all provided by the cloud service. Software as a service (SaaS) runs applications in the cloud environment, allowing customers to access those applications via the Internet.

Explain the two types of hypervisors.   Type I hypervisors run directly on the system hardware. They act as a mediator between the hardware and the guest operating systems. Type I hypervisors allocate resources to each guest operating system, ensuring that each one gets enough. Type II hypervisors run on top of a host operating system. The host operating system interacts with the server hardware; the hypervisor software must go through the host operating system to access resources. Guest operating systems still only interact with the hypervisor software.

Describe how containers differ from virtual machines.   Most container packages don't include a full operating system, but virtual machines do. Container packages only include the library files and application runtime files necessary to run a specific application. This makes the containers lightweight and easy to deploy.

Review Questions

1. Which cloud service method utilizes only servers owned and operated by a third party?

   A. Private

   B. Public

   C. Hybrid

   D. Type II

   E. Type I

2. Tom currently runs a cloud for his company on internal servers but needs some extra processing power to run a new application. What method of cloud service can he check out to leverage his existing cloud without needing to buy more internal servers?

   A. Private

   B. Public

   C. Hybrid

   D. Type I

   E. Type II

3. Sally is interested in developing her application in the cloud without having to worry about administering an operating system. What type of cloud service should she buy?

   A. PaaS

   B. Private cloud

   C. IaaS

   D. SaaS

   E. Hybrid cloud

4. Which type of cloud service allows you to spin up your own operating systems on infrastructure provided by the cloud?

   A. PaaS

   B. Private cloud

   C. IaaS

   D. SaaS

   E. Hybrid cloud

5. Which type of hypervisor interfaces directly with the host system hardware?

   A. Private

   B. Public

   C. Type II

   D. Type I

   E. Hybrid

6. Henry already has installed Red Hat Linux on his server but now needs to install virtual machines. What type of hypervisor package should he use?

    A. Private

    B. Public

    C. Type II

    D. Type I

    E. Hybrid

7. Which type of hypervisor template bundles all of the configuration files into a single file for distribution?

    A. XML

    B. JSON

    C. OVA

    D. OVF

    E. YAML

8. Fred wants to package his application so that it's guaranteed to run the same way no matter what Linux distribution his customers use. How can he do this?

    A. Package the application as a container.

    B. Package the application as a hypervisor.

    C. Deploy the application to a private cloud.

    D. Deploy the application as a virtual machine.

    E. Bundle the application as a `tar` file and deploy it.

9. What method should you use to easily move an application from a development environment to a production environment without having to duplicate the operating system?

    A. Public cloud

    B. Private cloud

    C. Type I hypervisor

    D. Type II hypervisor

    E. Container

10. Which Linux container package runs an engine as a process on the host operating system and provides a command-line interface to control containers?

    A. Snap

    B. Docker

    C. KVM

    D. XEN

    E. VirtualBox

Chapter

29

Inspecting Cloud and Virtualization Services

✓ **Objective 3.5: Summarize container, cloud, and orchestration concepts**

When designing and managing various cloud and virtualization system configurations, you need to understand how virtual and physical networks interoperate, the various disk storage choices available, how to automate booting a system, and how you can quickly install Linux distributions on your virtual machines. In addition, you need to be aware of some basic virtual machine creation and management tools. In this chapter, we'll continue our journey, which started in Chapter 28, into cloud and virtualization topics.

Focusing on VM Tools

Various virtual machine utilities allow you to create, destroy, boot, shut down, and configure your guest VMs. There are many open source alternatives from which to choose. Some work only at the command line and sometimes are used within shell scripts, whereas others are graphical. In the following sections, we'll look at a few of these tools.

Looking at *libvirt*

A popular virtualization management software collection is the libvirt library. This assortment includes the following elements:

- An application programming interface (API) library that is incorporated into several open source VMMs (hypervisors), such as KVM

- A daemon, libvirtd, that operates on the VM host system and executes any needed VM guest system management tasks, such as starting and stopping the VM

- Command-line utilities, such as virt-install and virsh, that operate on the VM host system and are used to control and manage VM guest systems

While typically most command-line utilities that start with vir or virt employ the libvirt library, you can double-check this using the ldd command. An example is shown in Listing 29.1 on a Rocky Linux distribution that has hypervisor packages installed.

Listing 29.1: Checking for libvirt using the ldd command

```
$ which virsh
/usr/bin/virsh
$
$ ldd /usr/bin/virsh | grep libvirt
```

```
libvirt-lxc.so.0 => /lib64/libvirt-lxc.so.0 (0x00007f4a3a10c000)
libvirt-qemu.so.0 => /lib64/libvirt-qemu.so.0 (0x00007f4a39f08000)
libvirt.so.0 => /lib64/libvirt.so.0 (0x00007f4a39934000)
$
```

A primary goal of the `libvirt` project is to provide a single way to manage virtual machines. It supports a number of hypervisors, such as KVM, QEMU, Xen, and VMware ESXi. You can find out more about the `libvirt` project at the `Libvirt.org` website.

Viewing *virsh*

One handy tool that uses the `libvirt` library is the `virsh` shell. It is a basic shell you can employ to manage your system's virtual machines.

If you'd like to try out the `virsh` shell, you can obtain it through the `libvirt-client` or `libvirt-clients` package. For older distributions, it may be located in the `libvirt-bin` package. Package installation was covered in Chapter 13, "Governing Software." Be aware that additional software packages are needed to create virtual machines.

If you have a VMM (hypervisor) product installed, you can employ the `virsh` shell to create, remove, start, stop, and manage your virtual machines. An example of entering and exiting the `virsh` shell is shown in Listing 29.2. Keep in mind that super user privileges are typically needed for shell commands involving virtual machines.

Listing 29.2: Exploring the `virsh` shell

```
$ virsh
Welcome to virsh, the virtualization interactive terminal.

Type:  'help' for help with commands
       'quit' to quit

virsh #
virsh # exit

$
```

You don't have to enter the `virsh` shell in order to manage your virtual machines. The various `virsh` commands can be entered directly from the Bash shell, which makes it useful for those who wish to use the commands in shell scripts to automate virtual machine administration. An example of using the `virsh` utility interactively is shown in Listing 29.3.

Listing 29.3: Using the virsh utility interactively

```
$ virsh help setvcpus
  NAME
    setvcpus - change number of virtual CPUs

  SYNOPSIS
    setvcpus <domain> <count> [--maximum] [--config]
[--live] [--current] [--guest] [--hotpluggable]

  DESCRIPTION
    Change the number of virtual CPUs in the guest domain.

  OPTIONS
    [--domain] <string>  domain name, id or uuid
    [--count] <number>   number of virtual CPUs
    --maximum            set maximum limit on next boot
    --config             affect next boot
    --live               affect running domain
    --current            affect current domain
    --guest              modify cpu state in the guest
    --hotpluggable       make added vcpus hot(un)pluggable


$
```

An easier utility than virsh to use for creating virtual machines at the command line is the virt-install utility. It is a Python program and is typically available from either the virtinst or virt-install package, depending on your distribution.

Managing with Virtual Machine Manager

Not to be confused with a hypervisor (VMM), the *Virtual Machine Manager* (also called *VMM*) is a lightweight desktop application for creating and managing virtual machines. It is a Python program available on many distributions that employ a GUI and is obtainable from the virt-manager package.

The Virtual Machine Manager can be initiated from a terminal emulator within the graphical environment via the virt-manager command. The VMM user interface is shown on a Rocky Linux 8 distribution in Figure 29.1.

FIGURE 29.1 Virtual Machine Manager

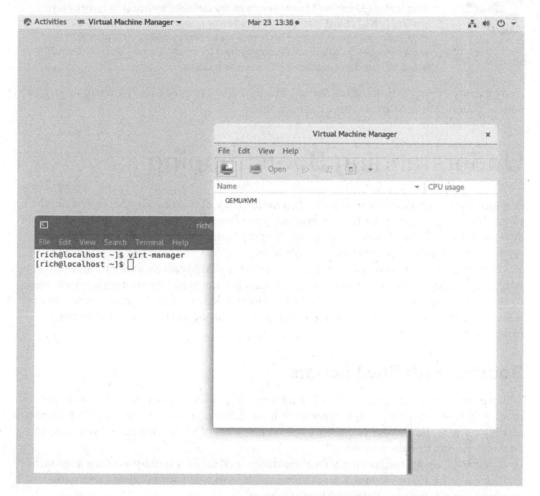

You do need to use super user privileges to run the Virtual Machine Manager, and if the `virt-manager` command is not issued from an account with those privileges, it will open a pop-up window asking for the root account password or something similar, depending on the distribution.

One nice feature the Virtual Machine Manager provides through its View menu is performance statistic graphs. In addition, the GUI interface allows modification of guest virtual machines' configurations, such as their virtual networks (virtual network configurations are covered later in this chapter).

The Virtual Machine Manager offers, by default, a virtual network computing (VNC) client viewer (`virt-viewer`). Thus, a graphical (desktop environment) console can be attached to any running virtual machine. However, SPICE also can be configured to do the same. VNC and SPICE were covered in Chapter 8, "Comparing GUIs."

You can view screenshots of the Virtual Machine Manager, read its documentation, and peruse its code at the `Virt-manager.org` website.

Understanding Bootstrapping

A bootstrap is a small fabric or leather loop on the back of a shoe. Nowadays you use them to help pull a shoe onto your foot by hooking your finger in the loop and tugging. A phrase developed from that little tool, "Pick yourself up by your bootstraps," which means to recover from a setback without any outside help.

Over time, the computer industry began mimicking that phrase with the terms *bootstrapping* and *booting*. They are often used interchangeably, but typically booting a system refers to powering up a system and having it start via its bootloader code. Bootstrapping a system refers to installing a new system using a configuration file or image of an earlier system installation.

Booting with Shell Scripts

Whether you are creating guest virtual machines in the cloud or on your own local host machine, there are various ways to get them booted. Starting a few VMs via a GUI is not too terribly difficult, but if your company employs hundreds of virtual machines, you need to consider automating the process.

Using shell scripts for booting virtual machines is typically a build-your-own approach, though there are many examples on the Internet. It works best for booting guest virtual machines on a company-controlled host machine.

If you prefer not to start from scratch, take a look at GitHub for available scripts. One popular project, which has several forks, is `http://github.com/giovtorres/kvm-install-vm`.

You can create configuration files for your various virtual machines and read them into the shell script(s) for booting as needed. The guest can be booted, when the host system starts, at predetermined times, or on demand. This is a flexible approach that allows a great deal of customization.

🌐 Real World Scenario

Booting School VMs with Shell Scripts

A school environment is an excellent setting for using guest virtual machines, especially in computer science classes. VMs provide an economical and highly flexible solution.

On the servers, guest VMs are configured to employ either temporary or permanent storage, depending on class needs. For example, students who do not need long-term storage for their files on the VM are provided with guest virtual machines with transitory virtual disks. Students who do need to store and later access their files, such as programming students, are provided with guest machines with persistent storage.

These guest virtual machines are booted as needed via scripts. The scripts can be initiated by an instructor prior to class or scheduled via a `cron` job (covered in Chapter 26, "Automating Jobs") or even via systemd timers (systemd was covered in Chapter 6, "Maintaining System Startup and Services").

In the classroom, either thin clients or student (or school-provided) laptops are available for accessing the guest virtual machines. The configuration and deployment of such machines simplifies many school computing environment complications and typically lowers associated costs.

Kickstarting with Anaconda

You can quickly and rather easily bootstrap a new system (physical or virtual) using the *kickstart installation method*. This RHEL-based technique for setting up and conducting a system installation consists of the following:

1. Create a kickstart file to configure the system.
2. Store the kickstart file on the network or on a detachable device, such as a USB flash drive.
3. Place the installation source (e.g., ISO file) where it is accessible to the kickstart process.
4. Create a boot medium that will initiate the kickstart process.
5. Kick off the kickstart installation.

Creating the Kickstart File

A *kickstart file* is a text file that contains all the installation choices you desire for a new system. While you could manually create this file with a text editor, it is far easier to use an *anaconda file*. For Red Hat–based distros, at installation, this file is created and stored in the

/root directory and is named anaconda-ks.cfg. It contains all the installation choices that were made when the system was installed.

 Ubuntu distributions do not create anaconda files at system installation. Instead you have to install the system-config-kickstart utility (the package name is system-config-kickstart) and use it to create your kickstart file. Ubuntu has a native bootstrapping product called *preseed*. It may be wise to use it, as opposed to the Red Hat–based kickstart method. Also, openSUSE distributions have their own utility called AutoYaST, which is another bootstrap alternative to kickstart.

An example of a Rocky Linux 8 distribution's anaconda file is shown snipped in Listing 29.4.

Listing 29.4: Looking at the anaconda-ks.cfg file

```
# cat /root/anaconda-ks.cfg
#version=RHEL8
# Use graphical install
graphical

repo --name="AppStream" --baseurl=file:///run/install/sources/mount-0000-
cdrom/AppStream

%packages
@^workstation-product-environment
@gnome-apps
@graphical-admin-tools
@office-suite
@system-tools
kexec-tools

%end

# Keyboard layouts
keyboard --xlayouts='us'
# System language
lang en_US.UTF-8
```

```
# Network information
network  --bootproto=dhcp --device=enp0s3 --ipv6=auto --activate
network  --hostname=localhost.localdomain

# Use CDROM installation media
cdrom

# Run the Setup Agent on first boot
firstboot --enable

ignoredisk --only-use=sda
autopart
# Partition clearing information
clearpart --none --initlabel

# System timezone
timezone America/New_York --isUtc

# Root password
rootpw --iscrypted $6$0/.K9AvlGaortpbn4$g0caaipRohs6RRx9pkyNucLSgj0Zee4mkWS
MmaVcCIRZgl2ooRNU21Lcr3MMGPSTcGjrqd8IT8CL2WUwz6KtN0
%addon com_redhat_kdump --enable --reserve-mb='auto'

%end


%anaconda
pwpolicy root --minlen=6 --minquality=1 --notstrict --nochanges --notempty
pwpolicy user --minlen=6 --minquality=1 --notstrict --nochanges --emptyok
pwpolicy luks --minlen=6 --minquality=1 --notstrict --nochanges --notempty
%end
$
```

Notice in Listing 29.4 that the root password is stored in this file. If other user accounts are created at installation time, those are stored here as well. While the values are encrypted, the file should still be kept secured so as not to compromise any of your virtual or physical systems this file is used to bootstrap.

In order to create the kickstart file for a system installation, start with the anaconda file and copy it for your new machines. Typically ks.cfg is used as the kickstart filename. After that, open the file in a text editor and make any necessary modifications.

Kickstart files use a special syntax, and unfortunately there are no man pages describing it. Your best option is to open your favorite web browser and enter **Kickstart Syntax Reference** to find a Fedora or Red Hat documentation site.

> Don't let kickstart file typographical errors cause installation problems. Besides giving the file a team review, use the `ksvalidator` utility to find syntax issues in a kickstart file.

Storing the Kickstart File

For regular physical system installations, typically a configured kickstart file is stored on removable media (such as a USB flash drive) or somewhere on the network, if you plan on using a PXE or TFTP boot process. For virtual machine creation, you can store it locally on the host system. In any case, make sure the file is properly protected.

Placing the Installation Source

The installation source is typically the ISO file you are employing to install the Linux distribution. However, you can also use an *installation tree*, which is a directory tree containing the extracted contents of an installation ISO file.

Often for a regular physical system, the ISO is stored on removable media or a network location. However, for a virtual machine, simply store the ISO or installation tree on the host system. You can even place it in the same directory as the kickstart file, as was done on the system shown in Listing 29.5.

Listing 29.5: Viewing the `ks.cfg` and ISO files' location

```
# ls VM-Install/
ks.cfg  ubuntu-20.04.1-live-server-amd64.iso
#
```

Creating a Boot Medium

For a physical installation, the method and medium you choose depend on the various system boot options as well as the type of system on which you will be performing the installation. A simple method for servers that have the ability to boot from USB drives or DVDs is to store a bootable live ISO on one of these choices.

For a virtual machine installation, such as a virtual machine on a KVM hypervisor, there is no need to create a boot medium. This just gets easier and easier!

Kicking Off the Installation

After you have everything in place, start the kickstart installation. For a physical system, start the boot process, reach a boot prompt, and enter a command like **linux ks=hd:sdc1:/ ks.cfg**, depending on your hardware environment, your bootloader, and the location of your kickstart file.

For a virtual system, you can simply employ the `virt-install` command if it's available on your host machine. Along with the other options used to create a virtual machine, you add two options similar to these:

```
--initrd-inject /root/VM-Install/ks.cfg
--extra-args="ks=file:/ks.cfg console=tty0 console=ttyS0,115200n8"
```

If desired, you can create a shell script with a loop and have it reissue the `virt-install` command multiple times to create/install as many virtual machines as you need.

Initializing with Cloud-init

Cloud-init is a Canonical product (the same people who produce the Ubuntu distributions). It provides a way to bootstrap virtualized machines. On its Cloud-init.io website, Canonical describes it best: "Cloud images are operating system templates and every instance starts out as an identical clone of every other instance. It is the user data that gives every cloud instance its personality and cloud-init is the tool that applies user data to your instances automatically."

The cloud-init service is written in Python and is available for cloud-based virtualization services, such as Amazon Web Services (AWS), Microsoft Azure, and Digital Ocean as well as with cloud-based management operating systems, like OpenStack. And your virtual machines don't have to be in a cloud to use cloud-init. It can also bootstrap local virtual machines using VMM (hypervisor) products like VMware and KVM. In addition, it is supported by most major Linux distributions. It is called an *industry standard* for a reason.

Cloud-init allows you to configure the virtual machine's hostname, temporary mount points, and the default locale. Even better, pregenerated OpenSSH private keys can be created to provide encrypted access to the virtualized system. Customized scripts can be employed to run when the virtual machine is bootstrapped. This is all done through what is called `user-data`, which is either a string of information or data stored in files that are typically Yet Another Markup Language (YAML)-formatted files.

> If you would like to take a look at the cloud-init utility, you can install it through the `cloud-init` package (package installation was covered in Chapter 13). It is available on most major Linux distributions.

The `/etc/cloud/cloud.cfg` file is the primary cloud-init configuration file. The command-line utility name is, as you might suspect, the `cloud-init` command. An example of using `cloud-init` to get help is shown in Listing 29.6.

Listing 29.6: Employing the –h option to get help on the `cloud-init` command

```
$ cloud-init -h
usage: /usr/bin/cloud-init [-h] [--version] [--file FILES] [--debug] [--force]

 {init,modules,single,query,dhclient-hook,features,analyze,devel,
collect-logs,clean,status}
                    ...


optional arguments:
  -h, --help               show this help message and exit
```

```
--version, -v          show program's version number and exit
--file FILES, -f FILES
                       additional yaml configuration files to use
--debug, -d            show additional pre-action logging (default: False)
--force                force running even if no datasource is found (use at
                       your own risk)

Subcommands:
  {init,modules,single,query,dhclient-hook,features,analyze,devel,
collect-logs,clean,status}
    init               initializes cloud-init and performs initial modules
    modules            activates modules using a given configuration key
    single             run a single module
    query              Query standardized instance metadata from the command
                       line.
    dhclient-hook      run the dhclient hookto record network info
    features           list defined features
    analyze            Devel tool: Analyze cloud-init logs and data
    devel              Run development tools
    collect-logs       Collect and tar all cloud-init debug info
    clean              Remove logs and artifacts so cloud-init can re-run.
    status             Report cloud-init status or wait on completion.
$
```

 You would only employ the cloud-init command on a host machine, where virtual machines are created. For cloud-based virtualization services, such as AWS or Microsoft Azure, you provide the user-data file or information via their virtualization management interface to bootstrap newly created virtual machines.

Exploring Storage Issues

It is easy to forget that your virtual machines don't use real disks. Instead, their virtual disks are simply files on a physical host's disk. Depending on the VMM (hypervisor) employed and the set configuration, a single virtual disk may be represented by a single physical file or multiple physical files.

When setting up your virtual system, it is critical to understand the various virtual disk configuration options. The choices you make will directly affect the virtual machine's performance. Several virtualization services and products have a few terms you need to understand before making these configurations.

Provisioning   When a virtual machine is created, you choose the amount of disk storage. However, it is a little more complicated than simply selecting the size. Virtual disks are provisioned either thinly or thickly.

Thick provisioning is a static setting where the virtual disk size is selected and the physical file(s) created on the physical disk is preallocated. Thus, if you select 700 GB as your virtual disk size, 700 GB of space is consumed on the physical drive. Some hypervisors (VMMs) have various versions of thick provisioning, such as lazy zero thick, that have performance implications.

Thin provisioning is grown dynamically, which causes the hypervisor to consume only the amount of disk space actually used for the virtual drive. Thus, if you select 700 GB as your virtual disk size but only 300 GB of space is written to the virtual drive, then only 300 GB of space is consumed on the physical drive. As more data is written to the virtual drive, more space is utilized on the physical drive up to the 700 GB setting. Be aware that the reverse is not necessarily true—when you delete data from the virtual drive, it does not automatically free up disk space from the physical drive.

Thin provisioning is often done to allow *overprovisioning*. In this scenario, more disk space is assigned virtually than is available physically. The idea is that you can scale up the physical storage as needed. For example, if the host system is using LVM (covered in Chapter 11, "Handling Storage"), additional volumes are added as needed to the physical logical volume to meet virtual machine demand.

Persistent Volumes   The term *persistent volume* is used by many virtualization products, such as OpenStack and Kubernetes. In essence, a virtualized persistent volume is similar to a physical disk in how it operates. Data is kept on the disk until the system or user overwrites it. The data stays on the disk, whether the virtual machine is running or not, and with some virtualization products, it can remain even after the virtual machine using it is destroyed.

Blobs   *Blob storage* is a Microsoft Azure cloud platform term. Blob storage is large unstructured data, which is offered over the Internet and can be manipulated with .NET code. Typically, a blob consists of images, streaming video and audio, big data, and so on.

Blob data items are grouped together into a container for a particular user account and can be one of three different types:

- **Block blobs** are blocks of text and binary data. The blobs are not managed as a group but instead are handled independently of one another. Their size limit is 4.7 TB.

- **Append blobs** are also blocks of text and binary data. However, their storage is enhanced to allow for efficient appending operations. Thus, this blob type is often used for logging data.

- **Page blobs** are simply random access files, which can be up to 8 TB in size. They are also used as virtual disks for Azure virtual machines.

Considering Network Configurations

Applications on physical systems are able to reach the outside world via a network interface card (NIC) and an attached network. With virtualized systems and virtualized networks, the landscape is a little different. Virtualized machines can have any number of virtualized NICs, the hypervisor may provide virtualized internal switches, and the NIC configuration choices are plentiful. The right configuration results in greater network and application performance as well as increased security.

Virtualizing the Network

Network virtualization has been evolving over the last few years. While it used to mean the virtualization of switches and routers running at OSI levels 2 and 3, it can now incorporate firewalls, server load balancing, and more at higher OSI levels. Some cloud providers are even offering network as a service (NaaS).

Two basic network virtualization concepts are virtualized local area networks (VLANs) and overlay networks:

VLAN   To understand a VLAN, it is best to start with a local area network (LAN) description. Systems and various devices on a LAN are typically located in a small area, such as an office or building. They share a common communications line or wireless link, they are often broken up into different network segments, and their network traffic travels at relatively high speeds.

A *VLAN* consists of systems and various devices on a LAN, too. However, this group of systems and various devices can be physically located across various LAN subnets. Instead of physical locations and connections, VLANs are based on logical and virtualized connections and use layer 2 to broadcast messages. Routers, which operate at layer 3, are used to implement this LAN virtualization.

Overlay Network   An *overlay network* is a network virtualization method that uses encapsulation and communication channel bandwidth tunneling. A network's communication medium (wired or wireless) is virtually split into different channels. Each channel is assigned to a particular service or device. Packets traveling over the channels are first encapsulated inside another packet for the trip. When the receiving end of the tunneled channel gets the encapsulated packet, the packet is removed from its capsule and handled.

With an overlay network, applications manage the network infrastructure. Besides the typical network hardware, this network type employs virtual switches, tunneling protocols, and *software-defined networking (SDN)*. Software-defined networking is a method for controlling and managing network communications via software. It consists of an SDN controller program as well as two application programming interfaces called *northbound* and *southbound*. Other applications on the network see the SDN as a logical network switch.

Overlay networks offer better flexibility and utilization than nonvirtualized network solutions. They also reduce costs and provide significant scalability.

Configuring Virtualized NICs

Virtual NICs (adapters) are sometimes directly connected to the host system's physical NIC. Other times they are connected to a virtualized switch, depending on the configuration and the hypervisor used. An example of a VM's adapter using a virtual switch is shown in Figure 29.2.

FIGURE 29.2   Virtual machine using a virtual switch

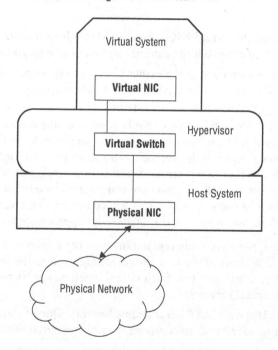

When configuring a virtual machine's NIC, you have lots of choices. It is critical to understand your options in order to make the correct selections.

Host-Only   A *host-only adapter* (sometimes called a *local adapter*) connects to a virtual network contained within the virtual machine's host system. There is no connection to the external physical (or virtual) network to which the host system is attached.

The result is speed. If the host system has two or more virtual machines, the network speed between the VMs is rather fast. This is because VMs' network traffic does not travel along wires or through the air but instead takes place in the host system's RAM.

This configuration also provides enhanced security. A virtual proxy server is a good example. Typically, a proxy server is located between a local system and the Internet. Any web requests sent to the Internet by the local system are intercepted by the proxy server, which then forwards them. It can cache data to enhance performance, act as a firewall, and provide privacy and security. One virtual machine on the host can act as a proxy server utilizing a different NIC configuration and have the ability to access the external network. The other virtual machine employing the host-only adapter sends/receives its web requests through the VM proxy server, increasing its protection.

Bridged   A *bridged NIC* makes the virtual machine like a node on the LAN or VLAN to which the host system is attached. The VM gets its own IP address and can be seen on the network.

In this configuration, the virtual NIC is connected to a host machine's physical NIC. It transmits its own traffic to/from the external physical (or virtual) network.

This configuration is employed in the earlier virtual proxy server example. The proxy server's NIC is configured as a bridged host, so it can reach the external network and operate as a regular system node on the network.

NAT   A *network address translation (NAT)* adapter configuration operates in a way that's similar to how NAT operates in the physical world. NAT in the physical networking realm uses a network device, such as a router, to "hide" a LAN computer system's IP address when that computer sends traffic out onto another network segment. All the other LAN systems' IP addresses are translated into a single IP address to other network segments. The router tracks each LAN computer's external traffic, so when traffic is sent back to that system, it is routed to the appropriate computer.

With virtualization, the NAT table is maintained by the hypervisor instead of a network device. Also, the IP address of the host system is employed as the single IP address that is sent out onto the external network. Each virtual machine has its own IP address within the host system's virtual network.

Physical and virtual system NAT has the same benefits. One of those is enhanced security by keeping internal IP addresses private from the external network.

Dual-Homed   In the physical world, a *dual-homed system* (sometimes called a *multihomed system*) is a computer that has one or more active network adapters. Often a physical host is configured with multiple NICs. This configuration provides redundancy. If one physical NIC goes bad, the load is handled by the others. In addition, it provides load balancing of external network traffic.

In the virtual world, many virtual machines are dual-homed or even multihomed, depending on the virtual networking environment configuration and goals. Looking back to our virtual proxy server example, it is dual-homed, with one internal network NIC (host-only) to communicate with the protected virtual machine, and it has a bridged adapter to transmit and receive packets on the external network. Figure 29.3 shows the complete network picture of this virtual proxy server.

FIGURE 29.3   Virtual proxy server

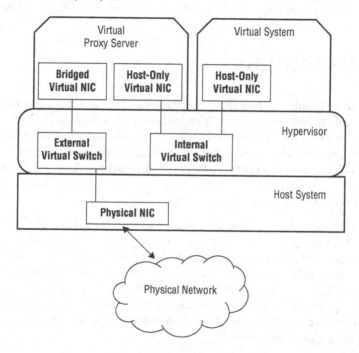

The physical and virtual machine network adapter configuration has performance and security implications. Understanding your internal virtual and external physical networks and goals is an important part of making these choices.

NOTE   Most container packages such as Kubernetes and Docker allow you to create a *service mesh* between applications. The service mesh is a dedicated infrastructure layer on top of the network that helps facilitate service-to-service communication. This enables separate parts of an application to communicate with each other in a high-speed manner.

Summary

Configuring your cloud and/or virtualization environment requires knowledge concerning networking and storage options. In addition, you need to understand how to quickly boot large numbers of virtual machines as well as bootstrap new ones. Discerning some of the various virtual and cloud machine tools is important as well. With a firm grasp on these concepts, you can participate in cloud and virtual system planning teams, which can successfully migrate a company's physical systems to a more modern and cost-effective environment.

Exam Essentials

Describe various VM tools.   The `libvirt` library is a popular software collection of virtualization management components. It includes an API, a daemon (`libvirtd`), and command-line utilities, such as `virt-install` and `virsh`. The `virsh` shell is one such tool provided by the `libvirt` library that allows you to manage a system's virtual machines. The Virtual Machine Manager (also called *VMM*) is a lightweight desktop application for creating and managing virtual machines. You can initiate it from the command line by issuing the **virt-manager** command in a terminal emulator.

Explain bootstrapping utilities.   The kickstart installation method employs a kickstart file that contains all the bootstrap choices desired for a new system. Instead of starting from scratch, the anaconda file, `/root/anaconda-ks.cfg`, is available on Red Hat–based distros and can be modified to configure a kickstart file. Ubuntu distributions do not employ the kickstart installation method by default. Instead they use a bootstrapping product named preseed. openSUSE distros also have their own alternative, which is AutoYaST. The Canonical product, cloud-init, is a bootstrap utility that is available for local virtual machines as well as cloud-based ones.

Detail the various virtual storage options.   Virtual disks can be provisioned either thick or thin. Thick provisioning is a static setting where the virtual disk size is selected and the physical file(s) created on the physical disk is preallocated. Thin provisioning is grown dynamically, which causes the hypervisor to consume only the amount of disk space actually used for the virtual drive. Drives can be either persistent or temporary. Temporary volumes are discarded when the virtual machine is stopped, whereas persistent disks are kept not only when the VM is shut down but sometimes even after it is deleted. Blob storage refers to unstructured data offered on the Microsoft Azure cloud platform. This storage typically consists of images, streaming video and audio, big data, and so on. There are three blob types— block, append, and page.

Summarize virtual network configurations.   One network type is an overlay network. This network virtualization method uses encapsulation and communication channel bandwidth tunneling. Besides the typical network hardware, this network type employs virtual switches, tunneling protocols, and software-defined networking (SDN). Network adapters (NICs) also have many configuration virtualization options. A dual-homed virtual machine has two virtualized NICs. A host-only adapter connects to a virtual network contained within the virtual machine's host system, and there is no connection to the external network. A bridged NIC makes the virtual machine like a node on the network to which the host system is attached. A NAT adapter creates a virtualized NAT router for the VM.

Review Questions

1. Which of the following is true concerning the `libvirt` library software collection? (Choose all that apply.)

   A. Provides an API library for hypervisors

   B. Provides a complete hypervisor (VMM) application

   C. Provides the `virsh` and `virsh-install` utilities

   D. Provides the anaconda file used for bootstrapping

   E. Provides the `libvirtd` daemon for host systems

2. Carol wants to automate the management of her virtual machines via a Bash shell script. Which of the following utilities can she use in this script? (Choose all that apply.)

   A. `virsh`

   B. `virtinst`

   C. `virt-manage`

   D. `virt-install`

   E. `setvcpus`

3. Nick is setting up a bootstrapping process on a RHEL system. He needs to store the installation tree. Which of the following are locations where he could store it? (Choose all that apply.)

   A. Network location

   B. USB flash drive

   C. On AutoYaST

   D. Within the preseed directory

   E. With the kickstart file

4. Which of the following is true concerning the cloud-init product? (Choose all that apply.)

   A. It was created and maintained by Microsoft.

   B. It is usable by cloud-based virtualization services.

   C. It is usable by cloud-based management operating systems.

   D. It is supported by most major Linux distributions.

   E. It is a bootstrap product.

5. Ms. Danvers is designing a set of virtual machines for her company, Miracle. Currently, her host machine uses LVM but only has enough disk space for 1 TB of data. Her three VMs will need 200 GB of disk space immediately but are projected to grow to 300 GB each within the next year. What should she do?

   A. Configure the three VMs to use persistent storage.

   B. Configure the three VMs to use temporary storage.

    C. Configure the three VMs to use thick provisioned storage.

    D. Configure the three VMs to use thin provisioned storage.

    E. Configure the three VMs to use blob storage.

6. Mr. Fury is a programming professor at Galactic University. This next semester he has chosen to use virtual machines for his students' labs. The students will be creating a single program that they'll work on throughout the entire semester. What is the best choice of disk storage for Mr. Fury's student virtual machines?

    A. Persistent storage

    B. Temporary storage

    C. Thick provisioned storage

    D. Thin provisioned storage

    E. Blob block storage

7. Which of the following is true about an overlay network? (Choose all that apply.)

    A. It is a storage virtualization method.

    B. It is a network virtualization method.

    C. It is a method that employs encapsulation.

    D. It is a method that employs bandwidth tunneling.

    E. It is a method that employs page blobs.

8. Carol needs her virtual machines to all act as nodes on her host machine's LAN and get their own IP address that they will use to send/receive network traffic. Which virtual NIC type should she configure on them?

    A. Host-only

    B. Bridged

    C. NAT

    D. Multihomed

    E. Dual-homed

9. Ms. Danvers wants her three virtual machines' IP address to be kept private, but she also wants them to communicate on the host machine's network using its IP address. Which virtual NIC type should she configure on them?

    A. Host-only

    B. Bridged

    C. NAT

    D. Multihomed

    E. Dual-homed

10. Nick has created five virtual machines on his host system. One virtual machine is employed as a firewall for the other four machines, which are confined with host-only adapters. The firewall VM operates on the host system's network as a node. Which of the following describe his firewall adapter configuration? (Choose all that apply.)

- **A.** Host-only
- **B.** Bridged
- **C.** NAT
- **D.** Multihomed
- **E.** Dual-homed

Chapter

30

Orchestrating the Environment

✓ **Objective 3.4: Summarize common infrastructure as code technologies**

Orchestration refers to the organization of a process that is balanced and coordinated and that achieves consistency in the results. In music, an orchestra conductor helps to organize the process that the musicians must traverse to produce beautiful music. The conductor analyzes the musical score (music recipe), determines the desired sound, and orchestrates the various individual musicians to reach the desired and consistent results.

Orchestration in the computing world has great similarities to a music orchestra, except instead of musicians, the process involves technologies. For example, a few IT processes that need orchestration are as follows:

- Application development
- Configuration management
- Disaster recovery
- Server monitoring
- Security

Notice in this list that many of these processes overlap. For example, security is an important item not just in server monitoring, but for the other list members as well. Thus, IT orchestration often involves multiple technology layers and tools. In this chapter, we'll take a look at the IT process orchestration subsets covered by the certification.

Understanding Orchestration Concepts

One particular IT orchestration process that is getting a lot of attention these days is DevOps. This method improves software delivery operations. DevOps includes the following components:

- Continuous integration
- Continuous testing
- Continuous delivery (or deployment)
- Infrastructure as code
- Infrastructure automation
- Monitoring and logging

The name *DevOps* comes from melding two job titles together. A software developer and a system administrator (also called *tech operations*) come together to work as a team in order to create a DevOps environment.

Probing Procedures

In DevOps, the idea is to quickly and continually provide new software features, bug fixes, and desired modifications to the customer. The focus is on continual small changes to the app as opposed to large, monolithic updates:

Continual App Processing   One DevOps layer involves software revision control (see Chapter 27, "Controlling Versions with Git") that quickly integrates app changes into the main software branch (*continuous integration*). In addition, these changes undergo automated testing to avoid breaking the app when the branch merges (*continuous testing*). With the help of the two previous components, software is delivered to the customer on a continual basis (*continuous delivery*).

Controlling the App Environment   To support this continuous app processing layer, it is critical in DevOps that the development and production environments match. This includes equivalent hardware, device drivers, operating system versions, software libraries, and so on. The requirement provides a software development environment that creates production code free from bugs and complications due to mismatched environments.

In addition, environment changes must be controlled and tested in a manner similar to how software revisions are orchestrated. For example, if a controlled update to the Linux kernel in the development environment introduces an unforeseen app bug, the environment can be rolled back to its previous version until the bug is addressed. Environment updates are typically done in small chunks, much like app revisions are handled, so that each environment modification can be properly and discretely managed. Tested new environments are added to a registry where older environments are also maintained in case a rollback to an earlier environment is needed.

Defining the App Environment   In DevOps, the development and production environments (infrastructure) have predefined specifications, such as what hardware to employ, the essential operating system, and any needed software packages as well as critical code libraries. The non-hardware specifications are typically implemented into the environment via automated code (*configuration management*).

Besides an environment's configuration, security measures, such as firewall ACLs (Chapter 18, "Overseeing Linux Firewalls") and authentication policies (Chapter 16, "Looking at Access and Authentication Methods"), must also be orchestrated. This too is implemented into the environment via automated code (*policy as code*).

Configuration management and policy as code fall under the umbrella term *infrastructure as code*. A benefit of using infrastructure as code is that the environments are repeatable. Also, they can be versioned, which is needed to implement revision control in the app environments for both policies and configuration. This DevOps component is covered more in depth later in this chapter.

Deploying the App Environment   The app and its development environment are often moved to a production status (production environment) in a continual manner. The "continual manner" can be hourly, daily, weekly, or whatever meets the app's business requirements.

The benefit of employing infrastructure as code techniques is that the process of deploying the app and its environment can be easily automated (*infrastructure automation*). Red Hat's Ansible product is one tool used for this DevOps deployment.

Monitoring the App Environment   When the app is operating in its production environment, it needs to be monitored and logged. Software metrics, infrastructure resource usage, and performance statistics are just a few of the items to monitor and log. The goal is to track the app environment and ensure that it is meeting predetermined conditions (environment health). Often this monitoring is automated as well.

As business needs change, the logged data can be valuable for future desired environment states. It provides threshold and performance measurements that make much easier decisions as to what app or environment infrastructure modifications are needed.

In addition, monitoring can provide alerts to potential failures or resource depletion events. If a particular preset limit is crossed, the monitoring software can issue an alert or even handle the event itself using predefined event rules.

Orchestration is the key to agile DevOps. Besides the methodology, various orchestration tools provide additional speed needed to succeed in the continual software delivery business setting.

Keep in mind that we are only covering a few DevOps concepts here. There are several other interesting DevOps topics, including microservices. For a deep dive into DevOps, consider *The DevOps Adoption Playbook* by Sanjeev Sharma (Wiley, 2017).

Analyzing Attributes

Virtualization, and more specifically containers (covered in Chapter 28, "Understanding Cloud and Virtualization Concepts"), greatly assist in the DevOps process. Containers in DevOps provide the following:

Static Environment   Containers provide a predetermined app environment (also called a *container image*) that does not change through time (immutable). The container is created with preset library and operating system versions and security settings. All these settings are recorded. No software updates (such as via a `sudo apt-get dist-upgrade` command) are issued within the image.

Version Control   After the software development process and prior to moving a modified app container image into production, the container and its recorded configuration are registered with a version control system. The version control system can contain previous app container images, including the one currently in production. Some companies use a manual version control system implemented with backups.

Replace Not Update   After registration, the app container is ready to move into production. Instead of the production app container image being updated to match the development image, the production container is stopped. The development app container image then replaces the production container and starts as the production environment. Thus, an environment switch occurs.

High Availability   *Replication* is the process of creating multiple copies of the production app container image and running them. This allows you to stop old currently unused production app containers and replace them with the new production app containers, which provides continual uptime for your app users. With containers and replication, the old method of shutting down your production environment to update it during a time period in the wee hours of the morning is gone.

To accomplish these tasks with container images, you need orchestration. Orchestration principles provide tools, utilities, and guidance for implementing app container images in a fast-paced environment, such as one that uses DevOps.

 Real World Scenario

Moving to DevOps and Orchestration

Marty is a tech ops lead. He is in charge of managing the systems that support his company's primary application, called Future.

Jennifer is lead programmer on the Future app. She and her team make desired enhancements and fix bugs in its software. When her team has completed its modifications and testing of the app, it is moved into production on Marty's systems.

Unfortunately, in this environment, problems ensue. Jennifer's development computers are not kept in sync with Marty's production systems as far as server, operating system versions, and libraries are concerned. This introduces additional bugs into the Future app code and causes lots of extra work for both Jennifer and Marty. In addition, customer-desired modifications are very slow to move into production. Marty and Jennifer tend to blame each other.

A coworker, Dr. Brown, has come back from DevOps training and proposes a radical (at least for them) way to shift their company's development and production process. He suggests the following:

1. The development team employs a container for their environment to create Future app changes.

2. The production application environment is also moved to a container, and its image is put into a registry for container version control.

3. The Future app production container is replicated, with each replication running to meet customer demand using a tool such as Kubernetes.

4. The development container's configuration and security policies are determined by Marty and Jennifer's team and recorded (infrastructure as code) in a tool, such as Puppet or SaltStack.

5. Instead of massive changes to the Future app, Jennifer's team will create small incremental changes to the code and use a version control system, such as Git.

6. These small software code changes are tested automatically via a tool, such as CircleCI or Jenkins.

7. The tested modifications are released on a weekly basis.

8. After the testing and development have been completed on the app development image, it is moved into the container registry for version control.

9. The current Future app production container images are stopped and the development containers take their places. This is done so that the Future app users experience no outages. If needed, Marty can roll back to the old production container image should problems arise.

10. On the production containers, the Future app is monitored and data logged to track performance and other metrics, using a tool such as Splunk. Performance events or container outages may automatically trigger the replication of additional production containers.

11. Jennifer and her development team create a new Future app development container image for more customer-requested modifications, and the process is started all over again.

The result of this DevOps implementation greatly reduces the Future app's software errors, increases the speed of desired customer modifications into production, and improves the communication between the tech ops and software development team. Overall, it is a win-win, as many companies are discovering today.

Provisioning the Data Center

When implemented correctly, container orchestration provides a way to increase the speed and agility of application deployment. Whether your company's data center is local or in the cloud, you can use orchestration concepts to quickly set up your app's required infrastructure. A few important infrastructure provisioning concepts are covered in the following sections.

Coding the Infrastructure

Much like a physical data center, a container infrastructure needs to be managed and controlled. In orchestration, the container's configuration is treated in a manner similar to how software revisions are treated:

Determine the infrastructure.   Along with the app requirements, the environment on which the app is executed must be preplanned. This activity is a mutual one between software development and tech ops. In this mutual activity, the container's operating system, libraries, services, security configuration, and any other supporting software or networking utilities are chosen.

The determined infrastructure is frozen to provide a nonchanging (immutable) environment for development and then production. Typically this app container infrastructure is only accessible via the app's or developer's API. Remote access services such as OpenSSH are not provided in order to protect its immutable environment.

Document the infrastructure.   The preset app container infrastructure is typically documented through an orchestration tool. The configuration management and policy as code settings (covered earlier in this chapter) are loaded into the utility's infrastructure as code portal, in a process called *automated configuration management.* The data is later used to deploy and replicate the app containers through *build automation.*

Provide revision control.   The infrastructure as code information is not just documented—it is also inserted into an orchestration tool registry, providing version control. Every time a change occurs in the container image infrastructure, its modifications are tracked.

Troubleshoot the infrastructure.   If an app container is deployed into production and problems occur, tech ops, software developers, or both handle the troubleshooting process. One item to check is the production container's documented configuration (as well as its revisions) to determine if any infrastructure items may be to blame.

This provides an easier method for tracking down that pesky new software library that caused all the problems. Various orchestration tools allow a quick determination of modified infrastructure components and quicker problem resolution.

Handling the application's infrastructure in this manner increases the agility of your app container deployment. It also improves the time to production speed. The basic life cycle of an orchestrated app container image is shown in Figure 30.1.

Notice that at the end of the container's life cycle (typically when the new app container image is ready), the container image is removed. However, the old app container image's configuration should be stored within a version control system (or backup storage) and thus redeployed if any problems occur with the new app container image.

FIGURE 30.1 Basic app container life cycle

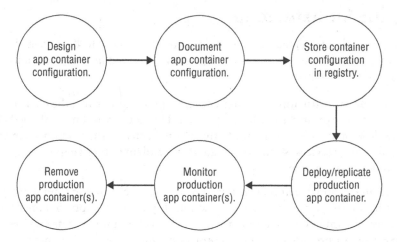

Automating the Infrastructure

With automated configuration management, not only can you troubleshoot the infrastructure more easily and roll the environment back to an earlier version, the deployment is automated. Often more than one app container is needed for both performance and balance loading. Your environment may require hundreds of running production app containers.

Manually configuring this infrastructure is tedious and certainly not fast or cost effective. With orchestration tools and automated configuration management, you can easily replicate the production app container and don't even have to be involved in the process (build automation). You simply let your orchestration tool know that you need X number of production app container images running at any one time.

Here are a few popular automation utilities in use today:

- **Ansible:** Owned by Red Hat, its main selling point is that remotely controlled servers don't need to run a separate agent software package. Ansible uses OpenSSH and Python to communicate using JSON-based protocols to remote servers. The configuration file is a standard text file, which can be stored in an encrypted vault.

- **Chef:** A Ruby-based package that uses Ruby-based "recipes" for defining server configurations; can run in either a client-server mode or a stand-alone mode.

- **Puppet:** Uses its own language to define system configurations for remote servers, thus requiring little to no programming knowledge to configure. It uses a client-server architecture, requiring remotely controlled servers to run a client application in the background. Currently is available in both commercial and open source versions.

- **SaltStack:** Owned by VMWare, this is a Python-based configuration management tool that stores server configuration data in a YAML data structures.

- **Terraform:** Owned by HashiCorp, this uses its own declarative language for storing server configurations, which you can define using the standard JSON data format. It has the ability to graph all resources, allowing operators to view infrastructure dependencies.

Comparing Agent and Agentless

Orchestration monitoring, logging, and reporting tools let you track app containers' health (how well they are performing, and if each one is still alive). Concerns over how these tools may adversely affect an app container's health gave rise to the agent versus agentless dispute.

Agent monitoring tools are orchestration utilities that require software (an agent) to be installed in the app container being monitored. These agents collect the data and transmit it to another location, such as a monitor server. The monitor server manages the information, provides analysis reporting, and also sends alerts for events, such as a container crashing.

Agentless monitoring tools are also orchestration utilities. In this case, an agent is not installed in the app container being monitored. Instead, the tool uses preexisting and/or embedded software in the container or the container's external environment to conduct its monitoring activity.

 Besides monitoring, logging, and reporting utilities, several high-level orchestration engines provide agentless orchestration too. One such example is Red Hat's Ansible.

Whether to use an agent-based or an agentless orchestration utility is hotly debated. Some people feel that an agent is detrimental to an app container's performance, whereas others see only minor effects. Some tech ops insist that agentless tools are inflexible; others believe installing and maintaining an agent in their containers is an unnecessary hassle. Whatever side you choose, realize that most companies use a combination of agent and agentless orchestration tools.

Investigating the Inventory

Orchestration monitoring utilities can automatically deal with an app container's untimely demise. When an app container shuts down, this triggers an event and the *desired state* is no longer met. A desired state is a predetermined setting that declares how many containers should be deployed and running.

For example, imagine that your software application needs to have 10 production app containers running to efficiently handle the workload. If one of those containers crashes, the container inventory now switches to 9. This triggers an event in the monitoring utility that the desired state is no longer being met.

Many orchestration utilities employ *self-healing*. With self-healing, if the desired state is not currently being achieved, the orchestration tool can automatically deploy additional production app containers. In the previous example, this means that the orchestration tool would immediately start up an additional production app container using the container's stored configuration settings (build automation). No human involvement is needed.

When a new production app container is first deployed, the self-healing orchestration property will cause containers to be deployed automatically until the desired state is met. That's handy.

Looking at Container Orchestration Engines

Orchestration of containers, whether the containers are on your local servers or in the cloud, requires various orchestration engines (also called *orchestration systems*). No one system can do it all. The best combination is a set of general and specialized orchestration tools.

Embracing Kubernetes

Originally designed and used by Google, Kubernetes is an open source orchestration system that is considered by many to be the de facto standard. Not only is Kubernetes very popular and free, it is also highly scalable, fault tolerant, and (relatively) easy to learn.

> NOTE   In some documentation, you will see the word *k8s* in reference to Kubernetes. The 8 replaces the "ubernete" portion of the Kubernetes name.

This system contains years of Google's orchestration experience, and because it is open source, additional community-desired features have been added. This is one reason so many companies have adopted its use for container orchestration.

Each Kubernetes managed service or application has the following primary components:

- **Cluster service:** Uses a YAML file to deploy and manage app pods
- **Pod:** Contains one or more running app containers
- **Worker:** Pod host system that uses a kubelet (agent) to communicate with cluster services
- **YAML file:** Contains a particular app container's automated configuration management and desired state settings

This distributed component configuration allows high scalability and great flexibility. It also works very well for continuous software delivery desired by companies employing the DevOps model.

Inspecting Docker Swarm

Docker, the popular app container management utility, created its own orchestration system, called Docker Swarm (also called *Swarm*). A group of Docker containers is referred to as a *cluster*, which appears to a user as a single container. To orchestrate a Docker cluster, you can employ Swarm.

With the Swarm system, you can monitor the cluster's health and return the cluster to the desired state should a container within the cluster fail. You can also deploy additional Docker containers if the desired app performance is not currently being met. Swarm is typically faster than Kubernetes when it comes to deploying additional containers.

Though not as popular as the Kubernetes orchestration system, Docker Swarm has its place. It is often used by those who are new to orchestration and already familiar with Docker tools.

Surveying Mesos

Apache Mesos is not a container orchestration system. Instead, Apache Mesos, created at the University of California, Berkeley, is a distributed systems kernel. It is similar to the Linux kernel, except that it operates at a higher construct level. One of its features is the ability to create containers. The bottom line is that Apache Mesos combined with another product, Marathon, does provide a type of container orchestration system framework. You could loosely compare Mesos with Marathon to Docker with Swarm.

Mesos with Marathon provides high availability and health monitoring integration and can support both Mesos and Docker containers. This orchestration framework has a solid history for large container deployment environments.

To find out more about Mesos with Marathon, don't use search engine terms like **Mesos orchestration**. Instead, go straight to the source at `https://mesosphere.github .io/marathon`.

Summary

Orchestration can involve processes in and out of the computing world, since many systems require harmonious, balanced, and coordinated procedures that achieve consistency in the results. DevOps is an IT method that benefits greatly from orchestration, including app container orchestration. The gains from these items allow such things as continuous delivery of software. Even outside of DevOps, app container orchestration is beneficial for many corporate environments.

Exam Essentials

Describe orchestration procedures.   An app container is first designed with a chosen operating system, libraries, and supporting software installed as security and authentication policies. After the image design is complete, it is documented and stored, typically in a version control registry. The app container is deployed and replicated as needed. At this point, the app container moves into the monitoring phase, where it continues until the container images are no longer needed.

Explain orchestrated app container attributes.   App container images are static (immutable) and do not change after they have been designed and documented. For a development app container, only the app is modified, not the infrastructure or policies. A container image is registered with a version control system to assist in troubleshooting as well as rollbacks, if needed. When a new app container image is ready, the old production container image is stopped, not updated. The new app container is started in its place. App containers can be replicated. Thus, if additional app containers are needed, the new image is replicated to meet the needs.

Summarize container monitoring.   Orchestration monitoring tools can have software installed on the app container (agent) or use already embedded or other preexisting container software (agentless). The monitoring utilities gather performance data and software metrics and watch the app containers' health. If the container inventory should drop below the desired state, the orchestration tool can use automated configuration management and build automation to replicate the number of containers to bring the app container inventory back to the desired state.

Review Questions

1. Which of the following can use orchestration? (Choose all that apply.)
    A. Software development
    B. Music production
    C. Server monitoring
    D. DevOps
    E. Containers

2. Connie, the tech ops lead, provides the development team with a development environment that currently matches the production environment. She insists that besides the app modifications, the environment should not change. What attribute should this development environment have to meet Connie's requirement?
    A. Self-replicating
    B. Immutable
    C. Kubernetes
    D. Infrastructure as code
    E. Self-healing

3. Bill, the software development team leader, understands Connie's (tech ops lead) desire for a static and matching development environment. However, since they are employing containers, Bill suggests a better improvement. Which of the following should he suggest?
    A. Modify the production container so that it matches the development container when the app is ready for production.
    B. Move the app from the development container to the production container when the app is ready for production.
    C. Stop any software updates on the development container from occurring before the app is ready for production.
    D. Replace the production container with the development container when the app is ready for production.
    E. Remove any updates on the development container that are not on the production container when the app is ready for production.

4. Which of the following orchestrated container attributes best provides high availability to an app user?
    A. Immutability
    B. Version control
    C. Replication
    D. Automation
    E. Documentation

5. In DevOps and container orchestration, non-hardware items such as the operating system and libraries and security policies are documented within the orchestration tool, implemented into the desired environment, and are called what?

   A. Marathon

   B. Build automation

   C. A development environment

   D. A container

   E. Infrastructure as code

6. Ms. Ward needs to move an app container into production. She employs an orchestration tool, which uses the predefined infrastructure as code to deploy and replicate the needed production container images. What orchestration concept did Ms. Ward use?

   A. Monitoring

   B. Build automation

   C. Replication

   D. Version control

   E. Docker Swarm

7. Which of the following is a benefit of automated configuration management in container orchestration? (Choose all that apply.)

   A. Containers can be deployed automatically.

   B. Containers can be replicated automatically.

   C. Troubleshooting infrastructure issues is easier.

   D. Continuous software delivery is enabled.

   E. Infrastructure modifications are tracked.

8. Mr. Abbot is recording requirements for the new orchestration tool. He needs the tool to automatically deploy and replicate any containers that have crashed. What is this called?

   A. Self-healing

   B. Build automation

   C. Continuous integration

   D. Infrastructure as code

   E. Pod builds

9. Which of the following are items that may be collected, used, or watched by an orchestration monitoring tool? (Choose all that apply.)

   A. Version control errors

   B. App container performance

   C. App metrics

   D. App container health

   E. Default states

10. Connie has picked an agentless orchestration monitoring utility for her app containers. Which of the following reasons might she have used in reaching this decision? (Choose all that apply.)

A. Connie wanted monitoring software installed on each app container.

B. She did not want monitoring software installed on each app container.

C. Connie was concerned about container performance being adversely affected by the monitoring software.

D. She was not concerned about container performance being adversely affected by the monitoring software.

E. Connie wanted to use what most companies use for orchestration monitoring.

Appendix

Answers to the Review Questions

Chapter 2: Introduction to Services

1. **B.** The Apache web server has gained popularity as being combined with the Linux OS, the MySQL database server, and the PHP programming server, making the LAMP stack. The nginX server is a newer web server that is gaining in popularity but is not part of the LAMP stack. The Lighthttpd web server has a small memory and CPU footprint, making it ideal for embedded systems but not for large-scale LAMP applications. The PostgreSQL package is a database server and not a web server.

2. **A.** A daemon is a single application that runs in background listening for client connection requests, so option A is the correct answer. A super-server listens for more than one application, so option B doesn't apply. The shell doesn't listen for network connections; it launches applications interactively, so option C is incorrect. The graphical desktop also allows you to launch applications, but it doesn't listen for client connection requests, so option D is incorrect.

3. **C.** When first released, the MySQL database server focused on speed, making it a popular choice for high-volume Internet web applications, so option C is correct. The MongoDB database server provides object-oriented database features but doesn't focus on performance, so option A is incorrect. The PostgreSQL database focused on implementing fancy database features instead of speed, so option B is incorrect. NoSQL is a database storage method that incorporates object-oriented data records and is not a database server package itself, so option D is incorrect.

4. **B.** Linux services listen on well-known ports for requests from clients, so option B is correct. A server normally has a single IP address to support multiple applications, so option A is incorrect. The server also normally has only a single Ethernet address, so option C is incorrect. The clients can't launch individual services on the server, so option D is incorrect.

5. **A.** The nginX web server can serve as a load balancer and send client requests to multiple backend web servers, so option A is correct. The Apache and lighthttpd web servers don't support this feature, so options B and D are incorrect. The PostgreSQL server is a database and not a web server, so option C is incorrect.

6. **C.** The MongoDB database server uses the JSON format for storing data records. The relational database is a type of database system and not a method for storing data, so option A is incorrect. YaML is a plaintext method for creating configuration files, but it is not used in MongoDB for storing data, so option B is incorrect. The MongoDB data is not normally encrypted, so option D is also incorrect.

7. **B.** The MTA package is responsible for connecting with remote mail hosts to deliver email messages, so option B is correct. The MUA allows clients to connect to the email server to read their messages, so option A is incorrect. The MDA allows you to create rules for processing mail locally, not to remote servers, so option C is incorrect. Evolution is an email MUA client application, not a server MTA package. The Evolution package is a graphical email client, so option D is incorrect.

8. C. The MDA allows you to create filters to match email messages to redirect to other folders, so option C is correct. The MUA is the user interface and doesn't control how incoming mail is delivered by the server, so option A is incorrect. The MTA delivers email to remote hosts and accepts mail from remote hosts, so option B is incorrect. The Evolution package is a graphical MUA package for clients and does not allow you to create filters to deliver email messages, so option D is incorrect.

9. D. The NFS protocol is used to share folder areas on the network with clients, so option D is correct. SNMP is a network protocol used for managing remote devices, so option A is incorrect. NTP is a network protocol used for setting the time on servers, so option B is incorrect. DHCP is a network program used for assigning IP addresses to network devices, so option C is incorrect.

10. B. The Samba software package allows a Linux server to communicate with Windows servers and clients using the SMB protocol, so option B is correct. The ntpd daemon listens for requests from a remote time server, so option A is incorrect. The DHCPd package provides DHCP services on the Linux server to assign network IP addresses; it doesn't allow workstations to map folders on the Linux server, so option C is incorrect. The Evolution package is a graphical desktop program used to access email in the mail folder and is not a server service, so option D is incorrect.

11. A, B. The rsyslogd program is used by SysV init systems to log events, and the journald program is used by Systemd systems to log events, so options A and B are the correct answers. The ntpd program provides time services and not logging services, so option C is incorrect. The DHCPd program is used for assigning IP addresses on a local network and not for logging services, so option D is incorrect.

12. C. The ntpd service uses NTP to synchronize the server time with a remote system, so option C is correct. The DHCPd program assigns IP addresses to devices on the local network but not time, so option A is incorrect. The BIND program provides hostname resolution services but not time services, so option B is incorrect. The Samba package allows a Linux server to interact with Windows clients and servers, but it doesn't provide time services, so option D is incorrect.

13. D. The CUPS application provides printer drivers and services that allow Linux systems to connect with local and remote printers, so option D is correct. The DHCPd program assigns IP addresses to devices on the local network but doesn't connect to remote printers, so option A is incorrect. The BIND application provides hostname resolution services but can't connect to printers, so option B is incorrect. The ntpd program allows you to synchronize the server time with a remote time clock but doesn't connect to network printers, so option C is incorrect.

14. B. The named program is part of the BIND application, which provides hostname resolution services, so option B is correct. The ntpd program is what provides network time, so option A is incorrect. The DHCPd program provides dynamic IP address allocation on a local network, so option C is incorrect. The CUPS application provides printing services on a Linux system, so option D is incorrect.

15. C. The NIS package was formerly called Yellow Pages (YP), but the name had to be changed due to trademark issues, so option C is correct. The Samba package, which provides Windows client and server services in Linux, refers to a popular Latin dance, not the Yellow Pages, so option A is incorrect. The Kerberos package, which does provide authentication services in Linux, refers to the three-headed hound that guards Hades, not the Yellow Pages, so option B is incorrect. The BIND application refers to binding a name to an IP address, which is a similar function to the Yellow Pages, but it wasn't formerly called Yellow Pages, so option D is incorrect.

16. A. The DHCPd program provides DHCP server services on a local network, so option A is correct. The BIND package provides hostname resolution services; it doesn't assign IP addresses, so option B is incorrect. The ntpd package provides network time services but not address services, so option C is incorrect. Evolution is a client MUA package for reading email; it doesn't provide IP addresses to clients, so option D is incorrect.

17. C. The OpenSSH package allows you to use certificates to establish a secure connection between two devices on the network, so option C is correct. The BIND package provides hostname resolution, not secure connections, so option A is incorrect. The ntpd package provides time services on the network, not secure connections, so option B is incorrect. The OpenSSL package allows you to create certificates used for encrypted communication but doesn't perform the communication itself, so option D is incorrect.

18. C. A web proxy server allows you to intercept client web requests and block any requests based on rules you define, so option C is correct. A DHCP server assigns IP addresses to devices on the local network; it doesn't intercept web requests, so option A is incorrect. A web server hosts websites but doesn't intercept requests made by local clients, so option B is incorrect. A container allows developers to easily deploy web applications in different environments but doesn't intercept web requests from local clients, so option D is incorrect.

19. A. A load balancer sends client requests to one server within a cluster of servers to balance traffic among the servers, so option A is correct. A web proxy server intercepts web requests from clients but can only filter or pass the request to the destination host, so option B is incorrect. A DHCP server assigns IP addresses to devices on a local network but doesn't help increase performance of network applications, so option C is incorrect. A container allows a developer to easily deploy web applications to different environments but can't control what traffic goes to which server, so option D is incorrect.

20. C. A container allows developers to develop applications in a controlled environment that can easily be deployed to other servers, so option C is correct. A web proxy intercepts web requests from clients but doesn't control how applications are deployed, so option A is incorrect. A DHCP server assigns IP addresses to devices on the local network but doesn't control how applications are deployed, so option B is incorrect. A cluster can help with application performance by spreading the load among multiple servers but doesn't control how developers deploy the application to the servers, so option D is incorrect.

Chapter 3: Managing Files, Directories, and Text

1. C. Option C will append an indicator code of / to every directory name, so therefore it is the best choice. The mkdir -v command creates a directory and lets you know whether or not it was successful, but it does not indicate directories, so option A is a wrong answer. The ls command only displays file and directory names, so option B is also a wrong answer. The ls -i command will display filenames along with their inode number, but it does not indicate directories, so option D is incorrect. While option E will work on some distributions to produce a long listing that can indicate directories, this command is not aliased to ls -l on every distribution, so therefore it is not the best command to use.

2. B. The -d switch on the ls command will allow you to view a directory file's metadata instead of seeing metadata for the files managed by that directory. Therefore, option B is the correct choice. Option A is a wrong answer because the -a switch forces the ls command to display hidden files, which are files starting with a dot (.). The -F switch will append an indicator code to each file but not allow you to view a directory's metadata, so option C is a wrong choice. The -l option is already being employed because you are viewing metadata, so it does not need to be added. Therefore, option D is an incorrect answer. The -R switch allows you to view file information recursively through a directory tree, and thus option E is also a wrong choice.

3. A. The mkdir -v command creates a directory and lets you know whether or not it was successful, so option A is the correct answer. The touch command creates blank and empty files, so option B is incorrect. The cp -R command will recursively copy an entire directory full of files to another directory. Since you do not know if the directory TheDir is empty or not, you most likely did not use this command, so option C is a wrong answer. The mv -r command will rename a directory to a new directory name. Again, you do not know if the directory TheDir is empty or not, so you most likely did not use this command, and thus, option D is also a wrong answer. Option E is an incorrect answer because the rmdir command deletes empty directories.

4. E. The rsync utility allows you to perform fast local copies, so for a big file it is the best utility to use in this case. Therefore, option E is the correct answer. The readlink -f command finds the file being pointed to via a series of soft links, so option A is an incorrect answer. The mv command will rename a file instead of creating a backup copy, so option B is incorrect. The cp command does create a file copy. However, it is not as fast as the rsync utility and therefore is not the best choice, making option C a wrong answer. The scp command also creates a file copy; however, it also is not as fast as the rsync utility and therefore is not the best choice, making option D a wrong answer.

5. E. The rm -rI command will recursively delete the files in the /home/Zoe directory tree, and it will ask before it starts, so you know you are deleting the correct tree. Therefore, option E is the best answer. Option A is incorrect because the cp command simply copies

files; it does not remove them. Option B is incorrect because not only is part of the directory name using the wrong case, but there is no verification the correct directory is being moved to the black hole device, /dev/null/. The rm -Rf command would work, but it is not the best command to use because it does not ask before it starts, so you do not know if you are deleting the correct tree. In fact, the -f option suppresses error messages, so option C is wrong. Option D would also work, but it is not the best answer because it employs the -i option. If Zoe has years of files in her home directory, you may be sitting there for a long time deleting files due to the fact that you must confirm each file before it is deleted. Therefore, option D is an incorrect answer.

6. B, C, E. When renaming a directory, you only need to employ the mv command. However, it is wise to use the -i option, so if the new directory name already exists, the utility will stop and ask permission prior to proceeding. Even better is to use the -n option; that way, if the new name you select is already being used, the mv command does not allow you to overwrite it. Also, the -v option is worthwhile, so the mv command operates in verbose mode, telling you what is going on. Therefore, options B, C, and E are all correct choices. The -f option is not a wise choice because it forces the directory's renaming, even if a directory already exists that has that name. Therefore, option A is a wrong answer. Also, there is no -r switch, because renaming a directory using the mv command does not require any recursive action. Thus, option D is an incorrect choice.

7. B. Option B is the correct answer because the hard links will prevent the three other command-line interface users from accidentally deleting the data. If they delete their link's name, they will not delete the data. Option A is an incorrect choice because hard-linked files must reside on the same filesystem together. Option C is also an incorrect choice because if you do not provide the symbolic links to the other three data users, they will have to access the data file directly and could delete it. While creating symbolic links will protect the data by letting it reside on a different filesystem, if it is mission-critical data, the filesystem employed should be rigorous enough to protect the data, and therefore your only threat would be human. Thus, option D is an incorrect answer. Symbolic linked files do not share an inode number. Therefore, option E is an incorrect choice.

8. A. The cat -v command will show any nonprinting characters that may have gotten embedded in the control file causing it to be corrupted, and therefore option A is the correct answer. The -z option only lets you see end-of-line characters if they are NULL, and thus, option B is a wrong choice. The -n option only numbers the text lines in output, so option C is also a wrong answer. The cat -s command will display multiple blank lines in the file as one blank line. This will not help in the investigation, so option D is an incorrect answer. The -E option displays a $ whenever a newline linefeed is encountered, and while possibly helpful, it is not the best option to use in this case. Therefore, option E is a wrong answer.

9. D. Option D is the correct answer because the best command to use is the pr -mtl 20 command. This will display the files side by side, remove any file headers or trailers, and set the page length to 20 lines so the files do not scroll off your screen. Of course, you may need to adjust the line length depending on your screen's resolution. Option A is incorrect because, while it will display the files side by side, the display may scroll off your screen. Option B is also incorrect, because the command will not display your files side by side. Option C is a wrong answer choice because the cat command will not display the files side by side.

Option E's command may work for you, but it is not the best choice because file headers or trailers will not be removed. Therefore, option E is an incorrect answer.

10. C. The head command can use either the -n 15 switch or the -15 switch to display a file's first 15 lines. Therefore, option C is the correct answer. To display all but the last 15 lines of the file, you would need to employ the -n -15 switch, so option A is incorrect. To display all but the first 15 lines, you need to use the tail command instead of the head command, so option B is a wrong answer. Also, you need to use tail to display the last 15 lines of the file, so option D is also an incorrect answer. Option E is a wrong choice because the command will not generate an error message in this case.

11. E. It is possible that the account name Hal is listed in the generated text file as hal. Therefore, your best next step is to employ the -i option on the grep command. This will quickly search the text file for the word Hal while ignoring case. Thus, option E is the correct answer. Option A is a wrong choice because the tail command will not allow you to search the file. Option B is also an incorrect answer, because the cat command will just display the entire text file to the screen and is not an efficient method for finding a few text lines. While you may end up having to regenerate the text file, prior to doing so you should check for Hal, ignoring case. If you find the records, then you have saved yourself some time. Thus, option C is also a wrong choice. Finally, the -d skip option on the grep command allows the search to skip any directory files. This option is useless in this situation, and therefore option D is an incorrect answer.

12. B. A pager utility allows you to view one text page at a time and move through the text at your own pace. Therefore, option B is the correct answer. A utility that only allows you to view the first few lines of a file would not be useful in this case, and these utilities are not called pagers. Therefore, option A is a wrong answer. While the less utility is a pager and will allow you to search through the text file, the coworker mentioned pagers, which includes the more utility. With the more utility you cannot search through text, so option C is an incorrect choice. You do not need to filter out text in the file, and filter utilities are not called pagers, so option D is a wrong answer. A utility that only allows you to view the last few lines of a file would not be useful in this case, and these utilities are not called pagers. Therefore, option E is an incorrect choice.

13. E. You need to use the q key to exit from the less pager utility; therefore, only option E does not describe less and is the correct answer. Option A is a wrong answer because less does not read the entire file prior to displaying the file's first page. You can also employ the up and down arrow keys to traverse the file as well as the spacebar to move forward a page and the Esc+V key combination to move backward a page, so options B, C, and D are incorrect answers.

14. B. The -q (or --brief) option used with the diff command will allow you to quickly determine if two text files are different from each other. Thus, option B is the correct answer. The -e switch allows you to create an ed script to use later on, so option A is an incorrect choice. The -s option does allow you to see if the files are the same and shows a simple message stating this fact. However, it is focused on file differences, so it is not the best switch to use. Therefore, option C is also a wrong answer. The diff command's -W option allows you to set a display width, and thus, option D is an incorrect choice. The -y switch displays the two files in two columns, so option E is also a wrong selection.

15. C. Option C is the correct answer because the `which` command will allow you to quickly see the location of the program you provide as an argument. If you see no response, you can go on to the next troubleshooting step of determining if the program is not installed. Option A is not correct because these actions will simply recall the original `diff` command and try it again. Logging out and then back in again may reset some variables you accidentally created, but it is not a good first step in this troubleshooting process. Therefore, option B is a wrong answer. Entering the `whereis diff` command will provide additional information concerning the `diff` command, such as program location and source code file locations as well as man page locations. This additional information is not needed, so option D is an incorrect choice. Rebooting a server just because a command does not work is not a good first troubleshooting step. Therefore, option E is also a wrong answer.

16. E. By default, the `locate` command uses file globbing, which adds wildcards to the pattern you enter. Thus, `conf` is turned into `*conf*`. Therefore, option E best explains the results and is the correct answer. The `locate` command will search for both file and directory names for specified patterns unless options are provided to modify this behavior. Therefore, option A is an incorrect answer. The `locate` command does not use the `-d skip` switch (the `grep` command does use it, though), and thus, option B is a wrong answer. Because the command operated normally, there is not a problem with the `locate` database, so option C is an incorrect choice. Also, a regular expression switch was not used in the `locate` command, so option D is also a wrong choice.

17. A. The `locate` utility searches the `mlocate.db` database, which is typically only updated one time per day via a `cron` job. Therefore, for this newly created file, the first thing you should do is update `mlocate.db` via the `updatedb` command, using super user privileges. Thus, option A is the correct answer. After you have updated the database, any of the commands in option B, C, or E should work fairly well, with option B's command being the best choice. However, for the first step, options B, C, and E are wrong answers. Downloading the file again is tedious and time-consuming and can possibly consume disk space unnecessarily. Therefore, option D is an incorrect choice.

18. D. When using the `locate` command, the *path* argument is listed first, which is a starting point directory. The `find` utility will search through that directory and all its subdirectories (recursively) for the file or files you seek. Also, the `-name` switch allows you to search for a file by name, so option D is the correct answer. Option A is incorrect because there is no `-r` switch, and no need for one. Option B is not the best command to use in this case because the starting directory is `/`, which is the root of the virtual directory structure. It is much better to start at the `/etc` directory, since the file is most likely located somewhere in that directory tree. Using the `-maxdepth` switch may hamper the search because it sets the subdirectory level to stop the search. Therefore, option C is a wrong answer. Option E is an incorrect choice, because the *path* and filename are flip-flopped and the `-name` switch is missing.

19. E. The `find / -nouser` command will search through the entire virtual directory structure looking for any files that do not have a username associated with them. Since Michael's account and home directory were deleted, any files he owned out in the virtual directory structure will not have a username associated with them, only a user ID (UID). Thus, option E is the best answer. Option A is incorrect because the `-name` switch is for file names, not usernames. Option B is also an incorrect answer, because the `-user` switch is used to search for files owned by a particular account. Since Michael's account was deleted, his username would no longer be associated with any files. Option C is a wrong answer because you do not know when his files may have experienced data changes, as indicated by the `-mmin` switch, and thus this is a bad method for trying to identify them. Option D is an incorrect choice because the `find` command is starting the search process in the user's home directory instead of the root (`/`) of the virtual directory structure.

20. C. The `grep` utility will allow you to search file contents quickly and effectively. Therefore, option C is the correct answer. The `which` utility can help you locate a program's location by its name, but it does not search its contents, so option A is an incorrect choice. The `whereis` command will search for a file's program location, source code files, and man pages, but it cannot search a file's contents, so option B is also a wrong choice. The `locate` utility will search for a file's location using its name, but it cannot search a file's contents, so option D is an incorrect answer. The `find` command can find files using a file's metadata, but it does not search inside a file, so option E is a wrong choice.

Chapter 4: Searching and Analyzing Text

1. C. A text file record is considered to be a single file line that ends in a newline linefeed that is the ASCII character LF. You can see if your text file uses this end-of-line character by issuing the `cat -E` command. Therefore, option C is the correct answer. The text file may have been corrupted, but this command does not indicate it, so option A is an incorrect choice. The text file records end in the ASCII character LF and not NUL or $. Therefore, options B and D are incorrect. The text file records may very well contain a $ at their end, but you cannot tell by the situation description, so option E is a wrong answer.

2. E. To properly use some of the `cut` command options, fields must exist within each text file record. These fields are data that is separated by a delimiter, which is one or more characters that create a boundary between different data items within a record. Therefore, option E best describes a delimiter and is the correct answer. Option A is made up and is a wrong answer. Option B describes an end-of-line character, such as the ASCII LF. Option C is made up and is a wrong answer. While a single space and a colon can be used as a delimiter, option D is not the best answer and is therefore a wrong choice.

3. C, D. Recall that many utilities that process text do not change the text within a file unless redirection is employed to do so. The only utilities in this list that will allow you to modify text are the text editors `vim` and `nano`. Therefore, options C and D are the correct answers. The `cut`, `sort`, and `sed` utilities gather the data from a designated text file(s), modify it according to the options used, and display the modified text to standard output. The text in the file is not modified. Therefore, options A, B, and E are incorrect choices.

4. A. The `cut` command gathers data from the text file, listed as its last argument, and displays it according to the options used. To define field delimiters as a comma and display each data center monitor's monitor ID, serial number, and location, the options to use are `-d "," -f 1,3,4`. Also, since the text file's records end with an ASCII LF character, no special options, such as the `-z` option, are needed to process these records. Therefore, option A is

the correct choice. Option B uses the unneeded -z option and is therefore a wrong answer. Option C is an incorrect choice because it reverses the -f and -d options. Options D and E are wrong answers because they put the filename before the command switches.

5. D. Option D is the best answer because a regular expression is a pattern template you define for a utility, such as grep, which uses the pattern to filter text. While you may use a series of characters in a grep *PATTERN*, they are not called regular expressions, so option A is a wrong answer. Option B is describing end-of-line characters, and not regular expression characters, so it also is an incorrect answer. While the ? is used in basic regular expressions, the * is not (however, .* is used). Therefore, option C is a wrong choice. Quotation marks may be employed around a *PATTERN*, but they are not considered regular expression characters, and therefore option E is an incorrect answer.

6. B. Option B is the best command because this grep command employs the correct syntax. It uses the quotation marks around the *pattern* to avoid unexpected results and uses the .* regular expression characters to indicate that anything can be between May 30 and the IPv4 address. No additional switches are necessary. Option A is not the best grep command because it uses the wrong regular expression of ?, which only allows one character to exist between May 30 and the IPv4 address. Options C and D are not the best grep commands because they employ the -i switch to ignore case, which is not needed in this case. The grep command in option E is an incorrect choice, because it uses the -v switch, which will display text records that do not match the *PATTERN*.

7. A, B, C, E. A BRE is a basic regular expression that describes certain patterns you can use with the grep command. An ERE is an extended regular expression and it requires the use of grep -e or the egrep command. Options A, B, C, and E are all BRE patterns that can be used with the grep command, so they are correct choices. The only ERE is in option D, and therefore, it is an incorrect choice.

8. E. To meet the search requirements, option E is the ERE to use with the egrep command. Therefore, option E is the correct answer. Option A will return either a record that ends with Luke or a record that ends with Laura. Thus, option A is the wrong answer. Option B is an incorrect choice because it will return either a record that begins with Luke or a record that begins with Laura and has one character between Laura and the Father is phrase. Option C has the Luke and Laura portion of the ERE correct, but it only allows one character between the names and the Father is phrase, which will not meet the search requirements. Thus, option C is a wrong choice. Option D will try to return either a record that ends with Luke or a record that ends with Laura and contains the Father is phrase, so the egrep command will display nothing. Thus, option D is an incorrect choice.

9. A, B. To sort the data.txt file numerically and save its output to the new file, newdata .txt, you can either use the -o switch to save the file or employ standard output redirection with the > symbol. In both cases, however, you need to use the -n switch to properly enact a numerical sort. Therefore, both options A and B are correct. Option C is a wrong answer because the command has the newdata.txt and data.txt flipped in the command's syntax. Options D and E do not employ the -n switch, so they are incorrect answers as well.

10. C, E. The commands in both options C and E will display the data.txt and datatoo .txt files' content one after the other to STDOUT. The cat -n command will also append line numbers to it, but it will still concatenate the files' content to standard output. Therefore, options C and E are correct. Option A will just display the files' names to STDOUT, so it is a wrong answer. Option B will numerically sort the data.txt, wipe out the datatoo .txt file's contents, and replace it with the numerically sorted contents from the data.txt file. Therefore, option B is an incorrect answer. Option D will show the two files' metadata to STDOUT instead of their contents, so it also is a wrong choice.

11. C. The pr command's primary purpose in life is to specially format a text file for printing, and it can accomplish the required task fairly quickly. Therefore, option C is the best choice. While the pr utility can handle formatting entire text files, the printf command is geared toward formatting the output of a single text line. While you could write a shell script to read and format each text file's line via the printf command, it would not be the quickest method to employ. Therefore, option A is a wrong answer. Option B's wc command will perform counts on a text file and does not format text file contents, so it is also an incorrect answer. The paste command will "sloppily" put together two or more text files side by side. Thus, option D is a wrong answer. Option E is an incorrect choice because the nano text editor would force you to manually format the text file, which is not the desired action.

12. E. The printf FORMAT "%.2f\n" will produce the desired result of 42.78, and therefore option E is the correct answer. The FORMAT in option A will simply output 42.777, so it is an incorrect choice. The FORMAT in option B will output 42 and therefore is a wrong answer. The printf FORMAT setting in option C will produce an error, and therefore, it is an incorrect choice. Option D's printf FORMAT "%.2c\n" will display 42 and thus is also an incorrect answer.

13. A, C. The first item output by the wc utility is the number of lines within a designated text file. Therefore, option A is correct. Option C is also correct, because the second item output by the wc utility is the number of words within a designated text file. Option B is a wrong answer because the file contains 2,020 lines and not characters. Option D is an incorrect choice because you do not know whether or not the Unicode subset of ASCII is used for the text file's encoding. You should always assume the last number is the number of bytes within the file. Use the -m or --chars switch on the wc command to get a character count. Therefore, the file could have 11,328 bytes in it instead of characters. Option E is also a wrong choice because the file has 2,020 lines in it.

14. B. A file descriptor is a number that represents a process's open files. Therefore, option B is the correct answer. A file type code is a letter that represents the file's type, displayed as the first item in the ls -l output line. Therefore, option A is a wrong answer. Option C is also wrong, because it is a made-up answer. Option D is incorrect because it describes only STDOUT, which has a file descriptor number of 1 and is only one of several file descriptors. A file indicator code is a symbol that indicates the file's classification, and it is generated by the ls -F command. Therefore, option E is also a wrong choice.

15. D. By default, STDOUT goes to your current terminal, which is represented by the /dev/ tty file. Therefore, option D is the correct answer. The /dev/ttyn file, such as /dev/ tty2, may be your current terminal at a particular point in time, but /dev/tty always represents your current terminal, so option A is a wrong answer. Option C is incorrect because it

is the symbol used at the command line to redirect STDOUT away from its default behavior. The pwd command displays your present working directory, so option E is a wrong choice.

16. A. The command in option A will display the SpaceOpera.txt file to output as well as save a copy of it to the SciFi.txt file. Therefore, option A is the correct answer. Option B is a wrong answer because it will only put a copy of SpaceOpera.txt into the SciFi .txt file. Option C is an incorrect choice because this will display the SpaceOpera.txt file to output and put any error messages into the SciFi.txt file. The cp command will only copy one text file to another. It will not display the original file to output, so option D is a wrong answer. Option E is a wrong choice because it will put a copy of SpaceOpera.txt into the SciFi.txt file and include any error messages that are generated.

17. D. The /dev/null file is also called the black hole, because anything you put into it cannot be retrieved. If you do not wish to see any error messages while issuing a command, you can redirect STDERR into it. Thus, option D is the correct answer. Options A, B, and C are wrong answers because they perform redirection to a file called BlackHole instead of /dev/null. Option E is also incorrect, because it redirects STDOUT to the /dev/null file, and any error messages will be displayed.

18. C. To find records within the Problems.txt file that contain the word error at least one time, the grep command is employed. The correct syntax is grep error Problems.txt. To count the records, the grep command's STDOUT is piped as STDIN into the wc utility. The correct syntax to count the records is wc -l. Therefore, option C is the correct answer. The command in option A is incorrect because its wc command is counting the number of bytes within each input record. Option B is a wrong answer, because its wc command is counting the number of words within each input record. The command in option D has two problems. First, its grep command syntax has the item for which to search and the file to search backward. Also, its wc command is counting the number of words within each input record. Therefore, option D is a wrong choice. Option E is an incorrect answer because its grep command syntax has the item for which to search and the file to search backward.

19. B, C, E. The xargs command, $() method, backticks (`), and brace expansion all allow you to build a command-line command on the fly. In this case, only options B, C, and E are using the correct command syntax to find any file named 42.tmp, which exists somewhere in your current directory's tree structure and display its contents to STDOUT. Therefore, options B, C, and E are correct answers. Option A is using the wrong syntax for the xargs command, and this command will generate an error message. Therefore, option A is a wrong answer. Option D is using the wrong syntax for brace expansion, and thus, it is an incorrect choice as well.

20. A, C, D, E. The three modes of the vim editor are command (also called normal mode), insert (also called edit or entry mode), and ex (sometimes called colon commands) mode. Therefore, options A, C, D, and E are correct answers. The only incorrect choice for this question is option B.

Chapter 5: Explaining the Boot Process

1. A. The workstation firmware looks for the bootloader program to load an operating system. The `fsck` program (option B) is used to check and repair damage to hard drives, so it isn't useful until after the Linux system has started. The Windows operating system only starts after a Windows bootloader program can run, so option C is incorrect. The `mount` program is a Linux tool for attaching a partition to the virtual directory, which isn't available until after the Linux system starts, so option D is also incorrect. The `mkinitrd` program is used to create an initrd RAM disk used for booting, but it isn't run when the workstation starts up, so option E is incorrect.

2. B. The workstation firmware looks at the first sector of the first hard drive to load the bootloader program. This is called the Master Boot Record, so option A is correct. The bootloader program itself can use the chainloader feature to look for another bootloader in a boot partition, but the firmware can't do that, so option D is incorrect. Option A specifies the configuration folder used to store the GRUB configuration file and the kernel image file, but the actual GRUB bootloader program can't be stored there. Option C specifies the common log file folder, but that doesn't contain the GRUB bootloader program. Option E also specifies a common Linux configuration file directory, but it's not used to store the GRUB bootloader program that the firmware can access.

3. D. The kernel ring buffer, which you can view by typing **dmesg**, contains messages from the boot messages from the kernel; thus, option D is correct. The `fsck` program (option A) fixes corrupted partitions, and the `mount` program (option C) is used to attach partitions to the virtual directory, so neither of those is correct. Option B, the `init` program, is used to start programs from the kernel, not display boot messages, so it also is incorrect. Option E, the `mkinitrd` program, is used to create a new initrd RAM disk and is not related to the boot messages, so it too is incorrect.

4. C. Most Linux distributions store boot log files in the `/var/log` folder. The `/etc` folder is most often used for storing system and application configuration files, not boot logs, so option A is incorrect. Some Unix systems use the `/var/messages` folder for storing log files, but Linux has not adopted this standard, so option B is also incorrect. The `/boot` folder contains the GRUB configuration files along with the image files necessary to boot the system, but it's not where Linux stores boot logs and is thus incorrect. The `/proc` folder is unique in that the Linux kernel dynamically stores information about the system there, but it doesn't store boot log information there.

5. A, B, C, D, E. The BIOS firmware can look in multiple locations for a bootloader program. Most commonly it looks at the internal hard drive installed on the system; however, if none is found, it can search other places. Most workstations allow you to boot from an external hard drive or from a DVD drive. Modern workstations now also provide the option to boot from a USB memory stick inserted into a USB port on the workstation. Finally, many workstations provide the PXE boot option, which allows the workstation to boot remotely from a network server.

6. A. The Master Boot Record (MBR) is only located in one place: on the first sector of the first hard drive on the workstation; thus, option A is the only correct answer. The boot partition in any hard drive may contain a bootloader, but it is not the Master Boot Record, which is run first by the firmware; thus, option B is incorrect. The other locations are not valid locations for the Master Boot Record, so options C, D, and E are all incorrect.

7. D. The ESP is stored in the `/boot/efi` directory on Linux systems. The UEFI firmware always looks for the `/boot/efi` directory for bootloader programs, so option D is correct. The `/etc` directory is used to store application and system configuration files, not bootloader programs, so option B is incorrect. The `/var` folder is used to store variable files such as log files, not bootable files, so option C is incorrect. Option E, the `/boot/grub` file, is used in GRUB Legacy and GRUB2 to store the bootloader configuration files, as well as the kernel image files. However, it is not used to store the bootloader files themselves, so option E is incorrect.

8. E. The UEFI specification doesn't require a specific extension for UEFI bootloader files, but it has become somewhat common in Linux to use the `.efi` file extension to identify them; thus, option E is correct. Option A and option D specify file extensions used to identify GRUB2 (option A) and GRUB Legacy (option D) configuration files, not UEFI bootloader files, so they are both incorrect. Option C specifies the `.lst` file extension, which is also used for GRUB Legacy configuration files, so it too is incorrect. The `.uefi` file extension is not used in Linux, so option B is incorrect.

9. B. The Linux Loader (LILO) bootloader program was the first bootloader used in Linux, so option B is correct. The GRUB Legacy bootloader, despite its name, wasn't the first bootloader, but the second bootloader commonly used in Linux. The GRUB2 bootloader was a later improvement over the GRUB Legacy bootloader, so options A and C are incorrect. Option D, the SYSLINUX bootloader, provides features for use with Microsoft FAT partitions, so that you can boot Linux from a floppy drive or USB memory stick, but it is a later creation and not the first Linux bootloader. Option E, ISOLINUX, is also a later bootloader that allows us to boot Linux from a CD or DVD drive.

10. A. The GRUB Legacy configuration files are stored in the `/boot/grub` directory, so option A is correct. Option B, the `/boot/efi` directory, is used to store UEFI bootloader programs, not GRUB configuration files, so it is incorrect. Option C, the `/etc` directory, stores many application and system configuration files, but not the GRUB Legacy configuration files. The `/var` directory stores variable files such as log files but not configuration files, so option D is incorrect. Likewise, Linux uses the `/proc` directory to provide dynamic kernel runtime data and not configuration files.

11. B, C. The GRUB2 bootloader stores configuration files in both the `/boot/grub` directory and the `/etc/grub.d` directory, so options B and C are correct. Linux uses the `/proc` directory to provide dynamic kernel runtime data and not configuration files, so option A is incorrect. Option D, `/boot/efi`, stores UEFI bootloader program files, not GRUB2 configuration files, so it is also incorrect. Option E, `/var`, is used to store variable files, such as log files, and not configuration files, so it is incorrect.

12. C. The `grub-mkconfig` command combines the configurations defined in the `/etc/default/grub` file and all of the files in the `/etc/grub.d` folder into a single grub `.cfg` configuration file. The `mkinitrd` command (option A) is used to create a new initrd RAM disk image file, so it is incorrect. Likewise, the `mkinitramfs` command (option B) is also used to create initrd image files on Debian systems, so it too is incorrect. The `grub-install` program is used by the GRUB Legacy bootloader to install the bootloader in the MBR or a boot partition, but isn't used to generate the GRUB2 configuration files, and is thus incorrect. Option E is the `fsck` program, which checks and repairs hard drive partitions, and is an incorrect answer for this question.

13. D. The `grub-install` command installs any configuration changes into the GRUB MBR, so option D is correct. The `mkinitrd` command creates a new initrd RAM disk image file, so option A is incorrect. Likewise, the `mkinitramfs` command (option B) is also used to create initrd image files on Debian systems, so it too is incorrect. The `grub-mkconfig` command is used in GRUB2 systems to create an updated configuration file but not in GRUB Legacy systems, so option C is incorrect. The `fsck` program checks and repairs hard drive partitions, so option E is incorrect.

14. B. The UEFI firmware method has replaced the BIOS in most IBM-compatible computers, so option B is correct. FTP, PXE, NFS, and HTTPS are not firmware methods, but methods for loading the Linux bootloader, so options A, C, D, and E are all incorrect.

15. E. The kernel ring buffer is an area in memory reserved for storing output messages as the Linux system boots, so option E is correct. Option A, BIOS, is firmware on the workstation, not an area in memory, so it is incorrect. The GRUB bootloader, option B, is a program that starts the Linux system and is not in memory, so it is also incorrect. The MBR is a location on the hard drive to store the Linux bootloader, so option C is incorrect. The initrd RAM disk is an area in memory that stores modules required for the boot process, but it doesn't store the boot messages as the system starts, so option D is incorrect.

16. A. The `single` command parameter instructs the Linux system to start in single-user mode after booting, so option A is correct. The `fsck` command checks and repairs hard drive partitions, so option B is incorrect. Both the `mkinitrd` and `mkinitramfs` commands create initrd RAM disk files, so options C and D are incorrect. The `dmesg` command displays the boot messages from the kernel ring buffer, so option E is incorrect.

17. A. A kernel panic occurs when a Linux system halts unexpectedly due to a system error, so option A is the correct term. The kernel ring buffer stores boot messages at boot time, so option B is incorrect. The initrd RAM disk is an area in memory that stores module files required to boot the system, so option C is incorrect. The bootloader and firmware are part of the Linux boot process and don't refer to when the system halts, so options D and E are both incorrect.

18. B. The `grub-mkconfig` command processes GRUB2 directives stored in the `/etc/grub.d` folder to create the `/etc/grub2.cfg` configuration file, so option B is correct. The `mkinitrd` and `mkinitramfs` commands are used to create an initrd RAM disk to store module files, so options A and D are incorrect. The `grub-install` command is used in GRUB Legacy to install the GRUB configuration file in the correct location but isn't used in GRUB2, so option C is incorrect. The `dmesg` command displays the system boot messages and isn't part of the GRUB2 bootloader, so option E is incorrect.

19. C. The `fsck` program can perform a filesystem check and repair multiple types of filesystems on partitions. You should use it on any partition that can't be mounted due to errors. The `mount` program (option A) is used to append a partition to a virtual directory; it can't correct a partition that contains errors (and will usually refuse to mount them). The `umount` command (option B) is also incorrect. It is used to remove a mounted partition from the virtual directory. Option D (the `dmesg` command) displays boot messages, and option E (the `mkinitrd` command) crates an initrd RAM disk, so both are incorrect.

20. A. The `mount` command allows you to specify both the partition and the location in the virtual directory where to append the partition files and folders. The files and folders contained in the partition then appear at that location in the virtual directory. The `umount` command (option B) is used to remove a mounted partition. Option C, the `fsck` command, is used to fix a hard drive that is corrupted and can't be mounted; it doesn't actually mount the drive itself. The `dmesg` command in option D is used to view boot messages for the system, which may tell you where a hard drive is appended to the virtual directory, but it doesn't actually do the appending. Option E, the `kninitramfs` command, creates an initrd RAM disk and doesn't directly handle mounting hard drives to the virtual directory.

Chapter 6: Maintaining System Startup and Services

1. B, C, E. The `init` program may exist in the `/etc/`, `/sbin/`, or `/bin/` directory, depending on your distribution and its version, so therefore options B, C, and E are correct. The `/etc/rc.d/` directory is used in SysVint systems and is not a location for the `init` program, so option A is a wrong answer. The `/etc/lib/systemd/` directory is the location of the `systemd` program, and thus option D is also an incorrect choice.

2. A, B, C, D, E. This is a tricky question, because all of these statements are true concerning systemd service units. It makes you realize that systemd-managed systems are very flexible.

3. A. There is no `runlevel7.target`. The legitimate systemd targets, which provide backward SysV init compatibility, go from `runlevel0.target` through `runlevel6.target`. Therefore, option A is the correct answer. The `emergency.target` is a special systemd target unit used to enter emergency mode. When your system goes into emergency mode, the system only mounts the root filesystem and mounts it as read-only. Therefore, option B is a systemd target unit and not a correct answer. The `graphical.target` is a legitimate systemd target, which provides multiple users access to the system via local terminals and/or through the network and offers a GUI. Thus, option C is an incorrect choice. The `multi-user.target` is also a legitimate systemd target, just like the `graphical.target`, except that it does not offer a GUI. Therefore, option D is also a wrong answer. The `rescue.target` is like `emergency.target`, but it mounts the root filesystem for reading and writing. Therefore, option E is an incorrect choice.

4. C. Any modified systemd service unit configuration file should be stored in the `/etc/systemd/system/` directory. This will prevent any package upgrades from overwriting it and keep the directory precedence from using the unmodified service unit copy, which may reside in the `/usr/lib/systemd/system/` directory. The directories in options A and B are made up. The `/usr/lib/systemd/system/` directory should only store unmodified unit files, which are provided by default, and thus option D is an incorrect answer. The `/run/system/systemd/` directory is also made up.

5. E. For starting Service-B immediately before starting Service-A, the Service-A unit configuration file will need to employ the `After` directive, set to something like `After=Service-B.unit`. Therefore, option E is the correct answer. The `Conflicts` directive sets the unit to not start with the designated units. If any of the designated units start, this unit is not started. Therefore, option A is a wrong answer. The `Wants` directive sets the unit to start together with the designated units. If any of the designated units do not start, this unit is still started. Therefore, option B is also an incorrect answer. The `Requires` directive sets the unit to start together with the designated units. If any of the designated units do not start, this unit is not started. Thus, option C is a wrong choice. The `Before` directive sets this unit to start before the designated units. While this should be set in Service-B's unit configuration file, it does not apply, in this case, to Service-A's configuration file. Therefore, option D is also an incorrect answer.

6. B, D. Linux systems use environment variables to store information about the shell session and working environment. If you need to ensure that a particular environment variable is set properly for your service, you need to use the `Environment` directive and/or the `EnvironmentFile` directive for setting environment parameters. Therefore, options B and D are correct answers. The `Type` directive sets the unit startup type, which can be, for example, `forking`. Thus, option A is a wrong answer. The `EnvironmentParam` is a made-up directive. `PATH` is an environment variable, which you may modify for your unit's environmental parameters. However, it is not a directive.

7. D. If a target unit file has the `AllowIsolate=no` setting, the target cannot be used with the `systemctl isolate` command. Therefore, option D is the correct answer. Option A's `static` is an enablement state displayed for a unit file via the `systemctl --list-unit-files` command. Thus, option A is a wrong answer. The `AllowIsolate=yes` directive permits the target to be used with the `systemctl isolate` command. Therefore, option B is also an incorrect choice. The `Type=oneshot` is a service unit directive, and you would not find it in a target unit file. Thus, option C is a wrong answer. Option E's `disabled` is also an enablement state, like `static`, making option E a wrong choice as well.

8. A. The best command to make the modified file take immediate effect for the OpenSSH service is `systemctl reload`. This command will load the service configuration file of the running designated service without stopping the service. Therefore, option A is the best answer. A `daemon-reload` will load the unit configuration file and not the service configuration file. The `restart` command will stop and immediately restart the service. While this will load the modified service configuration file, it will also disrupt the service for current service users. The `mask` command prevents a particular service from starting; the `unmask` command undoes the mask command's effects.

9. E. To set a particular service unit to start at boot time, you need to use the `systemctl enable` command followed by the service unit name. Therefore, option E is the correct answer. The `restart` command will stop and immediately restart the service but does not control whether or not a service unit is started at system boot. The `start` command will start the service but does not control whether or not a service unit is started at system boot. The `isolate` command is used with systemd target units, not service units. Option D's `disable` command will set a particular service unit to *not* start at boot time (disable it from starting).

10. B. To change the system's default target, you need to employ the `systemctl set-default` command, passing the target name as an argument and using super user privileges. The `get-default` command will show you the system's current default target. The `isolate` command is used to jump to new targets and not to set default targets. The `is-enabled` command displays `enabled` for any service that is configured to start at system boot and `disabled` for any service that is not configured to start at system boot. It only deals with services, and therefore option D is a wrong choice. The `is-active` command also only deals with services.

11. D. The `blame` command displays the amount of time each running unit took to initialize, and the units and their times are listed starting from the slowest to the fastest. That way, you can start investigating the units at the list's top. The `time` command displays the amount of time system initialization spent for the kernel, and the initial RAM filesystem, as well as the time it took for normal system user space to initialize. However, it does not help you determine which unit configurations may be to blame for the slow boot. The `dump` command displays data concerning all the units and the data is not in a format that lets you easily track down what unit takes the most time to initialize at boot. Therefore, option B is an incorrect choice. Option C's `failure` is a service state, indicating that the service has failed. The `verify` command is handy in that it scans unit files and displays warning messages if any errors are found. However, it does not provide configuration information that can assist you in uncovering the reason a system is slow to boot.

12. C, E. Debian-based Linux distributions that use SysV init only use runlevels from 0 through 2. The `runlevel` command shows the previous runlevel, or N for newly booted. Therefore, the only options that this `runlevel` command would show on an older Debian-based Linux distribution system, which uses SysV init, are C and E. Option A is incorrect, because it shows 5 as the current runlevel, and Debian-based distros don't use that runlevel. Option B is also incorrect, because it also shows 5 as the current runlevel. Option D is incorrect because it shows 3 as the current runlevel, and the Debian-based distros do not use that runlevel either.

13. A. For SysV init systems, the default runlevel is stored within the `/etc/inittab` file within the `initdefault` record. Therefore, option A is the correct answer. The `/etc/rc.d` is a directory and not a file. Thus, option B is a wrong answer. The `rc` file is a script that can reside in either the `/etc/init.d/` or the `/etc/rc.d/` directory. It runs the scripts that start the various system services when jumping runlevels or booting the system. However, this script does not contain any information concerning the default runlevel. Therefore, options C and D are incorrect choices. The `/etc/rc.local` file allows you to issue certain commands or run any scripts as soon as system initialization is completed. However, this script also does not contain any information concerning the default runlevel.

14. C. The directory that stores the service startup scripts for an old (and a new) SysV init system is the `/etc/init.d/` directory. Therefore, option C is the correct answer. The `/etc/rc.d/rcn.d/` directories are used on a SysV init system, but they contain symbolic links to the scripts within the `/etc/init.d/` directory. Thus, option B is an incorrect answer. Options A, D, and E are all systemd directories. Therefore, they are incorrect choices.

15. A, B, D, E. Runlevel 1 is also called single-user mode. You can employ either the `init` or the `telinit` command to jump to that runlevel and pass them one of the three following arguments: 1, s, or S. Therefore, options A, B, D, and E are correct answers. You cannot use the one argument to reach runlevel 1, and therefore option C is the only wrong choice.

16. B. The best command to use is the `service status` command, passing the service name to it as an argument. This will display the service's current status and allow you to start the troubleshooting process quickly. Therefore, option B is the correct answer. The `service start` command will start the designated service, but you do not know whether or not this service was stopped. Thus it is not the best command to use, and option A is an incorrect choice. The `service --status-all` command is not the best command to use because it shows the status of all the various services. Thus, option C is a wrong answer. The `service stop` command will stop the designated service and provide a `FAILED` status if it was already stopped. However, this is not the best way to check a service's status on a SysV init system. The `service reload` command will load the designated service's configuration file and provide a `FAILED` status if the service is stopped. Yet again, this is not the proper way to check a service's status.

17. D. To enable the DHCP service on your Red Hat–based SysV init system for runlevels 3 and 5, the correct command to use is the `chkconfig --levels 35 dhcp on` command. Therefore, option D is the correct answer. Options A and E are incorrect, because you cannot use the `service` command to enable SysV init services. Option B is a wrong answer because you cannot use a delimiter, such as a comma, to separate the runlevel list. Option C is an incorrect choice because this command has its service name and the `on` argument flip-flopped.

18. E. To enable the DHCP service on your Debian-based SysV init system for default runlevels, the correct command to use is `update-rc.d dhcp defaults`. Therefore, option E is the correct answer. Option A is incorrect because the last command argument should be `defaults` and not `default`. Option B is a wrong answer because you cannot use the `chkconfig` command on a Debian-based distribution. Option C is an incorrect choice because this command has the service name and the `default` argument flip-flopped. Also, it is using the wrong argument—the argument should be `defaults`. The command used in option D is incorrect because this command has the service name and the `defaults` argument flip-flopped.

19. C. The mount unit filenames are created by having the absolute directory reference's preceding forward slash (/) removed, subsequent forward slashes are converted to dashes (–), and trailing forward slashes are removed. Mount unit filenames also have a `.mount` extension. Therefore, the mount unit file for the `/var/log/` mount point would be `var-log.mount`. Thus, option C is the correct answer. The `/var/log.mount` unit filename is incorrect because the forward slashes were not removed or replaced. The `/var/log.unit` base name is incorrect because the forward slashes were not removed or replaced. Also, the wrong file extension is used. The `var-log.unit` base name is incorrect because the wrong file extension is used. The `var/log.mount` unit filename is incorrect because the middle forward slash was not replaced by a dash.

20. A, C, D. For systemd automount unit files, the only directives that can be included in the `[Automount]` file section are `Where`, `DirectoryMode`, and `TimeOutIdleSec`. Thus, options A, C, and D are correct answers. The `Options` and `What` directives are ones you would see in a mount unit file's `[Mount]` section. Therefore, options B and E are incorrect choices.

Chapter 7: Configuring Network Connections

1. C, D. The `nmtui` command provides an interactive text menu for selecting a network interface and setting the network parameters, and the `ip` command provides a command-line tool for setting network parameters, so both options C and D are correct. The `netstat` command displays information about network connections, but it doesn't set the network parameters, so option A is incorrect. The `ping` command can send ICMP packets to a remote host but doesn't set the local network parameters, so option B is incorrect. The `route` command sets the routing network parameters, but not the IP address or subnet mask, so option E is incorrect.

2. B. Starting with version 17.04, Ubuntu has switched to using the Netplan tool to set network address information, so option B is the correct answer. The `netstat` command doesn't set network information, but instead displays active network connections, so option A is incorrect. The `iwconfig` command sets wireless network parameters, but not network address information, so option C is incorrect. The `route` command sets default router information, but not network address information, so option D is incorrect. The `ifconfig` command does set network address information, but it isn't used by the newer versions of Ubuntu, so option E is incorrect.

3. A. The `ethtool` command displays features and parameters for network cards, so option A is the correct answer. The `netstat` command displays network statistics and connections, so option B is incorrect. The `iwconfig` and `iwlist` commands are used to set wireless network parameters and not Ethernet card settings, so options C and D are incorrect. The `route` command sets or displays routing information and not Ethernet card settings, so option E is incorrect.

4. E. The `ss` command displays a list of the open ports on a Linux system, along with the processes associated with each port, so option E is correct. The `iwconfig` command sets wireless network information, not open ports, so option A is incorrect. The `ip` command displays or sets network information on a network interface but doesn't display open ports, so option B is incorrect. The `ping` command sends ICMP messages to a remote host but doesn't display any open ports, so option C is incorrect. The `nmtui` command allows you to configure network parameters for a network interface but doesn't display the open ports on the system, so option D is incorrect.

5. A, C. The `nmcli` and the `ip` commands both allow you to set and change network settings from the command line, so options A and C are both correct. The `iwconfig` command only sets wireless network information, so option B is incorrect. The `netstat` command displays open ports but doesn't change any network settings, so option D is incorrect. The `ping` command sends ICMP packets to remote hosts for testing, but it also doesn't set any network settings, so option E is incorrect.

6. A. The default router is used to send packets from the local network to remote networks, so to communicate with a remote host you need to define the default router address, making option A correct. The netmask only defines the local network; it doesn't define what to do with packets for remote hosts, so option B is incorrect. The hostname and IP address only define features of the local host, so options C and D are incorrect. The DNS server defines how to retrieve the IP address of a host based on its domain name, so option E is incorrect.

7. E. The DNS server maps the hostname to an IP address, so you must have a DNS server defined in your network configuration to be able to use hostnames in your applications. Thus, option E is correct. The default router only defines how to send packets to remote hosts; it doesn't map the host name to the IP address, so option A is incorrect. The netmask value defines the local network, but not how to map hostnames to IP addresses, so option B is incorrect. The hostname and IP address define features of the local host, so options C and D are incorrect.

8. B. The Dynamic Host Configuration Protocol (DHCP) is used to assign dynamic IP addresses to client workstations on a network, so option B is correct. The default router can't assign addresses to devices, so option B is incorrect. The ARP table maps the hardware address of the network card to IP addresses but doesn't assign the IP addresses, so option C is incorrect. The netmask value determines the network address but not the IP address of the host, so option D is incorrect. The `ifconfig` command can set the static IP address of the host but doesn't automatically assign the IP address, so option E is incorrect.

9. B. The loopback address is a special address assigned to the loopback interface that allows local applications to communicate with each other, making option B the correct answer. Dynamic and static IP addresses are assigned to network interfaces, which interact with remote systems, not local applications, so options A and C are incorrect. The hostname identifies the local host for remote connections, not for local applications, so option D is incorrect. The MAC address identifies the network card hardware address but isn't used by local applications, so option E is incorrect.

10. A. The `dig` command can display individual host records for a domain, which you can use to find the MX mail host for the domain, so option A is correct. The `host` command only displays host IP address information; it can't determine the server type from the DNS records, so option D is incorrect. The `netstat` and `ss` commands display active network connections, but not the remote host types, so options B and E are both incorrect. The `ping6` command sends IPv6 ICMP packets to test remote hosts but can't tell if the remote host is a mail server, so option C is incorrect.

11. B. The `ss` command can display both open ports and the applications that own them, so option B is correct. The `ip` and `ifconfig` commands just display or set network settings, so options A and E are incorrect. The `host` and `dig` commands only display hostname information, so options C and D are also incorrect.

12. A. Red Hat–based systems use separate files to store the IP address and router information. Those files are stored in the `/etc/sysconfig/network-scripts` folder, making option A correct. Option B is where Debian-based systems store the interfaces file, which contains the network configuration settings. The `ifcfg-eth0` is a file used to store the configuration, not a folder, so option C is incorrect. The `ifconfig` and `iwconfig` are commands and not folders, so options D and E are incorrect.

13. B. The Debian system uses the `iface` setting to set features for an interface, and you must specify the `dhcp` option to dynamically obtain an IP address, making option B correct. Options C and E are incorrect since they don't use the `iface` setting. Option A sets a static IP address for the interface and not a dynamic address, so it's incorrect. Option D sets a link local IPv6 address and not a dynamic IP address, so it's incorrect.

14. B. The DNS servers are listed in the `/etc/resolv.conf` configuration file using the nameserver setting, so option B is correct. The `/etc/dhcpd.conf` file defines configuration settings for a DHCP server, so option A is incorrect. The `/etc/nsswitch.conf` file defines the order in which the system searches for a hostname, not the list of DNS servers used, so option C is incorrect. The `/etc/network/interfaces` file defines the network interfaces for a Debian-based system, not the list of DNS servers, so option D is also incorrect. The `/etc/sysctl.conf` file defines kernel network parameters and not a list of DNS servers, so option E is incorrect.

15. A. The `ifconfig` command must specify the network interface, the IP address, then the `netmask` option before the netmask address. You can use the `up` or `down` option to place the network card in an active or inactive state by default, but it's not required. Option A is the only option that uses the correct values in the correct order. Option C is close but fails to specify the network interface. Option B is not in the correct format, and options D and E fail to list the necessary configuration settings.

16. A. The `iwlist` command displays the available wireless network access points detected by the wireless network card, so option A is correct. The `iwconfig` command configures the network card to connect to a specific access point but doesn't list all of the detected access points, making option B incorrect. Option C specifies the `ifconfig` command, which is used to assign an IP address to a wireless network card but doesn't list the access points. The `ip` command specified in option D likewise can be used to set the IP address of the card but doesn't list the access points. Option E, the `arp` command, maps hardware addresses to IP addresses so that you can find duplicate IP addresses on your network, but it doesn't list the wireless access points.

17. D. The SSID value defines the access point name, and it is set using the `essid` option in the `iwconfig` command, making option D the correct answer. The `key` option specifies the encryption key required to connect to the access point but not the access point name, making option A incorrect. The `netmask` and `address` values aren't set by the `iwconfig` command, so options B and C are incorrect. The `channel` option defines the radio frequency the access point uses, not the access point name, so option E is also incorrect.

18. E. The `ip` command allows you to both display and set the IP address, netmask, and default router values for a network interface, so option E is correct. The `ifconfig` command can set the IP address and netmask values, but not the default router. The `iwconfig` command is used to set the wireless access point settings, and the `router` command is used to set the default router but not the IP address or netmask values. The `ifup` command only activates the network interface; it can't set the address values.

19. C. The `ping` command sends ICMP packets to a specified remote host and waits for a response, making option C the correct answer. The `netstat` command displays statistics about the network interface, so it's incorrect. The `ifconfig` command displays or sets network information but doesn't send ICMP packets, making option B incorrect. The `iwconfig` command displays or sets wireless network information, but it doesn't handle ICMP packets, making option D incorrect. The `ss` command displays information about open connections and ports on the system, so option E is also incorrect.

20. B. The `tcpdump` command displays network packets that traverse the system network interface, so you can use that for monitoring application packets on the network, making option B the correct answer. The `nc` command allows you to manually send packets on the network, but it doesn't allow you to monitor application packets, so option A is incorrect. The `ping` and `traceroute` commands only send ICMP packets to remote servers; they don't monitor packets, so options C and D are incorrect. The `mtr` command can display the connectivity status to a remote server, but it doesn't allow you to view application packets going to the server, so option E is incorrect.

Chapter 8: Comparing GUIs

1. C. A desktop environment is a series of components that work together to provide the graphical setting for the user interface. Therefore, option C is the correct answer. A graphical user interface (GUI) is a set of programs that allow a user to interact with the system via icons, windows, and various other visual elements. Thus, option A is a wrong answer. A display manager operates the screen where you choose a username and enter a password to gain system access. Therefore, option B is an incorrect choice. A file manager is the program that allows you to perform file maintenance activities graphically. Thus, option D is also a wrong choice. A window manager is a set of programs that determine how the windows are presented on the desktop. Therefore, option E is also an incorrect choice.

2. A, B, C, E. A favorites bar, file manager, icons, and a system tray are all part of a graphical UI. Therefore, options A, B, C, and E are correct choices. A command line is a location to enter text-based commands, and while you can reach it from the GUI using a terminal emulator, it is not considered to be part of the graphical UI. Therefore, option D is the only incorrect choice.

3. A. SDDM (Simple Desktop Display Manager) is the default display manager for the KDE Plasma desktop environment. Therefore, option A is the correct answer. Files, also called GNOME files, is the file manager within the GNOME Shell desktop environment. Therefore, option B is a wrong answer. Mutter is the GNOME shell window manager, and thus option C is an incorrect answer. GDM stands for the GNOME Display Manager. Therefore, option D is a wrong choice. Dock is another name for the GNOME Shell Dash, which is the favorites bar within GNOME Shell. Thus, option E is also an incorrect choice.

4. C. The KDE Plasma's file manager is named Dolphin. Therefore, option C is the correct answer. Nautilus is the file manager on the Unity desktop environment, and therefore, option A is a wrong answer. Plasmoid is another name for a KDE Plasma widget. Thus, option B is an incorrect answer. Kwin is the KDE Plasma's window manager, and therefore option D is a wrong choice. Nemo is the default file manager on the Cinnamon desktop environment. Thus, option E is an incorrect choice.

5. C, D. MATE's display manager is LightDM, and its file manager is Caja. Therefore, options C and D are correct answers. MATE was a fork of the GNOME 2 desktop environment and not GNOME Shell, so option A is a wrong answer. MATE uses a fork of Metacity, called Marco, as its window manager, so option B is also a wrong choice. At the time this book was being written, MATE was being actively developed, so option E is an incorrect choice.

6. A. The sound keys accessibility setting provides beeps whenever the Caps Lock or Num Lock key is turned on or off. Therefore, option A is the correct answer. A program that reads the GUI aloud, such as Orca, is a screen reader. Thus, option B is a wrong answer. The cursor blinking setting modifies the cursor blink rate to make it easier to locate the cursor on the screen. Therefore, option C is also an incorrect answer. Output to a refreshable braille display is provided by the Orca screen reader, which is a screen reader. Thus, option D is a wrong choice. Zoom settings allow the screen or a screen portion to be amplified to different magnification levels. Therefore, option E is also an incorrect choice.

7. D. The braille display device would be using the `brltty` service. The proper `systemctl` command to restart the services is in option D. Options A, B, and C all use incorrect names for the braille service. The command in option E would reload any modified `brltty` configuration files but not restart the service. Therefore, option E is also an incorrect choice.

8. A. Slow keys are a keyboard option that modifies how long a key must be pressed down to acknowledge the key. Therefore, option A is the correct answer. Sticky keys are a keyboard option that sets keyboard modifier keys, such as Ctrl and Shift, to maintain their pressed status until a subsequent key is pressed. Thus, option B is a wrong answer. Repeat keys are a keyboard option that modifies how long a key must be pressed down and that defines a delay to acknowledge the key repeat. Therefore, option C is also a wrong choice. Simulated secondary click is actually a mouse option, and it sets a primary key to be pressed along with a mouse click to emulate secondary mouse clicks. Thus, option D is an incorrect answer. A screen keyboard is a keyboard option that displays a visual keyboard on the UI that can be manipulated by a mouse or other pointing device to emulate keystrokes. Therefore, option E is also an incorrect choice.

9. E. The display server uses a communication protocol to transmit the desires of the UI to the operating system, and vice versa. Therefore, option E is the correct answer. A window manager is a program that communicates with the display server on behalf of the UI. Thus, option A is a wrong answer. A display manager controls the desktop environment's login screen, where you choose a username and enter a password to gain system access. Therefore, option B is also a wrong choice. A desktop environment is a user environment that provides a predetermined look and feel to a GUI, but it does not transmit the desires of the UI to the operating system, so option C is a wrong answer. A window server is another name for a window manager, and thus, option D is also an incorrect answer.

10. A, C, D, E. A compositor arranges various display elements within a window to create a screen image. Therefore, option A is a correct answer. Both Mutter and Kwin, even though their primary duty is as a window manager, also contain compositors. Thus, options C and D are correct answers too. Weston is a compositor for the Wayland display server, so option E is also a correct choice. Wayland is a display server and not a compositor. Thus, option B is the only wrong answer.

11. B, D. Wayland does use the $WAYLAND_DISPLAY environment variable, so option B is a correct answer. Also, XWayland supports legacy X11 programs. Therefore, option D is an additional correct answer. Wayland is a replacement for the X11 display server, and it is designed to be more secure. Thus, option A is a wrong answer. Wayland's compositor is swappable and there are several other compositors besides Weston available for use with Wayland. Therefore, option C is a wrong choice. In order to disable Wayland in GNOME Shell, you edit the /etc/gdm3/custom.conf file and set WaylandEnable to false. Thus, option E is also an incorrect answer.

12. C. The loginctl command will help you determine your current GUI session number. You can then use the loginctl command again along with your session number to determine if your GUI session is Wayland or X11. Thus, option C is the correct answer. While you can issue the command echo $WAYLAND_DISPLAY to help determine if your GUI session is Wayland or X11, $WAYLAND_DISPLAY by itself does nothing. Therefore, option A is a wrong answer. AccessX is a program that originally provided many universal access settings. There is no environment variable used by Wayland or X11 called $AccessX, and thus, option B is an incorrect answer. The $X11 environment variable is made up, so option D is a wrong choice. The runlevel command allows you to determine your system's current run level and is not used in determining display servers. Therefore, option E is also an incorrect choice.

13. C. When your display server is Wayland, some commands, such as gnome-shell --replace, do not work in your GUI session. Therefore, option C is the correct answer. The scenario does not indicate that the X11 display server is hung. So please don't reboot your server and know that option A is a wrong answer. The error message does not indicate that the -R option should be used instead. Thus, option B is an incorrect answer. If XWayland was being used, you would not receive an error message. Therefore, option D is also a wrong choice. If Wayland was disabled for the session, the command would not generate an error message. Thus, option E is an incorrect choice.

14. B, C, E. The X.Org foundation does develop an X server, called X11. The X server is being replaced by Wayland. X is short for X Window System, which is a display server. So options B, C, and E are correct. XFree86 was the dominant server implementing X until 2004. Now the dominant server is the X.Org foundation's X11 server, so option A is a wrong answer. The X.Org's server implements the X Window System version 11, and that is why it is sometimes called X11. It is not due to the number of graphical sessions a particular user can have. Therefore, option D is also an incorrect choice.

15. A, D. The xwininfo and xdpyinfo commands provide information about the X server, including the different screen types available, the default communication parameter values, and protocol extension information as well as individual window information. These two utilities would be the best ones to start diagnosing the problem. Therefore, options A and D are correct answers. Xorg -configure creates a new X11 configuration file for your perusal, which may be useful later on in the troubleshooting process. However, this is not the best command to start diagnosis. Therefore, option B is a wrong answer. The xcpyinfo command is made up, making option C an incorrect answer. The loginctl command can help you determine whether or not the user is using X11 or Wayland, but since you already know that the X display server is running, issuing this command will not help. Thus, option E is an incorrect answer as well.

16. A, B, C, D. SPICE, NX, Xrdp, and VNC are all remote desktops. Therefore, options A, B, C, and D are correct answers. Caja is the file manager in the MATE desktop environment and not a remote desktop. Thus, option E is the only incorrect answer.

17. A, D. SPICE and VNC are the remote desktops, which are typically used with virtual machines. By default, VNC is used with KVM virtual machines. However, you can replace VNC with SPICE. Thus, options A and D are the correct answers. NX and Xrdp are not typically used with virtual machines, and thus, options B, C, and E are not correct answers.

18. E. The Xrdp remote desktop software uses the Remote Desktop Protocol (RDP). Thus, option E is the correct answer. The Remote Frame Buffer (RFB) protocol is used by VNC. Thus, option A is a wrong answer. The Wayland protocol is used by the Wayland display server. Therefore, option B is also a wrong choice. Option C is also an incorrect answer, because the NX technology protocol is used by the NX remote desktop. The Simple protocol for ICEs, or Simple Protocol for Independent Computing Environments (SPICE), is used by the Spice remote desktop. Thus, option D is also an incorrect choice.

19. A, C, E. You need to indicate to the openSSH server that no terminal is required because you are only establishing a tunnel. Therefore, the -N switch is needed. The -f switch will send the openSSH tunnel into the background, freeing up your command-line interface so that you can type remote desktop commands. The local mode of the ssh command requires that you use the -L switch to specify the local system as well as the local and remote ports to be used. Therefore, options A, C, and E are correct. The -X switch is not used in SSH port forwarding, so option B is a wrong answer. The -R switch is used for remote mode SSH port forwarding. Therefore, option D is also an incorrect choice.

20. B. You need to employ X11 forwarding. To properly and securely access the remote Linux system and run an X11-based application, the command in option B is the best choice. The command in option A uses the trusted X11 via the -Y switch, which is not secure. Therefore, option A is a wrong answer. The command in option C also uses the -Y switch, so option C is also an incorrect answer. The command in option D uses the correct command switch but sends the connection to the laptop instead of the rack-mounted Linux server. Thus, option D is a wrong answer. The command in option E is using the -L switch, which is for local SSH port forwarding, and it uses the wrong syntax for that switch and attempts to send the connection to the laptop. Thus, option E is a *very* incorrect answer.

Chapter 9: Adjusting Localization Options

1. C. The ASCII character set uses a 7-bit code to store English language characters, so option C is correct. The UTF-8 character set uses 1 byte (8 bits) to store characters, so option A is incorrect. The UTF-16 character set uses 2 bytes (16 bits) to store characters, so option B is incorrect. The Unicode character set uses 3 bytes (24 bits) to store characters, so option D is incorrect, and the UTF-32 character set uses 4 bytes (32 bits) to store characters, so option E is incorrect.

2. A, B. The UTF-8 and UTF-16 character sets use a transformation process to reduce the Unicode character set into 1 byte (UTF-8) or 2 byte (UTF-16) values, so options A and B are correct. The ASCII character set doesn't transform any characters, so option C is incorrect. The Unicode character set also doesn't transform characters, so option D is incorrect. `locale` is a Linux command and not a character set, so option E is incorrect.

3. E. The Unicode character set uses 3 bytes to store characters, which provides enough space to represent all the characters in the known world languages, so option E is correct. The ASCII character set only supports English language characters, so option A is incorrect. The `LC_ALL` environment variable defines a character set to use for the Linux system but isn't a character set in itself, so option B is incorrect. Both the UTF-8 and UTF-16 character sets are a subset of the Unicode character set, so they can't represent all the language characters in use in the world, so options C and D are incorrect.

4. E. The `locale` command displays all of the `LC_` environment variables and their values, so option E is correct. The `date` command only displays the time and date, not the localization information, so option A is incorrect. The `time` command displays the amount of time an application uses on the system, not the localization information, so option B is incorrect. The `hwclock` command displays the hardware clock time, not the localization information, so option C is incorrect. The `LANG` environment variable allows you to set all the `LC_` environment variables in one place, but it doesn't display all their settings, so option D is incorrect.

5. C, E. The `LANG` and `LC_ALL` environment variables control all the localization environment variable settings, so options C and E are correct. The `LC_MONETARY`, `LC_NUMBERIC`, and `LC_CTYPE` environment variables each control a single category of localization environment variables, but not all of the localization environment variables, so options A, B, and D are all incorrect.

6. B. Localization is the process of adapting a Linux system's character set to use a local language, so option B is correct. The `locale` command allows you to view the character sets, but it doesn't adapt the Linux system to the locale environment, so option A is incorrect. The character set is used to specify language characters, but it doesn't adapt the Linux system to a specific language, so option C is incorrect. Unicode and ASCII are two types of character sets, and they don't adapt the Linux system to a specific language, so options D and E are incorrect.

7. D. The `localectl` command is part of the Systemd package and allows you to display and change the localization settings for your Linux system, so option D is correct. The `timedatectl` command is also part of the Systemd package, but it only applies to time and date changes and not the localization changes, so option A is incorrect. The `time`, `date`, and `locale` programs are legacy programs and not part of the Systemd package, so options B, C, and E are incorrect.

8. B. The `export` command sets the value associated with an environment variable, so option B is correct. The `time` command displays the amount of time an application used on the system, not the values of an environment variable, so option A is incorrect. The `locale` command displays the values of the localization environment variables but doesn't allow you to change them, so option C is incorrect. The `date` command displays and sets the time and date values but not the localization environment variables, so option D is incorrect. The `hwclock` command displays and sets the hardware clock but not the localization environment variables, so option E is incorrect.

9. B. The `LC_MONETARY` environment variable determines the character set used for displaying monetary values, so option B is correct. The `LC_NUMERIC` environment variable determines how Linux displays numeric values, so option A is incorrect. The `LC_CTYPE` environment variable determines the default character set used by programs but not necessarily only for monetary values, so option C is incorrect. The `LC_TIME` environment variable determines how the Linux system displays time, not monetary values, so option D is incorrect. The `LC_COLLATE` environment variable determines how Linux sorts alpha characters, not how it displays monetary values, so option E is incorrect.

10. A. Each time zone determines the offset from UTC that applies to a specific location, so option A is correct. The localization determines the character set used to display language characters but not the time, so option B is incorrect. The character set determines how to display the language characters but not the time, so option C is incorrect. The locale determines how Linux displays the time but not the actual time setting, so option D is incorrect. The hardware clock is the time the physical workstation or server is set to in BIOS or UEFI; it doesn't necessarily represent the time relative to UTC and can even be stored as a UTC value, so option E is incorrect.

11. B, E. Both the `hwclock` and `timedatectl` commands retrieve the time and date from the physical workstation or server, so options B and E are correct. The `date` command displays the system time and date, not the time and date set on the physical hardware, so option A is incorrect. The `time` command displays the amount of time a program uses on the system, not the physical hardware time and date on the workstation or server, so option C is incorrect. The `locale` command displays the localization environment variables and their values, not the hardware time and date, so option D is incorrect.

12. A. Red Hat–based systems use the `/etc/localtime` file to store the appropriate time zone file for the location where the system is running, so option A is correct. The `/etc/timezone` file is normally used by Debian-based systems, so option B is incorrect. The `/usr/share/zoneinfo` folder stores time zone files that you must copy to the `/etc/localtime` file, so option C is incorrect. The `/usr/share/timezone` and `/usr/share/localtime` folders are incorrect folder names, so options D and E and incorrect.

13. B. The `/usr/share/zoneinfo` folder contains template files for each of the time zones supported in Linux, so option B is correct. The `/etc/localtime` and `/etc/timezone` files are the locations where you copy or link the appropriate time zone file to, but neither of them is the template folder, so options A and C are incorrect. The `$HOME` folder contains the user environment settings and user files but not the time zone template files, so option D is incorrect. The `/usr/share/timezone` folder is an incorrect folder name, so option E is incorrect.

14. B. The `timedatectl` command from the Systemd package displays the current date, the Linux system time, the hardware clock time, and the time zone, so option B is correct. The `date` command displays the current system time, date, and time zone but not the hardware time, so option A is incorrect. The `time` command displays the amount of time an application uses on the CPU, not the current date and time, so option C is incorrect. The `hwclock` command displays the current hardware time but not the system time, date, or time zone, so option D is incorrect. The `localectl` command displays the localization settings for the system but not the time, date, hardware time, or time zone, so option E is incorrect.

15. A. The `date` command allows you to specify a format for displaying the time and date, so option A is correct. The `time` command displays the amount of CPU time an application consumes, not the current time and date, so option B is incorrect. The `timedatectl` command displays the current time and date but doesn't allow you to format the output, so option C is incorrect. The `localectl` command displays the localization settings for the system, but not the current time and date, so option D is incorrect. The `hwclock` command displays the current hardware time but doesn't allow you to specify the format, so option E is incorrect.

16. A, D. The `hwclock` and `timedatectl` commands allow you to synchronize the Linux system time to the workstation BIOS time, so options A and D are correct. The `date` command allows you to change the date and time, but it doesn't allow you to synchronize it with the workstation BIOS time, so option B is incorrect. The `time` command allows you to display the amount of CPU time an application consumes, but it doesn't allow you to synchronize the system time with the workstation BIOS time, so option C is incorrect. The `localectl` command is used for localization, not for setting the time, so option E is incorrect.

17. B. Red Hat–based Linux systems utilize the `chrony` software package for connecting to network time servers. The `ntpd` package is a legacy software package and not often used, so option A is incorrect. The `localectl` command isn't used for setting time, so option C is incorrect. While you can set the local time using the `timedatectl` command, you can't use it to set the time using a network time server, so option D is incorrect. Although Red Hat–based systems utilize the Systemd utilities, they don't use the `timesyncd` program for network time, so option E is incorrect.

18. E. The `TZ` environment variable overrides the default system time zone for session applications, so option E is correct. The `LANG` and `LC_ALL` environment variables set the entire system time zone, not just the programming environment, so options A and D are incorrect. The `LC_MONETARY` and `LC_NUMERIC` environment variables set the localization for money values and numeric values, but they don't change the time zone setting, so options B and C are incorrect.

19. C. The UTF-8 character set duplicates the ASCII character set, and it's the default used in most U.S. Linux installations, so option C is correct. The Unicode, UTF-16, and UTF-32 character sets use more than 1 byte to represent characters, so they are not often used for English language characters, making options A, B, and D incorrect. The `locale` command displays the localization environment variables and their values—it is not a character set code, so option E is incorrect.

20. B. The `localectl` command uses the `list-locales` option to display all the localizations installed on the Linux system, so option B is correct. The `timedatectl` command displays the local time and date, but it doesn't provide information on which localization files are installed, so option A is incorrect. The `locale` command displays the localization environment variable settings but doesn't list which localizations are installed, so option C is incorrect. The `LANG` and `LC_ALL` environment variables set the current localization but can't display which ones are installed on the system, so options D and E are incorrect.

Chapter 10: Administering Users and Groups

1. A, B, E. The user account's username, password (though it typically only contains an x), and UID are all legitimate fields in an `/etc/passwd` file record. Therefore, options A, B, and E are correct answers. The password change date and special flag are fields in the `/etc/shadow` file. Thus, options C and D are incorrect choices.

2. A, B, C. The password expiration date, account expiration date, and password are all legitimate fields in a `/etc/shadow` file record. Therefore, options A, B, and C are correct answers. The comment and default shell are fields in the `/etc/passwd` file. Thus, options D and E are incorrect choices.

3. E. The user account's username is the only field within an `/etc/passwd` and an `/etc/shadow` record that contains the same data. Therefore, option E is the correct answer. While both files have a password field, they do not contain the same data. The password can only exist in one of the two files, preferably the `/etc/shadow` file. Thus, option A is a wrong answer. The account expiration date only exists in the `/etc/shadow` file, so option B is also a wrong choice. The UID and GID fields only exist in the `/etc/passwd` file, so options C and D are also incorrect answers.

4. B, D, E. Though not very efficient, the `cat /etc/passwd` command would allow you to view the NUhura account's record within the `/etc/passwd` file. The `grep NUhura /etc/passwd` and `getent passwd NUhura` commands also would allow you to see the NUhura record. So options B, D, and E are correct choices. The `getent` command in option A has got the username and filename flip-flopped, so it is an incorrect choice. Also, the `passwd NUhura` command attempts to change the account's password instead of display its file record, so option C is also an incorrect answer.

5. E. The `useradd -D` command allows you to view the account creation configuration directives in the `/etc/default/useradd` file. Therefore, option E is the correct answer. The `/etc/passwd`, `/etc/shadow`, and `/etc/group` files do not contain account creation configuration directives, so options A, B, and C are wrong answers. While the `/etc/login.defs` file does contain account creation configuration directives, you cannot display it with the `useradd -D` command. Therefore, option D is also an incorrect choice.

6. C. If the `CREATE_HOME` directive is not set or it is set to `no`, when a user account is created no home directory will be created by default. Most likely this caused the problem, so option C is the correct answer. The `HOME` directive determines what base directory name is used when creating home directories for new accounts, so option A is a wrong answer. If you did not employ super user privileges, you would not have been able to even create the account, so option B is a wrong choice. The `INACTIVE` directive pertains to when an account will be considered inactive, so option D is also an incorrect answer. The `EXPIRE` directive is involved with account expiration and not home directory creation. Therefore, option E is also an incorrect choice.

7. D. To immediately remove the `KSingh` account and all his home directory files, using super user privileges you would use the `userdel -r KSingh` command. Therefore, option D is the correct answer. There is no `-r` option for the `usermod` command, so option A is a wrong answer. The `rm -r /home/KSingh` command would only remove the account's home directory files and not delete the user account. Therefore, option B is an incorrect answer. The `userdel` command without any options would only delete the account and not remove any of its home directory files, so option C is a wrong choice. The `-d` option on the `usermod` command is for changing an account's home directory. Therefore, option E is also an incorrect choice.

8. A, B, C, E. The `passwd`, `usermod`, `userdel`, and `chage` commands can all manipulate (or remove) an account's `/etc/shadow` file record data in some way. Therefore, options A, B, C, and E are all correct. While the `getent` command will allow you to display selected records from the `/etc/shadow` file, it will not allow you to manipulate data records within the file. Therefore, option D is the only incorrect choice.

9. B. The `newgrp` command will let you switch temporarily from your account's default group to another group with whom you have membership. Therefore, option B is the correct answer. The `usermod` command could make that switch, but it is not best for temporary situations, so it is an incorrect choice. The `groups` command allows you to display group information, but not change groups, so it also is a wrong answer. The `groupadd` and `groupmod` commands deal with group management, but not temporarily switching an account's default group. Therefore, options D and E are also incorrect choices.

10. C. The `usermod -aG NCC-1701 JKirk` command would add `JKirk` to the `NCC-1701` group as a member and not remove any of the account's previous group memberships. Therefore, option C is the correct answer. The `usermod -g NCC-1701 JKirk` command would change the `JKirk` account's primary group membership, so option A is a wrong answer. The command in option B would add the `JKirk` account as a member to the `NCC-1701` group, but it would remove any of the account's previous group memberships. Thus, option B is an incorrect answer. The `groupadd NCC-1701` command would only add the NCC-1701 group. Therefore, option D is a wrong answer as well. The `groupmod` command is for modifying groups, and so the command in option E would have undesirable results. Thus, option E is an incorrect choice.

11. B, D. The `getent group NCC-1701` and `grep NCC-1701 /etc/group` commands would both allow you to see the various NCC-1701 group members. Therefore, options B and D are correct answers. The `groups` command is for viewing an account's various group memberships. Therefore, option A is a wrong answer. It is always tempting to add an s to the `/etc/group` filename, because of the `groups` command. However, it is the `group` file and *not* the `groups` file. Thus, options C and E are incorrect choices.

12. A. The skeleton directory, `/etc/skel`, typically contains the user environment files that are copied to the account's home directory when it is created. Therefore, option A is the correct answer. Options B, C, and D all contain references to home (or potential home) directories. That is where the user environment files end up, but not where they come from. Thus options B, C, and D are wrong answers. The `/etc/` directory is where the global environment files reside. Therefore, option E is also an incorrect choice.

13. E. The `.bash_profile` user environment file is run first if it is found in the user account's home directory. Therefore, option E is the right answer. The `.bash_login` and `.profile` user environment files would be ignored if they existed alongside the `.bash_profile` file within the user's home directory. Thus, options A and C are wrong answers. The `.bashrc` file is typically called to execute from one of the other user environment files for an interactive login session. Thus, option B is also an incorrect answer. The `.bash.bashrc` file, though similar in name to a global environment file, does not exist. Therefore, option D is an incorrect choice.

14. B, C, D, E. Depending on the Linux distribution currently in use, the files (and directory) in options B, C, D, and E may be involved in setting up the global environment. The directory in option A, while similar to a user environment filename, is made up. Therefore, option A is the only incorrect choice.

15. A, B, E. The `whoami`, `who am i`, and `id` commands will all display information about the current account that is issuing the commands. Therefore, options A, B, and E are correct answers. While the `cat` commands may display user environment files in the account's home directory, they do not display information concerning the account. Thus, options C and D are incorrect choices.

16. D. The `w` command displays CPU load information for the last 1, 5, and 15 minutes as well as data about users who are currently accessing the system. Therefore, option D is the correct answer. The `who` command will display information concerning users who are currently logged into the system, but not CPU load data. Thus, option A is a wrong answer. The `id` command displays user account information, not CPU load data or active user info. Therefore, option B is also a wrong choice. The `whoami` command only displays the username of the current user issuing the command. Thus, option C is an incorrect answer. The `last` command displays past and present system access information for user accounts but nothing concerning CPU load data. Thus, option E is an incorrect choice.

17. B. The `last` command by default pulls its data from the `/var/log/wtmp` file. Therefore, option B is the correct answer. The `w` command uses data from the `/var/run/utmp` file, so option A is a wrong choice. The `last` command can pull information from an older saved `wtmp` file, such as `/var/log/wtmp.1`, but it does not do so by default. Thus, option C is a wrong choice. The `/etc/shadow` and `/etc/passwd` files do not contain any data that can be used with the `last` command. Therefore, options D and E are incorrect answers.

18. A, C. The `usrquota` and `grpquota` options are `/etc/fstab` settings used to enable user and group quotas for a filesystem. Therefore, options A and C are correct answers. Options B and D contain commands that are used with managing filesystem quotas. Thus, options B and D are wrong answers. The `aquota.user` is a file that is created when the `quotacheck -cu` command is employed. Therefore, option E is an incorrect choice.

19. B. To quickly remove quota limits on all filesystems, you would use the `quotaoff -a` command. Therefore, option B is the correct answer. Editing the `/etc/fstab` would take too long because you would have to remove the quota options and then unmount and remount all the filesystems. Thus, option A is a wrong answer. The `quotacheck` utility creates either the `aquota.group` file, if the `-cg` options are used, or the `aquota.user` file, if the `-cu` switches are used, or both files if `-cug` is employed. However, it does nothing for quickly turning off filesystems' quotas. Thus, options C and D are incorrect answers. The `umount` command will not turn off filesystems' quotas, and therefore option E is also an incorrect choice.

20. C. The `edquota -t` command will edit quota grace periods. Therefore, option C is the right answer. The `edquota -u` command edits a designated user's quota limits. Thus, option A is a wrong answer. The `edquota -g` command edits a designated group's quota limits. Therefore, option B is also an incorrect answer. The `edquota -G` command and `edquota --grace` command are made up. Thus, both options D and E are incorrect choices.

Chapter 11: Handling Storage

1. A. The solid-state drive (SSD) storage device uses an integrated circuit to store data, so option A is correct. SATA, SCSI, and PATA are drive connection types and not storage device types, so options B, C, and E are all incorrect. The hard disk drive (HDD) storage devices use disk platters and a read/write head to store data, not an integrated circuit, so option D is incorrect.

2. B. Linux creates files named `sdx` in the `/dev` folder for SCSI devices. For the second SCSI device, Linux would create the file `/dev/sdb`, so option B is correct. The `/dev/hdb` file would represent the second HDD drive connected to the system, so option A is incorrect, and `/dev/sda` would represent the first SCSI device connected to the system, so option E is incorrect. Options C and D both represent partitions and not entire drives, so they are both incorrect.

3. E. The udev program runs in the background on Linux systems and detects and mounts storage devices as they're connected to the system, so option E is correct. The mkfs program creates a filesystem on partitions; it doesn't mount them, so option A is incorrect. The fsck program repairs filesystems but doesn't mount them, so option B is incorrect. The umount program unmounts filesystems, not mounts them, so option C is incorrect. The mount program manually mounts filesystems but doesn't run in the background and automatically detect them, so option D is incorrect.

4. C. The udev program creates files in the /dev/disk/by-id folder that are linked to the raw device files for storage devices. These files are identified by manufacturer information, including the serial number assigned to the device, so option C is correct. The /dev/disk/by-path folder links files based on the drive's connection to the system, so option A is incorrect. The /dev/sdb file represents the raw device file assigned to the device, not a permanent link file, so option B is incorrect. The /dev/disk/by-uuid folder contains permanent link files based on the device UUID value, not the serial number, so option D is incorrect. The /dev/mapper folder contains files for virtual drives for LVM and multipath systems, not permanent links to raw device files, so option E is incorrect.

5. B. The GNU gparted program provides a graphical window for managing device partitions, so option B is correct. The gdisk, fdisk, and parted programs are all command-line partitioning tools, so options A, C, and D are all incorrect. The fsck program is a tool to repair filesystems, not create or modify partitions, so option E is incorrect.

6. A. Linux uses mount points to insert a filesystem on a storage device to the virtual directory, so option A is correct. Unlike Windows, Linux doesn't assign drive letters to storage devices, so option B is incorrect. The /dev files are used as raw devices for storage devices; they don't access the filesystem, so option C is incorrect. The /proc and /sys folders are used by the kernel to display and change storage device information, not add the filesystem to the virtual directory, so options D and E are incorrect.

7. D. The ext filesystem was the original filesystem used in Linux, and ext4 is the latest version of it, so option D is correct and option C is incorrect. The reiserFS and btrfs filesystems are specialty filesystems created separately from the ext filesystem, so options A and B are also incorrect. The nfs filesystem was created to allow sharing files and folders across networks and wasn't the original Linux filesystem, so option E is incorrect.

8. B. The mkfs program allows you to create a new filesystem on a partition, so option B is correct. The fdisk, gdisk, and parted programs are used to create or modify partitions but not to work with the filesystem installed on them, so options A, D, and E are all incorrect. The fsck program repairs filesystems but can't create them, so option C is incorrect.

9. B. The mount program allows you to insert the filesystem on a partition into the virtual directory, so option B is correct. The fsck program repairs filesystems but doesn't insert them into the virtual directory, so option A is incorrect. The umount program removes filesystems from the virtual directory, as opposed to inserting them, so option C is incorrect. The fdisk program partitions devices but doesn't create filesystems or insert them into the virtual directory, so option D is incorrect. The mkfs program creates filesystems but doesn't insert them into the virtual directory, so option E is also incorrect.

10. A. The `fsck` program repairs corrupted filesystems, so option A is correct. The `mount` program inserts filesystems into the virtual directory, but it can't repair them, so option B is incorrect. The `umount` program removes filesystems from the virtual directory but can't repair them, so option C is also incorrect. The `fdisk` program creates and modifies partitions but doesn't work with filesystems, so option D is incorrect. The `mkfs` program creates filesystems but doesn't repair them, so option E is incorrect.

Chapter 12: Protecting Files

1. E. Scheduling a full archive weekly and implementing a differential backup daily (which backs up all the data that is new or modified since the last full archive) will meet the requirements. Therefore, option E is the correct answer. Since you only want to create a full backup one time per week, option A is a wrong answer. Doing an incremental every day without a periodic full archive would result in a long time period to restore data. So option B does not match the requirements and is an incorrect choice. Doing a differential archive daily also does not fully match the requirements, because you are not conducting a full archive weekly. Thus, option C is a wrong answer. Option D is not as time efficient for a data restore as option E, because you would have to apply each incremental to restore data instead of one differential archive. Therefore, option D is also an incorrect choice.

2. B. The `gzip` utility compresses data files and gives them the `.gz` file extension. Therefore, option B is the correct answer. The `xz`, `bzip2`, and `zip` compression utilities compress a data file and give it a different file extension, so options A, C, and D are wrong answers. The `dd` utility is not a compression program. Therefore, option E is also a wrong choice.

3. D. To quickly create an archive of disparate files around the virtual directory structure, the best utility to use is the `cpio` program. This is because you can employ the `find` command to locate the files and then pipe the results into the `cpio` utility. Therefore, option D is the correct answer. While the `tar` utility uses SNAR files, it is not the most efficient program to use in this scenario, and thus, option A is a wrong answer. The `dd` utility is used for entire disks or partitions, and therefore, option B is an incorrect answer. The `rsync` and `zip` programs are not the most efficient utilities to use in this scenario, so options C and E are also incorrect choices.

4. E. The `tar` options `-cJvf` will create a tarball using the highest compression utility, `xz`, and allow the administrator to view the files via the verbose option while they are being copied into the compressed archive. Thus, option E is the correct answer. The switches in options A and B perform extracts (`-x`) and do not create, so they are wrong answers. The only thing wrong with option C is that it employs `gzip` compression via the `-z` switch, so it is an incorrect choice. Option D leaves out the verbose switch, so it too is an incorrect choice.

5. A. The `dd` command in option A will accomplish the job correctly and is the correct answer. The `dd` commands in options B through D have the input and output files flip-flopped, so they would destroy the data on the `/dev/sdc` drive. Therefore, options B, C, and D are wrong answers. The `dd` command in option E would wipe the `/dev/sdc` drive using zeros. Therefore, option E is also an incorrect choice.

6.   C. The -a switch allows you to recursively back up a directory tree and preserves all the file metadata. It is equivalent to using the -rlptgoD switches. Therefore, option C is the correct answer. The -r switch only allows recursive operations but does not preserve metadata, such as file ownership. Therefore, option A is a wrong answer. The -z switch employs compression and nothing else, so option B is a wrong choice. The -e and --rsh switches are used to designate a remote program to use when sending files to a remote system. Thus, options D and E are also incorrect choices.

7.   E. When you use the -z switch in conjunction with the rsync utility, you are employing compression from the zlib library. Therefore, option E is correct. And thus, options A, B, C, and D are incorrect choices.

8.   A, B, E. Options A, B, and E are all true statements regarding the scp utility and therefore are correct answers. The scp program is not an interactive utility, and so option C is a wrong answer. Also, the scp utility cannot be interrupted without ill effects (you have to start all over), so option D is also an incorrect choice.

9.   E. The reput command will resume your interrupted operation of uploading a local backup to a remote system. Therefore, option E is the correct answer. The progress command toggles on and off the progress display, so option A is a wrong answer. The get command and the reget command involve downloading a file from a remote system to a local system. Thus, options B and C are wrong choices. Though the put command was probably used prior to the operation's start, it will not resume an upload, so option D is also an incorrect choice.

10.   B. In this scenario, the most likely cause is that the archive got corrupted when it was transferred to the remote system. Therefore, option B is correct. If the local archive was corrupted when it was created, transferring would either corrupt it more or leave it the same. Therefore, option A is a wrong answer. Using incorrect commands within the sftp utility or wrong switches on the md5sum program will not typically cause corruption. Therefore, options C and E are wrong choices. The numbers only match if corruption has not occurred, and thus, option D is also an incorrect choice.

Chapter 13: Governing Software

1.   A, B. When developers distribute their applications as source code tarballs using the tar and gzip utilities, you often need to download the file from a website. The wget and cURL programs allow you to download files from the command line, so options A and B are correct. The dpkg tool is used for installing DEB package files, not tarballs, so option C is incorrect. The rpm and yum tools are used for installing RPM package files, so options D and E are incorrect.

2.   D. The make script runs the necessary compiler steps to compile all of the source code and library files necessary to build the application executable file, so option D is correct. The dpkg tool installs DEB package files, not source code files, so option A is incorrect. The rpm and yum tools are used to install RPM package files, so options B and C are incorrect. The wget program is used to download source code bundles, but not build them, so option E is incorrect.

3. C. The `configure` tool assesses your Linux system to ensure that any dependencies are met and that the proper compiler tools are installed and then builds the `make` script, so option C is correct. The `make` script along with the `install` option runs the `make` script but doesn't create it, so options A and B are incorrect. The `gcc` program compiles the source code and library files but doesn't create the `make` script, so option D is incorrect. The `dpkg` installs DEB package files but doesn't create a `make` script, so option E is incorrect.

4. A. The GNU Compiler Collection (`gcc`) is the most popular compiler used in Linux, so option A is correct. The `make` utility runs make scripts to help build applications using `gcc`, but it doesn't compile the source code directly, so option B is incorrect. The `configure` utility helps build the `make` script based on the location of the compiler program, but it doesn't compile the source code, so option C is incorrect. The `dpkg` and `rpm` programs are package tools for installing DEB and RPM package files, respectively, and aren't used to compile source code files, so options D and E are both incorrect.

5. E. The tape archive, or `tar`, application is often used for bundling source code projects into a single distributable file, so option E is correct. The `dpkg`, `rpm`, `yum`, and `apt-get` programs all work with package management files, and are not for archiving source code files, so options A, B, C, and D are all incorrect.

6. B. The `-zxvf` command-line options for the `tar` program are commonly used to decompress and extract files from a tarball file, so option B is correct. The `-Uvh` option group is commonly used for the `rpm` program to install packages, but it's not valid for the `tar` program, so option A is incorrect. The `-xvf` command-line option combination extracts files from a tarball but doesn't decompress them, so option C is incorrect. The `-zcvf` option group will create a new tarball and compress it, not extract and decompress the files, so option D is incorrect. The `-cvf` option group creates a new tarball file, but it doesn't extract files from an existing file, so option E is incorrect.

7. B. The Rocky Linux distribution uses the Red Hat package management system, which uses RPM files, so option B is correct. The `.deb` filename extension is used to identify Debian-based package management files, so option A is incorrect. The `.tgz` filename extension is used to identify compressed tar archive files, so option C is incorrect. The `.tar` filename extension is used to identify tar archive files, so option D is incorrect, and the `.gz` filename extension is used to identify files compressed with the `gzip` utility, so option E is incorrect.

8. D. The `dpkg` program is used to install DEB package files on Debian-based systems, so option D is correct. The `rpm`, `yum`, and `dnf` programs are all tools used for Red Hat–based package management systems, not Debian-based systems, so options A, B, and C are all incorrect. The `tar` program is used for creating and extracting tarball archive files, not DEB files, so option E is incorrect.

9. C, E. The `yum` and `dnf` programs are used to install RPM packages from Red Hat–based repositories, so options C and E are correct. The `dpkg` and `apt-get` programs are used for installing DEB files on Debian-based package management systems, so options A and D are incorrect. The `tar` program is used for creating and extracting archive files, so option B is incorrect.

10. A. Red Hat–based Linux distributions use the flatpak application container format to install containers, making option A correct. The snap application container format is used in Ubuntu, but not Red Hat, so option D is incorrect. The rpm and dpkg formats are used in package management, not application containers, so options B and C are incorrect. The gcc program is used for compiling source code into executable programs, so option E is incorrect.

Chapter 14: Tending Kernel Modules

1. A, C, D, E. A kernel module is a self-contained driver library file, which is not precompiled into the Linux kernel. It can be loaded and unloaded as needed, which provides additional functionality when required. These kernel modules keep the Linux kernel lighter and more agile. Therefore, options A, C, D, and E are all correct answers. The only incorrect answer is option B, and it is wrong because kernel modules are not compiled into the kernel.

2. B, D. Kernel module files, depending on the distribution, can be stored in a subdirectory of /lib/modules/*KernelVersion*/ or /usr/lib/modules/*KernelVersion*/. If the /usr/lib/modules/*KernelVersion*/ directory is used, it is typically hard-linked to the /lib/modules/KernelVersion/ directory. Therefore, options B and D are correct answers. The other directory names are made up. Thus, options A, C, and E are incorrect choices.

3. A, B, D, E. Older Linux distributions store module configuration information in a single configuration file, /etc/modules.conf. On more modern distributions, configuration information is stored in *.conf files within the /etc/modprobe.d/, /lib/modprobe.d/, /usr/lib/modprobe.d/, and run/modprobe.d/ directories. Therefore, options A, B, D, and E are all correct answers. The /etc/modules.d/ directory is made up, and thus option C is an incorrect choice.

4. E. The modinfo utility will allow you to view detailed information concerning a module passed as a command argument. This detailed information includes any dependencies. Therefore, option E is the correct answer. The dmesg command is helpful for viewing any kernel messages concerning module failures but does not display module dependency information. Thus, option A is a wrong answer. The insmod utility is used for loading modules dynamically, and therefore, option B is a wrong choice. The lsmod command displays currently loaded modules. While it does show other modules that are currently using the module, because it does not list dependencies or show information for unloaded modules, it is not the best choice. Thus, option C is also an incorrect answer. The modprobe utility is used for loading and unloading kernel modules, and therefore, it is not the best choice either. Thus, option D is an incorrect choice.

5. C. The modprobe utility will dynamically load the xyz utility, if you pass it as an argument to the command, and also load any of its needed dependencies. Therefore, option C is the correct answer. The insmod utility is used for loading modules dynamically. However, it will not load any of the module's dependencies, and therefore, option A is an incorrect choice. The modinfo utility allows you to view detailed information concerning a module passed as a command argument, but it does not load modules. Therefore, option B is a wrong answer. The lsmod command displays currently loaded modules, and thus option D is an incorrect

answer. The `depmod` command is used for scanning through the system in order to update the `modules.dep` file. Therefore, option E is also an incorrect choice.

6. D. The Linux system typically will automatically detect new hardware and load any needed modules. The `depmod` command will scan through the system looking for any hardware that was not automatically detected. It determines any needed modules, reviews the modules' dependencies, and updates the appropriate file. Therefore, option D is the correct answer. The `lsmod` command displays currently loaded modules, and thus option A is an incorrect answer. The `modinfo` utility allows you to view detailed information concerning a module passed as a command argument. However, if you don't know the device's associated module, this utility is of little use. Therefore, option B is a wrong choice. The `dmesg` command is helpful for viewing any kernel messages concerning module failures, so if it is a module failure issue, you can view it using this command. However, since the device was not detected, it is not the best command to start the troubleshooting process. Therefore, option C is a wrong answer. The `insmod` utility is used for loading modules dynamically, and therefore, option E is an incorrect choice.

7. A. The `modprobe` utility uses the `modules.dep` file to determine any module dependencies. Therefore, option A is the correct answer. The other options contain directories involved in the kernel module management, and thus options B, C, D, and E are wrong choices.

8. E. The `insmod` utility will allow you to quickly insert a module, whose name is passed as an argument to the command, into the Linux kernel. Therefore, option E is the correct answer. The `lsmod` command displays currently loaded modules, and thus option A is an incorrect answer. The `modinfo` utility allows you to view detailed information concerning a module passed as a command argument, but it does not load modules. Therefore, option B is a wrong answer. The `dmesg` utility displays the kernel's ring buffer but does not allow you to insert modules into it. Thus, option C is also a wrong choice. The `depmod` command is used for scanning through the system in order to update the `modules.dep` file. Therefore, option D is also an incorrect choice.

9. C. The `rmmod` command will quickly unload a module, but none of its dependencies, from the Linux kernel. Since the `abc` module does not have any dependencies, option C is the best answer. The `insmod` utility is used for loading (inserting) a module and not unloading one. Therefore, option A is a wrong answer. The `unload` command is made up, and thus option B is also an incorrect answer. The `modprobe` command used without any switches is for loading (inserting) modules, not unloading them. Thus, option D is a wrong choice. The `rm -f` command is used in removing files, not unloading modules. Therefore, option E is an incorrect answer.

10. B. The `modprobe -r` command will remove the module whose name is passed to it as an argument and any of its dependent modules. Therefore, option B is the best answer. The `dmesg` command is helpful for viewing kernel messages related to module failures but not for unloading modules. Thus, option A is a wrong answer. The `lsmod` utility shows brief module information for loaded modules but is not involved in the unlinking process. Therefore, option C is also an incorrect answer. The `paste` command allows you to sloppily put together two files side by side to STDOUT. However, it is not involved with kernel modules, so option D is also a wrong choice. The `groupdel` utility is used for removing user groups, and it also is not used with kernel modules. Therefore, option E is an incorrect choice.

Chapter 15: Applying Ownership and Permissions

1. A, B, E. The basic Linux security permissions that you can set are read, write, and execute access, so options A, B, and E are correct. To delete a file a user must have write access because there is no delete access permission, so option C is incorrect. To modify a file a user must also have write access because there is no specific modify access permissions, so option D is incorrect.

2. B, C, D. The three categories Linux uses for assigning permissions are the owner, the group, and all others on the system; thus answers B, C, and D are correct. The root user account already has full permissions on all files and folders, so it's not specified as a separate category, so option A is incorrect. Linux doesn't use a department category because departments must be defined as groups, so option E is also incorrect.

3. B. The Set User ID bit (SUID) allows all users to run applications as the root user account, so option B is correct. The sticky bit prevents users from deleting files for which they have group permissions but don't own. It doesn't allow users to run the file with root privileges, so option A is incorrect. The GUID bit directs Linux to set all files in a directory with the directory's group assignment and not that of the user account creating the file. However, it doesn't allow users to run files as the root user account, so option C is incorrect. The execute and write bits set those permissions for the standard category of users, groups, or others. They don't allow users to run files as the root user account, so both options D and E are incorrect.

4. E. The octal mode permission 644 represents read/write for the owner and read only for the group and other categories. In symbolic mode that would be rw-r--r--, so option E is correct. Option A, rwxrw-r--, would be octal mode 764, so it is incorrect. Option B, -w--w--w-, would be octal mode 222, so it is incorrect. Option C, -w-r--r--, would be octal mode 244, so it is also incorrect. Option D, rwxrw-rw-, would be octal mode 766, so it too is incorrect.

5. A, B. The chgrp command is used to change the group assigned to a file or directory; however, you can also specify a new group with the chown command to change the owner and the group at the same time, so both options A and B are correct. The chmod command changes the permissions assigned to a file or directory but not the group, so option C is incorrect. The chage command is used to control the password of user accounts, not the group assigned to a file or directory, so option D is incorrect. The ulimit command is used to restrict the system resources a user account can use, not to set the group assignment of a file or directory, so option E is incorrect.

6. C. The getfacl command retrieves all of the ACL permissions assigned to a file or directory, so option C is correct. The -Z option added to the ls command displays SELinux context settings, not ACL permissions, so option A is incorrect. The -l option of the ls command displays the standard Linux file permissions, not the ACL permissions, so option B is incorrect. The chmod command allows you to change the standard permissions assigned to

a file or directory, not display the ACL permissions, so option D is incorrect. The `setfacl` command allows you to change the ACL permissions for a file or directory, but not view them, so option E is incorrect.

7. D. The permissive mode in SELinux logs policy violations but doesn't prevent the action from happening, so option D is correct. The disabled mode allows all actions to happen but doesn't log them, so option A is incorrect. The enforcing mode logs policy violations and enforces them, so option B is incorrect. Options C and E, targeted and MLS, are not SELinux modes but rather define what types of daemons to monitor; they are both incorrect.

8. C. The `-Z` option of the `ls` command displays the SELinux security context assigned to a file or directory, so option C is correct. The `getsebool` command displays the current setting for a policy rule, not the security context of files, so option A is incorrect. The `setsebool` command enables or disables a policy rule, and it doesn't display the security context of a file, so option B is incorrect. The `getenforce` command displays the current SELinux mode, not the security context of files, so option D is incorrect. The `-l` option of the `ls` command displays the standard permissions assigned to a file, not the SELinux security context of the file, so option E is incorrect.

9. A, D. The `su` command allows you to run an application as another user, including the root user account, and the `sudo` command allows you to run an application as the root user account, so options A and D are both correct. Both `wheel` and `adm` are user groups that provide administrator privileges, but they aren't commands that run applications themselves, so options B and E are both incorrect. The `visudo` command opens an editor to edit the sudoers file so you can edit it, but it can't run other applications, so option C is incorrect.

10. C, D. Red Hat–based distributions use the `wheel` group and Debian-based distributions use the `sudo` group to allow members to gain administrator privileges on the system to run applications, so options C and D are correct. The `lp` group is used to grant access to system printers, not run applications with administrator privileges, so option A is incorrect. The `adm` group is commonly used in Debian-based systems to grant access to log files, but not run applications with administrator privileges, so option B is incorrect. Option E, `su`, is a command-line command for running commands as another user, not a user group, so it is incorrect.

Chapter 16: Looking at Access and Authentication Methods

1. D. For an application to use PAM, it must be compiled with the `libpam` (also called `libpam.so`) library. Thus, option D is the correct answer. Option A lists the `ldd` command, which allows you to view modules compiled with various applications. Therefore, option A is a wrong answer. Options B, C, and E are all PAM modules, but none are the PAM library module needed to make an application PAM-aware. Therefore, options B, C, and E are incorrect choices.

2. A, B, D, E. `requisite`, `required`, `sufficient`, and `optional` are all PAM control flags you may find in a PAM `/etc/pam.d/` configuration file. Therefore, options A, B, D, and E are correct. Option C, `allowed`, is made up and thus an incorrect choice.

3. B, E. The `pam_tally2` and `faillock` commands display failed login attempts, and therefore options B and E are correct answers. The `tally2` command does not exist, and thus option A is a wrong answer. The `pam_tally2.so` module is involved with locking out accounts due to failed login attempts, but it does not display failed logins. Therefore, option C is a wrong choice. The `pam_faillock` is made up, and thus, option D is also an incorrect choice.

4. B, C. Asymmetric, or public/private, key encryption involves a message sender encrypting a message with the receiver's public key. When the receiver obtains the encrypted message, it is then decrypted using the receiver's private key. Therefore, options B and C are correct answers. Symmetric key encryption is also called secret or private key encryption. It involves the sender and receiver using the same secret key to encrypt and decrypt a message. Therefore, options A, D, and E are incorrect choices.

5. E. Option E best describes a digital signature and is therefore the correct answer. Option A describes encryption and is thus a wrong answer. Option B describes decryption and is also an incorrect choice. PKI is described in option C, and thus option C is a wrong answer. Option D describes a self-signed digital certificate, and therefore it is an incorrect choice as well.

6. A. The OpenSSH application keeps track of any previously connected hosts and their public keys in each user's `~/.ssh/known_hosts` file. Therefore, option A is the correct answer. The `~/.ssh/authorized_keys` file is used on an SSH server to keep track of authorized public keys used for password-less authentication. Therefore, option B is a wrong answer. Options C and D are made up and therefore incorrect choices. Option E is an RSA public key that could be created by the `ssh-keygen` utility, so it is a wrong choice as well.

7. A, B, C. The `~./ssh/config`, `/etc/ssh/ssh_config`, and `/etc/ssh/sshd_config` files are all OpenSSH configuration files. Therefore, options A, B, and C are correct choices. The files listed in options D and E are made up and therefore incorrect answers.

8. E. The only correct answer is option E. These identity keys are created with the filenames of `id_type` for the private key and `id_type.pub` for the public key. The key in option E is a private key using the RSA algorithm. Option A's key is an RSA private key used in establishing a password authenticated SSH connection, so it is a wrong answer. The key listed in option B is a public version of option A's key, so it too is a wrong choice. The keys listed in options C and D are made up, and thus they are wrong choices as well.

9. A, C, D, E. Options A, C, D, and E are all true statements concerning TCP wrappers and therefore are correct choices. You would never want to place `ALL: ALL` in the `/etc/hosts.allow` file because it would block everyone from accessing the service. Instead, you would want to place this record in the `/etc/hosts.deny` file to provide the best security because it is checked last. Therefore, option B is a wrong choice.

10.   B, D, E.   Options B and E are protocols that may be involved in using VPN software as a client, and therefore they are correct choices. IPSec is a framework, which may be involved at the Network layer when using VPN software as a client, and thus option D is also a correct answer. Tunnel and transport are modes of IPSec, but not frameworks or protocols, so options A and C are incorrect choices.

Chapter 17: Implementing Logging Services

1.   D.   The syslog protocol created by the Sendmail project has become the de facto standard for logging system event messages in Linux, so option D is correct. SMTP is a mail protocol, and FTP stands for File Transfer Protocol, so both options A and B are incorrect. NTP stands for Network Time Protocol, so option C is incorrect. Option E, `journalctl`, is a tool used to read `systemd-journald` journal files, not a protocol for logging event messages, so it is also incorrect.

2.   A.   The `cron` application schedules jobs on Linux systems, so the `cron` facility keyword represents event messages received from the job scheduler, so option A is correct. The `user` keyword represents events received from users, so option B is incorrect. The `kern` keyword represents events received from the kernel, so option C is incorrect. The `console` keyword represents events received from a console on the system, so option D is incorrect. The `local0` keyword is not defined in the standard and is normally defined within the system but doesn't normally receive events from the job scheduler, so option E is incorrect.

3.   C.   The `emerg` severity level has a priority of 0, the highest level in syslog, so option C is correct. The `crit` severity level is at level 2, so it's not the highest level and therefore option A is incorrect. The `alert` keyword is assigned level 1, but it's not the highest level, so option B is incorrect. The `notice` keyword is assigned level 5 and is not the highest level, so option D is incorrect. The `err` keyword is assigned level 3 and is not the highest level, so option E is incorrect.

4.   B.   The `notice` severity level represents system event messages that are significant but normal, so option B is correct. The `crit` and `alert` keywords represent event messages that are critical or that require special attention, so options A and D are incorrect. The `info` keyword represents event messages that are only informational but not significant, so option C is incorrect. The `local0` keyword is not defined in the syslog protocol but by the local system, so option E is incorrect.

5.   E.   The `rsyslogd` application was designed to be a faster version of the `syslogd` application, so option E is correct. The `syslogd` application is the original syslog application and was not known for its speed, so option A is incorrect. The `syslog-ng` application was designed to be more versatile than `syslogd`, but not faster, so option B is incorrect. The `systemd-journald` application is known for faster queries in reading journal entries but wasn't designed to be faster in handling event messages, so option C is incorrect. The `klogd` application is part of the original `sysklogd` application and is also not fast, so option D is incorrect.

6. A. The `rsyslogd` application uses the `rsyslog.conf` configuration file by default, so option A is correct. Option D, `rsyslog.d`, is commonly used as a folder for storing additional `rsyslogd` configuration files, but it isn't the default configuration filename, so it is incorrect. Options B and C are configuration files for other logging applications, not `rsyslogd`, so they are incorrect. Option E is not a valid logging application configuration filename.

7. D. The `rsyslogd` application priorities log event messages with the defined severity or higher, so option D would log all kernel event messages at the `warn`, `alert`, or `emerg` severities and therefore it is correct. The option A facility and priority setting would only log kernel messages with a severity of warning, so it is incorrect. Option B would log all kernel event messages, not just warnings or higher, so it is incorrect. Option C would log all facility type event messages but include the information or higher level severity, so it is incorrect. Option E would log kernel event messages but only at the alert or emerg severity levels, not the warning level, so it is incorrect.

8. B. The `Storage` setting controls how `systemd-journald` manages the journal file. Setting the value to `persistent` ensures that the journal file will remain in the `/var/log/journal` directory, so option B is correct. Setting the value to `auto` only ensures that the journal file will be persistent if the `/var/log/journal` directory exists, so option A is incorrect. Setting the value to `volatile` ensures that the file does not persist, so option D is incorrect. Options C and E refer to settings that control whether or not event messages are passed to the `rsyslogd` application, so they are both incorrect.

9. C. The `-r` option displays the journal entries in reverse order, so the most recent entry will appear first. Thus, option C is correct. The `-a` option displays all of the data fields, but in the normal order, so option A is incorrect. The `-l` option displays all printable data fields, but in the normal order, so option B is incorrect. The `-e` option jumps to the end of the journal file but displays the remaining entries in normal order instead of reverse order, so option D is incorrect. The `-n` option displays a specified number of entries, but in normal order, so option E is incorrect.

10. A. The `journalctl` application allows you to filter event messages related to a specific application by the application process ID (PID) using the `OBJECT_PID` match, so option A is correct. The `Kernel` match retrieves event messages generated by the system kernel and not applications, so option B is incorrect. The `_TRANSPORT` option filters event messages based on how they were received and not by application, so option C is incorrect. Option D, `_UID`, filters event messages based on the user ID value, not the application, so it is incorrect. Option E, `_UDEV`, filters events by device ID and not by application, so it too is incorrect.

Chapter 18: Overseeing Linux Firewalls

1. A, C, E. The Linux firewall applications covered in this chapter use access control lists (ACLs) to identify which network packets are allowed in or out of the system. Therefore, option A is a correct answer. They identify the network packets by inspecting their control information along with other network data. Thus, option C is also a correct choice.

In addition, the Linux firewall applications use configuration files to maintain persistency, which allows the firewall configuration to survive system reboots and/or the firewall application being started or reloaded. Therefore, option E is also a correct answer. These firewalls cannot detect malicious behavior; they only follow predefined rules. Therefore, option B is a wrong answer. In addition, they use `netfilter` embedded in the Linux kernel and not `iptables` (which is instead a firewall service), so option D is also an incorrect choice.

2. B. Option B best describes packet filtering. Option A describes how packets are identified but only allows them into the system, and therefore is not the best answer. A packet's payload refers to the data it is carrying. In packet filtering, packets are identified by their control information, such as their source IP address. Therefore, option C is not the correct answer either. Network packets can be identified by much more than just their source address, making option D a wrong answer. Option E is also a wrong answer because it focuses on the packet's payload and not its control information.

3. C, D. A stateful firewall uses a memory table to track an established connection's packets, making it faster for those connections. In addition, it can tell if packets are fragmented and thus protects the system from attacks that spread among multiple packets. Therefore, options C and D are the correct answers. Stateless firewalls operate faster overall, and they are not as vulnerable to DDoS attacks. Thus, options A and B are wrong answers. While stateful firewalls are vulnerable to DDoS attacks, it is not a benefit. Therefore, option E is also an incorrect choice.

4. E. With `firewalld`, network traffic is grouped into a zone, which is a predefined rule set, also called a trust level. Therefore, option E is the correct answer. While `firewalld` does employ the `netfilter` and the `firewall-cmd` commands, those items are not predefined rule sets, so options A and B are wrong answers. A service is a predefined configuration set for a particular service, such as DNS. Therefore, option C is an incorrect answer as well. Option D is an incorrect choice because the zone that rejects packets is called `block`.

5. D. The `firewalld`'s runtime environment is the active firewall, but if the configuration is not saved as the permanent environment, it is not persistent. Therefore, after his successful tests, he should issue the `firewall-cmd --runtime-to-permanent` command to save the runtime environment to the permanent environment. Thus, option D is the correct answer. Rebooting the system would lose the tested runtime environment, so option A is a wrong answer. The `--panic-on` option blocks all incoming traffic, so option B is also an incorrect answer. The runtime environment is different than the permanent environment in this situation, so option C is a wrong choice. While the `--permanent` option will allow you to modify the runtime and permanent environment at the same time, Peter did not do this, so option E is also an incorrect answer.

6. C. To achieve the desired result, Peter will need to modify the iptables `INPUT` chain for the protocol `ping` uses, which is ICMP. Also, the target will need to be set to DROP, in order to not send any rejection message. Therefore, option C is the correct `iptables` command to use. The command in option A will set the policy to DROP for all incoming packets that do not have a rule in the `INPUT` chain, but that does not target `ping` packets. Therefore, option A is a wrong answer. The command in option B will send a rejection message, which is not desired, so it is also an incorrect answer. The command in option D is attempting to delete a rule, not add one. Therefore, option D is a wrong choice. The command in option E

is modifying the OUTPUT chain instead of the INPUT chain, which will affect outbound network packets. Thus, option E is an incorrect choice.

7. D. The sudo ufw status numbered command will display the UFW firewall's ACL rules with their associated numbers. Therefore, option D is the correct answer. Option A is made up and thus is a wrong answer. Both options B and C will show any rules, but they will not include their numbers, so those options are incorrect answers. The UFW command in option E enables the firewall but does not display ACL rules, so it is an incorrect choice as well.

8. A. While all these options use simple syntax, the ufw command in option A will block all incoming and outgoing OpenSSH connections and not send a blocking (rejection) message. Thus, option A is the correct answer. There is no drop argument in the ufw command, so option B is a wrong answer. The command in option C would send a rejection message. Thus, it is a wrong choice. The command in option D will allow OpenSSH connections, and therefore it is an incorrect answer. There is no block argument in the ufw command, so option E is also an incorrect choice.

9. A, B. Options A and B are true statements concerning both DenyHosts and Fail2Ban. DenyHosts only works with OpenSSH traffic, while Fail2Ban can handle many different types of traffic. So option C is a wrong answer. Fail2Ban's configuration file is named /etc/fail2ban/jail.conf, but the configuration file for DenyHosts is not. Therefore, option D is an incorrect answer as well. DenyHosts can only work with TCP Wrappers, whereas Fail2Ban can work with iptables, TCP Wrappers, firewalld, and so on. Thus, option E is an incorrect choice.

10. E. The command in option E will properly add the new IP address to the BlockThem IPset. Thus, it is the correct answer. The commands in options A and B create the IPset and do not add new addresses to it. Therefore, those options are wrong answers. The command in option C will save the current IPset configuration to the IPset configuration file. While this is something Virginia should do after the new address is added, it is not the currently needed command. Thus, option C is a wrong answer. The command in option D adds an entire subnet of addresses to the IPset and not a single IP address. Thus it is an incorrect answer as well.

Chapter 19: Embracing Best Security Practices

1. B. The Kerberos authentication method uses a ticket-granting system to assign a ticket to the user account after a successful authentication. Any server on the network that uses Kerberos can then authenticate the user account using that ticket. Thus, option B is correct. The LDAP, RADIUS, and TACACS+ authentication methods don't use tickets for user authentication, so options A, C, and D are all incorrect. The biometrics authentication method uses user physical features to authenticate user accounts but doesn't issue a ticket to allow single sign-on, so option E is incorrect.

2. C. Biometrics uses physical features of users to authenticate them on the Linux system, so option C is correct. LDAP and Kerberos are only single-factor authentication methods, so options A and E are incorrect. Tokens and PKI are both two-factor authentication methods but use digital tokens instead of physical features for authentication, so options B and D are incorrect.

3. A. The LDAP authentication method allows administrators to create a distributed database that not only authenticates user accounts but tracks user authorization of network resources, so option A is correct. The Kerberos and RADIUS authentication methods don't use a distributed database, nor can they authorize users to access network resources, so options B and D are incorrect. Tokens and PKI are two-factor authentication methods that don't use distributed databases, nor do they authorize users to access network resources, so options C and E are incorrect.

4. E. When you specify the `nologin` utility as the default shell for a user account, users will receive a message upon successful login that they aren't allowed to access the system, so option E is correct. Biometrics, tokens, and Kerberos are all authentication methods that won't prevent the root user account from logging in, so options A, B, and C are all incorrect. Removing the root user account from the `/etc/passwd` file removes the root user account from the system, which will break applications that require the root user account to run, so option D is incorrect.

5. B. All user data is normally stored under the `/home` directory structure on Linux systems, so placing the `/home` directory on a separate disk partition would separate user data from system data, making option B correct. The `/usr`, `/etc`, `/sbin`, and `/bin` directories all contain system data and not user data, so options A, C, D, and E are all incorrect.

6. D. The `chroot` program restricts an application to a specific area within the virtual filesystem structure, so option D is correct. Blocking the application network port would prevent guests from connecting to the application, so option A is incorrect. Moving the application to a private port number wouldn't restrict access to directories, so option B is incorrect. Placing the application in an encrypted partition or on a separate partition wouldn't prevent the application from accessing data outside of the application, so options C and E are incorrect.

7. A. The Linux Unified Key Setup (LUKS) feature provides disk-level encryption so that all files stored in a partition are automatically encrypted when written and decrypted when read, so option A is correct. The `chroot` utility restricts an application to a specific location in the virtual filesystem but doesn't encrypt files, so option B is incorrect. The `auditd` utility creates detailed logs of system activity such as user file access but doesn't encrypt files or disks, so option D is incorrect. Both PKI and Kerberos are authentication methods and not disk encryption methods, so both options D and E are incorrect.

8. C. The `/etc/cron.deny` file is a list of user accounts prevented from scheduling jobs, so adding the user to that file would stop them from scheduling the job, making option C correct. The `chroot` program restricts applications to a specific location in the virtual filesystem; it doesn't block users from scheduling jobs, so option A is incorrect. The `nologin` program prevents user accounts from logging into the system, which is an extreme solution to the problem, so option B isn't a good solution. The `/etc/hosts.deny` file blocks hosts from accessing the system and not users from scheduling jobs, so option D is incorrect.

The /etc/motd file displays a message to all users as they log into the system, but it won't block them from scheduling jobs, so option E is incorrect.

9. D. The fastest way to deter an attacker is to place their IP address in the /etc/hosts .deny file, preventing them from accessing the system, so option D is correct. Placing applications into a chroot jail prevents the application from accessing files outside of the jail filesystem but doesn't prevent the attacker from continuing to access a user account, so option A is incorrect. Adding the nologin shell to the user account will prevent the attacker from accessing the user account but will also block the valid user from accessing the account, so option B is incorrect. Implementing two-factor authentication will help stop the attacker but isn't a quick solution, so option C is incorrect. Adding the user account to the /etc/cron .deny file prevents the user account from scheduling jobs but won't stop the attacker from trying to log in as the user account, so option E is incorrect.

10. E. Disabling the FTP application network ports will prevent users from being able to use the FTP service, so option E is correct. Placing a message in the /etc/motd file to display when users log in won't prevent them from using the FTP service, so option A is incorrect. Moving the FTP application to a different network port may temporarily solve the problem, but once users find the alternative ports, they can continue using FTP, so option B is incorrect. The /etc/hosts.deny file contains IP addresses or hostnames of remote hosts to block, not user accounts, so option C is incorrect. The /etc/cron.deny file blocks users from scheduling jobs, not accessing network applications, so option D is incorrect.

Chapter 20: Analyzing System Properties and Remediation

1. B, C. A network socket is a single endpoint of a network connection's two endpoints. That single endpoint is on the local system, bound to a particular port, and uses a combination of an IP address and a port number. Therefore, options B and C are correct answers. Ports use numbers to identify which service or application is transmitting data, and thus option A is a wrong answer. Unix sockets are endpoints between processes on a local system and provide better interprocess communication (IPC) than localhost. Therefore, options D and E are incorrect choices.

2. A, B, E. The iperf, ping, and traceroute utilities will help test the network for high latency (slowness) in order to determine the cause. Thus, options A, B, and E are correct answers. The ip neigh command is used to check the routing tables and is often employed in situations where a duplicate or incorrect MAC address is causing problems on a local network segment. Therefore, option C is a wrong answer. The dig utility checks name server resolutions, not high latency. Thus, option D is also an incorrect choice.

3. A, D, E. The mtr, tracepath, and traceroute utilities all allow Mr. Scott to view router packets traveling through certain network segments and isolate which routers may be dropping packets. Therefore, options A, D, and E are correct answers. The ifconfig tool is for viewing and configuring network adapters. Therefore, option B is a wrong answer.

The `ethtool -s` command will show adapter statistics but not router information, and therefore option C is also an incorrect choice.

4. D. The `nslookup` utility can be used along with the `time` command to test new name servers to see if they are more efficient (faster). Thus, option D is the correct answer. Option A's `dnsmasq` is caching-only name server software, so it is a wrong answer. The `whois` utility performs queries of Whois servers, not name servers. Thus, option B is an incorrect answer. The `nmap` utility is used for network mapping and analysis (or pentesting), and therefore, option C is a wrong choice. The `ipset list` command displays the various IPsets on a system but is not involved with name resolution. Thus, option E is an incorrect choice.

5. A. The `iostat` command displays I/O wait, which is a performance statistic showing the amount of time a processor must wait on disk I/O. Therefore, option A is the correct answer. The `ioping` utility is more for testing new disks on performance items such as disk I/O latency, seek rates, sequential speeds, and so on. Therefore, option B is a wrong answer. The `du` and `df` commands are useful for situations where disk space is an issue but do not provide I/O wait statistics. Therefore, options C and D are incorrect answers. The `iotop` utility is helpful in locating an application or process causing high I/O but not CPU latency due to high I/O. Thus, option E is also an incorrect answer.

6. B. The `deadline` I/O scheduler is good for situations where increased database I/O and overall reduced I/O latency are needed, and/or an SSD is employed, and/or a real-time application is in use. Therefore, option B is the correct answer. Option A is the I/O scheduler configuration file's name, and therefore it is a wrong answer. Option C is one of the subdirectories in the directory that contains the I/O scheduler configuration file, such as `/sys/block/sdc/queue/`. Thus, option C is also an incorrect answer. The `cfq` scheduler is best for situations where more balanced I/O handling is needed and/or the system has a multiprocessor. Therefore, option D is a wrong answer. The `noop` I/O scheduler is good for situations where an SSD is employed but less CPU usage is needed. Therefore, option E is an incorrect choice.

7. A, B, D. The `uptime` command displays CPU load averages in 1-, 5-, and 15-minute increments. Thus, options A, B, and D are correct answers and options C and E are incorrect choices.

8. C. The `sar` utility is the best one for viewing a system's processor performance over time. It uses data stored by the `sadc` program in the `/var/log/sa/` directory, which contains up to a month's worth of data. Therefore, option C is the correct answer. The `uptime` utility is handy to view processor performance, but `sar` is a better one for viewing it over time. Thus, option A is a wrong answer. `sysstat` is a package that provides the `sar` utility, and therefore, option B is an incorrect answer. The `/proc/cpuinfo` file contains detailed processor information, but it is not the best for viewing CPU performance. Thus, option D is also a wrong choice. The `sysctl` utility is used to view or tweak kernel parameters. Therefore, option E is an incorrect choice.

9. E. The `swapon -s` command will allow Gertie to view a swap space element's type, name, and priority. Therefore, option E is the correct answer. The `vmstat` utility provides a lot of memory statistics, including disk I/O specific to swapping as well as total blocks in and blocks out to the device. However, it does not provide the information Gertie needs, so

option A is a wrong answer. The free command shows memory items such as free memory, used memory, and buffer/cache usage. Thus, option B is an incorrect answer. fstab is not a command, but a file. This file is where swap partitions/files must have records in order for the swap space to remain persistent through reboots. Therefore, option C is a wrong choice. The swapoff utility disengages a partition/file from swap space, and thus, option D is an incorrect choice.

10. E. In this scenario, since multiple swap spaces already exist and the one swap partition or file is on a logical volume, Elliot should add more swap space by using LVM tools to increase the logical volume. Thus, option E is the correct answer. While Elliot would need to employ mkswap and swapon on the logical volume after it is extended, options A, B, C, and D are using those utilities on files or partitions, instead of logical volumes. Therefore, those options are incorrect choices.

Chapter 21: Optimizing Performance

1. A, C, D. The GNU ps command in Linux supports parameters that were supported by the legacy BSD and Unix ps command, along with new options created by GNU, so options A, C, and D are correct. There are no Linux style options used by the ps command, so option B is incorrect. The ps command doesn't support numeric options, so option E is also incorrect.

2. B. The Unix style command-line options for the GNU ps command are identified by placing a single dash in front of the option, so option B is correct. The newer GNU options are identified by using a double dash, so option A is incorrect. The legacy BSD style options are identified by not placing anything in front of the option letter, so option C is incorrect. Unix style options still use letters, not decimal or hexadecimal numbers, so options D and E are both incorrect.

3. D. With no command-line options, the GNU ps command displays only processes run by the current shell, so option D is correct. To display all processes running on a specific terminal, you need to add the -t option, so option A is incorrect. To display all active processes, you must add the -A option, so option B is incorrect. To display the sleeping processes, you need to use the -ef option, so option C is incorrect. To display all processes run by the current user account, you need to add the -x option, so option E is incorrect.

4. A. The top command displays the currently running processes on the system and updates every 3 seconds, so option A is correct. The ps command displays currently running processes but doesn't update in real time, so option B is incorrect. The lsof command displays files currently opened by processes but not the processes themselves, so option C is incorrect. The pkill and kill commands are used to stop running processes, not display them, so options D and E are both incorrect.

5. E. The S command displays the processes based on the cumulative CPU time for each process, so option E is correct. The l command displays the processes based on the load average, so option A is incorrect. The F command allows you to select the field used to sort the

display, so option B is incorrect. The r command reverses the sort order of the display, so option C is incorrect. The y command highlights running tasks, so option D is incorrect.

6. B. The RES column in the top output displays the amount of physical memory used by the applications, so option B is correct. The VIRT column displays the amount of virtual memory, not physical memory, so option A is incorrect. The SHR column displays the amount of shared memory used, so option C is incorrect. The S column displays the status of the application process, so option D is incorrect. The %MEM column displays the percentage of physical memory the application is using but not the amount of physical memory, so option E is incorrect.

7. C. The nice command allows you to specify the priority level for an application, so option C is correct. The renice command allows you to change the priority level of an application that's already running, but not one that hasn't started yet, so option A is incorrect. The pkill and kill commands are used to stop running processes, not change their priority levels, so options B and D are incorrect. The pgrep command displays the application processes matching a search term; it doesn't change the priority level of the processes, so option E is incorrect.

8. A. The renice command allows you to change the priority level assigned to an application that's already running on the system, so option A is correct. The pkill and kill commands allow you to stop an application but not change the priority level, so options B and D are both incorrect. The nice command allows you to start an application with a specified priority level but not change the priority level of an application that's already running, so option C is incorrect. The pgrep command allows you to search for a running application based on a search term but not change the priority level of it, so option E is incorrect.

9. B. The pkill command allows you to send a HUP signal to a running process based on a search term for the process name, so option B is correct. The renice command allows you to change the priority level of an application that's already running but not stop it, so option A is incorrect. The nice command allows you to start an application at a specified priority level but not stop an application that's already running, so option C is incorrect. The kill command allows you to stop an application that's running, but you need to use the process ID number and not the name, so option D is incorrect. The pgrep command allows you to search for running applications based on their name but not stop them, so option E is incorrect.

10. D. The kill command allows you to stop an application that's already running by specifying its process ID, so option D is correct. The renice command allows you to change the priority level of an application but not stop it, so option A is incorrect. The pkill command allows you to stop an application, but by specifying its process name and not its process ID, so option B is incorrect. The nice command allows you to start an application using a specified priority level but not stop an application, so option C is incorrect. The pgrep command allows you to display running applications based on a search term for the application name but not stop them, so option E is incorrect.

Chapter 22: Investigating User Issues

1. C. Since Lamar is a contractor, his account should have an expiration date set. Thus, the first thing to check for his particular local access problem is whether or not the account has expired. Option C is the correct answer. GUI services may not be running, but this is not the first thing to check (and no one else is having problems, just Lamar). Thus, option A is an incorrect choice. Lamar is not employing a utility such as OpenSSH, so option B is a wrong answer. The account might be locked, but this is not the first thing to check, so option D is an incorrect answer. SELinux policy violations also may be a problem, but you don't know if the system is running SELinux or AppArmor. Therefore, option E is also an incorrect choice.

2. E. Since Irene normally logs into the system using the tty4 terminal and is having trouble today but can log in using the tty3 terminal, the first thing to check is whether or not the tty4 device file is corrupted. Therefore, option E is the correct answer. If getty services were not running, Irene could not log into the tty3 terminal, so option A is a wrong answer. Option B is not the first item to check, so it is an incorrect answer. The account is not locked because Irene can log in via the tty3 terminal. Thus, option C is an incorrect answer. Using the `last` command is not helpful in this scenario, unless you think Irene is confused, so option D is an incorrect choice as well.

3. B. To enlist Vincent's help, have him add the `-vvv` option on to his `ssh` command. This will provide a great deal of information that will assist you as you track down the problem. Therefore, option B is the correct answer. The `/etc/ssh/sshd_config` configuration file is on the server side, and Vincent cannot reach the system, so option A is the wrong answer. The `-X` option will only help if your system is forwarding X11 GUI servers over the network, so option C is an incorrect answer. If Vincent is using token-based authentication via `ssh`, then this will need to be checked, but it's not the first item to address. Thus, option D is a wrong choice. The `config` file may need to be checked, but it's not the first item to address, so option E is an incorrect choice as well.

4. D, E. The best log files for Anton to peruse in this situation are `/var/log/secure` and `/var/log/lastlog` using the `lastlog` command. Therefore, options D and E are the correct answers. Since `auditd` is not employed, the file in option A is not available and is a wrong answer. Since SELinux is not used, the file in option B is also an incorrect answer. This system, Rocky Linux, is a Red Hat–based system and not Debian, so the `/var/log/auth` file is not available. Thus option C is also an incorrect choice.

5. A, D. From the choices listed, to allow Tarissa to run the script, add her to the `wheel` group and add execute (x) to the shell script file's permissions. Thus, options A and D are the correct answers. Option B will do nothing for this situation and is a wrong answer. Adding write (w) to the group permissions will not allow her (or the `wheel` group members) to execute the file. Thus, option C is a wrong choice. Actions need to take place, so option E is incorrect.

6. B. For Miles to change his present working directory to `/home/miles`, the other section must have the execute (x) permission. Therefore, option B is the correct answer. You do not know Miles's home directory configuration, so you cannot assume it is `/home/miles`. Thus, option A is the wrong answer. The write (w) and read (r) permissions don't allow a user to change his present working directory to this directory. Therefore, options C and D

are incorrect answers. The dash (-) in a file permission listing is not a permission but instead shows the absence of a permission. Thus, option E is also an incorrect choice.

7. A, B, D, E. Options A, B, D, and E contain potential causes of Sarah's file creation problem and are therefore correct answers. A file with an immutable bit cannot be deleted, and thus option C is the only incorrect choice.

8. E. The `lsattr` command used on the file will display whether or not the immutable bit is set. If this bit is set, the user cannot delete the file until it is removed. Therefore, option E is the correct answer. The `chown` command changes a file's ownership, and thus option A is the wrong answer. The `chattr` command can add or remove certain file attributes, such as the immutable bit, but is not helpful at this point, so option B is an incorrect answer. The `chmod` utility changes file permissions (modes), but it does not help in this situation, so option C is a wrong choice. The `umask` command displays or sets what permissions are removed from default permissions when a file or directory is created. This is not helpful here, so option D is an incorrect choice.

9. D. When the `export EDITOR='vim'` line is put in her `~/.profile` file, the default editor will be set to the `vim` editor for Melissa. It will also stay set when she enters a sub-shell. Thus, option D is the correct answer. If option A or B was completed, then everyone on the system would have the `vim` editor as their default editor. Therefore, options A and B are incorrect answers. Option C would set the `vim` editor as Melissa's default editor, but it would not be set when she entered a subshell due to the missing `export` command. Thus, option C is also an incorrect answer. The `.bash.bashrc` file does not reside in the user's local directory (it is located in the `/etc` directory) and is also not a hidden file, so option E is an incorrect choice.

10. B, C, E. The `echo $SHELL` command will show Mark his current shell. Though it could be a modified environment variable, this will help to determine if his default shell has been changed. Thus, option B is a correct answer. The `sudo grep tcsh$ /etc/passwd` command will display any `/etc/passwd` file records that have `/bin/tcsh` as their default shell, including Mark's. Thus, option C is a correct answer too. The `sudo getent passwd MW2015` command will show Mark's account's password file setting, including its default shell. Therefore, option E is also a correct answer. The option A command will display the settings in the profile environment configuration file, but since Mark is the only one experiencing the problem, the `SHELL` environment variable is not set with this method. Thus, option A is a wrong answer. The command in option D will show the shadow file records and not the password file records. Therefore, option D is an incorrect choice.

Chapter 23: Dealing with Linux Devices

1. C. PCI boards use interrupts, I/O ports, and DMA channels to send and receive data with the PC motherboard, so option C is correct. USB devices transmit data using a serial bus connected to the motherboard and don't use DMA channels, so option A is incorrect. The GPIO interface uses memory-mapped specialty IC chips and not interrupts and I/O ports, so option B is incorrect. Monitors and printers are hardware devices and not hardware interfaces, so options D and E are incorrect.

2. **A.** The Linux kernel uses the `/proc/ioports` file to track the I/O ports used by the installed PCI boards on the system, so option A is correct. The kernel uses the `/proc/interrupts` and `/proc/dma` files to track interrupts and the DMA channel, not I/O ports, so options B and E are incorrect. The `/sys` directory contains files used to track kernel, module, and system features, not I/O ports, so option C is incorrect. The `/dev` directory contains files used to transfer data to and from devices, not track their I/O ports, so option D is incorrect.

3. **D.** The kernel creates files in the `/dev` directory for each device on the Linux system. These files are used to send data to the device and read data from the device. Thus, option D is correct. The `/sys` and `/proc` directories are used by the kernel to display system information, not transfer data, so options A and B are incorrect. The `/etc` directory is used for configuration files, not for transferring data, so option C is incorrect. The `/dev/mapper` directory is used by virtual systems such as LVM and LUKS to create virtual files that indirectly interface with devices through another application, not directly, so option E is incorrect.

4. **B.** The kernel uses the `/dev/mapper` directory to create virtual files that interface with applications that manipulate data on a virtual LVM volume before being sent to a physical hard drive device, so option B is correct. The `/dev` directory contains the physical device files, not virtual files, so option A is incorrect. The kernel uses the `/proc` and `/sys` directories to display kernel and system information, not virtual files for LVM volumes, so options C and D are incorrect. The `/etc` directory contains configuration files for applications, not LVM volumes, so option E is incorrect.

5. **A.** The `lsdev` command displays all the hardware information about all the devices connected to the system, so option A is correct. The `lsblk` command only displays information on block devices, so option B is incorrect. The `lspci` command only displays information about PCI devices, so option C is incorrect. The `lsusb` command only displays information about USB devices, so option D is incorrect. The `dmesg` command displays messages from the kernel ring buffer, not information about the current devices, so option E is incorrect.

6. **E.** The `dmesg` command displays the kernel event messages contained in the kernel ring buffer, so option E is correct. The `lsdev` command displays hardware information about devices, but not messages from the kernel, so option A is incorrect. The `lsblk` command only displays information about block devices, not kernel event messages, so option B is incorrect. The `lspci` command only displays information about PCI devices, not kernel event messages, so option C is incorrect. The `lsusb` command only displays information about USB devices, not kernel event messages, so option D is incorrect.

7. **A, C.** The `X.org` and Wayland software packages implement the X Windows graphical system for Linux, so options A and C are correct. The CUPS software package implements PostScript printing for Linux, not X Windows graphical systems, so option B is incorrect. X11 is an X Windows standard but not a software package, so option D is incorrect. The `udev` program is used to detect hot-pluggable devices, not implement the X Windows graphical system, so option E is incorrect.

8. B. The CUPS software package provides an interface to convert PostScript documents and send them to common printers, so option B is correct. The X.org and Wayland software packages are used to implement the X Windows graphical system in Linux, not interface with printers, so options A and C are incorrect. X11 is a standard for X Windows, not a software package for printers, so option D is incorrect. The udev program detects hot-pluggable devices but doesn't interact directly with the printers, so option E is incorrect.

9. E. The udev program runs in the background and monitors the kernel ring buffer for event messages from new devices, so option E is correct. The X.org and Wayland software packages implement the X Windows graphical system but don't listen for new devices, so options A and C are incorrect. The CUPS package interfaces with printers on the Linux system and doesn't listen for new devices, so option B is incorrect. X11 is a standard for X Windows and not a software package that listens for new devices, so option D is incorrect.

10. A. The udevadm program allows you to send control messages to the udev application running in background, signaling it to reload the rules defined in the /etc/udev/rules.d directory, so option A is correct. The udev application can't direct itself to reload the rules, so option B is incorrect. The lsusb, lspci, and lsdev programs are used for displaying hardware information for the system, not for directing the udev program to reload defined rules, so options C, D, and E are all incorrect.

Chapter 24: Troubleshooting Application and Hardware Issues

1. B. Due to this application that is memory intensive and experiencing performance issues, the system's swap space is most likely receiving high I/O from RAM. SSDs have a finite number of program/erase (PE) cycles, and continually writing and removing data from them, such as occurs in swap, will cause them to become degraded storage faster than normal. Thus, option B is the correct answer. Degraded mode refers to the mode a RAID enters when one or more of its member disks have failed. Since it is not stated whether the application data is stored on a RAID array, option A is a wrong answer. Only NVMe SSDs need to have a namespace in their device filenames. Since it is not stated whether these SSDs are NVMe disks, option C is also an incorrect answer. A missing volume occurs when a disk that is part of a logical volume fails or is accidentally removed. Since it is not stated whether these SSDs are involved with a logical volume, option D is a wrong choice. Resource exhaustion occurs when a system's finite resources are committed and unavailable to others. For disks, this includes running out of inode numbers or disk space. While it is possible that at some point in time the SSDs will experience resource exhaustion, there is not enough information provided to declare that they will. Therefore, option E is also an incorrect choice.

2. A, C. Since this is this system's first SCSI disk and it is not being recognized, it is possible that the appropriate modules (drivers) are not loaded. Thus, Mary should check to see if the drivers are on the system via the command in option A and check if they are currently loaded into the kernel using the command in option C. The pvscan utility is used for physical volumes being used for a logical volume's volume group. Therefore, option B is a wrong answer. The `hdparm` and `smartctl` commands in options D and E are employed for checking and resetting power management configurations on a SATA device. Thus, they are incorrect choices.

3. B, C, D. For Norman to begin the process of troubleshooting this application permission issue, he'll need to either know or determine the information listed in options B, C, and D. The disk type, where the program resides, does not assist in this troubleshooting process, so option A is a wrong answer. The program's name is also not helpful here, so option E is an incorrect choice.

4. D. Because the application can create the file in a particular directory with no problem but cannot write to the file, it is most likely a permission inheritance issue via default directory ACLs. Therefore, option D is the correct answer. If the directory ownership and their permissions were a problem, the application could not create a file in that directory. Therefore, option A is a wrong answer. File ownership and group membership would have to be manually changed by the application in order to cause this issue. Therefore, options B and C are incorrect answers. Executable privileges are involved with being able to run a program file or change a process's present working directory, and thus, option E is an incorrect choice.

5. E. The upgrade may have broken the Apache package by breaking a dependency. The `sudo apt-get check` command will check for such a thing. Thus, option E is the correct answer. The commands in options A and B will clean up the repository database and any temporary download files but not help to troubleshoot this issue. Therefore, options A and B are wrong answers. The command in option C shows library files used by the Apache service, but it does not help troubleshoot the problem and is therefore an incorrect answer. Option D's command checks for broken dependencies, but on a Red Hat–based system, and thus it is an incorrect choice.

6. C. If Peter cannot compile a flawlessly written C++ application, then the problem must lie with the compiler, GCC. Thus, option C is the correct answer. Application and file permissions would not cause this particular issue, so options A and B are wrong answers. A missing or outdated device would not be the problem for this situation, so option D is also an incorrect answer. Since Peter wrote this application, instead of trying to obtain one from a package repository, option E is an incorrect choice as well.

7. B. The `sealert` utility is used to check the audit log file for SELinux context violations. Therefore, the issue here revolves around SELinux. The `ls -Z` command will allow Mary to view the `flash.txt` file's SELinux context to determine if it needs to have it changed. Thus, option B is the correct answer. The option A command will not show the file's SELinux context and is therefore a wrong answer. While the `flash.txt` directory might have a context problem, the `ls -l` command will not show it, and thus option C is a wrong choice as well. Option D's `setroubleshoot` is a package and not a command, so it is a wrong answer. Option E's `restorecon` will fix SELinux labels, which may be used in the repair process but not in troubleshooting, so it is an incorrect choice.

8. A, B, D, E. For troubleshooting this issue, the firewall ACLs on both the NTP server and the application server must be checked. Either side could be dropping or rejecting packets, so options A and B are correct answers. If you do not have the NTP ports and transport

protocols memorized, the `/etc/services` file needs checking. That information is critical for reviewing server- and client-side firewall ACLs. Thus, option D is a correct answer too. It is a good idea to view the firewall log entries because they may point to the exact cause of the problem or provide valuable information. Therefore, option E is a right choice. The `firewall-cmd` command is specific only to those systems that employ the `firewalld` firewall. Therefore, option C is the only incorrect choice.

9. B. The communications port is a serial port, represented by the `/dev/ttyS#` device files. To find the right number (#), use the `dmesg` command to start the troubleshooting process. Thus, option B is the correct answer. Since a serial port is not represented by files named `/dev/COM#`, both options A and C are wrong answers. The `setserial` command is used after you determined the appropriate filename for the serial device, so it is not the first step and option D is an incorrect answer. The `cat /proc/interrupts` command is performed after you find the correct IRQ via the `setserial` command, so option E is an incorrect choice as well.

10. C, D, E. The activities in options C, D, and E are all steps that may be included in troubleshooting this USB printer issue. A CUPS system uses the `/etc/cups/printers.conf` file instead of the `/etc/printcap` file, so option A is a wrong answer. The `lpinfo -m` command allows you to view available printer drivers, not USB ports, so option B is an incorrect choice as well.

Chapter 25: Deploying Bash Scripts

1. B. The `#!` character combination defines the shebang, which tells the Linux shell what shell to use to run the shell script code, so option B is correct. The `>>` character combination appends the output of a command to a file, so option A is incorrect. The `|` character pipes the output of a command to another command, so option C is incorrect. The `>` character redirects the output of a command to a new file or overwrites an existing file, so option D is incorrect. The `2>` character combination redirects error messages from a command to a file, so option E is incorrect.

2. D. The `>` character redirects all of the output from a command to a new file, or overwrites an existing file, so option D is correct. The `>>` character combination appends all of the output from a command to an existing file, so option A is incorrect. The `#!` combination defines the shell to use, so option B is incorrect. The `|` character pipes output from one command to another command, so option C is incorrect. The `2>` character combination redirects only error messages from a command to a new file, not all of the output, so option E is incorrect.

3. C. The `u+x` chmod permission assigns execute permissions to the file owner so that you can run the file at the command prompt, which makes option C correct. The 644 octal permission assigns only read and write permissions to the file owner, not execute permissions, so option A is incorrect. The `u+r` permission assigns read permissions, not execute permissions, so option B is incorrect. The `u+w` permission assigns only write permissions and not execute permissions, so option D is incorrect. The `u=wr` permission assigns both read and write permissions but not execute permissions to the file owner, so option E is incorrect.

4.   A. The $USER environment variable contains the text username of the user account that started the shell, so option A is correct. The $UID environment variable contains the numeric user ID, not the text username, so option B is incorrect. The $HOME environment variable contains the home directory location of the user account, not the username, so option C is incorrect. The $BASH environment variable contains the location of the Bash shell executable file, not the username of the user who started the shell, so option D is incorrect. The $1 variable is a positional variable, not an environment variable. It's used to retrieve data from the command-line command that launched the shell, not to identify the user who started the shell, so option E is incorrect.

5.   C. To assign a value to a variable, you use the equal sign, but no spaces must be used between the variable name, the equal sign, and the value, so option C is correct. Option A uses the command substitution format, which doesn't assign a value to a variable but to the output of a command, so option A is incorrect. Option B places spaces between the variable name, equal sign, and the value, so option B is incorrect. Option D places quotes around the value, making it a string value and not a numeric value, so option D is incorrect. Option E uses backtick characters around the value, which attempts to run it using command substitution, which is incorrect.

6.   B. The -f *file* test checks if the specified object exists, and if it's a file, so option B is correct. The -e *file* test checks if the object exists, not the object type, so option A is incorrect. The -d *file* test checks if the object exists but is a directory, not a file, so option C is incorrect. The -x *file* test checks if the current user account has execute permissions for the file, not that the object exists and is a file, so option D is incorrect. The -w *file* test checks if the current user account has write permissions for the file, not that the object exists and is a file, so option E is incorrect.

7.   C. The bar character (|) pipes the output of one command to the input of another command, so option C is correct. The >> character combination appends the output of a command to an existing file, not to another command, so option A is incorrect. The shebang (#!) is used to identify the shell to use to run the script, not to redirect output from a command to another command, so option B is incorrect. The > character redirects the output of a command to a new file, not to another command, so option D is incorrect. The 2> character combination redirects the error messages from a command to a new file, not to another command, so option E is incorrect.

8.   D. The exit command allows us to return a specific error status when the shell script exits, so option D is correct. The #! shebang defines the shell to use to run the shell script, not the exit status, so option A is incorrect. The $? character combination displays the exit status from the last command; it doesn't return a specific exit status, so option B is incorrect. The $1 variable contains the first command-line parameter used when the shell script is launched from the command line; it doesn't set the exit status for the shell script, so option C is incorrect. The while command allows us to iterate through a set of commands until a specific condition is met; it doesn't return a specific exit status when the shell exits, so option E is incorrect.

9.   E. The $() command assigns the output of a command to a specified variable in the shell script, so option E is correct. The > character redirects the output of a command to a file, not to a variable, so option A is incorrect. The >> character combination appends the output of a command to an existing file, not to a variable, so option B is incorrect. The $[] command performs integer mathematical operations in the Bash shell, so option C is incorrect. The | character redirects the output of a command to another command, not to a variable, so option D is incorrect.

10. C. The $[] command performs simple integer mathematical operations in the Bash shell, so option C is correct. The > character redirects the output of a command to a new file, so option A is incorrect. The >> character combination appends the output of a command to an existing file, so option B is incorrect. The | character redirects the output of a command to another command, so option D is incorrect. The $() command redirects the output of a command to a variable in the shell script, so option E is incorrect.

Chapter 26: Automating Jobs

1.   B. The ampersand character (&) tells the shell to start the command in background mode from the console session, so option B is correct. The greater-than sign (>) redirects the output from the command to a file, so option A is incorrect. The pipe symbol (|) redirects the output from the command to another command, so option C is incorrect. The double greater-than sign (>>) appends the output from the command to a file, so option D is incorrect. The nohup command disconnects the session from the console session, so option E is incorrect.

2.   E. The nohup command disconnects the shell script from the current console session, so option E is correct. The greater-than sign (>) redirects the output from the command to a file, so option A is incorrect. The ampersand sign (&) runs the shell script in background mode, so option B is incorrect. The pipe symbol (|) redirects the output from the command to another command, so option C is incorrect. The double greater-than symbol (>>) appends the output from the command to a file, so option D is incorrect.

3.   C. The Ctrl+C key combination stops the job currently running in foreground mode on the console session, so option C is correct. Starting a command with the nohup command disconnects the job from the console session, so you can't stop it from the console with a key command, making option A incorrect. Starting a job with the ampersand (&) command places the job in background mode but doesn't allow you to stop the job from running, so option B is incorrect. The pipe symbol redirects the output from a shell script to another command, so option D is incorrect. The kill command will stop a running shell script, but if the shell script is running in your console session, you won't be able to submit the kill command from the command prompt, so option E is incorrect.

4.   A. The Ctrl+Z key combination pauses the job currently running in foreground mode on the console session, so option A is correct. The Ctrl+C key combination stops the job currently running in the foreground in the console session, rather than pauses it, so

option B is incorrect. The `nohup` command disconnects a job from the console session but doesn't pause the job, so option C is incorrect. The ampersand sign (&) runs a job in background mode in the console session, so option D is incorrect. The `fg` command resumes a stopped job in foreground mode, so option E is incorrect.

5. C. When you list the current jobs using the `jobs` command, there will be a plus sign next to the default job number, so option C is correct. The minus sign next to a job number indicates the job next in line to become the default job, so option D is incorrect. Neither the PID nor the job number indicates the default job, so options A and B are both incorrect. The `ps` command lists the running jobs but doesn't indicate the default job in a console session, so option E is incorrect.

6. B. The `fg` command allows you to change a currently running or stopped job to run in foreground mode on the current console session, so option B is correct. The `bg` command changes a currently running or stopped job to run in background mode, so option A is incorrect. The `nohup` command disconnects a job from the console session, so option C is incorrect. The ampersand sign (&) places a job in background mode, not foreground mode, so option D is incorrect. The `at` command runs a job in background mode at a specific time, so option E is incorrect.

7. C. The `at` command allows you to schedule a job to run at a specific time, so option C is correct. The `nohup` command disconnects a job from the console session, so option A is incorrect. The ampersand sign (&) runs a job in background mode, so option B is incorrect. The pipe symbol (|) and the greater-than symbol redirect the job output to either a command or a file, so options D and E are both incorrect.

8. D. The `cron` program checks the cron tables for each user account and runs any scheduled jobs automatically, so option D is correct. The `at` command only runs a specified command once at a scheduled time, so option A is incorrect. The `nohup` and ampersand (&) commands do not schedule jobs to run, so both options B and C are incorrect. The `atq` command displays the jobs already scheduled to run from the `at` command, so option E is incorrect.

9. E. The times specified in the cron table are listed in the order of minute, hour, day of month, month, and day of week. The hour is in 24-hour format, so the specified entry would run the job at 5:10 a.m. every day, making option E correct. Options A, B, C, and D are all incorrect times based on the specified entry.

10. C. The `crontab` command allows you to list or edit the cron table for your own user account, so option C is correct. The `cron` command is what reads the cron tables for each user account and runs the specified jobs; it doesn't list the jobs, so option A is incorrect. The `at` command allows you to schedule a job to run at a specific time, so option B is incorrect. The `jobs` command allows you to view the currently running or stopped jobs in your console session, so option D is incorrect. The `nohup` command disconnects the job from the console session, so option E is incorrect.

Chapter 27: Controlling Versions with Git

1. **A, C, D, E.** Options A, C, D, and E all contain true statements concerning version control and are therefore correct answers. Version control does not require filenames to contain version numbers, and thus, option B is an incorrect choice.

2. **B, C, D, E.** Conceptually Git is broken up into distinct areas, which are the working directory, the staging area (also called the index), the local repository, and the remote repository. Therefore, options B, C, D, and E are correct answers. A blob is another name for an object stored by Git in the `.git/objects/` directory. Thus, option A is an incorrect choice.

3. **A, B, C, E.** The steps listed in options A, B, C, and E are all involved in setting up a Git environment for the first time. Adding files to the staging area is done after the environment is set up and files have been created in the working directory. Therefore, option D is the only incorrect choice.

4. **D.** Because Natasha is setting up her Git environment, she should next create and initialize the `.git/` directory in her working directory, via the `git init` command. Therefore, option D is the correct answer. The `mkdir` command is employed to create the working directory, which is already done, so option A is a wrong answer. The `git config --list` command shows configuration data, which should be done after the `.git/` directory is initialized, so option B is a wrong choice. While Natasha could set up her GitHub repository now, it is not the best next step, so option C is a wrong answer. Starting to create program files is an incorrect choice since Natasha is still setting up her Git environment. Therefore, option E is incorrect.

5. **B.** Since Bruce employed the `--global` option when setting his Git configuration options, the information is stored in the global `~/.gitconfig` file. Therefore, option B is the correct answer. This Git configuration information is not stored on GitHub, and GitHub may not even be employed as the remote repository in this case, so option A is a wrong answer. The working directory's `.git/config` file is the local file, not the global one, so option C is a wrong choice. The `.git/index` file and `.git/objects` directory do not store this type of data, so options D and E are incorrect choices.

6. **A.** The next step Bruce should take is to add his new script to the staging area (index) via the `git add GreenMass.sh` command. Therefore, option A is the correct answer. The `git init` command is used to initialize the `.git/` directory in the working directory and is part of setting up the Git environment, so option B is a wrong answer. The script cannot yet be committed to the local repository because it has not been added to the staging area. Thus, option C is an incorrect choice. The `git log` command shows the commit history and is not appropriate at this point, so option D is a wrong answer. The script cannot be committed to the remote repository until it is committed to the local repository. Therefore, option E is an incorrect choice.

7.   D. Natasha is being efficient by employing the `git add .` command, which will add all the files within the working directory to the staging area (index). To stay efficient, she should create a `.gitignore` file in the working directory and add the names of the three files that she wishes to keep out of the index to that file. This will prevent them from being added. Therefore, option D is the correct answer. While Natasha could move the three files out of her working directory, that is a sloppy and inefficient choice, so option A is a wrong answer. She also could add the 22 files individually to the index, but that too is very inefficient, as is creating a new working directory for the three files. Thus, options B and C are incorrect answers. Temporarily deleting the three files would force Natasha to re-create them after the other files are added to the index. This too is sloppy, and therefore option E is an incorrect choice.

8.   C. Natasha is ready to push her project to the remote repository, so option C is the correct answer. While she may go home and relax later, if the project is released to the public, she must upload it to the remote repository first. Therefore, option A is a wrong answer. Cloning a remote repository is done when someone wants all the project files as well as the VCS history. In this scenario, Natasha already has that data, so option B is a wrong choice. Since the project is complete, there is no need to pull down any files from the remote repository. Therefore, option D is also an incorrect answer. The `remote add origin` *URL* command is used to configure the remote repository's address (URL), which Natasha has already accomplished. Thus, option E is an incorrect choice.

9.   E. The `git checkout testing` command will allow you to switch to a new Git branch called `testing`. Thus, option E is the correct answer. The `git branch testing` command creates a new branch called `testing` instead of switching to it. Thus, option A is a wrong answer. The command in option B allows you to view the names of any files managed by the `testing` branch, so it is an incorrect answer. The `git branch` command shows you the current branches within this project and designates which one is current via an asterisk, but it does not allow you to switch branches. Thus, option C is an incorrect answer. The command in option D will perform a commit to the local repository and add a comment of `testing` to the log file. Therefore, option D is also an incorrect choice.

10. B. The `git merge report` command will merge the `report` branch into the `master` branch as desired, so option B is the correct answer. The `git merge master` command will attempt to merge the `master` branch into another branch, but since Tony is already in the `master` branch, this will not work (and is not desired), so option A is a wrong answer. The `rebase` arguments will attempt to perform a rebase instead of a merge. Thus, options C and D are incorrect answers. The `git checkout master` command was already used by Tony to reach the master branch, and thus option E is an incorrect choice.

Chapter 28: Understanding Cloud and Virtualization Concepts

1.   B. Public cloud services utilize servers hosted by a third-party company, so option B is correct. Private cloud services use servers hosted internally by the company, not by a third party, so option A is incorrect. Hybrid cloud services utilize servers hosted both internally and externally, not just by a third party, so option C is incorrect. Type I and Type II are types of hypervisors and not cloud services, so options D and E are incorrect.

2. C. A hybrid cloud service utilizes servers internal to the company as well as external at a third-party location. This provides an easy way to increase server capabilities without having to purchase your own hardware, so option C is correct. The entire private cloud is hosted internally, so Tom would need to purchase additional servers to support the application, so option A is incorrect. A public cloud is hosted in its entirety externally on a third-party network, so Tom wouldn't be able to use his current cloud servers, so option B is incorrect. Type I and Type II are types of hypervisors and not cloud services, so options D and E are incorrect.

3. A. The platform-as-a-service (PaaS) cloud type provides a complete development environment for customers, so option A is correct. The private and hybrid clouds are methods of implementing a cloud and not types of clouds, so options B and E are incorrect. The infrastructure-as-a-service (IaaS) cloud type provides only hardware to build an operating system, so Sally would need more to develop her applications, making option C incorrect. The software-as-a-service (SaaS) cloud type provides the full application—it doesn't allow you to develop your own applications—so option D is incorrect.

4. C. The infrastructure-as-a-service (IaaS) cloud type allows you to install your own operating systems on the cloud hardware, so option C is correct. The private and hybrid clouds are methods of implementing clouds and not cloud types, so options B and E are incorrect. The platform-as-a-service (PaaS) and software-as-a-service (SaaS) cloud types provide the operating system, so you can't install your own, making options A and D incorrect.

5. D. Type I hypervisors interface directly with the system hardware and act as a go-between, controlling resources for the guest virtual machines, making option D correct. Type II hypervisors run on top of a host operating system and don't directly interface with the system hardware, so option C is incorrect. Private, public, and hybrid are methods for implementing cloud services and not hypervisors, so options A, B, and E are all incorrect.

6. C. Type II hypervisors install on a host operating system and receive resources from the host operating system, so option C is correct. Type I hypervisors install directly on the server hardware without a host operating system, so option D is incorrect. Private, public, and hybrid are methods of implementing cloud services and not types of hypervisors, so options A, B, and E are all incorrect.

7. C. The Open Virtualization Appliance (OVA) file format bundles all of the virtual machine configuration files into a single `tar` file for distribution, so option C is correct. The Open Virtualization Format (OVF) format defines several separate files for storing configuration values, not a single file, so option D is incorrect. XML, JSON, and YAML are all configuration file formats and not methods to bundle the configuration files, so options A, B, and E are all incorrect.

8. A. Containers bundle the application runtime files along with any library files required to run the application. This ensures that the application will run in any environment, so option A is correct. A hypervisor manages virtual machines on a system and doesn't deploy applications, so option B is incorrect. Deploying the application to a private cloud would make the application available to Fred's internal network, but customers outside of his network wouldn't be able to run the application, so option C is incorrect. Deploying the application as a virtual machine would make the application run consistently but would also require each customer to install the same hypervisor package on their operating system, so option D is incorrect. Bundling the application files as a `tar` file doesn't ensure that the required system library will be present on all of the customer workstations, so option E is incorrect.

9. E. Containers include all of the files necessary to run an application, no matter what the host system, so option E is the correct answer. Public and private clouds don't guarantee the same development and production environments directly, so options A and B are both incorrect. Type I and Type II hypervisors don't host applications directly but need a virtual machine, so options C and D are both incorrect.

10. B. The Docker container package runs as a process on the host operating system and provides a command-line interface for controlling containers, so option B is correct. The Snap package provides software application containers but doesn't provide a command-line interface to control them, so option A is incorrect. The KVM, XEN, and VirtualBox packages are all hypervisor packages, not containers, so options C, D, and E are all incorrect.

Chapter 29: Inspecting Cloud and Virtualization Services

1. A, C, E. Options A, C, and E all contain true statements concerning the `libvert` library software collection and are therefore correct answers. This software collection does not provide a complete hypervisor application (though many hypervisors incorporate it), so option B is a wrong answer. Also the `libvert` library does not provide an anaconda file. Thus, option D is also an incorrect choice.

2. A, D. The `virsh` and `virt-install` utilities are ones that Carol can incorporate into her Bash shell script for managing her virtual machines. Therefore, options A and D are correct answers. `virtinst` is the name of a package file, which provides utilities such as `virsh`, and thus, option B is a wrong answer. Option C, `virt-manage`, is a made-up utility, making option C an incorrect answer. `setvcpus` is an argument you can use with the `virsh` utility, as opposed to a utility itself, so option E is an incorrect choice.

3. A, B, E. The question does not indicate whether this system will be a virtual one or not. Typically for a physical installation, using the kickstart method, the installation tree is stored in a network location or removable media, such as a USB flash drive. Therefore, options A and B are correct answers. For a virtual machine installation, often the installation tree (or ISO) is stored alongside the kickstart file. Thus, option E is also a correct choice. AutoYaST and preseed are alternatives to kickstart for the openSUSE and Ubuntu distributions, so options C and D are incorrect choices.

4. B, C, D, E. Options B, C, D, and E are true statements about the cloud-init application and thus are correct answers. The only untrue is statement is in option A—the cloud-init product was created and is maintained by Canonical.

5. D. Ms. Danvers' best choice is to configure the three virtual machines to use thin provisioned storage. This method will allow the VMs to immediately consume 600 GB of the 1 TB of host disk space and grow over time as needed (which is called overprovisioning). As the VMs' data grows, she can purchase additional disk space for her host machine and add it to the logical volume. Thus, option D is the correct answer. There is not enough information

provided to determine whether or not the virtual machines' disks should be configured as permanent or temporary, so options A and B are wrong answers. Thick provisioning would cause the three virtual machines to allocate 1.2 TB of disk space, which is not available, and thus, option C is an incorrect answer. Blob storage is used on Microsoft Azure virtual machines, and the question does not indicate that this is the cloud provider environment Ms. Danvers is using. Thus, option E is an incorrect choice.

6. **A.** Because Mr. Fury's programming students will be creating a single program that they are working on for the entire semester, the virtual machine storage needs to be configured as persistent. This will allow the students to access and modify their program on the virtual machine without having to re-create it each time their VM boots. Thus, option A is the correct choice. If Mr. Fury uses temporary storage, the students would have to re-create their program each time the VM boots, so option B is a wrong answer. Thickly or thinly provisioned storage needs are not discussed in this question, so options C and D are also incorrect answers. Blob storage is used on Microsoft Azure virtual machines, and the question does not indicate that this is the cloud provider environment Mr. Fury is using. Therefore, option E is an incorrect choice.

7. **B, C, D.** Overlay networking is a network virtualization method that employs encapsulation as well as channel bandwidth tunneling. Therefore, options B, C, and D are correct answers. It is not a storage virtualization method, so option A is a wrong answer. Also, it does not employ page blobs (which are a Microsoft Azure platform storage option), so option E is also an incorrect choice.

8. **B.** In order for Carol's virtual machines to all act as nodes on her host machine's LAN and get their own IP address that they will use to send/receive network traffic, she needs to configure them as bridged adapters. Thus, option B is the correct answer. A host-only configured NIC will not be able to communicate on the external network, so option A is a wrong answer. A NAT adapter will not allow the VMs to each operate as a node on the host machine's network, so option C is a wrong choice. Multihomed and dual-homed are descriptions of the number of NICS employed by a VM, so options D and E are incorrect choices.

9. **C.** A virtual machine with a NAT configured adapter will have its IP address kept private and use the host machine's IP address to communicate on the host machine's network. Thus, option C is the correct answer. A host-only configured NIC will not be able to communicate on the external network, so option A is a wrong answer. A bridged adapter will not keep its assigned IP address private, so option B is also an incorrect answer. Multihomed and dual-homed are descriptions of the number of NICs employed by a VM, so options D and E are incorrect choices.

10. **A, B, E.** For Nick's firewall VM to act as a firewall to the other four virtual machines, it would need a host-only adapter to communicate with the other machines on the local internal network. The firewall VM would also need a bridged NIC to act as a node on the host machine's network. Because this firewall VM has two virtual NICs, it is considered to be dual-homed. Thus, options A, B, and E are correct choices. The NAT configuration type is not needed or employed in this scenario, so option C is a wrong answer. Also, since there are no more than two virtual adapters needed, it is not a multihomed (more than two) configuration, and option D is an incorrect choice.

Chapter 30: Orchestrating the Environment

1. A, B, C, D, E. All these choices contain items that can use orchestration and are correct choices. Since orchestration refers to the organization of a process that is balanced and coordinated and achieves consistency in the results, there are not many things that cannot use orchestration. An exception would be a situation where you are trying to simulate random chaos.

2. B. To meet Connie's requirement, the development environment must be immutable (not modifiable). Therefore, option B is the correct answer. Self-replication will not assist in reaching Connie's requirement for an unchanging environment, so option A is a wrong answer. Kubernetes is an orchestration engine, not an attribute, so option C is also an incorrect choice. Infrastructure as code does not provide an unchanging environment, so option D is a wrong answer. In orchestration, self-healing refers to a different issue than an unchanging environment, so option E is also an incorrect choice.

3. D. With container orchestration and DevOps, to keep the production and development environment matching so that problems do not occur when an app is moved into production, you simply replace the old production environment with the development environment. In the case of containers, this means you stop the old production container and start the new development container as the production container in its place. Thus, option D is the correct answer and follows the "replace, not update" attribute. While the answer in option A would work, it is terribly tedious, time-consuming, and full of potential problems. Therefore, it is a wrong answer. The answer in option B is the old-school method of moving an app into production, and it does not meet Connie's desire for a static and matching environment. Thus, it is also an incorrect answer. If before the app is ready for production, you stop any software updates on the development container from occurring, that does not make the development environment match the production environment alone. Thus, option C is a wrong choice. Option E also would work but is even more tedious and full of potential problems than the answer in option A. Therefore, it too is an incorrect choice.

4. C. Replication allows an orchestrated container to be built and deployed in multiple copies automatically. This provides high availability when a container crashes as well as when a new app container is being deployed. Therefore, option C is the correct answer. Immutability prevents environment issues from causing application problems, but it is not the best proponent of high availability, and thus, option A is a wrong answer. Version control allows you to roll back and troubleshoot problems in a production environment, which does help provide higher availability, but again it's not the best attribute toward doing so. Therefore, option B is also an incorrect answer. Option D provides speed in the orchestrated environment, which also helps provide high availability to an app user, but it too is not the best advocate. Thus, option D is also a wrong answer. While documentation helps in the troubleshooting process and slightly contributes to higher availability, it is not the best either. Therefore, option E is also an incorrect choice.

5. E. *Infrastructure as code* is an umbrella term that encompasses both the configuration management settings (operating system, libraries, additional software) and the policy as code items (security policies, authentication settings). Thus, option E is the correct choice. Marathon is the orchestration tool used with the Mesos application. Therefore, option A is a wrong answer. Build automation uses infrastructure as code. Thus, option B is an incorrect answer. A development environment can be built using infrastructure as a code. Therefore, option C is also a wrong answer. A container also can be built using infrastructure as a code but is not the code itself, so option D is an incorrect choice too.

6. B. Ms. Ward is using build automation. Thus, option B is the correct answer. Monitoring comes after containers are deployed, so option A is a wrong answer. Replication is part of the process Ms. Ward used, but it does not describe the container deployment, so option C is not the best answer and is an incorrect choice. Version control was hopefully used by Ms. Ward so she can roll back or troubleshoot her application, if needed, but option D is not a correct answer. Docker Swarm is an orchestration system, and thus, option E is also an incorrect answer.

7. A, B, C, E. In container orchestration, automated configuration management allows containers to be deployed and replicated automatically (build automation). Also, troubleshooting infrastructure issues is easier because the modifications are tracked in a version control system. Thus, options A, B, C, and E are all correct answers. While automated configuration management and orchestrated containers may be part of continuous software delivery, they are not directly related. Therefore, option D is the only incorrect choice.

8. A. Mr. Abbot needs an orchestration tool that can perform self-healing. Therefore, option A is the correct answer. Build automation may be involved in self-healing, but it does not describe the ability to deploy and replicate containers after they have crashed. Thus, option B is a wrong answer. Continuous integration is a DevOps software revision control method that encourages quickly integrating app changes into the main branch. Therefore, option C is an incorrect answer. Infrastructure as code may be employed by build automation but does not describe the ability to self-heal. Thus, option D is wrong choice. Pods are a component of the Kubernetes orchestration engine. Thus, option E is also an incorrect answer.

9. B, C, D, E. App container performance, metrics, container health, and default states are all collected, watched, or used by an orchestration monitoring tool. Therefore, options B, C, D, and E are all correct answers. Option A is the only incorrect choice because the version control system is not used or watched by an orchestration monitoring utility.

10. B, C. Those who choose agentless orchestration monitoring tools typically do not want to install monitoring software (an agent) on their app containers. Also, they are concerned about this installed agent adversely affecting performance. Therefore, options B and C are the correct answers. Since the answers in options A and D are opposite of options B and C, they are wrong answers. Also, the industry is divided on which is the best to use (agent or agentless) for orchestration monitoring, so option E is also an incorrect choice.

Index

Online Test Bank

Register to gain one year of FREE access after activation to the online interactive test bank to help you study for your CompTIA Linux+ certification exam—included with your purchase of this book! All of the chapter review questions and the practice tests in this book are included in the online test bank so you can practice in a timed and graded setting.

Register and Access the Online Test Bank

To register your book and get access to the online test bank, follow these steps:

1. Go to www.wiley.com/go/sybextestprep.
2. Select your book from the list.
3. Complete the required registration information, including answering the security verification to prove book ownership. You will be emailed a pin code.
4. Follow the directions in the email or go to www.wiley.com/go/sybextestprep.
5. Find your book on that page and click the "Register or Login" link with it. Then enter the pin code you received and click the "Activate PIN" button.
6. On the Create an Account or Login page, enter your username and password, and click Login or, if you don't have an account already, create a new account.
7. At this point, you should be in the test bank site with your new test bank listed at the top of the page. If you do not see it there, please refresh the page or log out and log back in.